sociology

readings

8

sociology

exploring the architecture of everyday life │readings│

8

david m. newman
DePauw University

jodi o'brien
Seattle University

PINE FORGE PRESS
An Imprint of SAGE Publications, Inc.
Los Angeles • London • New Delhi • Singapore • Washington DC

For information:

Pine Forge Press
A Sage Publications Company
2455 Teller Road
Thousand Oaks, California 91320
E-mail: order@sagepub.com

SAGE Publications Ltd.
1 Oliver's Yard
55 City Road
London EC1Y 1SP
United Kingdom

SAGE Publications India Pvt. Ltd.
B 1/I 1 Mohan Cooperative
    Industrial Area
Mathura Road, New Delhi 110 044
India

SAGE Publications Asia-Pacific Pte. Ltd.
33 Pekin Street #02-01
Far East Square
Singapore 048763

Printed in the United States of America

Library of Congress Cataloging-in-Publication Data

Sociology : Exploring the architecture of everyday life readings / editors, David M. Newman, Jodi O'Brien. — 8th ed.
    p. cm.
Includes bibliographical references.
ISBN 978-1-4129-7942-9 (pbk.)
    1. Sociology. I. Newman, David M., 1958- II. O'Brien, Jodi.

HM586.S64 2010
301—dc22   2009038198

Printed on acid-free paper

09   10   11   12   13   10   9   8   7   6   5   4   3   2   1

Acquiring Editor:	David Repetto
Editorial Assistant:	Nancy Scrofano
Production Editor:	Sarah K. Quesenberry
Proofreader:	Jenifer Kooiman
Typesetter:	C&M Digitals (P) Ltd.
Cover Designer:	Candice Harman
Marketing Manager:	Jennifer Reed Banando

Contents

PART III
SOCIAL STRUCTURE, INSTITUTIONS, AND EVERYDAY LIFE

Preface

One of the greatest challenges we face as teachers of sociology is getting our students to see the relevance of the course material to their own lives and to fully appreciate its connection to the larger society. We teach our students to see that sociology is all around us. It's in our families, our careers, our media, our jobs, our classrooms, our goals, our interests, our desires, even our minds. Sociology can be found at the neighborhood pub, in conversation with the clerk at 7-Eleven, on a date, and in the highest offices of government. It's with us when we're alone and when we're in a group of people. Sociology focuses on questions of global significance as well as private concern. For instance, sociologists study how some countries create and maintain dominance over others and also why we find some more people attractive and than others. Sociology is an invitation to understand yourself within the context of your historical and cultural circumstances.

We have compiled this collection of short articles, chapters, and excerpts with the intent of providing comprehensive examples of the power of sociology for helping us to make sense of our lives and our times. The readings are organized in a format that demonstrates:

- the uniqueness of the sociological perspective
- tools of sociological analysis
- the significance of different cultures in a global world
- social factors that influence identity development and self-management
- social rules about family, relationships, and belonging
- the influence of social institutions and organizations on everyday life
- the significance of socioeconomic class, gender, and racial/ethnic backgrounds in everyday life
- the significance of social demographics such as aging populations and migration
- the power of social groups and social change

In general, our intent is to demonstrate the significance of sociology in everyday life and to show that what seems "obvious" is often not so obvious when subjected to rigorous sociological analysis. The metaphor of "architecture" used in the title for this reader illustrates the sociological idea that as social beings we are constantly building and rebuilding our own social environment. The sociological promise is that if we understand these processes and how they affect us, we will be able to make more informed choices about how to live our lives and engage in our communities.

As in the first seven editions of the reader, the selections in this edition are intended to be vivid, provocative, and eye-opening examples of the practice of sociology. The readings represent a variety of styles. Some use common, everyday experiences and phenomena (such as drug use, disability, employment, athletic performance, religious devotion, eating fast food, the balance of work and family) to illustrate the relationship between the individual and society. Others focus on important social issues or problems (medical social control, race relations, poverty, educational inequalities, sexuality, immigration, global economics, environmental degradation, political extremism) or on specific historical events (massacres during war, drug scares, and 9/11). Some were written quite recently; others are sociological "classics." In addition to accurately representing the sociological perspective and providing rigorous coverage of the discipline, we hope the selections are thought-provoking, generate lots of discussion, and are enjoyable to read.

There are 40 selections in this reader and 17 of them are new. These new readings focus on current, important social issues such as diversity among same-sex couples, inner-city violence among teenage girls, the effect of pregnancy and post-pregnancy on women's body image, ethnicity and youth identity, language across generations in immigrant families, the social construction of legal and illegal drugs, compassion and poverty, teen childbearing in poor communities, the plight of Muslim Americans after 9/11, gentrification in African American neighborhoods, social contact between youth and older people, and the immigrant rights movement.

Most of the new readings are based on research studies that were written in the past 5 years. In recent editions of this reader we have increased the number of selections drawn from contemporary social research. In doing so we hope to provide you with illustrations of the ways in which social researchers combine theories and empirical studies to gain a better understanding of social patterns and processes. Although the professional language of some of these selections may seem challenging for introductory readers, we are confident that you will find them highly relevant and come away with a sense of being immersed in the most significant details of contemporary sociology.

To help you get the most out of these selections, we've written brief introductions that provide the sociological context for each chapter. We also included reflection points that can be used for comparing and contrasting the readings in each section and across sections. For those of you who are also reading the accompanying textbook, these introductions will furnish a quick intellectual link between the readings and information in the textbook. We have also included in these introductions brief instructions on what to look for when you read the selections in a given chapter. After each reading you will find a set of discussion questions to ponder. Many of these questions ask you to apply a specific author's conclusions to some contemporary issue in society or to your own life experiences. It is our hope that these questions will generate a lot of classroom debate and help you see the sociological merit of the readings.

A Web site established for this eighth edition includes do-it-yourself reviews and tests for students, Web-based activities designed to enhance learning, and a chat room where students and teachers can post messages and debate matters of sociological significance. The site can be accessed via the Pine Forge Web site at www.pineforge.com.

Books like these are enormous projects. We would like to thank David Repetto, Nancy Scrofano, Sarah Quesenberry , and the rest of the staff at Pine Forge Press for their useful advice and assistance in putting this reader together. It's always a pleasure to work with this very professional group. We are especially grateful to Shasti Conrad and Jennifer Hamann for research assistance in selecting new readings and to Carly Chillmon for assistance in editing this edition of the manuscript.

Enjoy!

David M. Newman
Department of Sociology/Anthropology
DePauw University
Greencastle, IN 46135
E-mail: dnewman@depauw.edu

Jodi O'Brien
Department of Sociology
Seattle University
Seattle, WA 98122
E-mail: jobrien@seattleu.edu

About the Editors

David M. Newman (Ph.D., University of Washington) is Professor of Sociology at DePauw University. In addition to the introductory course, he teaches courses in research methods, family, social psychology, and deviance. He has won teaching awards at both the University of Washington and DePauw University. His other written work includes *Identities and Inequalities: Exploring the Intersections of Race, Class, Gender, and Sexuality* (2005).

Jodi O'Brien (Ph.D., University of Washington) is Professor of Sociology at Seattle University. She teaches courses in social psychology, sexuality, inequality, and classical and contemporary theory. She writes and lectures on the cultural politics of transgressive identities and communities. Her other books include *Everyday Inequalities* (1998), *Social Prisms: Reflections on Everyday Myths and Paradoxes* (1999), and *The Production of Reality: Essays and Readings on Social Interaction, Fourth Edition* (2005).

PART I

The Individual and Society

Taking a New Look at a Familiar World

The primary claim of sociology is that our everyday feelings, thoughts, and actions are the product of a complex interplay between massive social forces and personal characteristics. We can't understand the relationship between individuals and their societies without understanding the connection between both. As C. Wright Mills discusses in the introductory article, the "sociological imagination" is the ability to see the impact of social forces on our private lives. When we develop a sociological imagination, we gain an awareness that our lives unfold at the intersection of personal biography and social history. The sociological imagination encourages us to move beyond individualistic explanations of human experiences to an understanding of the mutual influence between individuals and society. So, rather than study what goes on within people, sociologists study what goes on between and among people, as individuals, groups, organizations, or entire societies. Sociology teaches us to look beyond individual personalities and focus instead on the influence of social phenomena in shaping our ideas of who we are and what we think we can do.

Peter Berger, another well-known sociologist, invites us to consider the uniqueness of the sociological enterprise. According to Berger, the sociologist is driven by an insatiable curiosity to understand the social conditions that shape human behavior. The sociologist is also prepared to be surprised, disturbed, and sometimes even bored by what he or she discovers. In this regard, the sociologist is driven to make sense of the seemingly "obvious" with the understanding that once explored, it may not be so obvious after all. One example of the "non-obvious" is the influence that social institutions have on our behavior. It's not always easy to see this influence. We have a tendency to see people's behavior in individualistic, sometimes even biological terms. This tendency toward "individualistic" explanations is particularly pronounced in U.S. society.

The influence of social institutions on our personal lives is often felt most forcefully when we are compelled to obey the commands of someone who is in a position of institutional authority. The social institution with the most explicit hierarchy of authority is the military. In "The My Lai Massacre: A Military Crime of Obedience," Herbert Kelman and V. Lee Hamilton describe a specific example of a crime in which the individuals involved attempted to deny responsibility for their actions by claiming that they were following the orders of a military officer who had the legitimate right to command them. This incident occurred in the midst of the Vietnam War. Arguably, people do things under such trying conditions that they wouldn't ordinarily do, even—as in this case—kill defenseless people. Kelman and Hamilton make a key sociological point by showing that these soldiers were not necessarily psychological misfits who were especially mean or violent. Instead, the researchers argue, they were ordinary people caught up in tense circumstances that made obeying the brutal commands of an authority seem like the normal and morally acceptable thing to do.

Something to Consider as You Read

As you read these selections, consider the effects of social context and situation on behavior. Even though it might appear extreme, how might the behavior of these soldiers be similar to other examples of social influence? Consider occasions in which you have done something publicly that you didn't feel right about personally. How do you explain your behavior? How might a sociologist explain your behavior?

The Sociological Imagination

C. Wright Mills

(1959)

"The individual can . . . know his own chances in life only by becoming aware of those of all individuals in his circumstances."

Nowadays men often feel that their private lives are a series of traps. They sense that within their everyday worlds, they cannot overcome their troubles, and in this feeling, they are often quite correct: What ordinary men are directly aware of and what they try to do are bounded by the private orbits in which they live; their visions and their powers are limited to the close-up scenes of job, family, neighborhood; in other milieux, they move vicariously and remain spectators. And the more aware they become, however vaguely, of ambitions and of threats which transcend their immediate locales, the more trapped they seem to feel.

Underlying this sense of being trapped are seemingly impersonal changes in the very structure of continent-wide societies. The facts of contemporary history are also facts about the success and the failure of individual men and women. When a society is industrialized, a peasant becomes a worker; a feudal lord is liquidated or becomes a businessman. When classes rise or fall, a man is employed or unemployed; when the rate of investment goes up or down, a man takes new heart or goes broke. When wars happen, an insurance salesman becomes a rocket launcher; a store clerk, a radar man; a wife lives alone; a child grows up without a father. Neither the life of an individual nor the history of a society can be understood without understanding both.

Yet men do not usually define the troubles they endure in terms of historical change and institutional contradiction. The well-being they enjoy, they do not usually impute to the big ups and downs of the societies in which they live. Seldom aware of the intricate connection between the patterns of their own lives and the course of world history, ordinary men do not usually know what this connection means for the kinds of men they are becoming and for the kinds of history-making in which they might take part. They do not possess the quality of mind essential to grasp the interplay of man and society, of biography and history, of self and world. They cannot cope with their personal troubles in such ways as to control the structural transformations that usually lie behind them.

Surely it is no wonder. In what period have so many men been so totally exposed at so fast a pace to such earthquakes of change? That Americans have not known such catastrophic changes as have the men and women of other societies is due to historical facts that are now quickly becoming "merely history." The history that now affects every man is world history. Within this scene and this period, in the course of a single generation, one-sixth of mankind is transformed from all that is feudal and backward into all that is modern, advanced, and fearful. Political colonies are freed, new and less visible forms of imperialism installed. Revolutions occur; men feel the intimate grip of new kinds of authority. Totalitarian societies rise, and are smashed to bits—or succeed fabulously. After two centuries of ascendancy, capitalism is shown up as only one way to make society into an industrial apparatus. After two centuries of hope, even formal democracy is restricted to a quite small portion of mankind.

4

Everywhere in the underdeveloped world, ancient ways of life are broken up and vague expectations become urgent demands. Everywhere in the overdeveloped world, the means of authority and of violence become total in scope and bureaucratic in form. Humanity itself now lies before us, the supernation at either pole concentrating its most coordinated and massive efforts upon the preparation of World War Three.

The very shaping of history now outpaces the ability of men to orient themselves in accordance with cherished values. And which values? Even when they do not panic, men often sense that older ways of feeling and thinking have collapsed and that newer beginnings are ambiguous to the point of moral stasis. Is it any wonder that ordinary men feel they cannot cope with the larger worlds with which they are so suddenly confronted? That they cannot understand the meaning of their epoch for their own lives? That—in defense of selfhood—they become morally insensible, trying to remain altogether private men? Is it any wonder that they come to be possessed by a sense of the trap?

It is not only information that they need—in this Age of Fact, information often dominates their attention and overwhelms their capacities to assimilate it. It is not only the skills of reason that they need—although their struggles to acquire these often exhaust their limited moral energy.

What they need, and what they feel they need, is a quality of mind that will help them to use information and to develop reason in order to achieve lucid summations of what is going on in the world and of what may be happening within themselves. It is this quality, I am going to contend, that journalists and scholars, artists and publics, scientists and editors are coming to expect of what may be called the sociological imagination.

The sociological imagination enables its possessor to understand the larger historical scene in terms of its meaning for the inner life and the external career of a variety of individuals. It enables him to take into account how individuals, in the welter of their daily experience, often become falsely conscious of their social positions. Within that welter, the framework of modern society is sought, and within that framework the psychologies of a variety of men and women are formulated. By such means the personal uneasiness of individuals is focused upon explicit troubles and the indifference of publics is transformed into involvement with public issues.

The first fruit of this imagination—and the first lesson of the social science that embodies it—is the idea that the individual can understand his own experience and gauge his own fate only by locating himself within his period, that he can know his own chances in life only by becoming aware of those of all individuals in his circumstances. In many ways it is a terrible lesson; in many ways a magnificent one. We do not know the limits of man's capacities for supreme effort or willing degradation, for agony or glee, for pleasurable brutality or the sweetness of reason. But in our time we have come to know that the limits of "human nature" are frighteningly broad. We have come to know that every individual lives, from one generation to the next, in some society; that he lives out a biography, and that he lives it out within some historical sequence. By the fact of his living he contributes, however minutely, to the shaping of this society and to the course of its history, even as he is made by society and by its historical push and shove.

The sociological imagination enables us to grasp history and biography and the relations between the two within society. That is its task and its promise. To recognize this task and this promise is the mark of the classic social analyst. It is characteristic of Herbert Spencer—turgid, polysyllabic, comprehensive; of E. A. Ross—graceful, muckraking, upright; of Auguste Comte and Emile Durkheim; of the intricate and subtle Karl Mannheim. It is the quality of all that is intellectually excellent in Karl Marx; it is the clue to Thorstein Veblen's brilliant and ironic insight, to Joseph Schumpeter's many-sided constructions of reality; it is the basis of the psychological sweep of W. E. H. Lecky no less than of the profundity and clarity of Max Weber. And it is the signal of what is best in contemporary studies of man and society.

No social study that does not come back to the problems of biography, of history, and of their intersections within a society has completed its intellectual journey. Whatever the specific problems of the classic social analysts, however limited or however broad the features of social reality they have examined, those who have been imaginatively aware of the promise of their work have consistently asked three sorts of questions:

1. What is the structure of this particular society as a whole? What are its essential components, and how are they related to one another? How does it differ from other varieties of social order? Within it, what is the meaning of any particular feature for its continuance and for its change?

2. Where does this society stand in human history? What are the mechanics by which it is changing? What is its place within and its meaning for the development of humanity as a whole? How does any particular feature we are examining affect, and how is it affected by, the historical period in which it moves? And this period—what are its essential features? How does it differ from other periods? What are its characteristic ways of history making?

3. What varieties of men and women now prevail in this society and in this period? And what varieties are coming to prevail? In what ways are they selected and formed, liberated and repressed, made sensitive and blunted? What kinds of "human nature" are revealed in the conduct and character we observe in this society in this period? And what is the meaning for "human nature" of each and every feature of the society we are examining?

Whether the point of interest is a great power state or a minor literary mood, a family, a prison, a creed—these are the kinds of questions the best social analysts have asked. They are the intellectual pivots of classic studies of man in society—and they are the questions inevitably raised by any mind possessing the sociological imagination. For that imagination is the capacity to shift from one perspective to another—from the political to the psychological; from examination of a single family to comparative assessment of the national budgets of the world; from the theological school to the military establishment; from considerations of an oil industry to studies of contemporary poetry. It is the capacity to range from the most impersonal and remote transformations to the most intimate features of the human self—and to see the relations between the two. Back of its use there is always the urge to know the social and historical meaning of the individual in the society and in the period in which he has his quality and his being.

That, in brief, is why it is by means of the sociological imagination that men now hope to grasp what is going on in the world, and to understand what is happening in themselves as minute points of the intersections of biography and history within society. In large part, contemporary man's self-conscious view of himself as at least an outsider, if not a permanent stranger, rests upon an absorbed realization of social relativity and of the transformative power of history. The sociological imagination is the most fruitful form of this self-consciousness. By its use men whose mentalities have swept only a series of limited orbits often come to feel as if suddenly awakened in a house with which they had only supposed themselves to be familiar. Correctly or incorrectly, they often come to feel that they can now provide themselves with adequate summations, cohesive assessments, comprehensive orientations. Older decisions that once appeared sound now seem to them products of a mind unaccountably dense. Their capacity for astonishment is made lively again. They acquire a new way of thinking, they experience a transvaluation of values: in a word, by their reflection and by their sensibility, they realize the cultural meaning of the social sciences.

Perhaps the most fruitful distinction with which the sociological imagination works is between "the personal troubles of milieu" and "the public issues of social structure." This distinction is an essential tool of the sociological imagination and a feature of all classic work in social science.

Troubles occur within the character of the individual and within the range of his immediate relations with others; they have to do with his self and with those limited areas of social life of which he is directly and personally aware. Accordingly, the statement and the resolution of troubles properly lie within the individual as a biographical entity and within the scope of his immediate milieu—the social setting that is directly open to his personal experience and to some extent his willful activity. A trouble is a private matter: values cherished by an individual are felt by him to be threatened.

Issues have to do with matters that transcend these local environments of the individual and the range of his inner life. They have to do with the organization of many such milieux into the institutions of an historical society as a whole, with the ways in which various milieux overlap and interpenetrate to form the larger structure of social and historical life. An issue is a public matter: some value cherished by publics is felt to be threatened. Often there is a debate about what that value really is and about what it is that really threatens it. This debate is often without focus if only because it is the very nature of an issue, unlike even widespread trouble, that it cannot very well be defined in terms of the immediate and everyday environments of ordinary men. An issue, in fact, often involves a crisis in institutional arrangements, and often too it involves what Marxists call "contradictions" or "antagonisms."

In these terms, consider unemployment. When, in a city of 100,000, only one man is unemployed, that is his personal trouble, and for its relief we properly look to the character of the man, his skills, and his immediate opportunities. But when in a nation of 50 million employees, 15 million men are unemployed, that is an issue, and we may not hope to find its solution within the range of opportunities open to any one individual. The very

structure of opportunities has collapsed. Both the correct statement of the problem and the range of possible solutions require us to consider the economic and political institutions of the society, and not merely the personal situation and character of a scatter of individuals.

Consider war. The personal problem of war, when it occurs, may be how to survive it or how to die in it with honor; how to make money out of it; how to climb into the higher safety of the military apparatus; or how to contribute to the war's termination. In short, according to one's values, to find a set of milieux and within it to survive the war or make one's death in it meaningful. But the structural issues of war have to do with its causes; with what types of men it throws up into command; with its effects upon economic and political, family, and religious institutions, with the unorganized irresponsibility of a world of nation-states.

Consider marriage. Inside a marriage a man and a woman may experience personal troubles, but when the divorce rate during the first four years of marriage is 250 out of every 1,000 attempts, this is an indication of a structural issue having to do with the institutions of marriage and the family and other institutions that bear upon them.

Or consider the metropolis—the horrible, beautiful, ugly, magnificent sprawl of the great city. For many upper-class people, the personal solution to "the problem of the city" is to have an apartment with private garage under it in the heart of the city, and forty miles out, a house by Henry Hill, garden by Garrett Eckbo, on a hundred acres of private land. In these two controlled environments—with a small staff at each end and a private helicopter connection—most people could solve many of the problems of personal milieux caused by the facts of the city. But all this, however splendid, does not solve the public issues that the structural fact of the city poses. What should be done with this wonderful monstrosity? Break it all up into scattered units, combining residence and work? Refurbish it as it stands? Or, after evacuation, dynamite it and build new cities according to new plans in new places? What should those plans be? And who is to decide and to accomplish whatever choice is made? These are structural issues; to confront them and to solve them requires us to consider political and economic issues that affect innumerable milieux.

Insofar as an economy is so arranged that slumps occur, the problem of unemployment becomes incapable of personal solution. Insofar as war is inherent in the nation-state system and in the uneven industrialization of the world, the ordinary individual in his restricted milieu will be powerless—with or without psychiatric aid—to solve the troubles this system or lack of system imposes upon him. Insofar as the family as an institution turns women into darling little slaves and men into their chief providers and unweaned dependents, the problem of a satisfactory marriage remains incapable of purely private solution. Insofar as the overdeveloped megalopolis and the overdeveloped automobile are built-in features of the overdeveloped society, the issues of urban living will not be solved by personal ingenuity and private wealth.

What we experience in various and specific milieux, I have noted, is often caused by structural changes. Accordingly, to understand the changes of many personal milieux we are required to look beyond them. And the number and variety of such structural changes increase as the institutions within which we live become more embracing and more intricately connected with one another. To be aware of the idea of social structure and to use it with sensibility is to be capable of tracing such linkages among a great variety of milieux. To be able to do that is to possess the sociological imagination. . . .

THINKING ABOUT THE READING

Consider the political, economic, familial, and cultural circumstances into which you were born. Make a list of some of these circumstances and also some of the major historical events that have occurred in your lifetime. How do you think these historical and social circumstances may have affected your personal "biography"? Can you think of ways in which your actions have influenced the course of other people's lives? Identify some famous people and consider how the intersection of "history and biography" led them to their particular position. How might the outcome have differed if some of the circumstances in their lives were different?

Invitation to Sociology

Peter Berger

(1963)

We would say then that the sociologist (that is, the one we would really like to invite to our game) is a person intensively, endlessly, shamelessly interested in the doings of men. His natural habitat is all the human gathering places of the world, wherever men* come together. The sociologist may be interested in many other things. But his consuming interest remains in the world of men, their institutions, their history, their passions. He will naturally be interested in the events that engage men's ultimate beliefs, their moments of tragedy and grandeur and ecstasy. But he will also be fascinated by the commonplace, the everyday. He will know reverence, but this reverence will not prevent him from wanting to see and to understand. He may sometimes feel revulsion or contempt. But this also will not deter him from wanting to have his questions answered. The sociologist, in his quest for understanding, moves through the world of men without respect for the usual lines of demarcation. Nobility and degradation, power and obscurity, intelligence and folly—these are equally *interesting* to him, however unequal they may be in his personal values or tastes. Thus his questions may lead him to all possible levels of society, the best and the least known places, the most respected and the most despised. And, if he is a good sociologist, he will find himself in all these places because his own questions have so taken possession of him that he has little choice but to seek for answers.

We could say that the sociologist, but for the grace of his academic title, is the man who must listen to gossip despite himself, who is tempted to look through keyholes, to read other people's mail, to open closed cabinets. What interests us is the curiosity that grips any sociologist in front of a closed door behind which there are human voices. If he is a good sociologist, he will want to open that door, to understand these voices. Behind each closed door he will anticipate some new facet of human life not yet perceived and understood.

The sociologist will occupy himself with matters that others regard as too sacred or as too distasteful for dispassionate investigation. He will find rewarding the company of priests or of prostitutes, depending not on his personal preferences but on the questions he happens to be asking at the moment. He will also concern himself with matters that others may find much too boring. He will be interested in the human interaction that goes with warfare or with great intellectual discoveries, but also in the relations between people employed in a restaurant or between a group of little girls playing with their dolls. His main focus of attention is not the ultimate significance of what men do, but the action in itself, as another example of the infinite richness of human conduct.

In these journeys through the world of men the sociologist will inevitably encounter other professional Peeping Toms. Sometimes these will resent his presence, feeling that he is poaching on their preserves. In some places the sociologist will meet up with the economist, in others with the political scientist, in

---

*To be understood as people or persons.

yet others with the psychologist or the ethnologist. Yet chances are that the questions that have brought him to these same places are different from the ones that propelled his fellow trespassers. The sociologist's questions always remain essentially the same: "What are people doing with each other here?" "What are their relationships to each other?" "How are these relationships organized in institutions?" "What are the collective ideas that move men and institutions?" In trying to answer these questions in specific instances, the sociologist will, of course, have to deal with economic or political matters, but he will do so in a way rather different from that of the economist or the political scientist. The scene that he contemplates is the same human scene that these other scientists concern themselves with. But the sociologist's angle of vision is different.

Much of the time the sociologist moves in sectors of experience that are familiar to him and to most people in his society. He investigates communities, institutions and activities that one can read about every day in the newspapers. Yet there is another excitement of discovery beckoning in his investigations. It is not the excitement of coming upon the totally unfamiliar, but rather the excitement of finding the familiar becoming transformed in its meaning. The fascination of sociology lies in the fact that its perspective makes us see in a new light the very world in which we have lived all our lives. This also constitutes a transformation of consciousness. Moreover, this transformation is more relevant existentially than that of many other intellectual disciplines, because it is more difficult to segregate in some special compartment of the mind. The astronomer does not live in the remote galaxies, and the nuclear physicist can, outside his laboratory, eat and laugh and marry and vote without thinking about the insides of the atom. The geologist looks at rocks only at appropriate times, and the linguist speaks English with his wife. The sociologist lives in society, on the job and off it. His own life, inevitably, is part of his subject matter. Men

being what they are, sociologists too manage to segregate their professional insights from their everyday affairs. But it is a rather difficult feat to perform in good faith.

The sociologist moves in the common world of men, close to what most of them would call real. The categories he employs in his analyses are only refinements of the categories by which other men live—power, class, status, race, ethnicity. As a result, there is a deceptive simplicity and obviousness about some sociological investigations. One reads them, nods at the familiar scene, remarks that one has heard all this before and don't people have better things to do than to waste their time on truisms—until one is suddenly brought up against an insight that radically questions everything one had previously assumed about this familiar scene. This is the point at which one begins to sense the excitement of sociology.

Let us take a specific example. Imagine a sociology class in a Southern college where almost all the students are white Southerners. Imagine a lecture on the subject of the racial system of the South. The lecturer is talking here of matters that have been familiar to his students from the time of their infancy. Indeed, it may be that they are much more familiar with the minutiae of this system than he is. They are quite bored as a result. It seems to them that he is only using more pretentious words to describe what they already know. Thus he may use the term "caste," one commonly used now by American sociologists to describe the Southern racial system. But in explaining the term he shifts to traditional Hindu society, to make it clearer. He then goes on to analyze the magical beliefs inherent in caste tabus, the social dynamics of *commensalism* and *connubium*, the economic interests concealed within the system, the way in which religious beliefs relate to the tabus, the effects of the caste system upon the industrial development of the society and vice versa—all in India. But suddenly India is not very far away at all. The lecture then goes back to its Southern theme. The familiar now seems not quite so familiar anymore. Questions are raised that are new, perhaps raised angrily, but raised all the same. And at least some of the students have begun to understand that there are functions involved in this business of race that they have not read about in the newspapers (at least not those in their hometowns) and that their parents have not told them—partly, at least, because neither the newspapers nor the parents knew about them.

It can be said that the first wisdom of sociology is this—things are not what they seem. This too is a deceptively simple statement. It ceases to be simple after a while. Social reality turns out to have many layers of meaning. The discovery of each new layer changes the perception of the whole.

Anthropologists use the term "culture shock" to describe the impact of a totally new culture upon a newcomer. In an extreme instance such shock will be experienced by the Western explorer who is told, halfway through dinner, that he is eating the nice old lady he had been chatting with the previous day—a shock with predictable physiological if not moral consequences. Most explorers no longer encounter cannibalism in their travels today. However, the first encounters with polygamy or with puberty rites or even with the way some nations drive their automobiles can be quite a shock to an American visitor. With the shock may go not only disapproval or disgust but a sense of excitement that things can *really* be that different from what they are at home. To some extent, at least, this is the excitement of any first travel abroad. The experience of sociological discovery could be described as "culture shock" minus geographical displacement. In other words, the sociologist travels at home—with shocking results. He is unlikely to find that he is eating a nice old lady for dinner. But the discovery, for instance, that his own church has considerable money invested in the missile industry or that a few blocks from his home there are people who engage in cultic orgies may not be drastically different in emotional impact. Yet we would not want to imply that sociological discoveries are always or even

usually outrageous to moral sentiment. Not at all. What they have in common with exploration in distant lands, however, is the sudden illumination of new and unsuspected facets of human existence in society. This is the excitement and . . . the humanistic justification of sociology.

People who like to avoid shocking discoveries, who prefer to believe that society is just what they were taught in Sunday School, who like the safety of the rules and the maxims of what Alfred Schuetz has called the "world-taken-for-granted," should stay away from sociology. People who feel no temptation before closed doors, who have no curiosity about human beings, who are content to admire scenery without wondering about the people who live in those houses on the other side of that river, should probably also stay away from sociology. They will find it unpleasant or, at any rate, unrewarding. People who are interested in human beings only if they can change, convert or reform them should also be warned, for they will find sociology much less useful than they hoped. And people whose interest is mainly in their own conceptual constructions will do just as well to turn to the study of little white mice. Sociology will be satisfying, in the long run, only to those who can think of nothing more entrancing than to watch men and to understand things human.

It may now be clear that we have, albeit deliberately, understated the case in the title of this chapter. To be sure, sociology is an individual pastime in the sense that it interests some men and bores others. Some like to observe human beings, others to experiment with mice. The world is big enough to hold all kinds and there is no logical priority for one interest as against another. But the word "pastime" is weak in describing what we mean. Sociology is more like a passion. The sociological perspective is more like a demon that possesses one, that drives one compellingly, again and again, to the questions that are its own. An introduction to sociology is, therefore, an invitation to a very special kind of passion.

THINKING ABOUT THE READING

Peter Berger claims that sociologists are tempted to listen to gossip, peek through key-holes, and look at other people's mail. This can be interpreted to mean that the sociologist has an insatiable curiosity about other people. What are some other behaviors and situations that might capture the attention of the sociologist? How does the sociologist differ from the psychologist or the economist or the historian? Are these fields of study likely to be in competition with sociology or to complement it?

The My Lai Massacre

A Military Crime of Obedience

Herbert Kelman and V. Lee Hamilton

(1989)

March 16, 1968, was a busy day in U.S. history. Stateside, Robert F. Kennedy announced his presidential candidacy, challenging a sitting president from his own party—in part out of opposition to an undeclared and disastrous war. In Vietnam, the war continued. In many ways, March 16 may have been a typical day in that war. We will probably never know. But we do know that on that day a typical company went on a mission—which may or may not have been typical—to a village called Son (or Song) My. Most of what is remembered from that mission occurred in the subhamlet known to Americans as My Lai 4.

The My Lai massacre was investigated and charges were brought in 1969 and 1970. Trials and disciplinary actions lasted into 1971. Entire books have been written about the army's year-long cover-up of the massacre (for example, Hersh, 1972), and the cover-up was a major focus of the army's own investigation of the incident. Our central concern here is the massacre itself—a crime of obedience—and public reactions to such crimes, rather than the lengths to which many went to deny the event. Therefore this account concentrates on one day: March 16, 1968.

Many verbal testimonials to the horrors that occurred at My Lai were available. More unusual was the fact that an army photographer, Ronald Haeberle, was assigned the task of documenting the anticipated military engagement at My Lai—and documented a massacre instead. Later, as the story of the massacre emerged, his photographs were widely distributed and seared the public conscience. What might have been dismissed as unreal or exaggerated was depicted in photographs of demonstrable authenticity. The dominant image appeared on the cover of *Life*: piles of bodies jumbled together in a ditch along a trail—the dead all apparently unarmed. All were Oriental, and all appeared to be children, women, or old men. Clearly there had been a mass execution, one whose image would not quickly fade.

So many bodies (over twenty in the cover photo alone) are hard to imagine as the handi-work of one killer. These were not. They were the product of what we call a crime of obedience. Crimes of obedience begin with orders. But orders are often vague and rarely survive with any clarity the transition from one authority down a chain of subordinates to the ultimate actors. The operation at Son My was no exception.

"Charlie" Company, Company C, under Lt. Col. Frank Barker's command, arrived in Vietnam in December 1967. As the army's investigative unit, directed by Lt. Gen. William R. Peers, characterized the personnel, they "contained no significant deviation from the average" for the time. Seymour S. Hersh (1970) described the "average" more explicitly: "Most of the men in Charlie Company had volunteered for the draft; only a few had gone to college for even one year. Nearly half were black, with a few Mexican-Americans. Most were eighteen to twenty-two years old. The favorite reading matter of Charlie Company, like that of other line infantry units in Vietnam, was comic books" (p. 18). The action at My Lai, like that throughout Vietnam, was fought by a cross-section of those Americans who either believed in the war or lacked the social resources to avoid participating in it. Charlie Company was indeed average for that time, that place, and that war.

Two key figures in Charlie Company were more unusual. The company's commander, Capt. Ernest Medina, was an upwardly mobile Mexican-American who wanted to make the army his career, although he feared that he might never advance beyond captain because of his lack of formal education. His eagerness had earned him a nickname among his men: "Mad Dog Medina." One of his admirers was the platoon leader Second Lt. William L. Calley, Jr., an undistinguished, five-foot-three-inch junior-college dropout who had failed four of the seven courses in which he had enrolled his first year. Many viewed him as one of those "instant officers" made possible only by the army's then-desperate need for manpower. Whatever the cause, he was an insecure leader whose frequent claim was "I'm the boss." His nickname among some of the troops was "Surfside 5½," a reference to the swashbuckling heroes of a popular television show, "Surfside 6."

The Son My operation was planned by Lieutenant Colonel Barker and his staff as a search-and-destroy mission with the objective of rooting out the Forty-eighth Viet Cong Battalion from their base area of Son My village. Apparently no written orders were ever issued. Barker's superior, Col. Oran Henderson, arrived at the staging point the day before. Among the issues he reviewed with the assembled officers were some of the weaknesses of prior operations by their units, including their failure to be appropriately aggressive in pursuit of the enemy. Later briefings by Lieutenant Colonel Barker and his staff asserted that no one except Viet Cong was expected to be in the village after 7 A.M. on the following day. The "innocent" would all be at the market. Those present at the briefings gave conflicting accounts of Barker's exact orders, but he conveyed at least a strong suggestion that the Son My area was to be obliterated. As the army's inquiry reported: "While there is some conflict

in the testimony as to whether LTC Barker ordered the destruction of houses, dwellings, livestock, and other foodstuffs in the Song My area, the preponderance of the evidence indicates that such destruction was implied, if not specifically directed, by his orders of 15 March" (Peers Report, in Goldstein et al., 1976, p. 94).

Evidence that Barker ordered the killing of civilians is even more murky. What does seem clear, however, is that—having asserted that civilians would be away at the market—he did not specify what was to be done with any who might nevertheless be found on the scene. The Peers Report therefore considered it "reasonable to conclude that LTC Barker's minimal or nonexistent instructions concerning the handling of noncombatants created the potential for grave misunderstandings as to his intentions and for interpretation of his orders as authority to fire, without restriction, on all persons found in target area" (Goldstein et al., 1976, p. 95). Since Barker was killed in action in June 1968, his own formal version of the truth was never available.

Charlie Company's Captain Medina was briefed for the operation by Barker and his staff. He then transmitted the already vague orders to his own men. Charlie Company was spoiling for a fight, having been totally frustrated during its months in Vietnam—first by waiting for battles that never came, then by incompetent forays led by inexperienced commanders, and finally by mines and booby traps. In fact, the emotion-laden funeral of a sergeant killed by a booby trap was held on March 15, the day before My Lai. Captain Medina gave the orders for the next day's action at the close of that funeral. Many were in a mood for revenge.

It is again unclear what was ordered. Although all participants were alive by the time of the trials for the massacre, they were either on trial or probably felt under threat of trial. Memories are often flawed and self-serving at such times. It is apparent that Medina relayed to the men at least some of Barker's general message—to expect Viet Cong resistance, to burn, and to kill livestock. It is not clear that he ordered the slaughter of the inhabitants, but some of the men who heard him thought he had. One of those who claimed to have heard such orders was Lt. William Calley.

As March 16 dawned, much was expected of the operation by those who had set it into motion. Therefore a full complement of "brass" was present in helicopters overhead, including Barker, Colonel Henderson, and their superior, Major General Koster (who went on to become commandant of West Point before the story of My Lai broke). On the ground, the troops were to carry with them one reporter and one photographer to immortalize the anticipated battle.

The action for Company C began at 7:30 as their first wave of helicopters touched down near the subhamlet of My Lai 4. By 7:47 all of Company C was present and set to fight. But instead of the Viet Cong Forty-eighth Battalion, My Lai was filled with the old men, women, and children who were supposed to have gone to market. By this time, in their version of the war, and with whatever orders they thought they had heard, the men from Company C were nevertheless ready to find Viet Cong everywhere. By nightfall, the official tally was 128 VC killed and three weapons captured, although later, unofficial body counts ran as high as 500. The operation at Son My was over. And by nightfall, as Hersh reported: "the Viet Cong were back in My Lai 4, helping the survivors bury the dead. It took five days. Most of the funeral speeches were made by the Communist guerrillas. Nguyen Bat was not a Communist at the time of the massacre, but the incident changed his mind. 'After the shooting,' he said, 'all the villagers became Communists'" (1970, p. 74). To this day, the memory of the massacre is kept alive by markers and plaques designating the spots where groups of villagers were killed, by a large statue, and by the My Lai Museum, established in 1975 (Williams, 1985).

But what could have happened to leave American troops reporting a victory over Viet Cong when in fact they had killed hundreds of noncombatants? It is not hard to explain the report of victory; that is the essence of a cover-up. It is harder to understand how the killings came to be committed in the first place, making a cover-up necessary.

Mass Executions and the Defense of Superior Orders

Some of the atrocities on March 16, 1968, were evidently unofficial, spontaneous acts: rapes, tortures, killings. For example, Hersh (1970) describes Charlie Company's Second Platoon as entering "My Lai 4 with guns blazing" (p. 50); more graphically, Lieutenant "Brooks and his men in the second platoon to the north had begun to systematically ransack the hamlet and slaughter the people, kill the livestock, and destroy the crops. Men poured rifle and machine-gun fire into huts without knowing—or seemingly caring—who was inside" (pp. 49–50).

Some atrocities toward the end of the action were part of an almost casual "mopping-up," much of which was the responsibility of Lieutenant LaCross's Third Platoon of Charlie Company. The Peers Report states: "The entire 3rd Platoon then began moving into the western edge of My Lai (4), for the mop-up operation. . . . The squad . . . began to burn the houses in the southwestern portion of the hamlet" (Goldstein et al., 1976, p. 133). They became mingled with other platoons during a series of rapes and killings of survivors for which it was impossible to fix responsibility. Certainly to a Vietnamese all GIs would by this point look alike: "Nineteen-year-old Nguyen Thi Ngoc Tuyet watched a baby trying to open her slain mother's blouse to nurse. A soldier shot the infant while it was struggling with the blouse, and then slashed it with his bayonet." Tuyet also said she saw another baby hacked to death by GIs wielding their bayonets. "Le Tong, a twenty-eight-year-old rice farmer, reported seeing one woman raped after GIs killed her children. Nguyen Khoa, a thirty-seven-year-old peasant, told of a thirteen-year-old girl who was raped before being killed. GIs then attacked Khoa's wife, tearing off her clothes. Before they could rape her, however, Khoa said, their six-year-old son, riddled with bullets, fell and saturated her with blood. The GIs left her alone" (Hersh, 1970, p. 72). All of Company C was implicated in a pattern of death and destruction throughout the hamlet, much of which seemingly lacked rhyme or reason.

But a substantial amount of the killing was organized and traceable to one authority: the First Platoon's Lt. William Calley. Calley was originally charged with 109 killings, almost all of them mass executions at the trail and other locations. He stood trial for 102 of these killings, was convicted of 22 in 1971, and at first received a life sentence. Though others—both superior and subordinate to Calley—were brought to trial, he was the only one convicted for the My Lai crimes. Thus, the only actions of My Lai for which anyone was ever convicted were mass executions, ordered and committed. We suspect that there are commonsense reasons why this one type of killing was singled out. In the midst of rapidly moving events with people running about, an execution of stationary targets is literally a still life that stands out and whose participants are clearly visible. It can be proven that specific people committed specific deeds. An execution, in contrast to the shooting of someone on the run, is also more likely to meet the legal definition of an act resulting from intent—with malice aforethought. Moreover, American military law specifically forbids the killing of unarmed civilians or military prisoners, as does the Geneva Convention between nations. Thus common sense, legal standards, and explicit doctrine all made such actions the likeliest target for prosecution.

When Lieutenant Calley was charged under military law it was for violation of the Uniform Code of Military Justice (UCMJ) Article 118 (murder). This article is similar to civilian codes in that it provides for conviction if an accused:

> without justification or excuse, unlawfully kills a human being, when he—

1. has a premeditated design to kill;

2. intends to kill or inflict great bodily harm;

3. is engaged in an act which is inherently dangerous to others and evinces a wanton disregard of human life; or

4. is engaged in the perpetration or attempted perpetration of burglary, sodomy, rape, robbery, or aggravated arson. (Goldstein et al., 1976, p. 507)

For a soldier, one legal justification for killing is warfare; but warfare is subject to many legal limits and restrictions, including, of course, the inadmissibility of killing unarmed noncombatants or prisoners whom one has disarmed. The pictures of the trail victims at My Lai certainly portrayed one or the other of these. Such an action would be illegal under military law; ordering another to commit such an action would be illegal; and following such an order would be illegal.

But following an order may provide a second and pivotal justification for an act that would be murder when committed by a civilian. American military law assumes that the subordinate is inclined to follow orders, as that is the normal obligation of the role. Hence, legally, obedient subordinates are protected from unreasonable expectations regarding their capacity to evaluate those orders:

> An order requiring the performance of a military duty may be inferred to be legal. An act performed manifestly beyond the scope of authority, or pursuant to an order that a man of ordinary sense and understanding would know to be illegal, or in a wanton manner in the discharge of a lawful duty, is not excusable. (Par. 216, Subpar. *d*, Manual for Courts Martial, United States, 1969 Rev.)

Thus what *may* be excusable is the good-faith carrying out of an order, as long as that order appears to the ordinary soldier to be a legal one. In military law, invoking superior orders moves the question from one of the action's consequences—the body count—to one of evaluating the actor's motives and good sense.

In sum, if anyone is to be brought to justice for a massacre, common sense and legal codes decree that the most appropriate targets are those who make themselves executioners. This is the kind of target the government selected in prosecuting Lieutenant Calley with the greatest fervor. And in a military context, the most promising way in which one can redefine one's undeniable deeds into acceptability is to invoke superior orders. This is what Calley did in attempting to avoid conviction. Since the core legal issues involved points of mass execution—the ditches and trail where America's image of My Lai was formed—we review these events in greater detail.

The day's quiet beginning has already been noted. Troops landed and swept unopposed into the village. The three weapons eventually reported as the haul from the operation were picked up from three apparent Viet Cong who fled the village when the troops arrived and were pursued and killed by helicopter gunships. Obviously the Viet Cong did frequent the area. But it appears that by about 8:00 A.M. no one who met the troops was aggressive, and no one was armed. By the laws of war Charlie Company had no argument with such people.

As they moved into the village, the soldiers began to gather its inhabitants together. Shortly after 8:00 A.M. Lieutenant Calley told Pfc. Paul Meadlo that "you know what to do with" a group of villagers Meadlo was guarding. Estimates of the numbers in the group ranged as high as eighty women, children, and old men, and Meadlo's own estimate under oath was thirty to fifty people. As Meadlo later testified, Calley returned after ten or fifteen minutes: "He [Calley] said, 'How come they're not dead?' I said, 'I didn't know we were supposed to kill them.' He said, 'I want them dead.' He backed off twenty or thirty feet and started shooting into the people—the Viet Cong—shooting automatic. He was beside me. He burned four or five magazines. I burned off a few, about three. I helped shoot 'em" (Hammer, 1971, p. 155). Meadlo himself and others testified that Meadlo cried as he fired; others reported him later to be sobbing and

"all broke up." It would appear that to Lieutenant Calley's subordinates something was unusual, and stressful, in these orders.

At the trial, the first specification in the murder charge against Calley was for this incident; he was accused of premeditated murder of "an unknown number, not less than 30, Oriental human beings, males and females of various ages, whose names are unknown, occupants of the village of My Lai 4, by means of shooting them with a rifle" (Goldstein et al., 1976, p. 497).

Among the helicopters flying reconnaissance above Son My was that of CWO Hugh Thompson. By 9:00 or soon after, Thompson had noticed some horrifying events from his perch. As he spotted wounded civilians, he sent down smoke markers so that soldiers on the ground could treat them. They killed them instead. He reported to headquarters, trying to persuade someone to stop what was going on. Barker, hearing the message, called down to Captain Medina. Medina, in turn, later claimed to have told Calley that it was "enough for today." But it was not yet enough.

At Calley's orders, his men began gathering the remaining villagers—roughly seventy-five individuals, mostly women and children—and herding them toward a drainage ditch. Accompanied by three or four enlisted men, Lieutenant Calley executed several batches of civilians who had been gathered into ditches. Some of the details of the process were entered into testimony in such accounts as Pfc. Dennis Conti's: "A lot of them, the people, were trying to get up and mostly they was just screaming and pretty bad shot up. . . . I seen a woman tried to get up. I seen Lieutenant Calley fire. He hit the side of her head and blew it off" (Hammer, 1971, p. 125).

Testimony by other soldiers presented the shooting's aftermath. Specialist Four Charles Hall, asked by Prosecutor Aubrey Daniel how he knew the people in the ditch were dead, said: "There was blood coming from them. They were just scattered all over the ground in the ditch, some in piles and some scattered out 20, 25 meters perhaps up the ditch. . . . They were very old people, very young children, and mothers. . . . There was blood all over them" (Goldstein et al., 1976, pp. 501–502). And Pfc. Gregory Olsen corroborated the general picture of the victims: "They were—the majority were women and children, some babies. I distinctly remember one middle-aged Vietnamese male dressed in white right at my feet as I crossed. None of the bodies were mangled in any way. There was blood. Some appeared to be dead, others followed me with their eyes as I walked across the ditch" (Goldstein et al., 1976, p. 502).

The second specification in the murder charge stated that Calley did "with premeditation, murder an unknown number of Oriental human beings, not less than seventy, males and females of various ages, whose names are unknown, occupants of the village of My Lai 4, by means of shooting them with a rifle" (Goldstein et al., 1976, p. 497). Calley was also charged with and tried for shootings of individuals (an old man and a child); these charges were clearly supplemental to the main issue at trial—the mass killings and how they came about.

It is noteworthy that during these executions more than one enlisted man avoided carrying out Calley's orders, and more than one, by sworn oath, directly refused to obey them. For example, Pfc. James Joseph Dursi testified, when asked if he fired when Lieutenant Calley ordered him to: "No I just stood there. Meadlo turned to me after a couple of minutes and said 'Shoot! Why don't you shoot! Why don't you fire!' He was crying and yelling. I said, 'I can't! I won't!' And the people were screaming and crying and yelling. They kept firing for a couple of minutes, mostly automatic and semi-automatic" (Hammer, 1971, p. 143). . . .

Disobedience of Lieutenant Calley's own orders to kill represented a serious legal and moral threat to a defense *based* on superior orders, such as Calley was attempting. This defense had to assert that the orders seemed reasonable enough to carry out; that they appeared to be legal orders. Even if the orders in question were not legal, the defense had to assert that an ordinary individual could not and should not be expected to see the distinction. In short, if what happened was "business as usual," even though it might be bad business, then the defendant stood a chance of acquittal. But under direct command from "Surfside 5½," some ordinary enlisted men managed to refuse, to avoid, or at least to stop doing what they were ordered to do. As "reasonable men" of "ordinary sense and understanding," they had apparently found something awry that morning; and it would have been hard for an officer to plead successfully that he was more ordinary than his men in his capacity to evaluate the reasonableness of orders.

Even those who obeyed Calley's orders showed great stress. For example, Meadlo eventually began to argue and cry directly in front of Calley. Pfc. Herbert Carter shot himself in the foot, possibly because he could no longer take what he was doing. We were not destined to hear a sworn version of the incident, since neither side at the Calley trial called him to testify.

The most unusual instance of resistance to authority came from the skies. CWO Hugh Thompson, who had protested the apparent carnage of civilians, was Calley's inferior in rank but was not in his line of command. He was also watching the ditch from his helicopter and noticed some people moving after the first round of slaughter—chiefly children who had been shielded by their mothers' bodies. Landing to rescue the wounded, he also found some villagers hiding in a nearby bunker. Protecting the Vietnamese with his own body, Thompson ordered his men to train their guns on the Americans and to open fire if the Americans fired on the Vietnamese. He then radioed for additional rescue helicopters and stood between the Vietnamese and the Americans under Calley's command until the Vietnamese could be evacuated. He later returned to the ditch to unearth a child buried, unharmed, beneath layers of bodies. In October 1969, Thompson was awarded the Distinguished Flying Cross for heroism at

My Lai, specifically (albeit inaccurately) for the rescue of children hiding in a bunker "between Viet Cong forces and advancing friendly forces" and for the rescue of a wounded child "caught in the intense crossfire" (Hersh, 1970, p. 119). Four months earlier, at the Pentagon, Thompson had identified Calley as having been at the ditch.

By about 10:00 A.M., the massacre was winding down. The remaining actions consisted largely of isolated rapes and killings, "clean-up" shootings of the wounded, and the destruction of the village by fire. We have already seen some examples of these more indiscriminate and possibly less premeditated acts. By the 11:00 A.M. lunch break, when the exhausted men of Company C were relaxing, two young girls wandered back from a hiding place only to be invited to share lunch. This surrealist touch illustrates the extent to which the soldiers' action had become dissociated from its meaning. An hour earlier, some of these men were making sure that not even a child would escape the executioner's bullet. But now the job was done and it was time for lunch—and in this new context it seemed only natural to ask the children who had managed to escape execution to join them. The massacre had ended. It remained only for the Viet Cong to reap the political rewards among the survivors in hiding.

The army command in the area knew that something had gone wrong. Direct commanders, including Lieutenant Colonel Barker, had firsthand reports, such as Thompson's complaints. Others had such odd bits of evidence as the claim of 128 Viet Cong dead with a booty of only three weapons. But the cover-up of My Lai began at once. The operation was reported as a victory over a stronghold of the Viet Cong Forty-eighth. . . .

William Calley was not the only man tried for the event at My Lai. The actions of over thirty soldiers and civilians were scrutinized by investigators; over half of these had to face charges or disciplinary action of some sort. Targets of investigation included Captain Medina, who was tried, and various higher-ups, including General Koster. But Lieutenant Calley was the only person convicted, the only person to serve time.

The core of Lieutenant Calley's defense was superior orders. What this meant to him—in contrast to what it meant to the judge and jury—can be gleaned from his responses to a series of questions from his defense attorney, George Latimer, in which Calley sketched out his understanding of the laws of war and the actions that constitute doing one's duty within those laws:

Latimer: Did you receive any training which had to do with the obedience to orders?

Calley: Yes, sir.

Latimer: . . . what were you informed [were] the principles involved in that field?

Calley: That all orders were to be assumed legal, that the soldier's job was to carry out any order given him to the best of his ability.

Latimer: . . . what might occur if you disobeyed an order by a senior officer?

Calley: You could be court-martialed for refusing an order and refusing an order in the face of the enemy, you could be sent to death, sir.

Latimer: [I am asking] whether you were required in any way, shape or form to make a determination of the legality or illegality of an order?

Calley: No, sir. I was never told that I had the choice, sir.

Latimer: If you had a doubt about the order, what were you supposed to do?

Calley: . . . I was supposed to carry the order out and then come back and make my complaint. (Hammer, 1971, pp. 240–241)

Lieutenant Calley steadfastly maintained that his actions within My Lai had constituted, in his mind, carrying out orders from Captain Medina. Both his own actions and the orders he gave to others (such as the instruction to Meadlo to "waste 'em") were entirely in response to superior orders. He denied any intent to kill individuals and any but the most passing awareness of distinctions among the individuals: "I was ordered to go in there and destroy the enemy. That was my job on that day. That was the mission I was given. I did not sit down and think in terms of men, women, and children. They were all classified the same, and that was the classification that we dealt with, just as enemy soldiers." When Latimer asked if in his own opinion Calley had acted "rightly and according to your understanding of your directions and orders," Calley replied, "I felt then and I still do that I acted as I was directed, and I carried out the orders that I was given, and I do not feel wrong in doing so, sir" (Hammer, 1971, p. 257).

His court-martial did not accept Calley's defense of superior orders and clearly did not share his interpretation of his duty. The jury evidently reasoned that, even if there had been orders to destroy everything in sight and to "waste the Vietnamese," any reasonable person would have realized that such orders were illegal and should have refused to carry them out. The defense of superior orders under such conditions is inadmissible under international and military law. The U.S. Army's *Law of Land Warfare* (Dept. of the Army, 1956), for example, states that "the fact that the law of war has been violated pursuant to an order of a superior authority, whether military or civil, does not deprive the act in question of its character of a war crime, nor does it constitute a defense in the trial of an accused individual, unless he did not know and could not reasonably have been expected to know that the act was unlawful" and that "members of the armed forces are bound to obey only lawful orders" (in Falk et al., 1971, pp. 71–72).

The disagreement between Calley and the court-martial seems to have revolved around the definition of the responsibilities of a subordinate to obey, on the one hand, and to evaluate, on the other. This tension . . . can best be captured via the charge to the jury in the Calley court-martial, made by the trial judge, Col. Reid Kennedy. The forty-one pages of the charge include the following:

> Both combatants captured by and noncombatants detained by the opposing force . . . have the right to be treated as prisoners. . . . Summary execution of detainees or prisoners is forbidden by law. . . . I therefore instruct you . . . that if unresisting human beings were killed at My Lai (4) while within the effective custody and control of our military forces, their deaths cannot be considered justified. . . . Thus if you find that Lieutenant Calley received an order directing him to kill unresisting Vietnamese within his control or within the control of his troops, *that order would be an illegal order.*

A determination that an order is illegal does not, of itself, assign criminal responsibility to the person following the order for acts done in compliance with it. Soldiers are taught to follow orders, and special attention is given to obedience of orders on the battlefield. Military effectiveness depends on obedience to orders. On the other hand, the obedience of a soldier is not the obedience of an automaton. A soldier is a reasoning agent, obliged to respond, not as a machine, but as a person. The law takes these factors into account in assessing criminal responsibility for acts done in compliance with illegal orders.

> The acts of a subordinate done in compliance with an unlawful order given him by his superior are excused and impose no criminal liability upon him unless the superior's order is one which a man of *ordinary sense and understanding* would, under the circumstances, know to be unlawful, or if the order in question is actually known to the accused to be unlawful. (Goldstein et al., 1976, pp. 525–526; emphasis added)

By this definition, subordinates take part in a balancing act, one tipped toward obedience but tempered by "ordinary sense and understanding."

A jury of combat veterans proceeded to convict William Calley of the premeditated murder of no less than twenty-two human beings. (The army, realizing some unfortunate connotations in referring to the victims as "Oriental human beings," eventually referred to them as "human beings.") Regarding the first specification in the murder charge, the bodies on the trail, [Calley] was convicted of premeditated murder of not less than one person. (Medical testimony had been able to pinpoint only one person whose wounds as revealed in Haeberle's photos were sure to be immediately fatal.) Regarding the second specification, the bodies in the ditch, Calley was convicted of the premeditated murder of not less than twenty human beings. Regarding additional specifications that he had killed an old man and a child, Calley was convicted of premeditated murder in the first case and of assault with intent to commit murder in the second.

Lieutenant Calley was initially sentenced to life imprisonment. That sentence was reduced: first to twenty years, eventually to ten (the latter by Secretary of Defense Callaway in 1974). Calley served three years before being released on bond. The time was spent under house arrest in his apartment, where he was able to receive visits from his girlfriend. He was granted parole on September 10, 1975.

Sanctioned Massacres

The slaughter at My Lai is an instance of a class of violent acts that can be described as sanctioned massacres (Kelman, 1973): acts of indiscriminate, ruthless, and often systematic mass violence, carried out by military or paramilitary personnel while engaged in officially sanctioned campaigns, the victims of which are defenseless and unresisting civilians, including old men, women, and children. Sanctioned massacres have occurred throughout history. Within American history, My Lai had its precursors in the Philippine war around the turn of the century (Schirmer, 1971) and in the massacres of American Indians. Elsewhere in the world, one recalls the Nazis' "final solution" for European Jews, the massacres and deportations of Armenians by Turks, the liquidation of the kulaks and the great purges in the Soviet Union, and more recently the massacres in Indonesia and Bangladesh, in Biafra and Burundi, in South Africa and Mozambique, in Cambodia and Afghanistan, in Syria and Lebanon. . . .

The occurrence of sanctioned massacres cannot be adequately explained by the existence of psychological forces—whether these be characterological dispositions to engage in murderous violence or profound hostility against the target—so powerful that they must find expression in violent acts unhampered by moral restraints. Instead, the major instigators for this class of violence derive from the policy process. The question that really calls for psychological analysis is why so many people are willing to formulate, participate in, and condone policies that call for the mass killings of defenseless civilians. Thus it is more instructive to look not at the motives for violence but at the conditions under which the usual moral inhibitions against violence become weakened. Three social processes that tend to create such conditions can be identified: authorization, routinization, and dehumanization. Through authorization, the situation becomes so defined that the individual is absolved of the responsibility to make personal moral choices. Through routinization, the action becomes so organized that there is no opportunity for raising moral questions. Through dehumanization, the actors' attitudes toward the target and toward themselves become so structured that it is neither necessary nor possible for them to view the relationship in moral terms.

Authorization

Sanctioned massacres by definition occur in the context of an authority situation, a situation in which, at least for many of the participants, the moral principles that generally govern human relationships do not apply. Thus, when acts of violence are explicitly ordered, implicitly encouraged, tacitly approved, or at least permitted by legitimate authorities, people's readiness to commit or condone them is enhanced. That such acts are authorized seems to carry automatic justification for them. Behaviorally, authorization obviates the necessity of making judgments or choices. Not only do normal moral principles become inoperative, but—particularly when the actions are explicitly ordered—a different kind of morality, linked to the duty to obey superior orders, tends to take over.

In an authority situation, individuals characteristically feel obligated to obey the orders of the authorities, whether or not these correspond with their personal preferences. They see themselves as having no choice as long as they accept the legitimacy of the orders and of the authorities who give them. Individuals differ considerably in the degree to which—and the conditions under which—they are prepared to challenge the legitimacy of an order on the grounds that the order itself is illegal, or that those giving it have overstepped their authority, or that it stems from a policy that violates fundamental societal values. Regardless of such individual differences, however, the basic structure of a situation of legitimate authority requires subordinates to respond in terms of their role obligations rather than their personal preferences; they can openly disobey only by challenging the legitimacy of the authority. Often people obey without question even though the behavior they engage in may entail great personal sacrifice or great harm to others.

An important corollary of the basic structure of the authority situation is that actors often do not see themselves as personally responsible for the consequences of their actions. Again, there are individual differences, depending on actors' capacity and readiness to evaluate the legitimacy of orders received. Insofar as they see themselves as having had no choice in their actions, however, they do not feel personally responsible for them. They were not personal agents, but merely extensions of the authority. Thus, when their actions cause harm to others, they can feel relatively free of guilt. A similar mechanism operates when a person engages in antisocial behavior that was not ordered by the authorities but was tacitly encouraged and approved by them—even if only by making it clear that such behavior will not be punished. In this situation, behavior that was formerly illegitimate is legitimized by the authorities' acquiescence.

In the My Lai massacre, it is likely that the structure of the authority situation contributed to the massive violence in both ways—that is, by conveying the message that acts of violence against Vietnamese villagers were *required,* as well as the message that such acts, even if not ordered, were *permitted* by the authorities in charge. The actions at My Lai represented, at least in some respects, responses to explicit or implicit orders. Lieutenant Calley indicated, by orders and by example, that he wanted large numbers of villagers killed. Whether Calley himself had been ordered by his superiors to "waste" the whole area, as he claimed, remains a matter of controversy. Even if we assume, however, that he was not explicitly ordered to wipe out the village, he had reason to believe that such actions were expected by his superior officers. Indeed, the very nature of the war conveyed this expectation. The principal measure of military success was the "body count"—the number of enemy soldiers killed—and any Vietnamese killed by the U.S. military was commonly defined as a "Viet Cong." Thus, it was not totally bizarre for Calley to believe that what he was doing at My Lai was to increase his body count, as any good officer was expected to do.

Even to the extent that the actions at My Lai occurred spontaneously, without reference to superior orders, those committing them had reason to assume that such actions might be tacitly approved of by the military authorities. Not only had they failed to punish such acts in most cases, but the very strategies and tactics that the authorities consistently devised were based on the proposition that the civilian population of South Vietnam—whether "hostile" or "friendly"—was expendable. Such policies as search-and-destroy missions, the establishment of free-shooting zones, the use of antipersonnel weapons, the bombing of entire villages if they were suspected of harboring guerrillas, the forced migration of masses of the rural population, and the defoliation of vast forest areas helped legitimize acts of massive violence of the kind occurring at My Lai.

Some of the actions at My Lai suggest an orientation to authority based on unquestioning obedience to superior orders, no matter how destructive the actions these orders call for. Such obedience is specifically fostered in the course of military training and reinforced by the structure of the military authority situation. It also reflects, however, an ideological orientation that may be more widespread in the general population. . . .

Routinization

Authorization processes create a situation in which people become involved in an action without considering its implications and without really making a decision. Once they have taken the initial step, they are in a new psychological and social situation in which the pressures to continue are powerful. As Lewin (1947) has pointed out, many forces that might originally have kept people out of a situation reverse direction once they have made a commitment (once they have gone through the "gate region") and now serve to keep them in the situation. For example, concern about the criminal nature of an action, which might originally have inhibited a person from becoming involved, may now lead to deeper involvement in efforts to justify the action and to avoid negative consequences.

Despite these forces, however, given the nature of the actions involved in sanctioned massacres, one might still expect moral scruples to intervene; but the likelihood of moral resistance is greatly reduced by transforming the action into routine, mechanical, highly programmed operations. Routinization fulfills two functions. First, it reduces the necessity of making decisions, thus minimizing the occasions in which moral questions may arise. Second, it makes it easier to avoid the implications of the action, since the actor focuses on the details of the job rather than on its meaning. The latter effect is more readily achieved among those who participate in sanctioned massacres from a distance—from their desks or even from the cockpits of their bombers.

Routinization operates both at the level of the individual actor and at the organizational level. Individual job performance is broken down into a series of discrete steps, most of them carried out in automatic, regularized fashion. It becomes easy to forget the nature of the product that emerges from this process. When Lieutenant Calley said of My Lai that it was "no great deal," he probably implied that it was all in a day's work. Organizationally, the task is divided among different offices, each of which has responsibility for a small portion of it. This arrangement diffuses responsibility and limits the amount and scope of decision making that is necessary. There is no expectation that the moral implications will be considered at any of these points, nor is there any opportunity to do so. The organizational processes also help further legitimize the actions of each participant. By proceeding in routine fashion—processing papers, exchanging memos, diligently carrying out their assigned tasks—the different units mutually reinforce each other in the view that what is going on must be perfectly normal, correct, and legitimate. The shared illusion that they are engaged in a legitimate enterprise helps the participants assimilate their activities to other purposes, such as the efficiency of their performance, the productivity of their unit, or the cohesiveness of their group (see Janis, 1972).

Normalization of atrocities is more difficult to the extent that there are constant reminders of the true meaning of the enterprise. Bureaucratic inventiveness in the use of language helps to cover up such meaning. For example, the SS had a set of *Sprachregelungen,* or "language rules," to govern descriptions of their extermination program. As Arendt (1964) points out, the term *language rule* in itself was "a code name; it meant what in ordinary language would be called a lie" (p. 85). The code names for killing and liquidation were "final solution," "evacuation," and "special treatment." The war in Indochina produced its own set of euphemisms, such as "protective reaction," "pacification," and "forced-draft urbanization and modernization." The use of euphemisms allows participants in sanctioned massacres to differentiate their actions from ordinary killing and destruction and thus to avoid confronting their true meaning.

Dehumanization

Authorization processes override standard moral considerations; routinization processes reduce the likelihood that such considerations will arise. Still, the inhibitions against murdering one's fellow human beings are generally so strong that the victims must also be stripped of their human status if they are to be subjected to systematic killing. Insofar as they are dehumanized, the usual principles of morality no longer apply to them.

Sanctioned massacres become possible to the extent that the victims are deprived in the perpetrators' eyes of the two qualities essential to being perceived as fully human and included in the moral compact that governs human relationships: *identity*—standing as independent, distinctive individuals, capable of making choices and entitled to live their own lives— and *community*—fellow membership in an interconnected network of individuals who care for each other and respect each other's individuality and rights (Kelman, 1973; see also Bakan, 1966, for a related distinction between "agency" and "communion"). Thus, when a group of people is defined entirely in terms of a category to which they belong, and when this category is excluded from the human family, moral restraints against killing them are more readily overcome.

Dehumanization of the enemy is a common phenomenon in any war situation. Sanctioned massacres, however, presuppose a more extreme degree of dehumanization, insofar as the killing is not in direct response to the target's threats or provocations. It is not what they have done that marks such victims for death but who they are— the category to which they happen to belong. They are the victims of policies that regard their systematic destruction as a desirable end or an acceptable means. Such extreme dehumanization becomes possible when the target group can readily be identified as a separate category of people who have historically been stigmatized and excluded by the victimizers; often the victims belong to a distinct racial, religious, ethnic, or political group regarded as inferior or sinister. The traditions, the habits, the images, and the vocabularies for dehumanizing such groups are already well established and can be drawn upon when the groups are selected for massacre. Labels help deprive the victims of identity and community, as in the epithet "gooks" that was commonly used to refer to Vietnamese and other Indochinese peoples.

The dynamics of the massacre process itself further increase the participants' tendency to dehumanize their victims. Those who participate as part of the bureaucratic apparatus increasingly come to see their victims as bodies to be counted and entered into their reports, as faceless figures that will determine their productivity rates and promotions. Those who participate in the massacre directly—in the field, as it were—are reinforced in their perception of the victims as less than human by observing their very victimization. The only way they can justify what is being done to these people—both by others and by themselves—and the only way they can extract some degree of meaning out of the absurd events in which they find themselves participating (see Lifton, 1971, 1973) is by coming to believe that the victims are subhuman and deserve to be rooted out. And thus the process of dehumanization feeds on itself.

REFERENCES

Arendt, H. (1964). *Eichmann in Jerusalem: A report on the banality of evil.* New York: Viking Press.

Bakan, D. (1966). *The duality of human existence.* Chicago: Rand McNally.

Department of the Army. (1956). *The law of land warfare* (Field Manual, No. 27-10). Washington, DC: U.S. Government Printing Office.

Falk, R. A., Kolko, G., & Lifton, R. J. (Eds.). (1971). *Crimes of war.* New York: Vintage Books.

French, P. (Ed.). (1972). *Individual and collective responsibility: The massacre at My Lai.* Cambridge, MA: Schenkman.

Goldstein, J., Marshall, B., & Schwartz, J. (Eds.). (1976). *The My Lai massacre and its cover-up:*

Beyond the reach of law? (The Peers Report with a supplement and introductory essay on the limits of law). New York: Free Press.

Hammer, R. (1971). *The court-martial of Lt. Calley.* New York: Coward, McCann, & Geoghegan.

Hersh, S. (1970). *My Lai 4: A report on the massacre and its aftermath.* New York: Vintage Books.

_____. (1972). *Cover-up.* New York: Random House.

Janis, I. L. (1972). *Victims of groupthink: A psychological study of foreign-policy decisions and fiascoes.* Boston: Houghton Mifflin.

Kelman, H. C. (1973). Violence without moral restraint: Reflections on the dehumanization of victims and victimizers. *Journal of Social Issues, 29*(4), 25–61.

Lewin, K. (1947). Group decision and social change. In T. M. Newcomb & E. L. Hartley (Eds.), *Readings in social psychology.* New York: Holt.

Lifton, R. J. (1971). Existential evil. In N. Sanford, C. Comstock, & Associates, *Sanctions for evil: Sources of social destructiveness.* San Francisco: Jossey-Bass.

_____. (1973). *Home from the war—Vietnam veterans: Neither victims nor executioners.* New York: Simon & Schuster.

Manual for courts martial, United States (Rev. ed.). (1969). Washington, DC: U.S. Government Printing Office.

Schirmer, D. B. (1971, April 24). My Lai was not the first time. *New Republic,* pp. 18–21.

Williams, B. (1985, April 14–15). "I will never forgive," says My Lai survivor. *Jordan Times* (Amman), p. 4.

THINKING ABOUT THE READING

According to Kelman and Hamilton, social processes can create conditions under which usual restraints against violence are weakened. What social processes were in evidence during the My Lai massacre? The incident they describe provides us with an uncomfortable picture of human nature. Do you think most people would have reacted the way the soldiers at My Lai did? Are we all potential massacrers? Does the phenomenon of obedience to authority go beyond the tightly structured environment of the military? Can you think of incidents in your own life when you've done something—perhaps harmed or humiliated another person—because of the powerful influence of others? How might Kelman and Hamilton explain the actions of the individuals who carried out the hijackings and attacks of September 11, 2001, or of the American soldiers who abused Iraqi prisoners in their custody?

Seeing and Thinking Sociologically

2

Where is society located? This is an intriguing question. Society shapes our behavior and beliefs through social institutions such as religion, law, education, economics, and family. At the same time, we shape society through our interactions with one another and our participation in social institutions. In this way, we can say that society exists as an objective entity that transcends us. But it is also a construction that is created, reaffirmed, and altered through everyday interactions and behavior. Humans are social beings. We constantly look to others to help define and interpret the situations in which we find ourselves. Other people can influence what we see, feel, think, and do. But it's not just other people who influence us. We also live in a *society*, which consists of socially recognizable combinations of individuals—relationships, groups, and organizations—as well as the products of human action—statuses, roles, culture, and institutions. When we behave, we do so in a social context that consists of a combination of institutional arrangements, cultural influences, and interpersonal expectations. Thus, our behavior in any given situation is our own, but the reasons we do what we do are rooted in these more complex social factors.

This social structure provides us with a sense of order in our daily lives. But sometimes that order breaks down. In "Culture of Fear," Barry Glassner shows us how the news media function to *create* a culture that the public takes for granted. He focuses, in particular, on the emotion of fear in U.S. society. We constantly hear horror stories about such urgent social problems as deadly diseases, violent strangers, and out-of-control teens. But Glassner points out that the terrified public concern over certain issues is often inflated by the media and largely unwarranted. Ironically, when we live in a culture of fear, our most serious problems often go ignored.

Sociologists work to shed light on taken-for-granted social problems, but acquiring trustworthy information is often difficult. Patricia Adler provides an interesting example of how sociologists do research on controversial topics in "Researching Dealers and Smugglers." To many people, the sellers and users of illegal drugs are a dangerous scourge on American society. Adler was interested in understanding the upper echelons of the illicit drug trade—a small, secretive group of people condemned by most people in society but understood by few. Given the illegal and potentially dangerous activities involved, it is unlikely that drug smugglers would willingly answer questions about their trade on a survey or in an interview. So Adler and her husband established close friendships with dealers and smugglers and used a research technique called participant observation to collect inside information about their activities. Putting oneself in the world of one's research subjects can provide rich information, but it can also cause serious potential dangers.

Something to Consider as You Read

When reading the selections in this section, consider the kinds of rules sociologists use in deciding if something is worth studying. What rules do media journalists use in deciding whether a story is interesting? What role might politics play in decisions of both science and the media about what topics to focus on? How do such decisions shape our perception of important social problems?

Culture of Fear

Barry Glassner

(1999)

Why are so many fears in the air, and so many of them unfounded? Why, as crime rates plunged throughout the 1990s, did two-thirds of Americans believe they were soaring? How did it come about that by mid-decade 62 percent of us described ourselves as "truly desperate" about crime—almost twice as many as in the late 1980s, when crime rates were higher? Why, on a survey in 1997, when the crime rate had already fallen for a half dozen consecutive years, did more than half of us disagree with the statement "This country is finally beginning to make some progress in solving the crime problem"?[1]

In the late 1990s the number of drug users had decreased by half compared to a decade earlier; almost two-thirds of high school seniors had never used any illegal drugs, even marijuana. So why did a majority of adults rank drug abuse as the greatest danger to America's youth? Why did nine out of ten believe the drug problem is out of control, and only one in six believe the country was making progress?[2]

Give us a happy ending and we write a new disaster story. In the late 1990s the unemployment rate was below 5 percent for the first time in a quarter century. People who had been pounding the pavement for years could finally get work. Yet pundits warned of imminent economic disaster. They predicted inflation would take off, just as they had a few years earlier—also erroneously—when the unemployment rate dipped below 6 percent.[3]

We compound our worries beyond all reason. Life expectancy in the United States has doubled during the twentieth century. We are better able to cure and control diseases than

any other civilization in history. Yet we hear that phenomenal numbers of us are dreadfully ill. In 1996 Bob Garfield, a magazine writer, reviewed articles about serious diseases published over the course of a year in the *Washington Post,* the *New York Times,* and *USA Today.* He learned that, in addition to 59 million Americans with heart disease, 53 million with migraines, 25 million with osteoporosis, 16 million with obesity, and 3 million with cancer, many Americans suffer from more obscure ailments such as temporomandibular joint disorders (10 million) and brain injuries (2 million). Adding up the estimates, Garfield determined that 543 million Americans are seriously sick—a shocking number in a nation of 266 million inhabitants. "Either as a society we are doomed, or someone is seriously double-dipping," he suggested.[4]

Garfield appears to have underestimated one category of patients: for psychiatric ailments his figure was 53 million. Yet when Jim Windolf, an editor of the *New York Observer,* collated estimates for maladies ranging from borderline personality disorder (10 million) and sex addiction (11 million) to less well-known conditions such as restless leg syndrome (12 million) he came up with a figure of 152 million. "But give the experts a little time," he advised. "With another new quantifiable disorder or two, everybody in the country will be officially nuts."[5]

Indeed, Windolf omitted from his estimates new-fashioned afflictions that have yet to make it into the *Diagnostic and Statistical Manual of Mental Disorders* of the American Psychiatric Association: ailments such as road rage, which afflicts more than half of

Americans, according to a psychologist's testimony before a congressional hearing in 1997.[6]

The scope of our health fears seems limitless. Besides worrying disproportionately about legitimate ailments and prematurely about would-be diseases, we continue to fret over already refuted dangers. Some still worry, for instance, about "flesh-eating bacteria," a bug first rammed into our consciousness in 1994 when the U.S. news media picked up on a screamer headline in a British tabloid, "Killer Bug Ate My Face." The bacteria, depicted as more brutal than anything seen in modern times, was said to be spreading faster than the pack of photographers outside the home of its latest victim. In point of fact, however, we were not "terribly vulnerable" to these "superbugs," nor were they "medicine's worst nightmares," as voices in the media warned.

Group A strep, a cyclical strain that has been around for ages, had been dormant for half a century or more before making a comeback. The British pseudoepidemic had resulted in a total of about a dozen deaths in the previous year. Medical experts roundly rebutted the scares by noting that of 20 to 30 million strep infections each year in the United States fewer than 1 in 1,000 involve serious strep A complications, and only 500 to 1,500 people suffer the flesh-eating syndrome, whose proper name is necrotizing fasciitis. Still the fear persisted. Years after the initial scare, horrifying news stories continued to appear, complete with grotesque pictures of victims. A United Press International story in 1998 typical of the genre told of a child in Texas who died of the "deadly strain" of bacteria that the reporter warned "can spread at a rate of up to one inch per hour."[7]

Killer Kids

When we are not worrying about deadly diseases we worry about homicidal strangers. Every few months for the past several years it seems we discover a new category of people to fear: government thugs in Waco, sadistic cops on Los Angeles

freeways and in Brooklyn police stations, mass-murdering youths in small towns all over the country. A single anomalous event can provide us with multiple groups of people to fear. After the 1995 explosion at the federal building in Oklahoma City first we panicked about Arabs. "Knowing that the car bomb indicates Middle Eastern terrorists at work, it's safe to assume that their goal is to promote free-floating fear and a measure of anarchy, thereby disrupting American life," a *New York Post* editorial asserted. "Whatever we are doing to destroy Mideast terrorism, the chief terrorist threat against Americans, has not been working," wrote A. M. Rosenthal in the *New York Times*.[8]

When it turned out that the bombers were young white guys from middle America, two more groups instantly became spooky: right-wing radio talk show hosts who criticize the government—depicted by President Bill Clinton as "purveyors of hatred and division"— and members of militias. No group of disgruntled men was too ragtag not to warrant big, prophetic news stories.[9]

We have managed to convince ourselves that just about every young American male is a potential mass murderer—a remarkable achievement, considering the steep downward trend in youth crime throughout the 1990s. Faced year after year with comforting statistics, we either ignore them—adult Americans estimate that people under eighteen commit about half of all violent crimes when the actual number is 13 percent—or recast them as "The Lull Before the Storm" (*Newsweek* headline). "We know we've got about six years to turn this juvenile crime thing around or our country is going to be living with chaos," Bill Clinton asserted in 1997, even while acknowledging that the youth violent crime rate had fallen 9.2 percent the previous year.[10]

The more things improve the more pessimistic we become. Violence-related deaths at the nation's schools dropped to a record low during the 1996–97 academic year (19 deaths out of 54 million children), and only one in ten public schools reported *any* serious crime. Yet

Time and *U.S. News & World Report* both ran headlines in 1996 referring to "Teenage Time Bombs." In a nation of "Children Without Souls" (another *Time* headline that year), "America's beleaguered cities are about to be victimized by a paradigm shattering wave of ultraviolent, morally vacuous young people some call 'the superpredators,'" William Bennett, the former Secretary of Education, and John DiIulio, a criminologist, forecast in a book published in 1996.[11]

Instead of the arrival of superpredators, violence by urban youths continued to decline. So we went looking elsewhere for proof that heinous behavior by young people was "becoming increasingly more commonplace in America" (CNN). After a sixteen-year-old in Pearl, Mississippi, and a fourteen-year-old in West Paducah, Kentucky, went on shooting sprees in late 1997, killing five of their classmates and wounding twelve others, these isolated incidents were taken as evidence of "an epidemic of seemingly depraved adolescent murderers" (Geraldo Rivera). Three months later in March 1998 all sense of proportion vanished after two boys ages eleven and thirteen killed four students and a teacher in Jonesboro, Arkansas. No longer, we learned in *Time,* was it "unusual for kids to get back at the world with live ammunition." When a child psychologist on NBC's "Today" show advised parents to reassure their children that shootings at schools are rare, reporter Ann Curry corrected him. "But this is the fourth case since October," she said.[12]

Over the next couple of months young people failed to accommodate the trend hawkers. None committed mass murder. Fear of killer kids remained very much in the air nonetheless. In stories on topics such as school safety and childhood trauma, reporters recapitulated the gory details of the killings. And the news media made a point of reporting every incident in which a child was caught at school with a gun or making a death threat. In May, when a fifteen-year-old in Springfield, Oregon, did open fire in a cafeteria filled with students, killing two and wounding twenty-three others,

the event felt like a continuation of a "disturbing trend" (*New York Times*). The day after the shooting, on National Public Radio's "All Things Considered," the criminologist Vincent Schiraldi tried to explain that the recent string of incidents did not constitute a trend, that youth homicide rates had declined by 30 percent in recent years, and more than three times as many people were killed by lightning than by violence at schools. But the show's host, Robert Siegel, interrupted him. "You're saying these are just anomalous events?" he asked, audibly peeved. The criminologist reiterated that *anomalous* is precisely the right word to describe the events, and he called it "a grave mistake" to imagine otherwise.

Yet given what had happened in Mississippi, Kentucky, Arkansas, and Oregon, could anyone doubt that today's youths are "more likely to pull a gun than make a fist," as Katie Couric declared on the "Today" show?[13]

Roosevelt Was Wrong

We had better learn to doubt our inflated fears before they destroy us. Valid fears have their place; they cue us to danger. False and overdrawn fears only cause hardship.

Even concerns about real dangers, when blown out of proportion, do demonstrable harm. Take the fear of cancer. Many Americans overestimate the prevalence of the disease, underestimate the odds of surviving it, and put themselves at greater risk as a result. Women in their forties believe they have a 1 in 10 chance of dying from breast cancer, a Dartmouth study found. Their real lifetime odds are more like 1 in 250. Women's heightened perception of risk, rather than motivating them to get checkups or seek treatment, can have the opposite effect. A study of daughters of women with breast cancer found an inverse correlation between fear and prevention: the greater a daughter's fear of the disease the less frequent her breast self-examination. Studies of the general population—both men and women—find that large numbers of people who believe they have symptoms of cancer delay going to a doctor, often for several months. When asked why, they report they are terrified about the pain and financial ruin cancer can cause as well as poor prospects for a cure. The irony of course is that early treatment can prevent precisely those horrors they most fear.[14]

Still more ironic, if harder to measure, are the adverse consequences of public panics. Exaggerated perceptions of the risks of cancer at least produce beneficial by-products, such as bountiful funding for research and treatment of this leading cause of death. When it comes to large-scale panics, however, it is difficult to see how potential victims benefit from the frenzy. Did panics a few years ago over sexual assaults on children by preschool teachers and priests leave children better off? Or did they prompt teachers and clergy to maintain excessive distance from children in their care, as social scientists and journalists who have studied the panics suggest? How well can care givers do their jobs when regulatory agencies, teachers' unions, and archdioceses explicitly prohibit them from any physical contact with children, even kindhearted hugs?[15]

Was it a good thing for children and parents that male day care providers left the profession for fear of being falsely accused of sex crimes? In an article in the *Journal of American Culture,* sociologist Mary DeYoung has argued that day care was "refeminized" as a result of the panics. "Once again, and in the time-honored and very familiar tradition of the family, the primary responsibility for the care and socialization of young children was placed on the shoulders of low-paid women," she contends.[16]

We all pay one of the costs of panics: huge sums of money go to waste. Hysteria over the ritual abuse of children cost billions of dollars in police investigations, trials, and imprisonments. Men and women went to jail for years "on the basis of some of the most fantastic claims ever presented to an American jury," as Dorothy Rabinowitz of the *Wall Street Journal* demonstrated in a series of investigative articles for which she became a Pulitzer Prize finalist in 1996. Across the nation expensive

surveillance programs were implemented to protect children from fiends who reside primarily in the imaginations of adults.[17]

The price tag for our panic about overall crime has grown so monumental that even law-and-order zealots find it hard to defend. The criminal justice system costs Americans close to $100 billion a year, most of which goes to police and prisons. In California we spend more on jails than on higher education. Yet increases in the number of police and prison cells do not correlate consistently with reductions in the number of serious crimes committed. Criminologists who study reductions in homicide rates, for instance, find little difference between cities that substantially expand their police forces and prison capacity and others that do not.[18]

The turnabout in domestic public spending over the past quarter century, from child welfare and antipoverty programs to incarceration, did not even produce reductions in *fear* of crime. Increasing the number of cops and jails arguably has the opposite effect: it suggests that the crime problem is all the more out of control.[19]

Panic-driven public spending generates over the long term a pathology akin to one found in drug addicts. The more money and attention we fritter away on our compulsions, the less we have available for our real needs, which consequently grow larger. While fortunes are being spent to protect children from dangers that few ever encounter, approximately 11 million children lack health insurance, 12 million are malnourished, and rates of illiteracy are increasing.[20]

I do not contend, as did President Roosevelt in 1933, that "the only thing we have to fear is fear itself." My point is that we often fear the wrong things. In the 1990s middle-income and poorer Americans should have worried about unemployment insurance, which covered a smaller share of workers than twenty years earlier. Many of us have had friends or family out of work during economic downturns or as a result of corporate restructuring. Living in a nation with one of the largest income gaps of any industrialized country, where the bottom 40 percent of the population is worse off financially than their counterparts two decades earlier, we might also have worried about income inequality. Or poverty. During the mid- and late 1990s 5 million elderly Americans had no food in their homes, more than 20 million people used emergency food programs each year, and one in five children lived in poverty—more than a quarter million of them homeless. All told, a larger proportion of Americans were poor than three decades earlier.[21]

One of the paradoxes of a culture of fear is that serious problems remain widely ignored even though they give rise to precisely the dangers that the populace most abhors. Poverty, for example, correlates strongly with child abuse, crime, and drug abuse. Income inequality is also associated with adverse outcomes for society as a whole. The larger the gap between rich and poor in a society, the higher its overall death rates from heart disease, cancer, and murder. Some social scientists argue that extreme inequality also threatens political stability in a nation such as the United States, where we think of ourselves not as "haves and have nots" but as "haves and will haves." "Unlike the citizens of most other nations, Americans have always been united less by a shared past than by the shared dreams of a better future. If we lose that common future," the Brandeis University economist Robert Reich has suggested, "we lose the glue that holds our nation together."[22] . . .

Two Easy Explanations

In the following discussion I will try to answer two questions: Why are Americans so fearful lately, and why are our fears so often misplaced? To both questions the same two-word answer is commonly given . . . [One] popular explanation blames the news media. We have so many fears, many of them off-base, the argument goes, because the media bombard us with sensationalistic stories designed to

increase ratings. This explanation, sometimes called the media-effects theory . . . contains sizable kernels of truth. When researchers from Emory University computed the levels of coverage of various health dangers in popular magazines and newspapers they discovered an inverse relationship: much less space was devoted to several of the major causes of death than to some uncommon causes. The leading cause of death, heart disease, received approximately the same amount of coverage as the eleventh-ranked cause of death, homicide. They found a similar inverse relationship in coverage of risk factors associated with serious illness and death. The lowest-ranking risk factor, drug use, received nearly as much attention as the second-ranked risk factor, diet and exercise.[23]

Disproportionate coverage in the news media plainly has effects on readers and viewers. When Esther Madriz, a professor at Hunter College, interviewed women in New York City about their fears of crime they frequently responded with the phrase "I saw it in the news." The interviewees identified the news media as both the source of their fears and the reason they believed those fears were valid. Asked in a national poll why they believe the country has a serious crime problem, 76 percent of people cited stories they had seen in the media. Only 22 percent cited personal experience.[24]

When professors Robert Blendon and John Young of Harvard analyzed forty-seven surveys about drug abuse conducted between 1978 and 1997, they too discovered that the news media, rather than personal experience, provide Americans with their predominant fears. Eight out of ten adults say that drug abuse has never caused problems in their family, and the vast majority report relatively little direct experience with problems related to drug abuse. Widespread concern about drug problems emanates, Blendon and Young determined, from scares in the news media, television in particular.[25]

Television news programs survive on scares. On local newscasts, where producers live by the dictum "if it bleeds, it leads," drug, crime, and disaster stories make up most of the news portion of the broadcasts. Evening newscasts on the major networks are somewhat less bloody, but between 1990 and 1998, when the nation's murder rate declined by 20 percent, the number of murder stories on network newscasts increased 600 percent (*not* counting stories about O.J. Simpson).[26]

After the dinnertime newscasts the networks broadcast newsmagazines, whose guiding principle seems to be that no danger is too small to magnify into a national nightmare. Some of the risks reported by such programs would be merely laughable were they not hyped with so much fanfare: "Don't miss *Dateline* tonight or YOU could be the next victim!" Competing for ratings with drama programs and movies during prime-time evening hours, newsmagazines feature story lines that would make a writer for "Homicide" or "ER" wince.[27]

"It can happen in a flash. Fire breaks out on the operating table. The patient is surrounded by flames," Barbara Walters exclaimed on ABC's "20/20" in 1998. The problem— oxygen from a face mask ignited by a surgical instrument—occurs "more often than you might think," she cautioned in her introduction, even though reporter Arnold Diaz would note later, during the actual report, that out of 27 million surgeries each year the situation arises only about a hundred times. No matter, Diaz effectively nullified the reassuring numbers as soon as they left his mouth. To those who "may say it's too small a risk to worry about" he presented distraught victims: a woman with permanent scars on her face and a man whose son had died.[28]

The gambit is common. Producers of TV newsmagazines routinely let emotional accounts trump objective information. In 1994 medical authorities attempted to cut short the brouhaha over flesh-eating bacteria by publicizing the fact that an American is fifty-five times more likely to be struck by lightning than die of the suddenly celebrated microbe. Yet TV journalists brushed this fact aside with

remarks like, "whatever the statistics, it's devastating to the victims" (Catherine Crier on "20/20"), accompanied by stomach-turning videos of disfigured patients.[29]

Sheryl Stolberg, then a medical writer for the *Los Angeles Times,* put her finger on what makes the TV newsmagazines so cavalier: "Killer germs are perfect for prime time," she wrote. "They are invisible, uncontrollable, and, in the case of Group A strep, can invade the body in an unnervingly simple manner, through a cut or scrape." Whereas print journalists only described in words the actions of "billions of bacteria" spreading "like underground fires" throughout a person's body, TV newsmagazines made use of special effects to depict graphically how these "merciless killers" do their damage.[30]

In Praise of Journalists

Any analysis of the culture of fear that ignored the news media would be patently incomplete, and of the several institutions most culpable for creating and sustaining scares the news media are arguably first among equals. They are also the most promising candidates for positive change. Yet by the same token critiques such as Stolberg's presage a crucial shortcoming in arguments that blame the media. Reporters not only spread fears, they also debunk them and criticize one another for spooking the public. A wide array of groups, including businesses, advocacy organizations, religious sects, and political parties, promote and profit from scares. News organizations are distinguished from other fear-mongering groups because they sometimes bite the scare that feeds them.

A group that raises money for research into a particular disease is not likely to negate concerns about that disease. A company that sells alarm systems is not about to call attention to the fact that crime is down. News organizations, on the other hand, periodically allay the very fears they arouse to lure audiences. Some newspapers that ran stories about child murderers, rather than treat every incident as evidence of a shocking trend, affirmed the opposite. After the schoolyard shooting in Kentucky the *New York Times* ran a sidebar alongside its feature story with the headline "Despite Recent Carnage, School Violence Is Not on Rise." Following the Jonesboro killings they ran a similar piece, this time on a recently released study showing the rarity of violent crimes in schools.[31]

Several major newspapers parted from the pack in other ways. *USA Today* and the *Washington Post,* for instance, made sure their readers knew that what should worry them is the availability of guns. *USA Today* ran news stories explaining that easy access to guns in homes accounted for increases in the number of juvenile arrests for homicide in rural areas during the 1990s. While other news outlets were respectfully quoting the mother of the thirteen-year-old Jonesboro shooter, who said she did not regret having encouraged her son to learn to fire a gun ("it's like anything else, there's some people that can drink a beer and not become an alcoholic"), *USA Today* ran an op-ed piece proposing legal parameters for gun ownership akin to those for the use of alcohol and motor vehicles. And the paper published its own editorial in support of laws that require gun owners to lock their guns or keep them in locked containers. Adopted at that time by only fifteen states, the laws had reduced the number of deaths among children in those states by 23 percent.[32]

The *Washington Post,* meanwhile, published an excellent investigative piece by reporter Sharon Walsh showing that guns increasingly were being marketed to teenagers and children. Quoting advertisements and statistics from gun manufacturers and the National Rifle Association, Walsh revealed that by 1998 the primary market for guns—white males—had been saturated and an effort to market to women had failed. Having come to see children as its future, the gun industry has taken to running ads like the one Walsh found in a Smith & Wesson catalog: "Seems like only yesterday that your father brought you here for the first time," reads the copy beside a photo of a child aiming a handgun, his father by his side. "Those sure were the good times—just you, dad and his Smith & Wesson."[33]

As a social scientist I am impressed and somewhat embarrassed to find that journalists, more often than media scholars, identify the jugglery involved in making small hazards appear huge and huge hazards disappear from sight. Take, for example, the scare several years ago over the Ebola virus. Another *Washington Post* reporter, John Schwartz, identified a key bit of hocus-pocus used to sell that scare. Schwartz called it "the Cuisinart Effect," because it involves the mashing together of images and story lines from fiction and reality. A report by *Dateline NBC* on death in Zaire, for instance, interspersed clips from *Outbreak,* a movie whose plot involves a lethal virus that threatens to kill the entire U.S. population. Alternating between Dustin Hoffman's character exclaiming, "We can't stop it!" and real-life science writer Laurie Garrett, author of *The Coming Plague,* proclaiming that "HIV is not an aberration… it's part of a trend," *Dateline*'s report gave the impression that swarms of epidemics were on their way.[34]

Another great journalist-debunker, Malcolm Gladwell, noted that the book that had inspired *Outbreak,* Richard Preston's *The Hot Zone,* itself was written "in self-conscious imitation of a sci-fi thriller." In the real-world incident that occasioned *The Hot Zone,* monkeys infected in Zaire with a strain of Ebola virus were quarantined at a government facility in Reston, Virginia. The strain turned out not to be lethal in humans, but neither Preston in his book nor the screenwriters for *Outbreak* nor TV producers who sampled from the movie let that anticlimax interfere with the scare value of their stories. Preston speculates about an airborne strain of Ebola being carried by travelers from African airports to European, Asian, and American cities. In *Outbreak* hundreds of people die from such an airborne strain before a cure is miraculously discovered in the nick of time to save humanity. In truth, Gladwell points out in a piece in *The New Republic,* an Ebola strain that is both virulent to humans and airborne is unlikely to emerge and would mutate rapidly if it did, becoming far less potent before it had a chance to infect large numbers of people on a single continent, much less throughout the globe. "It is one of the ironies of the analysis of alarmists such as Preston that they are all too willing to point out the limitations of human beings, but they neglect to point out the limitations of microscopic life forms," Gladwell notes.[35]

Such disproofs of disease scares appear rather frequently in general-interest magazines and newspapers, including in publications where one might not expect to find them. The *Wall Street Journal,* for instance, while primarily a business publication and itself a retailer of fears about governmental regulators, labor unions, and other corporate-preferred hobgoblins, has done much to demolish medical myths. Among my personal favorites is an article published in 1996 titled "Fright by the Numbers," in which reporter Cynthia Crossen rebuts a cover story in *Time* magazine on prostate cancer. One in five men will get the disease, *Time* thundered. "That's scary. But it's also a lifetime risk—the accumulated risk over some 80 years of life," Crossen responds. A forty-year-old's chance of coming down with (not dying of) prostate cancer in the next ten years is 1 in 1,000, she goes on to report. His odds rise to 1 in 100 over twenty years. Even by the time he's seventy, he has only a 1 in 20 chance of *any* kind of cancer, including prostate.[36]

In the same article Crossen counters other alarmist claims as well, such as the much-repeated pronouncement that one in three Americans is obese. The number actually refers to how many are overweight, a less serious condition. Fewer are *obese* (a term that is less than objective itself), variously defined as 20 to 40 percent above ideal body weight as determined by current standards.[37]

Morality and Marketing

To blame the media is to oversimplify the complex role that journalists play as both proponents and doubters of popular fears. . . . Why do news organizations and their audiences find themselves drawn to one hazard rather than another?

Mary Douglas, the eminent anthropologist who devoted much of her career to studying how people interpret risk, pointed out that every society has an almost infinite quantity of potential dangers from which to choose. Societies differ both in the types of dangers they select and the number. Dangers get selected for special emphasis, Douglas showed, either because they offend the basic moral principles of the society or because they enable criticism of disliked groups and institutions. In *Risk and Culture,* a book she wrote with Aaron Wildavsky, the authors give an example from fourteenth-century Europe. Impure water had been a health danger long before that time, but only after it became convenient to accuse Jews of poisoning the wells did people become preoccupied with it.

Or take a more recent institutional example. In the first half of the 1990s U.S. cities spent at least $10 billion to purge asbestos from public schools, even though removing asbestos from buildings posed a greater health hazard than leaving it in place. At a time when about one-third of the nation's schools were in need of extensive repairs the money might have been spent to renovate dilapidated buildings. But hazards posed by seeping asbestos are morally repugnant. A product that was supposed to protect children from fires might be giving them cancer. By directing our worries and dollars at asbestos we express outrage at technology and industry run afoul.[38]

From a psychological point of view extreme fear and outrage are often projections. Consider, for example, the panic over violence against children. By failing to provide adequate education, nutrition, housing, parenting, medical services, and child care over the past couple of decades we have done the nation's children immense harm. Yet we project our guilt onto a cavalcade of bogeypeople—pedophile preschool teachers, preteen mass murderers, and homicidal au pairs, to name only a few.[39]

When Debbie Nathan, a journalist, and Michael Snedeker, an attorney, researched the evidence behind publicized reports in the 1980s and early 1990s of children being ritually raped and tortured they learned that although seven out of ten Americans believed that satanic cults were committing these atrocities, few of the incidents had actually occurred. At the outset of each ritual-abuse case the children involved claimed they had not been molested. They later changed their tunes at the urging of parents and law enforcement authorities. The ghastly tales of abuse, it turns out, typically came from the parents themselves, usually the mothers, who had convinced themselves they were true. Nathan and Snedeker suggest that some of the mothers had been abused themselves and projected those horrors, which they had trouble facing directly, onto their children. Other mothers, who had not been victimized in those ways, used the figure of ritually abused children as a medium of protest against male dominance more generally. Allegations of children being raped allowed conventional wives and mothers to speak out against men and masculinity without having to fear they would seem unfeminine. "The larger culture," Nathan and Snedeker note, "still required that women's complaints about inequality and sexual violence be communicated through the innocent, mortified voice of the child."

Diverse groups used the ritual-abuse scares to diverse ends. Well-known feminists such as Gloria Steinem and Catharine MacKinnon took up the cause, depicting ritually abused children as living proof of the ravages of patriarchy and the need for fundamental social reform.[40]

This was far from the only time feminist spokeswomen have mongered fears about sinister breeds of men who exist in nowhere near the high numbers they allege. Another example occurred a few years ago when teen pregnancy was much in the news. Feminists helped popularize the frightful but erroneous statistic that two out of three teen mothers had been seduced and abandoned by adult men. The true figure is more like one in ten, but some feminists continued to cultivate the scare well after the bogus stat had been definitively debunked.[41] . . .

Final Thoughts

The short answer to why Americans harbor so many misbegotten fears is that immense power and money await those who tap into our moral insecurities and supply us with symbolic substitutes. . . .

[Other tactics include] (1) Statements of alarm by newscasters; (2) glorification of wannabe experts are two telltale tricks of the fear mongers' trade; (3) the use of poignant anecdotes in place of scientific evidence; (4) the christening of isolated incidents as trends; and (5) depletions of entire categories of people as innately dangerous.

If journalists would curtail such practices, there would be fewer anxious and misinformed Americans. Ultimately, though, neither the ploys that narrators use nor what Cantril termed "the sheer dramatic excellence" of their presentations fully accounts for why people in 1938 swallowed a tall tale about martians taking over New Jersey or why people today buy into tales about perverts taking over cyberspace, unionizing employees taking over workplaces, heroin dealers taking over middle-class suburbs, and so forth.[42] . . .

Fear mongers have knocked the optimism out of us by stuffing us full of negative presumptions about our fellow citizens and social institutions. But the United States is a wealthy nation. We have the resources to feed, house, educate, insure, and disarm our communities if we resolve to do so.

There should be no mystery about where much of the money and labor can be found—in the culture of fear itself. We waste tens of billions of dollars and person-hours every year on largely mythical hazards like road rage, on prison cells occupied by people who pose little or no danger to others, on programs designed to protect young people from dangers that few of them ever face, on compensation for victims of metaphorical illnesses, and on technology to make airline travel—which is already safer than other means of transportation—safer still.

We can choose to redirect some of those funds to combat serious dangers that threaten large numbers of people. At election time we can choose candidates that proffer programs rather than scares.[43]

Or we can go on believing in martian invaders.

NOTES

1. Crime data here and throughout are from reports of the Bureau of Justice Statistics unless otherwise noted. Fear of crime: Esther Madriz, *Nothing Bad Happens to Good Girls* (Berkeley: University of California Press, 1997), ch. 1; Richard Morin, "As Crime Rate Falls, Fears Persist," *Washington Post* National Edition, 16 June 1997, p. 35; David Whitman, "Believing the Good News," *U.S. News & World Report*, 5 January 1998, pp. 45–46.

2. Eva Bertram, Morris Blachman et al., *Drug War Politics* (Berkeley: University of California Press, 1996), p. 10; Mike Males, *Scapegoat Generation* (Monroe, ME: Common Courage Press, 1996), ch. 6; Karen Peterson, "Survey: Teen Drug Use Declines," *USA Today*, 19 June 1998, p. A6; Robert Blendon and John Young, "The Public and the War on Illicit Drugs," *Journal of the American Medical Association* 279 (18 March 1998): 827–32. In presenting these statistics and others I am aware of a seeming paradox: I criticize the abuse of statistics by fearmongering politicians, journalists, and others but hand down precise-sounding numbers myself. Yet to eschew all estimates because some are used inappropriately or do not withstand scrutiny would be as foolhardy as ignoring all medical advice because some doctors are quacks. Readers can be assured I have interrogated the statistics presented here as factual. As notes throughout the book make clear, I have tried to rely on research that appears in peer-reviewed scholarly journals. Where this was not possible or sufficient, I traced numbers back to their sources, investigated the research methodology utilized to produce them, or conducted searches of the popular and scientific literature for critical commentaries and conflicting findings.

3. Bob Herbert, "Bogeyman Economics," *New York Times*, 4 April 1997, p. A15; Doug Henwood, "Alarming Drop in Unemployment," *Extra*, September 1994, pp. 16–17; Christopher Shea, "Low Inflation and Low Unemployment Spur Economists to Debate 'Natural Rate' Theory," *Chronicle of Higher Education*, 24 October 1997, p. A13.

4. Bob Garfield, "Maladies by the Millions," *USA Today*, 16 December 1996, p. A15.

5. Jim Windolf, "A Nation of Nuts," *Wall Street Journal*, 22 October 1997, p. A22.

6. Andrew Ferguson, "Road Rage," *Time*, 12 January 1998, pp. 64–68; Joe Sharkey, "You're Not Bad, You're Sick. It's in the Book," *New York Times*, 28 September 1997, pp. Nl, 5.

7. Malcolm Dean, "Flesh-eating Bugs Scare," *Lancet* 343 (4 June 1994): 1418; "Flesh-eating Bacteria," *Science* 264 (17 June 1994): 1665; David Brown, "The Flesh-eating Bug," *Washington Post* National Edition, 19 December 1994, p. 34; Sarah Richardson, "Tabloid Strep," *Discover* (January 1995): 71; Liz Hunt, "What's Bugging Us," *The Independent*, 28 May 1994, p. 25; Lisa Seachrist, "The Once and Future Scourge," *Science News* 148 (7 October 1995): 234–35. Quotes are from Bernard Dixon, "A Rampant Non-epidemic," *British Medical Journal* 308 (11 June 1994): 1576–77; and Michael Lemonick and Leon Jaroff, "The Killers All Around," *Time*, 12 September 1994, pp. 62–69. More recent coverage: "Strep A Involved in Baby's Death," UPI, 27 February 1998; see also, e.g., Steve Carney, "Miracle Mom," *Los Angeles Times*, 4 March 1998, p. A6; KTLA, "News at Ten," 28 March 1998.

8. Jim Naureckas, "The Jihad That Wasn't," *Extra*, July 1995, pp. 6–10, 20 (contains quotes). See also Edward Said, "A Devil Theory of Islam," *Nation*, 12 August 1996, pp. 28–32.

9. Lewis Lapham, "Seen but Not Heard," *Harper's*, July 1995, pp. 29–36 (contains Clinton quote). See also Robin Wright and Ronald Ostrow, "Illusion of Immunity Is Shattered," *Los Angeles Times*, 20 April 1995, pp. Al, 18; Jack Germond and Jules Witcover, "Making the Angry White Males Angrier," column syndicated by Tribune Media Services, May 1995; and articles by James Bennet and Michael Janofsky in the *New York Times*, May 1995.

10. Tom Morganthau, "The Lull Before the Storm?" *Newsweek*, 4 December 1995, pp. 40–42; Mike Males, "Wild in Deceit," *Extra*, March 1996,

pp. 7–9; *Progressive,* July 1997, p. 9 (contains Clinton quote); Robin Templeton, "First, We Kill All the 11-Year-Olds," *Salon,* 27 May 1998.

11. Statistics from "Violence and Discipline Problems in U.S. Public Schools: 1996–97," National Center on Education Statistics, U.S. Department of Education, Washington, DC, March 1998; CNN, "Early Prime," 2 December 1997; and Tamar Lewin, "Despite Recent Carnage, School Violence Is Not on Rise," *New York Times,* 3 December 1997, p. A14. Headlines: *Time,* 15 January 1996; *U.S. News & World Report,* 25 March 1996; Margaret Carlson, "Children Without Souls," *Time,* 2 December 1996, p. 70. William J. Bennett, John J. Dilulio, and John Walters, *Body Count* (New York: Simon & Schuster, 1996).

12. CNN, "Talkback Live," 2 December 1997; CNN, "The Geraldo Rivera Show," 11 December 1997; Richard Lacayo, "Toward the Root of Evil," *Time,* 6 April 1998, pp. 38–39; NBC, "Today," 25 March 1998. See also Rick Bragg, "Forgiveness, After 3 Die in Shootings in Kentucky," *New York Times,* 3 December 1997, p. A14; Maureen Downey, "Kids and Violence," 28 March 1998, *Atlanta Journal and Constitution,* p. A12.

13. Jocelyn Stewart, "Schools Learn to Take Threats More Seriously," *Los Angeles Times,* 2 May 1998, pp. Al, 17; "Kindergarten Student Faces Gun Charges," *New York Times,* 11 May 1998, p. A11; Rick Bragg, "Jonesboro Dazed by Its Darkest Day" and "Past Victims Relive Pain as Tragedy Is Repeated," *New York Times,* 18 April 1998, p. A7, and idem, 25 May 1998, p. A8. Remaining quotes are from Tamar Lewin, "More Victims and Less Sense in Shootings," *New York Times,* 22 May 1998, p. A20; NPR, "All Things Considered," 22 May 1998; NBC, "Today," 25 March 1998. See also Mike Males, "Who's Really Killing Our Schoolkids," *Los Angeles Times,* 31 May 1998, pp. M1, 3; Michael Sniffen, "Youth Crime Fell in 1997, Reno Says," Associated Press, 20 November 1998.

14. Overestimation of breast cancer: William C. Black et al., "Perceptions of Breast Cancer Risk and Screening Effectiveness in Women Younger Than 50," *Journal of the National Cancer Institute* 87 (1995): 720–31; B. Smith et al., "Perception of Breast Cancer Risk Among Women in Breast and Family History of Breast Cancer," *Surgery* 120 (1996): 297–303. Fear and avoidance: Steven Berman and Abraham Wandersman, "Fear of Cancer and Knowledge of Cancer," *Social Science and Medicine* 31 (1990): 81–90; S. Benedict et al.,

"Breast Cancer Detection by Daughters of Women with Breast Cancer," *Cancer Practice* 5 (1997): 213–19; M. Muir et al., "Health Promotion and Early Detection of Cancer in Older Adults," *Cancer Oncology Nursing Journal* 7 (1997): 82–89. For a conflicting finding see Kevin McCaul et al., "Breast Cancer Worry and Screening," *Health Psychology* 15 (1996): 430–33.

15. Philip Jenkins, *Pedophiles and Priests* (New York: Oxford University Press, 1996), see esp. ch. 10; Debbie Nathan and Michael Snedeker, *Satan's Silence* (New York: Basic Books, 1995), see esp. ch. 6; Jeffrey Victor, "The Danger of Moral Panics," *Skeptic* 3 (1995): 44–51. See also Noelle Oxenhandler, "The Eros of Parenthood," *Family Therapy Networker* (May 1996): 17–19.

16. Mary DeYoung, "The Devil Goes to Day Care," *Journal of American Culture* 20 (1997): 19–25.

17. Dorothy Rabinowitz, "A Darkness in Massachusetts," *Wall Street Journal,* 30 January 1995, p. A20 (contains quote); "Back in Wenatchee" (unsigned editorial), *Wall Street Journal,* 20 June 1996, p. A18; Dorothy Rabinowitz, "Justice in Massachusetts," *Wall Street Journal,* 13 May 1997, p. A19. See also Nathan and Snedeker, *Satan's Silence;* James Beaver, "The Myth of Repressed Memory," *Journal of Criminal Law and Criminology* 86 (1996): 596–607; Kathryn Lyon, *Witch Hunt* (New York: Avon, 1998); Pam Belluck, "'Memory' Therapy Leads to a Lawsuit and Big Settlement," *New York Times,* 6 November 1997, pp. A1, 10.

18. Elliott Currie, *Crime and Punishment in America* (New York: Metropolitan, 1998); Tony Pate et al., *Reducing Fear of Crime in Houston and Newark* (Washington, DC: Police Foundation, 1986); Steven Donziger, *The Real War on Crime* (New York: HarperCollins, 1996); Christina Johns, *Power, Ideology and the War on Drugs* (New York: Praeger, 1992); John Irwin et al., "Fanning the Flames of Fear," *Crime and Delinquency* 44 (1998): 32–48.

19. Steven Donziger, "Fear, Crime and Punishment in the U.S.," *Tikkun* 12 (1996): 24–27, 77.

20. Peter Budetti, "Health Insurance for Children," *New England Journal of Medicine* 338 (1998): 541–42; Eileen Smith, "Drugs Top Adult Fears for Kids' Well-being," *USA Today,* 9 December 1997, p. D1. Literacy statistic: Adult Literacy Service.

21. "The State of America's Children," report by the Children's Defense Fund, Washington, DC,

March 1998; "Blocks to Their Future," report by the National Law Center on Homelessness and Poverty, Washington, DC, September 1997; reports released in 1998 from the National Center for Children in Poverty, Columbia University, New York; Douglas Massey, "The Age of Extremes," *Demography* 33 (1996): 395–412; Notes Trudy Lieberman, "Hunger in America," *Nation,* 30 March 1998, pp. 11–16; David Lynch, "Rich Poor World," *USA Today,* 20 September 1996, p. B1; Richard Wolf, "Good Economy Hasn't Helped the Poor," *USA Today,* 10 March 1998, p. A3; Robert Reich, "Broken Faith," *Nation,* 16 February 1998, pp. 11–17.

22. Inequality and mortality studies: Bruce Kennedy et al., "Income Distribution and Mortality," *British Medical Journal* 312 (1996): 1004–7; Ichiro Kawachi and Bruce Kennedy, "The Relationship of Income Inequality to Mortality," *Social Science and Medicine* 45 (1997): 1121–27. See also Barbara Chasin, *Inequality and Violence in the United States* (Atlantic Highlands, NJ: Humanities Press, 1997). Political stability: John Sloan, "The Reagan Presidency, Growing Inequality, and the American Dream," *Policy Studies Journal* 25 (1997): 371–86 (contains Reich quotes and "will haves" phrase). On both topics see also Philippe Bourgois, *In Search of Respect: Selling Crack in El Barrio* (Cambridge: Cambridge University Press, 1996); William J. Wilson, *When Work Disappears* (New York, Knopf, 1996); Richard Gelles, "Family Violence," *Annual Review of Sociology* 11 (1985): 347–67; Sheldon Danziger and Peter Gottschalk, *America Unequal* (Cambridge, MA: Harvard University Press, 1995); Claude Fischer et al., *Inequality by Design* (Princeton, NJ: Princeton University Press, 1996).

23. Karen Frost, Erica Frank et al., "Relative Risk in the News Media," *American Journal of Public Health* 87 (1997): 842–45. Media-effects theory: Nancy Signorielli and Michael Morgan, eds., *Cultivation Analysis* (Newbury Park, CA: Sage, 1990); Jennings Bryant and Dolf Zillman, eds., *Media Effects* (Hillsdale, NJ: Erlbaum, 1994); Ronald Jacobs, "Producing the News, Producing the Crisis," *Media, Culture and Society* 18 (1996): 373–97.

24. Madriz, *Nothing Bad Happens to Good Girls,* see esp. pp. 111–14; David Whitman and Margaret Loftus, "Things Are Getting Better? Who Knew," *U.S. News & World Report,* 16 December 1996, pp. 30–32.

25. Blendon and Young, "War on Illicit Drugs." See also Ted Chiricos et al., "Crime, News and Fear of Crime," *Social Problems* 44 (1997): 342–57.

26. Steven Stark, "Local News: The Biggest Scandal on TV," *Washington Monthly* (June 1997): 38–41; Barbara Bliss Osborn, "If It Bleeds, It Leads," *Extra,* September–October 1994, p. 15; Jenkins, *Pedophiles and Priests,* pp. 68–71; "It's Murder," *USA Today,* 20 April 1998, p. D2; Lawrence Grossman, "Does Local TV News Need a National Nanny?" *Columbia Journalism Review* (May 1998): 33.

27. Regarding fearmongering by news-magazines, see also Elizabeth Jensen et al., "Consumer Alert," *Brill's Content* (October 1998): 130–47.

28. ABC, "20/20," 16 March 1998.

29. Thomas Maugh, "Killer Bacteria a Rarity," *Los Angeles Times,* 3 December 1994, p. A29; Ed Siegel, "Roll Over, Ed Murrow," *Boston Globe,* 21 August 1994, p. 14. Crier quote from ABC's "20/20," 24 June 1994.

30. Sheryl Stolberg, "'Killer Bug' Perfect for Prime Time," *Los Angeles Times,* 15 June 1994, pp. A1, 30–31. Quotes from Brown, "Flesh-eating Bug"; and Michael Lemonick and Leon Jaroff, "The Killers All Around," *Time,* 12 September 1994, pp. 62–69.

31. Lewin, "More Victims and Less Sense"; Tamar Lewin, "Study Finds No Big Rise in Public-School Crimes," *New York Times,* 25 March 1998, p. A18.

32. "Licensing Can Protect," *USA Today,* 7 April 1998, p. A11; Jonathan Kellerman, "Few Surprises When It Comes to Violence," *USA Today,* 27 March 1998, p. A13; Gary Fields, "Juvenile Homicide Arrest Rate on Rise in Rural USA," *USA Today,* 26 March 1998, p. A11; Karen Peterson and Glenn O'Neal, "Society More Violent, So Are Its Children," *USA Today,* 25 March 1998, p. A3; Scott Bowles, "Armed, Alienated and Adolescent," *USA Today,* 26 March 1998, p. A9. Similar suggestions about guns appear in Jonathan Alter, "Harnessing the Hysteria," *Newsweek,* 6 April 1998, p. 27.

33. Sharon Walsh, "Gun Sellers Look to Future—Children," *Washington Post,* 28 March 1998, pp. A1, 2.

34. John Schwartz, "An Outbreak of Medical Myths," *Washington Post* National Edition, 22 May 1995, p. 38.

35. Richard Preston, *The Hot Zone* (New York: Random House, 1994); Malcolm Gladwell, "The Plague Year," *New Republic,* 17 July 1995, p. 40.

36. Erik Larson, "A False Crisis: How Workplace Violence Became a Hot Issue," *Wall*

Street Journal, 13 October 1994, pp. A1, 8; Cynthia Crossen, "Fright By the Numbers," *Wall Street Journal,* 11 April 1996, pp. B1, 8. See also G. Pascal Zachary, "Junk History," *Wall Street Journal,* 19 September 1997, pp. A1, 6.

37. On variable definitions of obesity see also Werner Cahnman, "The Stigma of Obesity," *Sociological Quarterly* 9 (1968): 283–99; Susan Bordo, *Unbearable Weight* (Berkeley: University of California Press, 1993); Joan Chrisler, "Politics and Women's Weight," *Feminism and Psychology* 6 (1996): 181–84.

38. Mary Douglas and Aaron Wildavsky, *Risk and Culture* (Berkeley: University of California Press, 1982), see esp. pp. 6–9; Mary Douglas, *Risk and Blame* (London: Routledge, 1992). See also Mary Douglas, *Purity and Danger* (New York: Praeger, 1966). Asbestos and schools: Peter Cary, "The Asbestos Panic Attack," *U.S. News & World Report,* 20 February 1995, pp. 61–64; Children's Defense Fund, "State of America's Children."

39. See Marina Warner, "Peroxide Mug-shot," *London Review of Books,* 1 January 1998, pp. 10–11.

40. Nathan and Snedeker, *Satan's Silence* (quote from p. 240). See also David Bromley, "Satanism: The New Cult Scare," in James Richardson et al., eds., *The Satanism Scare* (Hawthorne, NY: Aldine de Gruyter, 1991), pp. 49–71.

41. Of girls ages fifteen to seventeen who gave birth, fewer than one in ten were unmarried and had been made pregnant by men at least five years older. See Steven Holmes, "It's Awful, It's Terrible, It's . . . Never Mind," *New York Times,* 6 July 1997, p. E3.

42. CNN, "Crossfire," 27 August 1995 (contains Huffington quote); Ruth Conniff, "Warning: Feminism Is Hazardous to Your Health," *Progressive,* April 1997, pp. 33–36 (contains Sommers quote). See also Susan Faludi, *Backlash* (New York: Crown, 1991); Deborah Rhode, "Media Images, Feminist Issues," *Signs* 20 (1995): 685–710; Paula Span, "Did Feminists Forget the Most Crucial Issues?" *Los Angeles Times,* 28 November 1996, p. E8.

43. See Katha Pollitt, "Subject to Debate," *Nation,* 26 December 1994, p. 788, and idem, 20 November 1995, p. 600.

THINKING ABOUT THE READING

Glassner originally wrote this piece nearly a decade ago. What are some contemporary examples of cultural fears that he might include if he were writing this today? How do you determine if the fear is a cultural myth or something that should be taken seriously as a social problem? According to Glassner, how are these cultural myths created, and why are we so inclined to believe in them? Do you think a culture less organized by the medium of television would be more or less likely to support such myths?

Researching Dealers and Smugglers

Patricia A. Adler

(1985)

I strongly believe that investigative field research (Douglas 1976), with emphasis on direct personal observation, interaction, and experience, is the only way to acquire accurate knowledge about deviant behavior. Investigative techniques are especially necessary for studying groups such as drug dealers and smugglers because the highly illegal nature of their occupation makes them secretive, deceitful, mistrustful, and paranoid. To insulate themselves from the straight world, they construct multiple false fronts, offer lies and misinformation, and withdraw into their group. In fact, detailed, scientific information about upper-level drug dealers and smugglers is lacking precisely because of the difficulty sociological researchers have had in penetrating into their midst. As a result, the only way I could possibly get close enough to these individuals to discover what they were doing and to understand their world from their perspectives (Blumer 1969) was to take a membership role in the setting. While my different values and goals precluded my becoming converted to complete membership in the sub-culture, and my fears prevented my ever becoming "actively" involved in their trafficking activities, I was able to assume a "peripheral" membership role. I became a member of the dealers' and smugglers' social world and participated in their daily activities on that basis. . . .

Getting In

When I moved to Southwest County [California] in the summer of 1974, I had no idea that I would soon be swept up in a sub-culture of vast drug trafficking and unending partying, mixed with occasional cloak-and-dagger subterfuge. I had moved to California with my husband, Peter, to attend graduate school in sociology. We rented a condominium townhouse near the beach and started taking classes in the fall. We had always felt that socializing exclusively with academicians left us nowhere to escape from our work, so we tried to meet people in the nearby community. One of the first friends we made was our closest neighbor, a fellow in his late twenties with a tall, hulking frame and gentle expression. Dave, as he introduced himself, was always dressed rather casually, if not sloppily, in T-shirts and jeans. He spent most of his time hanging out or walking on the beach with a variety of friends who visited his house, and taking care of his two young boys, who lived alternately with him and his estranged wife. He also went out of town a lot. We started spending much of our free time over at his house, talking, playing board games late into the night, and smoking marijuana together. We were glad to find someone from whom we could buy marijuana in this new place, since we did not know too many people. He also began treating us to a fairly regular supply of cocaine, which was a thrill because this was a drug we could rarely afford on our student budgets. We noticed right away, however, that there was something unusual about his use and knowledge of drugs: while he always had a plentiful supply and was fairly expert about marijuana and cocaine, when we tried to buy a small bag of marijuana from him he had little idea of the going price. This incongruity piqued our curiosity and raised suspicion. We wondered if he might be dealing in larger quantities.

Keeping our suspicions to ourselves, we began observing Dave's activities a little more closely. . . . Dave, in fact, had no visible means of financial support. When we asked him what he did for a living, he said something vague about being a real estate speculator, and we let it go at that. We never voiced our suspicions directly since he chose not to broach the subject with us.

We did discuss the subject with our mentor, Jack Douglas, however. He was excited by the prospect that we might be living among a group of big dealers, and urged us to follow our instincts and develop leads into the group. . . . We decided that if anything did develop out of our observations of Dave, it might make a nice paper for a field methods class or independent study. . . .

We thus watched Dave and continued to develop our friendship with him. We also watched his friends and got to know a few of his more regular visitors. We continued to build friendly relations by doing, quite naturally, what Becker (1963), Polsky (1969), and Douglas (1972) had advocated for the early stages of field research: we gave them a chance to know us and form judgments about our trustworthiness by jointly pursuing those interests and activities which we had in common.

Then one day something happened which forced a breakthrough in the research. Dave had two guys visiting him from out of town and, after snorting quite a bit of cocaine, they turned their conversation to a trip they had just made from Mexico, where they piloted a load of marijuana back across the border in a small plane. Dave made a few efforts to shift the conversation to another subject, telling them to "button their lips," but they apparently thought that he was joking. They thought that anybody as close to Dave as we seemed to be undoubtedly knew the nature of his business. They made further allusions to his involvement in the operation and discussed the outcome of the sale. We could feel the wave of tension and awkwardness from Dave when this conversation began, as he looked toward us to see if we understood the implications of what was being said, but then he just shrugged it off as done. Later, after the two guys left, he discussed with us what happened. He admitted to us that he was a member of a smuggling crew and a major marijuana dealer on the side. He said that he knew he could trust us, but that it was his practice to say as little as possible to outsiders about his activities. This inadvertent slip, and Dave's subsequent opening up, were highly significant in forging our entry into Southwest County's drug world. From then on he was open in discussing the nature of his dealing and smuggling activities with us.

He was, it turned out, a member of a smuggling crew that was importing a ton of marijuana weekly and 40 kilos of cocaine every few months. During that first winter and spring, we observed Dave at work and also got to know the other members of his crew, including Ben, the smuggler himself. . . .

Once we realized the scope of Ben's and his associates' activities, we saw the enormous research potential in studying them. This scene was different from any analysis of drug trafficking that we had read in the sociological literature because of the amounts they were dealing and the fact that they were importing it themselves. We decided that, if it was at all possible, we would capitalize on this situation, to "opportunistically" (Riemer 1977) take advantage of our prior expertise and of the knowledge, entree, and rapport we had already developed with several key people in this setting. We therefore discussed the idea of doing a study of the general subculture with Dave and several of his closest friends (now becoming our friends). We assured them of the anonymity, confidentiality, and innocuousness of our work. They were happy to reciprocate our friendship by being of help to our professional careers. In fact, they basked in the subsequent attention we gave their lives.

We began by turning first Dave, then others, into key informants and collecting their life histories in detail. We conducted a series of taped, in-depth interviews with an unstructured, open-ended format. We questioned them about such topics as their backgrounds, their recruitment into the occupation, the stages of their dealing careers, their relations with others, their motivations, their lifestyle, and their general impressions about the community as a whole.

We continued to do taped interviews with key informants for the next six years until 1980, when we moved away from the area. After that, we occasionally did follow-up interviews when we returned for vacation visits. These later interviews focused on recording the continuing unfolding of events and included detailed probing into specific conceptual areas, such as dealing networks, types of dealers, secrecy, trust, paranoia, reputation, the law, occupational mobility, and occupational stratification. The number of taped interviews we did with each key informant varied, ranging between 10 and 30 hours of discussion.

Our relationship with Dave and the others thus took on an added dimension—the research relationship. As Douglas (1976), Henslin (1972), and Wax (1952) have noted, research relationships involve some form of mutual exchange. In our case, we offered everything that friendship could entail. We did routine favors for them in the course of our everyday lives, offered them insights and advice about their lives from the perspective of our more respectable position, wrote letters on their behalf to the authorities when they got in trouble, testified as character witnesses at their non-drug-related trials, and loaned them money when they were down and out. When Dave was arrested and brought to trial for check-kiting, we helped [his ex-wife] Jean organize his defense and raise the money to pay his fines. We spelled her in taking care of the children so that she could work on his behalf. When he was eventually sent to the state prison we maintained close ties with her and discussed our mutual efforts to buoy Dave up and secure his release. We also visited him in jail. . . .

Dave's eventual release from prison three months later brought our involvement in the research to an even deeper level. He was broke and had nowhere to go. When he showed up on our doorstep, we took him in. We offered to let him stay with us until he was back on his feet again and could afford a place of his own. He lived with us for seven months, intimately sharing his daily experiences with us. During this time we witnessed, firsthand, his transformation from a scared ex-con who would never break the law again to a hard-working legitimate employee who only dealt to get money for his children's Christmas presents, to a full-time dealer with no pretensions at legitimate work. Both his process of changing attitudes and the community's gradual reacceptance of him proved very revealing.

We socialized with Dave, Jean, and other members of Southwest County's dealing and smuggling community on a near-daily basis, especially during the first four years of the research (before we had a child). We worked in their legitimate businesses, vacationed together, attended their weddings, and cared for their children. Throughout their relationship with us, several participants became co-opted to the researcher's perspective and actively sought out instances of behavior which filled holes in the conceptualizations we were developing. Dave, for one, became so intrigued by our conceptual dilemmas that he undertook a "natural experiment" entirely on his own, offering an unlimited supply of drugs to a lower-level dealer to see if he could work up to higher levels of dealing, and what factors would enhance or impinge upon his upward mobility.

In addition to helping us directly through their own experiences, our key informants aided us in widening our circle of contacts. For instance, they let us know when someone in whom we might be interested was planning on dropping by, vouching for our trustworthiness and reliability as friends who could be included in business conversations. Several times we were even awakened in the night by phone calls informing us that someone had dropped by for a visit, should we want to "casually" drop over too. We rubbed the sleep from our eyes, dressed, and walked or drove over, feeling like sleuths out of a television series. We thus were able to snowball, through the active efforts of our key informants, into an expanded study population. This was supplemented by our own efforts to cast a research net and befriend other dealers, moving from contact to contact slowly and carefully through the domino effect.

The Covert Role

The highly illegal nature of dealing in illicit drugs and dealers' and smugglers' general level of suspicion made the adoption of an overt research role highly sensitive and problematic. In discussing this issue with our key informants, they all agreed that we should be extremely discreet (for both our sakes and theirs). We carefully approached new individuals before we admitted that we were studying them. With many of these people, then, we took a covert posture in the research setting. As nonparticipants in the business activities which bound members together into the group, it was difficult to become fully accepted as peers. We therefore tried to establish some sort of peripheral, social membership in the general crowd, where we could be accepted as "wise" (Goffman 1963) individuals and granted a courtesy membership. . . .

Developing Trust

Like achieving entree, the process of developing trust with members of unorganized deviant groups can be slow and difficult. In the absence of a formal structure separating members from outsiders, each individual must form his or her own judgment about whether new persons can be admitted to their confidence. No gatekeeper existed to smooth our path to being trusted, although our key informants acted in this role whenever they could by providing introductions and references. In addition, the unorganized

nature of this group meant that we met people at different times and were constantly at different levels in our developing relationships with them. We were thus trusted more by some people than by others, in part because of their greater familiarity with us. But as Douglas (1976) has noted, just because someone knew us or even liked us did not automatically guarantee that they would trust us.

We actively tried to cultivate the trust of our respondents by tying them to us with favors. Small things, like offering the use of our phone, were followed with bigger favors, like offering the use of our car, and finally really meaningful favors, like offering the use of our home. Here we often trod a thin line, trying to ensure our personal safety while putting ourselves in enough of a risk position, along with our research subjects, so that they would trust us. While we were able to build a "web of trust" (Douglas 1976) with some members, we found that trust, in large part, was not a simple status to attain in the drug world. Johnson (1975) has pointed out that trust is not a one-time phenomenon, but an ongoing developmental process. From my experiences in this research I would add that it cannot be simply assumed to be a one-way process either, for it can be diminished, withdrawn, reinstated to varying degrees, and requestioned at any point. Carey (1972) and Douglas (1972) have remarked on this waxing and waning process, but it was especially pronounced for us because our subjects used large amounts of cocaine over an extended period of time. This tended to make them alternately warm and cold to us. We thus lived through a series of ups and downs with the people we were trying to cultivate as research informants.

The Overt Role

After this initial covert phase, we began to feel that some new people trusted us. We tried to intuitively feel when the time was right to approach them and go overt. We used two means of approaching people to inform them that we were involved in a study of dealing and smuggling: direct and indirect. In some cases our key informants approached their friends or connections and, after vouching for our absolute trustworthiness, convinced these associates to talk to us. In other instances, we approached people directly, asking for their help with our project. We worked our way through a progression with these secondary contacts, first discussing the dealing scene overtly and later moving to taped life history interviews. Some people reacted well to us, but others responded skittishly, making appointments to do taped interviews only to break them as the day drew near, and going through fluctuating stages of being honest with us or putting up fronts about their dealing activities. This varied, for some, with their degree of active involvement in the business. During the times when they had quit dealing, they would tell us about their present and past activities, but when they became actively involved again, they would hide it from us.

This progression of covert to overt roles generated a number of tactical difficulties. The first was the problem of *coming on too fast* and blowing it. Early in the research we had a dealer's old lady (we thought) all set up for the direct approach. We knew many dealers in common and had discussed many things tangential to dealing with her without actually mentioning the subject. When we asked her to do a taped interview of her bohemian lifestyle, she agreed without hesitation. When the interview began, though, and she found out why we were interested in her, she balked, gave us a lot of incoherent jumble, and ended the session as quickly as possible. Even though she lived only three houses away we never saw her again. We tried to move more slowly after that.

A second problem involved simultaneously *juggling our overt and covert roles* with different people. This created the danger of getting our cover blown with people who did not know about our research (Henslin 1972). It was very confusing to separate the people who knew about our study from those who did

not, especially in the minds of our informants. They would make occasional veiled references in front of people, especially when loosened by intoxicants, that made us extremely uncomfortable. We also frequently worried that our snooping would someday be mistaken for police tactics. Fortunately, this never happened. . . .

Problems and Issues

Reflecting on the research process, I have isolated a number of issues which I believe merit additional discussion. These are rooted in experiences which have the potential for greater generic applicability.

The first is the *effect of drugs on the data-gathering process.* Carey (1972) has elaborated on some of the problems he encountered when trying to interview respondents who used amphetamines, while Wax (1952, 1957) has mentioned the difficulty of trying to record field notes while drinking sake. I found that marijuana and cocaine had nearly opposite effects from each other. The latter helped the interview process, while the former hindered it. Our attempts to interview respondents who were stoned on marijuana were unproductive for a number of reasons. The primary obstacle was the effects of the drug. Often, people became confused, sleepy, or involved in eating to varying degrees. This distracted them from our purpose. At times, people even simulated overreactions to marijuana to hide behind the drug's supposed disorienting influence and thereby avoid divulging information. Cocaine, in contrast, proved to be a research aid. The drug's warming and sociable influence opened people up, diminished their inhibitions, and generally increased their enthusiasm for both the interview experience and us.

A second problem I encountered involved *assuming risks while doing research.* As I noted earlier, dangerous situations are often generic to research on deviant behavior. We were most afraid of the people we studied. As Carey

(1972), Henslin (1972), and Whyte (1955) have stated, members of deviant groups can become hostile toward a researcher if they think that they are being treated wrongfully. This could have happened at any time from a simple occurrence, such as a misunderstanding, or from something more serious, such as our covert posture being exposed. Because of the inordinate amount of drugs they consumed, drug dealers and smugglers were particularly volatile, capable of becoming malicious toward each other or us with little warning. They were also likely to behave erratically owing to the great risks they faced from the police and other dealers. These factors made them moody, and they vacillated between trusting us and being suspicious of us.

At various times we also had to protect our research tapes. We encountered several threats to our collection of taped interviews from people who had granted us these interviews. This made us anxious, since we had taken great pains to acquire these tapes and felt strongly about maintaining confidences entrusted to us by our informants. When threatened, we became extremely frightened and shifted the tapes between different hiding places. We even ventured forth one rainy night with our tapes packed in a suitcase to meet a person who was uninvolved in the research at a secret rendezvous so that he could guard the tapes for us.

We were fearful, lastly, of the police. We often worried about local police or drug agents discovering the nature of our study and confiscating or subpoenaing our tapes and field notes. Sociologists have no privileged relationship with their subjects that would enable us legally to withhold evidence from the authorities should they subpoena it. For this reason we studiously avoided any publicity about the research, even holding back on publishing articles in scholarly journals until we were nearly ready to move out of the setting. The closest we came to being publicly exposed as drug researchers came when a former sociology graduate student (turned dealer, we had heard from inside sources) was arrested at the scene of a cocaine deal. His lawyer wanted us to testify about the dangers of doing drug-related research, since he was using his research status as his defense. Fortunately, the crisis was averted when his lawyer succeeded in suppressing evidence and had the case dismissed before the trial was to have begun. Had we been exposed, however, our respondents would have acquired guilt by association through their friendship with us.

Our fear of the police went beyond our concern for protecting our research subjects, however. We risked the danger of arrest ourselves through our own violations of the law. Many sociologists (Becker 1963; Carey 1972; Polsky 1969; Whyte 1955) have remarked that field researchers studying deviance must inevitably break the law in order to acquire valid participant observation data. This occurs in its most innocuous form from having "guilty knowledge": information about crimes that are committed. Being aware of major dealing and smuggling operations made us an accessory to their commission, since we failed to notify the police. We broke the law, secondly, through our "guilty observations," by being present at the scene of a crime and witnessing its occurrence (see also Carey 1972). . . .

Another methodological issue arose from the *cultural clash between our research subjects and ourselves*. While other sociologists have alluded to these kinds of differences (Humphreys 1970, Whyte 1955), few have discussed how the research relationships affected them. Relationships with research subjects are unique because they involve a bond of intimacy between persons who might not ordinarily associate together, or who might otherwise be no more than casual friends. When fieldworkers undertake a major project, they commit themselves to maintaining a long-term relationship with the people they study. However, as researchers try to get depth involvement, they are apt to come across fundamental differences in character, values, and attitudes between their subjects and themselves. In our case, we were most strongly confronted by differences in present versus future orientations, a desire for risk versus security, and feelings of spontaneity versus self-discipline. These differences often caused us great frustration. We repeatedly saw dealers act irrationally, setting themselves up for failure. We wrestled with our desire to point out their patterns of foolhardy behavior and offer advice, feeling competing pulls between our detached, observer role which advised us not to influence the natural setting, and our involved, participant role which called for us to offer friendly help whenever possible. . . .

The final issue I will discuss involved the various *ethical problems* which arose during this research. Many fieldworkers have encountered ethical dilemmas or pangs of guilt during the course of their research experiences (Carey 1972; Douglas 1976; Humphreys 1970; Johnson 1975; Klockars 1977, 1979; Rochford 1985). The researchers' role in the field makes this necessary because they can never fully align themselves with their subjects while maintaining their identity and personal commitment to the scientific community. Ethical dilemmas, then, are directly related to the amount of deception researchers use in gathering the data, and the degree to which they have accepted such acts as necessary and therefore neutralized them.

Throughout the research, we suffered from the burden of intimacies and confidences. Guarding secrets which had been told to us during taped interviews was not always easy or pleasant. Dealers occasionally revealed things about themselves or others that we had to pretend not to know when interacting with their close associates. This sometimes meant that we had to lie or build elaborate stories to cover for some people. Their fronts therefore became our fronts, and we had to weave our own web of deception to guard their performances. This became especially disturbing during the writing of the research report, as I was torn by conflicts between using details to enrich the data and glossing over descriptions to guard confidences.

Using the covert research role generated feelings of guilt, despite the fact that our key informants deemed it necessary, and thereby condoned it. Their own covert experiences were far more deeply entrenched than ours, being a part of their daily existence with non-drug world members. Despite the universal presence of covert behavior throughout the setting, we still felt a sense of betrayal every time we ran home to write research notes on observations we had made under the guise of innocent participants. . . .

REFERENCES

Becker, Howard. 1963. *Outsiders.* New York: Free Press.

Blumer, Herbert. 1969. *Symbolic Interactionism.* Englewood Cliffs, NJ: Prentice Hall.

Carey, James T. 1972. "Problems of access and risk in observing drug scenes." In Jack D. Douglas, ed., *Research on Deviance*, pp. 71–92. New York: Random House.

Douglas, Jack D. 1972. "Observing deviance." In Jack D. Douglas, ed., *Research on Deviance*, pp. 3–34. New York: Random House.

_____. 1976. *Investigative Social Research.* Beverly Hills, CA: Sage.

Goffman, Erving. 1963. *Stigma.* Englewood Cliffs, NJ: Prentice Hall.

Henslin, James M. 1972. "Studying deviance in four settings: research experiences with cabbies, suicides, drug users and abortionees." In Jack D. Douglas, ed., *Research on Deviance*, pp. 35–70. New York: Random House.

Humphreys, Laud. 1970. *Tearoom Trade.* Chicago: Aldine.

Johnson, John M. 1975. *Doing Field Research.* New York: Free Press.

Klockars, Carl B. 1977. "Field ethics for the life history." In Robert Weppner, ed., *Street Ethnography*, pp. 201–26. Beverly Hills, CA: Sage.

_____. 1979. "Dirty hands and deviant subjects." In Carl B. Klockars and Finnbarr W. O'Connor, eds., *Deviance and Decency*, pp. 261–82. Beverly Hills, CA: Sage.

Polsky, Ned. 1969. *Hustlers, Beats, and Others.* New York: Doubleday.

Riemer, Jeffrey W. 1977. "Varieties of opportunistic research." *Urban Life* 5:467–77.

Rochford, E. Burke, Jr. 1985. *Hare Krishna in America.* New Brunswick, NJ: Rutgers University Press.

Wax, Rosalie. 1952. "Reciprocity as a field technique." *Human Organization* 11:34–37.

_____. 1957. "Twelve years later: an analysis of a field experience." *American Journal of Sociology* 63: 133–42.

Whyte, William F. 1955. *Street Corner Society.* Chicago: University of Chicago Press.

THINKING ABOUT THE READING

Many of the issues sociologists try to understand are phenomena that occur under highly secretive circumstances. Patricia A. Adler chose a research method that brought her and her husband face to face with people involved in serious criminal activities. Only from this vantage point could they fully understand the social forces at play. What does she mean when she says that researchers want to understand criminals from their own perspective? Do you think this tactic is ethical? Should social researchers be obligated to report criminal activity to the proper authorities, or is it appropriate to conceal such information in the name of scientific inquiry? Can you think of a better way to acquire accurate information about drug dealers and smugglers?

PART II

The Construction of Self and Society

Building Reality

The Social Construction of Knowledge

3

Sociologists often talk about reality as a *social construction*. What they mean is that truth and knowledge are discovered, communicated, reinforced, and changed by members of society. Truth doesn't just fall from the sky and hit us on the head. What is considered truth or knowledge is specific to a given culture. All cultures have specific rules for determining what counts as good and right and true. As social beings, we respond to our interpretations and definitions of situations, not to the situations themselves. We learn from our cultural environment what sorts of ideas and interpretations are reasonable and expected. Thus, we make sense of situations and events in our lives by applying culturally shared definitions and interpretations. In this way, we distinguish fact from fantasy, truth from fiction, myth from reality. This process of interpretation or "meaning making" is tied to interpersonal interaction, group membership, culture, history, power, economics, and politics.

Discovering patterns and determining useful knowledge are the goals of any academic discipline. The purpose of an academic field such as sociology is to provide the public with useful and relevant information about how society works. This task is typically accomplished through systematic social research—experiments, field research, unobtrusive observation, and surveys. But gathering trustworthy data can be difficult. People sometimes lie or have difficulty recalling past events in their lives. Sometimes the simple fact of observing people's behavior changes that behavior. And, as you saw in the previous chapter, sometimes the information needed to answer questions about important, controversial issues is hard to obtain without raising ethical issues.

Moreover, sometimes the characteristics and phenomena we're interested in understanding are difficult to observe and measure. Unlike other disciplines in, say, the natural sciences, sociologists deal with concepts that can't be seen or touched. In "Concepts, Indicators, and Reality," Earl Babbie gives us a brief introduction to some of the problems researchers face when they try to transform important, but abstract, concepts into *indicators* (things that researchers can systematically quantify so they can generate statistical information). In so doing, he shows us that although sociologists provide us with useful empirical findings about the world in which we live, an understanding of the measurement difficulties they face will provide us with the critical eye of an informed consumer as we go about digesting research information.

In a similar vein, Howard Schuman, in "Sense and Nonsense About Surveys," provides us with some guidance about how to interpret the information the media provide us every day. In particular, he focuses on the pitfalls of poor sampling and the dilemmas raised by poorly worded survey questions. In doing so, Schuman provides us with useful guidance on how to interpret the information that most people unquestioningly accept as truth. As a result, we become more informed consumers of socially constructed reality.

Something to Consider as You Read

Babbie's and Schuman's comments remind us that even scientists must make decisions about how to interpret information. Thus, scientists, working within academic communities, define truth and knowledge. This knowledge is often significant and useful, but we need to remember that it is the construction of a group of people following particular rules, not something that is just "out there." As you read these selections, think about the kind of information you would need or would want that might convince you to question some truth that you have always taken for granted.

Concepts, Indicators, and Reality

Earl Babbie

(1986)

Measurement is one of the fundamental aspects of social research. When we describe science as logical/empirical, we mean that scientific conclusions should (1) make sense and (2) correspond to what we can observe. It is the second of these characteristics I want to explore in this essay.

Suppose we are interested in learning whether education really reduces prejudice. To do that, we must be able to measure both prejudice and education. Once we've distinguished prejudiced people from unprejudiced people and educated people from uneducated people, we'll be in a position to find out whether the two variables are related.

Social scientific measurement operates in accordance with the following implicit model:

- Prejudice exists as a *variable*: some people are more prejudiced than others.
- There are numerous *indicators* of prejudice.
- None of the indicators provides a perfect reflection of prejudice as it "really" is, but they can point to it at least approximately.
- We should try to find better and better indicators of prejudice—indicators that come ever closer to the "real thing."

This model applies to all of the variables social scientists study. Take a minute to look through the following list of variables commonly examined in social research.

Arms race	Tolerance
Religiosity	Fascism
Urbanism	Parochialism
TV watching	Maturity
Susceptibility	Solidarity
Stereotyping	Instability
Anti-Semitism	Education
Voting	Liberalism
Dissonance	Authoritarianism
Pessimism	Race
Anxiety	Happiness
Revolution	Powerlessness
Alienation	Mobility
Social class	Consistency
Age	Delinquency
Self-esteem	Compassion
Idealism	Democracy
Prestige	Influence

Even if you've never taken a course in social science, many of these terms are at least somewhat familiar to you. Social scientists study things that are of general interest to everyone. The nuclear arms race affects us all, for example, and it is a special concern for many of us. Differences in *religiosity* (some of us are more religious than others) are also of special interest to some people. As our country has evolved from small towns to large cities, we've all thought and talked more about *urbanism*—the good and bad associated with city life. Similar interests can be identified for all of the other terms.

My point is that you've probably thought about many of the variables mentioned in the list. Those you are familiar with undoubtedly have the quality of reality for you: that is, you know they exist. Religiosity, for example, is real. Regardless of whether you're in favor of it, opposed to it, or don't care much one way or the other, you at least know that religiosity exists. Or does it?

This is a particularly interesting question for me, since my first book, *To Comfort and to Challenge* (with Charles Glock and Benjamin Ringer), was about this subject. In particular, we wanted to know why some people were more religious than others (the sources of religiosity) and what impact differences in religiosity had on other aspects of life (the consequences of religiosity). Looking for the sources and consequences of a particular variable is a conventional social scientific undertaking; the first step is to develop a measure of that variable. We had to develop methods for distinguishing religious people, nonreligious people, and those somewhere in between.

The question we faced was, if religiosity is real, how do we know that? How do we distinguish religious people from nonreligious people? For most contemporary Americans, a number of answers come readily to mind. Religious people go to church, for example. They believe in the tenets of their faith. They pray. They read religious materials, such as the Bible, and they participate in religious organizations.

Not all religious people do all of these things, of course, and a great deal depends on their particular religious affiliation, if any. Christians believe in the divinity of Jesus; Jews do not. Moslems believe Mohammed's teachings are sacred; Jews and Christians do not. Some signs of religiosity are to be found in seemingly secular realms. Orthodox Jews, for example, refrain from eating pork; Seventh-Day Adventists don't drink alcohol.

In our study, we were interested in religiosity among a very specific group: Episcopal churchmembers in America. To simplify our present discussion, let's look at that much narrower question: How can you distinguish religious from nonreligious Episcopalians in America?

As I've indicated above, we are likely to say that religious people attend church, whereas nonreligious people do not. Thus, if we know someone who attends church every week, we're likely to think of that person as religious; indeed, religious people joke about churchmembers who only attend services on Easter and at Christmas. The latter are presumed to be less religious.

Of course, we are speaking rather casually here, so let's see whether church attendance would be an adequate measure of religiosity for Episcopalians and other mainstream American Christians. Would you be willing to equate religiosity with church attendance? That is, would you be willing to call religious everyone who attended church every week, let's say, and call nonreligious everyone who did not?

I suspect that you would not consider equating church attendance with religiosity a wise policy. For example, consider a political figure who attends church every Sunday, sits in the front pew, puts a large contribution in the collection plate with a flourish, and by all other evidence seems only interested in being known as a religious person for the political advantage that may entail. Let's add that the politician in question regularly lies and cheats, exhibits no Christian compassion toward others, and ridicules religion in private. You'd probably consider it inappropriate to classify that person as religious.

Now imagine someone confined to a hospital bed, who spends every waking minute reading in the Bible, leading other patients in prayer, raising money for missionary work abroad—but never going to church. Probably this would fit your image of a religious person.

These deviant cases illustrate that, while church attendance is somehow related to religiosity, it is not a sufficient indicator in and of itself. So how can we distinguish religious from nonreligious people?

Prayer is a possibility. Presumably, people who pray a lot are more religious than those who don't. But wouldn't it matter what they prayed for? Suppose they were only praying for money. How about the Moslem extremist praying daily for the extermination of the Jews? How about the athlete praying for an opponent to be hit by a truck? Like church attendance, prayer seems to have something to do with religiosity, but we can't simply equate the two.

We might consider religious beliefs. Among Christians, for example, it would seem to make sense that a person who believes in God is more religious than one who does not. However, this would require that we consider the person who says, "I'll believe anything they say just as long as I don't rot in Hell" more religious than, say, a concerned theologian who completes a lifetime of concentrated and devoted study of humbly concluding that who or what God is cannot be known with certainty. We'd probably decide that this was a misclassification.

Without attempting to exhaust all the possible indicators of religiosity, I hope it's clear that we would never find a single measure that will satisfy us as tapping the real essence of religiosity. In recognition of this, social researchers use a combination of indicators to create a *composite measure*—an index or a scale—of variables such as religiosity. Such a measure might include all of the indicators discussed so far: church attendance, prayer, and beliefs.

While composite measures are usually a good idea, they do not really solve the dilemma I've laid out. With a little thought, we could certainly imagine circumstances in which a "truly" religious person nonetheless didn't attend church, pray, or believe, and we could likewise imagine a nonreligious person who did all of those things. In either event, we would have demonstrated the imperfection of the composite measure.

Recognition of this often leads people to conclude that variables like religiosity are simply beyond empirical measurement. This conclusion is true and false and even worse.

The conclusion is false in that we can make any measurement we want. For example, we can ask people if they attend church regularly and call that a measure of religiosity just as easily as Yankee Doodle called the feather in his hat macaroni. In our case, moreover, most people would say that what we've measured is by no means irrelevant to religiosity.

The conclusion is true in that no empirical measurement—single or composite—will satisfy all of us as having captured the essence of religiousness. Since that can never happen, we can never satisfactorily measure religiosity.

The situation is worse than either of these comments suggests in that the reason we can't measure religiosity is that it doesn't exist! Religiosity isn't real. Neither is prejudice, love, alienation, or any of those other variables. Let's see why.

There's a very old puzzle I'm sure you're familiar with: when a tree falls in the forest, does it make a sound if no one is there to hear it? High school and college students have struggled with that one for centuries. There's no doubt that the unobserved falling tree will still crash through the branches of its neighbors, snap its own limbs into pieces, and slam against the ground. But would it make a sound?

If you've given this any thought before, you've probably come to the conclusion that the puzzle rests on the ambiguity of the word *sound*. Where does sound occur? In this example, does it occur in the falling tree, in the air, or in the ear of the beholder? We can be reasonably certain that the falling tree generates turbulent waves in the air; if those waves in the air strike your ear, you will experience something we call *hearing*. We say you've heard a sound. But do the waves in the air per se qualify as sound?

The answer to this central question is necessarily arbitrary. We can have it be whichever way we want. The truth is that (1) a tree fell; (2) it created waves in the air; and (3) if the waves reached someone's ear, they would cause an experience for that person. Humans created the idea of *sound* in the context of that whole process. Whenever waves in the air cause an experience by way of our ears, we use the term *sound* to identify that experience. We're usually not too precise about where the sound happens: in the tree, in the air, or in our ears.

Our imprecise use of the term *sound* produces the apparent dilemma. So what's the truth? What's really the case? Does it make a sound or not? The truth is that (1) a tree fell; (2) it created waves in the air; and (3) if the waves reached someone's ear, they would cause an experience for that person. That's it. That's the final and ultimate truth of the matter.

I've belabored this point, because it sets the stage for understanding a critical issue in social research—one that often confuses students. To move in the direction of that issue, let's shift from sound to sight for a moment. Here's a new puzzle for you: are the tree's leaves green if no one is there to see them? Take a minute to think about that, and then continue reading.

Here's how I'd answer the question. The tree's leaves have a certain physical and chemical composition that affects the reflection of light rays off of them; specifically, they only reflect the green portion of the light spectrum. When rays from that portion of the light spectrum hit our eyes, they create an experience we call the color green.

"But are the leaves green if no one sees them?" you may ask. The answer to that is whatever we want it to be, since we haven't specified where the color green exists: in the physical/chemical composition of the leaf, in the light rays reflected from the leaf, or in our eyes.

While we are free to specify what we mean by the color green in this sense, nothing we do can change the ultimate truth, the ultimate reality of the matter. The truth is that (1) the leaves have a certain physical and chemical composition; (2) they reflect only a portion of the light spectrum; and (3) that portion of the light spectrum causes an experience if it hits our eyes. That's the ultimate truth of the universe in this matter.

By the same token, the truth about religiosity is that (1) some people to go church more than others; (2) some pray more than others; (3) some believe more than others; and so forth. This is observably the case.

At some point, our ancestors noticed that the things we're discussing were not completely independent of one another. People who went to church seemed to pray more, on the whole, than people who didn't go to church. Moreover, those who went to church and prayed seemed to believe more of the church's teachings than did those who neither went to church nor prayed. The observation of relationships such as these led them to conclude literally that "there is more here than meets the eye." The term *religiosity* was created to represent the *concept* that all the concrete observables seemed to have in common. People gradually came to believe that the concepts were real and the "indicators" only pale reflections.

We can never find a "true" measure of religiosity, prejudice, alienation, love, compassion, or any other such concepts, since none of them exists except in our minds. Concepts are "figments of our imaginations." I do not mean to suggest that concepts are useless or should be dispensed with. Life as we know it depends on the creation and use of concepts, and science would be impossible without them. Still, we should recognize that they are fictitious, then we can trade them in for more useful ones whenever appropriate.

THINKING ABOUT THE READING

Define the following terms: "poverty," "happiness," "academic effort," "love." Now consider what indicators you would use to determine people's levels of each of these concepts. The indicator must be something that will allow you to clearly determine whether or not someone is in a particular state (such as: poor or not poor; happy or not happy; in love or not in love). For example, you might decide that "blushing" in the presence of someone is one indicator of being "in love" or that the number of hours a person spends studying for a test is an indicator of "academic effort." What's wrong with simply asking people if they're poor, if they're in love, if they're happy, or if they work hard? Consider the connection between how a concept is defined and how it can be measured. Is it possible that sociology sometimes uses concepts that seem meaningless because they are easier to "see" and measure?

Sense and Nonsense About Surveys

Howard Schuman

(2002)

Surveys draw on two human propensities that have served us well from ancient times. One is to gather information by asking questions. The first use of language around 100,000 years ago may have been to utter commands such as "Come here!" or "Wait!" Questions must have followed soon after: "Why?" or "What for?" From that point, it would have been only a short step to the use of interrogatives to learn where a fellow hominid had seen potential food, a dangerous animal, or something else of importance. Asking questions continues to be an effective way of acquiring information of all kinds, assuming of course that the person answering is able and willing to respond accurately.

The other inclination, learning about one's environment by examining a small part of it, is the sampling aspect of surveys. A taste of something may or may not point to appetizing food. A first inquiry to a stranger, a first glance around a room, a first date—each is a sample of sorts, often used to decide whether it is wise to proceed further. As with questions, however, one must always be aware of the possibility that the sample may not prove adequate to the task.

Sampling: How Gallup Achieved Fame

Only within the past century—and especially in the 1930s and 1940s—were major improvements made in the sampling process that allowed the modern survey to develop and flourish. A crucial change involved recognition that the value of a sample comes not simply from its size but also from the way it is obtained. Every serious pursuit likes to have a morality tale that supports its basic beliefs: witness Eve and the apple in the Bible or Newton and his apple in legends about scientific discovery. Representative sampling has a marvelous morality tale also, with the additional advantage of its being true.

The story concerns the infamous *Literary Digest* poll prediction—based on 10 million questionnaires sent out and more than two million received back—that Roosevelt would lose decisively in the 1936 presidential election. At the same time, George Gallup, using many fewer cases but a much better method, made the more accurate prediction that FDR would win. Gallup used quotas in choosing respondents in order to represent different economic strata, whereas the *Literary Digest* had worked mainly from telephone and automobile ownership lists, which in 1936 were biased toward wealthy people apt to be opposed to Roosevelt. (There were other sources of bias as well.) As a result, the *Literary Digest* poll disappeared from the scene, and Gallup was on his way to becoming a household name.

Yet despite their intuitive grasp of the importance of representing the electorate accurately, Gallup and other commercial pollsters did not use the probability sampling methods that were being developed in the same decades and that are fundamental to social science surveys today. Probability sampling in its simplest form calls for each person in the population to have an equal chance of being selected. It can also be used in more complex applications where the chances are deliberately made to be unequal, for example, when oversampling a minority group in order

57

to study it more closely; however, the chances of being selected must still be known so that they can later be equalized when considering the entire population.

Intuitions and Counterintuitions About Sample Size

Probability sampling theory reveals a crucial but counterintuitive point about sample size: the size of a sample needed to accurately estimate a value for a population depends very little on the size of the population. For example, almost the same size sample is needed to estimate, with a given degree of precision, the proportion of left-handed people in the United States as is needed to make the same estimate for, say, Peoria, Illinois. In both cases a reasonably accurate estimate can be obtained with a sample size of around 1,000. (More cases are needed when extraordinary precision is called for, for example, in calculating unemployment rates, where even a tenth of a percent change may be regarded as important.)

The link between population size and sample size cuts both ways. Although huge samples are not needed for huge populations like those of the United States or China, a handful of cases is not sufficient simply because one's interest is limited to Peoria. This implication is often missed by those trying to save time and money when sampling a small community.

Moreover, all of these statements depend on restricting your interest to overall population values. If you are concerned about, say, left-handedness among African Americans, then African Americans become your population, and you need much the same sample size as for Peoria or the United States.

Who Is Missing?

A good sample depends on more than probability sampling theory. Surveys vary greatly in their quality of implementation, and this variation is not captured by the "margin of error" plus/minus percentage figures that accompany most media reports of polls. Such percentages reflect the size of the final sample, but they do not reveal the sampling method or the extent to which the targeted individuals or households were actually included in the final sample. These details are at least as important as the sample size.

When targeted members of a population are not interviewed or do not respond to particular questions, the omissions are a serious problem if they are numerous and if those missed differ from those who are interviewed on the matters being studied. The latter difference can seldom be known with great confidence, so it is usually desirable to keep omissions to a minimum. For example, sampling from telephone directories is undesirable because it leaves out those with unlisted telephones, as well as those with no telephones at all. Many survey reports are based on such poor sampling procedures that they may not deserve to be taken seriously. This is especially true of reports based on "focus groups," which offer lots of human interest but are subject to vast amounts of error. Internet surveys also cannot represent the general population adequately at present, though this is an area where some serious attempts are being made to compensate for the inherent difficulties. . . .

The percentage of people who refuse to take part in a survey is particularly important. In some federal surveys, the percentage is small, within the range of 5 to 10 percent. For even the best nongovernment surveys, the refusal rate can reach 25 percent or more, and it can be far larger in the case of poorly executed surveys. Refusals have risen substantially from earlier days, becoming a major cause for concern among serious survey practitioners. Fortunately, in recent years research has shown that moderate amounts of nonresponse in an otherwise careful survey seem in most cases not to have a major effect on results. Indeed, even the *Literary Digest*, with its abysmal sampling and massive nonresponse rate, did well predicting elections before the dramatic realignment of the electorate in 1936. The problem is that one can never be certain as to the effects of refusals and other forms of non-response, so obtaining a high response rate remains an important goal.

Questions About Questions

Since survey questions resemble the questions we ask in ordinary social interaction, they may seem less problematic than the counterintuitive and technical aspects of sampling. Yet survey results are every bit as dependent on the form, wording, and context of the questions asked as they are on the sample of people who answer them.

No classic morality tale like the *Literary Digest* fiasco highlights the question-answer process, but an example from the early days of surveys illustrates both the potential challenges of question writing and the practical solutions.

In 1940 Donald Rugg asked two slightly different questions to equivalent national samples about the general issue of freedom of speech:

- Do you think the United States should forbid public speeches against democracy?
- Do you think the United States should allow public speeches against democracy?

Taken literally, forbidding something and not allowing something have the same effect, but clearly the public did not view the questions as identical. Whereas 75 percent of the public would not allow such speeches, only 54 percent would forbid them, a difference of 21 percentage points. This finding was replicated several times in later years, not only in the United States but also (with appropriate translations) in Germany and the Netherlands. Such "survey-based experiments" call for administering different versions of a question to random subsamples of a larger sample. If the results between the subsamples differ by more than can be easily explained by chance, we infer that the difference is due to the variation in wording.

In addition, answers to survey questions always depend on the form in which a question is asked. If the interviewer presents a limited set of alternatives, most respondents will choose one, rather than offering a different alternative of their own. In one survey-based experiment, for example, we asked a national sample of Americans to name the most important problem facing the country. Then we asked a comparable sample a parallel question that provided a list of four problems from which to choose the most important; this list included none of the four problems mentioned most often by the first sample but instead provided four problems that had been mentioned by fewer than 3 percent of the earlier respondents. The list question also invited respondents to substitute a different problem if they wished (see table 1). Despite the invitation, the majority of respondents (60 percent) chose one of the rare problems offered, reflecting their reluctance to go outside the frame of reference provided by the question. The form of a question provides the "rules of the game" for respondents, and this must always be kept in mind when interpreting results.

Other difficulties occur with survey questions when issues are discussed quite generally, as though there is a single way of framing them and just two sides to the debate. For example, what is called "the abortion issue" really consists of different issues: the reasons for an abortion, the trimester involved, and so forth. In a recent General Social Survey, nearly 80 percent of the national sample supported legal abortion in the case of "a serious defect in the baby," but only 44 percent supported it "if the family has a low income and cannot afford any more children." Often what is thought to be a conflict in findings between two surveys is actually a difference in the aspects of the general issue that they queried. In still other cases an inconsistency reflects a type of illogical wish fulfillment in the public itself, as when majorities favor both a decrease in taxes and an increase in government services if the questions are asked separately.

Table 1   Experimental Variation Between Open and Closed Questions

A. Open Question "What do you think is the most important problem facing this country today [1986]?"

B. Closed Question "Which of the following do you think is the most important problem facing this country today [1986]—the energy shortage, the quality of public schools, legalized abortion, or pollution—or, if you prefer, you may name a different problem as most important."

    1. Energy shortage

    2. Quality of public schools

    3. Legalized abortion

    4. Pollution

SOURCE: Adapted from H. Schuman and I. Scott, "Problems in the Use of Survey Questions to Measure Public Opinion," *Science* v. 236, pp. 957–59, May 22, 1987.

Solutions to the Question Wording Problem

All these and still other difficulties (including the order in which questions are asked) suggest that responses to single survey questions on complex issues should be viewed with considerable skepticism. What to do then, other than to reject all survey data as unusable for serious purposes? One answer can be found from the replications of the forbid/allow experiment above: Although there was a 21 percentage points difference based on question wording in 1940 and a slightly larger difference (24 percentage points) when the experiment was repeated some 35 years later, both the forbid and the allow wordings registered similar declines in Americans' intolerance of speeches against democracy. . . . No matter which question was used—as long as it was the same one at both times—the conclusion about the increase in civil libertarian sentiments was the same.

More generally, what has been called the "principle of form-resistant correlations" holds in most cases: if question wording (and meaning) is kept constant, differences over time, differences across educational levels, and most other careful comparisons are not seriously affected by specific question wording.

Indeed, the distinction between results for single questions and results based on comparisons or associations holds even for simple factual inquiries. Consider, for example, a study of the number of rooms in American houses. No God-given rule states what to include when counting the rooms in a house (bathrooms? basements? hallways?); hence the average number reported for a particular place and time should not be treated as an absolute truth. What we can do, however, is try to apply the same definitions over time, across social divisions, even across nations. That way, we gain confidence in the comparisons we make—who has more rooms than who, for example. . . .

We still face the task of interpreting the meaning of questions and of associations among questions, but that is true in all types of research. Even an index constructed from a large number of questions on the basis of a sophisticated statistical calculation called factor analysis inevitably requires the investigator to interpret what it is that he or she has measured. There is no escaping this theoretical challenge, fundamental to all research, whether using surveys or other methods such as field observations.

Survey researchers should also ask several different questions about any important issue.

In addition to combining questions to increase reliability, the different answers can be synthesized rather than depending on the angle of vision provided by any single question. A further safeguard is to carry out frequent experiments like that on the forbid/allow wordings. By varying the form, wording, and context of questions, researchers can gain insight into both the questions and the relevant issues. Sometimes variations turn out to make no difference, and that is also useful to learn. For example, I once expected support for legalized abortion to increase when a question substituted *end pregnancy* for the word *abortion* in the phrasing. Yet no difference was found. Today, more and more researchers include survey-based experiments as part of their investigations, and readers should look for these sorts of safeguards when evaluating survey results.

The Need for Comparisons

To interpret surveys accurately, it's important to use a framework of comparative data in evaluating the results. For example, teachers know that course evaluations can be interpreted best against the backdrop of evaluations from other similar courses: a 75 percent rating of lectures as "excellent" takes on a quite different meaning depending on whether the average for other lecture courses is 50 percent or 90 percent. Such comparisons are fundamental for all survey results, yet they are easily overlooked when one feels the urge to speak definitively about public reactions to a unique event.

Comparative analysis over time, along with survey-based experiments, can also help us understand responses to questions about socially sensitive subjects. Experiments have shown that expressions of racial attitudes can change substantially for both black and white Americans depending on the interviewer's race. White respondents, for instance, are more likely to support racial intermarriage when speaking to a black than to a white interviewer.

Such self-censoring mirrors variations in cross-race conversations outside of surveys, reflecting not a methodological artifact of surveys but rather a fact of life about race relations in America. Still, if we consider time trends, with the race of interviewer kept constant, we can also see that white responses supporting intermarriage have clearly increased over the past half century (see table 2), that actual intermarriage rates have also risen (though from a much lower level) over recent years, and that the public visibility of cross-race marriage and dating has also increased. It would be foolish to assume that the survey data on racial attitudes reflect actions in any literal sense, but they do capture important *trends* in both norms and behavior. . . .

Surveys remain our best tool for learning about large populations. One remarkable advantage surveys have over some other methods is the ability to identify their own limitations, as illustrated by the development of both probability theory in sampling and experiments in questioning. In the end, however, with surveys as with all research methods, there is no substitute for both care and intelligence in the way evidence is gathered and interpreted. What we learn about society is always mediated by the instruments we use, including our own eyes and ears. As Isaac Newton wrote long ago, error is not in the art but in the artificers.

Table 2   Percent of White Americans Approving or Disapproving of Racial Intermarriage, 1958–1997

"Do you approve or disapprove of marriage between blacks and whites?"

Year	Approve	Disapprove
1958	4	96
1978	34	66
1997	67	33

SOURCE: Gallup Poll.

THINKING ABOUT THE READING

Schuman offers a few examples of how we all use sampling in our everyday lives. Come up with some examples of your own. For instance, how many students did you meet or talk with when considering whether to attend your current school? How confident are you about the ability of this "sample" to represent your school climate? What kinds of techniques and knowledge might make a social science survey more accurate than this kind of informal sampling? Schuman says that certain contemporary domains, such as the Internet, are difficult to survey representatively. What does he mean by this? What is the "wording problem"? In your opinion, do you think that people are inclined to give answers to survey questions even if they have never thought about the issue before? If so, what kind of information does this provide about human beliefs and motivations? What kinds of methods might be used to gather accurate information about human social life? What are some of the advantages and disadvantages of these methods?

Building Order

Culture and History

4

Culture provides members of a society with a common bond and a set of shared rules and beliefs for making sense of the world in similar ways. Shared cultural knowledge makes it possible for people to live together in a society. Sociologists refer to shared cultural expectations as social norms. Norms are the rules and standards that govern all social encounters and the mechanisms that provide order in our day-to-day lives. Shared norms make it possible to know what to expect from others and what others can expect from us. When norms are violated, we are reminded of the boundaries of social behavior. These violations lead us to notice otherwise taken-for-granted rules about what is considered right and wrong.

When we examine the social influences on our behavior, things that were once familiar and taken for granted suddenly become unfamiliar and curious. During the course of our lives, we are rarely forced to examine *why* we do the common things we do; we just do them. But if we take a step back and examine our common customs and behaviors, they begin to look as strange as the "mystical" rituals of some far-off, exotic land. It is for this reason that Horace Miner's article, "Body Ritual Among the Nacirema," has become a classic in sociology and anthropology. As you read this selection, consider the process of using the sociological imagination to understand your own life and the lives of others. When you think about other cultures, how can you be sure that your perceptions, as an outsider, are not as bizarre as Miner's perspective on the Nacirema? When done well, sociological research helps us to understand different points of view and different cultural contexts from the perspective of insiders.

Cultural clashes can be quite confusing and painful for newly arrived immigrants from countries with vastly different cultural traditions. In the article "The Melting Pot," Anne Fadiman examines the experiences of Hmong refugees in the United States. Hundreds of thousands of Hmong people have fled Laos since that country fell to communist forces in 1975. Most have settled in the United States. Virtually every element of Hmong culture and tradition stands in stark contrast to the highly modernized culture of U.S. society. The Hmong have been described in the U.S. media as simplistic, primitive, and throwbacks to the Stone Age. This article vividly portrays the everyday conflicts immigrants face as they straddle two vastly different cultures.

What happens when an industry is transported from one culture to another, especially if the cultures are very different? In the third reading for the section, James L. Watson addresses this question in the context of the transportation of the fast food industry, specifically McDonald's, to Hong Kong. McDonald's epitomizes Western cultural patterns of fast food consumption and other norms of consumer capitalism. What happens when this industry arrives in Asia? Watson observes that the result is cultural changes that reflect both globalization processes and also local resistance to those processes. Accordingly, this article demonstrates the importance of looking closely at local cultures in studying the effects of globalization.

Something to Consider as You Read

How do cultural practices provide social order? Where is this order located? In our minds? In our interactions with others? Think about what happens to your own sense of order when you become immersed in a different culture. What are some of the challenges you might face in trying to maintain your own cultural beliefs and practices while living in a completely different culture? Are some cultural practices easier to export than others? Why? As you read and compare these selections, think about why some cultures consider their ways to be better and more "real" than others. Do you think this ethnocentrism is a hallmark of all cultures, or just some? As processes of globalization increase, what are the consequences for local cultures?

Body Ritual Among the Nacirema

Horace Miner

(1956)

The anthropologist has become so familiar with the diversity of ways in which different peoples behave in similar situations that he is not apt to be surprised by even the most exotic customs. In fact, if all of the logically possible combinations of behavior have not been found somewhere in the world, he is apt to suspect that they must be present in some yet undescribed tribe. This point has, in fact, been expressed with respect to clan organization by Murdock (1949, p. 71). In this light, the magical beliefs and practices of the Nacirema present such unusual aspects that it seems desirable to describe them as an example of the extremes to which human behavior can go.

Professor Linton first brought the ritual of the Nacirema to the attention of anthropologists twenty years ago (1936, p. 326), but the culture of this people is still very poorly understood. They are a North American group living in the territory between the Canadian Cree, the Yaqui and Tarahumara of Mexico, and the Carib and Arawak of the Antilles. Little is known of their origin, although tradition states that they came from the east. According to Nacirema mythology, their nation was originated by a culture hero, Notgnihsaw, who is otherwise known for two great feats of strength—the throwing of a piece of wampum across the river Pa-To-Mac and the chopping down of a cherry tree in which the Spirit of Truth resided.

Nacirema culture is characterized by a highly developed market economy which has evolved in a rich natural habitat. While much of the people's time is devoted to economic pursuits, a large part of the fruits of these labors and a considerable portion of the day are spent in ritual activity. The focus of this activity is the human body, the appearance and health of which loom as a dominant concern in the ethos of the people. While such a concern is certainly not unusual, its ceremonial aspects and associated philosophy are unique.

The fundamental belief underlying the whole system appears to be that the human body is ugly and that its natural tendency is to debility and disease. Incarcerated in such a body, man's only hope is to avert these characteristics through the use of the powerful influences of ritual and ceremony. Every household has one or more shrines devoted to this purpose. The more powerful individuals in this society have several shrines in their houses and, in fact, the opulence of a house is often referred to in terms of the number of such ritual centers it possesses. Most houses are of wattle and daub construction, but the shrine rooms of the more wealthy are walled with stone. Poorer families imitate the rich by applying pottery plaques to their shrine walls.

While each family has at least one such shrine, the rituals associated with it are not family ceremonies but are private and secret. The rites are normally only discussed with children, and then only during the period when they are being initiated into these mysteries. I was able, however, to establish sufficient rapport with the natives to examine these shrines and to have the rituals described to me.

The focal point of the shrine is a box or chest which is built into the wall. In this chest are kept the many charms and magical potions without which no native believes he could live. These preparations are secured from a variety of specialized practitioners. The most powerful of these are the medicine men, whose assistance must be rewarded with substantial gifts. However, the medicine men do not provide the curative potions for their clients, but decide what the ingredients should be and then write them down in an ancient and secret language. This writing is understood only by the medicine men and by the herbalists who, for another gift, provide the required charm.

The charm is not disposed of after it has served its purpose, but is placed in the charm-box of the household shrine. As these magical materials are specific for certain ills, and the real or imagined maladies of the people are many, the charm-box is usually full to overflowing. The magical packets are so numerous that people forget what their purposes were and fear to use them again. While the natives are very vague on this point, we can only assume that the idea in retaining all the old magical materials is that their presence in the charm-box, before which the body rituals are conducted, will in some way protect the worshipper.

Beneath the charm-box is a small font. Each day every member of the family, in succession, enters the shrine room, bows his head before the charm-box, mingles different sorts of holy water in the font, and proceeds with a brief rite of ablution. The holy waters are secured from the Water Temple of the community, where the priests conduct elaborate ceremonies to make the liquid ritually pure.

In the hierarchy of magical practitioners, and below the medicine men in prestige, are specialists whose designation is best translated "holy-mouth-men." The Nacirema have an almost pathological horror of and fascination with the mouth, the condition of which is believed to have a supernatural influence on all social relationships. Were it not for the rituals of the mouth, they believe that their teeth would fall out, their gums bleed, their jaws shrink, their friends desert them, and their lovers reject them. They also believe that a strong relationship exists between oral and moral characteristics. For example, there is a ritual ablution of the mouth for children which is supposed to improve their moral fiber.

The daily body ritual performed by everyone includes a mouth-rite. Despite the fact that these people are so punctilious about care of the mouth, this rite involves a practice which strikes the uninitiated stranger as revolting. It was reported to me that the ritual consists of inserting a small bundle of hog hairs into the mouth, along with certain magical powders, and then moving the bundle in a highly formalized series of gestures.

In addition to the private mouth-rite, the people seek out a holy-mouth-man once or twice a year. These practitioners have an impressive set of paraphernalia, consisting of a variety of augers, awls, probes, and prods. The use of these objects in the exorcism of the evils of the mouth involves almost unbelievable ritual torture of the client. The holy-mouth-man opens the client's mouth and, using the above-mentioned tools, enlarges any holes which decay may have created in the teeth. Magical materials are put into these holes. If there are no naturally occurring holes in the teeth, large sections of one or more teeth are gouged out so that the supernatural substance can be applied. In the client's view, the purpose of these ministrations is to arrest decay and to draw friends. The extremely sacred and traditional character of the rite is evident in the fact that the natives return to the holy-mouth-man year after year, despite the fact that their teeth continue to decay.

It is to be hoped that, when a thorough study of the Nacirema is made, there will be careful inquiry into the personality structure of these people. One has but to watch the gleam in the eye of a holy-mouth-man, as he jabs an awl into an exposed nerve, to suspect that a certain amount of sadism is involved. If this can be established, a very interesting pattern emerges, for most of the population shows definite masochistic tendencies. It was to these that Professor Linton referred in discussing a distinctive part of the daily body ritual which is performed only by men. This part of the rite involves scraping and lacerating the surface of the face with a sharp instrument. Special women's rites are performed only four times during each lunar month, but what they lack in frequency is made up in barbarity. As part of this ceremony, women bake their heads in small ovens for about an hour. The theoretically interesting point is that what seems to be a preponderantly masochistic people have developed sadistic specialists.

The medicine men have an imposing temple, or *latipso,* in every community of any size. The more elaborate ceremonies required to treat very sick patients can only be performed at this temple. These ceremonies involve not only the thaumaturge but a permanent group of vestal maidens who move sedately about the temple chambers in distinctive costume and headdress.

The *latipso* ceremonies are so harsh that it is phenomenal that a fair proportion of the really sick natives who enter the temple ever recover. Small children whose indoctrination is still incomplete have been known to resist attempts to take them to the temple because "that is where you go to die." Despite this fact, sick adults are not only willing but eager to undergo the protracted ritual purification, if they can afford to do so. No matter how ill the supplicant or how grave the emergency, the guardians of many temples will not admit a client if he cannot give a rich gift to the custodian. Even after one has gained admission and survived the ceremonies, the guardians will not permit the neophyte to leave until he makes still another gift.

The supplicant entering the temple is first stripped of all his or her clothes. In everyday life the Nacirema avoids exposure of his body and its natural functions. Bathing and excretory acts are performed only in the secrecy of the household shrine, where they are ritualized as part of the body-rites. Psychological shock results from the fact that body secrecy is suddenly lost upon entry into the *latipso.* A man, whose own wife has never seen him in an excretory act, suddenly finds himself naked and assisted by a vestal maiden while he performs his natural functions into a sacred vessel. This sort of ceremonial treatment is necessitated by the fact that the excreta are used by a diviner to ascertain the course and nature of the client's sickness. Female clients, on the other hand, find their naked bodies are subjected to the scrutiny, manipulation, and prodding of the medicine men.

Few supplicants in the temple are well enough to do anything but lie on their hard beds. The daily ceremonies, like the rites of the holy-mouth-men, involve discomfort and torture. With ritual precision, the vestals awaken their miserable charges each dawn and roll them about on their beds of pain while performing ablutions, in the formal movements of which the maidens are highly trained. At other times they insert magic wands in the supplicant's mouth or force him to eat substances which are supposed to be healing. From time to time the medicine men come to their clients and jab magically treated needles into their flesh. The fact that these temple ceremonies may not cure, and may even kill the neophyte, in no way decreases the people's faith in the medicine men.

There remains one other kind of practitioner, known as a "listener." This witch-doctor has the power to exorcise the devils that lodge in the heads of people who have been bewitched. The Nacirema believe that parents bewitch their own children. Mothers are particularly suspected of putting a curse on children while teaching them the secret body rituals. The counter-magic of the witch-doctor is unusual in its lack of ritual. The patient simply tells the "listener" all his troubles and fears, beginning with the earliest difficulties he can remember. The memory displayed by the Nacirema in these exorcism sessions is truly remarkable. It is not uncommon for the patient to bemoan the rejection he felt upon being weaned as a babe, and a few individuals even see their troubles going back to the traumatic effects of their own birth.

In conclusion, mention must be made of certain practices which have their base in native esthetics but which depend upon the pervasive aversion to the natural body and its functions. There are ritual fasts to make fat people thin and ceremonial feasts to make thin people fat. Still other rites are used to make women's breasts larger if they are small, and smaller if they are large. General dissatisfaction with breast shape is symbolized in the fact that the ideal form is virtually outside the range of human variation. A few women afflicted with almost inhuman hypermammary development are so idolized that they make a handsome living by simply going from village to village and permitting the natives to stare at them for a fee.

Reference has already been made to the fact that excretory functions are ritualized, routinized, and relegated to secrecy. Natural reproductive functions are similarly distorted. Intercourse is taboo as a topic and scheduled as an act. Efforts are made to avoid pregnancy by the use of magical materials or by limiting intercourse to certain phases of the moon. Conception is actually very infrequent. When pregnant, women dress so as to hide their condition. Parturition takes place in secret, without friends or relatives to assist, and the majority of women do not nurse their infants.

Our review of the ritual life of the Nacirema has certainly shown them to be a magic-ridden people. It is hard to understand how they have managed to exist so long under the burdens which they have imposed upon themselves. But even such exotic customs as these take on real meaning when they are viewed with the insight provided by Malinowski when he wrote (1948, p. 70):

> Looking from far and above, from our high places of safety in the developed civilization, it is easy to see all the crudity and irrelevance of magic. But without its power and guidance early man could not have mastered his practical difficulties as he has done, nor could man have advanced to the higher stages of civilization.

REFERENCES

Linton, R. (1936). *The study of man.* New York: Appleton-Century.

Malinowski, B. (1948). *Magic, science, and religion.* Glencoe, IL: Free Press.

Murdock, G. P. (1949). *Social structure.* New York: Macmillan.

THINKING ABOUT THE READING

What do you think of this culture? Do their ways seem very foreign or are there some things that seem familiar? This article was written more than 50 years ago and, of course, much has changed since then. How might you update this description of the "Nacirema" to account for current values and rituals? Imagine you are an anthropologist from a culture completely unfamiliar with Western traditions. Using your own life as a starting point, think of common patterns of work, leisure, learning, intimacy, eating, sleeping, and so forth. Are there some customs that distinguish your group (religious, racial, ethnic, friendship, etc.) from others? See if you can find the reasons why these customs exist, which customs serve an obvious purpose (e.g., health), which might seem arbitrary and silly to an outside observer?

The Melting Pot

Anne Fadiman

(1997)

The Lee family—Nao Kao, Foua, Chong, Zoua, Cheng, May, Yer, and True—arrived in the United States on December 18, 1980. Their luggage consisted of a few clothes, a blue blanket, and a wooden mortar and pestle that Foua had chiseled from a block of wood in Houaysouy. They flew from Bangkok to Honolulu, and then to Portland, Oregon, where they were to spend two years before moving to Merced. Other refugees told me that their airplane flights—a mode of travel that strained the limits of the familiar Hmong concept of migration—had been fraught with anxiety and shame: they got airsick, they didn't know how to use the bathroom but were afraid to soil themselves, they thought they had to pay for their food but had no money, they tried to eat the Wash'n Dris. The Lees, though perplexed, took the novelties of the trip in stride. Nao Kao remembers the airplane as being "just like a big house."

Their first week in Portland, however, was miserably disorienting. Before being placed by a local refugee agency in a small rented house, they spent a week with relatives, sleeping on the floor. "We didn't know anything so our relatives had to show us everything," Foua said. "They knew because they had lived in America for three or four months already. Our relatives told us about electricity and said the children shouldn't touch those plugs in the wall because they could get hurt. They told us that the refrigerator is a cold box where you put meat. They showed us how to open the TV so we could see it. We had never seen a toilet before and we thought maybe the water in it was to drink or cook with. Then our relatives told us what it was, but we didn't know whether we should sit or whether we should stand on it. Our relatives took us to the store

but we didn't know that the cans and packages had food in them. We could tell what the meat was, but the chickens and cows and pigs were all cut up in little pieces and had plastic on them. Our relatives told us the stove is for cooking the food, but I was afraid to use it because it might explode. Our relatives said in America the food you don't eat you just throw away. In Laos we always fed it to the animals and it was strange to waste it like that. In this country there were a lot of strange things and even now I don't know a lot of things and my children have to help me, and it still seems like a strange country."

Seventeen years later, Foua and Nao Kao use American appliances, but they still speak only Hmong, celebrate only Hmong holidays, practice only the Hmong religion, cook only Hmong dishes, sing only Hmong songs, play only Hmong musical instruments, tell only Hmong stories, and know far more about current political events in Laos and Thailand than about those in the United States. When I first met them, during their eighth year in this country, only one American adult, Jeanine Hilt, had ever been invited to their home as a guest. It would be hard to imagine anything further from the vaunted American ideal of assimilation, in which immigrants are expected to submerge their cultural differences in order to embrace a shared national identity. *E pluribus unum:* from many, one.

During the late 1910s and early 1920s, immigrant workers at the Ford automotive plant in Dearborn, Michigan, were given free, compulsory "Americanization" classes. In addition to English lessons, there were lectures on work habits, personal hygiene, and table manners. The first sentence they memorized was "I am a good American." During their graduation ceremony they gathered next to a gigantic wooden pot, which their teachers stirred with ten-foot ladles. The students walked through a door into the pot, wearing traditional costumes from their countries of origin and singing songs in their native languages. A few minutes later, the door in the pot opened, and the students walked out again, wearing suits and ties, waving American flags, and singing "The Star-Spangled Banner."

The European immigrants who emerged from the Ford Motor Company melting pot came to the United States because they hoped to assimilate into mainstream American society. The Hmong came to the United States for the same reason they had left China in the nineteenth century: because they were trying to *resist* assimilation. As the anthropologist Jacques Lemoine has observed, "they did not come to our countries only to save their lives, they rather came to save their selves, that is, their Hmong ethnicity." If their Hmong ethnicity had been safe in Laos, they would have preferred to remain there, just as their ancestors—for whom migration had always been a problem-solving strategy, not a footloose impulse—would have preferred to remain in China. Unlike the Ford workers who enthusiastically, or at least uncomplainingly, belted out the "The Star-Spangled Banner" (of which Foua and Nao Kao know not a single word), the Hmong are what sociologists call "involuntary migrants." It is well known that involuntary migrants, no matter what pot they are thrown into, tend not to melt.

What the Hmong wanted here was to be left alone to be Hmong: clustered in all-Hmong enclaves, protected from government interference, self-sufficient, and agrarian. Some brought hoes in their luggage. General Vang Pao has said, "For many years, right from the start, I tell the American government that we need a little bit of land where we can grow vegetables and build homes like in Laos. . . . I tell them it does not have to be the best land, just a little land where we can live." This proposal was never seriously considered. "It was just out of the question," said a spokesman for the State Department's refugee program. "It would cost too much, it would be impractical, but most of all it would set off wild protests from [other Americans] and from other refugees who weren't getting land for themselves." . . .

Just as newly arrived immigrants in earlier eras had been called "FOBs"—Fresh Off the Boat—some social workers nicknamed the incoming Hmong, along with the other Southeast Asian refugees who entered the United States after the Vietnam War, "JOJs": Just Off the Jet. Unlike the first waves of Vietnamese and Cambodian refugees, most of whom received several months of vocational and language training at regional "reception centers," the Hmong JOJs, who arrived after the centers had closed, were all sent directly to their new homes. (Later on, some were given "cultural orientation" training in Thailand before flying to the United States. Their classes covered such topics as how to distinguish a one-dollar bill from a ten-dollar bill and how to use a peephole.) The logistical details of their resettlement were contracted by the federal government to private nonprofit groups known as VOLAGs, or national voluntary resettlement agencies, which found local sponsors. Within their first few weeks in this country, newly arrived families were likely to deal with VOLAG officials, immigration officials, public health officials, social service officials, employment officials, and public assistance officials. The Hmong are not known for holding bureaucrats in high esteem. As one proverb puts it, "To see a tiger is to die; to see an official is to become destitute." In a study of adaptation problems among Indochinese refugees, Hmong respondents rated "Difficulty with American Agencies" as a more serious problem than either "War Memories" or "Separation from Family." Because many of the VOLAGs had religious affiliations, the JOJs also often found themselves dealing with Christian ministers, who, not surprisingly, took a dim view of shamanistic animism. A sponsoring pastor in Minnesota told a local newspaper, "It would be wicked to just bring them over and feed and clothe them and let them go to hell. The God who made us wants them to be converted. If anyone thinks that a gospel-preaching church would bring them over and not tell them about the Lord, they're out of their mind." The proselytizing backfired. According to a study of Hmong mental health problems, refugees sponsored by this pastor's religious organization were significantly more likely, when compared to other refugees, to require psychiatric treatment.

The Hmong were accustomed to living in the mountains, and most of them had never seen snow. Almost all their resettlement sites had flat topography and freezing winters. The majority were sent to cities, including Minneapolis, Chicago, Milwaukee, Detroit, Hartford, and Providence, because that was where refugee services—health care, language classes, job training, public housing—were concentrated. To encourage assimilation, and to avoid burdening any one community with more than its "fair share" of refugees, the Immigration and Naturalization Service adopted a policy of dispersal rather than clustering. Newly arrived Hmong were assigned to fifty-three cities in twenty-five different states: stirred into the melting pot in tiny, manageable portions, or, as John Finck, who worked with Hmong at the Rhode Island Office of Refugee Resettlement, put it, "spread like a thin layer of butter throughout the country so they'd disappear." In some places, clans were broken up. In others, members of only one clan were resettled, making it impossible for young people, who were forbidden by cultural taboo from marrying within their own clan, to find local marriage partners. Group solidarity, the cornerstone of Hmong social organization for more than two thousand years, was completely ignored.

Although most Hmong were resettled in cities, some nuclear families, unaccompanied by any of their extended relations, were placed in isolated rural areas. Disconnected from traditional supports, these families exhibited unusually high levels of anxiety, depression, and paranoia. In one such case, the distraught and delusional father of the Yang family—the only Hmong family sponsored by the First Baptist Church of Fairfield, Iowa—attempted to hang himself in the basement of his wooden bungalow along with his wife and four children. His wife changed her mind at the last minute and cut the family down, but she acted too late to save their only son. An Iowa grand jury declined to indict either parent, on the grounds that the father was suffering from Post-Traumatic Stress Disorder, and the mother, cut off from all sources of information except her husband, had no way to develop an independent version of reality.

Reviewing the initial resettlement of the Hmong with a decade's hindsight, Lionel Rosenblatt, the former United States Refugee Coordinator in Thailand, conceded that it had been catastrophically mishandled. "We knew at the start their situation was different, but we just couldn't make any special provisions for them," he said. "I still feel it was no mistake to bring the Hmong here, but you look back now and say, 'How could we have done it so shoddily?'" Eugene Douglas, President Reagan's ambassador-at-large for refugee affairs, stated flatly, "It was a kind of hell they landed into. Really, it couldn't have been done much worse."

The Hmong who sought asylum in the United States were, of course, not a homogeneous lump. A small percentage, mostly the high-ranking military officers who were admitted first, were multilingual and cosmopolitan, and a larger percentage had been exposed in a desultory fashion to some aspects of American culture and technology during the war or while living in Thai refugee camps. But the experience of tens of thousands of Hmong was much like the Lees'. It is possible to get some idea of how monumental the task of adjustment was likely to be by glancing at some of the pamphlets, audiotapes, and videos that refugee agencies produced for Southeast Asian JOJs. For example, "Your New Life in the United States," a handbook published by the Language and Orientation Resource Center in Washington, D.C., included the following tips:

Learn the meaning of "WALK"–"DON'T WALK" signs when crossing the street.

To send mail, you must use stamps.

To use the phone:

1) Pick up the receiver
2) Listen for dial tone
3) Dial each number separately
4) Wait for person to answer after it rings
5) Speak.

The door of the refrigerator must be shut.

Never put your hand in the garbage disposal.

Do not stand or squat on the toilet since it may break.

Never put rocks or other hard objects in the tub or sink since this will damage them.

Always ask before picking your neighbor's flowers, fruit, or vegetables.

In colder areas you must wear shoes, socks, and appropriate outerwear. Otherwise, you may become ill.

Always use a handkerchief or a kleenex to blow your nose in public places or inside a public building.

Never urinate in the street. This creates a smell that is offensive to Americans. They also believe that it causes disease.

Spitting in public is considered impolite and unhealthy. Use a kleenex or handkerchief.

Picking your nose or your ears in public is frowned upon in the United States.

The customs they were expected to follow seemed so peculiar, the rules and regulations so numerous, the language so hard to learn, and the emphasis on literacy and the decoding of other unfamiliar symbols so strong, that many Hmong were overwhelmed. Jonas Vangay told me, "In America, we are blind because even though we have eyes, we cannot see. We are deaf because even though we have ears, we cannot hear." Some newcomers wore pajamas as street clothes; poured water on electric stoves to extinguish them; lit charcoal fires in their living rooms; stored blankets in their refrigerators; washed rice in their toilets; washed their clothes in swimming pools; washed their hair with Lestoil; cooked with motor oil and furniture polish; drank Clorox; ate cat food; planted crops in public parks; shot and ate skunks, porcupines, woodpeckers, robins, egrets, sparrows, and a bald eagle; and hunted pigeons with crossbows in the streets of Philadelphia.

If the United States seemed incomprehensible to the Hmong, the Hmong seemed equally incomprehensible to the United States. Journalists seized excitedly on a label that is still trotted out at regular intervals: "the most primitive refugee group in America." (In an angry letter to the *New York Times,* in which that phrase had appeared in a 1990 news article, a Hmong computer specialist observed, "Evidently, we were not too primitive to fight as proxies for United States troops in the war in Laos.") Typical phrases from newspaper and magazine stories in the late seventies and eighties included "low-caste hill tribe," "Stone Age," "emerging from the mists of time," "like Alice falling down a rabbit hole." Inaccuracies were in no short supply. A 1981 article in the *Christian Science Monitor* called the Hmong language "extremely simplistic"; declared that the Hmong, who have been sewing *paj ntaub* [embroidered cloth] with organic motifs for centuries, make "no connection between a picture of a tree and a real tree"; and noted that "the Hmong have no oral tradition of literature. . . . Apparently no folk tales exist." Some journalists seemed to shed all inhibition, and much of their good sense as well, when they were loosed on the Hmong. . . .

Timothy Dunnigan, a linguistic anthropologist who has taught a seminar at the University of Minnesota on the media presentation of Hmong and Native Americans, once remarked to me, "The kinds of metaphorical language that we use to describe the Hmong say far more about us, and our attachment to our own frame of reference, than they do about the Hmong." . . .

It could not be denied that the Hmong were genuinely mysterious—far more so, for instance, than the Vietnamese and Cambodians who were streaming into the United States at the same time. Hardly anyone knew how to pronounce the word "Hmong." Hardly anyone—except the anthropology graduate students who suddenly realized they could write dissertations on patrilineal exogamous clan structures without leaving their hometowns—knew what role the Hmong had played during the war, or even what war it had been, since our government had succeeded all too well in keeping the Quiet War quiet. Hardly anyone knew they had a rich history, a complex culture, an efficient social system, and enviable family values. They were therefore an ideal blank surface on which to project xenophobic fantasies. . . .

Not everyone who wanted to make the Hmong feel unwelcome stopped at slander. In the words of the president of a youth center in Minneapolis, his Hmong neighbors in the mid-eighties were "prime meat for predators." In Laos, Hmong houses had no locks. Sometimes they had no doors. Cultural taboos against theft and intra-community violence were poor preparation for life in the high-crime, inner-city neighborhoods in which most Hmong were placed. Some of the violence directed against them had nothing to do with their ethnicity; they were simply easy marks. But a good deal of it was motivated by resentment, particularly in urban areas, for what was perceived as preferential welfare treatment.

In Minneapolis, tires were slashed and windows smashed. A high school student getting off a bus was hit in the face and told to "go back to China." A woman was kicked in the thighs, face, and kidneys, and her purse, which contained the family's entire savings of $400, was stolen; afterwards, she forbade her children to play outdoors, and her husband, who had once commanded a fifty-man unit in the Armée Clandestine, stayed home to guard the family's belongings. In Providence, children were beaten walking home from school. In Missoula,

teenagers were stoned. In Milwaukee, garden plots were vandalized and a car was set on fire. In Eureka, California, two burning crosses were placed on a family's front lawn. In a random act of violence near Springfield, Illinois, a twelve-year-old boy was shot and killed by three men who forced his family's car off Interstate 55 and demanded money. His father told a reporter, "In a war, you know who your enemies are. Here, you don't know if the person walking up to you will hurt you."

In Philadelphia, anti-Hmong muggings, robberies, beatings, stonings, and vandalism were so commonplace during the early eighties that the city's Commission on Human Relations held public hearings to investigate the violence. One source of discord seemed to be a $100,000 federal grant for Hmong employment assistance that had incensed local residents, who were mostly unemployed themselves and believed the money should have been allocated to American citizens, not resident aliens. . . .

One thing stands out in all these accounts: the Hmong didn't fight back. . . .

Although on the battlefield the Hmong were known more for their fierceness than for their long livers, in the United States many were too proud to lower themselves to the level of the petty criminals they encountered, or even to admit they had been victims. An anthropologist named George M. Scott, Jr., once asked a group of Hmong in San Diego, all victims of property damage or assault, why they had not defended themselves or taken revenge. Scott wrote, "several Hmong victims of such abuse, both young and old, answered that to have done so, besides inviting further, retaliatory, abuse, would have made them feel 'embarrassed' or ashamed. . . . In addition, the current president of Lao Family [a Hmong mutual assistance organization], when asked why his people did not 'fight back' when attacked here as they did in Laos, replied simply, 'because nothing here is worth defending to us.'"

In any case, Hmong who were persecuted by their neighbors could exercise a time-honored alternative to violence: flight. . . . Between 1982 and 1984, three quarters of the Hmong population of Philadelphia simply left town and joined relatives in other cities. During approximately the same period, one third of all the Hmong in the United States moved from one city to another. When they decided to relocate, Hmong families often lit off without notifying their sponsors, who were invariably offended. If they couldn't fit one of their possessions, such as a television set, in a car or bus or U-Haul, they left it behind, seemingly without so much as a backward glance. Some families traveled alone, but more often they moved in groups. When there was an exodus from Portland, Oregon, a long caravan of overloaded cars motored together down Interstate 5, bound for the Central Valley of California. With this "secondary migration," as sociologists termed it, the government's attempt to stir the Hmong evenly into the melting pot was definitively sabotaged.

Although local violence was often the triggering factor, there were also other reasons for migrating. In 1982, when all refugees who had lived in the United States for more than eighteen months stopped receiving Refugee Cash Assistance—the period of eligibility had previously been three years—many Hmong who had no jobs and no prospects moved to states that provided welfare benefits to two-parent families. Their original host states were often glad to get rid of them. For a time, the Oregon Human Resources Department, strapped by a tight state budget, sent refugees letters that pointedly detailed the levels of welfare benefits available in several other states. California's were among the highest. Thousands of Hmong also moved to California because they had heard it was an agricultural state where they might be able to farm. But by far the most important reason for relocating was reunification with other members of one's clan. Hmong clans are sometimes at odds with each other, but within a clan, whose thousands of members are regarded as siblings, one can always count on support and sympathy. A Hmong who tries to gain acceptance to a kin

group other than his own is called a *puav,* or bat. He is rejected by the birds because he has fur and by the mice because he has wings. Only when a Hmong lives among his own subspecies can he stop flitting restlessly from group to group, haunted by the shame of not belonging.

The Hmong may have been following their venerable proverb, "There's always another mountain," but in the past, each new mountain had yielded a living. Unfortunately, the most popular areas of secondary resettlement all had high unemployment rates, and they got higher. . . .

By 1985, at least eighty percent of the Hmong in Merced, Fresno, and San Joaquin counties were on welfare.

That didn't halt the migration. Family reunification tends to have a snowball effect. The more Thaos or Xiongs there were in one place, the more mutual assistance they could provide, the more cultural traditions they could practice together, and the more stable their community would be. Americans, however, tended to view secondary migration as an indication of instability and dependence. . . .

Seeing that the Hmong were redistributing themselves as they saw fit, and that they were becoming an economic burden on the places to which they chose to move, the federal Office of Refugee Resettlement tried to slow the migratory tide. The 1983 Highland Lao Initiative, a three-million-dollar "emergency effort" to bolster employment and community stability in Hmong communities outside California, offered vocational training, English classes, and other enticements for the Hmong to stay put. Though the initiative claimed a handful of modest local successes, the California migration was essentially unstoppable. By this time, most Hmong JOJs were being sponsored by relatives in America rather than by voluntary organizations, so the government no longer had geographic control over their placements. The influx therefore came—and, in smaller increments, is still coming—from Thailand as well as from other parts of America. Therefore, in addition to trying to prevent the Hmong from moving to high-welfare states, the Office of Refugee Resettlement started trying to encourage the ones who were already there to leave. Spending an average of $7,000 per family on moving expenses, job placement, and a month or two of rent and food subsidies, the Planned Secondary Resettlement Program, which was phased out in 1994, relocated about 800 unemployed Hmong families from what it called "congested areas" to communities with "favorable employment opportunities"—i.e., unskilled jobs with wages too low to attract a full complement of local American workers.

Within the economic limitations of blue-collar labor, those 800 families have fared well. Ninety-five percent have become self-sufficient. They work in manufacturing plants in Dallas, on electronics assembly lines in Atlanta, in furniture and textile factories in Morganton, North Carolina. More than a quarter of them have saved enough money to buy their own houses, as have three quarters of the Hmong families who live in Lancaster County, Pennsylvania, where the men farm or work in food-processing plants, and the women work for the Amish, sewing quilts that are truthfully advertised as "locally made." Elsewhere, Hmong are employed as grocers, carpenters, poultry processors, machinists, welders, auto mechanics, tool and die makers, teachers, nurses, interpreters, and community liaisons. In a survey of Minnesota employers, the respondents were asked "What do you think of the Hmong as workers?" Eighty-six percent rated them "very good." . . .

Some younger Hmong have become lawyers, doctors, dentists, engineers, computer programmers, accountants, and public administrators. Hmong National Development, an association that promotes Hmong self-sufficiency, encourages this small corps of professionals to serve as mentors and sponsors for other Hmong who might thereby be induced to follow suit. The cultural legacy of mutual assistance has been remarkably adaptive. Hundreds of Hmong students converse electronically, trading gossip and information—opinions on the relevance of traditional customs, advice on college admissions, personal ads—via the Hmong Channel on the Internet Relay Chat system. . . . There is also a Hmong Homepage on the World Wide Web (http://www.stolaf.edu/people/cdr/hmong/) and several burgeoning Hmong electronic mailing lists, including Hmongnet, Hmongforum, and Hmong Language Users Group.

The M.D.s and J.D.s and digital sophisticates constitute a small, though growing, minority. Although younger, English-speaking Hmong who have been educated in the United States have better employment records than their elders, they still lag behind most other Asian-Americans. . . .

For the many Hmong who live in high-unemployment areas, questions of advancement are often moot. They have no jobs at all. This is the reason the Hmong are routinely called this country's "least successful refugees." It is worth noting that the standard American tests of success that they have flunked are almost exclusively economic. If one applied social indices instead—such as rates of crime, child abuse, illegitimacy, and divorce—the Hmong would probably score better than most refugee groups (and also better than most Americans), but those are not the forms of success to which our culture assigns its highest priority. Instead, we have trained the spotlight on our best-loved index of failure, the welfare rolls. In California, Minnesota, and Wisconsin, where, not coincidentally, benefits tend to be relatively generous and eligibility requirements relatively loose, the percentages of Hmong on welfare are approximately forty-five, forty, and thirty-five (an improvement over five years ago, when they were approximately sixty-five, seventy, and sixty). The cycle of dependence that began with rice drops in Laos and reinforced with daily handouts at Thai refugee camps has been completed here in the United States. The conflicting structures of the Hmong culture and the American welfare system make it almost impossible for the average family to become independent. . . .

Few things gall the Hmong more than to be criticized for accepting public assistance.

For one thing, they feel they deserve the money. Every Hmong has a different version of what is commonly called "The Promise": a written or verbal contract, made by CIA personnel in Laos, that if they fought for the Americans, the Americans would aid them if the Pathet Lao won the war. After risking their lives to rescue downed American pilots, seeing their villages flattened by incidental American bombs, and being forced to flee their country because they had supported the "American War," the Hmong expected a hero's welcome here. According to many of them, the first betrayal came when the American airlifts rescued only the officers from Long Tieng, leaving nearly everyone else behind. The second betrayal came in the Thai camps, when the Hmong who wanted to come to the United States were not all automatically admitted. The third betrayal came when they arrived here and found they were ineligible for veterans' benefits. The fourth betrayal came when Americans condemned them for what the Hmong call "eating welfare." The fifth betrayal came when the Americans announced that the welfare would stop.

Aside from some older people who consider welfare a retirement benefit, most Hmong would prefer almost any other option—if other options existed. What right-thinking Hmong would choose to be yoked to one of the most bureaucratic institutions in America? . . .

In a study of Indochinese refugees in Illinois, the Hmong exhibited the highest degree of "alienation from their environment." According to a Minnesota study, Hmong refugees who had lived in the United States for a year and a half had "very high levels of depression, anxiety, hostility, phobia, paranoid ideation, obsessive compulsiveness and feelings of inadequacy." (Over the next decade, some of these symptoms moderated, but the refugees' levels of anxiety, hostility, and paranoia showed little or no improvement.) The study that I found most disheartening was the 1987 California Southeast Asian Mental Health Needs Assessment, a statewide epidemiological survey funded by the Office of Refugee Resettlement and the National Institute of Mental Health. It was shocking to look at the bar graphs comparing the Hmong with the Vietnamese, the Chinese-Vietnamese, the Cambodians, and the Lao—all of whom, particularly the Cambodians, fared poorly compared to the general population—and see how the Hmong stacked up: Most depressed. Most psychosocially dysfunctional. Most likely to be severely in need of mental health treatment. Least educated. Least literate. Smallest percentage in labor force. Most likely to cite "fear" as a reason for immigration and least likely to cite "a better life." . . .

"Full" of both past trauma and past longing, the Hmong have found it especially hard to deal with present threats to their old identities. I once went to a conference on Southeast Asian mental health at which a psychologist named Evelyn Lee, who was born in Macao, invited six members of the audience to come to the front of the auditorium for a role-playing exercise. She cast them as a grandfather, a father, a mother, an eighteen-year-old son, a sixteen-year-old daughter, and a twelve-year-old daughter. "Okay," she told them, "line up according to your status in your old country." Ranking themselves by traditional notions of age and gender, they queued up in the order I've just mentioned, with the grandfather standing proudly at the head of the line. "Now they come to America," said Dr. Lee. "Grandfather has no job. Father can only chop vegetables. Mother didn't work in the old country, but here she gets a job in a garment factory. Oldest daughter works there too. Son drops out of high school because he can't learn English. Youngest daughter learns the best English in the family and ends up at U.C. Berkeley. Now you line up again." As the family reshuffled, I realized that its power structure had turned completely upside down, with the twelve-year-old girl now occupying the head of the line and the grandfather standing forlornly at the tail.

Dr. Lee's exercise was an eloquent demonstration of what sociologists call "role loss." Of all the stresses in the Hmong community, role loss . . . may be the most corrosive to the ego. . . .

And in this country the real children have assumed some of the power that used to belong to their elders. The status conferred by speaking English and understanding American conventions is a phenomenon familiar to most immigrant groups, but the Hmong, whose identity has always hinged on tradition, have taken it particularly hard. . . .

Although Americanization may bring certain benefits—more job opportunities, more money, less cultural dislocation—Hmong parents are likely to view any earmarks of assimilation as an insult and a threat. "In our families, the kids eat hamburger and bread," said Dang Moua sadly, "whereas the parents prefer hot soup with vegetables, rice, and meat like tripes or liver or kidney that the young ones don't want." . . .

Sukey Waller, Merced's maverick psychologist, once recalled a Hmong community meeting she had attended. "An old man of seventy or eighty stood up in the front row," she said, "and he asked one of the most poignant questions I have ever heard: 'Why, when what we did worked so well for two hundred years, is everything breaking down?'" When Sukey told me this, I understood why the man had asked the question, but I thought he was wrong. Much has broken down, but not everything. Jacques Lemoine's analysis of the postwar hegira—that the Hmong came to the West to save not only their lives but their ethnicity—has been at least partially confirmed in the United States. I can think of no other group of immigrants whose culture, in its most essential aspects, has been so little eroded by assimilation. Virtually all Hmong still marry other Hmong, marry young, obey the taboo against marrying within their own clans, pay bride-prices, and have large families. Clan and lineage structures are intact, as is the ethic of group solidarity and mutual assistance. On most weekends in Merced, it is possible to hear a death drum beating at a Hmong funeral or a *txiv neeb's* gong and rattle sounding

at a healing ceremony. Babies wear strings on their wrists to protect their souls from abduction by *dabs*. People divine their fortunes by interpreting their dreams. (If you dream of opium, you will have bad luck; if you dream you are covered with excrement, you will have good luck; if you dream you have a snake on your lap, you will become pregnant.) Animal sacrifices are common, even among Christian converts, a fact I first learned when May Ying Xiong told me that she would be unavailable to interpret one weekend because her family was sacrificing a cow to safeguard her niece during an upcoming open-heart operation. When I said, "I didn't know your family was so religious," she replied, "Oh yes, we're Mormon." . . .

I was able to see the whole cycle of adjustment to American life start all over again during one of my visits to Merced. When I arrived at the Lees' apartment, I was surprised to find it crammed with people I'd never met before. These turned out to be a cousin of Nao Kao's named Joua Chai Lee, his wife, Yeng Lor, and their nine children, who ranged in age from eight months to twenty-five years. They had arrived from Thailand two weeks earlier, carrying one piece of luggage for all eleven of them. In it were packed some clothes, a bag of rice, and, because Joua is a *txiv neeb's* assistant, a set of rattles, a drum, and a pair of divinatory water-buffalo horns. The cousins were staying with Foua and Nao Kao until they found a place of their own. The two families had not seen each other in more than a decade, and there was a festive atmosphere in the little apartment, with small children dashing around in their new American sneakers and the four barefooted adults frequently throwing back their heads and laughing. Joua said to me, via May Ying's translation, "Even though there are a lot of us, you can spend the night here too." May Ying explained to me later that Joua didn't really expect me to lie down on the floor with twenty of his relatives. It was simply his way, even though he was in a strange country where he owned almost nothing, of extending a face-saving bit of Hmong hospitality.

I asked Joua what he thought of America. "It is really nice but it is different," he said, "It is very flat. You cannot tell one place from another. There are many things I have not seen before, like that"—a light switch—"and that"—a telephone—"and that"—an air conditioner. "Yesterday our relatives took us somewhere in a car and I saw a lady and I thought she was real but she was fake." This turned out to have been a mannequin at the Merced Mall.

"I couldn't stop laughing all the way home," he said. And remembering how funny his mistake had been, he started to laugh again.

Then I asked Joua what he hoped for his family's future here. "I will work if I can," he said, "but I think I probably cannot. As old as I am, I think I will not be able to learn one word of English. If my children put a heart to it, they will be able to learn English and get really smart. But as for myself, I have no hope."

THINKING ABOUT THE READING

Why has it been so difficult for Hmong refugees to adjust to life in the United States? How do the experiences of younger Hmong compare to those of their elders? Why are the Hmong such a popular target of anti-immigrant violence and persecution? Why is the U.S. government so unwilling to grant the Hmong their wish to be "left alone"? In other words, why is there such a strong desire to assimilate them into American culture? On a more general level, why is there such distaste in this society when certain ethnic groups desire to retain their traditional way of life? Consider the differences that might emerge between different generations within immigrant families. What aspects of culture are the most difficult to maintain through the generations?

McDonald's in Hong Kong

Consumerism, Dietary Change, and the Rise of a Children's Culture

James L. Watson

(1997)

Transnationalism and the Fast Food Industry*

Does the roaring success of McDonald's and its rivals in the fast food industry mean that Hong Kong's local culture is under siege? Are food chains helping to create a homogenous, "global" culture better suited to the demands of a capitalist world order? Hong Kong would seem to be an excellent place to test the globalization hypothesis, given the central role that cuisine plays in the production and maintenance of a distinctive local identity. Man Tso-chuen's great-grandchildren are today avid consumers of Big Macs, pizza, and Coca-Cola; does this somehow make them less "Chinese" than their grandfather?

The people of Hong Kong have embraced American-style fast foods, and by so doing they might appear to be in the vanguard of a worldwide culinary revolution. But they have not been stripped of their cultural traditions, nor have they become "Americanized" in any but the most superficial of ways. Hong Kong in the late 1990s constitutes one of the world's most heterogeneous cultural environments. Younger people, in particular, are fully conversant in transnational idioms, which include language, music, sports, clothing, satellite television, cyber-communications, global travel, and—of course—cuisine. It is no longer possible to distinguish what is local and what is not. In Hong Kong, the transnational *is* the local.

Eating Out: A Social History of Consumption

By the time McDonald's opened its first Hong Kong restaurant in 1975, the idea of fast food was already well established among local consumers. Office workers, shop assistants, teachers, and transport workers had enjoyed various forms of take-out cuisine for well over a century; an entire industry had emerged to deliver mid-day meals direct to workplaces. In the 1960s and 1970s thousands of street vendors produced snacks and simple meals on demand, day or night. Time has always been money in Hong Kong; hence, the dual keys to success in the catering trade were speed and convenience. Another essential characteristic was that the food, based primarily on rice or noodles, had to be hot. Even the most cosmopolitan of local consumers did not (and many still do not) consider cold foods, such as sandwiches and salads, to be acceptable meals. Older people in South China associate cold food with offerings to the dead and are understandably hesitant to eat it.

The fast food industry in Hong Kong had to deliver hot items that could compete with

---

*Seven of the world's ten busiest McDonald's restaurants are located in Hong Kong. When McDonald's first opened in 1975, few thought it would survive more than a few months. By January 1, 1997, Hong Kong had 125 outlets, which means that there was one McDonald's for every 51,200 residents, compared to one for every 30,000 people in the United States.

traditional purveyors of convenience foods (noodle shops, dumpling stalls, soup carts, portable grills).

McDonald's mid-1970s entry corresponded to an economic boom associated with Hong Kong's conversion from a low-wage, light-industrial outpost to a regional center for financial services and high-technology industries. McDonald's takeoff thus paralleled the rise of a new class of highly educated, affluent consumers who thrive in Hong Kong's ever-changing urban environment—one of the most stressful in the world. These new consumers eat out more often than their parents and have created a huge demand for fast, convenient foods of all types. In order to compete in this market, McDonald's had to offer something different. That critical difference, at least during the company's first decade of operation, was American culture packaged as all-American, middle-class food.

***

Mental Categories: Snack Versus Meal

As in other parts of East Asia, McDonald's faced a serious problem when it began operation in Hong Kong: Hamburgers, fries, and sandwiches were perceived as snacks (Cantonese *siu sihk*, literally "small eats"); in the local view these items did not constitute the elements of a proper meal. This perception is still prevalent among older, more conservative consumers who believe that hamburgers, hot dogs, and pizza can never be "filling." Many students stop at fast food outlets on their way home from school; they may share hamburgers and fries with their classmates and then eat a full meal with their families at home. This is not considered a problem by parents, who themselves are likely to have stopped for tea and snacks after work. Snacking with friends and colleagues provides a major opportunity for socializing (and transacting business) among southern Chinese. Teahouses, coffee shops, bakeries, and ice cream parlors are popular precisely because they provide a

structured yet informal setting for social encounters. Furthermore, unlike Chinese restaurants and banquet halls, snack centers do not command a great deal of time or money from customers.

Contrary to corporate goals, therefore, McDonald's entered the Hong Kong market as a purveyor of snacks. Only since the late 1980s has its fare been treated as the foundation of "meals" by a generation of younger consumers who regularly eat non-Chinese food. Thanks largely to McDonald's, hamburgers and fries are now a recognized feature of Hong Kong's lunch scene. The evening hours remain, however, the weak link in McDonald's marketing plan; the real surprise was breakfast, which became a peak traffic period.

The mental universe of Hong Kong consumers is partially revealed in the everyday use of language. Hamburgers are referred to, in colloquial Cantonese, as *han bou bao*—*han* being a homophone for "ham" and *bao* the common term for stuffed buns or bread rolls. *Bao* are quintessential snacks, and however excellent or nutritious they might be, they do not constitute the basis of a satisfying (i.e., filling) meal. In South China that honor is reserved for culinary arrangements that rest, literally, on a bed of rice (*fan*). Foods that accompany rice are referred to as *sung*, probably best translated as "toppings" (including meat, fish, and vegetables). It is significant that hamburgers are rarely categorized as meat (*yuk*); Hong Kong consumers tend to perceive anything that is served between slices of bread (Big Macs, fish sandwiches, hot dogs) as *bao*. In American culture the hamburger is categorized first and foremost as a meat item (with all the attendant worries about fat and cholesterol content), whereas in Hong Kong the same item is thought of primarily as bread.

From Exotic to Ordinary: McDonald's Becomes Local

Following precedents in other international markets, the Hong Kong franchise promoted McDonald's basic menu and did not introduce items that would be more recognizable to Chinese consumers (such as rice dishes, tropical fruit, soup noodles). Until recently the food has been indistinguishable from that served in Mobile, Alabama, or Moline, Illinois. There are, however, local preferences: the best-selling items in many outlets are fish sandwiches and plain hamburgers; Big Macs tend to be the favorites of children and teenagers. Hot tea and hot chocolate outsell coffee, but Coca-Cola remains the most popular drink.

McDonald's conservative approach also applied to the breakfast menu. When morning service was introduced in the 1980s, American-style items such as eggs, muffins, pancakes, and hash brown potatoes were not featured. Instead, the local outlets served the standard fare of hamburgers and fries for breakfast. McDonald's initial venture into the early morning food market was so successful that Mr. Ng [managing director of McDonald's Hong Kong], hesitated to introduce American-style breakfast items, fearing that an abrupt shift in menu might alienate consumers who were beginning to accept hamburgers and fries as a regular feature of their diet. The transition to eggs, muffins, and hash browns was a gradual one, and today most Hong Kong customers order breakfasts that are similar to those offered in American outlets. But once established, dietary preferences change slowly: McDonald's continues to feature plain hamburgers (but not the Big Mac) on its breakfast menu in most Hong Kong outlets.

Management decisions of the type outlined above helped establish McDonald's as an icon of popular culture in Hong Kong. From 1975 to approximately 1985, McDonald's became the "in" place for young people wishing to associate themselves with the laid-back, nonhierarchical dynamism they perceived American society to embody. The first generation of consumers patronized McDonald's precisely because it was *not* Chinese and was *not* associated with Hong Kong's past as a backward-looking colonial outpost where (in their view) nothing of consequence ever happened. Hong Kong was changing and, as noted earlier, a new consumer culture was beginning to take shape. McDonald's

caught the wave of this cultural movement and has been riding it ever since.

Today, McDonald's restaurants in Hong Kong are packed—wall-to-wall—with people of all ages, few of whom are seeking an American cultural experience. Twenty years after Mr. Ng opened his first restaurant, eating at McDonald's has become an ordinary, everyday experience for hundreds of thousands of Hong Kong residents. The chain has become a local institution in the sense that it has blended into the urban landscape; McDonald's outlets now serve as rendezvous points for young and old alike.

What's in a Smile? Friendliness and Public Service

American consumers expect to be served "with a smile" when they order fast food, but this is not true in all societies. In Hong Kong people are suspicious of anyone who displays what is perceived to be an excess of congeniality, solicitude, or familiarity. The human smile is not, therefore, a universal symbol of openness and honesty. "If you buy an apple from a hawker and he smiles at you," my Cantonese tutor once told me, "you know you're being cheated."

Given these cultural expectations, it was difficult for Hong Kong management to import a key element of the McDonald's formula—service with a smile—and make it work. Crew members were trained to treat customers in a manner that approximates the American notion of "friendliness." Prior to the 1970s, there was not even an indigenous Cantonese term to describe this form of behavior. The traditional notion of friendship is based on loyalty to close associates, which by definition cannot be extended to strangers. Today the concept of *public* friendliness is recognized—and verbalized—by younger people in Hong Kong, but the term many of them use to express this quality is "friendly," borrowed directly from English. McDonald's, through its television advertising, may be partly responsible for this innovation, but to date it has had little effect on workers in the catering industry.

During my interviews it became clear that the majority of Hong Kong consumers were uninterested in public displays of congeniality from service personnel. When shopping for fast food most people cited convenience, cleanliness, and table space as primary considerations; few even mentioned service except to note that the food should be delivered promptly. Counter staff in Hong Kong's fast food outlets (including McDonald's) rarely make great efforts to smile or to behave in a manner Americans would interpret as friendly. Instead, they project qualities that are admired in the local culture: competence, directness, and unflappability. In a North American setting the facial expression that Hong Kong employees use to convey these qualities would likely be interpreted as a deliberate attempt to be rude or indifferent. Workers who smile on the job are assumed to be enjoying themselves at the consumer's (and management's) expense: In the words of one diner I overheard while standing in a queue, "They must be playing around back there. What are they laughing about?"

Consumer Discipline?

[A] hallmark of the American fast food business is the displacement of labor costs from the corporation to the consumers. For the system to work, consumers must be educated—or "disciplined"—so that they voluntarily fulfill their side of an implicit bargain: We (the corporation) will provide cheap, fast service, if you (the customer) "earn" your own tray, seat yourself, and help clean up afterward. Time and space are also critical factors in the equation: Fast service is offered in exchange for speedy consumption and a prompt departure, thereby making room for others. This system has revolutionized the American food industry and has helped to shape consumer expectations in other sectors of the economy. How has it fared in Hong Kong? Are Chinese customers conforming to disciplinary models devised in Oak Brook, Illinois?

The answer is both yes and no. In general Hong Kong consumers have accepted the basic elements of the fast food formula, but with "localizing" adaptations. For instance, customers generally do not bus their own trays, nor do they depart immediately upon finishing. Clearing one's own table has never been an accepted part of local culinary culture, owing in part to the low esteem attaching to this type of labor. During McDonald's first decade in Hong Kong, the cost of hiring extra cleaners was offset by low wages. A pattern was thus established, and customers grew accustomed to leaving without attending to their own rubbish. Later, as wages escalated in the late 1980s and early 1990s. McDonald's tried to introduce self-busing by posting announcements in restaurants and featuring the practice in its television advertisements. As of February 1997, however, little had changed. Hong Kong consumers have ignored this aspect of consumer discipline.

What about the critical issues of time and space? Local managers with whom I spoke estimated that the average eating time for most Hong Kong customers was between 20 and 25 minutes, compared to 11 minutes in the United States fast food industry. This estimate confirms my own observations of McDonald's consumers in Hong Kong's central business districts (Victoria and Tsimshatsui). A survey conducted in the New Territories city of Yuen Long—an old market town that has grown into a modern urban center—revealed that local McDonald's consumers took just under 26 minutes to eat.

Perhaps the most striking feature of the American-inspired model of consumer discipline is the queue. Researchers in many parts of the world have reported that customers refuse, despite "education" campaigns by the chains involved, to form neat lines in front of cashiers. Instead, customers pack themselves into disorderly scrums and jostle for a chance to place their orders. Scrums of this nature were common in Hong Kong when McDonald's opened in 1975. Local managers discouraged this practice by stationing queue monitors near the registers during busy hours and, by the 1980s, orderly lines were the norm at McDonald's. The disappearance of the scrum corresponds to a general change in Hong Kong's public culture as a new generation of residents, the children of refugees, began to treat the territory as their home. Courtesy toward strangers was largely unknown in the 1960s: Boarding a bus during rush hour could be a nightmare and transacting business at a bank teller's window required brute strength. Many people credit McDonald's with being the first public institution in Hong Kong to enforce queuing, and thereby helping to create a more "civilized" social order. McDonald's did not, in fact, introduce the queue to Hong Kong, but this belief is firmly lodged in the public imagination.

Hovering and the Napkin Wars

Purchasing one's food is no longer a physical challenge in Hong Kong's McDonald's but finding a place to sit is quite another matter. The traditional practice of "hovering" is one solution: Choose a group of diners who appear to be on the verge of leaving and stake a claim to their table by hovering nearby, sometimes only inches away. Seated customers routinely ignore the intrusion; it would, in fact, entail a loss of face to notice. Hovering was the norm in Hong Kong's lower- to middle-range restaurants during the 1960s and 1970s, but the practice has disappeared in recent years. Restaurants now take names or hand out tickets at the entrance; warning signs, in Chinese and English, are posted: "Please wait to be seated." Customers are no longer allowed into the dining area until a table is ready.

Fast food outlets are the only dining establishments in Hong Kong where hovering is still tolerated, largely because it would be nearly impossible to regulate. Customer traffic in McDonald's is so heavy that the standard restaurant design has failed to reproduce American-style dining routines: Rather than ordering first and finding a place to sit afterward, Hong Kong consumers usually arrive in groups and delegate one or two people to claim a table while someone else joins the counter queues. Children make ideal hoverers and learn to scoot through packed restaurants, zeroing in on diners who are about to finish. It is one of the wonders of comparative ethnography to witness the speed with which Hong Kong children perform this reconnaissance duty. Foreign visitors are sometimes unnerved by hovering, but residents accept it as part of everyday life in one of the world's most densely populated cities. It is not surprising, therefore, that Hong Kong's fast food chains have made few efforts to curtail the practice.

Management is less tolerant of behavior that affects profit margins. In the United States fast food companies save money by allowing (or requiring) customers to collect their own napkins, straws, plastic flatware, and condiments. Self-provisioning is an essential feature of consumer discipline, but it only works if the system is not abused. In Hong Kong napkins are dispensed, one at a time, by McDonald's crew members who work behind the counter; customers who do not ask for napkins do not receive any. This is a deviation from the corporation's standard operating procedure and adds a few seconds to each transaction, which in turn slows down the queues. Why alter a well-tested routine? The reason is simple: napkins placed in public dispensers disappear faster than they can be replaced.

***

Buffets, like fast food outlets, depend upon consumers to perform much of their own labor in return for reduced prices. Abuse of the system—wasting food or taking it home—is taken for granted and is factored into the price of buffet meals. Fast food chains, by contrast, operate at lower price thresholds where consumer abuse can seriously affect profits.

Many university students of my acquaintance reported that they had frequently observed older people pocketing wads of paper napkins, three to four inches thick, in restaurants that permit self-provisioning. Management efforts to stop this behavior are referred to, in the Cantonese-English slang of Hong Kong youth, as the "Napkin Wars." Younger people were appalled by what they saw as the waste of natural resources by a handful of customers. As they talked about the issue, however, it became obvious that the Napkin Wars represented more—in their eyes—than a campaign to conserve paper. The sight of diners abusing public facilities reminded these young people of the bad old days of their parents and grandparents, when Hong Kong's social life was dominated by refugees who had little stake in the local community. During the 1960s and 1970s, economic insecurities were heightened by the very real prospect that Red Guards might take over the colony at any moment. The game plan was simple during those decades: Make money as quickly as possible and move on. In the 1980s a new generation of local-born youth began treating Hong Kong as home and proceeded to build a public culture better suited to their vision of life in a cosmopolitan city. In this new Hong Kong, consumers are expected to be sophisticated and financially secure, which means that it would be beneath their dignity to abuse public facilities. Still, McDonald's retains control of its napkins.

***

Children as Consumers

During the summer of 1994, while attending a business lunch in one of Hong Kong's fanciest hotels, I watched a waiter lean down to consult with a customer at an adjoining table. The object of his attention was a six-year-old child who studied the menu with practiced skill. His parents beamed as their prodigy performed; meanwhile, sitting across the table, a pair of grandparents sat bolt upright, scowling in obvious disapproval. Twenty years ago the sight of a child commanding such attention would have shocked the entire restaurant into silence. No one, save the immediate party (and this observer), even noticed in 1994.

Hong Kong children rarely ate outside their home until the late 1970s, and when they did, they were expected to eat what was put in front of them. The idea that children might actually order their own food or speak to a waiter would have outraged most adults; only foreign youngsters (notably the offspring of British and American expatriates) were permitted to make their preferences known in public. Today, Hong Kong children as young as two or three participate in the local economy as full-fledged consumers, with their own tastes and brand loyalties. Children now have money in their pockets and they spend it on personal consumption, which usually means snacks. In response, new industries and a specialized service sector has emerged to "feed" these discerning consumers. McDonald's was one of the first corporations to recognize the potential of the children's market; in effect, the company started a revolution by making it possible for even the youngest consumers to *choose* their own food.

***

Many Hong Kong children of my acquaintance are so fond of McDonald's that they refuse to eat with their parents or grandparents in Chinese-style restaurants or *dim sam* teahouses. This has caused intergenerational distress in some of Hong Kong's more conservative communities. In 1994, a nine-year-old boy, the descendant of illustrious ancestors who settled in the New Territories eight centuries ago, talked about his concerns as we consumed Big Macs, fries, and shakes at McDonald's: "A-bak [uncle], I like it here better than any place in the world. I want to come here every day." His father takes him to McDonald's at least twice a week, but his grandfather, who accompanied them a few times in the late 1980s, will no longer do so. "I prefer to eat *dim sam*," the older man told me later. "That place [McDonald's] is for kids." Many grandparents have resigned themselves to the new consumer trends and take their preschool grandchildren to McDonald's for mid-morning snacks—precisely the time of day that local teahouses were once packed with retired people. Cantonese grandparents have always played a prominent role in child minding, but until recently the children had to accommodate to the proclivities of their elders. By the 1990s grandchildren were more assertive and the mid-morning *dim sam* snack was giving way to hamburgers and Cokes.

***

Ronald McDonald and the Invention of Birthday Parties

Until recently most people in Hong Kong did not even know, let alone celebrate, their birthdates in the Western calendrical sense; dates of birth according to the lunar calendar were recorded for divinatory purposes but were not noted in annual rites. By the late 1980s, however, birthday parties, complete with cakes and candles, were the rage in Hong Kong. Any child who was anyone had to have a party, and the most popular venue was a fast food restaurant, with McDonald's ranked above all competitors. The majority of Hong Kong people live in overcrowded flats, which means that parties are rarely held in private homes.

Except for the outlets in central business districts, McDonald's restaurants are packed every Saturday and Sunday with birthday parties, cycled through at the rate of one every hour. A party hostess, provided by the restaurant, leads the children in games while the parents sit on the sidelines, talking quietly among themselves. For a small fee celebrants receive printed invitation cards, photographs, a gift box containing toys and a discount coupon for future trips to McDonald's. Parties are held in a special enclosure, called the Ronald Room, which is equipped with low tables and tiny stools—suitable only for children. Television commercials portray Ronald McDonald leading birthday celebrants on exciting safaris and expeditions. The clown's Cantonese name, Mak Dong Lou Suk-Suk ("Uncle McDonald"), plays on the intimacy of kinship and has helped transform him into one of Hong Kong's most familiar cartoon figures.

***

McDonald's as a Youth Center

Weekends may be devoted to family dining and birthday parties for younger children, but on weekday afternoons, from 3:00 to 6:00 P.M., McDonald's restaurants are packed with teenagers stopping for a snack on their way home from school. In many outlets 80 percent of the late afternoon clientele appear in school uniforms, turning the restaurants into a sea of white frocks, light blue shirts, and dark trousers. The students, aged between 10 and 17, stake out tables and buy snacks that are shared in groups. The noise level at this time of day is deafening; students shout to friends and dart from table to table. Few adults, other than restaurant staff, are in evidence. It is obvious that McDonald's is treated as an informal youth center, a recreational extension of school where students can unwind after long hours of study.

***

In contrast to their counterparts in the United States, where fast food chains have devised ways to discourage lingering, McDonald's in Hong Kong does not set a limit on table time. When I asked the managers of several Hong Kong outlets how they coped with so many young people chatting at tables that might otherwise be occupied by paying customers, they all replied that the students were "welcome." The obvious strategy is to turn a potential liability into an asset: "Students create a good atmosphere which is good for our business," said one manager as he watched an army of teenagers—dressed in identical school uniforms—surge into his restaurant. Large numbers of students also use McDonald's as a place to do homework and prepare for exams, often in groups. Study space of any kind, public or private, is hard to find in overcrowded Hong Kong.

* * *

Conclusions:
Whose Culture Is It?

In what sense, if any, is McDonald's involved in these cultural transformations (the creation of a child-centered consumer culture, for instance)? Has the company helped to create these trends, or merely followed the market? Is this an example of American-inspired, transnational culture crowding out indigenous cultures?

The deeper I dig into the lives of consumers themselves, in Hong Kong and elsewhere, the more complex the picture becomes. Having watched the processes of culture change unfold for nearly thirty years, it is apparent to me that the ordinary people of Hong Kong have most assuredly *not* been stripped of their cultural heritage, nor have they become the uncomprehending dupes of transnational corporations. Younger people—including many of the grandchildren of my former neighbors in the New Territories—are avid consumers of transnational culture in all of its most obvious manifestations: music, fashion, television, and cuisine. At the same time, however, Hong Kong has itself become a major center for the *production* of transnational culture, not just a sinkhole for its *consumption*. Witness, for example, the expansion of Hong Kong popular culture into China, Southeast Asia, and beyond: "Cantopop" music is heard on radio stations in North China, Vietnam, and Japan; the Hong Kong fashion industry influences clothing styles in Los Angeles, Bangkok, and Kuala Lumpur; and, perhaps most significant of all, Hong Kong is emerging as a center for the production and dissemination of satellite television programs throughout East, Southeast, and South Asia.

A lifestyle is emerging in Hong Kong that can best be described as postmodern, postnationalist, and flamboyantly transnational. The wholesale acceptance and appropriation of Big Macs, Ronald McDonald, and birthday parties are small, but significant aspects of this redefinition of Chinese cultural identity. In closing, therefore, it seems appropriate to pose an entirely new set of questions: Where does the transnational end and the local begin? Whose culture is it, anyway? In places like Hong Kong the postcolonial periphery is fast becoming the metropolitan center, where local people are consuming and simultaneously producing new cultural systems.

***

THINKING ABOUT THE READING

According to Watson's observations, the people in Hong Kong have adopted some of the characteristics of McDonald's "fast food" culture and resisted others. How has the presence of McDonald's changed Chinese culture? How have the Chinese changed this "fast food" culture to better fit their own? What does this reading suggest about the relationship between globalization and local cultures? Consider other examples of globalized industries and the impact on local cultures.

Building Identity

Socialization

5

S ociology teaches us that humans don't develop in a social vacuum. Other people, cultural practices, historical events, and social institutions shape what we do and say, what we value, and who we become. Our self-concept, identity, and sense of self-worth are derived from our interactions with other people. We are especially tuned into the reactions, real or imagined, of others.

Socialization is the process by which individuals learn their culture and learn to live according to the norms of their society. Through socialization, we learn how to perceive our world, gain a sense of our own identity, and discover how to interact appropriately with others. This learning process occurs within the context of several social institutions—schools, religious institutions, the media, and the family—and it extends beyond childhood. Adults must be resocialized into a new galaxy of norms, values, and expectations each time they leave or abandon current positions and enter new ones.

The conditions into which we are born shape our initial socialization in profound ways. Circumstances such as race, ethnicity, and social class are particularly significant factors in socialization processes. In "Life as the Maid's Daughter," sociologist Mary Romero describes a research interview with a young Chicana regarding her recollections of growing up as the daughter of a live-in maid for a white, upper-class family living in Los Angeles. Romero describes the many ways in which this girl learns to move between different social settings, adapt to different expectations, and occupy different social positions. This girl must constantly negotiate the boundaries of inclusion and exclusion, as she struggles between the socializing influence of her own ethnic group and that of the white, upper-class employers she and her mother live with. Through this juggling, she illustrates the ways in which we manage the different, often contradictory, identities that we take on in different situations.

Although ethnicity is an important factor in shaping our identities, the ways in which this work are complex. Zhou and Lee suggest that Asian American youth have a distinct culture and sense of identity that reflects their unique position as "in between" in a society that focuses on "black/white" racial identities. Immigration status, racism, and globalization are also significant features in shaping this unique identity. In a popular sociological article, "The Code of the Streets," Elijah Anderson looks at the complexities of socialization among young African American men living in the inner cities. Anderson is particularly interested in the development of "manhood" and respect among These young men and the relationship between violence and survival. To survive, one must adopt the "code"—a complex system of norms, dress, rituals, and expected behavior. The third reading for this section is a contemporary study focusing on inner-city girls and their relationship to the "code." Nikki Jones suggests that these girls are no more immune to violence than boys. She provides narrative descriptions of some of the ways in which street life shapes the behavior and identity of the young women in her study.

Something to Consider as You Read

According to sociologists, we are shaped by our cultural environment and by the influences of significant people and groups in our lives. Consider some of the people or groups whose opinions matter to you. Can you imagine them as a kind of audience in your head, observing and reacting to your behavior? Think about the desire to feel included. To what extent has this desire shaped your participation in a group that has had an impact on your self-image? How important are "role models" in the socialization process? If someone is managing conflicting identities and has no role models or others in similar situations, how might this conflict affect her or his sense of self and relationships with others? What do these readings suggest about the importance of being the "right person in the right place" even if that's not all you feel yourself to be? How do power and authority affect people's sense of self and their right to be whomever they want to be in any situation? How do social conditions shape our choices and opportunities?

Life as the Maid's Daughter

An Exploration of the Everyday Boundaries of Race, Class, and Gender

Mary Romero

(1995)

Introduction

. . . My current research attempts to expand the sociological understanding of the dynamics of race, class, and gender in the everyday routines of family life and reproductive labor. . . . I am lured to the unique setting presented by domestic service . . . and I turn to the realities experienced by the children of private household workers. This focus is not entirely voluntary. While presenting my research on Chicana private household workers, I was approached repeatedly by Latina/os and African Americans who wanted to share their knowledge about domestic service—knowledge they obtained as the daughters and sons of household workers. Listening to their accounts about their mothers' employment presents another reality to understanding paid and unpaid reproductive labor and the way in which persons of color are socialized into a class-based, gendered, racist social structure. The following discussion explores issues of stratification in everyday life by analyzing the life story of a maid's daughter. This life story illustrates the potential of the standpoint of the maid's daughter for generating knowledge about race, class, and gender. . . .

Social Boundaries Presented in the Life Story

The first interview with Teresa,[1] the daughter of a live-in maid, eventually led to a life history project. I am intrigued by Teresa's experiences with her mother's white, upper-middle-class employers while maintaining close ties to her relatives in Juarez, Mexico, and Mexican friends in Los Angeles. While some may view Teresa's life as a freak accident, living a life of "rags to riches," and certainly not a common Chicana/o experience, her story represents a microcosm of power relationships in the larger society. Life as the maid's daughter in an upper-middle-class neighborhood exemplifies many aspects of the Chicano/Mexicano experience as "racial ethnics" in the United States, whereby the boundaries of inclusion and exclusion are constantly changing as we move from one social setting and one social role to another.

Teresa's narrative contains descriptive accounts of negotiating boundaries in the employers' homes and in their community. As the maid's daughter, the old adage "Just like one of the family" is a reality, and Teresa has to learn when she must act like the employer's child and when she must assume the appropriate behavior as the maid's daughter. She has to recognize all the social cues and interpret social settings correctly—when to expect the same rights and privileges as the employer's children and when to fulfill the expectations and obligations as the maid's daughter. Unlike the employers' families, Teresa and her mother rely on different ways of obtaining knowledge. The taken-for-granted reality of the employers' families do not contain conscious experiences of negotiating race and class status, particularly not in the intimate setting of the home. Teresa's status is constantly changing in response to the wide range of social settings she encounters—from employers' dinner parties with movie

89

stars and corporate executives to Sunday dinners with Mexican garment workers in Los Angeles and factory workers in El Paso. Since Teresa remains bilingual and bicultural throughout her life, her story reflects the constant struggle and resistance to maintain her Mexican identity, claiming a reality that is neither rewarded nor acknowledged as valid.

Teresa's account of her life as the maid's daughter is symbolic of the way that racial ethnics participate in the United States; sometimes we are included and other times excluded or ignored. Teresa's story captures the reality of social stratification in the United States, that is, a racist, sexist, and class-structured society upheld by an ideology of equality. I will analyze the experiences of the maid's daughter in an upper-middle-class neighborhood in Los Angeles to investigate the ways that boundaries of race, class, and gender are maintained or diffused in everyday life. I have selected various excerpts from the transcripts that illustrate how knowledge about a class-based and gendered, racist social order is learned, the type of information that is conveyed, and how the boundaries between systems of domination impact everyday life. I begin with a brief history of Teresa and her mother, Carmen.

Learning Social Boundaries: Background

Teresa's mother was born in Piedras Negras, a small town in Aguas Calientes in Mexico. After her father was seriously injured in a railroad accident, the family moved to a small town outside Ciudad Juarez. . . . By the time she was fifteen she moved to Juarez and took a job as a domestic, making about eight dollars a week. She soon crossed the border and began working for Anglo families in the country club area in El Paso. Like other domestics in El Paso, Teresa's mother returned to Mexico on weekends and helped support her mother and sisters. In her late twenties she joined several of her friends in their search for better-paying jobs in Los Angeles. The women immediately

found jobs in the garment industry. Yet, after six months in the sweatshops, Teresa's mother went to an agency in search of domestic work. She was placed in a very exclusive Los Angeles neighborhood. Several years later Teresa was born. Her friends took care of the baby while Carmen continued working; childcare became a burden, however, and she eventually returned to Mexico. At the age of thirty-six Teresa's mother returned to Mexico with her newborn baby. Leaving Teresa with her grandmother and aunts, her mother sought work in the country club area. Three years later Teresa and her mother returned to Los Angeles.

Over the next fifteen years Teresa lived with her mother in the employer's (Smith) home, usually the two sharing the maid's room located off the kitchen. From the age of three until Teresa started school, she accompanied her mother to work. She continued to live in the Smiths' home until she left for college. All of Teresa's live-in years were spent in one employer's household. The Smiths were unable to afford a full-time maid, however, so Teresa's mother began doing day work throughout the neighborhood. After school Teresa went to whatever house her mother was cleaning and waited until her mother finished working, around 4 or 6 P.M., and then returned to the Smiths' home with her mother. Many prominent families in the neighborhood knew Teresa as the maid's daughter and treated her accordingly. While Teresa wanted the relationship with the employers to cease when she went to college and left the neighborhood, her mother continued to work as a live-in maid with no residence other than the room in the employer's home; consequently, Teresa's social status as the maid's daughter continued. . . .

One of the Family

As Teresa got older, the boundaries between insider and outsider became more complicated, as employers referred to her and Carmen as "one of the family." Entering into an employer's world as the maid's daughter, Teresa was not only subjected to the rules of an outsider but also had to recognize when the rules changed, making her momentarily an insider. While the boundaries dictating Carmen's work became blurred between the obligations of an employee and that of a friend or family member, Teresa was forced into situations in which she was expected to be just like one of the employer's children, and yet she remained the maid's daughter. . . .

Living under conditions established by the employers made Teresa and her mother's efforts to maintain a distinction between their family life and an employer's family very difficult. Analyzing incidents in which the boundaries between the worker's family and employer's family were blurred highlights the issues that complicate the mother-daughter relationship. Teresa's account of her mother's hospitalization was the first of numerous conflicts between the two that stemmed from the live-in situation and their relationships with the employer's family. The following excerpt demonstrates the difficulty in interacting as a family unit and the degree of influence and power employers exerted over their daily lives:

When I was about ten my mother got real sick. That summer, instead of sleeping downstairs in my mother's room when my mother wasn't there, one of the kids was gone away to college, so it was just Rosalyn, David and myself that were home. The other two were gone, so I was gonna sleep upstairs in one of the rooms. I was around eight or nine, ten I guess. I lived in the back room. It was a really neat room because Rosalyn was allowed to paint it. She got her friend who was real good, painted a big tree and clouds and all this stuff on the walls. So I really loved it and I had my own room. I was with the Smiths all the time, as my parents, for about two months. My mother was in the hospital for about a month. Then when she came home, she really couldn't do anything. We would all have dinner, the Smiths were really, really supportive. I went to summer school and I took math and English and stuff like that. I was in this drama class and I did drama and I got to do the leading role. Everybody really liked me and Ms. Smith

would come and see my play. So things started to change when I got a lot closer to them and I was with them alone. I would go see my mother everyday, and my cousin was there. I think that my cousin kind of resented all the time that the Smiths spent with me. I think my mother was really afraid that now that she wasn't there that they were going to steal me from her. I went to see her, but I could only stay a couple of hours and it was really weird. I didn't like seeing my mother in pain and she was in a lot of pain. I remember before she came home the Smiths said that they thought it would be a really good idea if I stayed upstairs and I had my own room now that my mother was going to be sick and I couldn't sleep in the same bed 'cause I might hurt her. It was important for my mother to be alone. And how did I feel about that? I was really excited about that [having her own room]— you know. They said, "Your mom she is probably not going to like it and she might get upset about it, but I think that we can convince her that it is ok." When my mom came home, she understood that she couldn't be touched and that she had to be really careful, but she wanted it [having her own room] to be temporary. Then my mother was really upset. She got into it with them and said, "No, I don't want it that way." She would tell me, "No, I want you to be down here. ¿Qué crees que eres hija de ellos? You're gonna be with me all the time, you can't do that." So I would tell Ms. Smith. She would ask me when we would go to the market together, "How does your mom seem, what does she feel, what does she say?" She would get me to relay that. I would say, "I think my mom is really upset about me moving upstairs. She doesn't like it and she just says no." I wouldn't tell her everything. They would talk to her and finally they convinced her, but my mom really, really resented it and was really angry about it. She was just generally afraid. All these times that my mother wasn't there, things happened and they would take me places with them, go out to dinner with them and their friends. So that was a real big change, in that I slept upstairs and had different rules. Everything changed. I was more independent. I did my own homework; they would open the back door and yell that dinner was ready—you know. Things were just real different.

The account illustrates how assuming the role of insider was an illusion because neither the worker's daughter nor the worker ever became a member of the white, middle-class family. Teresa was only allowed to move out of the maid's quarter, where she shared a bed with her mother, when two of the employer's children were leaving home, vacating two bedrooms. . . .

Teresa and Carmen did not experience the boundaries of insider and outsider in the same way. Teresa was in a position to assume a more active family role when employers made certain requests. Unlike her mother, she was not an employee and was not expected to clean and serve the employer. Carmen's responsibility for the housework never ceased, however, regardless of the emotional ties existing between employee and employers. She and her employers understood that, whatever family activity she might be participating in, if the situation called for someone to clean, pick up, or serve, that was Carmen's job. When the Smiths requested Teresa to sit at the dinner table with the family, they placed Teresa in a different class position than her mother, who was now expected to serve her daughter alongside her employer. Moving Teresa upstairs in a bedroom alongside the employer and their children was bound to drive a wedge between Teresa and Carmen. There is a long history of spatial deference in domestic service, including separate entrances, staircases, and eating and sleeping arrangements. Carmen's room reflected her position in the household. As the maid's quarter, the room was separated from the rest of the bedrooms and was located near the maid's central work area, the kitchen. The room was obviously not large enough for two beds because Carmen and Teresa shared a bed. Once Teresa was moved upstairs, she no longer shared the same social space in the employer's home as her mother. Weakening the bonds between the maid and her daughter permitted the employers to broaden their range of relationships and interaction with Teresa.

Carmen's feelings of betrayal and loss underline how threatening the employers'

actions were. She understood that the employers were in a position to buy her child's love. They had already attempted to socialize Teresa into Euro-American ideals by planning Teresa's education and deciding what courses she would take. Guided by the importance they place on European culture, the employers defined the Mexican Spanish spoken by Teresa and her mother as inadequate and classified Castillan Spanish as "proper" Spanish. As a Mexican immigrant woman working as a live-in maid, Carmen was able to experience certain middle-class privileges, but her only access to these privileges was through her relationship with employers. Therefore, without the employers' assistance, she did not have the necessary connections to enroll Teresa in private schools or provide her with upper-middle-class experiences to help her develop the skills needed to survive in elite schools. Carmen only gained these privileges for her daughter at a price; she relinquished many of her parental rights to her employers. To a large degree the Smiths determined Carmen's role as a parent, and the other employers restricted the time she had to attend school functions and the amount of energy left at the end of the day to mother her own child.

Carmen pointed to the myth of "being like one of the family" in her comment, "¿Qué crees que eres hija de ellos? You're gonna be with me all the time, you can't do that." The statement underlines the fact that the bond between mother and daughter is for life, whereas the pseudofamily relationship with employers is temporary and conditional. Carmen wanted her daughter to understand that taking on the role of being one of the employer's family did not relinquish her from the responsibility of fulfilling her "real" family obligations. The resentment Teresa felt from her cousin who was keeping vigil at his aunt's hospital bed indicated that she had not been a dutiful daughter. The outside pressure from an employer did not remove her own family obligations and responsibilities. Teresa's relatives expected a daughter to be at her mother's side providing any assistance possible as a caretaker, even if it was limited to companionship. The employer determined Teresa's activity, however, and shaped her behavior into that of a middle-class child; consequently, she was kept away from the hospital and protected from the realities of her mother's illness. Furthermore, she was submerged into the employer's world, dining at the country club and interacting with their friends.

Her mother's accusation that Teresa wanted to be the Smiths' daughter signifies the feelings of betrayal or loss and the degree to which Carmen was threatened by the employer's power and authority. Yet Teresa also felt betrayal and loss and viewed herself in competition with the employers for her mother's time, attention, and love. In this excerpt Teresa accuses her mother of wanting to be part of employers' families and community:

> I couldn't understand it—you know—until I was about eighteen and then I said, "It is your fault. If I treat the Smiths differently, it is your fault. You chose to have me live in this situation. It was your decision to let me have two parents, and for me to balance things off, so you can't tell me that I said this. You are the one who wanted this." When I was about eighteen we got into a huge fight on Christmas. I hated the holidays because I hated spending them with the Smiths. My mother always worked. She worked on every holiday. She loved to work on the holidays! She would look forward to working. My mother just worked all the time! I think that part of it was that she wanted to have power and control over this community, and she wanted the network, and she wanted to go to different people's houses.

As employers, Mr. and Mrs. Smith were able to exert an enormous amount of power over the relationship between Teresa and her mother. Carmen was employed in an occupation in which the way to improve working conditions, pay, and benefits was through the manipulation of personal relationships with employers. Carmen obviously tried to take advantage of her relationship with the Smiths in order to provide the best for her daughter.

The more intimate and interpersonal the relationship, the more likely employers were to give gifts, do favors, and provide financial assistance. Although speaking in anger and filled with hurt, Teresa accused her mother of choosing to be with employers and their families rather than with her own daughter. Underneath Teresa's accusation was the understanding that the only influence and status her mother had as a domestic was gained through her personal relationships with employers. Although her mother had limited power in rejecting the Smiths' demands, Teresa held her responsible for giving them too much control. Teresa argued that the positive relationship with the Smiths was done out of obedience to her mother and denied any familial feelings toward the employers. The web between employee and employers' families affected both mother and daughter, who were unable to separate the boundaries of work and family.

Maintaining Cultural Identity

A major theme in Teresa's narrative was her struggle to retain her Mexican culture and her political commitment to social justice. Rather than internalizing meaning attached to Euro-American practices and redefining Mexican culture and bilingualism as negative social traits, Teresa learned to be a competent social actor in both white, upper-middle-class environments and in working- and middle-class Chicano and Mexicano environments. To survive as a stranger in so many social settings, Teresa developed an acute skill for assessing the rules governing a particular social setting and acting accordingly. Her ability to be competent in diverse social settings was only possible, however, because of her life with the employers' children. Teresa and her mother maintained another life—one that was guarded and protected against any employer intrusion. Their other life was Mexican, not white, was Spanish speaking, not English speaking, was female dominated rather than male dominated, and was poor and working-class, not upper-middle-class. During the week Teresa and her mother visited the other Mexican maids in the neighborhoods, on weekends they occasionally took a bus into the Mexican barrio in Los Angeles to have dinner with friends, and every summer they spent a month in Ciudad Juarez with their family. . . .

Teresa's description of evening activity with the Mexican maids in the neighborhood provides insight into her daily socialization and explains how she learned to live in the employer's home without internalizing all their negative attitudes toward Mexican and working-class culture. Within the white, upper-class neighborhood in which they worked, the Mexican maids got together on a regular basis and cooked Mexican food, listened to Mexican music, and gossiped in Spanish about their employers. Treated as invisible or as confidants, the maids were frequently exposed to the intimate details of their employers' marriages and family life. The Mexican maids voiced their disapproval of the lenient child-rearing practices and parental decisions, particularly surrounding drug usage and the importance of material possessions:

> Raquel was the only one [maid] in the neighborhood who had her own room and own TV set. So everybody would go over to Raquel's. . . . This was my mother's support system. After hours, they would go to different people's [maid's] rooms depending on what their rooms had. Some of them had kitchens and they would go and cook all together, or do things like play cards and talk all the time. I remember that in those situations they would sit, and my mother would talk about the Smiths, what they were like. When they were going to negotiate for raises, when they didn't like certain things, I would listen and hear all the different discussions about what was going on in different houses. And they would talk, also, about the family relationships. The way they interacted, the kids did this and that. At the time some of the kids were smoking pot and they would talk about who was smoking marijuana. How weird it was that the parents didn't care. They would talk about what they saw as being wrong. The marriage relationship, or how weird it was they would go off to the beauty shop and spend all this money, go shopping and do all these weird things and the effect that it had on the kids.

The interaction among the maids points to the existence of another culture operating invisibly within a Euro-American and male-dominated community. The workers' support system did not include employers and addressed their concerns as mothers, immigrants, workers, and women. They created a Mexican-dominated domain for themselves. Here they ate Mexican food, spoke Spanish, listened to the Spanish radio station, and watched novellas on TV. Here Teresa was not a cultural artifact but, instead, a member of the Mexican community.

In exchanging gossip and voicing their opinions about the employers' lifestyles, the maids rejected many of the employers' priorities in life. Sharing stories about the employers' families allowed the Mexican immigrant women to be critical of white, upper-middle-class families and to affirm and enhance their own cultural practices and beliefs. The regular evening sessions with other working-class Mexican immigrant women were essential in preserving Teresa and her mother's cultural values and were an important agency of socialization for Teresa. For instance, the maids had a much higher regard for their duties and responsibilities as mothers than as wives or lovers. In comparison to their mistresses, they were not financially dependent on men, nor did they engage in the expensive and time-consuming activity of being an ideal wife, such as dieting, exercising, and maintaining a certain standard of beauty in their dress, makeup, and hairdos. Unlike the employers' daughters, who attended cotillions and were socialized to acquire success through marriage, Teresa was constantly pushed to succeed academically in order to pursue a career. The gender identity cultivated among the maids did not include dependence on men or the learned helplessness that was enforced in the employers' homes but, rather, promoted self-sufficiency.

However, both white women employers and Mexican women employees were expected to be nurturing and caring. These traits were further reinforced when employers asked Teresa to babysit for their children or to provide them with companionship during their husbands' absences.

So, while Teresa observed her mother adapting to the employers' standards in her interaction with their children, she learned that her mother did not approve of their lifestyle and understood that she had another set of expectations to adhere to. Teresa attended the same schools as employers' children, wore similar clothes, and conducted most of her social life within the same socio-economic class, but she remained the maid's daughter—and learned the limitations of that position. Teresa watched her mother uphold higher standards for her and apply a different set of standards to the employers' children; most of the time, however, it appeared to Teresa as if they had no rules at all.

Sharing stories about the Smiths and other employers in a female, Mexican, and worker-dominated social setting provided Teresa with a clear image of the people she lived with as employers rather than as family members. Seeing the employers through the eyes of the employees forced Teresa to question their kindness and benevolence and to recognize their use of manipulation to obtain additional physical and emotional labor from the employees. She became aware of the workers' struggles and the long list of grievances, including no annual raises, no paid vacations, no social security or health benefits, little if any privacy, and sexual harassment. Teresa was also exposed to the price that working-class immigrant women employed as live-in maids paid in maintaining white, middle-class, patriarchal communities. Employers' careers and lifestyles, particularly the everyday rituals affirming male privilege, were made possible through the labor women provided for men's physical, social, and emotional needs. Female employers depended on the maid's labor to assist in the reproduction

of their gendered class status. Household labor was expanded in order to accommodate the male members of the employers' families and to preserve their privilege. Additional work was created by rearranging meals around men's work and recreation schedules and by waiting on them and serving them. Teresa's mother was frequently called upon to provide emotional labor for the wife, husband, mother, and father within an employer's family, thus freeing members to work or increase their leisure time.

Discussion

Teresa's account offers insight into the ways racial ethnic women gain knowledge about the social order and use the knowledge to develop survival strategies. As the college-educated daughter of an immigrant Mexican woman employed as a live-in maid, Teresa's experiences in the employers' homes, neighborhood, and school and her experiences in the homes of working-class Mexicano families and barrios provided her with the skills to cross the class and cultural boundaries separating the two worlds. The process of negotiating social boundaries involved an evaluation of Euro-American culture and its belief system in light of an intimate knowledge of white, middle-class families. Being in the position to compare and contrast behavior within different communities, Teresa debunked notions of "American family values" and resisted efforts toward assimilation. Learning to function in the employers' world was accomplished without internalizing its belief system, which defined ethnic culture as inferior. Unlike the employers' families, Teresa's was not able to assume the taken-for-granted reality of her mother's employers because her experiences provided a different kind of knowledge about the social order.

While the employers' children were surrounded by positive images of their race and class status, Teresa faced negative sanctions against her culture and powerless images of her race. Among employers' families she quickly learned that her "mother tongue" was not valued and that her culture was denied. All the Mexican adults in the neighborhood were in subordinate positions to the white adults and were responsible for caring for and nurturing white children. Most of the female employers were full-time homemakers who enjoyed the financial security provided by their husbands, whereas the Mexican immigrant women in the neighborhood all worked as maids and were financially independent; in many cases they were supporting children, husbands, and other family members. By directly observing her mother serve, pick up after, and nurture employers and their families, Teresa learned about white, middle-class privileges. Her experiences with other working-class Mexicans were dominated by women's responsibility for their children and extended families. Here the major responsibility of mothering was financial; caring and nurturing were secondary and were provided by the extended family or children did without. Confronted with a working mother who was too tired to spend time with her, Teresa learned about the racial, class, and gender parameters of parenthood, including its privileges, rights, responsibilities, and obligations. She also learned that the role of a daughter included helping her mother with everyday household tasks and, eventually, with the financial needs of the extended family. Unlike her uncles and male cousins, Teresa was not exempt from cooking and housework, regardless of her financial contributions. Within the extended family Teresa was subjected to standards of beauty strongly weighted by male definitions of women as modest beings, many times restricted in her dress and physical movements. Her social worlds became clearly marked by race, ethnic, class, and gender differences.

Successfully negotiating movement from a white, male, and middle-class setting to one dominated by working-class, immigrant, Mexican women involved a socialization process that provided Teresa with the skills to be bicultural. Since neither setting was bicultural, Teresa had to become that in order to be a competent social actor in each. Being bicultural included having the ability to assess the rules governing each setting and to understand her ethnic, class, and gender position. Her early socialization in the employers' households was not guided by principles of creativity, independence, and leadership but, rather, was based on conformity and accommodation. Teresa's experiences in two different cultural groups allowed her to separate each and to fulfill the employers' expectations without necessarily internalizing the meaning attached to the act. Therefore, she was able to learn English without internalizing the idea that English is superior to Spanish or that monolingualism is normal. The existence of a Mexican community within the employers' neighborhood provided Teresa with a collective experience of class-based racism, and the maids' support system affirmed and enhanced their own belief system and culture. As Philomena Essed (1991, 294) points out, "The problem is not only how knowledge of racism is acquired but also what kind of knowledge is being transmitted."

Teresa's life story lends itself to a complex set of analyses because the pressures to assimilate were challenged by the positive interactions she experienced within her ethnic community. Like other bilingual persons in the United States, Teresa's linguistic abilities were shaped by the linguistic practices of the social settings she had access to. Teresa learned the appropriate behavior for each social setting, each marked by different class and cultural dynamics and in which women's economic roles and relationships to men were distinct. An overview of Teresa's socialization illustrates the process of biculturalism—a process that included different sets of standards and rules governing her actions as a woman, as a Chicana, and as the maid's daughter. . . .

NOTES

This essay was originally presented as a paper at the University of Michigan, "Feminist Scholarship: Thinking through the Disciplines," 30 January 1992. I want to thank Abigail J. Stewart and Donna Stanton for their insightful comments and suggestions.

1. The names are pseudonyms.

REFERENCE

Essed, Philomena. 1991. *Understanding Everyday Racism.* Newbury Park, Calif.: Sage Publications.

THINKING ABOUT THE READING

Teresa's childhood is unique in that she and her mother lived in the household of her mother's employer, requiring them to conform to the expectations of the employers even when her mother was "not at work." Her childhood was shaped by the need to read signals from others to determine her position in various social settings. What were some of the different influences in Teresa's early socialization? Did she accept people's attempts to mold her, or did she resist? How did she react to her mother's employers' referring to her as "one of the family"? Teresa came from a poor family, but she spent her childhood in affluent households. With respect to socialization, what advantages do you think these experiences provided her? What were the disadvantages? How do you think these experiences would have changed if she was a *son* of a live-in maid rather than a daughter? If she was a poor *white* girl rather than Latina?

The Making of Culture, Identity, and Ethnicity Among Asian American Youth

Min Zhou and Jennifer Lee

(2004)

Youth and Culture

In preindustrial societies, one's life course was roughly marked by two discrete stages—childhood and adulthood. However, in postindustrial societies, the duration of childhood has been prolonged and also includes the distinct, yet overlapping stages of adolescence and youth. Today, youth generally refer to those between the ages of 16 and 24 (and sometimes even 30). These young people are at the stage in their life cycles where they strive to find their own spaces, make their own choices, and form their own identities, while at the same time deterred by certain norms, rules, regulations, and social forces from accepting the myriad responsibilities that accompany full adulthood.

The delayed entrance into adulthood stems from two sources: on the one hand, societal constraints prohibit youth from partaking in certain adult activities; and on the other, youth also prolong this stage in their lives. For instance, while American youth may legally enter the labor force, those under the age of 18 are considered minors and therefore banned from participating in electoral politics or purchasing a pack of cigarettes. In addition, it is a criminal offense for an adult to have sex with a minor, even when the sex is consensual. Furthermore, while accorded the full rights of citizenship at the age of 18, those under the age of 21 are prohibited from buying or consuming alcoholic beverages and entering nightclubs that serve alcohol. While societal constraints play an active part in delaying the entrance into adulthood, American youth

themselves are increasingly active participants in prolonging this stage of their lives. For instance, it is becoming increasingly more common (and to some extent necessary in today's economy) for those under the age of 25 to continue with school full time after graduating from high school. Consequently, seeking higher education delays the transition to adulthood, which is typically characterized by a stable job, marriage, home life, and parenthood.

Today, to be young is to be hip, cool, fun loving, carefree, and able to follow one's heart's desires. As a significant social group, this age cohort is inherently ambiguous as it juxtaposes and strives to find balance between the dialectics of parental influence and individual freedom, dependence and independence, innocence and responsibility, and ultimately adolescence and adulthood. It is precisely the tension arising from this ambiguity that drives the public misrepresentation of youth as deviant, delinquent, deficient, and rebellious or resistant.

Culture, on the other hand, is defined as the ways, forms, and patterns of life in which socially identifiable groups interact with their environments and express their symbolic and material existences. Young people experience the conditions of their lives, define them, and respond to them, and in the process, they produce unique cultural forms and practices that become the expressions and products of their own experiences (Brake, 1985). Thus, youth culture is broadly referred to as a particular way of life, combined with particular patterns of beliefs, values, symbols, and activities that are shared, lived, or expressed by young people (Frith, 1984). As social scientists, our goal is not only to identify young people's shared activities but also to uncover the values that underlie their activities and behavior. As early as 1942, Talcott Parsons coined the phrase "youth culture" to describe a distinctive world of youth structured by age and sex roles with a value system in opposition to the adult world of productive work, responsibility, and routine (p. 606). While youth culture may oppose the adult values of conformity to adult culture and responsibilities, it also serves as an invaluable problem-solving resource—the development and use of day-to-day practices to help make sense of and cope with youth's shared problems (Frith, 1984).

Contemporary research on youth culture reveals a tendency to move youth out of class-based categories, and instead, emphasize the diversity of youth cultures as well as the multidimensional nature of resistance. The resurgent literature on youth culture, especially since the 1980s, turns our attention to the distinctive characteristics of youth, with a particular emphasis on the impacts of class, race/ethnicity, gender, and geography on their cultural expressions, signs, symbols, and activities.

We highlight several significant conceptual advancements in the recent literature on youth culture as they help provide some contextual background for our understanding of the Asian American youth culture. Instead of placing youth within a class framework or portraying them as delinquents, new research on youth in the United States focuses on the interactive processes between various macro and micro social forces in the formation and practice of culture and identity. Going beyond analyses of class, contemporary work recognizes the diversity of youth cultures, examining differences across a wide range of social categories, including class, race/ethnicity, gender, sexuality, and geography, and sometimes even making further distinctions within these categories. For example, the experiences of white and nonwhite youth, boys and girls, and

heterosexuals and homosexuals are now presumed to have distinct characteristics that interact with structural forces such as hegemony, racism, sexism, and homophobia. Their experiences shape their socialization, which in turn affect the ways in which members of each respective group express, represent, and identify themselves.

Intergenerational differences among Asians complicate intragroup dynamics and family relations. Most notably, native-born children and grandchildren of Asian ancestry feel a sense of ambivalence toward newer arrivals. Because about two-thirds of the Asian American population is first generation, native-born Asians must now confront renewed images of Asians as "foreigners." Resembling the new immigrants in phenotype, but not necessarily in behavior, language, and culture, the more "assimilated" native born find that they must actively and constantly distinguish themselves from the newer arrivals. The "immigrant shadow" looms large for Asian American youth and can weigh heavily on the identity formation of native-born youth. However, native- and foreign-born youth react differently to the "immigrant shadow." For instance, comments about one's "good English" or inquiries about where one comes from are often taken as insensitive at best, and offensive or even insulting at worst, to native-born Asian Americans. By stark contrast, similar encounters tend to be interpreted or felt more positively among foreign-born Asians. Different lived experiences between the native and foreign-born are thus not only generational but also cultural.

While recognizing the vast diversity among Asian Americans, we argue that intragroup dynamics and their consequences render the Asian American experience unique, and the imposed pan-ethnic category meaningful for analysis. However, we do not lose sight of the fact that "Asian American" is an imposed identity and most often, not adopted by either the first or second generation who are much more likely to identify with their national origins than other Americans.

Immigration

Immigration is the most immediate process that shapes the cultural formation of Asian American youth. As noted earlier, Asian Americans are a predominantly immigrant group, which in turn has an enormous impact on the experiences of Asian American youth. As they grow up, they are intimately influenced and often intensely constrained by the immigrant family, the ethnic community, and their parents' ancestral homeland. Research has illustrated how the immigrant family and ethnic community have been the primary sources of support as well as the primary sites of conflict (Zhou and Bankston, 1998).

Asian American children, despite their diverse origins, share certain common family experiences—most prominently the unduly familial obligation to obey their elders and repay parental sacrifices, along with the extraordinarily high parental expectations for educational and occupational achievement. Many Asian immigrant parents (especially those who had already secured middle-class status in their home countries) migrated to provide better opportunities for their children. As new immigrants, the first generation often endure difficulties associated with migration such as lack of English-language proficiency, American cultural literacy, and familiarity with the host society. Moreover, those who gave up their middle-class occupations often endure downward occupational mobility, relative deprivation, and discrimination from the host society (Lee, 2000). In their directed quest to achieve socioeconomic mobility, the first generation appears to their children as little more than one-dimensional hard workers who focus too much on material achievement and too little on leisure.

Although their children may feel that their immigrant parents have a narrow vision of success, the first generation are all too aware of their own limits in ensuring socioeconomic mobility for their children, and hence, turn to education as the surest path to move ahead. Thus, not only do they place an enormous amount of pressure on their children to excel in school, but they also provide the material means to assure success. For example, they move to neighborhoods with strong public schools, send their children to private after-school programs (including language programs, academic tutoring, and enrichment institutions in the ethnic community), spend time to seek out detailed academic information, and make decisions about schools and majors for their children (Zhou and Li, 2003).

Although the parents feel that they are doing what is best for their children, the children—whose frame of reference is "American"—see things differently. From their point of view, their parents appear rigid and "abnormal," that is, unacculturated, old-fashioned, and traditional disciplinarians who are incapable of having fun with them and unwilling to show respect for their individuality. The children view the immigrant family and ethnic community as symbols of the old world—strictly authoritarian, severely demanding, and overwhelmingly stifling.

At the same time, however, the children witness at first hand their parents' daily struggles as new immigrants trying to make it in America, and consequently, develop a unique respect and sensitivity toward them. One of the most prominent ways that they demonstrate their respect and sensitivity is through a subtle blend of conformity to and rebellion against their parents. Asian American youth are less likely to talk back or blatantly defy their parents than other American youth. For example, in her study of Nisei daughters during the years of Asian exclusion, Valerie Matsumoto depicts the tension between native-born daughters and their immigrant parents in the way they defined womanhood. However, rather than challenging their parents head-on, running away from the family, or leaving the ethnic community, the native-born daughters judiciously negotiated the roles assigned to them by their parents and the tightly knit community by creating various cultural forms—dances, dating, and courtship romances—to assert a gender identity that was simultaneously feminine, "Americanized," and "Japanese." Although this delicate balancing act may take a heavy emotional toll on Asian American youth, it is precisely their ambivalence toward their immigrant families that makes the youth culturally sensitive, which, in turn, expands their repertoire for cultural expression.

Racial Exclusion

Along with the experiences associated with immigration, racialization is a second important process that shapes the cultural formation of Asian American youth. The youth confront the consequences of racialization in a number of ways, the first of which is their encounter with racial exclusion. During the period of Asian exclusion, Asian Americans—who were considered an "inferior race"—were confined to ethnic enclaves. The youth who grew up in this era had few social, educational, or occupational options beyond the walls of the ethnic enclave and were barred from full participation in American life. Consequently, some Asian American youth turned their attention overseas to their parents' ancestral homeland for opportunities that were denied to them in the United States. For example, frustrated by their limited mobility options in America, native-born Chinese youth in the 1930s promoted the "Go West to China" movement to seek better opportunities in their ancestral homeland.

Cultural forms and expressions such as ethnic presses, dances, and beauty pageant contests not only affirmed ethnic identities but also inadvertently reinforced Asian Americans as the foreign "Other." While the days of racial segregation in ethnic enclaves have long since disappeared, the effects of racialization still remain a part of growing up in the United States for Asian American youth. For instance, today's Asian American youth develop an awareness of their nonwhite racial identity that functions as a marker of exclusion in some facets of American society, as Nazli

Kibria (2002) describes in her study of second-generation Chinese and Korean Americans.

Racial Stereotyping

Another way in which Asian American youth face the consequences of racialization is through racial stereotyping. Excluded from fair representation in mainstream American media, most portrayals of Asian Americans have been either insidious stereotypes of the "foreign" *other* or celebrated images of the "super" *other,* setting Asian Americans apart from other Americans. So pervasive are racial stereotypes of Asian Americans that Asian American youth culture is, in part, produced within the context of counteracting these narrowly circumscribed, one-dimensional images, most prominently that of the model minority.

The celebrated "model minority" image of Asian Americans was born in the mid-1960s, at the peak of the civil rights and ethnic consciousness movements, but *before* the rising waves of immigration and refugee influx from Asia. Two articles published in 1966—"Success Story, Japanese-American Style," by William Petersen in the *New York Times Magazine* and "Success of One Minority Group in U.S.," by the *U.S. News and World Report* staff—marked a significant departure from the portrayal of Asian Americans as aliens and foreigners, and changed the way that the media depicted Asian immigrants and their descendants. Both articles extolled Japanese and Chinese Americans for their persistence in overcoming extreme hardship and discrimination in order to achieve success (unmatched even by U.S.-born whites) with "their own almost totally unaided effort" and "no help from anyone else." The press attributed their winning wealth and ability to get ahead in American society to hard work, family solidarity, discipline, delayed gratification, nonconfrontation, and disdain for welfare.

Although the image of the model minority may seem laudatory, it has far-reaching consequences that extend beyond Asian Americans.

First, the model minority stereotype serves to buttress the myth that the United States is a country devoid of racism, and one that accords equal opportunity for all who take the initiative to work hard to get ahead. The image functions to blame those who lag behind and are not making it for their failure to work hard, their inability to delay gratification, and their inferior culture. Not only does the image thwart other racial/ethnic minorities' demands for social justice, it also pits minority groups against each other.

Perhaps one of the most devastating consequences of the model minority stereotype is its effect on Asian American youth who feel frustrated and burdened because others judge them by standards *different* from those of other American youth. Their rebellion against the image manifests itself in their adoption of cultural forms and styles that are influenced by other racial/ethnic minority youth, especially African American youth. For example, many Asian American youth adorn hip-hop style clothing, listen to rap music, and frequent hip-hop clubs. However, it would be a mistake to assume that Asian American youth simply imitate other youth cultures. While they borrow elements from other minority youth cultures, they consciously create unique Asian-American-style cultural forms and practices that manifest themselves in import car racing, DJ-ing and emceeing, raving, and film and theater.

A case in point is the recently released all-Asian-cast Hollywood film *Better Luck Tomorrow*, directed by Justin Lin (2003). Defiantly turning the model minority image on its head, the film exposes the dark side of living up to the meek, studious, overachiever stereotype. Moreover, it depicts a series of shocking scenarios that illustrates that Asian American adolescents are just as confused and disturbed as other disaffected American youth who are bored with life. The multifaceted portrayal of Asian American youth proves that they can be good-looking, smart, funny, susceptible to drugs and alcohol, prone to violence and other vices, capable of self-destructive behavior, and completely lacking in morals all at once. While the model minority stereotype still endures in the media and popular culture, Asian American youth use cultural expression to show that they are far more multidimensional, complex, and, in fact, normal than the stereotype allows.

Invisibility

Yet another way in which Asian American youth confront the consequences of racialization is with invisibility, or the lack of public/media exposure. While all American youth are marginalized in society, they are nevertheless highly visible in mainstream American culture. Stereotypical or not, images of white and black youth permeate the media—from high culture on television, film, theater, music, dance, and fashion, to low culture on the street. However, images of Asian American youth are virtually absent, and perceptibly so. Hence, their expression through cultural forms and practices is an avenue through which Asian American youth make their presence on the American scene.

For example, Asian Americans have never had a significant place in the American recording industry as performers, producers, or consumers. By contrast, whites and blacks, and more recently Latinos, have been highly visible in and targeted by the recording industry. To counter the invisibility, many Asian American cultural workers believe that "just by being there" is the first step to being recognized, but beyond that, Asian Americans need to take active steps to realize their full political and artistic potential (Wong, 1997). So invisible are Asian Americans in the recording industry that many Asian American cultural workers consider making a mark on this scene as an urgent political and revolutionary project.

Whereas cultural workers agree that Asians are invisible in the arts, they do not agree on the means by which to assert their presence. For instance, Fred Ho (1999), an Asian American jazz artist, argues that "just being there" is not enough. Moreover, Ho contends that because Asian American cultural work is revolutionary in nature, Asian Americans should be in control of the means of cultural production by establishing their own production companies. Only by establishing their own means of cultural production can Asian Americans problematize the ideology of assimilation, reject Eurocentric and essentialist forms, and draw upon the rich Asian, immigrant, and working-class traditions of Asian Americans.

Globalization and Transnationalism

Globalization and transnationalism provide yet another means through which Asian Americans confront the effects of racialization. Advancements in digital technologies and the Internet allow today's generation of Asian American youth to communicate and stay in close contact with their respective ancestral homelands through visual imagery, music, sounds, and words beyond the imagination of earlier generations. Globalization beyond national borders widens the cultural space in which Asian American youth are able to maneuver at relative ease to create new opportunities for cultural production and expression.

Cultural forms such as styles, music, dances, desires, and dreams among South Asian American youth, for example, are shaped not only by American influences but also through diasporic influences to create an empowering sense of identity (Maira, 2002). The opportunities presented by globalization for the identity formation of Asian American youth are not reserved only for the native born.

In sum, Asian American youths' adoption of cultural forms are the products of both opportunities and constraints presented to them from the larger processes of immigration and racialization. Because many Asian Americans are foreign born, the experiences of Asian American youth are inextricably linked to immigrant adaptation, the immigrant family, and the ethnic community, thereby making their experiences distinctive from those of other American youth. And while other racial/ethnic minority youth also experience the racialization of their identities, the effects of racialization and the way they manifest themselves in cultural expression are distinctive. Racial/ethnic minorities in the United States have suffered and continue to suffer from exclusion and stereotypes, but the stereotypes of each group are different and affect minority youth differently. The stereotype of the Asian model minority constrains and frustrates youth, pigeonholing them into a one-dimensional, superhuman mold. In other realms, Asian American youth experience the pangs of invisibility and attempt to make their mark through unique cultural practices such as import car racing, dance, theater, and clothing styles. Finally, today's advancements in technology offer Asian American youth influences beyond America, and also broaden the scope of their cultural terrain.

Asian American Identity and an "Emergent Culture of Hybridity"

A diverse lot, today's Asian American youth often adopt a number of different identities—ethnic, hyphenated-American, pan-ethnic, or multiracial—and these identities are not necessarily mutually exclusive. However, unlike white American youth whose choice of ethnic identities is symbolic, the identity choices among Asian American youth are far more limited and consequential. Previous research indicates that nativity, generational status, bilingualism, gender, neighborhood context, and perceptions of discrimination are important factors in determining the identity choices among today's Asian American youth (Lee and Bean, 2004; Portes and Rumbaut, 2001; Xie and Goyette, 1997; Zhou and Bankston, 1998). Perhaps most importantly, as nonwhite racial/ethnic minorities, Asian American youth are subject to outsiders' ascription, meaning that how others perceive them has a profound effect on the way they choose to identify themselves. Joane Nagel (1994) has long noted that the choice of identities is a dialectical process that involves both internal and external opinions and processes, that is, what *you* think your identity is versus what *they* think your identity is.

Yet another distinctive feature of Asian American identity is that Asians are neither black nor white, but occupy a position in between, at least at this moment in time. In a society that has long been divided by an impenetrable black-white color line, it is not at all clear that today's Asian Americans see themselves (or for that matter that others see them) as either black *or* white. While Asian Americans may be considered "people of color," the degree to which they view themselves and are viewed by others as closer to black or white is highly ambiguous (Lee and Bean, 2004). On the one hand, they are minorities and therefore subject to racial discrimination and prejudice. On the other, some Asian ethnic groups have achieved social status on a par with—and in some arenas, superseding—whites. Consequently, the "in-between" and "dual status" of Asians may provide greater flexibility in the identity choices for Asian American youth, especially for Asian multiracials.

Although the centrality of race, outsiders' ascription, and the black-white color line has a powerful effect on the identity choices of Asian American youth, also relevant is the fact that most Asian American youth are either immigrants or the children of immigrants. Hence, their identities are inextricably bound by the experiences of immigration, the immigrant family, and the ethnic community, as well as their interactions with mainstream institutions such as schools.

Asian American youth feel they are both a part of and yet apart from mainstream America. Asian American youth have successfully carved out a unique cultural space for themselves that is, in part, a consequence of their constant negotiation between the traditions of their immigrant families and the marginalization and exclusion they experience from the larger society. This does not mean that Asian American youth divorce themselves entirely from mainstream American culture. However, the unique dual status of Asian American youth combined with their immigrant backgrounds prompt them to actively craft a culture of their own that is distinctive both from their ethnic communities and from other American institutions and youth. In doing so, they negotiate between "American" and "Asian" traits, which often results in an "emergent culture of hybridity" that mixes elements of both worlds. By carving out a space and culture of their own through "grass roots cultural production" (Bielby, 2004), Asian American youth have been able to adopt an identity apart from the restraints imposed by the roles and expectations of the family, the ethnic community, work, and school. Consequently, this culture offers young Asian Americans a collective identity—a reference group from which they can develop an individual identity (Brake, 1985).

REFERENCES

Bielby, William T., "Rock in a Hard Place: Grass-Roots Cultural Production in the Post-Elvis Era," *American Sociological Review 69* (2004): 1–13.

Brake, Michael, *Comparative Youth Culture: The Sociology of Youth Cultures and Youth Subcultures in America, Britain, and Canada* (New York: Routledge, 1985).

Frith, Simon, *The Sociology of Youth* (Ormskirk, Lancashire: Causeway Press, 1984).

Ho, Fred, "Identity: Beyond Asian American Jazz: My Musical and Political Changes in the Asian American Movement," *Leonardo Musk Journal 9* (1999): 45–51.

Kibria, Nazli, *Becoming Asian American: Second Generation Chinese and Korean Identity* (Baltimore: Johns Hopkins University Press, 2002).

Lee, Jennifer, "Striving for the American Dream: Struggle, Success, and Intergroup Conflict among Korean Immigrant Entrepreneurs," in *Contemporary Asian America: A Multidisciplinary Reader,* ed. Min Zhou and James V. Gatewood (New York: New York University Press, 2000), 278–296.

Lee, Jennifer and Frank D. Bean, "America's Changing Color Lines: Immigration, Race/Ethnicity, and Multiracial Identification" *Annual Review of Sociology 30* (2004): 221–242.

Lin, Justin (Director), *Better Luck Tomorrow,* Hollywood, CA: Paramount Pictures, 2003.

Maira, Sunaina Marr, *Desis in the House: Indian American Youth Culture in New York City* (Philadelphia: Temple University Press, 2002).

Nagel, Joane, "Constructing Ethnicity: Creating and Recreating Ethnic Identity and Culture," *Social Problems 41* (1994): 152–171.

Parsons, Talcott, "Age and Sex in the Social Structure of the United States," *American Sociological Review 7* (1942): 604–616.

Petersen, William, "Success Story, Japanese-American Style," *New York Times Magazine,* January 9, 1966, pp. 20–21, 33, 36, 38, 40–41, 43.

Portes, Alejandro and Rubén G. Rumbaut, *Legacies: The Story of the Immigrant Second Generation* (Berkeley: University of California Press, 2001).

U.S. News & World Report, "Success Story of One Minority in the U.S.," December 26, 1966, pp. 73–78.

Wong, Deborah, "Just Being There: Making Asian American Space in the Recording Industry," in *Music of Multicultural America: A Study of Twelve Musical Communities,* ed. Kip Lornell and Anne K. Rasmussen (London: Schirmer Books, 1997), 287–316.

Xie, Yu and Kimberly Goyette, "The Racial Identification of Biracial Children with One Asian Parent: Evidence from the 1990 Census," *Social Forces 76* (1997): 547–570.

Zhou, Min and Carl L. Bankston, III., *Growing Up American: How Vietnamese Children Adapt to Life in the United States* (New York: Russell Sage Foundation, 1998).

Zhou, Min and Xiyuan Li, "Ethnic Language Schools and the Development of Supplementary Education in the Immigrant Chinese Community in the United States," *New Directions for Youth Development: Understanding the Social Worlds of Immigrant Youth* (Winter 2003): 57–73.

THINKING ABOUT THE READING

Zhou and Lee suggest that Asian American youth have created their own distinctive culture and identity. What are some examples of this culture? What are some of the factors that contribute to the construction of Asian American youth identities? What do the authors mean when they say that Asian American youth occupy a position between "black and white"? What are some of the implications of this position for their sense of identity and culture?

Working 'the Code'

On Girls, Gender, and Inner-City Violence

Nikki Jones

(2008)

In mainstream American society, it is commonly assumed that women and girls shy away from conflict, are not physically aggressive, and do not fight like boys and men.

In this article, I draw on field research among African-American girls in the United States to argue that the circumstances of inner-city life have encouraged the development of uniquely situated femininities that simultaneously encourage and limit inner-city girls' use of physical aggression and violence. First, I begin by arguing that, in the urban environments that I studied, gender—being a girl—does not protect inner-city girls from much of the violence experienced by inner-city boys. In fact, teenaged boys and girls are both preoccupied with 'survival' as an ongoing project. I use my analysis of interviews with young people involved in violent incidents to demonstrate similarities in how young people work 'the code of the street' across perceived gender lines. This in-depth examination of young people's use of physical aggression and violence reveals that while young men and young women fight, survival is still a gendered project.

Race, Gender, and Inner-City Violence

Inner-city life has changed dramatically over the last century and especially over the last 30 years.

In his ethnographic account of life in inner-city Philadelphia, Elijah Anderson writes that the code of the street is 'a set of prescriptions and proscriptions, or informal rules, of behaviour organised around a desperate search for respect that governs public social relations, especially violence among so many residents, particularly young men and women' (Anderson, 1999, p. 10). Furthermore, the code is 'a system of accountability that promises "an eye for an eye," or a certain "payback" for transgressions' (Anderson, 1999, p. 10). Fundamental elements of the code include respect and 'a credible reputation for vengeance that works to deter aggression' (Anderson, 1999, p. 10). According to Anderson, it is this complex relationship between masculinity, respect and violence that, at times, encourages poor, urban young men to risk their lives in order to be recognised and respected by others *as a man*.

Black feminist scholar Patricia Hill Collins considers Anderson's discussion of masculinity and the 'code of the street' in her recent analysis of the relationship between hegemonic (and racialised) masculinities and femininities, violence and dominance (Collins, 2004, pp. 188–212). Collins argues that the hyper-criminalisation of urban spaces is exacerbated by the culture of the code. As young men from distressed urban areas cycle in and out of correctional facilities at historically remarkable rates, she argues, urban public schools, street concerns and homes have become a ' . . . nexus of street, prison and youth culture,' which exerts 'a tremendous amount of pressure on Black men, especially young, working class men, to avoid being classified as "weak"' (Collins, 2004, p. 211).

What About Girls?

Over the last few decades, feminist criminologists and gender and crime scholars have examined women's and girls' experiences with aggression and violence with increasing complexity. Emphasising how particular material circumstances influence women's and girls' relationship to violence shifts the focus from the consideration of dichotomous gender differences to the empirical examination of gender similarities and differences in experiences with violence among young women and men who live in poor, urban areas (Simpson, 1991). The analysis presented here follows in this tradition by recognising the influence of shared life circumstances on young people's use of violence.

The young people from Philadelphia's inner-city neighbourhoods that I encountered generally share similar life circumstances, yet how they respond to these structural and cultural circumstances—that is, how they work the code of the street—is also gendered in ways that reflect differences among inner-city girls' and boys' understanding of what you 'got to' do to 'survive.'

Methods

Each of the respondents featured in this study was enrolled in a city hospital-based violence intervention project that targeted youth aged 12 to 24 who presented in the emergency department as a result of an intentional violent incident and were considered to be at either moderate or high risk for involvement in future violent incidents. As a consequence of patterns of racial segregation within the city, almost the entire population of young women and men who voluntarily enrolled in the hospital's violence intervention project were African-American.

My fieldwork for this study took place in three phases over 3 years (2001–2003). During the first phase of the study, which lasted about a year and a half, I conducted 'ride alongs' with intervention counsellors who met with young people in their homes shortly after their initial visit to the emergency room. I also conducted a series of interviews with members of the intervention counselling staff. Most of the staff grew up in Philadelphia and were personally familiar with many of the neighbourhoods we visited. During this time and throughout the study, I also observed interactions in the spaces and places that were significant in the lives of the young people I met. These spaces included trolley cars and buses (transportation to and from school), a neighbourhood high school nicknamed 'the Prison on the Hill,' the city's family and criminal court, and various correctional facilities in the area. I also intentionally engaged in extended conversations with grandmothers and mothers, sisters, brothers, cousins and friends of the young people I visited and interviewed. I recorded this information in my fieldnotes and used it to complement, supplement, test and, at times, verify the information collected during interviews.

Shared Circumstances, Shared Code

While the problem of inner-city violence is believed to impact boys and men only, my interviews with teenaged inner-city girls revealed that young women are regularly exposed to many of the same forms of violence that men are exposed to in their everyday lives and are deeply influenced by its normative order. In the inner-city neighbourhoods I visited, which were often quite isolated from the rest of the city, I encountered young men and young women who could quickly recall a friend, relative or 'associate' who had been shot, robbed or stabbed. In the public high school I visited, I watched adolescent girls and boys begin their school day with the same ritual: they dropped their bags on security belts, stepped through a metal detector, and raised their arms and spread their legs for a police-style 'pat down' before entering the building. Repeatedly, I encountered teenaged girls who, like the young men they share space with in the inner city, had stories to tell about getting 'rolled on,' or getting 'jumped,' or about the 'fair one' gone bad. It is these shared circumstances of life that engender a shared understanding about how to survive in a setting where your safety is never guaranteed. In the following sections, I provide portraits of four young people involved in violent incidents in order to illustrate what was revealed to me during the course of field research and interviews: an appreciation of 'the code of the street' that cut across gender lines. The first two respondents, Billy and DeLisha, tell stories of recouping from a very public loss in a street fight. The second set of respondents, Danielle and Robert, highlight how even those who are averse to fighting must sometimes put forth a 'tough front' to deter potentially aggressive challenges in the future.

Billy and DeLisha: 'I'm Not Looking Over My Shoulder'

Billy was 'jumped' by a group of young men while in 'their' neighbourhood, which is within walking distance of his own. He tells me this story as we sit in the living room of his row home. Billy recently reached his 20s, although he looks older than his age. He is White but shares a class background that is similar to many of the young people I interviewed. His block, like most of the others I visited during this study, is a collection of row homes in various states of disrepair. Billy spends more time here than he would like. He is unemployed and when asked how best the intervention project he enrolled in could help him his request was simple: I need a job. As we talk, I think that Billy is polite—he offers me a drink (a beer, which I decline) before we begin our interview—and even quiet. He recalls two violent battles within the last year, both of which ended with him in the emergency room, without wavering too far from a measured, even

tone. The first incident he recalls for me happened in South Philadelphia. He was walking down the block, when he came across a group of guys on the corner, guys who he had 'trouble' with in the past. As he stood talking to an acquaintance, Billy was approached from behind and punched in the back of the head. The force of the punch was multiplied exponentially by brass knuckles, 'splitting [his] head open.' Billy was knocked out instantly, fell face-first toward the ground and split his nose on a concrete step. The thin scar from this street-fight remains several months later.

In contrast to Billy's even tone, DeLisha is loud. She is thin with a medium-brown complexion. Her retelling of the story of her injury is more like a re-enactment as the adrenaline, anxiety and excitement of the day return. She comes across as fiercely independent, especially for a 17-year-old girl. DeLisha, a young mother with a 1-year-old daughter, has been unable to rely on her own drug-addicted mother for much of her life. After years of this independence, she is convinced that she does not need anyone's help to 'make it' in life. While she has been a 'fighter' for as long as she can remember, she was never hurt before. Not in school. Not in her neighbourhood, which is one of the most notorious in the city. And not like this. She had agreed to a fight with another neighbourhood girl. The younger girl, pressured by her family and peers to win the battle, shielded a box-cutter from DeLisha's sight until the very last minute. When it seemed that she would lose, the girl flashed the box-cutter and slashed DeLisha across the hand, tearing past skin and muscle into a tendon on her arm.

During my interviews with Billy and DeLisha, I asked each of them how these very public losses, which also resulted in serious physical injuries, would influence their mobility within the neighbourhood. Would they avoid certain people and places? Would or could they shrug their loss off or would they seek vengeance for their lost battle? Billy's and DeLisha's responses were strikingly similar in tone, nearly identical at some points, and equally revealing of two of the most basic elements of the code of the street: the commitment to maintaining a 'tough front' and 'payback.'

> Billy: I mean, just like I say, I walk around this neighbourhood. I'm not looking over my shoulder. . . . I'm not going to walk [and] look around my shoulder because I've got people looking for me. I mean you want me . . . you know where I live. They can call me at any time they want. That's how, that's how I think. . . . I'm not going to sit around my own neighbourhood and just say: 'Aww, I got to watch my back.' You want me? You got me.

> DeLisha: I'm not a scared type . . . I walk on the streets anytime I want to. I do anything I want to, anytime I want to do it. It's never been a problem walking on the street 3.00 in the morning. If I want to go home 3.00 in the morning, I'm going to go home. I'm not looking over my shoulder. My grandma never raised me to look over my shoulder. I'm not going to stop because of some little incident [being cut in the hand with a box cutter].

Billy and DeLisha's strikingly similar responses reveal their commitment to a shared 'system of accountability,' the code of the street, which, as Anderson argues, governs much of social life, especially violence, in distressed urban areas (Anderson, 1999). Billy and DeLisha hold themselves accountable to this system ('I'm not going to . . .') and are also aware that others will hold them accountable for their behaviours and actions. Billy and DeLisha are acutely aware that someone who 'looks over their shoulder' while walking down the street is perceived as weak, a moving target, and both are determined to reject such a fate. Instead, Billy and DeLisha remain committed to managing their 'presentation of self' (Goffman, 1959) in a way that masks any signs of vulnerability.

In addition to their commitment to 'not looking over their shoulder,' Billy and DeLisha are also sensitive to the fact that the fights they were in were not 'fair.' These street-level injustices inform Billy and DeLisha's expectations for retaliation. Consistent with the code, both Billy and DeLisha—equally armed with long fight histories—realise the importance of 'payback' and consider future battles with their challengers to be inevitable. When I asked DeLisha if she anticipated another fight with the young woman who cut her, she replied with a strong yes, 'because I'm taking it there with her.' Billy was also equally committed to retaliation, telling me: ' . . . one by one, I will get them.'

Danielle and Robert: 'Sometimes You Got to Fight'

In *Code of the Street* (1999), Anderson demonstrates how important it is for young people to prove publicly that they are not someone to be 'messed with.' One of the ways that young people prove this to others is by engaging in fights in public, when necessary. The following statements from Danielle and Robert, two young people who are adept at avoiding conflicts, illustrate teenaged girls' and boys' shared understanding of the importance of demonstrating that one is willing to fight as a way to deter ongoing challenges to one's well-being:

> Danielle: 'cause sometimes you got to fight, not fight, but get into that type of battle to let them know that I'm not scared of you and you can't keep harassing me thinking that it's okay.

> Robert: . . . you know, if someone keep picking on you like that, you gonna have to do something to prove a point to them: that you not going to be scared of them . . . So, sometimes you do got to, you do got to fight. Cause you just got to tell them that you not scared of them.

Like DeLisha and Billy, Danielle, a recent high-school graduate, and Robert, who is in the 11th grade, offer nearly identical explanations of the importance of physically protecting one's own boundaries by demonstrating to others that you will fight, if necessary. While neither Danielle nor Robert identify as 'fighters,' both are convinced that sometimes you 'got to fight.' Again, this shared language reveals an awareness and commitment to a shared system of accountability, 'the code of the street,' which encourages young people—teenaged girls and boys—to present a 'tough front' as a way to discourage on-going challenges to one's personal security. For the young people in this study, the value placed on maintaining a tough front or 'proving a point' cut across perceived gender lines.

In addition to possibly deterring future challenges, Anderson argues that presenting and ultimately proving oneself as someone who is not to be 'messed with' helps to build a young person's confidence and self-esteem: 'particularly for young men and perhaps increasingly among females . . . their identity, their self-respect, and their honor are often intricately tied up with the way they perform on the streets during and after such [violent] encounters' (Anderson, 1999, p. 76). Those young people who are able to perform well during these public encounters acquire a sense of confidence that will facilitate their movement throughout the neighbourhood. This boost to one's sense of self is not restricted to young men; young women who can fight and win may also demonstrate a strong sense of pride and confidence in their ability to 'handle' potentially aggressive or violent conflicts, as illustrated by the following interview with Nicole.

Nicole: 'I Feel Like I Can Defend Myself'

My conversation with Nicole typifies the confidence expressed by teenaged girls who can fight and win. Nicole is a smart, articulate young woman who attended some community college courses while still a senior in high school. She planned to attend a state university to study engineering after graduation. While in high school, she tells me, she felt confident in her ability to walk the hallways of her sometimes chaotic public school: 'I feel like I can defend myself.' Unlike some young women who walk the hallways constantly testing others, Nicole's was a quiet confidence: 'I don't, like, I mean, when I'm walking around school or something, I don't walk around talking about "yeah, I beat this girl up."' Nicole could, in fact, claim that she didn't beat up just one girl but several, at the same time. Nicole explained to me how her most recent fight began:

> We [she and another young woman] had got into two arguments in the hallway and then her friends were holding her back. So I just said, 'Forget it. I'm just going to my class.' So I'm in class, I'm inside the classroom and I hear Nina say, 'Is this that bitch's class?' I came to the door and was like, 'Yes, this is my class.' And she puts her hands up [in fighting position] and she swings . . . And me and her was fighting, and then I got her on the wall, and then I felt somebody pulling my hair, and it turns out to be Jessica. Right? And then we fighting, and then I see Tasha, and it's me and all these three people and then they broke it all up.

Nicole's only injury in the fight came from the elbow of the school police officer who eventually ended the battle. As Nicole recalls this fight, and her performance in particular, I notice that she is smiling. This smile, together with the tone in which she tells the story of her earlier battle, makes it clear that she is proud of her ability to meet the challenge presented to her by these young women. Impressed at her ability to fight off three teenaged girls at the same time, I ask Nicole: 'How did you manage not to get jumped?' She quickly corrects my definition of the situation: 'No. I managed to beat them up.' After retelling her fight story, Nicole shakes her head from side to side and says: 'I had to end up beating them up. So sad.' I notice her sure smile return. 'You don't really look like you feel bad about that,' I say. 'I don't,' she replies.

The level of self-confidence that Nicole displays in this brief exchange contrasts with the passivity and submissiveness that is commonly expected of women and girls, especially white, middle-class women and girls (Collins,

2004). It is young men, not teenaged girls, who are expected to exude such confidence as they construct a 'tough front' to deter would-be challengers (Anderson, 1999). Nicole's confidence is also more than an expressive performance. Nicole knows that she is physically able to fight and win, when necessary, because she has done so in the past. For teenaged girls like Nicole and Sharmaine, whom I discuss below, this confidence is essential to their evaluation of how best to handle potential interpersonal conflicts in their everyday lives.

Sharmaine: '... I Have One Hand Left'

Sharmaine, an 8th grader, displayed a level of self-confidence similar to Nicole's after a fight with a boy in her classroom. Moments before the fight, the boy approached Sharmaine while she was looking out her classroom window, and 'whispered something' in her ear. Sharmaine knew that this boy liked her, but she thought she had made it quite clear that she did not like him. Sharmaine quickly told him to back off and then looked to her teacher for reinforcement. Her teacher, Sharmaine recalls, just laughed at the boy's advances. After he whispered in Sharmaine's ear a second time, she turned around and punched him in the face. Sharmaine later ended up in the emergency room with a jammed finger from the punch. I asked Sharmaine if she was concerned about him getting back at her when she returned to school. She tells me that someone in the emergency room asked her the same question. 'What did you say?' I ask. 'I told them no . . . because I have one hand left.'

For young women like Nicole and Sharmaine, the proven ability to defend themselves translates into a level of self-confidence that is not typically expected in girls and young women. Those girls who are confident in their ability to 'take care of themselves' become more mobile as they come to believe, as DeLisha says, that they can 'do anything [they] want to, anytime [they] want to do it.' Girls who are able to gain and maintain this level of self-confidence are able to challenge the real and imagined gendered boundaries on space and place in the inner city.

'Boys Got to Go Get Guns'

The need to be 'distinguished as a man'—a benchmark of hegemonic masculinity—often fosters adolescent boys' preoccupation with distinguishing themselves *from* women (Anderson, 1999; Collins, 2004, p. 210; Connell & Messerschmidt, 2005). This is a gendered preoccupation that was not revealed in urban adolescent girls' accounts of physical aggression and violence. The following statement from Craig, a young man who has deliberately checked his readiness to fight after being shot in the hip, illustrates how the need to 'be a man' influences young men's consideration of violence:

> Yeah, I don't fight no more. I can't fight [because of injury]. So, I really stop and think about stuff because it isn't even worth it . . . unless, I mean, you really want it [a fight] to happen . . . I'm going to turn the other cheek. But, I'm not going to be, like, wearing a skirt. That's the way you got to look at it.

While Craig is prepared to exit his life as a 'fighter,' he predicts that his newfound commitment to avoid fights will not stand up to the pressure of proving his manhood to a challenger. Craig is well aware of how another young man can communicate that he 'really want [a fight] to happen.' Once a challenger publicly escalates a battle in this way, young men like Craig have few choices. At this moment, a young man will have to demonstrate to his challenger, and his audience, that he isn't 'wearing a skirt.' Not only must he fight, he must also fight *like a man.*

Craig's admission is revealing of how a young man's concern with not being 'like' a woman influences his consideration of the appropriate use of physical aggression. While a similar type of preoccupation with intergender distinctions was not typically revealed in young women's accounts, I found that teenaged girls were generally aware of at least one significant difference in how young women and men were expected to work the code of the street. As is revealed in my conversation with Shante, a teenaged girl who was hit in the head with a brick by a neighbourhood girl, young men are generally expected to use more serious or lethal forms of violence than girls or women. I asked Shante what people in her neighbourhood thought about girls fighting.

> 'Today,' she asked, 'you mean like people on the street?'
>
> 'Yeah.'
>
> 'If [a girl] get beat up, you just get beat up. That's on you.'
>
> 'Do you think it's different for boys?' I asked.
>
> 'Umm, boys got to go get guns. They got to blow somebody's head off. They got to shoot. They don't fight these days. They use guns.'

Shante's perception of what boys 'got to' do is informed by years of observation and experience. Shante has grown up in a neighbourhood marked by violence. Days before this interview, she saw a young man get shot in the head. She tells me he was dead by the time he hit the sidewalk. When I asked Shante whether or not girls used guns, she could recall just one young woman from the neighbourhood—the same young woman who hit Shante over the head with a brick—who had 'pistol whipped' another teenaged girl. While she certainly used the gun as a weapon, she didn't shoot her. These two incidents are actually quite typical of reported gender differences in the use of weapons in violent acts: boys and men are much more likely than girls and women to use guns to shoot and kill. Women and girls, like many of the young women I spoke with during this study, are far more likely to rely on knives and box-cutters, if they use a weapon at all (see also Miller, 1998 & 2001; Pastor, et al., 1996, p. 28). Those young women who did use a weapon, such as a knife

or box-cutter, explained that they did so for protection. For example, Shante told me that she carried a razor blade, 'because she doesn't trust people.'

Takeya: 'A Good Girl'

In contrast to the commitment to protecting one's manhood, which Craig alludes to and Elijah Anderson describes in great detail (Anderson, 1999), the young women I spoke to did not suggest that they fought because that's what *women* do. Furthermore, while young women deeply appreciated the utility of a 'tough front,' they were unlikely to use phrases like 'I don't want to be wearing a skirt.' In fact, while young men like Craig work to prove their manhood by distinguishing themselves from women, many of the young women I spoke with—including the 'toughest' among them—embraced popular notions of femininity, 'skirts' and all. For many of the girls I interviewed, an appreciation of some aspects of hegemonic femininity modulated their involvement in violent interactions.

My conversation with Takeya sheds light on how inner-city girls attempt to reconcile the contradictory concerns that emerge from intersecting survival and gender projects. When I asked Takeya, a slim 13-year-old girl with a light brown complexion, about her fighting history, she replied, 'I'm not in no fights. I'm a good girl.' 'You are a good girl?' I asked. 'Yeah, I'm a good girl and I'm-a be a pretty girl at 18.'

Takeya's concern with being a 'pretty girl' reflects an appreciation of aspects of hegemonic femininity that place great value on beauty. Her understanding of what it means to be beautiful is also influenced by the locally placed value on skin colour, hair texture and body figure. While brown skin and textured hair may not fit hegemonic (White, middle-class) conceptions of beauty, in this setting, a light-brown skinned complexion, 'straight' or 'good' hair, and a slim figure help to make one 'pretty' and 'good' (Banks, 2000). Yet, Takeya also knows that one's ability to stay pretty—to be a pretty girl at age 18—is directly influenced by one's involvement in interpersonal aggression or violence.

In order to be considered a 'pretty girl' by her peers, Takeya knows that she must avoid those types of interpersonal conflicts that tend to result in cuts and scratches to young women's faces, especially the ones that others consider beautiful (in *Code of the Street* [1999] Anderson writes that such visible scars often result in heightened status for the young women who leave their mark on pretty girls). Yet, Takeya is also aware that the culture of the code requires her to become an able fighter and to maintain a reputation as such. After expressing her commitment to being a 'good' girl, Takeya is sure to inform me that not only does she know how to fight, others also recognise her as an able fighter: 'I don't want you to think I don't know how to fight. I mean everybody always come get me [for fights]. [I'm] the number one [person they come to get].'

Takeya's simultaneous embrace of the culture of code and some aspects of normative femininity, Craig's concern with distinguishing himself from women, and Shante's convincing disclosure regarding what boys 'got to' do highlight how masculinity and femininity projects overlap and intersect with the project of survival for young people in distressed inner-city neighbourhoods. Both Craig and Takeya appreciate fundamental elements of 'the code,' especially the importance of being known as an able fighter. Yet, Craig's use of physical aggression is likely to be encouraged by his commitment to a distinctive aspect of hegemonic masculinity: being distinguished from a girl. Meanwhile, Takeya's use of physical aggression and violence is tempered—though not extinguished—by seemingly typical 'female' concerns: being a 'good' and 'pretty' girl. In contrast to the project of accomplishing masculinity, which overlaps and, at times, contradicts the project of survival for young men, the project of accomplishing femininity can, at times, facilitate young women's struggle to survive in this setting.

Gender, Survival, and 'the Code'

I have argued that gender does not protect young women from much of the violence young men experience in distressed inner-city neighbourhoods, and that given these shared circumstances, it becomes equally important for women and men to work 'the code of the street.' Like many adolescent boys, young women also recognise that reputation, respect and retaliation—the '3 Rs' of the code of the street—organise their social world (Anderson, 1999). Yet, as true as it is that, at times, young men and women work the code of the street in similar ways, it is also true that differences exist. These differences are rooted in the relationships between masculinity, femininity and the use of violence or aggression in distressed urban areas and emerge from overlapping and intersecting survival and gender projects.

In order to 'survive' in today's inner city, young women like DeLisha, Danielle, Shante and Takeya are encouraged to embrace some aspects of the 'code of the street' that organises much of inner-city life (Anderson, 1999). In doing so, these girls also embrace and accomplish some aspects of hegemonic masculinity that are embedded in the code. My analysis of interviews with teenaged girls and boys injured in intentional violent incidents reveals an appreciation of the importance of maintaining a tough front and demonstrating nerve across perceived gender lines. It is this appreciation of the cultural elements of the code that leads teenaged girls like Danielle to believe strongly that 'sometimes you got to fight.'

REFERENCES

Anderson, E. (1999). *Code of the street: Decency, violence and the moral life of the inner city.* New York: W.W. Norton.

Banks, I. (2000). *Hair matters: Beauty, power, and Black women's consciousness.* New York: New York University Press.

Collins, P. Hill. (2004). *Black sexual politics: African Americans, gender, and the new racism.* New York: Routledge.

Connell, R.W., & Messerschmidt, J.W. (2005). Hegemonic masculinity: Rethinking the concept. *Gender & Society,* 19(6), 829–859.

Goffman, E. (1959). *The presentation of self in everyday life.* New York: Anchor Books.

Miller, J. (1998). Up It up: Gender and the accomplishment of street robbery. *Criminology,* 36(1), 37–66.

Miller, J. (2001). *One of the guys: Girls, gangs, and gender.* Oxford: Oxford University Press.

Pastor, J., McCormick, J., & Fine, M. (1996). Makin' homes: An urban girl thing. In B.J. Ross Leadbeater & N. Way (Eds.), *Urban girls: Resisting stereotypes, creating identities.* New York: New York University Press.

Simpson, S.S. (1991). Caste, class, and violent crime: Explaining difference in female offending. *Criminology,* 29(1), 115–135.

THINKING ABOUT THE READING

This reading demonstrates that inner-city girls are also not as isolated from violence as is commonly thought. What are some of the reasons for their involvement with violence? What is the "code of the street"? How are violence and the "code" related to the ways in which these girls see themselves? How are they related to their survival? Does the way in which girls use and understand violence differ from the ways in which boys see it?

Supporting Identity

The Presentation of Self

6

Social behavior is highly influenced by the images we form of others. We typically form impressions of people based on an initial assessment of their social group membership (ethnicity, age, gender, etc.), their personal attributes (e.g., physical attractiveness), and the verbal and nonverbal messages they provide. These assessments are usually accompanied by a set of expectations we've learned to associate with members of certain social groups or people with certain attributes. Such judgments allow us to place people in broad categories and provide a degree of predictability in interactions.

While we are forming impressions of others, we are fully aware that they are doing the same thing with us. Early in life, most of us learn that it is to our advantage to have people think highly of us. In "The Presentation of Self in Everyday Life," Erving Goffman describes a process called *impression management* in which we attempt to control and manipulate information about ourselves to influence the impressions others form of us. Impression management provides the link between the way we perceive ourselves and the way we want others to perceive us. We've all been in situations—a first date, a job interview, meeting a girlfriend's or boyfriend's family for the first time—in which we've felt compelled to "make a good impression." What we often fail to realize, however, is that personal impression management may be influenced by larger organizational and institutional forces.

Impression management extends to control and presentation of the body. In "Maternity and Its Discontents," Upton and Han present research based on interviews with women who experience a loss of their sense of self when they become pregnant and "lose" their bodies. Not only do they gain significant weight in a culture that scrutinizes and punishes female weight gain, but they become "public" bodies, bodies that represent something that others feel entitled to touch and comment on. After pregnancy, women face another dilemma in trying to regain the expected physical form of presentation and feel pressure to "get the body back."

The third reading is likely to raise considerable discussion. Why do college-age men go on "girl hunts"? Sociologist David Grazian uses Goffman's framework to explain this behavior. He suggests that the urban nightlife girl hunt scene is actually a ritual of male bonding and masculine identity building. Getting a girl is not really the goal. Hanging out and bonding with other men and reinforcing patterns of masculinity is the point of these ritual-like practices. If this is the case, then what are the implications for the perpetuation of cultural practices that build masculinity by objectifying women?

Something to Consider as You Read

As you read these selections on the presentation of self and identity, consider where people get their ideas about whom and what they can be in various settings. Consider a setting in which everyone present may be trying to create a certain impression because that's what they all think everyone else wants. What would have to happen in order for the "impression script" to change in this setting? In what ways do material resources and authority influence the impression we're able to make? Are there certain types of people who needn't be concerned about the impressions they give off? Compare and contrast the readings on pregnancy and the "girl hunt." Are there similar cultural scripts operating in both these scenarios?

The Presentation of Self in Everyday Life
Selections

Erving Goffman

(1959)

Introduction

When an individual enters the presence of others, they commonly seek to acquire information about him or to bring into play information about him already possessed. They will be interested in his general socio-economic status, his conception of self, his attitude toward them, his competence, his trustworthiness, etc. Although some of this information seems to be sought almost as an end in itself, there are usually quite practical reasons for acquiring it. Information about the individual helps to define the situation, enabling others to know in advance what he will expect of them and what they may expect of him. Informed in these ways, the others will know how best to act in order to call forth a desired response from him.

For those present, many sources of information become accessible and many carriers (or "sign-vehicles") become available for conveying this information. If unacquainted with the individual, observers can glean clues from his conduct and appearance which allow them to apply their previous experience with individuals roughly similar to the one before them or, more important, to apply untested stereotypes to him. They can also assume from past experience that only individuals of a particular kind are likely to be found in a given social setting. They can rely on what the individual says about himself or on documentary evidence he provides as to who and what he is. If they know, or know of, the individual by virtue of experience prior to the interaction, they can rely on assumptions as to the persistence and generality of psychological traits as a means of predicting his present and future behavior. . . .

The expressiveness of the individual (and therefore his capacity to give impressions) appears to involve two radically different kinds of sign activity: the expression that he *gives,* and the expression that he *gives off.* The first involves verbal symbols or their substitutes which he uses admittedly and solely to convey the information that he and the others are known to attach to these symbols. This is communication in the traditional and narrow sense. The second involves a wide range of action that others can treat as symptomatic of the actor, the expectation being that the action was performed for reasons other than the information conveyed in this way. As we shall have to see, this distinction has an only initial validity. The individual does of course intentionally convey misinformation by means of both of these types of communication, the first involving deceit, the second feigning.

Taking communication in both its narrow and broad sense, one finds that when the individual is in the immediate presence of others, his activity will have a promissory character. The others are likely to find that they must accept the individual on faith, offering him a just return while he is present before them in exchange for something whose true value will not be established until after he has left their presence. (Of course, the others also live by inference in their dealings with the physical world, but it is only in the world of social interaction that the objects about which they make inferences will purposely facilitate and hinder this inferential process.) The security that they justifiably feel in making inferences about the individual will vary, of course, depending on such factors as the amount of information they already possess about him, but no amount of such past evidence can entirely obviate the necessity of acting on the basis of inferences. As William I. Thomas suggested:

> It is also highly important for us to realize that we do not as a matter of fact lead our lives, make our decisions, and reach our goals in everyday life either statistically or scientifically. We live by inference. I am, let us say, your guest. You do not know, you cannot determine scientifically, that I will not steal your money or your spoons. But inferentially I will not and inferentially you have me as a guest.[1]

Let us now turn from the others to the point of view of the individual who presents himself before them. He may wish them to think highly of him, or to think that he thinks highly of them, or to perceive how in fact he feels toward them, or to obtain no clear-cut impression; he may wish to ensure sufficient harmony so that the interaction can be sustained, or to defraud, get rid of, confuse, mislead, antagonize, or insult them. Regardless of the particular objective which the individual has in mind and of his motive for having this objective, it will be in his interests to control the conduct of the others, especially their responsive treatment of him.[2] This control is achieved largely by influencing the definition of the situation which the others come to formulate, and he can influence this definition by expressing himself in such a way as to give them the kind of impression that will lead them to act voluntarily in accordance with his own plan. Thus, when an individual appears in the presence of others, there will usually be some reason for him to mobilize his activity so that it will convey an impression to others which it is in his interests to convey. . . .

I have said that when an individual appears before others his actions will influence the definition of the situation which they come

to have. Sometimes the individual will act in a thoroughly calculating manner, expressing himself in a given way solely in order to give the kind of impression to others that is likely to evoke from them a specific response he is concerned to obtain. Sometimes the individual will be calculating in his activity but be relatively unaware that this is the case. Sometimes he will intentionally and consciously express himself in a particular way, but chiefly because the tradition of his group or social status require this kind of expression and not because of any particular response (other than vague acceptance or approval) that is likely to be evoked from those impressed by the expression. Sometimes the traditions of an individual's role will lead him to give a well-designed impression of a particular kind and yet he may be neither consciously nor unconsciously disposed to create such an impression. The others, in their turn, may be suitably impressed by the individual's efforts to convey something, or may misunderstand the situation and come to conclusions that are warranted neither by the individual's intent nor by the facts. In any case, in so far as the others act *as if* the individual had conveyed a particular impression, we may take a functional or pragmatic view and say that the individual has "effectively" projected a given definition of the situation and "effectively" fostered the understanding that a given state of affairs obtains. . . .

When we allow that the individual projects a definition of the situation when he appears before others, we must also see that the others, however passive their role may seem to be, will themselves effectively project a definition of the situation by virtue of their response to the individual and by virtue of any lines of action they initiate to him. Ordinarily the definitions of the situation projected by the several different participants are sufficiently attuned to one another so that open contradiction will not occur. I do not mean that there will be the kind of consensus that arises when each individual present candidly expresses what he really feels and honestly agrees with the expressed feelings of the others present. This kind of harmony is an optimistic ideal and in any case not necessary for the smooth working of society. Rather, each participant is expected to suppress his immediate heartfelt feelings, conveying a view of the situation which he feels the others will be able to find at least temporarily acceptable. The maintenance of this surface of agreement, this veneer of consensus, is facilitated by each participant concealing his own wants behind statements which assert values to which everyone present feels obliged to give lip service. Further, there is usually a kind of division of definitional labor. Each participant is allowed to establish the tentative official ruling regarding matters which are vital to him but not immediately important to others, e.g., the rationalizations and justifications by which he accounts for his past activity. In exchange for this courtesy he remains silent or noncommittal on matters important to others but not immediately important to him. We have then a kind of interactional *modus vivendi*. Together the participants contribute to a single overall definition of the situation which involves not so much a real agreement as to what exists but rather a real agreement as to whose claims concerning what issues will be temporarily honored. Real agreement will also exist concerning the desirability of avoiding an open conflict of definitions of the situation.[3] I will refer to this level of agreement as a "working consensus." It is to be understood that the working consensus established in one interaction setting will be quite different in content from the working consensus established in a different type of setting. Thus, between two friends at lunch, a reciprocal show of affection, respect, and concern for the other is maintained. In service occupations, on the other hand, the specialist often maintains an image of disinterested involvement in the problem of the client, while the client responds with a show of respect for the competence and integrity of the specialist. Regardless of such differences in content, however, the general form of these working arrangements is the same. . . .

. . . Given the fact that the individual effectively projects a definition of the situation when he enters the presence of others, we can assume that events may occur within the interaction which contradict, discredit, or otherwise throw doubt upon this projection. When these disruptive events occur, the interaction itself may come to a confused and embarrassed halt. Some of the assumptions upon which the responses of the participants had been predicated become untenable, and the participants find themselves lodged in an interaction for which the situation has been wrongly defined and is now no longer defined. At such moments the individual whose presentation has been discredited may feel ashamed while the others present may feel hostile, and all the participants may come to feel ill at ease, nonplussed, out of countenance, embarrassed, experiencing the kind of anomy that is generated when the minute social system of face-to-face interaction breaks down. . . .

We find that preventive practices are constantly employed to avoid these embarrassments and that corrective practices are constantly employed to compensate for discrediting occurrences that have not been successfully avoided. When the individual employs these strategies and tactics to protect his own projections, we may refer to them as "defensive practices"; when a participant employs them to save the definition of the situation projected by another, we speak of "protective practices" or "tact." Together, defensive and protective practices comprise the techniques employed to safe-guard the impression fostered by an individual during his presence before others. It should be added that while we may be ready to see that no fostered impression would survive if defensive practices were not employed, we are less ready perhaps to see that few impressions could survive if those who received the impression did not exert tact in their reception of it.

In addition to the fact that precautions are taken to prevent disruption of projected definitions, we may also note that an intense interest in these disruptions comes to play a significant role in the social life of the group. Practical jokes and social games are played in which embarrassments which are to be taken unseriously are purposely engineered.[4] Fantasies are created in which devastating exposures occur. Anecdotes from the past—real, embroidered, or fictitious—are told and retold, detailing disruptions which occurred, almost occurred, or occurred and were admirably resolved. There seems to be no grouping which does not have a ready supply of these games, reveries, and cautionary tales, to be used as a source of humor, a catharsis for anxieties, and a sanction for inducing individuals to be modest in their claims and reasonable in their projected expectations. The individual may tell himself through dreams of getting into impossible positions. Families tell of the time a guest got his dates mixed and arrived when neither the house nor anyone in it was ready for him. Journalists tell of times when an all-too-meaningful misprint occurred, and the paper's assumption of objectivity or decorum was humorously discredited. Public servants tell of times a client ridiculously misunderstood form instructions, giving answers which implied an unanticipated and bizarre definition of the situation.[5] Seamen, whose home away from home is rigorously he-man, tell stories of coming back home and inadvertently asking mother to "pass the fucking butter."[6] Diplomats tell of the time a near-sighted queen asked a republican ambassador about the health of his king.[7]

To summarize, then, I assume that when an individual appears before others he will have many motives for trying to control the impression they receive of the situation. This report is concerned with some of the common techniques that persons employ to sustain such impressions and with some of the common contingencies associated with the employment of these techniques. It will be convenient to end this introduction with some definitions. . . . For the purpose of this report, interaction (that is, face-to-face interaction) may be roughly defined as the reciprocal influence of individuals upon one another's actions when in one another's immediate physical presence. An interaction may be defined as all the interaction which occurs throughout any one occasion when a given set of individuals are in one another's continuous presence; the term "an encounter" would do as well. A "performance" may be defined as all the activity of a given participant on a given occasion which serves to influence in any way any of the other participants. Taking a particular participant and his performance as a basic point of reference, we may refer to those who contribute the other performances as the audience, observers, or co-participants. The pre-established pattern of action which is unfolded during a performance and which may be presented or played through on other occasions may be called a "part" or "routine."[8] These situational terms can easily be related to conventional structural ones. When an individual or performer plays the same part to the same audience on different occasions, a social relationship is likely to arise. Defining social role as the enactment of rights and duties attached to a given status, we can say that a social role will involve one or more parts and that each of these different parts may be presented by the performer on a series of occasions to the same kinds of audience or to an audience of the same persons. . . .

Performances

Front

I [use] the term "performance" to refer to all the activity of an individual which occurs during a period marked by his continuous presence before a particular set of observers and which has some influence on the observers. It will be convenient to label as "front" that part of the individual's performance which regularly functions in a general and fixed fashion to define the situation for those who observe the performance. Front, then, is the expressive equipment of a standard kind intentionally or unwittingly employed by the individual during his performance. For preliminary purposes, it will be convenient to distinguish and label what seem to be the standard parts of front.

First, there is the "setting," involving furniture, décor, physical layout, and other background items which supply the scenery and stage props for the spate of human action played out before, within, or upon it. A setting tends to stay put, geographically speaking, so that those who would use a particular setting as part of their performance cannot begin their act until they have brought themselves to the appropriate place and must terminate their performance when they leave it. It is only in exceptional circumstances that the setting follows along with the performers; we see this in the funeral cortège, the civic parade, and the dreamlike processions that kings and queens are made of. In the main, these exceptions seem to offer some kind of extra protection for performers who are, or who have momentarily become, highly sacred. . . .

It is sometimes convenient to divide the stimuli which make up personal front into "appearance" and "manner," according to the function performed by the information that these stimuli convey. "Appearance" may be taken to refer to those stimuli which function at the time to tell us of the performer's social statuses. These stimuli also tell us of the individual's temporary ritual state, that is, whether he is engaging in formal social activity, work, or informal recreation, whether or not he is celebrating a new phase in the season cycle or in his life-cycle. "Manner" may be taken to refer to those stimuli which function at the time to warn us of the interaction role the performer will expect to play in the oncoming situation. Thus a haughty, aggressive manner may give the impression that the performer expects to be the one who will initiate the verbal interaction and direct its course. A meek, apologetic manner may give the impression that the performer expects to follow the lead of others, or at least that he can be led to do so. . . .

Dramatic Realization

While in the presence of others, the individual typically infuses his activity with signs which dramatically highlight and portray confirmatory facts that might otherwise remain unapparent or obscure. For if the individual's activity is to become significant to others, he must mobilize his activity so that it will express *during the interaction* what he wishes to convey. In fact, the performer may be required not only to express his claimed capacities during the interaction but also to do so during a split second in the interaction. Thus, if a baseball umpire is to give the impression that he is sure of his judgment, he must forgo the moment of thought which might make him sure of his judgment; he must give an instantaneous decision so that the audience will be sure that he is sure of his judgment.[9] . . .

Similarly, the proprietor of a service establishment may find it difficult to dramatize what is actually being done for clients because the clients cannot "see" the overhead costs of the service rendered them. Undertakers must therefore charge a great deal for their highly visible product—a coffin that has been transformed into a casket—because many of the other costs of conducting a funeral are ones that cannot be readily dramatized.[10] Merchants, too, find that they must charge high prices for things that look intrinsically inexpensive in order to compensate the establishment for expensive things like insurance, slack periods, etc., that never appear before the customers' eyes. . . .

Idealization

. . . I want to consider here another important aspect of this socialization process— the tendency for performers to offer their observers an impression that is idealized in several different ways.

The notion that a performance presents an idealized view of the situation is, of course, quite common. Cooley's view may be taken as an illustration:

If we never tried to seem a little better than we are, how could we improve or "train ourselves from the outside inward"? And the same impulse to show the world a better or idealized aspect of ourselves finds an organized expression in the various professions and classes, each of which has to some extent a cant or pose, which its members assume unconsciously, for the most part, but which has the effect of a conspiracy to work upon the credulity of the rest of the world. There is a cant not only of theology and of philanthropy, but also of law, medicine, teaching, even of science—perhaps especially of science, just now, since the more a particular kind of merit is recognized and admired, the more it is likely to be assumed by the unworthy.[11]

Thus, when the individual presents himself before others, his performance will tend to incorporate and exemplify the officially accredited values of the society, more so, in fact, than does his behavior as a whole.

To the degree that a performance highlights the common official values of the society in which it occurs, we may look upon it, in the manner of Durkheim and Radcliffe-Brown, as a ceremony—as an expressive rejuvenation and reaffirmation of the moral values of the community. Furthermore, insofar as the expressive bias of performances comes to be accepted as reality, then that which is accepted at the moment as reality will have some of the characteristics of a celebration. To stay in one's room away from the place where the party is given, or away from where the practitioner attends his client, is to stay away from where reality is being performed. The world, in truth, is a wedding.

One of the richest sources of data on the presentation of idealized performances is the literature on social mobility. In most societies there seems to be a major or general system of stratification, and in most stratified societies there is an idealization of the higher strata and some aspiration on the part of those in low places to move to higher ones. (One must be careful to appreciate that this involves not merely a desire for a prestigeful place but also a desire for a place close to the sacred center of the common values of the society.) Commonly we find that upward mobility involves the presentation of proper performances and that efforts to move upward and efforts to keep from moving downward are expressed in terms of sacrifices made for the maintenance of front. Once the proper sign-equipment has been obtained and familiarity gained in the management of it, then this equipment can be used to embellish and illumine one's daily performances with a favorable social style.

Perhaps the most important piece of sign-equipment associated with social class consists of the status symbols through which material wealth is expressed. American society is similar to others in this regard but seems to have been singled out as an extreme example of wealth-oriented class structure—perhaps because in America the license to employ symbols of wealth and financial capacity to do so are so widely distributed. . . .

Reality and Contrivance

. . . Some performances are carried off successfully with complete dishonesty, others with complete honesty; but for performances in general neither of these extremes is essential and neither, perhaps, is dramaturgically advisable.

The implication here is that an honest, sincere, serious performance is less firmly connected with the solid world than one might first assume. And this implication will be strengthened if we look again at the distance usually placed between quite honest performances and quite contrived ones. In this connection take, for example, the remarkable phenomenon of stage acting. It does take deep skill, long training, and psychological capacity to become a good stage actor. But this fact should not blind us to another one: that almost anyone can quickly learn a script well enough to give a charitable audience some sense of realness in what is being contrived before them. And it seems this is so because ordinary social intercourse is itself put together as a scene is put together, by the exchange of dramatically inflated actions, counteractions, and terminating replies. Scripts even in the hands of unpracticed players can come to life because life itself is a dramatically enacted thing. All the world is not, of course, a stage, but the crucial ways in which it isn't are not easy to specify. . . .

When the individual does move into a new position in society and obtains a new part to perform, he is not likely to be told in full detail how to conduct himself, nor will the facts of his new situation press sufficiently on him from the start to determine his conduct without his further giving thought to it. Ordinarily he will be given only a few cues, hints, and stage directions, and it will be assumed that he already has in his repertoire a large number of bits and pieces of performances that will be required in the new setting. The individual will already have a fair idea of what modesty, deference, or righteous indignation looks like, and can make a pass at playing these bits when necessary. He may even be able to play out the part of a hypnotic subject[12] or commit a "compulsive" crime[13] on the basis of models for these activities that he is already familiar with.

A theatrical performance or a staged confidence game requires a thorough scripting of the spoken content of the routine; but the vast part involving "expression given off" is often determined by meager stage directions. It is expected that the performer of illusions will already know a good deal about how to manage his voice, his face, and his body, although he—as well as any person who directs him—may find it difficult indeed to provide a detailed verbal statement of this kind of knowledge. And in this, of course, we approach the situation of the straightforward man in the street. Socialization may not so much involve a learning of the many specific details of a single concrete part—often there could not be enough time or energy for this. What does seem to be required of the individual is that he learn enough pieces of expression to be able to "fill in" and manage, more or less, any part that he is likely to be given. The legitimate performances of everyday life are not "acted" or "put on" in the sense that the performer knows in advance just what he is going to do, and does this solely because of the effect it is likely to

have. The expressions it is felt he is giving off will be especially "inaccessible" to him.[14] But as in the case of less legitimate performers, the incapacity of the ordinary individual to formulate in advance the movements of his eyes and body does not mean that he will not express himself through these devices in a way that is dramatized and preformed in his repertoire of actions. In short, we all act better than we know how.

When we watch a television wrestler gouge, foul, and snarl at his opponent we are quite ready to see that, in spite of the dust, he is, and knows he is, merely playing at being the "heavy," and that in another match he may be given the other role, that of clean-cut wrestler, and perform this with equal verve and proficiency. We seem less ready to see, however, that while such details as the number and character of the falls may be fixed beforehand, the details of the expressions and movements used do not come from a script but from command of an idiom, a command that is exercised from moment to moment with little calculation or forethought. . . .

Personality-Interaction-Society

In recent years there have been elaborate attempts to bring into one framework the concepts and findings derived from three different areas of inquiry: the individual personality, social interaction, and society. I would like to suggest here a simple addition to these interdisciplinary attempts.

When an individual appears before others, he knowingly and unwittingly projects a definition of the situation, of which a conception of himself is an important part. When an event occurs which is expressively incompatible with this fostered impression, significant consequences are simultaneously felt in three levels of social reality, each of which involves a different point of reference and a different order of fact.

First, the social interaction, treated here as a dialogue between two teams, may come to an embarrassed and confused halt; the situation may cease to be defined. Previous positions may become no longer tenable, and participants may find themselves without a charted course of action. The participants typically sense a false note in the situation and come to feel awkward, flustered, and, literally, out of countenance. In other words, the minute social system created and sustained by orderly social interaction becomes disorganized. These are the consequences that the disruption has from the point of view of social interaction.

Secondly, in addition to these disorganizing consequences for action at the moment, performance disruptions may have consequences of a more far-reaching kind. Audiences tend to accept the self projected by the individual performer during any current performance as a responsible representative of his colleague-grouping, of his team, and of his social establishment. Audiences also accept the individual's particular performance as evidence of his capacity to perform the routine and even as evidence of his capacity to perform any routine. In a sense these larger social units—teams, establishments, etc.—become committed every time the individual performs his routine; with each performance the legitimacy of these units will tend to be tested anew and their permanent reputation put at stake. This kind of commitment is especially strong during some performances. Thus, when a surgeon and his nurse both turn from the operating table and the anesthetized patient accidentally rolls off the table to his death, not only is the operation disrupted in an embarrassing way, but the reputation of the doctor, as a doctor and as a man, and also the reputation of the hospital may be weakened. These are the consequences that disruptions may have from the point of view of social structure.

Finally, we often find that the individual may deeply involve his ego in his identification with a particular part, establishment, and group, and in his self-conception as someone who does not disrupt social interaction or let down the social units which depend upon that interaction. When a disruption occurs, then, we may find that the self-conceptions around which his personality has been built may become discredited. These are consequences that disruptions may have from the point of view of individual personality.

Performance disruptions, then, have consequences at three levels of abstraction: personality, interaction, and social structure. While the likelihood of disruption will vary widely from interaction to interaction, and while the social importance of likely disruptions will vary from interaction to interaction, still it seems that there is no interaction in which the participants do not take an appreciable chance of being slightly embarrassed or a slight chance of being deeply humiliated. Life may not be much of a gamble, but interaction is. Further, insofar as individuals make efforts to avoid disruptions or to correct for ones not avoided, these efforts, too, will have simultaneous consequences at the three levels. Here, then, we have one simple way of articulating three levels of abstraction and three perspectives from which social life has been studied.

Staging and the Self

The general notion that we make a presentation of ourselves to others is hardly novel; what ought to be stressed in conclusion is that the very structure of the self can be seen in terms of how we arrange for such performances in our Anglo-American society. . . .

The self, then, as a performed character, is not an organic thing that has a specific location, whose fundamental fate is to be born, to mature, and to die; it is a dramatic effect arising diffusely from a scene that is presented, and the characteristic issue, the crucial concern, is whether it will be credited or discredited.

In analyzing the self then we are drawn from its possessor, from the person who will profit or lose most by it, for he and his body merely provide the peg on which something of collaborative manufacture will be hung for a time. And the means for producing and maintaining selves do not reside inside the peg; in fact these means are often bolted down in social establishments. There will be a back region with its tools for shaping the body, and a front region with its fixed props. There will be a team of persons whose activity on stage in conjunction with available props will constitute the scene from which the performed character's self will emerge, and another team, the audience, whose interpretive activity will be necessary for this emergence. The self is a product of all of these arrangements, and in all of its parts bears the marks of this genesis.

The whole machinery of self-production is cumbersome, of course, and sometimes breaks down, exposing its separate components: back region control; team collusion; audience tact; and so forth. But, well oiled, impressions will flow from it fast enough to put us in the grips of one of our types of reality—the performance will come off and the firm self accorded each performed character will appear to emanate intrinsically from its performer.

Let us turn now from the individual as character performed to the individual as performer. He has a capacity to learn, this being exercised in the task of training for a part. He is given to having fantasies and dreams, some that pleasurably unfold a triumphant performance, others full of anxiety and dread that nervously deal with vital discreditings in a public front region. He often manifests a gregarious desire for teammates and audiences, a tactful considerateness for their concerns; and he has a capacity for deeply felt shame, leading him to minimize the chances he takes of exposure.

These attributes of the individual *qua* performer are not merely a depicted effect of particular performances; they are psychobiological in nature, and yet they seem to arise out of intimate interaction with the contingencies of staging performances.

And now a final comment. In developing the conceptual framework employed in this report, some language of the stage was used. I spoke of performers and audiences; of routines and parts; of performances coming off or falling flat; of cues, stage settings, and backstage; of dramaturgical needs, dramaturgical skills, and dramaturgical strategies. Now it should be admitted that this attempt to press a

mere analogy so far was in part a rhetoric and a maneuver. . . .

And so here the language and mask of the stage will be dropped. Scaffolds, after all, are to build other things with, and should be erected with an eye to taking them down.

This report is not concerned with aspects of theater that creep into everyday life. It is concerned with the structure of social encounters—the structure of those entities in social life that come into being whenever persons enter one another's immediate physical presence. The key factor in this structure is the maintenance of a single definition of the situation, this definition having to be expressed, and this expression sustained in the face of a multitude of potential disruptions.

A character staged in a theater is not in some ways real, nor does it have the same kind of real consequences as does the thoroughly contrived character performed by a confidence man; but the *successful* staging of either of these types of false figures involves use of *real* techniques—the same techniques by which everyday persons sustain their real social situations. Those who conduct face to face interaction on a theater's stage must meet the key requirement of real situations; they must expressively sustain a definition of the situation: but this they do in circumstances that have facilitated their developing an apt terminology for the interactional tasks that all of us share.

NOTES

1. Quoted in E. H. Volkart, editor, *Social Behavior and Personality,* Contributions of W. I. Thomas to Theory and Social Research (New York: Social Science Research Council, 1951), p. 9.

2. Here I owe much to an unpublished paper by Tom Burns of the University of Edinburgh. He presents the argument that in all interaction a basic underlying theme is the desire of each participant to guide and control the responses made by the others present. A similar argument has been advanced by Jay Haley in a recent unpublished paper, but in regard to a special kind of control, that having to do with defining the nature of the relationship of those involved in the interaction.

3. An interaction can be purposely set up as a time and place for voicing differences in opinion. But in such cases participants *must* be careful to agree not to disagree on the proper tone of voice, vocabulary, and degree of seriousness in which all arguments are to be phrased, and upon the mutual respect which disagreeing participants must carefully continue to express toward one another. This debaters' or academic definition of the situation may also be invoked suddenly and judiciously as a way of translating a serious conflict of views into one that can be handled within a framework acceptable to all present.

4. Goffman, *op. cit.*, pp. 319–27.

5. Peter Blau, "Dynamics of Bureaucracy" (Ph.D. dissertation, Department of Sociology, Columbia University, forthcoming, University of Chicago Press), pp. 127–29.

6. Walter M. Beattie, Jr., "The Merchant Seaman" (unpublished M.A. report, Department of Sociology, University of Chicago, 1950), p. 35.

7. Sir Frederick Ponsonby, *Recollections of Three Reigns* (New York: Dutton, 1952), p. 46.

8. For comments on the importance of distinguishing between a routine of interaction and any particular instance when this routine is played through, see John van Neumann and Oskar Morgenstern, *The Theory of Games and Economic Behaviour* (2nd ed.) (Princeton: Princeton University Press, 1947), p. 49.

9. See Babe Pinelli, as told to Joe King, *Mr. Ump* (Philadelphia: Westminster Press, 1953), p. 75.

10. Material on the burial business used throughout this report is taken from Robert W. Habenstein, "The American Funeral Director" (unpublished Ph.D. dissertation, Department of Sociology, University of Chicago, 1954). I owe much to Mr. Habenstein's analysis of a funeral as a performance.

11. Charles H. Cooley, *Human Nature and the Social Order* (New York: Scribner's, 1922), pp. 352–53.

12. This view of hypnosis is neatly presented by T. R. Sarbin, "Contributions to Role-Taking Theory. I: Hypnotic Behavior," *Psychological Review*, 57, pp. 255–70.

13. See D. R. Cressey, "The Differential Association Theory and Compulsive Crimes," *Journal of Criminal Law, Criminology and Police Science*, 45, pp. 29–40.

14. This concept derives from T. R. Sarbin, "Role Theory," in Gardner Lindzey, *Handbook of Social Psychology* (Cambridge: Addison-Wesley, 1954), Vol. 1, pp. 235–36.

THINKING ABOUT THE READING

According to Goffman, why must everyone engage in impression management? What are some of the reasons we do this? What does he mean by the terms, definition of the situation, working consensus, and preventative strategies? Consider a situation in which you were particularly aware of your own self-presentation. Do you think Goffman is interested primarily in the interactions between people or in their individual psychology? What is the source of the "scripts" that people use to determine what role they should play in a given situation or performance?

Maternity and Its Discontents
"Getting the Body Back" After Pregnancy

Rebecca L. Upton and Sallie S. Han

(2003)

"It's the most cataclysmic thing that will happen to a woman," Elena claimed. "Nothing—I mean, you could win a Nobel, you could go into space, but nothing else you do will so overturn your life." A year after the birth of her first son, Elena, thirty-nine, admitted that she still struggled with what it meant to be a mother, and in particular what had happened to her body and her self, in her own words, "how dislocating it is to have a child, how unbelievably—at every level, physically—it's exhausting, it wipes you out." Carolyn, thirty-two and the mother of one, also observed that "pregnancy *does* change everything, your body in particular—and then you have even more work, not just the work-work you did before, but all of a sudden you are like, Hey!? Where's my body?—it's like a whole other job, you have to *work* so hard to get it *back*." Later, when her daughter was almost one and a half years old, Carolyn recalled, "We thought we were pregnant again, and I was really happy and when I told my husband he was happy, too, but then he saw what I was thinking and just said, really sympathizing with me, '*ahhhh*, just when you got your body back.'"

As both Elena and Carolyn point out, losing the body, being wiped out, both literally and figuratively, is a profound and very real experience for many postpartum women. The pregnant body in particular is seemingly subject to far more social, public scrutiny than the body prior to pregnancy. Yet after delivery, when a woman is in a sense transformed into a different kind of person, literally a "new mother," a kind of tension exists between this new social self and the individual who is struggling to get a particular body and self back. In this article, we describe these transformations as they are experienced by a group of women who already struggled with tensions between a public and a private kind of identity—women in the paid labor force.

Pregnancy represents a particularly liminal stage in the life course, one in which the social family and the social individual are literally transformed. Yet at the conclusion of pregnancy, many women in the contemporary United States experience a profound sense of loss and even an increased sense of liminality. A loss of the pregnant self has occurred but also a loss of an even prior body, a previous identity. For many, the categories and identities of "mother" and "worker" come into direct conflict and this conflict is experienced, even played out on the body, the postpartum body, itself. As Elena suggested, one becomes invisible. As Carolyn suggested, the physical body itself had to be recaptured and even recast during this period.

As one woman told us, "Before I was just another one of the guys at work, we'd even joke about sex and stuff like that, but when I got pregnant, and was showing, you'd think that I was some total virgin . . . they all acted so shocked! I guess I brought sex into work!"

Certain clothes, foods, and behaviors became part of a new self, or identity, based on what was changing with one's body and on the external knowledge of that change.

Data and Method

Conducted in several small but relatively urban communities in southeast Michigan, the data for this article were gathered through in-depth ethnographic interviews that were largely open-ended. The interviews were conducted with a total of sixty individuals over the course of one year and focused on how individuals and couples negotiated changes in work, family, and gender obligations after childbirth.

We focused in particular on women who were actively employed in the paid labor force when they were pregnant. In part, we were interested in collecting data on what is often considered today to be the middle-class, dual-earning family, the contemporary typical American family.

Working Hard on the Body

The idea that the female body is controlled and subject to a constant barrage of social scrutiny is certainly not new. The idea that one must work hard to get a particular type of socially sanctioned body and that we actively "work" on bodies is a ubiquitous narrative in contemporary society and certainly among those who identify as middle class. From television, to magazines, to the kinds of foods and diets advertised throughout U.S. society, we know that the attention paid to a particular type of valued female form is great (Bordo 1993; Douglas 1995; Sault 1994). For many women in this study, women who defined themselves as middle class, the idea that one is constantly and actively "working" on the body was a pervasive theme. Carolyn, who spoke about "getting the body back" as a "whole other job" at the start of this article, talked often about what she saw as the constant maintenance of the body. She said,

> I would say that I spend many hours thinking about what I am doing that's either good or bad for my body. That was even before having a child, now . . . I'd say I think about it maybe more . . . mostly because I am anxious to keep myself fit but also it was a big push to get back into shape, to set a good example [for her daughter], feel like she was getting the right nutrition and all that, it was like I was constantly keeping track of what I was eating, what I had consumed . . . some days it drives me crazy.

Women work on the body. Society works on the body. The body is seemingly under constant construction and evaluation. For women who consider themselves middle class, who aspire to the kind of status and identity that such a social label implies, working on the body is an important aspect of their everyday lives. What happens during pregnancy? As the data from this study suggest, many women experience a time when they "lose" themselves in a pregnant body, yet the body itself is becoming crafted by external social mores. The social scrutiny of the body becomes even more increased, and yet many women spoke about how they became more "visible," gaining a different, new identity and body and how their identities as workers, as women, were more highlighted and in some ways more challenged as a result of this new state of being.

Losing the Body: Becoming a Pregnant Self

> It took me a long time to tell anyone at work. Well, anyone in general for that matter. I was more careful at the gym and all, and I just wore normal, regular clothes, actually up until about my fifth month. That's when things were getting tighter, you could tell that I was pregnant if you looked . . . [laughing] but of course there [at work], no one is really *supposed* to look, no one is supposed to notice until you tell them, as if they can't see!
>
> —Joelyn, thirty-three, mother of one, expecting a second

Bodies, and in particular, pregnant bodies, are public bodies. Without exception, the women in this study experienced the hand of a friend, family member, or even a stranger on her stomach while she was pregnant. Comments on body size and shape are open topics for discussion during pregnancy but for the most part are taboo topics in other places and times. As Isobel, the twenty-seven-year-old mother of two put it,

> People totally compliment each other when they lose weight, but what about when you put it on? You never see someone and say, "Gee! You look like you really are getting fat!" It's like we have these invisible bodies that suddenly, for this period in our lives, are really, really visible.

Isobel is representative of many of the women in this study who experienced and described a particular experience of "losing" the body when becoming pregnant. "It was as if suddenly the whole world had access to my body . . . not just the touching [of the belly] but like, what you could eat, wear, drink, even *say* . . . someone, somewhere had an opinion of how that was going to affect the baby," Isobel said.

As Isobel's statements point out, the pregnant body becomes subject to increased social control and scrutiny. Moral and value judgments were implied based upon what pregnant women choose to eat, wear, and say, and highlight the idea for some that the individual is now "lost." Joelyn, working in a busy law office, emphasized the role that clothing played in the construction of a pregnant body. She pointed out, as many women in this study did, that pregnancy can in fact be concealed. Concealing pregnancy was often desirable if women felt they would be (and in many cases they were) going to be treated differently in the workplace. Joelyn explained,

> Being really pregnant was like—you might as well bring the baby to work, it's hard to be discreet bringing a baby to work. I think the best advice is to be as professional as possible and dress like you mean it, not like you are just lounging around, being this pregnant person at work, you are at work and just happen to be pregnant. So for me, the best idea was to play it down as much as I could. I didn't tell anyone for a long time and even then I just tried to wear as much "normal" stuff as I could and just really act like my normal old self as much as possible. . . . I really didn't want to be treated any differently by anyone.

For Joelyn, being her "normal old self" was an important ideology while pregnant and one that hinted at the powerful social constructions of pregnant women in ways that are not one's "normal old self." Joelyn further explained that she had struggled for a long time with her legal career, trying to decide whether this was a good step for her and if it was something she wanted to do. She often felt that she was not taken seriously as a successful part of the practice after she took some time off to consider her options even though she returned to the practice and has pursued further education in this field. While clearly pregnancy indicates a kind of change in the life stage, for Joelyn, it was particularly important that she not lose her identity at the workplace as something other than a successful, productive worker. Pregnancy for her, and for others such as Isobel, demonstrated how the private body enters the public domain and called into sharp relief the idea of the body as subject to social and political control.

On the other hand, emphasizing and constructing the body as pregnant was a strategy employed by women to perhaps combat these difficult and often challenging boundaries of body and self. Rejecting the idea that her body was "lost," Desiree, thirty-nine and the mother of three, recalled how during each of her pregnancies, she "really played up her body and tried to call attention to it." As she continued,

> I work in a pretty busy office, I manage a bunch of guys and I could tell when I first got pregnant that they were all like "Whoa, what's going on here?" you know? Like how were they supposed to react to me, well, I suppose to my body, and what was going to happen. . . . Anyway, I didn't show right away after I told them, but what I did do was start wearing different kinds of clothes, you know, stuff that looks nice, not sloppy like sweats I might wear at home, but work clothes but ones that were obviously maternity clothes. I started even talking about shopping at maternity stores and what kinds of maternity clothes they make these days, stuff like that. . . . I think it was a way that I could say to everyone else "Hey, I'm pregnant" without them sort of having

to guess if they didn't know or just start talking to me in some weird way . . . like I suddenly had changed my whole personality, just because I was pregnant.

As Desiree chose to wear particularly marked maternity clothing, she asserted that she was still the individual in control of the body. While others might comment on the pregnancy, similar to Isobel and others' experiences, for Desiree, the individual construction and material labeling of her body as "pregnant" and therefore not necessarily "lost" was central. As she elaborated, "It didn't change who I was, my essential self anyway . . . [laughing] sure, I might've been more bitchy at times, nicer at others, but whatever, everyone has that and to say that someone is totally changed, it's like erasing who they are." As Elena noted at the start of the article, pregnancy has the potential to "wipe" you out. For Desiree, dressing and emphasizing the pregnant body was one strategy for resisting such loss and yet simultaneously and interestingly highlights how the pregnant body becomes much more "visible" in contemporary culture.

In contrast, how postpartum women are perceived and negotiate some of these boundaries between the private body and the public self often rests on narratives of invisibility. While pregnant, a certain identity has been lost, or replaced. Similarly, after delivery, conflicting ideologies about the necessity to regain a former self even as one has acquired a new identity exist.

Losing the Pregnant Body: Becoming a Postpartum Self

Don't get me wrong, I was really ready to *not* be pregnant anymore . . . particularly that last week or so, boy, did I just want to have her out—I was miserable and really, really uncomfortable—I felt huge! But I have to say that once I wasn't pregnant anymore, it was like I was back to being this woman who was just overweight, I wasn't pregnant, I was just fat.

Sharon, twenty-seven and the mother of a six-month-old daughter, Emily, described her experience of losing her pregnant identity, an experience which many women in this study emphasized as particularly important. For many, it was not necessarily a return to a former self, and certainly not a former body, although the latter was emphasized repeatedly as an important goal. As Sharon continued,

I was always kind of heavy, well, you know, I never worked out a whole lot, I was definitely self-conscious, but when I was pregnant, suddenly I didn't really have to feel badly if I wanted to eat chicken nuggets nonstop, it was like having license to eat whatever and whenever and I didn't have to feel like I was being judged. Afterwards, I felt like I was seen as really out of control if I ate like too many sweets, or whatever people brought into work, like I was supposed to just be eating healthy stuff and like foods that were good for the baby. It's not like I was ever that thin before I was pregnant but suddenly everyone, including me, thought that I should be getting back to something like that.

Sharon works as an administrative assistant in a large department at a local university. She was able to take four months off after Emily's birth and talked openly about her experiences while pregnant and postpartum in the workplace and at home. As she described, "I felt pretty lucky, I have a supportive work environment, a lot of people have children so had been through the whole process." On the other hand, the further along she was in her pregnancy, Sharon repeatedly stressed how she felt "like a belly" every time she walked into work. She said,

I definitely did feel like all the attention would go to my stomach which was getting bigger and bigger . . . particularly in that last trimester, I swear I put on a ton of weight! But the thing was, I didn't really mind it, for once it was okay that people were looking at me that way because I knew it was because I was pregnant. I sort of lost whatever low self-esteem I had before and now I could feel comfortable being however I wanted to be and people just had to be okay with that.

For Sharon, losing the body, the prepregnancy body, was a kind of liberation from the scrutiny she experienced previously. Growing up in what she described as "your typical middle-class home" and now living that lifestyle herself, Sharon argued that she

> never fit the mold, I never looked like the superwoman, beautiful, successful, all pulled together, nope, I was the slouchy, kind of quiet type, I wore nice clothes I guess, but not the super trendy stuff, I really didn't want to call attention to my body at all.

For Sharon, then, "losing the body" during pregnancy and the experience of more public attention to her individual, private body was almost welcome within the bounds of "pregnancy."

Postpregnancy for Sharon was another story entirely. Echoing Carolyn's earlier statements, she said,

> It was like I had double the work, an entirely new job where the goal was not just to take care of my new baby, my job, but now my body, I was back to square one, but worse.

The pressure to "get the body back" after delivery can be intense. The pregnant body is now lost, and while a new identity as a new mother emerges at the individual level, social norms insist on the importance of getting that body back—presumably some "ideal" body *a priori* to pregnancy. For Sharon this was clearly a contradiction in terms. She explained,

> I was really upset by all the weight I had put on. I know it was unrealistic, but I did sort of have the idea in my head, like poof, after giving birth, well somehow I'd go back to a different body, not a perfect body, but hey . . . not one that was now really overweight. I was breastfeeding which everyone said would help, you know, makes the uterus contract, it burns fat and all, but still, I really felt like I had to do something

else. So anyway I went on one of those diets, and I drank all these shakes and then had the one "sensible dinner" . . . it was awful. I felt totally hungry all of the time and like I said, back to square one where I was knocking myself out to try and look like some model, it wasn't like I had the perfect body to begin with.

Sharon's experience of "losing the pregnant body" and the need to regain or get some other type of body "back" was one that resonated in the narratives of many women in the study. While many women talked about how they knew the weight would eventually come off if they ate sensibly and were active, several women spoke about going on particular diets after delivery in order to do just that. One of the most popular and often referred to products by women in this study, Slim-Fast, has launched a recent advertising campaign to appeal to women who "can't wait to get back into pre-pregnancy clothes." In short, women such as Sharon are bombarded with the message that reattaining a certain self and body is paramount. Ironically, this message is concurrent with others that suggest that a woman's body and self have been profoundly and irrevocably changed by pregnancy. One is no longer just a woman or a working professional, but as the text on a Slim-Fast advertisement reads, "Being a new mom is exhilarating and exhausting, . . . you need to take care of yourself so you can take care of your baby." At the same time that the advertisement indicates this change of status, it poses the question, "When can you start dieting?" and offers, as Sharon pointed out, a sample Slim-Fast diet on the side, complete with carefully controlled "meal" times.

Getting the Body Back

Carolyn's husband had noted that Carolyn had "gotten her body back" when they had thought they might be pregnant a second time. But how did Carolyn know? Specifically, in the quest to regain a lost body, or a particular kind of identity through the body, how does one know when the body itself is actually back? As many women pointed out, "getting the body back" was a path, a trajectory toward a certain kind of ideal type, an ideal role. Carolyn suggested,

I would say I felt like I had my body back when I could go to a yoga class and I didn't feel like my hips were still stretched like crazy rubber bands. I could wear my old clothes and not feel super self-conscious in them. That was really important for me, to be able to wear my clothes again, not just for cost or whatever, but you know, you want to be able to say, heck, I got back down to that size, no problem, there's something of the old me there! I would also say that it was when I felt I could handle situations with Alissa [her daughter] and work and I wasn't quite so stressed out and not sleeping at all. So in that sense, I'd have to say it's about how you look but also how you feel—are you dealing with it all or are you just a mess.

For Sharon, who does not feel that she has been able to successfully "get the body back," her goals are similar, but she points out that a certain transition has occurred and that the divisions between being a certain kind of "self," a mom, a worker, or whatever may not be so easily separated from being a certain kind of "body,"

I am working on it, but it's almost like I know I am never going to get there. I will never be that perfect working mom who also has like tons of time to be there with the kids, I think that's what I think of when I hear about getting the body back and when women really dwell on that. I mean, you are a changed person, you are not the same old person you were going into this so why would you be the same kind of body?

For many women in this study, the impetus to get the body back was a social one. The message that getting the body back was important is one that can be seen in popular culture, magazines advertising diet products for women, and even in medical literature.

For women in this study, it was not just the attention that was paid to what they were eating while pregnant that became important and an object of scrutiny, but what they were eating and doing in the postpartum period to get that body back. Sharon described how her doctor emphasized repeatedly the need to get her body back due to health concerns and said,

I know it's true, that putting on all this weight is like creating a higher risk of disease for myself. I am worried about my blood pressure and getting diabetes and it's my doctor who is the one focused on that. I've gone for several check ups now and I honestly believe that she is telling her staff to put all these magazines and articles around about the risks of not getting that bod back!

While Carolyn notes that she feels like she has gotten her body back and that it was a hard won struggle for many other women, it is not clear what is meant by getting the body back. As Evelyne's and Sharon's concerns point out, it may be that that body is irrevocably changed. Breasts, hips, stomachs may be different after pregnancy and may never be "recaptured." On the other hand, if the struggle to get the body back is indicative of larger elements of identity, of control over certain aspects of the self in society, then achieving that goal may take various other forms. If getting the body back has more to do with becoming visible in a way that many postpartum women feel they are not, then observing the strategies and means through which women attempt to regain lost bodies and selves can illustrate important aspects about gender in U.S. society.

In the paid labor force, women are constantly negotiating what it means to be a working woman. When pregnant in the workplace, boundaries between what it means to work and what it means to be a woman center on the pregnant, sexually intrusive body and become part of public discourse. After pregnancy, the boundaries and rules that govern what it means to be a woman in U.S. society are again emphasized but center largely on negating the sexual, pregnant self in the search for a previous or even elusive body/self. By exploring the meaning of getting the body back and beginning to see the ways in which women view that goal can help illustrate just how social and individual controls over the body and boundaries between seeming dichotomies of public and private, self and society, operate in contemporary U.S. culture.

REFERENCES

Bordo, Susan. 1993. *Unbearable weight: Feminism, Western culture and the body*. Berkeley: University of California Press.

Douglas, Susan. 1995. *Where the girls are: Growing up female with the mass media*. New York: Times Books.

Sault, Nicole. 1994. *Many mirrors*. New Brunswick, NJ: Rutgers University Press.

THINKING ABOUT THE READING

Upton and Han focus on the pregnant body as an aspect of self-presentation. Consider some of the ways in which the private bodies of pregnant women become objects of public scrutiny. Why do the pregnant women interviewed here feel they lose themselves when they "lose" their bodies in pregnancy? What are some of the differences between pregnant women and men who gain weight? What other types of bodies might receive the kind of public attention described in this reading (e.g., the poor, disabled)? Why are some bodies more susceptible to public scrutiny than others?

The Girl Hunt

Urban Nightlife and the Performance of Masculinity as Collective Activity

David Grazian

(2007)

Young urbanites identify downtown clusters of nightclubs as *direct sexual marketplaces,* or markets for singles seeking casual encounters with potential sex partners (Laumann et al. 2004).

In this article I examine girl hunting—a practice whereby adolescent heterosexual men aggressively seek out female sexual partners in nightclubs, bars, and other public arenas of commercialized entertainment. In this article I wish to emphasize the performative nature of contemporary flirtation rituals by examining how male-initiated games of heterosexual pursuit function as strategies of impression management in which young men sexually objectify women to heighten their own performance of masculinity. While we typically see public sexual behavior as an interaction between *individuals,* I illustrate how these rituals operate as collective and homosocial group activities conducted in the company of men.

The Performance of Masculinity as Collective Activity

Girl hunting in nightclubs would not seem to serve as an especially efficacious strategy for locating sexual partners, particularly when compared with other methods (such as meeting through mutual friends, colleagues, classmates, or other trusted third parties; common participation in an educational or recreational activity; or shared membership in a civic or religious organization). In fact, the statistical rareness of the one-night stand may help explain why

successful lotharios are granted such glorified status and prestige among their peers in the first place (Connell and Messerschmidt 2005:851). But if this is the case, then why do adolescent men persist in hassling women in public through aggressive sexual advances and pickup attempts (Duneier and Molotch 1999; Snow et al. 1991; Whyte 1988), particularly when their chances of meeting sex partners in this manner are so slim?

I argue that framing the question in this manner misrepresents the actual sociological behavior represented by the girl hunt, particularly since adolescent males do not necessarily engage in girl hunting to generate sexual relationships, even on a drunken short-term basis. Instead, three counterintuitive attributes characterize the girl hunt. First, the girl hunt is as much *ritualistic* and *performative* as it is utilitarian—it is a social drama through which young men perform their interpretations of manhood. Second, as demonstrated by prior studies (Martin and Hummer 1989; Polk 1994; Sanday 1990; Thorne and Luria 1986), girl hunting is not always a purely heterosexual pursuit but can also take the form of an inherently *homosocial* activity. Here, one's male peers are the intended audience for competitive games of sexual reputation and peer status, public displays of situational dominance and rule transgression, and in-group rituals of solidarity and loyalty. Finally, the emotional effort and logistical deftness required by rituals of sexual pursuit (and by extension the public performance of masculinity itself) encourage some young men to seek out safety in numbers by participating in the girl hunt as a kind of *collective* activity, in which they enjoy the social and psychological resources generated by group cohesion and dramaturgical teamwork (Goffman 1959). Although tales of sexual adventure traditionally feature a single male hero, such as Casanova, the performance of heterosexual conquest more often resembles the exploits of the dashing Christian de Neuvillette and his better-spoken coconspirator Cyrano de Bergerac (Rostand 1897). By aligning themselves with similarly oriented accomplices, many young men convince themselves of the importance and efficacy of the girl hunt (despite its poor track record), summon the courage to pursue their female targets (however clumsily), and assist one another in "mobilizing masculinity" (Martin 2001) through a collective performance of gender and heterosexuality.

Methods and Data

I draw on firsthand narrative accounts provided by 243 heterosexual male college students attending the University of Pennsylvania, an Ivy League research university situated in Philadelphia. These data represent part of a larger study involving approximately 600 college students (both men and women).

Because young people are likely to self-consciously experiment with styles of public behavior (Arnett 1994, 2000), observing undergraduates can help researchers understand how young heterosexual men socially construct masculinity through gendered interaction rituals in the context of everyday life. But just as there is not one single mode of masculinity but many *masculinities* available to young men, respondents exhibited a variety of socially recognizable masculine roles in their accounts, including the doting boyfriend, dutiful son, responsible escort, and perfect gentleman. In the interests of exploring the girl hunt as *one among many types* of social orientation toward the city at night, the findings discussed

here represent only the accounts of those heterosexual young men whose accounts revealed commonalities relevant to the girl hunt, as outlined above.

The Girl Hunt and the Myth of the Pickup

It is statistically uncommon for men to successfully attract and "pick up" female sexual partners in bars and nightclubs. However, as suggested by a wide selection of mass media—from erotic films to hardcore pornography—heterosexual young men nevertheless sustain fantasies of successfully negotiating chance sexual encounters with anonymous strangers in urban public spaces (Bech 1998), especially dance clubs, music venues, singles bars, cocktail lounges, and other nightlife settings. According to Aaron, a twenty-one-year-old mixed-race junior:

> I am currently in a very awkward, sticky, complicated and bizarre relationship with a young lady here at Penn, where things are pretty open right now, hopefully to be sorted out during the summer when we both have more time. So my mentality right now is to go to the club with my best bud and seek out the ladies for a night of great music, adventure and female company off of the grounds of campus.

Young men reproduce these normative expectations of masculine sexual prowess—what I call *the myth of the pickup*—collectively through homosocial group interaction. According to Brian, a nineteen-year-old Cuban sophomore:

> Whether I would get any girl's phone number or not, the main purpose for going out was to try to get with hot girls. That was our goal every night we went out to frat parties on campus, and we all knew it, even though we seldom mention that aspect of going out. *It was implicitly known that tonight, and every night out, was a girl hunt.* Tonight, we were taking that goal to Philadelphia's nightlife. In the meanwhile, we

would have fun drinking, dancing, and joking around. (emphasis added)

For Brian and his friends, the "girl hunt" articulates a shared orientation toward public interaction in which the group collectively negotiates the city at night. The heterosexual desire among men for a plurality of women (hot *girls*, as it were) operates at the individual and group level. As in game hunting, young men frequently evaluate their erotic prestige in terms of their raw number of sexual conquests, like so many notches on a belt. Whereas traditional norms of feminine desire privilege the search for a singular and specified romantic interest (Prince Charming, Mr. Right, or his less attractive cousin, Mr. Right Now), heterosexual male fantasies idealize the pleasures of an endless abundance and variety of anonymous yet willing female sex partners (Kimmel and Plante 2005).

Despite convincing evidence to the contrary (Laumann et al. 2004), these sexual fantasies seem deceptively realizable in the context of urban nightlife. To many urban denizens, the city and its never-ending flow of anonymous visitors suggests a sexualized marketplace governed by transactional relations and expectations of personal noncommitment (Bech 1998), particularly in downtown entertainment zones where nightclubs, bars, and cocktail lounges are concentrated. The density of urban nightlife districts and their tightly packed venues only intensifies the pervasive yet improbable male fantasy of successfully attracting an imaginary surplus of amorous single women.

Adolescent men strengthen their belief in this fantasy of the sexual availability of women in the city—the myth of the pickup—through collective reinforcement in their conversations in the hours leading up to the girl hunt. While hyping their sexual prowess to the group, male peers collectively legitimize the myth of the pickup and increase its power as a model for normative masculine behavior. According to Dipak, an eighteen-year-old Indian freshman:

I finished up laboratory work at 5:00 pm and walked to my dormitory, eagerly waiting to "hit up a club" that night. . . . I went to eat with my three closest friends at [a campus dining hall]. We acted like high school freshmen about to go to our first mixer. We kept hyping up the night and saying we were going to meet and dance with many girls. Two of my friends even bet with each other over who can procure the most phone numbers from girls that night. Essentially, the main topic of discussion during dinner was the night yet to come.

Competitive sex talk is common in male homosocial environments (Bird 1996) and often acts as a catalyst for sexual pursuit among groups of adolescent and young adult males. For example, in his ethnographic work on Philadelphia's black inner-city neighborhoods, Anderson (1999) documents how sex codes among youth evolve in a context of peer pressure in which young black males "run their game" by women as a means of pursuing in-group status. Moreover, this type of one-upmanship heightens existing heterosexual fantasies and the myth of the pickup while creating a largely unrealistic set of sexual and gender expectations for young men seeking in-group status among their peers. In doing so, competitive sexual boasting may have the effect of momentarily energizing group participants. However, in the long run it is eventually likely to deflate the confidence of those who inevitably continue to fall short of such exaggerated expectations and who consequently experience the shame of a spoiled masculine identity (Goffman 1963).

Preparing for the Girl Hunt Through Collective Ritual

Armed with their inflated expectations of the nightlife of the city and its opportunities for sexual conquest, young men at Penn prepare for the girl hunt by crafting a specifically gendered and class-conscious nocturnal self (Grazian 2003)—a presentation of masculinity that relies on prevailing fashion cues and upper-class taste emulation. According to Edward, a twenty-year-old white sophomore, these decisions are made strategically:

I hadn't hooked up with a girl in a couple weeks and I needed to break my slump (the next girl you hook up with is commonly referred to as a "slump-bust" in my social circle). So I was willing to dress in whatever manner would facilitate in hooking up.

Among young college men, especially those living in communal residential settings (i.e., campus dormitories and fraternities), these preparations for public interaction serve as *collective rituals of confidence building*—shared activities that generate group solidarity and cohesion while elevating the personal resolve and self-assuredness of individual participants mobilizing for the girl hunt. Frank, a nineteen-year-old white sophomore, describes the first of these rituals:

> As I began observing both myself and my friends tonight, I noticed that there is a distinct pre-going-out ritual that takes place. I began the night by blasting my collection of rap music as loud as possible, as I tried to overcome the similar sounds resonating from my roommate's room. Martin seemed to play his music in order to build his confidence. It appears that the entire ritual is simply there to build up one's confidence, to make one more adept at picking up the opposite sex.

Frank explains this preparatory ritual in terms of its collective nature, as friends recount tall tales that celebrate character traits commonly associated with traditional conceptions of masculinity, such as boldness and aggression. Against a soundtrack of rap music—a genre known for its misogynistic lyrics and male-specific themes, including heterosexual boasting, emotional detachment, and masculine superiority (McLeod 1999)—these shared ritual moments of homosociality are a means of generating group resolve and bolstering the self-confidence of each participant. Again, according to Frank:

> Everyone erupted into stories explaining their "high-roller status." Martin recounted how he spent nine hundred dollars in Miami one weekend, while Lance brought up his cousins who spent twenty-five hundred dollars with

ease one night at a Las Vegas bachelor party. Again, all of these stories acted as a confidence booster for the night ahead.

Perhaps unsurprisingly, this constant competitive jockeying and one-upmanship so common in male-dominated settings (Martin 2001) often extends to the sexual objectification of women. While getting dressed among friends in preparation for a trip to a local strip club, Gregory, a twenty-year-old white sophomore, reports on the banter: "We should all dress rich and stuff, so we can get us some hookers!" Like aggressive locker-room boasting, young male peers bond over competitive sex talk by laughing about real and make-believe sexual exploits and misadventures (Bird 1996). This joking strengthens male group intimacy and collective heterosexual identity and normalizes gender differences by reinforcing dominant myths about the social roles of men and women (Lyman 1987).

After engaging in private talk among roommates and close friends, young men (as well as women) commonly participate in a more public collective ritual known among American college students as "pregaming." As Harry, an eighteen-year-old white freshman, explains,

> Pregaming consists of drinking with your "boys" so that you don't have to purchase as many drinks while you are out to feel the desired buzz. On top of being cost efficient, the actual event of pregaming can get any group ready and excited to go out.

The ritualistic use of alcohol is normative on college campuses, particularly for men (Martin and Hummer 1989), and students largely describe pregaming as an economical and efficient way to get drunk before going out into the city. This is especially the case for underage students who may be denied access to downtown nightspots. However, it also seems clear that pregaming is a bonding ritual that fosters social cohesion and builds confidence among young men in anticipation of the challenges that accompany the girl hunt.

According to Joey, an eighteen-year-old white freshman:

> My thoughts turn to this girl, Jessica. . . . I was thinking about whether or not we might hook up tonight. . . . As I turn to face the door to 301, I feel the handle, and it is shaking from the music and dancing going on in the room. I open the door and see all my best friends just dancing together. . . . I quickly rush into the center of the circle and start doing my "J-walk," which I have perfected over the years. My friends love it and begin to chant, "Go Joey—it's your birthday." I'm feeling connected with my friends and just know that we're about to have a great night. . . . Girls keep coming in and out of the door, but no one really pays close attention to them. Just as the "pregame" was getting to its ultimate height, each boy had his arms around each other jumping in unison, to a great hip-hop song by Biggie Smalls. One of the girls went over to the stereo and turned the power off. We yelled at her to turn it back on, but the mood was already lost and we decided it was time to head out.

In this example, Joey's confidence is boosted by the camaraderie he experiences in a male-bonding ritual in which women—supposedly the agreed-upon raison d'être for the evening—are ignored or, when they make their presence known, scolded. As these young men dance arm-in-arm with one another, they generate the collective effervescence and sense of social connectedness necessary to plunge into the nightlife of the city. As such, pregaming fulfills the same function as the last-minute huddle (with all hands in the middle) does for an athletic team (Messner 2002). It is perhaps ironic that Joey's ritual of "having fun with my boys" prepares him for the girl hunt (or more specifically in his case, an opportunity to "hook up" with Jessica) even as it requires those boys to exclude their female classmates. At the same time, this men-only dance serves the same function as the girl hunt: it allows its participants to expressively perform hegemonic masculinity through an aggressive display of collective identification.

During similar collective rituals leading up to the girl hunt, young men boost each other's confidence in their abilities of sexual persuasion by watching films about male heterosexual exploits in urban nightlife, such as Doug Liman's *Swingers* (1996), which chronicles the storied escapades of two best friends, Mike and Trent. According to Kevin, an eighteen-year-old white freshman:

> I knew that [my friend] Darryl needed to calm down if he wanted any chance of a second date. At about 8:15 pm, I sat him down and showed him (in my opinion), the movie that every man should see at least once—I've seen it six times—*Swingers*. . . . Darryl immediately related to Mike's character, the self-conscious but funny gentleman who is still on the rebound from a long-term relationship. At the same time, he took Trent's words for scripture (as I planned): "There's nothing wrong with showing the beautiful babies that you're money and that you want to party." His mind was clearly eased at the thought of his being considered "money." Instead of being too concerned with not screwing up and seeming "weird or desperate," Darryl now felt like he was in control. The three of us each went to our own rooms to get ready.

This collective attention to popular cultural texts helps peer groups generate common cultural references, private jokes, and speech norms as well as build in-group cohesion (Eliasoph and Lichterman 2003; Fine 1977; Swidler 2001).

Girl Hunting and the Collective Performance of Masculinity

Finally, once the locus of action moves to a more public venue such as a bar or nightclub, the much-anticipated "girl hunt" itself proceeds as a strategic display of masculinity best performed with a suitable game partner. According to Christopher, a twenty-two-year-old white senior, he and his cousin Darren "go out together a lot. We enjoy each other's company and we seem to work well together when trying to meet women." Reporting on his evening at a local dance club, Lawrence, a twenty-one-year-old white junior, illustrates how the girl hunt itself operates as collective activity:

> We walk around the bar area as we finish [our drinks]. After we are done, we walk down to the regular part of the club. We make the rounds around the dance floor checking out the girls. . . . We walk up to the glassed dance room and go in, but leave shortly because it is really hot and there weren't many prospects.

Lawrence and his friends display their elaborated performance of masculinity by making their rounds together as a pack in search of a suitable feminine target. Perhaps it is not surprising that the collective nature of their pursuit should also continue *after* such a prize has been located:

> This is where the night gets really interesting. We walk back down to the main dance floor and stand on the outside looking at what's going on and I see a really good-looking girl behind us standing on the other side of the wall with three friends. After pointing her out to my friends, I decide that I'm going to make the big move and talk to her. So I turn around and ask her to dance. She accepts and walks over. My friends are loving this, so they go off to the side and watch. . . .
>
> After dancing for a little while she brings me over to her friends and introduces me. They tell me that they are all freshman [*sic*] at [a local college], and we go through the whole small talk thing again. I bring her over to my two boys who are still getting a kick out of the whole situation . . . My boys tell me about some of the girls they have seen and talked to, and they inform me that they recognized some girls from Penn walking around the club.

Why do Lawrence and his dance partner both introduce each other to their friends? Lawrence seems to gain almost as much pleasure from his *friends'* excitement as from his own exploits, just as they are "loving" the vicarious

thrill of watching their comrade succeed in commanding the young woman's attention, as if their own masculinity is validated by his success.

In this instance, arousal is not merely individual but represents a collectively shared experience as well (Thorne and Luria 1986:181). For these young men the performance of masculinity does not necessarily require successfully meeting a potential sex partner as long as one enthusiastically participates in the ritual *motions* of the girl hunt in the company of men. When Lawrence brings over his new female friend, he does so to celebrate his victory with his buddies, and in return, they appear gratified by their *own* small victory by association. (And while Lawrence celebrates with them, perhaps he alleviates some of the pressure of actually conversing with her.)

As Christopher remarked above on his relationship with his cousin, the collective aspects of the girl hunt also highlight the efficacy of conspiring with peers to meet women: "We go out together a lot. We enjoy each other's company and we seem to work well together when trying to meet women." In the language of the confidence game, men eagerly serve as each other's shills (Goffman 1959; Grazian 2004; Maurer 1940) and sometimes get roped into the role unwittingly with varying degrees of success.

Among young people, the role of the passive accomplice is commonly referred to in contemporary parlance as a *wingman*. In public rituals of courtship, the wingman serves multiple purposes: he provides validation of a leading man's trustworthiness, eases the interaction between a single male friend and a larger group of women, serves as a source of distraction for the friend or friends of a more desirable target of affection, can be called on to confirm the wild (and frequently misleading) claims of his partner, and, perhaps most important, helps motivate his friends by building up their confidence. Indeed, men describe the role of the wingman in terms of loyalty, personal responsibility, and dependability, traits commonly associated with masculinity

(Martin and Hummer 1989; Mishkind et al. 1986). According to Nicholas, an eighteen-year-old white freshman:

> As we were beginning to mobilize ourselves and move towards the dance floor, James noticed Rachel, a girl he knew from Penn who he often told me about as a potential girlfriend. Considering James was seemingly into this girl, Dan and I decided to be good wingmen and entertain Rachel's friend, Sarah.

Hegemonic masculinity is not only expressed by competitiveness but camaraderie as well, and many young men will take their role as a wingman quite seriously and at a personal cost to their relationships with female friends. According to Peter, a twenty-year-old white sophomore:

> "It sounds like a fun evening," I said to Kyle, "but I promised Elizabeth I would go to her date party." I don't like to break commitments. On the other hand, I didn't want to leave Kyle to fend for himself at this club . . . Kyle is the type of person who likes to pick girls up at clubs. If I were to come see him, I would want to meet other people as well. Having Elizabeth around would not only prevent me from meeting (or even just talking to) other girls, but it would also force Kyle into a situation of having no "wing man."

In the end, Peter takes Elizabeth to a nightclub where, although he *himself* will not be able to meet available women, he will at least be able to assist Kyle in meeting them:

> Behind Kyle, a very attractive girl smiles at me. Yes! Oh, wait. Damnit, Elizabeth's here. . . . "Hey, Kyle," I whisper to him. "That girl behind you just smiled at you. Go talk to her." Perhaps Kyle will have some luck with her. He turns around, takes her by the hand, and begins dancing with her. She looks over at me and smiles again, and I smile back. I don't think Elizabeth noticed. I would have rather been in Kyle's position, but I was happy for him, and I was dancing with Elizabeth, so I was satisfied for the moment.

By the end of the night, as he and Kyle chat in a taxi on the way back to campus, Peter learns that he was instrumental in securing his friend's success in an additional way:

> "So what ever happened with you and that girl?" I ask. "I hooked up with her. Apparently she's a senior." I ask if she knew he was a freshman. "Oh, yeah. She asked how old you were, though. I said you were a junior. I had to make one of us look older."

Peter's willingness to serve as a wingman demonstrates his complicity in sustaining the ideals of hegemonic masculinity, which therefore allows him to benefit from the resulting "patriarchal dividends"—acceptance as a member of his male homosocial friendship network and its attendant prestige—even when he himself does not personally seek out the sexual rewards of the girl hunt.

In addition, the peer group provides a readily available audience that can provide emotional comfort to all group members, as well as bear witness to any individual successes that might occur. As demonstrated by the preceding examples, young men deeply value the erotic prestige they receive from their conspiratorial peers upon succeeding in the girl hunt. According to Zach, a twenty-year-old white sophomore:

> About ten minutes later, probably around 2:15 am, we split up into cabs again, with the guys in one and the girls in another. . . . This time in the cab, all the guys want to talk about is me hooking up on the dance floor. It turns out that they saw the whole thing. I am not embarrassed; in fact I am proud of myself.

As an audience, the group can collectively validate the experience of any of its members and can also internalize an individual's success as a shared victory. Since, in a certain sense, a successful sexual interaction must be recognized by one's peers to gain status as an in-group "social fact," the group can transform a private moment into a celebrated public event—thereby making it "count" for the male participant and his cohorts.

A participant's botched attempt at an ill-conceived pickup can solidify the male group's bonds as much as a successful one. According to Brian, the aforementioned nineteen-year-old Cuban sophomore:

> We had been in the club for a little more than half an hour, when the four of us were standing at the perimeter of the main crowd in the dancing room. It was then when Marvin finished his second Corona and by his body gestures, he let it be known that he was drunk enough and was pumped up to start dancing. He started dancing behind a girl who was dancing in a circle with a few other girls. Then the girl turned around and said "Excuse me!" Henry and I saw what happened. We laughed so hard and made so much fun of him for the rest of the night. I do not think any of us has ever been turned away so directly and harshly as that time.

In this instance, Marvin's abruptly concluded encounter with an unwilling female participant turns into a humorous episode for the rest of his peer group, leaving his performance of masculinity bruised yet intact. Indeed, in his gracelessness Marvin displays an enthusiastic male heterosexuality as emphasized by his drunken attempts to court an unsuspecting target before a complicit audience of his male peers. And as witnesses to his awkward sexual advance, Brian and Henry take pleasure in the incident, as it not only raises *their* relative standing within the group in comparison with Marvin but can also serve as a narrative focus for future "signifying" episodes (or ceremonial exchanges of insults) and other rituals of solidarity characteristic of joking relationships among male adolescents (Lyman 1987:155). Meanwhile, these young men can bask in their collective failure to attract a woman without ever actually challenging the basis of the girl hunt itself: the performance of adolescent masculinity.

In the end, young men may enjoy this performance of masculinity—the hunt itself—even more than the potential romantic or sexual rewards they hope to gain by its successful execution. In his reflections on a missed opportunity

to procure the phone number of a law student, Christopher, the aforementioned twenty-two-year-old senior, admits as much: "There's something about the chase that I really like. Maybe I subconsciously neglected to get her number. I am tempted to think that I like the idea of being on the look out for her better than the idea of calling her to go out for coffee." While Christopher's excuse may certainly function as a compensatory face-saving strategy employed in the aftermath of another lonely night (Berk 1977), it might also indicate a possible acceptance of the limits of the girl hunt despite its potential opportunities for male bonding and the public display of adolescent masculinity.

REFERENCES

Anderson, Elijah. 1999. *Code of the Street: Decency, Violence, and the Moral Life of the Inner City.* New York: Norton.

Arnett, Jeffrey Jensen. 1994. "Are College Students Adults? Their Conceptions of the Transition to Adulthood." *Journal of Adult Development* 1(4):213–24.

———. 2000. "Emerging Adulthood: A Theory of Development from the Late Teens through the Twenties." *American Psychologist* 55(5): 469–80.

Bech, Henning. 1998. "Citysex: Representing Lust in Public." *Theory, Culture & Society* 15(3–4): 215–41.

Berk, Bernard. 1977. "Face-Saving at the Singles Dance." *Social Problems* 24(5):530–44.

Bird, Sharon R. 1996. "Welcome to the Men's Club: Homosociality and the Maintenance of Hegemonic Masculinity." *Gender & Society* 10(2):120–32.

Connell, R. W. and James W. Messerschmidt. 2005. "Hegemonic Masculinity: Rethinking the Concept." *Gender & Society* 19(6):829–59.

Duneier, Mitchell and Harvey Molotch. 1999. "Talking City Trouble: Interactional Vandalism, Social Inequality, and the 'Urban Interaction Problem.'" *American Journal of Sociology* 104(5):1263–95.

Eliasoph, Nina and Paul Lichterman. 2003. "Culture in Interaction." *American Journal of Sociology* 108(4):735–94.

Fine, Gary Alan. 1977. "Poputar Culture and Social Interaction: Production, Consumption, and Usage." *Journal of Popular Culture 11*(2): 453–56.

Goffman, Erving. 1959. *The Presentation of Self in Everyday Life.* Garden City, NY: Anchor Books.

———. 1963. *Stigma: Notes on the Management of Spoiled Identity.* New York: Simon & Schuster.

Grazian, David. 2003. *Blue Chicago: The Search for Authenticity in Urban Blues Clubs.* Chicago: University of Chicago Press.

———. 2004. "The Production of Popular Music as a Confidence Game: The Case of the Chicago Blues." *Qualitative Sociology 27*(2):137–58.

Kimmel, Michael S. and Rebecca F. Plante. 2005. "The Gender of Desire: The Sexual Fantasies of Women and Men." In *The Gender of Desire: Essays on Male Sexuality,* edited by M. S. Kimmel. Albany: State University of New York Press.

Laumann, Edward O., Stephen Ellingson, Jenna Mahay, Anthony Paik, and Yoosik Youm, eds. 2004. *The Sexual Organization of the City.* Chicago: University of Chicago Press.

Lyman, Peter. 1987. "The Fraternal Bond as a Joking Relationship: A Case Study of the Role of Sexist Jokes in Male Group Bonding." In *Changing Men: New Directions in Research on Men and Masculinity,* edited by M. S. Kimmel. Newbury Park, CA: Sage.

Martin, Patricia Yancey. 2001. "'Mobilizing Masculinities': Women's Experiences of Men at Work." *Organization 8*(4):587–618.

Martin, Patricia Yancey and Robert A. Hummer. 1989. "Fraternities and Rape on Campus." *Gender & Society 3*(4):457–73.

Maurer, David W. 1940. *The Big Con: The Story of the Confidence Man.* New York: Bobbs-Merrill.

McLeod, Kembrew. 1999. "Authenticity within Hip-Hop and Other Cultures Threatened with Assimilation." *Journal of Communication 49*(4): 134–50.

Messner, Michael A. 2002. *Taking the Field: Women, Men, and Sports.* Minneapolis: University of Minnesota Press.

Mishkind, Marc, Judith Rodin, Lisa R. Silberstein, and Ruth H. Striegel-Moore. 1986. "The Embodiment of Masculinity." *American Behavioral Scientist 29*(5):545–62.

Polk, Kenneth. 1994. "Masculinity, Honor, and Confrontational Homicide." In *Just Boys Doing Business? Men, Masculinities, and Crime,* edited by T. Newburn and E. A. Stanko. London: Routledge.

Rostand, Edmond. 1897. *Cyrano de Bergerac.*

Sanday, Peggy Reeves. 1990. *Fraternity Gang Rape: Sex, Brotherhood, and Privilege on Campus.* New York: New York University Press.

Snow, David A., Cherylon Robinson, and Patricia L. McCall. 1991. "'Cooling Out' Men in Singles Bars and Nightclubs: Observations on the Interpersonal Survival Strategies of Women in Public Places." *Journal of Contemporary Ethnography 19*(4):423–19.

Swidler, Ann. 2001. *Talk of Love: How Culture Matters.* Chicago: University of Chicago Press.

Thorne, Barrie and Zella Luria. 1986. "Sexuality and Gender in Children's Daily Worlds." *Social Problems 33*(3):176–90.

Whyte, William H. 1988. *City: Rediscovering the Center.* New York: Doubleday.

THINKING ABOUT THE READING

What is the "girl hunt"? According to the author, the purpose of the girl hunt is male social bonding. What does he mean by this? The author uses Goffman's framework as a way to understand why men engage in these activities. What are some of the interaction rituals and performances these young men engage in when they go out to clubs? What are the implications of this kind of research for understanding social issues such as gender, dating, and sexual violence?

Building Social Relationships

Intimacy and Family

7

In this culture, close, personal relationships are the standard by which we judge the quality and happiness of our everyday lives. Yet in a complex, individualistic society like ours, these relationships are becoming more difficult to establish and sustain. Although we like to think that the things we do in our relationships are completely private experiences, they are continually influenced by large-scale political interests and economic pressures. Like every other aspect of our lives, close relationships are best understood within the broader social context. Laws, customs, and social institutions often regulate the form relationships can take, our behavior in them, and even the ways in which we can exit them. At a more fundamental level, societies determine which relationships can be considered "legitimate" and therefore entitled to cultural and institutional recognition. Relationships that lack societal validation are often scorned and stigmatized.

If you were to ask couples applying for a marriage license why they were getting married, most, if not all, would no doubt mention the love they feel for one another. But as Stephanie Coontz discusses in "The Radical Idea of Marrying for Love," love hasn't always been a prerequisite or even a justification for marriage. Until relatively recently, marriage was principally an economic arrangement, and love, if it existed at all, was a sometimes irrational emotion that was of secondary importance. In fact, in some past societies, falling in love before marriage was considered disruptive, even threatening, to the extended family. Today, however, it's hard to imagine a marriage that begins without love.

Paradoxically, many cultural critics discredit same sex couples who also seek marriage because they are in love and want to build a life and a family together. Gay and lesbian couples lobbying for marriage are portrayed as being frivolous and culturally inappropriate and are assumed to be undermining the deeper meaning of marriage. Using recent survey data, Gary Gates demonstrates that there is considerable diversity among same sex couples—just as there is among heterosexual, or differently gendered couples. It may surprise many readers to learn that same sex couples with children tend to be more disadvantaged than media portrayals suggest. According to Gates, these families need marriage for the same reasons that heterosexual families do, for the state benefits it provides.

One of the most pressing dilemmas that all types of families face these days is how to balance the demands of their work lives with those of their home lives. In "Coping with Commitment," Kathleen Gerson examines the strategies men and women use to emphasize one sphere of their lives over the other. Two of these strategic responses—the stay-at-home mother and breadwinner father—are quite traditional and, historically, have had tremendous cultural support. Two other strategies—the working mother and the caretaking father—are distinctly nontraditional and often carry extra burdens. Although many people believe that the choice to emphasize the domestic component of one's life or the work component is a matter of moral conviction, Gerson points out that these choices are often influenced by broader cultural barriers, economic shifts, and occupational opportunities.

Something to Consider as You Read

Each of these selections emphasizes the significance of external or structural components in shaping family experiences. As you read, keep track of factors such as income level and job opportunities and consider how these factors affect the choices families make. Consider some of the ways in which household income might be related to family choices. For example, consider what choices a family with a high income might have regarding how best to assist an ailing grandparent or how to deal with an unexpected teen pregnancy or in providing children with extracurricular activities. Consider how these choices are related to the appearance of "traditional family values." How does legal marriage support families? For instance, what kinds of benefits and social assistance do married couples receive that assists them in raising children?

The Radical Idea of Marrying for Love

Stephanie Coontz

(2005)

The Real Traditional Marriage

To understand why the love-based marriage system was so unstable and how we ended up where we are today, we have to recognize that for most of history, marriage was not primarily about the individual needs and desires of a man and woman and the children they produced. Marriage had as much to do with getting good in-laws and increasing one's family labor force as it did with finding a lifetime companion and raising a beloved child.

Marriage, a History

Reviewing the role of marriage in different societies in the past and the theories of anthropologists and archaeologists about its origins, I came to reject two widespread, though diametrically opposed, theories about how marriage came into existence among our Stone Age ancestors: the idea that marriage was invented so men would protect women and the opposing idea that it was invented so men could exploit women. Instead, marriage spoke to the needs of the larger group. It converted strangers into relatives and extended cooperative relations beyond the immediate family or small band by creating far-flung networks of in-laws. . . .

Certainly, people fell in love during those thousands of years, sometimes even with their own spouses. But marriage was not fundamentally about love. It was too vital an economic and political institution to be entered into solely on the basis of something as irrational as love. For thousands of years the theme song for most weddings could have been "What's Love Got to Do with It?" . . .

For centuries, marriage did much of the work that markets and governments do today. It organized the production and distribution of goods and people. It set up political, economic, and military alliances. It coordinated the division of labor by gender and age. It orchestrated people's personal rights and obligations in everything from sexual relations to the inheritance of property. Most societies had very specific rules about how people should arrange their marriages to accomplish these tasks.

Of course there was always more to marriage than its institutional functions. At the end of the day—or at least in the middle of the night—marriage is also a face-to-face relationship between individuals. The actual experience of marriage for individuals or for particular couples seldom conforms exactly to the model of marriage codified in law, custom, and philosophy in any given period. But institutions do structure people's expectations, hopes, and constraints. For thousands of years, husbands had the right to beat their wives. Few men probably meted out anything more severe than a slap. But the law upheld the authority of husbands to punish their wives physically and to exercise forcibly their "marital right" to sex, and that structured the relations between men and women in *all* marriages, even loving ones.

The Radical Idea of Marrying for Love

George Bernard Shaw described marriage as an institution that brings together two people "under the influence of the most violent, most insane, most delusive, and most transient of passions. They are required to swear that they will remain in that excited, abnormal, and exhausting condition continuously until death do them part."[1]

Shaw's comment was amusing when he wrote it at the beginning of the twentieth century, and it still makes us smile today, because it pokes fun at the unrealistic expectations that spring from a dearly held cultural ideal—that marriage should be based on intense, profound love and a couple should maintain their ardor until death do them part. But for thousands of years the joke would have fallen flat.

For most of history it was inconceivable that people would choose their mates on the basis of something as fragile and irrational as love and then focus all their sexual, intimate, and altruistic desires on the resulting marriage. In fact, many historians, sociologists, and anthropologists used to think romantic love was a recent Western invention. This is not true. People have always fallen in love, and throughout the ages many couples have loved each other deeply.[2]

But only rarely in history has love been seen as the main reason for getting married. When someone did advocate such a strange belief, it was no laughing matter. Instead, it was considered a serious threat to social order.

In some cultures and times, true love was actually thought to be incompatible with marriage. Plato believed love was a wonderful emotion that led men to behave honorably. But the Greek philosopher was referring not to the love of women, "such as the meaner men feel," but to the love of one man for another.[3]

Other societies considered it good if love developed after marriage or thought love should be factored in along with the more serious considerations involved in choosing a mate. But even when past societies did welcome or encourage married love, they kept it on a short leash. Couples were not to put their feelings for each other above more important commitments, such as their ties to parents, siblings, cousins, neighbors, or God.

In ancient India, falling in love before marriage was seen as a disruptive, almost anti-social act. The Greeks thought lovesickness was a type of insanity, a view that was adopted by medieval commentators in Europe. In the Middle Ages the French defined love as a "derangement of the mind" that could be cured by sexual intercourse, either with the loved one or with a different partner.[4] This cure assumed, as Oscar Wilde once put it, that the quickest way to conquer yearning and temptation was to yield immediately and move on to more important matters.

In China, excessive love between husband and wife was seen as a threat to the solidarity of the extended family. Parents could force a son to divorce his wife if her behavior or work habits didn't please them, whether or not he loved her. They could also require him take a concubine if his wife did not produce a son. If a son's romantic attachment to his wife rivaled his parents' claims on the couple's time and labor, the parents might even send her back to her parents. In the Chinese language the term *love* did not traditionally apply to feelings between husband and wife. It was used to describe an illicit, socially disapproved relationship. In the 1920s a group of intellectuals invented a new word for love between spouses because they thought such a radical new idea required its own special label.[5]

In Europe, during the twelfth and thirteenth centuries, adultery became idealized as the highest form of love among the aristocracy. According to the Countess of Champagne, it was impossible for true love to "exert its powers between two people who are married to each other."[6]

In twelfth-century France, Andreas Capellanus, chaplain to Countess Marie of Troyes, wrote a treatise on the principles of courtly love. The first rule was that "marriage is no real excuse for not loving." But he meant loving someone outside the marriage. As late as the eighteenth century the French essayist Montaigne wrote that any man who was in love with his wife was a man so dull that no one else could love him.[7]

Courtly love probably loomed larger in literature than in real life. But for centuries, noblemen and kings fell in love with courtesans rather than the wives they married for political reasons. Queens and noblewomen had to be more discreet than their husbands, but they too looked beyond marriage for love and intimacy.

This sharp distinction between love and marriage was common among the lower and middle classes as well. Many of the songs and stories popular among peasants in medieval Europe mocked married love.

The most famous love affair of the Middle Ages was that of Peter Abelard, a well-known theologian in France, and Héloïse, the brilliant niece of a fellow churchman at Notre Dame. The two eloped without marrying, and she bore him a child. In an attempt to save his career but still placate Héloïse's furious uncle, Abelard proposed they marry in secret. This would mean that Héloïse would not be living in sin, while Abelard could still pursue his church ambitions. But Héloïse resisted the idea, arguing that marriage would not only harm his career but also undermine their love.[8] . . .

"Happily Ever After"

Through most of the past, individuals hoped to find love, or at least "tranquil affection," in marriage.[9] But nowhere did they have the same recipe for marital happiness that prevails in most contemporary Western countries. Today there is general agreement on what it takes for a couple to live "happily ever after." First, they must love each other deeply and choose each other unswayed by outside pressure. From then on, each must make the partner the top priority in life, putting that relationship above any and all competing ties. A husband and wife, we believe, owe their highest obligations and deepest loyalties to each other and the children they raise. Parents and in-laws should not be allowed to interfere in the marriage. Married couples should be best friends, sharing their most intimate feelings and secrets.

They should express affection openly but also talk candidly about problems. And of course they should be sexually faithful to each other.

This package of expectations about love, marriage, and sex, however, is extremely rare. When we look at the historical record around the world, the customs of modern America and Western Europe appear exotic and exceptional. . . .

About two centuries ago Western Europe and North America developed a whole set of new values about the way to organize marriage and sexuality, and many of these values are now spreading across the globe. In this Western model, people expect marriage to satisfy more of their psychological and social needs than ever before. Marriage is supposed to be free of the coercion, violence, and gender inequalities that were tolerated in the past. Individuals want marriage to meet most of their needs for intimacy and affection and all their needs for sex.

Never before in history had societies thought that such a set of high expectations about marriage was either realistic or desirable. Although many Europeans and Americans found tremendous joy in building their relationships around these values, the adoption of these unprecedented goals for marriage had unanticipated and revolutionary consequences that have since come to threaten the stability of the entire institution.

The Era of Ozzie and Harriet: The Long Decade of "Traditional" Marriage

The long decade of the 1950s, stretching from 1947 to the early 1960s in the United States and from 1952 to the late 1960s in Western Europe, was a unique moment in the history of marriage. Never before had so many people shared the experience of courting their own mates, getting married at will, and setting up their own households. Never had married couples been so independent of extended family ties and community groups. And never before had so many people agreed that only one kind of family was "normal."

The cultural consensus that everyone should marry and form a male breadwinner family was like a steamroller that crushed every alternative view. By the end of the 1950s even people who had grown up in completely different family systems had come to believe that universal marriage at a young age into a male breadwinner family was the traditional and permanent form of marriage.

In Canada, says historian Doug Owram, "every magazine, every marriage manual, every advertisement . . . assumed the family was based on the . . . male wage-earner and the child-rearing, home-managing housewife." In the United States, marriage was seen as the only culturally acceptable route to adulthood and independence. Men who chose to remain bachelors were branded "narcissistic," "deviant," "infantile," or "pathological." Family advice expert Pat Landes argued that practically everyone, "except for the sick, the badly crippled, the deformed, the emotionally warped and the mentally defective," ought to marry. French anthropologist Martine Segalen writes that in Europe the postwar period was characterized by the overwhelming "weight of a single family model." Any departure from this model—whether it was late marriage, nonmarriage, divorce, single motherhood, or even delayed childbearing—was considered deviant. Everywhere psychiatrists agreed and the mass media affirmed that if a woman did not find her ultimate fulfillment in homemaking, it was a sign of serious psychological problems.[10]

A 1957 survey in the United States reported that four out of five people believed that anyone who preferred to remain single was "sick," "neurotic" or "immoral." Even larger majorities agreed that once married, the husband should be the breadwinner and the wife should stay home. As late as 1962 one survey of young women found that almost all expected to be married by age twenty-two, most hoped to have four children, and all expected to quit work permanently when the first child was born.[11]

During the 1950s even women who had once been political activists, labor radicals, or feminists—people like my own mother, still proud of her work to free the Scottsboro Boys from legal lynching in the 1930s and her job in the shipyards during the 1940s—threw themselves into homemaking. It's hard for anyone under the age of sixty to realize how profoundly people's hunger for marriage and domesticity during the 1950s was shaped by their huge relief that two decades of depression and war were finally over and by their amazed delight at the benefits of the first real mass consumer economy in history. "It was like a miracle," my mother once told me, to see so many improvements, so quickly, in the quality of everyday life. . . .

This was the first chance many people had to try to live out the romanticized dream of a private family, happily ensconced in its own nest. They studied how the cheery husbands and wives on their favorite television programs organized their families (and where the crabby ones went wrong). They devoured articles and books on how to get the most out of marriage and their sex lives. They were even interested in advertisements that showed them how to use home appliances to make their family lives better. . . .

Today strong materialist aspirations often corrode family bonds. But in the 1950s, consumer aspirations were an integral part of constructing the postwar family. In its April 1954 issue, *McCall's* magazine heralded the era of "togetherness," in which men and women were constructing a "new and warmer way of life . . . as a family sharing a common experience." In women's magazines that togetherness was always pictured in a setting filled with modern appliances and other new consumer products. The essence of modern life, their women readers learned, was "abundance, emancipation, social progress, airy house, healthy children, the refrigerator, pasteurised milk, the washing-machine, comfort, quality and accessibility."[12] And of course marriage.

Television also equated consumer goods with family happiness. Ozzie and Harriet hugged each other in front of their Hotpoint appliances. A man who had been a young father in the 1950s told a student of mine that he had no clue how to cultivate the family "togetherness" that his wife kept talking about until he saw an episode of the sitcom *Leave It to Beaver*, which gave him the idea of washing the car with his son to get in some "father-son" time.

When people could not make their lives conform to those of the "normal" families they saw on TV, they blamed themselves—or their parents. . . . "Why didn't she clean the house in high heels and shirtwaist dresses like they did on television?"[13]

At this early stage of the consumer revolution, people saw marriage as the gateway to the good life. Americans married with the idea of quickly buying their first home, with the wife working for a few years to help accumulate the down payment or furnish it with the conveniences she would use once she became a full-time housewife. People's newfound spending money went to outfit their homes and families. In the five years after World War II, spending on food in the United States rose by a modest 33 percent and clothing expenditures by only 20 percent, but purchases of household furnishings and appliances jumped by 240 percent. In 1961, Phyllis Rosenteur, the author of an American advice book for single women, proclaimed: "Merchandise plus Marriage equals our economy."[14]

In retrospect, it's astonishing how confident most marriage and family experts of the 1950s were that they were witnessing a new stabilization of family life and marriage. The idea that marriage should provide both partners with sexual gratification, personal intimacy, and self-fulfillment was taken to new heights in that decade. Marriage was the place not only where people expected to find the deepest meaning in their lives but also where they would have the most fun. Sociologists noted that a new "fun morality," very different "from the older 'goodness morality,'" pervaded society. "Instead of feeling guilty for having too much fun, one is inclined to feel ashamed if one does not have enough." A leading motivational researcher of the day argued that the challenge for a consumer society was "to demonstrate that the hedonistic approach to life is a moral, not an immoral, one."[15]

But these trends did not cause social commentators the same worries about the neglect of societal duties that milder ideas about the pleasure principle had triggered in the 1920s. Most 1950s sociologists weren't even troubled by the fact that divorce rates were *higher* than they had been in the 1920s, when such rates had been said to threaten the very existence of marriage. The influential sociologists Ernest Burgess and Harvey Locke wrote matter-of-factly that "the companionship family relies upon divorce as a means of rectifying a mistake in mate selection." They expressed none of the panic that earlier social scientists had felt when they first realized divorce was a permanent feature of the love-based marital landscape. Burgess and Locke saw a small amount of divorce as a safety valve for the "companionate" marriage and expected divorce rates to stabilize or decrease in the coming decades as "the services of family-life education and marriage counseling" became more widely available.[16]

The marriage counseling industry was happy to step up to the plate. By the 1950s Paul Popenoe's American Institute of Family Relations employed thirty-seven counselors and claimed to have helped twenty thousand people become "happily adjusted" in their marriages. "It doesn't require supermen or superwomen to succeed in marriage," wrote Popenoe in a 1960 book on saving marriages. "Success can be attained by almost anyone."[17]

There were a few dissenting voices. American sociologist Robert Nisbet warned in 1953 that people were loading too many "psychological and symbolic functions" on the nuclear family, an institution too fragile to bear such weight. In the same year, Mirra Komarovsky decried the overspecialization of gender roles in American marriage and its corrosive effects on women's self confidence.[18]

But even when marriage and family experts acknowledged that the male breadwinner family created stresses for women, they seldom supported any change in its division of labor. The world-renowned American sociologist Talcott Parsons recognized that because most women were not able to forge careers, they might feel a need to attain status in other ways. He suggested that they had two alternatives. The first was to be a "glamour girl" and exert sexual sway over men. The second was to develop special expertise in "humanistic" fields, such as the arts or community volunteer work. The latter, Parsons thought, was socially preferable, posing less of a threat to society's moral standards and to a woman's own self-image as she aged. He never considered the third alternative: that women might actually win access to careers. Even Komarovsky advocated nothing more radical than expanding part-time occupations to give women work that didn't interfere with their primary role as wives and mothers.[19]

Marriage counselors took a different tack in dealing with housewives' unhappiness. Popenoe wrote dozens of marital advice books, pamphlets, and syndicated newspaper columns, and he pioneered the *Ladies' Home Journal* feature "Can This Marriage Be Saved?," which was based on case histories from his Institute of Family Relations. The answer was almost always yes, so long as the natural division of labor between husbands and wives was maintained or restored. . . .

In retrospect, the confidence these experts expressed in the stability of 1950s marriage and gender roles seems hopelessly myopic. Not only did divorce rates during the 1950s never drop below the highs reached in 1929, but as early as 1947 the number of women entering the labor force in the United States had begun to surpass the number of women leaving it.[20] Why were the experts so optimistic about the future of marriage and the demise of feminism?

Some were probably unconsciously soothed into complacency by the mass media, especially the new television shows that delivered nightly images of happy female homemakers in stable male breadwinner families. . . .

When divorce did occur, it was seen as a failure of individuals rather than of marriage.

One reason people didn't find fault with the 1950s model of marriage and gender roles was that it was still so new that they weren't sure they were doing it right. Millions of people in Europe and America were looking for a crash course on how to attain the modern marriage. Confident that "science" could solve their problems, couples turned not just to popular culture and the mass media but also to marriage experts and advice columnists for help. If the advice didn't work, they blamed their own inadequacy.[21] . . .

At every turn, popular culture and intellectual elites alike discouraged women from seeing themselves as productive members of society. In 1956 a *Life* magazine article commented that women "have minds and should use them . . . so long as their primary interest is in the home." . . . Adlai Stevenson, the two-time Democratic Party candidate for president of the United States, told the all-female graduating class of Smith College that "most of you" are going to assume "the humble role of housewife," and "whether you like the idea or not just now," later on "you'll like it."[22]

Under these circumstances, women tried their best to "like it." By the mid-1950s American advertisers reported that wives were using housework as a way to express their individuality. It appeared that Talcott Parsons was right: Women were compensating for their lack of occupational status by expanding their role as consumer experts and arbiters of taste and style. First Lady Jackie Kennedy was the supreme exemplar of this role in the early 1960s.[23]

Youth in the 1950s saw nothing to rebel against in the dismissal of female aspirations for independence. The number of American high school students agreeing that it would be good "if girls could be as free as boys in asking for dates" fell from 37 percent in 1950 to 26 percent in 1961, while the percentage of those who thought it would be good for girls to share the expenses of dates declined from 25 percent to 18 percent. The popular image was that only hopeless losers would engage in such egalitarian behavior. A 1954 Philip Morris ad in the

Massachusetts Collegian made fun of poor Finster, a boy who finally found a girl who shared his belief in "the equity of Dutch treat." As a result, the punch line ran, "today Finster goes everywhere and shares expenses fifty-fifty with Mary Alice Hematoma, a lovely three-legged girl with side-burns."[24]

No wonder so many social scientists and marriage counselors in the 1950s thought that the instabilities associated with the love-based "near-equality" revolution in gender roles and marriage had been successfully contained. Married women were working outside the home more often than in the past, but they still identified themselves primarily as housewives. Men seemed willing to support women financially even in the absence of their older patriarchal rights, as long as their meals were on the table and their wives kept themselves attractive. Moreover, although men and women aspired to personal fulfillment in marriage, most were willing to stay together even if they did not get it. Sociologist Mirra Komarovsky interviewed working-class couples at the end of the 1950s and found that "slightly less than one-third [were] happily or very happily married." In 1957, a study of a cross section of all social classes found that only 47 percent of U.S. married couples described themselves as "very happy." Although the proportion of "very happy" marriages was lower in 1957 than it was to be in 1976, the divorce rate was also lower.[25]

What the experts failed to notice was that this stability was the result of a unique moment of equilibrium in the expansion of economic, political, and personal options. Ironically, this one twenty-year period in the history of the love-based "near-equality" marriage when people stopped predicting disaster turned out to be the final lull before the long-predicted storm.

The seeming stability of marriage in the 1950s was due in part to the thrill of exploring the new possibilities of married life and the size of the rewards that men and women received for playing by the rules of the postwar economic boom. But it was also due to the incomplete development of the "fun morality" and the consumer revolution. There were still many ways of penalizing nonconformity, tamping down aspirations, and containing discontent in the 1950s.

One source of containment was the economic and legal dependence of women. Postwar societies continued the century-long trend toward increasing women's legal and political rights outside the home and restraining husbands from exercising heavy-handed patriarchal power, but they stopped short of giving wives equal authority with their husbands. Legal scholar Mary Ann Glendon points out that right up until the 1960s, "nearly every legislative attempt to regulate the family decision-making process gave the husband and father the dominant role."[26]

Most American states retained their "head and master" laws, giving husbands the final say over questions like whether or not the family should move. Married women couldn't take out loans or credit cards in their own names. Everywhere in Europe and North America it was perfectly legal to pay women less than men for the same work. Nowhere was it illegal for a man to force his wife to have sex. One legal scholar argues that marriage law in the 1950s had more in common with the legal codes of the 1890s than the 1990s.[27]

Writers in the 1950s generally believed that the old-style husband and father was disappearing and that this was a good thing. The new-style husband, said one American commentator, was now "partner in the family firm, part-time man, part-time mother and part-time maid." Family experts and marital advice columnists advocated a "fifty-fifty design for living," emphasizing that a husband should "help out" with child rearing and make sure that sex with his wife was "mutually satisfying."[28]

But the 1950s definition of fifty-fifty would satisfy few modern couples. Dr. Benjamin Spock, the famous parenting advice expert, called for men to get more involved in parenting but added that he wasn't suggesting equal involvement. "Of course I don't mean that the father has to give just as many bottles, or change just as many diapers as the mother," he explained in a 1950s edition of his perennial bestseller *Baby and Child Care*. "But it's fine for him to do these things occasionally. He might make the formula on Sunday."[29]

The family therapist Paul Popenoe was equally cautious in his definition of what modern marriage required from the wife. A wife should be "sympathetic with her husband's work and a good listener," he wrote. But she must never consider herself "enough of an expert to criticize him."[30] . . .

Many 1950s men did not view male breadwinning as a source of power but as a burdensome responsibility made worthwhile by their love for their families. A man who worked three jobs to support his family told interviewers, "Although I am somewhat tired at the moment, I get pleasure out of thinking the family is dependent on me for their income." Another described how anxious he had been to finish college and "get to . . . acting as a husband and father should, namely, supporting my family." Men also remarked on how wonderful it felt to be able to give their children things their families had been unable to afford when they were young.[31]

A constant theme of men and women looking back on the 1950s was how much better their family lives were in that decade than during the Depression and World War II. But in assessing their situation against a backdrop of such turmoil and privation, they had modest expectations of comfort and happiness, so they were more inclined to count their blessings than to measure the distance between their dreams and their real lives.

Modest expectations are not necessarily a bad thing. Anyone who expects that marriage will always be joyous, that the division of labor will always be fair, and that the earth will move whenever you have sex is going to be often disappointed. Yet it is clear that in many 1950s marriages, low expectations could lead people to put up with truly terrible family lives.

Historian Elaine Tyler May comments that in the 1950s "the idea of 'working marriage' was

one that often included constant day-to-day misery for one or both partners." Jessica Weiss recounts interviews conducted over many years in the Berkeley study with a woman whose husband beat her and their children. The wife often threw her body between her husband and the young ones, taking the brunt of the violence on herself because "I can take it much easier than the kids can." Her assessment of the marriage strikes the modern observer as a masterpiece of understatement: "We're really not as happy as we should be." She was not even indignant that her neighbors rebuffed her children when they fled the house to summon help. "I can't say I blame the neighbors," she commented. "They didn't want to get involved." Despite two decades of such violence, this woman did not divorce until the late 1960s.[32]

A 1950s family that looked well functioning to the outside world could hide terrible secrets. Both movie star Sandra Dee and Miss America of 1958, Marilyn Van Derbur, kept silent about their fathers' incestuous abuse until many years had passed. If they had gone public in the 1950s or early 1960s, they might not even have been believed. Family "experts" of the day described incest as a "one-in-a-million occurrence," and many psychiatrists claimed that women who reported incest were simply expressing their own oedipal fantasies.[33]

In many states and countries a nonvirgin could not bring a charge of rape, and everywhere the idea that a man could rape his own wife was still considered absurd. Wife beating was hardly ever treated seriously. The trivialization of family violence was epitomized in a 1954 report of a Scotland Yard commander that "there are only about twenty murders a year in London and not all are serious—some are just husbands killing their wives."[34] . . .

Still, these signs of unhappiness did not ripple the placid waters of 1950s complacency. The male breadwinner marriage seemed so pervasive and popular that social scientists decided it was a necessary and inevitable result of modernization. Industrial societies, they argued, needed the division of labor embodied in the male breadwinner nuclear family to compensate for their personal demands of the modern workplace. The ideal family—or what Talcott Parsons called "the normal" family—consisted of a man who specialized in the practical, individualistic activities needed for subsistence and a woman who took care of the emotional needs of her husband and children.[35]

The close fit that most social scientists saw between the love-based male breadwinner family and the needs of industrial society led them to anticipate that this form of marriage would accompany the spread of industrialization across the globe and replace the wide array of other marriage and family systems in traditional societies. This view was articulated in a vastly influential 1963 book titled *World Revolution and Family Patterns,* by American sociologist William F. Goode. Goode's work became the basis for almost all high school and college classes on family life in the 1960s, and his ideas were popularized by journalists throughout the industrial world.[36]

Goode surveyed the most up-to-date family data in Europe and the United States, the Middle East, sub-Saharan Africa, India, China, and Japan and concluded that countries everywhere were evolving toward a conjugal family system characterized by the "love pattern" in mate selection. The new international marriage system, he said, focused people's material and psychic investments on the nuclear family and increased the "emotional demands which each spouse can legitimately make upon each other," elevating loyalty to spouse above obligations to parents. Goode argued that such ideals would inevitably eclipse other forms of marriage, such as polygamy. Monogamous marriage would become the norm all around the world.

The ideology of the love-based marriage, according to Goode, "is a radical one, destructive of the older traditions in almost every society." It "proclaims the right of the individual to choose his or her own spouse.... It

asserts the worth of the *individual* as against the inherited elements of wealth or ethnic group." As such, it especially appealed "to intellectuals, young people, women, and the disadvantaged." . . .

Despite women's legal gains and the "radical" appeal of the love ideology to women and youth, Goode concluded that a destabilizing "full equality" was not in the cards. Women had not become more "career-minded" between 1900 and the early 1960s, he said. In his 380-page survey of world trends, Goode did not record even one piece of evidence to suggest that women might become more career-minded in the future.

Most social scientists agreed with Goode that the 1950s family represented the wave of the future. They thought that the history of marriage had in effect reached its culmination in Europe and North America and that the rest of the world would soon catch up. As late as 1963 nothing seemed more obvious to most family experts and to the general public than the preeminence of marriage in people's lives and the permanence of the male breadwinner family.

But clouds were already gathering on the horizon.

When sustained prosperity turned people's attention from gratitude for survival to a desire for greater personal satisfaction . . .

When the expanding economy of the 1960s needed women enough to offer them a living wage . . .

When the prepared foods and drip-dry shirts that had eased the work of homemakers also made it possible for men to live comfortable, if sloppy bachelor lives . . .

When the invention of the birth control pill allowed the sexualization of love to spill over the walls of marriage . . .

When the inflation of the 1970s made it harder for a man to be the sole breadwinner for a family . . .

When all these currents converged, the love-based male-provider marriage would find itself buffeted from all sides.

NOTES

1. Quoted in John Jacobs, *All You Need Is Love and Other Lies About Marriage* (New York: HarperCollins, 2004), p. 9.

2. William Jankowiak and Edward Fischer, "A Cross-Cultural Perspective on Romantic Love," *Ethnology* 31 (1992).

3. Ira Reiss and Gary Lee, *Family Systems in America* (New York: Holt, Rinehart and Winston, 1988), pp. 91–93.

4. Karen Dion and Kenneth Dion, "Cultural Perspectives on Romantic Love," *Personal Relationships* 3 (1996); Vern Bullough, "On Being a Male in the Middle Ages," in Clare Less, ed., *Medieval Masculinities* (Minneapolis: University of Minnesota Press, 1994); Hans-Werner Goetz, *Life in the Middle Ages, from the Seventh to the Thirteenth Century* (Notre Dame, Ind.: University of Notre Dame Press, 1993).

5. Francis Hsu, "Kinship and Ways of Life," in Hsu, ed., *Psychological Anthropology* (Cambridge, U.K.: Schenkman, 1972), and *Americans and Chinese: Passage to Differences* (Honolulu: University Press of Hawaii, 1981); G. Robina Quale, *A History of Marriage Systems* (Westport, Conn.: Greenwood Press, 1988); Marilyn Yalom, "Biblical Models," in Yalom and Laura Carstensen, eds., *Inside the American Couple* (Berkeley: University of California Press, 2002).

6. Andreas Capellanus, *The Art of Courtly Love* (New York: W. W. Norton, 1969), pp. 106–07.

7. Ibid., pp.106–07, 184. On the social context of courtly love, see Theodore Evergates, ed., *Aristocratic Women in Medieval France* (Philadelphia: University of Pennsylvania Press, 1999); Montaigne, quoted in Olwen Hufton, *The Prospect Before Her: A History of Women in Western Europe, 1500–1800* (New York: Alfred A. Knopf, 1996), p. 148.

8. Betty Radice, trans., *Letters of Abelard and Heloise* (Harmondsworth, U.K.: Penguin, 1974).

9. The phrase is from Chiara Saraceno, who argues that until the end of the nineteenth century, Italian families defined love as the development of such feelings over the course of a marriage. Saraceno, "The Italian Family," in Antoine Prost and Gerard Vincent, eds., *A History of Private Life: Riddles of Identity in Modern Times* (Cambridge, Mass.: Belknap Press, 1991), p. 487.

10. Owram, *Born at the Right Time*, p. 22 (see chap. 13, n. 20); Elaine Tyler May, *Homeward Bound: American Families in the Cold War Era* (New York: Basic Books, 1988); Barbara Ehrenreich, *The Hearts of Men: American Dreams and the Flight from Commitment* (Garden City, N.Y.: Anchor Press, 1983), pp. 14–28; Douglas Miller and Marson Nowak, *The Fifties: The Way We Really Were* (Garden City, N.Y.: Doubleday, 1977), p. 154; Duchen, *Women's Rights* (see chap. 13, n. 28); Marjorie Ferguson, *Forever Feminine: Women's Magazines and the Cult of Femininity* (London: Heinemann, 1983); Moeller, *Protecting Motherhood* (see chap. 13, n. 22); Martine Segalen, "The Family in the Industrial Revolution," in Burguière et al., p. 401 (see chap. 8, n. 2).

11. Daniel Yankelovich, *New Rules: Searching for Self-Fulfillment in a World Turned Upside Down* (New York: Random House, 1981); Lois Gordon and Alan Gordon, *American Chronicle: Seven Decades in American Life, 1920–1989* (New York: Crown, 1990).

12. Alan Ehrenhalt, *The Lost City: Discovering the Forgotten Virtues of Community in the Chicago of the 1950s* (New York: Basic Books, 1995), p. 233; modernity quote from the French woman's magazine *Marie-Claire*, in Duchen, *Women's Rights and Women's Lives*, p. 73 (see chap. 13, n. 28).

13. Quoted in Ruth Rosen, *The World Split Open: How the Modern Women's Movement Changed America* (New York: Viking, 2000), p. 44.

14. Coontz, *The Way We Never Were*, p. 25; Rosenteur, quoted in Bailey, *From Front Porch to Back Seat*, p. 76 (see chap. 12, n. 11).

15. Martha Wolfenstein, "Fun Morality" [1955], in Warren Susman, ed., *Culture and Commitment, 1929–1945* (New York: George Braziller, 1973), pp. 84, 90; Coontz, *The Way We Never Were*, p. 171.

16. Ernest Burgess and Harvey Locke, *The Family: From Institution to Companionship* (New York: American Book Company, 1960), pp. 479, 985, 538.

17. Molly Ladd-Taylor, "Eugenics, Sterilisation and Modern Marriage in the USA," *Gender & History* 13 (2001), pp. 312, 318.

18. Nisbet, quoted in John Scanzoni, "From the Normal Family to Alternate Families to the Quest for Diversity with Interdependence," *Journal of Family Issues* 22 (2001); Mirra Komarovsky, *Women in the Modern World: Their Education and Their Dilemmas* (Boston: Little, Brown, 1953).

19. Talcott Parsons, "The Kinship System of the United States" in Parsons, *Essays in Sociological Theory* (Glencoe, Ill.: Free Press, 1954); Parsons and Robert Bales, *Family, Socialization, and Interaction Processes* (Glencoe, Ill.: Free Press, 1955).

20. *Historical Statistics of the United States: Colonial Times to the Present* (Washington, D.C.: U.S. Department of Commerce, Bureau of the Census, 1975); Sheila Tobias and Lisa Anderson, "What Really Happened to Rosie the Riveter," *Mss Modular Publications* 9 (1973).

21. Beth Bailey, "Scientific Truth . . . and Love: The Marriage Education Movement in the United States," *Journal of Social History* 20 (1987).

22. Miller and Nowak, *The Fifties*, pp. 164–65; Weiss, *To Have and to Hold*, p. 19 (see chap. 13, n. 29); Rosen, *World Split Open*, p. 41.

23. Glenna Mathews, *"Just a Housewife": The Rise and Fall of Domesticity in America* (New York: Oxford University Press, 1987); Betty Friedan, *The Feminine Mystique* (New York: Dell, 1963).

24. Bailey, *From Front Porch to Back Seat*, p. 111.

25. Mirra Komarovsky, *Blue-Collar Marriage* (New Haven: Vintage, 1962), p. 331. Mintz and Kellogg, *Domestic Revolutions*, p. 194; Norval Glenn, "Marital Quality," in David Levinson, ed., *Encyclopedia of Marriage and the Family* (New York: Macmillan, 1995), vol. 2, p. 449.

26. Mary Ann Glendon, *The Transformation of Family Law* (Chicago: University of Chicago Press, 1989), p. 88. On Europe, Gisela Bock, *Women in European History* (Oxford, U.K.: Blackwell Publishers, 2002), p. 248; Bonnie Smith, *Changing Lives: Women in European History Since 1700* (Lexington, Mass.: D. C. Heath, 1989), p. 492.

27. Sara Evans, *Tidal Wave: How Women Changed America at Century's End* (New York: Free Press, 2003), pp. 1–20; John Ekelaar, "The End of an Era?," *Journal of Family History* 28 (2003), p. 109. See also Lenore Weitzman, *The Marriage Contract* (New York: Free Press, 1981).

28. Ehrenhalt, *Lost City*, p. 233.

29. Quoted in Michael Kimmell, *Manhood in America: A Cultural History* (New York: Free Press, 1996), p. 246.

30. Ladd-Taylor, "Eugenics," p. 319.

31. Ibid., p. 32; Robert Rutherdale, "Fatherhood, Masculinity, and the Good Life During Canada's Baby Boom," *Journal of Family History* 24 (1999), p. 367.

32. May, *Homeward Bound*, p. 202; Weiss, *To Have and to Hold*, pp. 136–38.

33. Marilyn Van Derbur Atler, "The Darkest Secret," *People* (June 10, 1991); Dodd Darin, *The Magnificent Shattered Life of Bobby Darin and Sandra Dee* (New York: Warner Books, 1995); Elizabeth Pleck, *Domestic Tyranny* (New York: Oxford University Press, 1987); Linda Gordon, *Heroes of Their Own Lives: The Politics and History of Family Violence, 1880–1960* (New York: Viking, 1988).

34. Coontz, *The Way We Never Were*, p. 35; Leonore Davidoff et al., *The Family Story* (London: Longmans, 1999), p. 215.

35. Parsons, "The Kinship System of the United States"; Parsons, "The Normal American Family," in Seymour Farber, Piero Mustacchi, and Roger Wilson, eds., *Man and Civilization: The Family's Search for Survival* (New York: McGraw-Hill, 1965); Parsons and Bales, *Family, Socialization, and Interaction Processes*. For similar theories in British sociology, see Michael Young and Peter Willmott's *The Symmetrical Family* (London: Pelican, 1973), pp. 28–30; *Family and Kinship in East London* (Glencoe, Ill.: The Free Press, 1957); and *Family and Class in a London Suburb*.

36. The quotations and figures in this and the following paragraphs are from Goode, *World Revolution*.

THINKING ABOUT THE READING

According to Coontz, if not for romance, what are some of the common reasons throughout history that people marry? What are the characteristics of the "male breadwinner, love-based marriage"? What social conditions are necessary for this kind of family arrangement to prevail? Does Coontz think this family form is viable in the long-term future? Do you?

Diversity Among Same-Sex Couples and Their Children

Gary Gates

(2008)

Current controversies about marriage and parenting rights for lesbians and gay men provide a good example of why it is essential to take account of race and class in discussions of sexuality and family life, and why it is also necessary to integrate race and class into our discussion of issues such as marriage for same-sex couples. The success of television shows such as *Will & Grace* and *Queer Eye for the Straight Guy* contribute to an increasingly visible role for lesbians and gay men in American news media and in popular culture. Unfortunately, popular images rarely display the diversity of the lesbian and gay community in the United States, focusing disproportionately on relatively wealthy, white, and urban gay men. A recent analysis of American television broadcast media by the Gay and Lesbian Alliance Against Defamation (2007) found that the gay community was commonly portrayed as both white and male. But the real life world of the lesbian and gay community, especially those who are raising children, is often far removed from trendy lofts, expensive cocktails, and designer labels. To cite a few examples:

- Mississippi, not California, is the state where same-sex couples are most likely to be raising children.
- The median household income of same-sex couples with children is substantially lower than that of different-sex married couples with children.
- More than half of the children being raised by same-sex couples are non-white.

This essay explores the diversity of same-sex couples and their families, focusing primarily on analyses of data from the 2000 United States Census. In doing so, I offer a demographic portrait of lesbian and gay couples and their families that challenges stereotypes and myths about this under-studied population.

Child Rearing Among Lesbians and Gay Men

Perhaps the most intriguing finding from Census 2000 was that more than one in five same-sex couples were raising children—which translates into more than 250,000 children being raised by openly gay and lesbian couples (Gates and Ost, 2004).[1] Evidence from the 2002 National Survey of Family Growth (NSFG) demonstrates that these couples represent only the tip of the lesbian and gay child-rearing iceberg. Not only does the Census understate the actual number of same-sex couples currently raising children, but it also does not take into account the growing desire and ability of gays and lesbians to have children in the future (Figure 1).[2] Among childless lesbians and gay men, four in ten lesbians and fully half of gay men want to have a child. Furthermore, a third of lesbians and one in six gay men already have children, even if they are not presently raising them as part of a couple (Macomber, Badgett, Gates, and Chambers, 2007).

So where are all of these children coming from? Among children under age 18 living with same-sex couples, only 7 percent are adopted and 1.5 percent are foster children.[3] The vast majority, more than 70 percent, are either the "natural born" child or a "step-child"

Figure 1

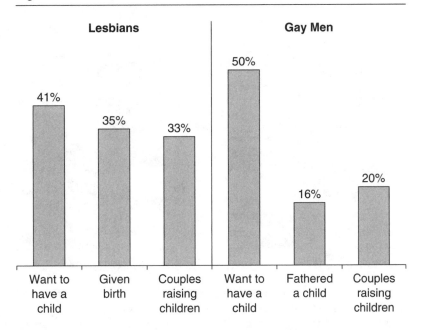

of the householder. An additional 5 percent are grandchildren, with another 5 percent other relatives such as siblings and cousins, and 10 percent are "non-relatives" (at least in relation to the householder). Clearly, a portion of the 70 percent of children who are "natural born" or "step-children" are likely the product of reproductive technologies like artificial insemination or surrogacy. Unfortunately, we have no way of estimating how common this practice is among same-sex couples or lesbian and gay people in general. However, given the expenses associated with these procedures and evidence regarding the economic disadvantage of many of these couples discussed below, it seems likely that a large portion of these children are the product of a prior heterosexual relationship. Not surprisingly, men and women in same-sex couples who were previously married are nearly twice as likely as their never-married counterparts to have a child under 18 in the home (Figure 2).

Contrary to most television images of same-sex couples raising children, diversity by race and ethnicity is one of the more striking demographic characteristics of such couples.

African-American and Latina women in same-sex couples are more than twice as likely as their white counterparts to be raising a child. And gay African-American men and Latinos are three times as likely to be raising children as are gay white men. Consistent with this finding, 40 percent of individuals in same-sex couples raising children are non-white. And more than half of the children of same-sex couples are non-white.

Same-sex couples raising children defy the stereotype of lesbian and gay people as wealthy, urban, sophisticates perhaps more than any segment of the lesbian and gay community. Across all racial and ethnic groups, same-sex couples raising children have lower median household incomes than do married couples raising children. The median household income of African-Americans in a same-sex couple raising children is more than 20 percent lower than that of their married counterparts. For Whites and Asian/Pacific Islanders, the comparable difference is about 10 percent (Sears and Gates, 2005). Clearly, same-sex couples raising children are not particularly wealthy (Figure 3).

Figure 2 Child under age 18 in the home

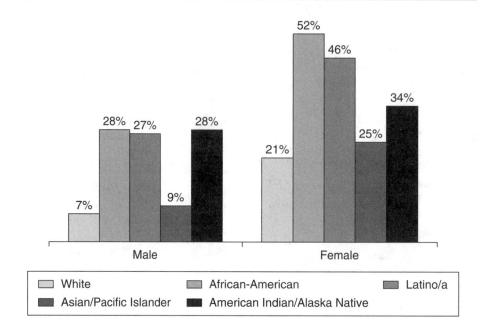

Figure 3 Median household income: Families raising children under age 18

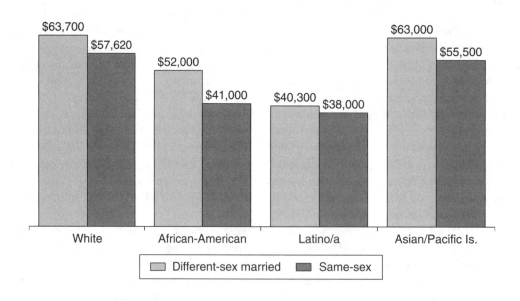

They also do not tend to live in areas known as gay enclaves. More than four in ten same-sex couples in Mississippi are raising children, making it the state where same-sex couples are most likely to have a child. Mississippi is followed by South Dakota, Alaska, South Carolina, and Louisiana. Among similarly ranking metropolitan areas, San Antonio, Texas, where more than 36 percent of same-sex couples are raising children, tops the list. The top five include Bergen-Passaic (New Jersey), Memphis, Houston, and Fort Worth (Gates and Ost, 2004).

Changes in the Future

As more gay men and lesbians feel free to come out about their identity and relationships, we are likely to see the similarities between gay and lesbian and heterosexual families become even greater. Polling from the last few decades demonstrates a marked change in American attitudes toward gay and lesbian people. In 1988, a Gallup poll found that only 33 percent of Americans thought that homosexual relations between consenting adults should be legal. By 2007, that figure had increased to 59 percent.[4] As the social stigma surrounding lesbians and gay men declines, more of them appear willing to "come out" on surveys and provide information about their sexual orientation and the nature of their relationships, and that process is now spreading beyond the urban areas where gays and lesbians historically felt freer to reveal their sexual orientation. In 1990, the first year that the Census used the "unmarried partner" category, there were more than 290,000 individuals who identified themselves as part of a same-sex couple in the United States (Smith and Gates, 2001). In 2000, the Census recorded nearly 1.2 million individuals in same-sex couples. By 2005, the figure had risen to more than 1.5 million (Gates, 2007). Analyses of the 2005 American Community Survey show that states throughout the Midwest have experienced the largest increases in same-sex couples since the Census 2000 (Gates, 2007). This offers further evidence that we need to alter our perception that lesbians and gay men are concentrated in the coastal regions of the country (Gates and Ost, 2004). As the proverbial closet doors open wider in areas such as the Midwest and the South, more gay men and lesbians will feel free to move to these regions and more long-term gay and lesbian residents in those regions will feel free to come out.

Changes in the location preferences of same-sex couples demonstrate this pattern. In 1990, 93 percent of self-identified same-sex couples were located in a metropolitan area, compared to just 80 percent of all American households. By 2000, this demographic gap had narrowed. While the rate at which all American households were located in a metropolitan area had not changed much (rising to 81 percent), the comparable figure for same-sex couples had dropped to 86 percent.[5] The U.S. Census Bureau defines "urban clusters" as areas with population densities that exceed 1,000 people per square mile. In 1990, about 75 percent of all American households lived in these urban areas compared to 90 percent of same-sex couples. By 2000, that gap too had narrowed, with 80 percent of all American households living in urban clusters compared to 84 percent of same-sex couples.

Child-rearing rates among same-sex couples are also on the rise, creating more convergence among heterosexual and same-sex couples. In 1990, only about 5 percent of same-sex male couples and 20 percent of same-sex female couples were raising children. By 2000, child-rearing rates had increased to nearly 20 percent of male couples and a third of female couples.

The racial and ethnic composition of same-sex couples provides a third example of the increasing similarity between the characteristics of same-sex and heterosexual couples. In 1990, 20 percent of Americans identified as non-white.[6] In that same year, only 13 percent of men and women who identified themselves as being in a same-sex couple were non-white. By Census 2000, the percentage of Americans who were non-white had risen to 30 percent. Among those in same-sex couples, the figure rose more dramatically to nearly a quarter who were non-white. The data suggest a demographic convergence of sorts. As lesbians and gay men in minority communities feel more comfortable in coming out, the "visible" gay community looks increasingly like the broader American population. Analyses of Census data provide clear evidence of a gay and lesbian community reflecting the diversity of America in family form, socio-economic status, and race and ethnicity.

Why Does This Matter?

Census data offer a portrait of lesbian and gay families that challenges monolithic and stereotyped images of them as wealthy, white, childless, and urban—an image that likely never reflected the truth about this diverse population. The demographic diversity of the lesbian and gay community has bearing on policy debates regarding marriage and adoption rights. Among other things, marriage provides legal and economic protections that cannot be completely replicated through non-marital legal contracts. For example, federal social security survival benefits are not awarded to same-sex partners nor can these partners file wrongful death lawsuits in states that do not recognize their relationships. These rights, so important to economic security in times of crisis like the death of a spouse, would certainly be even more important to lower-income same-sex couples.

Census analyses showing economic disadvantages among same-sex couples raising children are also cogent to these debates. Marriage and legal adoption provide myriad legal and economic protections specifically for parents and their children. In the absence of marriage or adoption, some partners in same-sex couples have no legal standing in relation to their children. Among other problems, this lack of standing could impact their ability to cover their children on employee healthcare plans and create difficulties in an emergency medical situation where the legal parent is not available to authorize appropriate care. Again, among lower-income lesbian and gay families, the rights and protections afforded by marriage and legal adoption can be even more critical.

Marriage and adoption rights for lesbians and gay men may be seen as luxuries by some members of the public, something that an affluent community wants as a whim or an abstract statement of principle. But these rights can be absolutely vital to lower-income people and their families, who, Census data confirm, comprise a large portion of the lesbian and gay community. The struggle for equal rights for sexual minorities should not be understood as merely a struggle among elites; it should be a key part of larger efforts promoting racial and social justice.

NOTES

1. Identification of same-sex couples in the 2000 U.S. Decennial Census relies on information provided about the nature of the relationship between the person who filled out the Census form and his or her relationship to other members of the household. If this person describes another adult of the same sex as his or her "unmarried partner" or "husband/wife," the couple counts as a same-sex unmarried partner household (see Gates and Ost, 2004 for a detailed explanation of counting same-sex couples). Because only couples are counted, the Census data do not capture single gay men, lesbians, or bisexuals nor do they offer a way to separately identify bisexuals or transgender individuals.

2. The Census most likely undercounts the population of same-sex couples. Concerns about revealing the nature of their relationships to the federal government may lead many same-sex couples not to use categories like "unmarried partner" or "husband/wife" to describe their partnerships. In addition, some couples may believe that "unmarried partner" or "husband/wife" does not accurately describe their relationship.

3. An estimated 65,500 adopted children and 14,000 foster children are living with a lesbian and gay parent, both single and partnered (Macomber, Badgett, Gates, and Chambers, 2007).

4. See http://www.galluppoll.com/content/?ci=27694 (accessed 5 July 2007).

5. Some caution should be noted in comparing same-sex couples identified in the 1990 and 2000 Census enumerations. The 2000 Census includes couples where one same-sex partner was identified as the "husband," "wife," or "unmarried partner" of the other partner. The 1990 counts only include couples where a same-sex partner is identified as an "unmarried partner." Same-sex spouses were not included in the 1990 counts.

6. Census Bureau figures report race and Hispanic/Latino(a) ethnicity separately. These figures for the percent of the non-white population are based only on reported race and therefore do not take ethnicity into account. Americans of any racial category may also be Hispanic or Latino/a.

REFERENCES

Gates, G.J., and Ost. J., *The Gay and Lesbian Atlas* (Washington: Urban Institute Press, 2004).

Gates, G.J., *Same-Sex Couples and the Gay, Lesbian, and Bisexual Population: New Estimates from the American Community Survey.* (Los Angeles: Williams Institute, University of California, 2007).

Gay and Lesbian Alliance Against Defamation. Network Responsibility Index, Primetime Programming 2006–2007, a special report. (2007).

Macomber, J.E., Badgett, M.V.L., Gates, G., and Chambers, K., *Adoption and Foster Care by Lesbian and Gay Parents in the United States.* (Washington, DC: The Urban Institute, The Williams Institute, UCLA School of Law, 2007).

Sears, R.B., and Gates, G.J., *Same-Sex Couples and Same-Sex Couples Raising Children in the United States: Data from Census 2000.* (Los Angeles: Williams Institute, University of California, 2005).

Smith, D., and Gates, G.J., *Gay and Lesbian Families in the United States: Same-Sex Unmarried Partner Households.* Human Rights Campaign Report (Washington, DC, 2001).

THINKING ABOUT THE READING

Gates uses social statistics to disprove many of the common stereotypes about gay and lesbian couples and their children. According to the data in this reading, what are some of the common characteristics of gay and lesbian couples with children? How does this social reality compare with the images of gays and lesbians seen on television and in movies? According to the logic in this reading, how would the legal and social benefits of marriage help these families?

Coping With Commitment

Dilemmas and Conflicts of Family Life

Kathleen Gerson

(1992)

Since 1950, when the breadwinner-homemaker household accounted for almost two-thirds of all American households, widespread changes have occurred in the structure of American family life. Rising rates of divorce, separation, and cohabitation outside of marriage have created a growing percentage of single-parent and single-adult households. The explosion in the percentage of employed women, and especially employed mothers, has produced a rising tide of dual-earner couples whose patterns of child rearing differ substantially from the 1950s' norm of the stay-at-home mother.... The breadwinner-homemaker model of family life has become only one of an array of alternatives that confront men and women as they build (and often change) their lives over the course of an expanded adulthood....

Incomplete and unequal social change has created new personal dilemmas over how to balance parental and employment commitments and new social conflicts between those who have developed "traditional" and "nontraditional" resolutions to the intransigent conflicts between family and workplace demands. These dilemmas and conflicts pose the central challenges to which new generations of women, men, and children must respond.

Personal Dilemmas and Family Diversity: The Consequences of Unequal Social Change

Social change in family structure remains inconsistent in two consequential ways. First, some social arrangements have changed significantly,

but others have not. Even though an increasing percentage of families depend on the earnings of wives and mothers, women continue to face discrimination at the workplace and still retain responsibility for the lion's share of household labor. Similarly, despite the growth of dual-earner and single-parent households, the structural conflicts between family and work continue to make it difficult for either women or men to combine child rearing with sustained employment commitment. The combination of dramatic change in some social arrangements (for example, women's influx into the labor force) and relatively little change in others (for example, employers' continuing expectation that job responsibilities should take precedence over family needs) has created new forms of gender inequality and new dilemmas for both women and men who confront the dual demands of employment and parenthood.

Second, social change is inconsistent because social groups differ greatly in how and to what degree they have been exposed to change. Not only are the alternatives that women and men face structured differently, but within each gender group, the alternatives vary significantly. A growing group of women, for example, have gained access to highly rewarded professional and managerial careers, but most women remain segregated in relatively ill-rewarded, female-dominated occupations. Similarly, the stagnation of real wages has eroded many men's ability to support wives and children on their paycheck alone, but most men still enjoy significant economic advantages. This variation in opportunities and constraints has, in turn, promoted contrasting orientations toward family change among differently situated groups of women and men. . . .

Choosing Between Employment and Motherhood

Although most women, including most mothers, now participate in the paid labor force, this apparent similarity masks important differences in women's responses to the conflicts between employment and motherhood. Not only do some mothers continue to stay home to rear children, but many employed women work part time or intermittently and continue to emphasize family over employment commitments. These "domestically oriented" women stand in contrast to a growing group of "nondomestic" women, who have developed employment ties that rival, and/or some surpass, family commitments. Women develop "domestic" or "nondomestic" orientations in response to specific sets of occupational and interpersonal experiences. These contrasting orientations to family life are not only rooted in different social circumstances; they also represent opposing responses to the conflict between motherhood and employment. . . .

All women face an altered social context, but they differ in how and to what extent they have been exposed to structural change. This uneven exposure to new opportunities and constraints has produced contrasting orientations toward employment and motherhood. . . .

Exposure to expanded opportunities outside the home (for example, upward employment mobility) and unanticipated insecurities within it (for example, marital instability or economic squeezes in the household) tends to promote a nondomestic orientation, even among women who once planned for full-time motherhood. Exposure to a more traditional package of opportunities and constraints (such as constricted employment options and stable marriage) tends, in contrast, to promote a domestic orientation even among those who felt ambivalent toward motherhood and domesticity as children. Both orientations reflect contextually sensible, if unexpected and largely unconscious, responses to the structural conflicts between employment and motherhood. . . .

Strategies of Domestically Oriented Women

Despite the forces leading other women out of the home, domestically oriented women confront ample reasons to avoid such a fate. Blocked occupational opportunities leave these women poorly positioned to enjoy the benefits of work outside the home. They have concluded that domestic pursuits offer significant advantages over workplace commitment. A homemaker and mother of two declared:

> I never plan to go back [to work]. I'm too spoiled now. I'm my own boss. I have independence; I have control; I have as much freedom as anyone is going to have in our society. No [paid] job can offer me those things.

Since their "freedom" depends on someone else's paycheck, domestically oriented women are willing to accept responsibility for the care of home and children in exchange for male economic support. As this disillusioned ex-schoolteacher and full-time mother of two pointed out, they have little desire to change places with their breadwinning husbands:

> I have met guys who were housepersons, but I can't see any reason [for it]. It would turn it all crazy for me to come home around five thirty, and he'd have to have things ready for me. I think if I thought that [bringing in a paycheck] was my role for the rest of my life, I would hate it. I don't want to be [my husband]; then I would have to go and fight the world. I don't want the pressures that he has to bear— supporting a family, a mortgage, putting in all those hours at the office. Ugh!

Whether or not they work, domestically oriented women put their family commitments first. When employed, they carefully define their work attachments as a discretionary choice that can be curtailed if necessary and that always comes second to their children's needs. A part-time clerk and mother of two defined paid work as a "job," not a career:

> I would never want to get us in a situation where I would *have* to work, because then I would really hate it. I don't work to have a career. Without a career, I can quit a job whenever I want. To have a career, you have to stick with it, and it takes a lot. I'd have to give up a lot of things my kids need, and it's not worth it to me. A job, I don't have to give up anything.

Although relatively insulated from the pushes and pulls that lead other women toward strong labor force attachment, domestically oriented women are nevertheless affected by the social changes taking place around them. The erosion of structural and ideological supports for a traditional arrangement has made their commitment to a family form based on a strict sexual division of labor problematic. The increased fragility of marriage, for example, poses an abiding, if unspoken, threat to domestic women's security. In the context of high divorce rates, homemaking women cannot assume that the relationships they depend on will last. This ex-clerk and mother of a young daughter complained:

> [Having a child] has made me more dependent on my husband. I think he was attracted to me because I was very independent, and now I'm very dependent. I don't know what I would do if things didn't work out between [us] and we had to separate and I had to go to work to support my child. I think I'd be going bananas. It's scary to me.

Even when their marriages are secure, domestically oriented women face other incursions on their social position. The rise of work-commitment among other women has not only provided an alternative to domesticity, it has also eroded the ideological hegemony that homemakers once enjoyed. Domestically oriented women feel unfairly devalued by others, as these ex-clerical workers explained:

> There are times when I have some trouble with my identity; that has to do with being a

mother. Because of society, sometimes the recognition or lack of it bothers me.

> People put no value on a housewife. If you have a job, you're interesting. If you don't you're really not very interesting, and sometimes I think people turn you off.

This ex-nurse added that even when economic pressures are weak, the social pressures to seek employment make domesticity a difficult choice:

> I have been feeling a lot of pressure . . . there's a lot of pressure on women now that you should feel like you want to work. Sometimes it's hard to know what you feel, because I really don't feel like I want to [work], but I think I *should* feel like I want to.

The erosion of the structural and ideological supports for domesticity has left domestically oriented women feeling embattled. They are now forced to defend a personal choice and family arrangement that was once considered sacrosanct. For these reasons, domestically oriented women cannot afford to take a neutral stance toward social change, and many have developed ideologies of opposition to other people's choices. Domestically oriented women tend to view employed mothers as either selfish and dangerous to children or overburdened and miserable, as these two homemakers suggested:

> I have a neighbor with young children who works just because she wants to. I get sort of angry . . . I think I resent the unfairness to the child. I don't know how to answer the argument that men can have families and work, but women can't. Maybe it's not fair, but that's the way it is.
>
> Most of the time all I hear from them is griping, and they're tired, and they're frantic to get everything done. It's a shame. I hate hurrying like that.

They viewed career-committed women as selfish, unattractive, and, at least in the case of childless women, unfulfilled:

> Women can [take on men's jobs], but it's a blood-and-guts type of a thing. Those who

make it are witches because they found out what they had to do to get there. [ex-saleswoman planning first child]

I feel like they're missing out on something. If they're going to make a long-term thing of it and never have children, I think they're missing something.

Finally, domestically oriented women support men's right and duty to be primary breadwinners. They frown on men who shirk their duties to support women and children. This homemaker and mother of two could not understand why "undependable" men were considered glamorous:

There's this mystique about the charismatic, not decent and dependable, sort of man. They're movie types. . . . My husband goes to work at eight and comes home at five, and [people] say, "Isn't that boring?" And I say, "No. Not at all," because it gives me time to do what I want.

Although their strategies have unfolded against the tide of social change, domestically oriented women illustrate the forces that not only limit the change but provide a powerful opposition to it. Their personal circumstances give them ample reason to view change as a dangerous threat to their own and their children's well-being, even when it leads in the direction of greater gender equality.

Strategies of Work-Committed Women

Work-committed women lack the option of domesticity, or the desire to opt for it, but they nevertheless face significant obstacles. Persistent wage inequality and occupational sex segregation continue to deny most employed women an equal opportunity to succeed at the workplace. In addition, limited change in the organization of work, especially in male-dominated occupations, combines with the "stalled revolution" in the sexual division of domestic work to make it difficult for employed women to integrate career-commitment with motherhood. Work-committed women have responded in several ways to this predicament. A small but significant proportion have decided to forgo childbearing altogether, but the majority of work-committed women are attempting to balance child rearing with strong labor force attachment.

Childless women have concluded that childbearing is an unacceptably dangerous choice in a world where marriage is fragile and motherhood threatens to undermine employment prospects. A strong skepticism regarding the viability of marriage led a divorced executive to reject childbearing:

[Having children] probably would set back my career . . . irretrievably. The real thing that fits in here is my doubts about men and marriage, because if I had real faith that the marriage would go on, and that this would be a family unit and be providing for these children, being set back in my career wouldn't be that big a deal. But I have a tremendous skepticism about the permanency of relationships, which makes me want to say, "Don't give anything up, because you're going to lose something that you're going to need later on, because [the man] won't be there.

Childless women also have considerable skepticism about men's willingness to assume the sacrifices and burdens of parenthood. Since gender equality in parenting seems out of reach, so does motherhood. For this childless physician, even avowedly egalitarian men appeared untrustworthy:

I would *never* curtail my career goals for a [child] . . . I would not subjugate my career any more than a man would subjugate his career. . . . [And] I don't know anybody who says he wants an egalitarian relationship. Among the married ones with children, everybody says, "Sure, we'll share with children equally." But nobody does.

Given the lack of structural supports for combining career commitment and childbearing, these women are convinced they must choose between the two. They have decided that the continuing obstacles to integrating employment and child rearing leave women facing a curiously "old-fashioned" choice between mutually exclusive alternatives:

> I think you either do one or the other. . . . You could have children and work, but you wouldn't really be a very senior sort of involved person. Although men can be presidents of companies and have children, women can't. [single interior designer]
>
> I just think that [children] are a responsibility, and you have to be willing to devote all your time to them. If you can't do that, I don't think you should have them. I know that's really old-fashioned, but I tend to believe it. [high school–educated secretary]

Most work-committed women, however, do eventually have children. Many hold the beliefs this lawyer voiced:

> I don't think it's fair that [working] women can't have kids. They make things fuller, more complete. I think it rounds out your life.

Work-committed mothers must create strategies to meet the competing demands of child rearing and employment. However, their strategic choices are severely limited by intransigence in the workplace. This aspiring banker lamented:

> [My bosses] figure that I'm to have my career, and what I do at home is my own business, but it better not interrupt the job. I've been pushed as far forward as I have because I was a maniac and I never went home.

Since most employers continue to penalize workers, regardless of gender, for parental involvement that interferes with the job, employed mothers have had to look elsewhere for relief from the competing demands of employment and child rearing. Three strategies, in particular, offer hope of easing their plight. First, employed mothers limit their demands by limiting family size. Although the two-child family remains the preferred alternative, the one-child family is gaining acceptance. This upwardly mobile office worker concluded:

> I know one child won't drive me crazy, and two might. I know I couldn't work and have two. . . . I don't think [one child] would affect [my work plans] at all. More than one would. That's one of the reasons I only want one.

Employed mothers must also reevaluate and alter the beliefs about child rearing they inherited from earlier generations, who frowned on working mothers. One work-committed office worker rejected the idea that children suffer when mothers work, despite having been raised by a full-time mother:

> I liked my mother being home, but I think it's okay for a mother to work. As long as she doesn't make her children give things up, and I don't think I'd make my children give anything up by me working.

Finally, work-committed mothers have engaged in a protracted struggle to bring men into the process of parenting. Their male partner's support of their independence gives them leverage to demand sharing, even if it doesn't guarantee that such sharing will be equal. A professor acknowledged:

> [My husband] respects my accomplishments. He wants me to keep doing something I enjoy. He wants me to be fairly independent, and he also wants his own independence . . . as long as he can support himself and half a child.

Some have decided that male parental involvement is a precondition to childbearing, as these upwardly mobile workers explained:

> I want [equal] participation, and without it I don't want children. I want it for the children, for myself. Without two people doing it, I think it would be a burden on one person. It's no longer a positive experience. [lawyer engaged to be married, in her early thirties]
>
> I think it's going to come to the point that if we're willing to have children, we work things out pretty much [equally] between ourselves.

And I think he would rather help out than to not have [children] at all. It's a two-way thing. [office manager in her late twenties]

In rejecting childlessness, most work-committed women have developed strategies to cope with the dual burdens of employment and motherhood. In addition to having smaller families, developing new ideologies about child rearing and mothering, and pressuring men to become involved fathers, work-committed mothers are challenging traditional work and family arrangements based on the assumption of a male worker with a wife at home or, at most, loosely tied to paid employment. Like their domestically oriented counterparts, the need to defend their choices against other people's disapproval encourages them to denigrate different resolutions to the conflict between employment and motherhood. From this perspective, it becomes tempting to define domestically oriented women as:

. . . kind of mentally underdeveloped and not too interesting. Let's face it, it's kind of boring. I guess I don't consider just having children as doing something.

Inconsistent and unequal social change has promoted differing strategic reactions among women that leave them socially divided and politically opposed. The contours of change, however, also depend on men's reactions to the emerging conflicts and dilemmas of family life.

Choosing Between Privilege and Sharing: Men's Responses to Gender and Family Change

While the transformation in women's lives has garnered the most attention, significant changes have also occurred in men's family patterns. The primary breadwinner who emphasizes economic support and constricted participation in child rearing persists, but this model—like its female counterpart, the homemaker—no longer predominates. Alongside this pattern, several alternatives have gained adherents. An increasing

proportion of men have moved away from family commitments—among them single and childless men who have chosen to forgo parenthood and divorced fathers who maintain weak ties to their offspring. Another group of men, however, has become more involved in the nurturing activities of family life. Although these "involved fathers" rarely assume equal responsibility for child rearing, they are nevertheless significantly more involved with their children than are primary breadwinners, past or present. Change in men's lives, while limited and contradictory, is nonetheless part of overall family change.

As with women's choices, men's family patterns reflect uneven exposure to structural change in family and work arrangements. . . .

Among men (as among women), different experiences and orientations promote contrasting strategies to cope with the tensions between maintaining male privilege and easing traditional male burdens.

Strategies of Primary Breadwinning Men

Just as domestically oriented women interpret the meaning of work through the lens of their family commitments, whether or not they are employed, so primary breadwinning men define their parental involvement in terms of income, whether or not their wives work. First, these men emphasize money, not time, in calculating their contributions to the household. For this surveyor, "good fathering" means being a good provider—that is, providing financial support, not participating in child rearing:

What is a good father? It's really hard to say. I always supported my children, fed them, gave them clothes, a certain amount of love when I had time. There was always the time factor. Maybe giving them money doesn't make you a good father, but not giving it probably makes you a bad father. I guess I could have done maybe a little more with them if financially I wasn't working all the time, but I've never hit my kids. I paid my daughter's tuition. I take them on vacation every year. Am I a good father? Yes, I would say so.

Even when their wives are employed, primary breadwinning men de-value the importance of wives' earnings. They define this income as "extra" and nonessential and thus also define a woman's job as secondary to her domestic responsibilities. Even though his wife worked hard as a waitress, this architect did not believe that she shared the duties of breadwinning:

> She took care of [our son], and I did all the breadwinning. When we got the house, she started working for extra money. She worked weekends, but her job doesn't affect us at all. Financially, my job takes care of everything plus. Her income is gravy, I guess you'd call it.

By defining fatherhood in terms of financial support and wives' income as supplementary and nonessential, primary breadwinners relieve themselves of the responsibility for domestic chores and of a sense of guilt that such an arrangement might generate. A park worker was proud to announce:

> I do nothing with the cooking or cleaning. I do no household, domestic anything. I could, but I won't, because I feel I shouldn't have to. If my wife's not sick, I see no reason why I should do it. I feel my responsibility is to bring home the money and her responsibility is to cook and clean.

And like the domestically oriented women who felt fortunate not to *have* to work, primary breadwinners see their wives as the fortunate recipients of personal freedom and material largesse. The park worker continued:

> My wife's got it made. The cat's got it made, too. I'm very good to my wife. She drives a new car, has great clothes, no responsibilities. She's very happy to be just around the house, do what she wants. She's got her freedom; what more could you want?

Although primary breadwinning men, like domestically oriented women, have been relatively insulated from the social-structural incentives that promote nontraditional choices among others, they, too, are affected by changes in others' lives. Despite stable employment and marriages, these men fear the erosion of the material and ideological supports for male privilege that their fathers could take for granted. As women have fought for equal rights at the workplace and other men have moved away from family patterns that emphasize separate spheres, those who remain committed to the "good provider" ethic feel embattled and threatened. Even the small gains made by women at the workplace are perceived as unfair as the historic labor market advantages of men undergo reconsideration, if not drastic alteration. A plumber and father of five resented the incursions some women are making into his field of expertise:

> Women have it a little easier as far as job-related [matters] is concerned [*sic*]. The tests are getting easier, classifications are going down [to let women in]. From what I hear in plants with women, they *can't* do the job. This isn't chauvinistic guys talking; this is guys talking in general. We pick up a 250-pound motor, but there's no way a young lady will pick it up unless she's a gorilla, a brute. But when she's got to do the job, two other guys have got to come along to help. I'm not saying women can't handle the job, [but] a woman comes to work for us, and they [the bosses] have got five men covering for her. Usually it's a hardship, but the guys bend over backwards for her. If she can't handle her job, why should she be there?

Similarly, primary breadwinners make a distinction between their situation and that of other men—especially childless, single men who, presumably, do not share their heavy economic responsibilities. They define their interests not just in terms of being a man, but a particular type of man who sacrifices for the good of his family and therefore needs to protect his interests in a hostile, changing world. The park worker explained:

> Being a father is a responsibility. If you don't have a wife, don't have children—you get fired, who cares? When you have someone who's depending on your salary, you protect your

interest on the job more. You become more afraid, and you become more practical. You realize you're out in the ocean, and nobody's going to help you. You're on your own, and you grow up real quick and start behaving like an adult.

In response to this perceived need to protect their interests, primary breadwinning men, like domestically oriented women, hold tightly to a set of social and political beliefs that emphasize the natural basis and moral superiority of gender differences and inequalities. Primary breadwinners argue that their own sexual division of labor is both natural and normal, as the plumber maintained:

As far as bread and butter is concerned, the man should have a little more [of] the responsibility than the woman. I'm not chauvinistic or anything, but it's basic, normal [that] it's a man. There aren't many men where the wife works full-time.
Who should take care of the children?
Again, you go back to whoever's home and whoever's working. Primary would be the mother. It's natural; it comes natural. In my house, it's my wife. She's doing it all.

If their own choices are viewed as natural and normal, then other patterns appear abnormal, unhealthy, and dangerous. Men who are unable or unwilling to meet the demands of breadwinning are judged to be moral and social failures, as the park worker pointed out.

The husband may not be able to provide. Just because he's a man, doesn't mean he can provide. There's a lot of losers out there, a lot of guys have a thirty-dollar-an-hour drug habit. How are they going to work? The wife might have to. Considering both people are normal, the breadwinner in my opinion should be the man.

Primary breadwinners hold similar beliefs about nondomestic patterns for women. Along with domestically oriented women, they tend to argue that career and motherhood are mutually exclusive alternatives for women and that responsible mothering requires forgoing a career. With five children and his own wife a homemaker, the plumber had little sympathy for mothers who feel the need for a life outside the home:

A career is a career; a family is a family. When you have a career, you donate your whole self to your career. If you have a family, you donate yourself to your family. [If a woman] has a career and no children, that's different. If she's a mother, her place should be at home. If she doesn't need the money, she has to have an ulterior motive for going to work. She's either tired of the kids or she's tired of being around the kids. If she's trying to keep her sanity, if she's unhappy at home, then she's got nobody to blame but herself, because she created that.

If a strict sexual division of caretaking and breadwinning is morally correct, it follows that current social changes are dangerous. Primary breadwinners tend to view these changes as hazardous for women as well as for men and children. Like their domestically oriented female counterparts, they argue, according to the park worker, that the decline of inequality threatens the historic protections women have enjoyed:

The woman should be protected, have a higher place. A mother is the most cherished thing you could be on this earth, and the woman should be respected and cared for. Equality would reduce that. A woman should be put on a pedestal above the man, and equality would put them on the same level. Why would they want to be equal with men who are dying earlier, under stress, who are really in the firing position? They already got it all. Equality for a woman would be the worst thing, because she already has the advantage. Women would lose from equality. Why would they want it? What is the need for it?

Despite their contrasting commitments, primary breadwinning men and domestically oriented women are interdependent in ways that lead their world views and political ideologies to converge. Their outlooks contrast not only with those of nondomestic women, but with those developed by nontraditional men as well.

Alternatives to Primary Breadwinning Among Men

Men who eschew primary breadwinning have concluded that the privileges afforded "good providers" are not worth the price that privilege entails. They view breadwinning responsibilities as burdensome and constricting, but their rejection of breadwinning poses its own dilemmas. The loosening bonds of marriage allow these men greater latitude to avoid parental responsibilities, both economic and social. On the other hand, the increasing number of work-committed women encourages and, indeed, pressures some nontraditional men to become more involved in the noneconomic aspects of family life than was typical of men a generation ago. These two patterns—forgoing parental commitments and becoming involved in caretaking—represent increasingly popular, if quite different, responses to the search for an alternative to traditional masculinity amid a contradictory and ambiguous set of options.

Forgoing Parental Commitments

Like permanently childless women, some men have opted to forgo parental responsibilities. This group includes childless men who do not wish or plan to become fathers and divorced fathers who have significantly curtailed their economic and social ties to their offspring in the wake of marital disruption. These men have come to value autonomy over commitment and to view children as a threat to their freedom of choice. A social service director, for example, was convinced that childlessness opened vocational options he would not have enjoyed as a breadwinning father:

What do you think things would be like if you did have kids?

Vocationally, I would have had to make other choices because the field I'm in just doesn't pay a terrific amount of money, and with children, you have expenses, and you have to look forward to a lot more future planning than I have to do with my current situation. So I've been able to sort of play with my career, and really just have a lot of fun in doing what I do, without having that responsibility.

Permanently childless men have decided that the potential benefits of fatherhood are not worth its risks. A childless psychologist admitted with some discomfort:

Does seeing other men with young children bring out any response in you?

Relief! [laughs] I don't just see the good parts; I see it all. I see the shit they have to wade through literally and figuratively, and very often I say to myself, "There but for the grace of God go I." It's a very ambivalent position I have about it.

This ambivalence toward fatherhood is not necessarily confined to childless men. Some divorced fathers also develop a relatively weak emotional and social attachment to their children. Whether their reaction is a defense against the pain of loss or an extension of their lack of involvement in child rearing prior to divorce, divorced fathers who become distant from their children tend to discount the importance of parenthood. A truck driver and divorced father of two, who sees his children and pays their child support sporadically, explained:

How would you feel if you had never had kids?

I don't think that would bother me. Being that I do have them, it's okay. I enjoy them when I see them. But if I never had them, I don't think I'd really miss them. I don't think it would be that important if they weren't there.

And even though this divorced dentist spent little time with his school-age daughter, who resided with her mother in another city, he envied his childless counterparts:

Men who don't have any children just seem to have more time to do the things they want to do and don't have to deal with the trials and tribulations of raising a child.

In contrast to traditional women and men, these men agree with work-committed women that traditional arrangements are neither inherently superior nor more natural family forms. Instead, they argue that primary bread-winning is oppressive to men and harmful to society. Though more vociferous than most, the psychologist, who at age 43 had never married, painted a vivid picture of the personal and social costs these men attach to male breadwinning:

> At this particular period in history, the woman is getting all the sympathy for her desperate position in the home by herself, lonely and isolated, taking care of these kids. I also have sympathy for the guy who has to be out getting his ass kicked by industrial tyrants and corporate assholes and the whole competitive complex. I think it's a tough life, and very often the man is tremendously underestimated, underrated.

Another confirmed bachelor, a childless free-lance writer, equated the woes of materialism with the "trap" of primary breadwinning:

> I just see these people, and they seem so closed and so materialistic, and it makes me sad for them. Because all this free spirit seems to go down the drain and they're trapped. I wrote a song called "When You're My Age, You'll Be Selling Insurance." It makes me happy that I managed to avoid it, that I haven't been trapped by that.

Although permanently childless men and uninvolved fathers have rejected the "good provider" ethos, they are less certain about what to put in its place. They reject traditional beliefs about gender, but they are also ambivalent about what gender equality should mean. In contrast to primary breadwinners and domestically oriented women, these men argue that gender differences are smaller, more malleable, and less desirable than traditional views suggest. A single, childless physician argued that perceived gender differences are socially constructed and reflect social evaluations of behavior rather than essential, sex-related characteristics:

> To me, the key to being a man, the same thing as being a woman, is being a good human being. For me, there's nothing that really defines being a man. It doesn't mean you can't cry. I could stay at home and be happy and have a lot of what would be quote feminine characteristics. In some situations, it helps to be macho, but a lot of that just reflects stereotypes. If it's a guy, he's aggressive; if it's a woman, she's a ball buster. One's negative; one's positive. And it can be the same behavior. Sometimes I wish it was a little clearer, but basically you've got to say, "What are you as an individual?"

If gender is socially constructed and thus malleable, it follows that it can be reconstructed in a different way. He believed that a change in the social definitions of gender is desirable:

> I look at the grief and anxiety my father had by being the sole provider. So if being a man is being the rock and support of your family, let's change that definition of being a man. Because that doesn't look very good to me.

Although men who have opted for freedom from parental commitments argue that gender differences are neither natural nor necessarily desirable, they remain ambivalent about what gender does or should mean. They believe that gender equality is a desirable goal, but equality defined in a specific and limited way. They emphasize women's equal responsibilities in the context of equal rights. For these men, equality means exactly what domestically oriented women fear it will mean—that women should relinquish the economic and legal "protections" that have accompanied their second-class status. As the divorced truck driver, quoted earlier, argued:

> [If] women want equal rights, let them pay child support, alimony. Let them get drafted.

You want to be equal, you do everything equal not just certain things. They got girls now in the sanitation department. God bless them if that's what [they] want to do, but when it comes down to it, you've got to pick up that pail and dump it in the truck. I'm not going to go over and help you. You want the job, you do what I do and that's it.

Similarly, these men support women's economic self-sufficiency, for their own ability to remain autonomous is closely linked to women's independence. A systems analyst who had never married declared:

I'm not really big on women who stay at home and just raise kids. I think everybody should be a fully functioning, self-supporting adult, and certainly economically that's necessity now. I believe, in terms of women's issues, that if they prepared themselves for the idea that they have to assume their financial burdens and responsibilities, they won't have to be emotional hostages to toxic relationships. And men won't either.

This vision of economic and social equality does not, however, easily extend to the domestic sphere. Because these men place a high value on their freedom, they resist applying the principle of equality to child rearing. Indeed, the paradox of espousing the equal right to be free while resisting the equal responsibility for parenthood leads them to avoid parental commitments. The systems analyst feared he would be drawn into what he deemed the least attractive aspects of parenting:

[If I had a child,] I could see that I would want to take a role in playing with the child, overseeing its training and schooling, providing that type of thing. I don't really see me wanting to do a lot in the way of getting up in the middle of the night, formulas, changing diapers. I'm not at all into that.

And so, these men are able to resolve the dilemma between their support of some aspects of gender equality and their resistance to its more threatening implications only by

forgoing both the burdens and the joys of raising a child.

Caretaking Fathers

A more equal sharing of both earning income and rearing children provides another alternative to primary breadwinning. While complete equality remains rare even among dual-earner couples, male participation in caretaking is nevertheless on the rise. Men who are married to work-committed women and divorced fathers who have retained either joint or sole custody of their children are particularly likely to participate in child rearing. In contrast to childless men, these men have placed family at the center of their lives. In contrast to primary breadwinners, they value spending time with their families as much as contributing money to them. A utility worker with a young daughter and a wife employed as a marketing manager insisted:

For me, being with my family is the major, the ultimate in my life—to be with them and share things with them. Money is secondary, but time with them is the important thing in life. That's why I put up with this job—because I can get home early. To me, spending time with [my daughter] makes up for it. I'm home at 3:40 and spend a lot of time with her, just like the long days when she was young and I was on unemployment.

Some involved fathers view the time spent in child care not as simply helping out, but as an incomparably pleasurable activity and an essential component of good parenting. This thirty-seven-year-old construction worker chose to work the night shift so that he could spend his days with his newborn daughter while his wife pursued a dancing career:

I take care of [my daughter] during the morning and the day. [My wife] takes care [of her] in the evenings. I work from three to eleven P.M. and wake up with the morning ahead of me, and that's important with a little one. Even if I'm pretty tired when I get up, all I have to do is look at that little face, and I feel good. It's not just a case of doing extra things. I'm not doing extra things. This is what has to be done when you have a baby. . . . You learn so much too. It's a thrill to watch the various senses start to come into play. She'll make a gurgling noise that's close to a vowel sound or an actual syllable, and I'll repeat it. I love the communication. The baby smiles more around me than she does around [her mother].

Unlike primary breadwinners or childless men, these "involved fathers" do not draw distinct boundaries between the tasks of mothers and fathers. The time constraints on their wives combine with their own need and preference for economic sharing to promote financial and social interdependence. Neither breadwinning nor nurturing is defined as one person's domain. As the utility worker pointed out:

It's not like, "Give me your money, and I hold it; or you take my money and hold it." We put it in one pot and take care of whatever we need. . . . We pull the same weight. . . . As far as time and being around the house is concerned, I can stay home more than [my wife] can stay home. I come home in the afternoon, and I'm here with [my daughter] after school. [My wife] can come home at night to be with her. She likes her job, and she likes the sharing. She's got both worlds. So it has worked out good.

Like employed mothers, involved fathers must juggle the dual demands of employment and parenthood. While men do not generally jeopardize their chances for workplace success by becoming fathers, those men who wish to spend time with their children must trade off between work and family in much the same kinds of ways that employed mothers do. A bank vice-president, married to a woman with a career in public relations, began to relax his obsessive work habits when his daughter was born:

They changed immediately, which is exactly what I expected would happen, and I've never really gone back to my old habits of working all the time. I still work long days in the office, but

I get home every night to relieve the babysitter by six. I hardly ever work on weekends, and I don't work at home. So, yes, my habits have changed.

These involved fathers come closest to embracing the "interdependent" vision of gender equality upheld by work-committed mothers. They see moral and practical advantages to shared caretaking. According to the construction worker quoted earlier, domestic as well as workplace equality is not only the most practical response to changed economic conditions but also the best way to avoid the resentment and conflict that too often occur between husbands and wives:

With the baby, we do everything even-steven. What other way can you go nowadays, the whole economy being what it is? But that's also the way it should be. Even if I had the money to take of things [myself], [my wife] has a calling, a vocation, that she needs to fulfill and I want her to fulfill. We're in this together; we both want to be an influence on the child. The next logical step is for both of us to spend time with her. . . . I feel there won't be any of this women-against-men in our marriage.

If work-committed women face numerous obstacles in their search for ways to combine career and motherhood, then nurturing fathers also face deeply rooted structural barriers to full equality in parenting. Even when the desire to participate in parenting is strong, these men encounter significant constraints on implementing their preferences. Role reversal, for example, is rarely a realistic option, since men's wages remain essential to the survival of the vast majority of households and few couples are comfortable with an arrangement in which a woman supports a man. The utility worker found being a "househusband" unacceptable, despite his preference for not working:

Is there an ideal job for you?
    Staying home. But, it's just not possible. I couldn't just quit and say, "You work, and I'll stay home." But if we were put into the

situation where we didn't have to work, I could tell her we could both quit. When I hit the Lotto . . . but right now, I'm stuck.

Were it not for the economic and psychological need to earn a steady income through paid employment, these men might be far more involved in child rearing than is currently possible. Yet, as the supports for homemaking mothers erode, supports for homemaking fathers have not arisen to offset the growing imbalance between children's needs and families' resources. Like domestically oriented women, a rehabilitation counselor defined paid work in terms of a "job," not a "career." Unlike such women, however, he lacked the option to trade his paid but tiresome job for the more personally fulfilling work of parenting:

> I don't like to work. I work because I need the money, and I want to give my family the best I could [sic], but work's not that important to me. I'm not the type that has career aspirations and [is] very goal-oriented. To tell you the truth, if I won the lottery, and I didn't have to work, I wouldn't. But I would volunteer. I would work in a nursery school. I would do a lot more volunteer work with my daughter's school. I would love to go on trips that the mothers who don't work get a chance go to on. I would like to be more active in the PTA, get my hands into a lot of different volunteer organizations. I would *love* that. But I can't.

In sum, while women grapple with the choice between motherhood and committed employment, men are generally denied such a choice. Even when a man wishes to be an involved father, rarely is he able to trade full-time employment for parental involvement. The primary breadwinning surveyor noted, with some envy, that although women remain disadvantaged, many still retain the option not to work—an option few men enjoy:

> Women can have the best of both worlds, whereas men can only have one choice. A woman has a choice of which way she wants to go. If she wants to be a successful lawyer, she has that choice. If she wants to stay home, she

also has that choice most of the time. Women have doors opened for them and their meals paid for. They have the best of both worlds; men are just stuck with one.

Structural and ideological barriers to men's participation in child rearing inhibit the prospects for genuine equality in parental and employment options. Limits on men's options constrain even the most feminist men's ability and willingness to embrace genuine symmetry in gender relations. The truncated range of choices available to men restricts the options open to women as well.

Beyond the Debate on the Family

Social change in family arrangements has expanded the range of options adult women and men encounter, but the inconsistent nature of change has also created new personal dilemmas, more complex forms of gender inequality, and a growing social and ideological cleavage between more traditional family forms and the emerging alternatives. Since people have different exposure to changes in the structure of marriage, the economy, and the workplace, they have developed contrasting responses. Some have developed new patterns of family life that emphasize either greater freedom from family commitments (for example, childless women and men and uninvolved divorced fathers) or more equal sharing of breadwinning responsibilities (for example, work-committed women and involved fathers). Others have endeavored to re-create a more traditional model of gender exchange in spite of the social forces promoting change (for example, women who are domestically oriented and men who are primary breadwinners). The growth of alternative patterns of family life amid the persistence of more traditional forms has not produced a new consensus to replace the old, but rather an increasing competition among a diverse range of family types. This range cuts across gender, as different groups of women and of men find themselves in opposing positions. The complex landscape of emerging family patterns defies generalizations about either the decline or persistence of American families. Instead, men and women are developing multiple "family strategies" and contradictory directions of change to cope with the contrasting dilemmas they confront.

If the uneven and inconsistent nature of change has produced social division and political conflict in the short run, then the long-run fate of American family life depends on finding genuine resolutions to the dilemmas and conflicts that make all family choices problematic. Such an approach would move beyond a "zero-sum" politics of the family to acceptance of and support for diversity in family life; it would reduce the barriers to integrating work and family for employed parents of either sex;

and it would promote gender equality in rights, responsibilities, and options regarding parenting and employment. The conflicts and dilemmas spawned by uneven social change can only be resolved by striving to make change itself more equal and consistent. . . .

In this context, the central political challenge should not be defined as how to halt the so-called decline of the family. Instead, we need to find a way to transcend the conflicts among the emerging array of "family groups." Surely, the first step is to abandon the search for one, and only one, correct family form in favor of addressing the full range of dilemmas and needs spawned by inevitable but unequal change. Only then will citizens and policymakers be able to forge a humane and just set of opportunities for all parents and their children.

THINKING ABOUT THE READING

Make a list of the factors that Gerson uses to explain the different choices people make about work and family. According to Gerson, do people usually end up taking the family role they planned, or do their lives shift as they cope with unexpected choices? Discuss the relationship between "family values" and economic structure. In your estimation, who benefits most from a traditional family arrangement? What kind of arrangement do you think would be most beneficial to all family members? What kind of employment and economic situation would support this arrangement? Do you think the current structure of the labor force in the United States reflects the realistic lives of most families? Explore some of the different arrangements in other countries. Do these differing arrangements suggest anything about the connection between cultural ideologies and law and economics?

Constructing
Difference

Social Deviance

8

According to most sociologists, deviance is not an inherent feature or personality trait. Instead, it is a consequence of a definitional process. Like beauty, it is in the eye of the beholder. Deviant labels can impede everyday social life by forming expectations in the minds of others. Some sociologists argue that the definition of deviance is a form of social control exerted by more powerful people and groups over less powerful ones.

At the structural level, the treatment of people defined as deviant is often more a function of *who* they are than of *what* they did. In particular, sex, age, class, ethnic, and racial stereotypes often combine to influence social reactions to individuals who have broken the law. In "Watching the Canary," Lani Guinier and Gerald Torres provide several explanations for the disproportionate number of black and brown young men in U.S. prisons. They examine the intersection of racial profiling tactics, the war on drugs, and our mass incarceration policies to illustrate why these men are at greater risk for arrest. On the basis of race, these men are already defined as deviant and often expected to be engaged in criminal activity.

Similarly, our perceptions of deviant social problems can also be influenced by the identities of people most closely associated with the behavior in question. The use of marijuana is frequently associated with the stereotype of the "pothead." Who uses marijuana for medical purposes and how do these individuals negotiate the deviant identity and politics associated with its use? It may surprise readers to learn that this group consists of children and older people as well as individuals who might normally be seen as possible "pot" users. In "Patients, 'Potheads,' and Dying to Get High" Wendy Chapkis describes the various strategies that providers and users of medical marijuana engage in to offset the impression of the deviant "pothead."

The definitional process that results in the labeling of some people as deviant can occur at the institutional as well as the individual level. Powerful institutions are capable of creating a conception of deviance that the public comes to accept as truth.

One such institution is the field of medicine. We usually think of medicine as a benevolent institution whose primary purpose is to help sick people get better. But in "Medicine as an Institution of Social Control," Peter Conrad and Joseph W. Schneider show how medical vocabularies and ideologies shape public perceptions of deviance.

They show how various types of problematic behavior, previously considered crimes or sins, come to be seen as illnesses. We usually think of the individuals and organizations that make up the criminal justice system (police, courts, prisons) as the agents responsible for controlling deviance. But a medicalized view of deviance has given rise to a system of social control made up of physicians, psychiatrists, psychologists, counselors, and other specialists. The authors describe the important social implications of conceiving of deviance as a "disorder" that can and should be "treated" and "cured."

Something to Consider as You Read

In reading and comparing these selections, consider who has the power to define others as deviant. Think about the role of social institutions in establishing definitions of deviance. For example, how does medicine or religion or law participate in describing certain behaviors as abnormal and/or immoral and/or illegal? Does it make a difference which social institution defines certain behaviors as deviant? Why do you think certain deviant behaviors fall under the domain of medicine and others fall under the domain of the law? For instance, over time, alcohol use has moved from being an illegal activity to being a medical condition. Who makes the decisions to define certain behaviors not only as deviant but as deviant within a particular social domain?

Watching the Canary

Lani Guinier and Gerald Torres

(2002)

"To my friends, I look like a black boy. To white people who don't know me I look like a wanna-be punk. To the cops I look like a criminal." Niko, now fourteen years old, is reflecting on the larger implications of his daily journey, trudging alone down Pearl Street, backpack heavy with books, on his way home from school. As his upper lip darkens with the first signs of a moustache, he is still a sweet, sometimes kind, unfailingly polite upper-middle-class black boy. To his mom and dad he looks innocent, even boyish. Yet his race, his gender, and his baggy pants shout out a different, more alarming message to those who do not know him. At thirteen, Niko was aware that many white people crossed the street as he approached. Now at fourteen, he is more worried about how he looks to the police. After all, he is walking while black.

One week after Niko made these comments to his mom, the subject of racial profiling was raised by a group of Cambridge eighth graders who were invited to speak in a seminar at Harvard Law School. Accompanied by their parents, teachers, and the school principal, the students read essays they had written in reaction to a statement of a black Harvard Law School student whose own arrest the year before in New York City had prompted him to write about racial profiling.[1] One student drew upon theories of John Locke to argue that "the same mindset as slavery provokes police officers to control black people today." Another explained a picture he had drawn showing a black police officer hassling a black woman because the officer assumed she was a prostitute. Black cops harass black people too, he said aloud. "It just seems like all the police are

angry and have a lot of aggression coming out." A third boy concluded that when the cops see a black person they see "the image of a thug." Proud that he knew the *American Heritage Dictionary*'s definition of a thug—a "cut-throat or ruffian"—he concluded that the cops are not the key to understanding racial profiling. Nor did he blame the white people who routinely crossed the street as he approached. If what these white people see is a thug, "they would normally want to pull their purse away." He blamed the media for this "psychological enslavement," as well as those blacks who allowed themselves to be used to "taint our image."

One boy spoke for fifteen minutes in a detached voice, showing little emotion; but he often strayed from his prepared text to describe in great detail the story of relatives who had been stopped by the police or to editorialize about what he had written. Only after all the students left did the professor discover why the boy had talked so long—and why so many adults had shown up for this impromptu class.

Several of the boys, including the one who had spoken at length, had already had personal encounters with the police. Just the week before, two of the boys had been arrested and had spent six hours locked in separate cells. . . .

Watching the Canary

Rashid and Jonathan (not their real names) are the sons of a lawyer and a transit employee, respectively. "Why don't you arrest *them*?" one of the boys asked the officer, referring to the white kids walking in the same area. "We only have two sets of cuffs," the officer replied. These cops knew whom to take in: the white kids were innocent; the black boys were guilty.

In the words of one of their classmates, black boys like Rashid and Jonathan are viewed as thugs, despite their class status. Aided by the dictionary and the media, our eighth-grade informant says this is racial profiling. Racial profiling, he believes, is a form of "psychological enslavement." . . .

But these black boys are not merely victims of racial profiling. They are canaries. And our political-race project asks people to pay attention to the canary. The canary is a source of information for all who care about the atmosphere in the mines—and a source of motivation for changing the mines to make them safer. The canary serves both a diagnostic and an innovative function. It offers us more than a critique of the way social goods are distributed. What the canary lets us see are the hierarchical arrangements of power and privilege that have naturalized this unequal distribution.

. . . We have urged those committed to progressive social change to watch the canary—and to assure the most vulnerable among us a space to experiment with democratic practice and discover their own power. Even though the canary is in a cage, it continues to have agency and voice. If the miners were watching the canary, they would not wait for it to fall off its perch, legs up. They would notice that it is talking to them. "I can't breathe, but you know what? You are being poisoned too. If you save me, you will save yourself. Why is that mine owner sending all of us down here to be poisoned anyway?" The miners might then realize that they cannot escape this life-threatening social arrangement without a strategy that disrupts the way things are.

What would we learn if we watched these particular two black boys? First, we would discover that from the moment they were born, each had a 30 percent chance of spending some portion of his life in prison or jail or under the supervision of the criminal justice system. . . . Among black men between the ages of 18 and 30 who drop out of high school,

more become incarcerated than either go on to attend college or hold a job.[2] . . .

In the United States, if young men are not tracked to college and they are black or brown, we wait for their boredom, desperation, or sense of uselessness to catch up with them. We wait, in other words, for them to give us an excuse to send them to prison. The criminal justice system has thus become our major instrument of urban social policy.

David Garland explains that imprisonment has ceased to be the incarceration of individual offenders and has instead become "the systematic imprisonment of whole groups of the population"—in this case, young black and Latino males in large urban municipalities. Or as the political scientist Mary Katzenstein observes, "Policies of incarceration in this country are fundamentally about poverty, about race, about addiction, about mental illness, about norms of masculinity and female accommodation among men and women who have been economically, socially, and politically demeaned and denied."[3] . . .

But how does this "race to incarcerate" happen disproportionately to young black and Latino boys? Why is it that increasingly the nation's prisons and jails have become temporary or permanent cages for our canaries? One reason is that white working-class youth enjoy greater opportunities in the labor market than do black and Latino boys, owing in part to lingering prejudice. . . .

A second reason for the disproportionate impact of incarceration on the black and brown communities is the increased discretion given to prosecutors and police officers and the decreased discretion given to judges, whose decisions are exposed to public scrutiny in open court, unlike the deals made by prosecutors and police. Media sensationalism and political manipulation around several high profile cases (notably Willie Horton and Polly Klaas) led to mandatory minimum sentences in many states. Meanwhile, laws such as "three strikes and you're out" channeled unreviewable discretion to prosecutors, who decide which strikes to call and which to ignore. . . .

A third and, according to some commentators, the most important explanation for the disproportionate incarceration of black and Latino young men is the war on drugs. In this federal campaign—one of the most volatile issues in contemporary politics—drug users and dealers are routinely painted as black or Latino, deviant and criminal. This war metaphorically names drugs as the enemy, but it is carried out in practice as a massive incarceration policy focused on black, Latino, and poor white young men. It has also swept increasing numbers of black and Latina women into prison. . . .

Presidents Ronald Reagan and George Bush had a distinct agenda, according to Marc Mauer: to "reduce the powers of the federal government," to "scale back the rights of those accused of crime," and to "diminish privacy rights."[4] Their goal was to shrink one branch of government (support for education and job training), while enlarging another (administration of criminal justice). Mauer concludes that the political and fiscal agendas of both the Reagan and first Bush administrations were quite successful. They reduced the social safety net and government's role in helping the least well off. Their success stemmed, in part, from their willingness to "polarize the debate" on a variety of issues, including drugs and prison.

Racial targeting by police (racial profiling) works in conjunction with the drug war to criminalize black and Latino men. Looking for drug couriers, state highway patrols use a profile, developed ostensibly at the behest of federal drug officials, that suggests black and Latinos are more likely to be carrying drugs. The disproportionate stops of cars driven by blacks or Latinos as well as the street sweeps of pedestrians certainly helps account for some of the racial disparity in sentencing and conviction rates. And because much of the drug activity in the black and Latino communities takes place in public, it is easier to target. . . .

A fourth explanation for the high rates of incarceration of black and brown young men is the economic boon that prison-building has brought to depressed rural areas. Prison construction has become—next to the military—our society's major public works program. And as prison construction has increased, money spent on higher education has declined, in direct proportion. Moreover, federal funds that used to go to economic or job training programs now go exclusively to building prisons. . . .

A fifth explanation is the need for a public enemy after the Cold War. Illegal drugs conveniently fit that role. President Nixon started this effort, calling drugs "public enemy number one." George Bush continued to escalate the rhetoric, declaring that drugs are "the greatest domestic threat facing our nation" and are turning our cities "into battlegrounds." By contrast, the use and abuse of alcohol and prescription drugs, which are legal, rarely result in incarceration. . . .

When drunk drivers do serve jail time, they are typically treated with a one- or two-day sentence for a first offense. For a second offense they may face a mandatory sentence of two to ten days. Compare that with a person arrested and convicted for *possession* of illegal drugs. Typical state penalties for a first-time offender are up to five years in prison and one to ten years for a second offense. . . .

We do not, by any means, claim to have exhaustively researched the criminal justice implications of racial profiling, the war on drugs, or our nation's mass incarceration policies. What we do claim is that canary watchers should pay attention to these issues if they want to understand what is happening in the United States. The cost of these policies is being subsidized by all taxpayers; one immediate result is that government support for other social programs has become an increasingly scarce resource.

NOTES

1. Bryonn Bain, "Walking While Black," *The Village Voice*, April 26, 2000, at 1, 42. Bain and his brother and cousin were arrested, held overnight and then released, with all charges eventually dropped, after the police in New York City, looking for young men who were throwing bottles on the

Upper West Side, happened upon Bain et al. as they exited a Bodega. Bain, at the time, had his laptop and law books in his backpack, because he was enroute to the bus station where he intended to catch a bus back to Cambridge. Bain's essay in *The Voice* generated 90,000 responses.

2. Bruce Western and Becky Pettit, "Incarceration and Racial Inequality in Men's Employment," 54 *Industrial and Labor Relations Review* 3 (2000).

3. "Remarks on Women and Leadership: Innovations for Social Change," sponsored by Radcliffe Association, Cambridge, Massachusetts, June 8, 2001. In her talk, Katzenstein cites David Garland. "Introduction: The Meaning of Mass Imprisonment," 3(1) *Punishment and Society* 5–9 (2001).

4. Marc Mauer. (1999) *Race to Incarcerate*, New York: New Press.

THINKING ABOUT THE READING

Make a list of the social factors that Guinier and Torres link to the high incarceration rate of African American and Latino men. Discuss why these factors may affect these men more than white men. Do you think economic opportunity is related to these factors? In other words, are all African American and Latino men equally at risk for incarceration? What other factors do you think might be part of this equation? Groups who oppose the death penalty often argue that it is applied unevenly and discriminates among certain groups of people. Discuss this argument in light of what you have just read. As you think about this, consider each of the phases of the judicial process: processes of arrest, the decision to charge with a crime, availability of legal defense, jury selection, and sentencing guidelines. Who or what is making the decisions in each of these instances? Do you think the different people and agencies involved in each step of the process are all in agreement, or might there be disagreement between, say, the police, judges, and lawmakers? How might these relationships affect the likelihood of a defendant being treated "justly"?

Patients, "Potheads," and Dying to Get High

Wendy Chapkis

(2006)

The Wo/Men's Alliance for Medical Marijuana (WAMM) is an organization that is not easily classified. WAMM is not, as the federal Drug Enforcement Administration (DEA) might suggest, a cover for illicit drug dealing to recreational users, but neither is it properly characterized as a pharmacy dispensing physician-recommended medicine. In this article, I describe briefly the origins of WAMM and then discuss the problem of trying to divide medical marijuana users into "real patients" and "potheads." Such classification is complicated further by the relationship between medicinal cannabis use and the experience of getting "high."

What Is WAMM?

WAMM was founded in California in 1993 by medical marijuana patient Valerie Corral and her husband, Michael Corral, a master gardener. In April 2004, WAMM drew national and international attention when it successfully won a temporary injunction against the U.S. Justice Department; as a result, the alliance now operates the only nongovernmental legal medical marijuana garden in the country. The organization is unique in other respects as well. It is organized as a *cooperative*. Marijuana is grown and distributed collectively and *without charge* to the 250 patient participants. Instead of paying for their marijuana, members are expected, as their health permits, to contribute volunteer hours to the organization by working in the garden; assisting with fund-raising; making cannabis tinctures,

milk, capsules, and muffins; or volunteering in the office.

Over a five-year period (from 1999 to 2004), I conducted more than three dozen interviews with WAMM members about their involvement with the organization and their therapeutic use of marijuana. The WAMM members interviewed for this article reported use of marijuana with a physician's recommendation for a range of conditions including nausea related to chemotherapy (for cancer and AIDS), spasticity (multiple sclerosis), seizures (epilepsy), and chronic and acute pain. In order to become members of WAMM, each of the patient participants had to discuss with his or her doctor the possible therapeutic value of marijuana and to have been told explicitly (and in writing) that cannabis might prove useful in managing the specific symptoms associated with his or her illness, disability, or course of treatment. The number of members the program can accommodate is limited by the amount of marijuana the organization is able to grow. There is an extensive waiting list to join the organization; with more than 80% of its members living with a life-threatening illness, the standing joke is that "people are literally dying to get into WAMM."

Financial support for the organization comes largely from external donations. In 1998, however, the federal government revoked WAMM's nonprofit status on the grounds that it was involved in supplying a federally prohibited substance. WAMM's struggle for survival further intensified in the fall of 2002 when the federal DEA raided the WAMM garden and arrested the two cofounders (to date, no charges have been filed against them). Despite these challenges, WAMM has continued to operate with the full support of California's elected officials and in close cooperation with local law enforcement. In April 2004, Judge Jeremy Fogel of the federal district court in San Jose (citing a recent Ninth Circuit Court of Appeals decision, *Raich v. Ashcroft,* soon to be reviewed by the U.S. Supreme Court) barred the Justice Department from interfering with the Corrals, WAMM patients, or the collective's garden. The federal injunction has provided at least temporary respite in the ongoing battle with the federal government.

Who Are the WAMM Members? "Worthy Patients" or "Unworthy Potheads"?

Dorothy Gibbs is the sort of patient voters are encouraged to imagine when the question of medical marijuana is before them. At ninety-four and confined to a bed in a Santa Cruz nursing home, this WAMM member is hardly the stereotypical "pothead" many critics believe to be hiding behind the medical marijuana movement. Cannabis, for Dorothy Gibbs, has never been anything but a medicine, a particularly effective analgesic that relieves severe pain associated with her post-polio syndrome:

> I never smoked marijuana before; I had no reason to. But the relief I got was wonderful and long lasting and pretty immediate, too. I didn't really have any misgivings about using marijuana; I figured it had to be better than what I'd got. They had me on lots of other medications, but I couldn't stand them; they made me so sick.

Most Americans (80% according to a recent CNN/Time poll; Stein, 2002) support the right of seriously ill patients like Dorothy Gibbs to access and use medical marijuana. This broad support is coupled, however, with lingering concerns that medical marijuana

may be, as described in *Time* magazine, largely "a kind of ruse" (Stein). From this perspective, medical marijuana campaigns are seen as a cover for drug legalization and most, if not all, "medicinal use" as nothing more than a recreational habit dressed up in a doctor's recommendation.

Tensions between medical and social uses of marijuana are unavoidable in a political context in which nonmedicinal use is at once widespread, formally prohibited, and often severely punished. Because of the social and legal penalties associated with recreational use, it is reasonable that some consumers would attempt to acquire a measure of legitimacy and protection by identifying a medical need for marijuana. Medical marijuana users, then, become divided in the public arena between patients, like Dorothy Gibbs, who have never used marijuana except as a medicine, and "pretenders" who have a social relationship to the drug. As with other discreditable identities (like the prostitute, the poor person, or the single mother), a line is then drawn between a small class of deserving "victims" and a much larger group of the willfully bad who are unworthy of protection or support.

Such divisions are both illusory and dangerous. In the case of marijuana use, the identities of medical and social users are not neatly dichotomous. Some medical users have had prior experience with marijuana as a means of enhancing pleasure before they had occasion to become familiar with its potential in relieving pain. Other patients discovered the reasons for the plant's popularity as a recreational drug only after being introduced to it for a more narrowly therapeutic purpose.

With the majority of WAMM members living with life-threatening conditions and many of the chronically ill confined to wheelchairs, this is an organization that presents the legitimate face of medical marijuana, the sick and dying who are widely seen as deserving of the drug. Yet even within this population, neat divisions between medical and social users are unworkable. "Di," for example, a WAMM member in her midforties living with AIDS, acknowledges,

> I'm just going to be totally honest—it wasn't AIDS that introduced me to pot. I had smoked marijuana as a kid and I liked it even then. When I tested positive in 1991, I felt that it was kind of a benefit that I got to use the term "medical marijuana," but I didn't quite own it as medicine because it had just been my lifestyle. But then, a few years ago, I traveled out of state [without access to marijuana]. I spent a week traveling and then went to Florida with my mom. By the time we got there, I was in so much pain from the neuropathy, I couldn't get up. We went to Urgent Care and they gave me morphine. The pain just wouldn't go away. I took the morphine for a week until I got back to California. When I got home, I started smoking pot again as normal and it took about three or four days and I stopped taking the morphine. I realized I had probably kept myself from having this really severe nerve pain for a long time by smoking every day. It was like this big validation that I really was using good medicine.

"Maria," a fifty-two-year-old single mother living with metastatic ovarian cancer, had no current relationship to marijuana when she fell ill, but she did associate the drug with the recreational use of her youth. This past association made it difficult for her to accept that cannabis might have therapeutic value:

> I don't even know if I would have believed [that marijuana was medicine] if I hadn't tried it for medical purposes myself. I hadn't smoked for many years since I had my daughter. But a good friend said that they had heard it was really good for the nausea [related to chemotherapy] and turned me on to WAMM. . . . What an incredible difference; the pharmaceuticals don't hold a candle [to marijuana] in terms of immediate relief . . . I don't think I would have believed it because it had always been recreational to me.

A Cover for Drug Dealing or an Alternative Pharmacy?

Because of confusions about the legitimacy of marijuana as medicine and of users as patients,

provider organizations such as WAMM are often misunderstood as well. Even within communities largely tolerant of marijuana use, such as Santa Cruz, suspicions remain about the role of a provider organization. "Betty," now a WAMM volunteer, initially assumed WAMM was little more than a cover for recreational users to obtain their drug of choice:

> A friend of the family developed stomach cancer, and when he got the prescription for marijuana he said to me, "I got into this organization; it's called WAMM." I had heard of WAMM but had never been involved with it or anything. Anyway, he says, "Everybody wants to be my caregiver but they all smoke and they're going to steal my pot. I know you don't do marijuana, so would you do this for me?" At first I said, "No, I don't think so." A couple of weeks later, he came back and asked again. So I said, "I'll tell you what—I'll go and check this out, but I'm not going to be sitting around with a bunch of potheads. I'm really not into that, I might as well be honest. But I'll go with you and check it out." So I went and I was really surprised at what I found. These people aren't potheads. These people aren't drug addicts. They're not derelicts. It's nothing like I had envisioned in my mind. I was very surprised . . . these people are really sick. And it's not like they all sit around and get stoned. I was amazed.

Similarly, "Hal," a seventy-year-old with severe neurological pain from failed back surgery, remembers that when a friend suggested he consider marijuana to manage the pain and WAMM as a way to access that marijuana, he was suspicious:

> Right, "medical" marijuana, sure. But [after trying it] I couldn't deny I felt better. I didn't know anything about WAMM; I'd never even heard of a cannabis buying club. I just wasn't in that world. I immediately jumped to the wrong conclusion. I thought "you're a bunch of potheads who are scamming the system." Right? So I'll be a pothead and scam the system. I don't care because I need it. I need it.

Hal's suspicion that WAMM was largely a cover for drug dealing to recreational users was shattered only when he attended his first weekly membership meeting:

> The first time I went to WAMM, with all these misconceptions in my mind, I looked around the room and thought, "My god, these people are really not well." I went home and said to my wife, "I'm going to have to rethink this whole thing. I'm going to have to stop jumping to conclusions here because this was an incredible experience."

Attending a WAMM meeting is indeed consciousness altering; new patients and guests enter expecting a room thick with marijuana smoke and instead find a room filled with human suffering and a collectively organized attempt to alleviate it. In fact, no marijuana is smoked at WAMM membership meetings. Rather, the hour-and-a-half gathering is spent building community: sharing news about the needs of the organization and the needs of the membership. Announcements are made not only about volunteer "opportunities" to work in the garden or the office, but also about members needing hospital visits, meals, or informal hospice support. Memorials are planned for those who have recently died, and holiday parties are organized for those with a desire to socialize and to celebrate. Information is exchanged about the practical dimensions of living with chronic or terminal illness and about coping with the often cascading challenges of pain, poverty, and social isolation. The meetings conclude with members picking up a week's supply of medical marijuana.

Neither Drug Dealing nor a Pharmacy: A New Model of Community Health Care

Although WAMM is not, then, a cover for recreational drug dealing, neither is it simply a pharmacy dispensing physician-recommended medicine. Indeed, by its very design, the organization does not "dispense" marijuana at all. Rather, members collectively grow, harvest,

clean, and store the plants; transform them into tinctures, baked goods, and other products; and draw their share throughout the year according to medical need. This is made all the more remarkable by the fact that WAMM never charges for that medicine. The paradigm-breaking phenomenon of patients collectively producing their own medicines not only challenges the "pharmaceuticalization" of healing, it also creates a therapeutic setting that effectively disrupts the atomized experience of illness and treatment characteristic of conventional medical practice. And, because WAMM members are on the front lines of legal and political battles around medical marijuana, the organization also necessarily facilitates civic engagement.

In short, WAMM approaches "health care" in the most expansive terms, addressing "afflictions" of the body, mind, and spirit, as well as those of the body politic. In this way, the organization more closely resembles women's health care cooperatives (originating in the feminist health care movement of the 1970s) and AIDS self-help and community support organizations (organized through the gay community in the 1980s and 1990s) than it does a pharmacy.

Like these earlier manifestations of community-based health initiatives, WAMM, too, deliberately challenges the monopoly of medical professionals, the pharmaceutical industry, and the state to determine the conditions of treatment, access to drugs, and even the terms of life and death. The objective of WAMM activists is not simply to add another drug to a patient's medicine cabinet but rather to create community. WAMM cofounder Valerie Corral observes:

> We came together around the marijuana, but it's not just the marijuana, it's the community. If the government has its way, and we have to go to a pharmacy to get our prescriptions filled, then we do it all alone. We would lack that coming together, and that is as important as anything else. Totally important. There is magic in joining together with other beings in suffering. That's the "joyful participation in the sorrows of the

world" that the Buddhists talk about. It's how you recognize something is bigger than you and it's a paradigm breaker.

Patient participants initially may join WAMM for no other reason than to access doctor-recommended medication. But it is difficult for members to relate to the organization as nothing more than a dispensary. Weekly attendance at a ninety-minute participants' meeting is required for pickup of marijuana. At a minimum, this means that members must become familiar with each other's faces, witness each other's suffering, and confront repeated requests for assistance by both the organization and by individual participants. In other words, just because the marijuana in WAMM is free and organic doesn't make it without cost, at least in terms of emotional investment. For some, like thirty-seven-year-old "John," living with HIV, the price feels very high indeed.

> I've had a strange relationship to WAMM because a dispensary is really what I would have rather had it be. I'm a matter-of-fact kind of person, and if I have to have this condition, and I have to use a substance, I want to be able to get it and go and not be a part of anything. I don't want to know who my pharmacist is. That's exactly how I feel about WAMM. I go to the meetings because it is a requirement, but it's not necessarily what I would opt to do. I bet everybody who goes just wants to pick up their medicine and leave. Basically, what we want is our medicine and to get on with our lives.

Indeed, those "with a life" and, perhaps more important, an income may prefer a dispensary or buyers' club over a demandingly intimate self-help collective. But for many who remain members, marijuana becomes only one of a number of threads tying them to the organization. "Joe," a forty-year-old man with a severe seizure disorder, explains:

> The medicine is actually turning into a secondary or tertiary part of what WAMM is all about for me now. It's more about the group

itself, the fellowship that goes on, the ways we help each other. Actually that's the biggest thing I want to rave about: that de-isolation that takes place. Isolation that accompanies illness gets to everybody eventually. Suddenly you are removed from any kind of social matrix, like being in school or at work so you don't have the day-to-day contacts with people that make all the difference in your life. WAMM takes you out of that isolation by putting you in contact with other people, like it or not. That's what I really like about the requirement that you come every week to get what you need. You have to be there. That's the only rule actually, and that's what makes it work. People get there whether they'd rather stay at home and then they start finding things in themselves that relate to other people. It's a way for patients to get a hold of their own lives and feel whole, feel human.

One of the most distinctive features of belonging to the WAMM community is, in the words of one participant, the possibility of "dying in the embrace of friends." Because the majority of members are living with life-threatening illness, death is a close companion. For the most active members, this is both the source of great social cohesion and, simultaneously, an almost unbearably painful aspect of collective life. "Kurt," a forty-two-year-old living with AIDS, explains:

> At first I came because I heard that this Mother Teresa was giving out the best medicinal marijuana in the fucking world. And I wanted to know what this was about. What I found was a collective. WAMM has become the most unique group I've belonged to in my whole life. Sometimes it's hard for me, though, because it's a place for the sick and dying. And I'm sick but I'm not dying. I've pulled away from WAMM these past years because every time I become close to someone, they've died. And I was like "fuck this. I'm not going to go through this every time." But what WAMM has done for me—and for everybody they've supplied—is what nobody could do. Whether it's the marijuana or the tincture, or Valerie just coming and sitting by your side. So many people have died, but at least they had somebody sitting by their side.

Dying to Get High

Given decades of condemnation in this country of "reefer madness" and the supposedly dangerously intoxicating high produced by marijuana, it is not surprising that medical marijuana advocates have steered away from any discussion of the consciousness-altering properties of the substance. In an effort to distinguish medical from recreational use, the medical marijuana movement has focused almost entirely on the utility of medical marijuana in physical symptom management (that is, on its effects on nausea, pain, appetite, muscle spasms, ocular pressure, and seizure disorders). It is as if the "high" that inspires recreational use either disappears with medicinal use or, at best, is an unintended and unfortunate side effect. The medical marijuana movement, in other words, seems to have decided that talking about the psychoactive properties of cannabis will serve only to further discredit the drug, working against efforts to transform it into a "medicine."

WAMM cofounder Valerie Corral has resisted this impulse. In addition to gathering data on how marijuana affects members' physical symptom management, Valerie has been encouraging members to reflect on how marijuana might be affecting their psychospiritual well-being. Valerie observes:

> I've gotten criticism for even talking about "consciousness"—I think people are afraid it will be used against us. But I really think it's interesting that the government is so determined to take the "high" out of marijuana before they legalize it as a prescription medicine. You never hear them talking about taking the "low" out of opiates; we allow medicine that relieves pain and is addictive but puts a veil over consciousness. So why is it so important to remove access to a drug that relieves pain and allows for an opening of consciousness?

My interviews suggest that living with severe and chronic pain and with an enhanced awareness of death is, in itself, profoundly consciousness altering. Medical interventions that ignore this dimension are increasingly recognized as inadequate by those involved in palliative care. "Healing," in such situations, is necessarily distinct from "curing" and involves interventions in body, mind, and spirit. Dr. Bal Mount, the founder and director of the Palliative Care Unit at the Royal Victorian Hospital in Montreal, argues, "Healing doesn't necessarily have to do with just the physical body. If one has a broader idea of what healing and wellness are, all kinds of people die as well people" (quoted in Webb, 1999, p. 317).

"Bill," a fifty-three-year-old gay man who has been a caregiver to several WAMM members living with and dying of AIDS, was a cofounder of the local AIDS project in the 1980s and has extensive experience with the medical use of marijuana. He reports:

> The gay community was well aware of marijuana, and early on in the AIDS epidemic we realized that it solved several major things: it solved problems of appetite when somebody wouldn't eat anymore; and it solved nausea, which I didn't think it would, but it did. And it seemed to really help somebody get past the stuck spot they were in of being sick and not being able to be helped, being in that all-alone space. Get them stoned and they got past that.

Deborah Silverknight, a fifty-one-year-old African American/Native American woman with chronic pain from a broken back, notes that this association between marijuana and a sense of enhanced well-being is an old one:

> My great-grandmother referred to marijuana as the "mother plant"—the one you smoke that helps you medicinally and spiritually. Marijuana is a meditative thing for me. It's not only about the physical pain, but relief of pain of the spirit. If I'm having a terrible back spasm, then it's mostly about the need for physical pain relief. But even then, it has that other dimension as well.

The psychospiritual effects of marijuana were frequently remarked upon by WAMM members who reported that the consciousness-altering properties of marijuana were a necessary component of its therapeutic value. Altered consciousness enhances physical symptom relief by helping them to deal with situational depression associated with chronic pain and illness.

"Barb," a forty-five-year-old white woman with post-polio syndrome, observes:

> When I get a pain flair, I smoke and it helps to relieve the pain and relieve the spasms but it also means I don't get as depressed. My attitude is more like, "oh, okay, I'm going to be in pain today, but I'm going to enjoy what I can enjoy and get through the day." Marijuana never fails to lift my mood. I smoke and think "okay, I'm just going to have to go with the pain today. It's beautiful outside and I'm going to go tool around the garden in my chair." It takes you to another level mentally of acceptance about being in this kind of pain. So when I'm in that "I can't handle this another minute stage," it produces a positive shift and I can go on to something else. The other drugs I'm prescribed have such major side effects, but if I smoke a joint, the biggest side effect is a mental lift. And that's a side effect I can live with.

"Hal," the seventy-year-old living with severe neuropathy, notes:

> When you are in constant pain, your focus is 100% on yourself: I can't move this way, I can't twist this way, I can't put my foot down that way. That kind of thing. It's terrible.
>
> I'd never been one who was self-absorbed to the extent that I would forget about other things. I became that way [because of the pain]. I don't know how my wife could stand it. But, I find at this point [with the marijuana], I am in a sense witnessing my pain; what's happened as a result is that I am no longer so absorbed in my pain. I can rise above it, and then I'm able to do whatever I have to do.

One common objection in antidrug literature to the "high" associated with psychoactive drug use is that it offers only a "distortion" or "escape" from reality. The implication is that escape is somehow unworthy or undesirable,

and the "alternative reality" accessed through drugs is illegitimate. But, in the context of chronic pain or terminal illness, one might question whether, in the words of Lily Tomlin, reality isn't "greatly overrated."

Pamela Cutler, a thirty-eight-year-old white woman in the final stages of living with metastatic breast cancer, observes:

> Marijuana kind of helps dull the reality of this situation. And anyone who says it's not a tough reality . . . I mean your mind will barely even take it in. It does dull it, and I don't think there is anything wrong with that if I want to dull it. That's fine . . . was diagnosed with breast cancer and had a radical mastectomy . . . the whole thing was a big shock. I mean I was thirty-six. I was like, "What?" And ever since then it's been like a roller coaster: okay, it's spread to your bones, and then it's spread to my lungs, and then my liver . . . [Marijuana] makes it easier to take for me. It doesn't really take it away. It just dulls the sharpness of it—like "oh my god, I'm going to be dead." I just think that's just incredible.

Although most of the individuals I interviewed commented on the therapeutic value of the psychoactive properties of marijuana, a number were careful to make a distinction between the psychoactive effect of marijuana when used medicinally and the effects when used recreationally. For many of them, the contrast between "getting loaded for fun" and medicinal use was described as profound. In part, this difference may be a question of, as Norman Zinberg (1984) has phrased it, the effects of "set" (the user's mindset) and "setting" (the context in which the drug is taken). A substance taken in expectation of pleasurable intoxication by a healthy individual may produce a substantially different effect from that experienced by an individual living with a life-threatening illness or in chronic pain.

"Kurt," the forty-two-year-old white man living with AIDS, notes:

> I used to smoke recreationally, but it became a whole different thing when I became HIV positive and needed it as a medicinal thing. I had

never had a life-threatening disease, and now I was watching everyone die in front of me. It wasn't just getting high anymore; it let me think about why I am still here after they are all gone.

Some individuals suggested that the different experience of marijuana when used medicinally was less about changed context and more about simple drug habituation. "Cher," a fifty-two-year-old white woman with chronic pain and seizure disorder, reports:

I have to use marijuana every day to deal with pain . . . I feel like I'm so habituated that it really doesn't do that much to my mood anymore or at least it's hard to tell . . . It was more fun being a big pothead than it is being a medical user, for me. You get higher when you are a recreational user. Anytime you use something every day, your system almost naturalizes it. And frankly, I do not really feel stoned anymore unless I smoke because I am so habituated to eating it. And when I smoke, I remember how wonderful it was when marijuana actually got you high. It's like any drug; your body gets habituated.

Hal too reports a diminishing "high" as he became more accustomed to the drug:

After a couple of months, I found that I wasn't getting high as much as I was getting calm. It took a couple of months though. At first, I'd smoke and get really high and have a wonderful afternoon or evening or whatever. But then it started to change and I just got calm.

Hal's shift from "high" to "calm" may be the result not only of biochemical tolerance but also the effect of increased familiarity with the altered state so that it becomes the quotidian reality rather than the "alter."

Interview subjects who had a history of drug abuse and recovery were especially insistent on making a clear distinction between a recreational "high" and the effects of medicinal marijuana use. By drawing a clear line between "getting loaded" and "taking medicine," these individuals were able to maintain their sense of sobriety while using cannabis therapeutically.

Inocencio Manjon-McFaline, a fifty-four-year-old African American/Latino man with cancer and a former cocaine addict who got sober in 1998, described the difference like this:

What's strange now is that I don't feel the effects [from marijuana] that I remember from when I would smoke it before, smoking to get loaded. It's a different time for me. I'm not smoking it looking for a high. Maybe it's just psychologically different knowing I'm smoking it for medicinal use. But I haven't felt loaded. I smoke only for the pain. It gets me out of there, out of that frame of mind. I'll smoke and I'll tend to focus on what I want to focus on. Generally, that's my breathing and my heartbeat. And I'll get really into plants. I just really get into that and forget about pain. . . . Every breath I take is a blessing. I don't fear death, but I don't look forward to it. I really treasure life.

Inocencio's comments raise an important question about what it means to get "high." Clearly he is no longer looking to "get loaded" and argues that he no longer gets "high." Yet, his description of his medicinal use suggests that the marijuana assists him not only in dealing with pain and nausea but also in "focusing" on his breath, on his heartbeat, on the blessings of being alive. This state may seem more "altered" when there are more conventional demands on one's time than when one is in a state of dying. The present-tense focus, which is an aspect of getting "high" that is often commented on, matches the needs of the end-of-life process and therefore may not feel "altering" but rather "confirming" or "enhancing."

Qualities associated with the psychoactive effects of cannabis—such as present-tense focus, mood elevation, and a deepened appreciation of the "minor miracles" of life—may be especially usefully enhanced in the face of anxiety over death or chronic pain. Given antidrug rhetoric in our culture, it is not surprising that some medical marijuana patients may downplay the psychoactive effects of cannabis use. And certainly some medical marijuana users may become habituated to the effects of the

THC and to the altered or enhanced state to which it provides access. But "habituation," "tolerance," or "familiarity" are not synonymous with "no effect." For those living with chronic pain, terminal illness, or both, the psychotherapeutic and metaphysical effects of marijuana may complement the mindset and setting in which the substance is used. As these accounts suggest, although medical marijuana use is most certainly not just about getting "loaded" in any conventional recreational sense, its therapeutic value may be strongly tied to the psychoactive properties of *the plant* (rather than "of cannabis"). This suggestion has significant implications for both the practice of medicine and the transformation of public policy.

REFERENCES

Stein, J. (2002, November 4). The new politics of pot. *Time*. Retrieved March 4, 2005, from http://www.time.com/time/archive/preview/0,10987,1101021104-384830,00.html

Webb, M. (1999). *The good death*. New York: Bantam.

Zinberg, N. (1984). *Drug, set, and setting*. New Haven, CT: Yale University Press.

THINKING ABOUT THE READING

People who routinely use marijuana are often considered socially deviant. How is this social conception of deviance applied to people who use marijuana for medical purposes? How do common conceptions of deviance affect the availability of medical marijuana? What are some of the strategies that health-care providers and users of medical marijuana use to reduce the stigma? What are the factors that determine why some drugs are considered medicinal (and therefore legal) and others considered recreational (and therefore illegal)? Can you think of other types of activities that may be considered beneficial in one social situation and deviant in another?

Medicine as an Institution of Social Control

Peter Conrad and Joseph W. Schneider

(1992)

In our society we want to believe in medicine, as we want to believe in religion and our country; it wards off collective fears and reduces public anxieties (see Edelman, 1977). In significant ways medicine, especially psychiatry, has replaced religion as the most powerful extralegal institution of social control. Physicians have been endowed with some of the charisma of shamans. In the 20th century the medical model of deviance . . . ascended with the glitter of a rising star, expanding medicine's social control functions. . . .

Types of Medical Social Control

Medicine was first conceptualized as an agent of social control by Talcott Parsons (1951) in his seminal essay on the "sick role." . . . Elliot Freidson (1970a) and Irving Zola (1972) have elucidated the jurisdictional mandate the medical profession has over anything that can be labeled an illness, regardless of its ability to deal with it effectively. The boundaries of medicine are elastic and increasingly expansive (Ehrenreich & Ehrenreich, 1975), and some analysts have expressed concern at the increasing medicalization of life (Illich, 1976). Although medical social control has been conceptualized in several ways, including professional control of colleagues (Freidson, 1975) and control of the micropolitics of physician-patient interaction (Waitzkin & Stoeckle, 1976), the focus here is narrower. Our concern . . . is with the medical control of deviant behavior, an aspect of the medicalization of deviance (Conrad, 1975; Pitts, 1968). Thus by medical social control we mean the ways in which

medicine functions (wittingly or unwittingly) to secure adherence to social norms—specifically, by using medical means to minimize, eliminate, or normalize deviant behavior. This section illustrates and catalogues the broad range of medical controls of deviance and in so doing conceptualizes three major "ideal types" of medical social control.

On the most abstract level medical social control is the acceptance of a medical perspective as the dominant definition of certain phenomena. When medical perspectives of problems and their solutions become dominant, they diminish competing definitions. This is particularly true of problems related to bodily functioning and in areas where medical technology can demonstrate effectiveness (e.g., immunization, contraception, antibacterial drugs) and is increasingly the case for behavioral and social problems (Mechanic, 1973). This underlies the construction of medical norms (e.g., the definition of what is healthy) and the "enforcement" of both medical and social norms. Medical social control also includes medical advice, counsel, and information that are part of the general stock of knowledge: for example, a well-balanced diet is important, cigarette smoking causes cancer, being overweight increases health risks, exercising regularly is healthy, teeth should be brushed regularly. Such directives, even when unheeded, serve as road signs for desirable behavior. At a more concrete level, medical social control is enacted through professional medical intervention [and] treatment (although it may include some types of self-treatment such as self-medication or medically oriented self-help groups). This intervention aims at returning sick individuals to compliance with health norms and to their conventional social roles, adjusting them to new (e.g., impaired) roles, or, short or these, making individuals more comfortable with their condition (see Freidson, 1970a; Parsons, 1951). Medical social control of deviant behavior is usually a variant of medical intervention that seeks to eliminate, modify, isolate, or regulate behavior socially defined as deviant, with medical means and in the name of health.

Traditionally, psychiatry and public health have served as the clearest examples of medical control. Psychiatry's social control functions with mental illness, especially in terms of institutionalization, have been described clearly (e.g., Miller, 1976; Szasz, 1970). Recently it has been argued that psychotherapy, because it reinforces dominant values and adjusts people to their life situations, is an agent of social control and a supporter of the status quo (Halleck, 1971; Hurvitz, 1973). Public health's mandate, the control and elimination of conditions and diseases that are deemed a threat to the health of community, is more diffuse. It operates as a control agent by setting and enforcing certain "health" standards in the home, workplace, and community (e.g., food, water, sanitation) and by identifying, preventing, treating, and, if necessary, isolating persons with communicable diseases (Rosen, 1972). A clear example of the latter is the detection of venereal disease. Indeed, public health has exerted considerable coercive power in attempting to prevent the spread of infectious disease.

There are a number of types of medical control of deviance. The most common forms of medical social control include medicalizing deviant behavior—that is, defining the behavior as an illness or a symptom of an illness or underlying disease—and subsequent direct medical intervention. . . .

Social Consequences of Medicalizing Deviance

Jesse Pitts (1968), one of the first sociologists to give attention to the medicalization of deviance, suggests that "medicalization is one of the most effective means of social control and that it is destined to become the main mode of *formal* social control" (p. 391, emphasis in original). . . .

In this section we discuss some of the more significant consequences and ramifications of defining deviant behavior as a medical problem. We must remind the reader that we are examining the *social* consequences of medicalizing deviance, which can be analyzed separately from the validity of medical definitions or diagnoses, the effectiveness of medical regimens, or their individual consequences. These variously "latent" consequences inhere in medicalization itself and occur *regardless* of how efficacious the particular medical treatment or social control mechanism. As will be apparent, our sociological analysis has left us skeptical of the social benefits of medical social control. We separate the consequences into the "brighter" and "darker" sides of medicalization. The "brighter" side will be presented first.

Brighter Side

The brighter side of medicalization includes the positive or beneficial qualities that are attributed to medicalization. We review briefly the accepted socially progressive aspects of medicalizing deviance. They are separated more for clarity of presentation than for any intrinsic separation in consequence.

First, medicalization is related to a long-time *humanitarian* trend in the conception and control of deviance. For example, alcoholism is no longer considered a sin or even a moral weakness; it is now a disease. Alcoholics are no longer arrested in many places for "public drunkenness"; they are now somehow "treated," if only to be dried out for a time. Medical treatment for the alcoholic can be seen as a more humanitarian means of social control. It is not retributive or punitive, but at least ideally, therapeutic. Troy Duster (1970, p. 10) suggests that medical definitions increase tolerance and compassion for human problems and they "have now been reinterpreted in an almost nonmoral fashion." (We doubt this, but leave the morality issue for a later discussion.) Medicine and humanitarianism historically developed concurrently and, as some have observed, the use of medical language and evidence increases the prestige of human proposals and enhances their acceptance (Wootton, 1959; Zola, 1975). Medical definitions are imbued with the prestige of the medical profession and are considered the "scientific" and humane way of viewing a problem. . . . This is especially true if an apparently "successful" treatment for controlling the behavior is available, as with hyperkinesis.

Second, medicalization allows for the extension of the *sick role* to those labeled as deviants. . . . Many of the perceived benefits of the medicalization of deviance stem from the assignment of the sick role. Some have suggested that this is the most significant element of adopting the medical model of deviant behavior (Sigler & Osmond, 1974). By defining deviant behavior as an illness or a result of illness, one is absolved of responsibility for one's behavior. It diminishes or *removes blame* from the individual for deviant actions. Alcoholics are no longer held responsible for their uncontrolled drinking, and perhaps hyperactive children are no longer the classroom's "bad boys" but children with a medical disorder. There is some clear secondary gain here for the individual. The label "sick" is free of the moral opprobrium and implied culpability of "criminal" or "sinner." The designation of sickness also may reduce guilt for drinkers and their families and for hyperactive children and their parents. Similarly, it may result in reduced stigma for the deviant. It allows for the development of more acceptable accounts of deviance: a recent film depicted a child witnessing her father's helpless drunken stupor; her mother remarked, "It's okay. Daddy's just sick."

The sick role allows for the "conditional legitimization" of a certain amount of deviance, so long as the individual fulfills the obligation of the sick role. As Renée Fox (1977) notes:

The fact that the exemptions of sickness have been extended to people with a widening arc of attitudes, experiences and behaviors in American society means primarily that what is regarded as "conditionally legitimated deviance" has increased. . . . So long as [the deviant] does not abandon himself to illness or eagerly embrace it, but works actively on his own or with medical professionals to improve his condition, he is considered to be responding appropriately, even admirably, to an unfortunate occurrence. Under these conditions, illness is accepted as legitimate deviance. (p. 15)

The deviant, in essence, is medically excused for the deviation. But, as Talcott Parsons (1972) has pointed out, "the conditional legitimization is bought at a 'price,' namely, the recognition that illness itself is an undesirable state, to be recovered from as expeditiously as possible" (p. 108). Thus the medical excuse for deviance is only valid when the patient deviant accepts the medical perspective of the inherent undesirability of his or her sick behavior and submits to a subordinate relationship with an official agent of control (the physician) toward changing it. This, of course, negates any threat the deviant may pose to society's normative structure, for such deviants do not challenge the norm; by accepting deviance as sickness and social control as "treatment," the deviant underscores the validity of the violated norm.

Third, the medical model can be viewed as portraying an *optimistic* outcome for the deviant. Pitts (1968) notes, "the possibility that a patient may be exploited is somewhat minimized by therapeutic ideology, which creates an optimistic bias concerning the Patient's fate" (p. 391). The therapeutic ideology, accepted in some form by all branches of medicine, suggests that a problem (e.g., deviant behavior) can be changed or alleviated if only the proper treatment is discovered and administered. Defining deviant behavior as an illness may also mobilize hope in the individual patient that with proper treatment a "cure" is possible (Frank, 1974). Clearly this could have beneficial results and even become a self fulfilling prophecy. Although the medical model is interpreted frequently as optimistic about individual change, under some circumstances it may lend itself to pessimistic interpretations. The attribution of physiological cause coupled with the lack of effective treatment engendered a somatic pessimism in the late 19th-century conception of madness. . . .

Fourth, medicalization lends the *prestige of the medical profession* to deviance designations and treatments. The medical profession is the most prestigious and dominant profession in American society (Freidson, 1970a). As just noted, medical definitions of deviance become imbued with the prestige of the medical profession and are construed to be the "scientific" way of viewing a problem. The medical mantle of science may serve to deflect definitional challenges. This is especially true if an apparently "successful" treatment for controlling the behavior is available. Medicalization places the problem in the hands of healing physicians. "The therapeutic value of professional dominance, from the patient's point of view, is that it becomes the *doctor's* problem" (Ehrenreich & Ehrenreich, 1975, p. 156, emphasis in original). Physicians are assumed to be beneficent and honorable. "The medical and paramedical professions," Pitts (1968) contends, "especially in the United States, are probably more immune to corruption than are the judicial and parajudicial professions and relatively immune to political pressure" (p. 391).

Fifth, medical social control is more *flexible* and often more *efficient* than judicial and legal controls. The impact of the flexibility of medicine is most profound on the "deviance of everyday life," since it allows "social pressures on deviance [to] increase without boxing the deviant into as rigid a category as 'criminal'" (Pitts, 1968, p. 391). Medical controls are adjustable to fit the needs of the individual patient, rather than being a response to the deviant act itself. It may be more efficient (and less expensive) to control opiate addiction with methadone maintenance than with long prison terms or mental hospitalization. The behavior of disruptive hyperactive children, who have been immune to all parental and teacher sanctions, may dramatically improve after treatment

with medications. Medical controls circumvent complicated legal and judicial procedures and may be applied more informally. This can have a considerable effect on social control structures. For example, it has been noted that defining alcoholism as a disease would reduce arrest rates in some areas up to 50%.

In sum, the social benefits of medicalization include the creation of humanitarian and nonpunitive sanctions; the extension of the sick role to some deviants; a reduction of individual responsibility, blame, and possible stigma for deviance; an optimistic therapeutic ideology; care and treatment rendered by a prestigious medical profession; and the availability of a more flexible and often more efficient means of social control.

Darker Side

There is, however, another side to the medicalization of deviant behavior. Although it may often seem entirely humanitarian to conceptualize deviance as sickness as opposed to badness, it is not that simple. There is a "darker" side to the medicalization of deviance. In some senses these might be considered as the more clearly latent aspects of medicalization. In an earlier work Conrad (1975) elucidated four consequences of medicalizing deviance; building on that work, we expand our analysis to seven. Six are discussed here; the seventh is described separately in the next section.

Dislocation of responsibility. As we have seen, defining behavior as a medical problem removes or profoundly diminishes responsibility from the individual. Although affixing responsibility is always complex, medicalization produces confusion and ambiguity about who is responsible. Responsibility is separated from social action; it is located in the nether world of biophysiology or psyche. Although this takes the individual officially "off the hook," its excuse is only a partial one. The individual, the putative deviant, and the undesirable conduct are still associated. Aside from where such conduct is "seated," the sick deviant is the medium of its expression.

With the removal of responsibility also comes the lowering of status. A dual-class citizenship is created: those who are deemed responsible for their actions and those who are not. The not-completely-responsible sick are placed in a position of dependence on the fully responsible nonsick (Parsons, 1975, p. 108). Kittrie (1971, p. 347) notes in this regard that more than half the American population is no longer subject to the sanctions of criminal law. Such persons, among others, become true "second-class citizens."

Assumption of the moral neutrality of medicine. Cloaked in the mantle of science, medicine and medical practice are assumed to be objective and value free. But this profoundly misrepresents reality. The very nature of medical practice involves value judgment. To call something a disease is to deem it undesirable. Medicine is influenced by the moral order of society— witness the diagnosis and treatment of masturbation as a disease in Victorian times—yet medical language of disease and treatment is assumed to be morally neutral. It is not, and the very technological-scientific vocabulary of medicine that defines disease obfuscates this fact.

Defining deviance as disease allows behavior to keep its negative judgment, but medical language veils the political and moral nature of this decision in the guise of scientific fact. There was little public clamor for moral definitions of homosexuality as long as it remained defined an illness, but soon after the disease designation was removed, moral crusaders (e.g., Anita Bryant) launched public campaigns condemning the immorality of homosexuality. One only needs to scratch the surface of medical designations for deviant behavior to find overtly moral judgments.

Thus, as Zola (1975) points out, defining a problem as within medical jurisdiction is not morally neutral precisely because in establishing its relevance as a key dimension for action, the moral issue is prevented from being squarely faced and occasionally from even being raised. By the acceptance of a specific behavior as an undesirable state the issue becomes not whether to treat an individual problem but how and when (p. 86).

Defining deviance as a medical phenomenon involves moral enterprise.

Domination of expert control. The medical profession is made up of experts; it has a monopoly on anything that can be conceptualized as an illness. Because of the way the medical profession is organized and the mandate it has from society, decisions related to medical diagnoses and treatment are controlled almost completely by medical professionals.

Conditions that enter the medical domain are not ipso facto medical problems, whether we speak of alcoholism, hyperactivity, or drug addiction. When a problem is defined as medical, it is removed from the public realm, where there can be discussion by ordinary people, and put on a plane where only medical people can discuss it. As Janice Reynolds (1973) succinctly states,

> The increasing acceptance, especially among the more educated segments of our populace, of technical solutions—solutions administered by disinterested and morally neutral experts—results in the withdrawal of more and more areas of human experience from the realm of public discussion. For when drunkenness, juvenile delinquency, sub par performance and extreme political beliefs are seen as symptoms of an underlying illness or biological defect the merits and drawbacks of such behavior or beliefs need not be evaluated. (pp. 220–221)

The public may have their own conceptions of deviant behavior, but those of the experts are usually dominant. Medical definitions have a high likelihood for dominance and hegemony: they are often taken as the last scientific word. The language of medical experts increases mystification and decreases the accessibility of public debate.

Medical social control. Defining deviant behavior as a medical problem allows certain things to be done that could not otherwise be considered; for example, the body may be cut open or psychoactive medications given. As we elaborated above, this treatment can be a form of social control.

In regard to drug treatment, Henry Lennard (1971) observes: "Psychoactive drugs, especially those legally prescribed, tend to restrain individuals from behavior and experience that are not complementary with the requirements of the dominant value system" (p. 57). These forms of medical social control presume a prior definition of deviance as a medical problem. Psychosurgery on an individual prone to violent outbursts requires a diagnosis that something is wrong with his brain or nervous system. Similarly, prescribing drugs to restless, overactive, and disruptive schoolchildren requires a diagnosis of hyperkinesis. These forms of social control, what Stephan Chorover (1973) has called "psychotechnology," are powerful and often efficient means of controlling deviance. These relatively new and increasingly popular forms of medical control could not be used without the prior medicalization of deviant behavior. As is suggested from the discovery of hyperkineses and to a lesser extent the development of methadone treatment of opiate addiction, if a mechanism of medical social control seems useful, then the deviant behavior it modifies will be given a medical label or diagnosis. We imply no overt malevolence on the part of the medical profession; rather, it is part of a larger process, of which the medical profession is only a part. The larger process might be called the individualization of social problems.

Individualization of social problems. The medicalization of deviance is part of a larger phenomenon that is prevalent in our society: the individualization of social problems. We tend to look for causes and solutions to complex social problems in the individual rather than in the social system. William Ryan (1971) has identified this process as "blaming the victim": seeing the causes of the problem in individuals (who are usually of low status) rather than as

endemic to the society. We seek to change the "victim" rather than the society. The medical practice of diagnosing an illness in an individual lends itself to the individualization of social problems. Rather than seeing certain deviant behaviors as symptomatic of social conditions, the medical perspective focuses on the individual, diagnosing and treating the illness itself and generally ignoring the social situation.

Hyperkinesis serves as a good example of this. Both the school and parents are concerned with the child's behavior; the child is difficult at home and disruptive in school. No punishments or rewards seem consistently effective in modifying the behavior, and both parents and school are at their wits' end. A medical evaluation is suggested. The diagnosis of hyperkinetic behavior leads to prescribing stimulant medications. The child's behavior seems to become more socially acceptable, reducing problems in school and home. Treatment is considered a medical success.

But there is an alternative perspective. By focusing on the symptoms and defining them as hyperkinesis, we ignore the possibility that the behavior is not an illness but an adaptation to a social situation. It diverts our attention from the family or school and from seriously entertaining the idea that the "problem" could be in the structure of the social system. By giving medications, we are essentially supporting the existing social and political arrangements in that it becomes a "symptom" of an individual disease rather than a possible "comment" on the nature of the present situation. Although the individualization of social problems aligns well with the individualistic ethic of American culture, medical intervention against deviance makes medicine a de facto agent of dominant social and political interests.

Depoliticization of deviant behavior. Depoliticization of deviant behavior is a result of both the process of medicalization and the individualization of social problems. Probably one of the clearest . . . examples of such depoliticization occurred when political dissidents in the [former]

Soviet Union were declared mentally ill and confined to mental hospitals (Conrad, 1977). This strategy served to neutralize the meaning of political protest and dissent, rendering it (officially, at least) symptomatic of mental illness.

The medicalization of deviant behavior depoliticizes deviance in the same manner. By defining the overactive, restless, and disruptive child as hyperkinetic, we ignore the meaning of the behavior in the context of the social system. If we focused our analysis on the school system, we might see the child's behavior as a protest against some aspect of the school or classroom situation, rather than symptomatic of an individual neurological disorder. Similar examples could be drawn of the opiate addict in the ghetto, the alcoholic in the workplace, and others. Medicalizing deviant behavior precludes us from recognizing it as a possible international repudiation of existing political arrangements.

There are other related consequences of the medicalization of deviance beyond the six discussed. The medical ideal of early intervention may lead to early labeling and secondary deviance (see Lemert, 1972). The "medical decision rule," which approximates "when in doubt, treat," is nearly the converse of the legal dictum "innocent until proven guilty" and may unnecessarily enlarge the population of deviants (Scheff, 1963). Certain constitutional safeguards of the judicial system that protect individuals' rights are neutralized or by-passed by medicalization (Kittrie, 1971). Social control in the name of benevolence is at once insidious and difficult to confront. Although these are all significant, we wish to expand on still another consequence of considerable social importance, the exclusion of evil.

Exclusion of Evil

Evil has been excluded from the imagery of modern human problems. We are uncomfortable with notions of evil; we regard them as primitive and nonhumanitarian, as residues from a theological era. Medicalization contributes to the exclusion of concepts of evil in our society. Clearly medicalization is not the sole cause of exclusion of evil, but it shrouds conditions, events, and people and prevents them from being confronted as evil. . . .

For example, Hitler orchestrated the greatest mass genocide in modern history, yet some have reduced his motivation for the destruction of the Jews (and others) to a personal pathological condition. To them and to many of us, Hitler was sick. But this portrays the horror of the Holocaust as a product of individual pathology; as Thomas Szasz frequently points out, it prevents us from seeing and confronting man's inhumanity to man. Are Son of Sam, Charles Manson, the assassins of King and the Kennedys, the Richard Nixon of Watergate, Libya's Muammar Kaddafi, or the all-too-common child beater sick? Although many may well be troubled, we argue that there is little to be gained by deploying such a medical vocabulary of motives. It only hinders us from comprehending the human element in the decisions we make, the social structures we create, and the actions we take. Hannah Arendt (1963), in her exemplary study of the banality of evil, contends that Nazi war criminal Adolph Eichmann, rather than being sick, was "terribly, terrifyingly normal."

Susan Sontag (1978) has suggested that on a cultural level, we use the metaphor of illness to speak of various kinds of evil. Cancer, in particular, provides such a metaphor: we depict slums and pornography shops as "cancers" in our cities; J. Edgar Hoover's favorite metaphor for communism was "a cancer in our midst"; and Nixon's administration was deemed "cancerous," rotting from within. In our secular culture, where powerful religious connotations of sin and evil have been obscured, cancer (and for that matter, illness in general) is one of the few available images of unmitigated evil and wickedness. As Sontag (1978) observes:

> But how to be . . . [moral] in the late twentieth century? How, when . . . we have a sense of evil but no longer the religious or philosophical language to talk intelligently about evil. Trying

to comprehend "radical" or "absolute" evil, we search for adequate metaphors. But the modern disease metaphors are all cheap shots.... Only in the most limited sense is any historical event or problem like an illness. It is invariably an encouragement to simplify what is complex.... (p. 85)

Thus we suggest that the medicalization of social problems detracts from our capability to see and confront the evils that face our world. In sum, the "darker" side of the medicalization of deviance has profound consequences for the putative or alleged deviant and society....

Medicalizing Deviance: A Final Note

The potential for medicalizing deviance has increased in the past few decades. The increasing dominance of the medical profession, the discovery of subtle physiological correlates of human behavior, and the creation of medical technologies (promoted by powerful pharmaceutical and medical technology industry interests) have advanced this trend. Although we remain skeptical of the overall social benefits of medicalization and are concerned about its "darker" side, it is much too simplistic to suggest a wholesale condemnation of medicalization. Offering alcoholics medical treatment in lieu of the drunk tank is undoubtedly a more humane response to deviance; methadone maintenance allows a select group of opiate addicts to make successful adaptations to society; some schoolchildren seem to benefit from stimulant medications for hyperkinesis; and the medical discovery of child abuse may well increase therapeutic intervention. Medicalization in general has reduced societal condemnation of deviants. But these benefits do not mean these conditions are in fact diseases or that the same results could not be achieved in another manner. And even in those instances of medical "success," the social consequences indicated . . . are still evident.

The most difficult consequence of medicalization for us to discuss is the exclusion of evil. In part this is because we are members of a culture that has largely eliminated evil from intellectual and public discourse. But our discomfort also stems from our ambivalence about what can meaningfully be construed as evil in our society. If we are excluding evil, what exactly are we excluding? We have no difficulty depicting such conditions as pain, violence, oppression, exploitation, and abject cruelty as evil. Social scientists of various stripes have been pointing to these evils and their consequences since the dawn of social science. It is also possible for us to conceive of "organizational evils" such as corporate price fixing, false advertising (or even all advertising), promoting life-threatening automobiles, or the wholesale drugging of nursing home patients to facilitate institutional management. We also have little trouble in seeing ideologies such as imperialism, chauvinism, and racial supremacy as evils. Our difficulty comes with seeing individuals as evil. While we would not adopt a Father-Flanagan-of-Boys-Town attitude of "there's no such thing as a bad boy," our own socialization and "liberal" assumptions as well as sociological perspective make it difficult for us to conceive of any individual as "evil." As sociologists we are more likely to see people as products of their psychological and social circumstances: there may be evil social structures, ideologies, or deeds, but not evil people. Yet when we confront a Hitler, an Idi Amin, or a Stalin of the forced labor camps, it is sometimes difficult to reach any other conclusion. We note this dilemma more as clarification of our stance than as a solution. There are both evils in society and people who are "victims" to those evils. Worthwhile social scientific goals include uncovering the evils, understanding and aiding the victims, and ultimately contributing to a more humane existence for all.

REFERENCES

Arendt, H. *Eichmann in Jerusalem*. New York: Viking Press, 1963.

Chorover, S. Big Brother and psychotechnology. *Psychol. Today*, 1973, 7, 43–54 (Oct.).

Conrad, P. The discovery of hyperkinesis: Notes on the medicalization of deviant behavior. *Social Prob.*, 1975, 23, 12–21 (Oct.).

Conrad, P. Soviet dissidents, ideological deviance, and mental hospitalization. Presented at Midwest Sociological Society Meetings, Minneapolis, 1977.

Duster, T. *The legislation of morality.* New York: The Free Press, 1970.

Edelman, M. *Political language: Words that succeed and policies that fail.* New York: Academic Press, Inc., 1977.

Ehrenreich, B., & Ehrenreich, J. Medicine and social control. In B. R. Mandell (Ed.), *Welfare in America: Controlling the "dangerous" classes.* Englewood Cliffs, N.J.: Prentice Hall, Inc., 1975.

Fox, Renée. The medicalization and demedicalization of American society. *Daedalus,* 1977, *106,* 9–22.

Frank, J. *Persuasion and healing.* (Rev. ed.). New York: Schocken Books, Inc., 1974.

Freidson, E. *Profession of medicine.* New York: Harper & Row, Publishers, Inc., 1970. (a)

Freidson, E. *Doctoring together.* New York: Elsevier North-Holland, Inc., 1975.

Halleck, S. L. *The politics of therapy.* New York: Science House, 1971.

Hurvitz, N. Psychotherapy as a means of social control. *J. Consult. Clin. Psychol.,* 1973, *40,* 232–239.

Ilich, I. *Medical nemesis.* New York: Pantheon Books, Inc., 1976.

Kittrie, N. *The right to be different: Deviance and enforced therapy.* Baltimore: Johns Hopkins University Press, 1971. Copyright The Johns Hopkins Press, 1971.

Lemert, E. M. *Human deviance, social problems and social control* (2nd ed.). Englewood Cliffs, N.J.: Prentice Hall, 1972.

Lennard, H. L., Esptein, L. J., Bernstein, A., & Ranson, D. C. *Mystification and drug misuse.* New York: Perennial Library, 1971.

Mechanic, D. Health and illness in technological societies. *Hastings Center Stud.* 1973, *1*(3), 7–18.

Miller, K. S. *Managing madness.* New York: The Free Press, 1976.

Parsons, T. *The social system.* New York: The Free Press, 1951.

Parsons, T. Definitions of illness and health in light of American values and social structure. In E. G. Jaco (Ed.), *Patients, physicians and illness.* (2nd ed.). New York: The Free Press, 1972.

Parsons, T. The sick role and the role of the physician reconsidered. *Health Society,* 1975, *53,* 257–278 (Summer).

Pitts, J. Social control: The concepts. In D. Sills (Ed.), *International encyclopedia of social sciences.* (Vol. 14). New York: Macmillan Publishing Co., Inc., 1968.

Reynolds, J. M. The medical institution: The death and disease-producing appendage. In L. T. Reynolds & J. M. Henslin (Eds.), *American society: A critical analysis.* New York: David McKay Co., Inc., 1973.

Rosen, G. The evolution of social medicine. In H. E. Freeman, S. Levine, & L. Reeder (Eds.), *Handbook of medical sociology* (2nd ed.). Englewood Cliffs, N.J.: Prentice Hall, Inc., 1972.

Ryan, W. *Blaming the victim.* New York: Vintage Books, 1971.

Scheff, T. J. Decision rules, types of errors, and their consequences in medical diagnosis. *Behav. Sci.,* 1963, *8,* 97–107.

Sigler, M., & Osmond, H. *Models of madness, models of medicine.* New York: Macmillan Publishing Co., Inc., 1974.

Sontag, S. *Illness as metaphor.* New York: Farrar, Straus & Giroux, 1978.

Szasz, T. *The manufacture of madness.* New York: Harper & Row, Publishers, Inc., 1970.

Waitzkin, H., & Stoeckle, J. Information control and the micropolitics of health care: Summary of an ongoing project. *Soc. Sci. Med.,* 1976, *10,* 263–276 (June).

Wootton, B. *Social science and social pathology.* London: George Allen & Unwin, 1959.

Zola, I. K. Medicine as an institution of social control. *Sociological Rev.,* 1972, *20,* 487–504.

Zola, I. K. In the name of health and illness: On some socio-political consequences of medical influence. *Soc. Sci. Med.,* 1975, *9,* 83–87.

THINKING ABOUT THE READING

How does medicine function as a means of social control? What do the authors mean when they say, "Evil has been excluded from the imagery of modern human problems"? Do you agree that perceiving troublesome behavior as an "illness" prevents us from confronting such behavior as evil? Why do you suppose we have such a profound desire to use the vocabulary of medicine to describe deviant behavior? Clearly some people are helped when their problematic behaviors are conceived as illnesses or disorders and they are prescribed drugs or some sort of surgical treatment. Do you think that Conrad and Schneider overstate the negative consequences of the medicalization of deviance?

PART III

Social Structure, Institutions, and Everyday Life

The Structure of Society

Organizations and Social Institutions

9

One of the great sociological paradoxes is that we live in a society that so fiercely extols the virtues of rugged individualism and personal accomplishment, yet we spend most of our lives responding to the influence of larger organizations and social institutions. These include both nurturing organizations, such as churches and schools, and larger, more impersonal bureaucratic institutions.

No matter how powerful and influential they are, organizations are more than structures, rules, policies, goals, job descriptions, and standard operating procedures. Each organization, and each division within an organization, develops its own norms, values, and language. This is usually referred to as organizational culture. Organizational cultures are usually pervasive and entrenched, yet, even so, individuals often find ways to exert some control over their lives within the confines of these organizations. Accordingly, organizations are dynamic entities in which individuals struggle for personal freedom and expression while also existing under the rules and procedures that make up the organization. Given this dynamic activity, an organization is rarely what it appears to be on the surface.

For example, many people are unaware of and unconcerned with the harsh conditions under which our most coveted products are made. William Greider, in "These Dark Satanic Mills," discusses the exploitative potential of relying on "third world" factories. He uses a particular tragedy, the 1993 industrial fire at the Kader Industrial Toy Company in Thailand, to illustrate how global economics create and sustain international inequality. Greider shows us the complex paradox of the global marketplace: While foreign manufacturing facilities free factory workers from certain poverty, they also ensnare the workers in new and sometimes lethal forms of domination.

Ellen Rosen brings the implications of global corporate capitalism closer to home in her observations of Wal-Mart management practices. She suggests that the Wal-Mart corporate goal of generating profit produces management tactics that intimidate and exploit the worker. Workers cannot directly talk back or challenge this work climate because they are likely to lose their jobs. At the same time, Wal-Mart attempts to soften its practices by persuading employees that they are part of the Wal-Mart "family." This type of organizational culture is frequently used to get employees to work harder (often for less pay) than they otherwise might.

Michael A. Messner and Suzel Bozada-Deas focus on an even more subtle form of organizational culture and socialization, youth sports clubs. Intrigued by the observation that youth sports teams generally have male coaches and female "team parents," they explore the underlying institutional dynamics that result in this persistent gender division. They find that even when adult coaches and parents don't intend this gender division, it occurs as a consequence of gender norms that are deeply embedded in our understanding of family, work, and sports.

Something to Consider as You Read

As you read these selections, think about a job you've had and the new procedures you had to learn when you started. Was the job just about the procedures, or did you also have to learn new (and perhaps informal) cultural norms? Think about some of the ways in which the organizational environment induces you to behave in ways that are very specific to that situation. As you read, compare some of these organizational environments to the ones discussed in this section—work and sports. How might other social institutions such as education and religion shape behavior and beliefs?

These Dark Satanic Mills

William Greider

(1997)

. . . If the question were put now to everyone, everywhere—do you wish to become a citizen of the world?—it is safe to assume that most people in most places would answer, no, they wish to remain who they are. With very few exceptions, people think of themselves as belonging to a place, a citizen of France or Malaysia, of Boston or Tokyo or Warsaw, loyally bound to native culture, sovereign nation. The Chinese who aspire to get gloriously rich, as Deng instructed, do not intend to become Japanese or Americans. Americans may like to think of themselves as the world's leader, but not as citizens of "one world."

The deepest social meaning of the global industrial revolution is that people no longer have free choice in this matter of identity. Ready or not, they are already of the world. As producers or consumers, as workers or merchants or investors, they are now bound to distant others through the complex strands of commerce and finance reorganizing the globe as a unified marketplace. The prosperity of South Carolina or Scotland is deeply linked to Stuttgart's or Kuala Lumpur's. The true social values of Californians or Swedes will be determined by what is tolerated in the factories of Thailand or Bangladesh. The energies and brutalities of China will influence community anxieties in Seattle or Toulouse or Nagoya.

. . . Unless one intends to withdraw from modern industrial life, there is no place to hide from the others. Major portions of the earth, to be sure, remain on the periphery of the system, impoverished bystanders still waiting to be included in the action. But the patterns of global interconnectedness are already the dominant reality. Commerce has leapt beyond social consciousness and, in doing so, opened up challenging new vistas for the human potential. Most people, it seems fair to say, are not yet prepared to face the implications. . . .

Two centuries ago, when the English industrial revolution dawned with its fantastic invention and productive energies, the prophetic poet William Blake drew back in moral revulsion. Amid the explosion of new wealth, human destruction was spread over England—peasant families displaced from their lands, paupers and poorhouses crowded into London slums, children sent to labor at the belching ironworks or textile looms. Blake delivered a thunderous rebuke to the pious Christians of the English aristocracy with these immortal lines:

> And was Jerusalem builded here
> Among these dark Satanic mills?

Blake's "dark Satanic mills" have returned now and are flourishing again, accompanied by the same question.[1]

On May 10, 1993, the worst industrial fire in the history of capitalism occurred at a toy factory on the outskirts of Bangkok and was reported on page 25 of the *Washington Post.* The *Financial Times* of London, which styles itself as the daily newspaper of the global economy, ran a brief item on page 6. The *Wall Street Journal* followed a day late with an account on page 11. The *New York Times* also put the story inside, but printed a dramatic photo on its front page: rows of small shrouded bodies on bamboo pallets—dozens of them—lined along the damp pavement, while dazed rescue workers stood awkwardly among the corpses. In the background, one could see the collapsed, smoldering structure of a mammoth factory where the Kader Industrial Toy Company of Thailand had employed three thousand workers manufacturing stuffed toys and plastic dolls, playthings destined for American children.[2]

The official count was 188 dead, 469 injured, but the actual toll was undoubtedly higher since the four-story buildings had collapsed swiftly in the intense heat and many bodies were incinerated. Some of the missing were never found; others fled home to their villages. All but fourteen of the dead were women, most of them young, some as young as thirteen years old. Hundreds of the workers had been trapped on upper floors of the burning building, forced to jump from third- or fourth-floor windows, since the main exit doors were kept locked by the managers, and the narrow stairways became clotted with trampled bodies or collapsed.

When I visited Bangkok about nine months later, physical evidence of the disaster was gone—the site scraped clean by bulldozers—and Kader was already resuming production at a new toy factory, built far from the city in a rural province of northeastern Thailand. When I talked with Thai labor leaders and civic activists, people who had rallied to the cause of the fire victims, some of them were under the impression that a worldwide boycott of Kader products was under way, organized by conscience-stricken Americans and Europeans. I had to inform them that the civilized world had barely noticed their tragedy.

As news accounts pointed out, the Kader fire surpassed what was previously the worst industrial fire in history—the Triangle Shirtwaist Company fire of 1911—when 146 young immigrant women died in similar circumstances at a garment factory on the Lower East Side of Manhattan. The Triangle Shirtwaist fire became a pivotal event in American politics, a public scandal that provoked citizen reform movements and energized the labor organizing that built the International Ladies Garment Workers Union and other unions. The fire in Thailand did not produce meaningful political responses or even shame among consumers. The indifference of the leading newspapers merely reflected the tastes of their readers, who might be moved by human suffering in their own communities but were inured to news of recurring calamities in distant places. A fire in Bangkok was like a typhoon in Bangladesh, an earthquake in Turkey.

The Kader fire might have been more meaningful for Americans if they could have seen the thousands of soot-stained dolls that spilled from the wreckage, macabre litter scattered among the dead. Bugs Bunny, Bart Simpson and the Muppets. Big Bird and other *Sesame Street* dolls. Playskool "Water Pets." Santa Claus. What the initial news accounts did not mention was that Kader's Thai factory produced most of its toys for American companies—Toys "R" Us, Fisher-Price, Hasbro, Tyco, Arco, Kenner, Gund and J. C. Penney—as well as stuffed dolls, slippers and souvenirs for Europe.[3]

Globalized civilization has uncovered an odd parochialism in the American character: Americans worried obsessively over the everyday safety of their children, and the U.S. government's regulators diligently policed the design of toys to avoid injury to young innocents. Yet neither citizens nor government took any interest in the brutal and dangerous conditions imposed on the people who manufactured those same toys, many of whom were mere adolescent children themselves. Indeed, the government position, both in Washington and Bangkok, assumed that there was no social obligation connecting consumers with workers, at least none that governments could enforce without disrupting free trade or invading the sovereignty of other nations.

The toy industry, not surprisingly, felt the same. Hasbro Industries, maker of Playskool, subsequently told the *Boston Globe* that it would no longer do business with Kader, but, in general, the U.S. companies shrugged off responsibility. Kader, a major toy manufacturer based in Hong Kong, "is extremely reputable, not sleaze bags," David Miller, president of the Toy Manufacturers of America, assured *USA Today*. "The responsibility for those factories," Miller told ABC News, "is in the hands of those who are there and managing the factory."[4]

The grisly details of what occurred revealed the casual irresponsibility of both companies and governments. The Kader factory compound consisted of four interconnected, four-story industrial barns on a three-acre lot on Buddhamondhol VI Road in the Sampran district west of Bangkok. It was one among Thailand's thriving new industrial zones for garments, textiles, electronics and toys. More than 50,000 people, most of them migrants from the Thai countryside, worked in the district at 7,500 large and small firms. Thailand's economic boom was based on places such as this, and Bangkok was almost choking on its own fantastic growth, dizzily erecting luxury hotels and office towers.

The fire started late on a Monday afternoon on the ground floor in the first building and spread rapidly upward, jumping to two adjoining buildings, all three of which swiftly collapsed. Investigators noted afterwards that the structures had been cheaply built, without concrete reinforcement, so steel girders and stairways crumpled easily in the heat. Thai law required that in such a large factory, fire-escape stairways must be sixteen to thirty-three feet wide, but Kader's were a mere four and a half feet. Main doors were locked and many windows barred to prevent pilfering by the employees. Flammable raw materials—fabric, stuffing, animal fibers—were stacked everywhere, on walkways and next to electrical boxes. Neither safety drills nor fire alarms and sprinkler systems had been provided.

Let some of the survivors describe what happened.

A young woman named Lampan Taptim: "There was the sound of yelling about a fire. I tried to leave the section but my supervisor told me to get back to work. My sister who worked on the fourth floor with me pulled me away and insisted we try to get out. We tried to go down the stairs and got to the second floor; we found that the stairs had already caved in. There was a lot of yelling and confusion. . . . In desperation, I went back up to the windows and went back and forth, looking down below. The smoke was thick and I picked the best place to jump in a pile of boxes. My sister jumped, too. She died."

A young woman named Cheng: "There is no way out [people were shouting], the security guard has locked the main door out! It was horrifying. I thought I would die. I took off my gold ring and kept it in my pocket and put on my name tag so that my body could be identifiable. I had to decide to die in the fire or from jumping down from a three stories' height." As the walls collapsed around her, Cheng clung to a pipe and fell downward with it, landing on a pile of dead bodies, injured but alive.

An older woman named La-iad Nadsnguen: "Four or five pregnant women jumped before me. They died before my eyes." Her own daughter jumped from the top floor and broke both hips.

Chauweewan Mekpan, who was five months pregnant: "I thought that if I jumped, at least my parents would see my remains, but if I stayed, nothing would be left of me." Though her back was severely injured, she and her unborn child miraculously survived.

An older textile worker named Vilaiwa Satieti, who sewed shirts and pants at a neighboring factory, described to me the carnage she encountered: "I got off work about five and passed by Kader and saw many dead bodies lying around, uncovered. Some of them I knew. I tried to help the workers who had jumped from the factory. They had broken legs and broken arms and broken heads. We tried to keep them alive until they got to the hospital, that's all you could do. Oh, they were teenagers, fifteen to twenty years, no more than that, and so many of them, so many."

This was not the first serious fire at Kader's factory, but the third or fourth. "I heard somebody yelling 'fire, fire,'" Tumthong Podhirun testified, " . . . but I did not take it seriously because it has happened before. Soon I smelled smoke and very quickly it billowed inside the place. I headed for the back door but it was locked. . . . Finally, I had no choice but to join the others and jumped out of the window. I saw many of my friends lying dead on the ground beside me."[5]

In the aftermath of the tragedy, some Bangkok activists circulated an old snapshot of two smiling peasant girls standing arm in arm beside a thicket of palm trees. One of them, Praphai Prayonghorm, died in the 1993 fire at Kader. Her friend, Kammoin Konmanee, had died in the 1989 fire. Some of the Kader workers insisted afterwards that their factory had been haunted by ghosts, that it was built on the site of an old graveyard, disturbing the dead. The folklore expressed raw poetic truth: the fire in Bangkok eerily resembled the now-forgotten details of the Triangle Shirtwaist disaster eighty years before. Perhaps the "ghosts" that some workers felt present were young women from New York who had died in 1911.

Similar tragedies, large and small, were now commonplace across developing Asia and elsewhere. Two months after Kader, another fire at a Bangkok shirt factory killed ten women. Three months after Kader, a six-story hotel collapsed and killed 133 people, injuring 351. The embarrassed minister of industry ordered special inspections of 244 large factories in the Bangkok region and found that 60 percent of them had basic violations similar to Kader's. Thai industry was growing explosively—12 to 15 percent a year—but workplace injuries and illnesses were growing even faster, from 37,000 victims in 1987 to more

than 150,000 by 1992 and an estimated 200,000 by 1994.

In China, six months after Kader, eighty-four women died and dozens of others were severely burned at another toy factory fire in the burgeoning industrial zone at Shenzhen. At Dongguan, a Hong Kong–owned raincoat factory burned in 1991, killing more than eighty people (Kader Industries also had a factory at Dongguan where two fires have been reported since 1990). In late 1993, some sixty women died at the Taiwanese-owned Gaofu textile plant in Fuzhou Province, many of them smothered in their dormitory beds by toxic fumes from burning textiles. In 1994, a shoe factory fire killed ten persons at Jiangmen; a textile factory fire killed thirty-eight and injured 160 at the Qianshan industrial zone.[6]

"Why must these tragedies repeat themselves again and again?" the *People's Daily* in Beijing asked. The official *Economic Daily* complained: "The way some of these foreign investors ignore international practice, ignore our own national rules, act completely lawlessly and immorally and lust after wealth is enough to make one's hair stand on end."[7]

America was itself no longer insulated from such brutalities. When a chicken-processing factory at Hamlet, North Carolina, caught fire in 1991, the exit doors there were also locked and twenty-five people died. A garment factory discovered by labor investigators in El Monte, California, held seventy-two Thai immigrants in virtual peonage, working eighteen hours a day in "sub-human conditions." One could not lament the deaths, harsh working conditions, child labor and subminimum wages in Thailand or across Asia and Central America without also recognizing that similar conditions have reappeared in the United States for roughly the same reasons.

Sweatshops, mainly in the garment industry, scandalized Los Angeles, New York and Dallas. The grim, foul assembly lines of the poultry-processing industry were spread across the rural South; the *Wall Street Journal*'s Tony Horwitz won a Pulitzer Prize for his harrowing description of this low-wage work. "In general," the U.S. Government Accounting Office reported in 1994, "the description of today's sweatshops differs little from that at the turn of the century."[8]

That was the real mystery: Why did global commerce, with all of its supposed modernity and wondrous technologies, restore the old barbarisms that had long ago been forbidden by law? If the information age has enabled multinational corporations to manage production and marketing spread across continents, why were their managers unable—or unwilling—to organize such mundane matters as fire prevention?

The short answer, of course, was profits, but the deeper answer was about power: Firms behaved this way because they could, because nobody would stop them. When law and social values retreated before the power of markets, then capitalism's natural drive to maximize returns had no internal governor to check its social behavior. When one enterprise took the low road to gain advantage, others would follow.

The toy fire in Bangkok provided a dramatic illustration for the much broader, less visible forms of human exploitation that were flourishing in the global system, including the widespread use of children in manufacturing, even forced labor camps in China or Burma. These matters were not a buried secret. Indeed, American television has aggressively exposed the "dark Satanic mills" with dramatic reports. ABC's *20/20* broadcast correspondent Lynn Sherr's devastating account of the Kader fire; CNN ran disturbing footage. Mike Wallace of CBS's *60 Minutes* exposed the prison labor exploited in China. NBC's *Dateline* did a piece on Wal-Mart's grim production in Bangladesh. CBS's *Street Stories* toured the shoe factories of Indonesia.

The baffling quality about modern communications was that its images could take us to people in remote corners of the world vividly and instantly, but these images have not as yet created genuine community with them. In terms of human consciousness, the "global village" was still only a picture on the TV screen.

Public opinion, moreover, absorbed contradictory messages about the global reality that were difficult to sort out. The opening stages of industrialization presented, as always, a great paradox: the process was profoundly liberating for millions, freeing them from material scarcity and limited life choices, while it also ensnared other millions in brutal new forms of domination. Both aspects were true, but there was no scale on which these opposing consequences could be easily balanced, since the good and ill effects were not usually apportioned among the same people. Some human beings were set free, while other lives were turned into cheap and expendable commodities.

Workers at Kader, for instance, earned about 100 baht a day for sewing and assembling dolls, the official minimum wage of $4, but the constant stream of new entrants meant that many at the factory actually worked for much less—only $2 or $3 a day—during a required "probationary" period of three to six months that was often extended much longer by the managers. Only one hundred of the three thousand workers at Kader were legally designated employees; the rest were "contract workers" without permanent rights and benefits, the same employment system now popularized in the United States.

"Lint, fabric, dust and animal hair filled the air on the production floor," the International Confederation of Free Trade Unions based in Brussels observed in its investigative report. "Noise, heat, congestion and fumes from various sources were reported by many. Dust control was nonexistent; protective equipment inadequate. Inhaling the dust created respiratory problems and contact with it caused skin diseases." A factory clinic dispensed antihistamines or other drugs and referred the more serious symptoms to outside hospitals. Workers paid for the medication themselves and were reimbursed, up to $6, only if they had contributed 10 baht a month to the company's health fund.

A common response to such facts, even from many sensitive people, was: yes, that was terrible, but wouldn't those workers be even worse off if civil standards were imposed on their employers since they might lose their jobs as a result? This was the same economic rationale offered by American manufacturers a century before to explain why American children must work in the coal mines and textile mills. U.S. industry had survived somehow (and, in fact, flourished) when child labor and the other malpractices were eventually prohibited by social reforms. Furthermore, it was not coincidence that industry always assigned the harshest conditions and lowest pay to the weakest members of a society—women, children, uprooted migrants. Whether the factory was in Thailand or the United States or Mexico's *maquiladora* zone, people who were already quite powerless were less likely to resist, less able to demand decency from their employers. . . .

After the fire Thai union members, intellectuals and middle-class activists from social rights organizations (the groups known in developing countries as nongovernmental organizations, or NGOs) formed the Committee to Support Kader Workers and began demanding justice from the employer. They sent a delegation to Hong Kong to confront Kader officials and investigate the complex corporate linkages of the enterprise. What they discovered was that Kader's partner in the Bangkok toy factory was actually a fabulously wealthy Thai family, the Chearavanonts, ethnic Chinese merchants who own the Charoen Pokphand Group, Thailand's own leading multinational corporation.

The CP Group owns farms, feed mills, real estate, air-conditioning and motorcycle factories, food-franchise chains—two hundred companies worldwide, several of them listed on the New York Stock Exchange. The patriarch and chairman, Dhanin Chearavanont, was said by *Fortune* magazine to be the seventy-fifth richest man in the world, with personal assets of $2.6 billion (or 65 billion baht, as the *Bangkok Post* put it). Like the other emerging "Chinese multinationals," the Pokphand Group operates through the informal networks of kinfolk and ethnic contacts spread around the world by the Chinese diaspora, while it also participates in the more rigorous accounting systems of Western economies. . . .

In the larger context, this tragedy was not explained by the arrogant power of one wealthy family or the elusive complexities of interlocking corporations. The Kader fire was ordained and organized by the free market itself. The toy industry—much like textiles and garments, shoes, electronics assembly and other low-wage sectors—existed (and thrived) by exploiting a crude ladder of desperate competition among the poorest nations. Its factories regularly hopped to new locations where wages were even lower, where the governments would be even more tolerant of abusive practices. The contract work assigned to foreign firms, including thousands of small sweatshops, fitted neatly into the systems of far-flung production of major brand names and distanced the capital owners from personal responsibility. The "virtual corporation" celebrated by some business futurists already existed in these sectors and, indeed, was now being emulated in some ways by advanced manufacturing—cars, aircraft, computers.

Over the last generation, toy manufacturers and others have moved around the Asian rim in search of the bottom-rung conditions: from Hong Kong, Korea and Taiwan to Thailand and Indonesia, from there to China, Vietnam and Bangladesh, perhaps on next to Burma, Nepal or Cambodia. Since the world had a nearly inexhaustible supply of poor people and suppliant governments, the market would keep driving in search of lower rungs; no one could say where the bottom was located. Industrial conditions were not getting better, as conventional theory assured the innocent consumers, but in many sectors were getting much worse. In America, the U.S. diplomatic opening to Vietnam was celebrated as progressive politics. In Southeast Asia, it merely opened another trapdoor beneath wages and working conditions.

A country like Thailand was caught in the middle: if it conscientiously tried to improve, it would pay a huge price. When Thai unions lobbied to win improvements in minimum-wage standards, textile plants began leaving for Vietnam and elsewhere or even importing cheaper "guest workers" from Burma. When China opened its fast-growing industrial zones in Shenzhen, Dongguan and other locations, the new competition had direct consequences on the factory floors of Bangkok.

Kader, according to the ICFTU, opened two new factories in Shekou and Dongguan where young people were working fourteen-hour days, seven days a week, to fill the U.S. Christmas orders for Mickey Mouse and other American dolls. Why should a company worry about sprinkler systems or fire escapes for a dusty factory in Bangkok when it could hire brand-new workers in China for only $20 a month, one fifth of the labor cost in Thailand?

The ICFTU report described the market forces: "The lower cost of production of toys in China changes the investment climate for countries like Thailand. Thailand competes with China to attract investment capital for local toy production. With this development, Thailand has become sadly lax in enforcing its own legislation. It turns a blind eye to health violations, thus allowing factory owners to ignore safety standards. Since China entered the picture, accidents in Thailand have nearly tripled."

The Thai minister of industry, Sanan Kachornprasart, described the market reality more succinctly: "If we punish them, who will want to invest here?" Thai authorities subsequently filed charges against three Kader factory managers, but none against the company itself nor, of course, the Cheara-vanont family.[9]

. . . The fire in Bangkok reflected the amorality of the marketplace when it has been freed of social obligations. But the tragedy also mocked the moral claims of three great religions, whose adherents were all implicated. Thais built splendid golden temples exalting Buddha, who taught them to put spiritual being before material wealth. Chinese claimed to have acquired superior social values, reverence for family and community, derived from the teachings of Confucius. Americans bought the toys from Asia to celebrate the birth of Jesus Christ. Their shared complicity was another of the strange convergences made possible by global commerce. . . .

In the modern industrial world, only the ignorant can pretend to self-righteousness since only the primitive are truly innocent. No advanced society has reached that lofty stage without enduring barbaric consequences and despoliation along the way; no one who enjoys the uses of electricity or the internal combustion engine may claim to oppose industrialization for others without indulging in imperious hypocrisy.

Americans, one may recall, built their early national infrastructure and organized large-scale agriculture with slave labor. The developing American nation swept native populations from their ancient lands and drained the swampy prairies to grow grain. It burned forests to make farmland, decimated wildlife, dammed the wild rivers and displaced people who were in the way. It assigned the dirtiest, most dangerous work to immigrants and children. It eventually granted political rights to all, but grudgingly and only after great conflicts, including a terrible civil war.

The actual history of nations is useful to remember when trying to form judgments about the new world. Asian leaders regularly remind Americans and Europeans of exactly how the richest nation-states became wealthy and observe further that, despite their great wealth, those countries have not perfected social relations among rich and poor, weak and powerful. The maldistribution of incomes is worsening in America, too, not yet as extreme as Thailand's, but worse than many less fortunate nations. . . .

Coming to terms with one's own history ought not only to induce a degree of humility toward others and their struggles, but also to clarify what one really believes about human society. No one can undo the past, but that does not relieve people of the burden of making judgments about the living present or facing up to its moral implications. If the global system has truly created a unified marketplace, then every worker, every consumer, every society is already connected to the other. The responsibility exists and invoking history is not an excuse to hide from the new social questions.

Just as Americans cannot claim a higher morality while benefiting from inhumane exploitation, neither can developing countries pretend to become modern "one world" producers and expect exemption from the world's social values. Neither can the global enterprises. The future asks: Can capitalism itself be altered and reformed? Or is the world doomed to keep renewing these inhumanities in the name of economic progress?

The proposition that human dignity is indivisible does not suppose that everyone will become equal or alike or perfectly content in his or her circumstances. It does insist that certain well-understood social principles exist internationally which are enforceable and ought to be the price of admission in the global system. The idea is very simple: every person—man, woman and child—regardless of where he or she exists in time and place or on the chain of economic development, is entitled to respect as an individual being.

For many in the world, life itself is all that they possess; an economic program that deprives them of life's precious possibilities is not only unjust, but also utterly unnecessary.

Peasants may not become kings, but they are entitled to be treated with decent regard for their sentient and moral beings, not as cheap commodities. Newly industrialized nations cannot change social patterns overnight, any more than the advanced economies did before them, but they can demonstrate that they are changing.

This proposition is invasive, no question, and will disturb the economic and political arrangements within many societies. But every nation has a sovereign choice in this matter, the sort of choice made in the marketplace every day. If Thailand or China resents the intrusion of global social standards, it does not have to sell its toys to America. And Americans do not have to buy them. If Singapore rejects the idea of basic rights for women, then women in America or Europe may reject Singapore—and multinational firms that profit from the subordination of women. If people do not assert these values in global trade, then their own convictions will be steadily coarsened.

In Bangkok, when I asked Professor Voravidh to step back from Thailand's problems and suggest a broader remedy, he thought for a long time and then said: "We need cooperation among nations because the multinational corporations can shift from one country to another. If they don't like Thailand, they move to Vietnam or China. Right now, we are all competing and the world is getting worse. We need a GATT on labor conditions and on the minimum wage, we need a standard on the minimum conditions for work and a higher standard for children."

The most direct approach, as Voravidh suggested, is an international agreement to incorporate such standards in the terms of trade, with penalties and incentives, even temporary embargoes, that will impose social obligations on the global system, the firms and countries. Most of the leading governments, including the United States, have long claimed to support this idea—a so-called social clause for GATT—but the practical reality is that they do not. Aside from rhetoric, when their negotiators are at the table, they always yield readily to objections from the multinational corporations and developing nations. Both the firms and the governing elites of poor countries have a strong incentive to block the proposition since both profit from a free-running system that exploits the weak. A countering force has to come from concerned citizens. Governments refuse to act, but voters and consumers are not impotent, and, in the meantime, they can begin the political campaign by purposefully targeting the producers—boycotting especially the well-known brand names that depend upon lovable images for their sales. Americans will not stop buying toys at Christmas, but they might single out one or two American toy companies for Yuletide boycotts, based on their scandalous relations with Kader and other manufacturers. Boycotts are difficult to organize and sustain, but every one of the consumer-goods companies is exquisitely vulnerable.

In India, the South Asian Coalition on Child Servitude, led by Kailash Satyarthi, has created a promising model for how to connect the social obligations of consumers and workers. Indian carpet makers are notorious for using small children at their looms—bonded children like Thailand's bonded prostitutes—and have always claimed economic necessity. India is a poor nation and the work gives wage income to extremely poor families, they insist. But these children will never escape poverty if they are deprived of schooling, the compulsory education promised by law.

The reformers created a "no child labor" label that certifies the rugs were made under honorable conditions and they persuaded major importers in Germany to insist upon the label. The exporters in India, in turn, have to allow regular citizen inspections of their workplaces to win the label for their rugs. Since this consumer-led certification system began, the carpet industry's use of children has fallen dramatically. A Textile Ministry official in New Delhi said: "The government is now contemplating the total eradication of child labor in the next few years."[10]

Toys, shoes, electronics, garments—many consumer sectors are vulnerable to similar approaches, though obviously the scope of manufacturing is too diverse and complex for consumers to police it. Governments have to act collectively. If a worldwide agreement is impossible to achieve, then groups of governments can form their own preferential trading systems, introducing social standards that reverse the incentives for developing countries and for capital choosing new locations for production.

The crucial point illustrated by Thailand's predicament is that global social standards will help the poorer countries escape their economic trap. Until a floor is built beneath the market's social behavior, there is no way that a small developing country like Thailand can hope to overcome the downward pull of competition from other, poorer nations. It must debase its citizens to hold on to what it has achieved. The path to improvement is blocked by the economics of an irresponsible marketplace.

Setting standards will undoubtedly slow down the easy movement of capital—and close down the most scandalous operations—but that is not a harmful consequence for people in struggling nations that aspire to industrial prosperity or for a global economy burdened with surpluses and inadequate consumption. When global capital makes a commitment to a developing economy, it ought not to acquire the power to blackmail that nation in perpetuity. Supported by global rules, those nations can begin to improve conditions and stabilize their own social development. At least they would have a chance to avoid the great class conflicts that others have experienced.

In the meantime, the very least that citizens can demand of their own government is that it no longer use public money to finance the brutal upheavals or environmental despoliation that has flowed from large-scale projects of the World Bank and other lending agencies. The social distress in the cities begins in the countryside, and the wealthy nations have often financed it in the name of aiding development. The World Bank repeatedly proclaims its new commitment to strategies that address the development ideas of indigenous peoples and halt the destruction of natural systems. But social critics and the people I encountered in Thailand and elsewhere have not seen much evidence of real change.

The terms of trade are usually thought of as commercial agreements, but they are also an implicit statement of moral values. In its present terms, the global system values property over human life. When a nation like China steals the property of capital, pirating copyrights, films or technology, other governments will take action to stop it and be willing to impose sanctions and penalty tariffs on the offending nation's trade. When human lives are stolen in the "dark Satanic mills," nothing happens to the offenders since, according to the free market's sense of conscience, there is no crime.

NOTES

1. William Blake's immortal lines are from "Milton," one of his "prophetic books" written between 1804 and 1808. *The Portable Blake*, Alfred Kazin, editor (New York: Penguin Books, 1976).

2. *Washington Post, Financial Times* and *New York Times*, May 12, 1993, and *Wall Street Journal*, May 13, 1993.

3. The U.S. contract clients for Kader's Bangkok factory were cited by the International Confederation of Free Trade Unions headquartered in Brussels in its investigatory report, "From the Ashes: A Toy Factory Fire in Thailand," December 1994. In the aftermath, the ICFTU and some nongovernmental organizations attempted to mount an "international toy campaign" and a few sporadic demonstrations occurred in Hong Kong and London, but there never was a general boycott of the industry or any of its individual companies. The labor federation met with associations of British and American toy manufacturers and urged them

to adopt a "code of conduct" that might discourage the abuses. The proposed codes were inadequate, the ICFTU acknowledged, but it was optimistic about their general adoption by the international industry.

4. Mitchell Zuckoff of the *Boston Globe* produced a powerful series of stories on labor conditions in developing Asia and reported Hasbro's reaction to the Kader fire, July 10, 1994. David Miller was quoted in *USA Today*, May 13, 1993, and on ABC News *20/20*, July 30, 1993.

5. The first-person descriptions of the Kader fire are but a small sampling from survivors' horrifying accounts, collected by investigators and reporters at the scene. My account of the disaster is especially indebted to the investigative report by the International Confederation of Free Trade Unions; Bangkok's English-language newspapers, the *Post* and *The Nation;* the Asia Monitor Resource Center of Hong Kong; and Lynn Sherr's devastating report on ABC's *20/20*, July 30, 1993. Lampan Taptim and Tumthong Podhirun, "From the Ashes," ICFTU, December 1994; Cheng: *Asian Labour Update*, Asia Monitor Resource Center, Hong Kong, July 1993; La-iad Nads-nguen: *The Nation*, Bangkok, May 12, 1993; and Chaweewan Mekpan: *20/20*.

6. Details on Thailand's worker injuries and the litany of fires in China are from the ICFTU report and other labor bulletins, as well as interviews in Bangkok.

7. The *People's Daily* and *Economic Daily* were quoted by Andrew Quinn of Reuters in *The Daily Citizen* of Washington, DC, January 18, 1994.

8. Tony Horwitz described chicken-processing employment as the second fastest growing manufacturing job in America: *Wall Street Journal*, December 1, 1994. U.S. sweatshops were reviewed in "Garment Industry: Efforts to Address the Prevalence and Conditions of Sweatshops," U.S. Government Accounting Office, November 1994.

9. Sanan was quoted in the *Bangkok Post*, May 29, 1993.

10. The New Delhi–based campaign against child labor in the carpet industry is admittedly limited to a narrow market and expensive product, but its essential value is demonstrating how retailers and their customers can be connected to a distant factory floor. See, for instance, Hugh Williamson, "Stamp of Approval," *Far Eastern Economic Review*, February 2, 1995, and N. Vasuk Rao in the *Journal of Commerce*, March 1, 1995.

THINKING ABOUT THE READING

Greider argues that the tragedy of the Kader industrial fire cannot be explained simply by focusing on greedy families and multinational corporations. Instead, he blames global economics and the organization of the international toy industry. He writes, "The Kader fire was ordained and organized by the free market itself." What do you suppose he means by this? Given the enormous economic pressures that this and other multinational industries operate under, are such tragedies inevitable? Why have attempts to improve the working conditions in "third world" factories been so ineffective?

How to Squeeze More out of a Penny

Ellen Israel Rosen

(2006)

This chapter focuses on the structure of Wal-Mart's store operations in an effort to analyze how the firm's technology, culture, store policies, and covert and overt management practices shape the experience of Wal-Mart's workers. While men and women are employed at Wal-Mart, almost two-thirds of all employees are women (64 percent). Among hourly sales workers, even more (70.2 percent) are women. Most hourly workers at Wal-Mart stack merchandise, help customers, and work as cashiers.

Business analysts explain Wal-Mart's tremendous growth and productivity as a result of its sophisticated information technology (IT) and unique logistics systems. Wal-Mart's efficiency, profitability, and size are seen as a function of the system's potential to gather information and for management to use it to rapidly distribute low-priced consumer goods to stores. Only infrequently do they look at the quality of work this produces for employees, the assumption being that the jobs require little education and are easy to learn. Yet, as I will argue, these new systems operate within the context of a management practice and a company culture which intensify work pressures on Wal-Mart's retail staff and lead to a form of "management by intimidation." Ultimately, these practices may contribute to illegal activities, particularly sex discrimination and wage abuse, issues that have publicly plagued Wal-Mart for several years.

Centralization

Wal-Mart's success is partly a result of its centralization. Even before the advent of computer technology, the firm had always sought to centralize operations and authority. Executives at Wal-Mart headquarters at Bentonville, Arkansas, traditionally sent out managers to monitor each store through regular visits. Then field managers made weekly reports to company headquarters. Today's computer technology allows Bentonville to collect vast quantities of information not previously available, which has greatly increased the firm's ability to centralize and standardize Wal-Mart's operation.

Wal-Mart is a traditional bureaucracy, autocratically run from the top down, from Bentonville, Arkansas, where the CEO and his closest associates make decisions for the company. All directives and policy changes decided at this level flow through the employment pyramid to all of Wal-Mart's stores and distribution centers, from the store managers to those at the very bottom of the pyramid, where "sales associates" unload merchandise and deal with customers, and cashiers check out merchandise. Managers of stores and distribution centers send data directly to the home office. The technology is specifically designed to allow corporate headquarters to be constantly abreast of information about its suppliers and its stores, so top management can respond to any event that affects Wal-Mart's stores.

Why pick on Wal-Mart? Other large retailers engage in many of the same practices, those both legal and illegal. Yet Wal-Mart's rapid growth, size, and power have made it the leader—a change agent, or as Nelson Lichtenstein argues, "a template of the new global capitalism." With a market power unequaled by any of its competitors, Wal-Mart has been the model on which America's, and a new kind of global, capitalism is now being built. Where Wal-Mart leads, others follow.

The Store Manager

The store manager provides the basic connection between the demands of corporate headquarters and the hierarchy of store management and hourly employees. He is also the face of Bentonville on the ground. The most important job of the store manager is to reduce the store's costs and increase the store's sales. Store managers may not always be able to control sales, but they can reduce the store's operating costs by the choices they make deploying personnel to manage the merchandise.

Bill Thomas is a former manager of a Wal-Mart supercenter in Kentucky. One of the most important jobs he did was to figure out the "labor budget" for his store: how many employees he could schedule for the next three weeks, each at particular rates of pay, based on when they were available for work. After making this calculation, he forwarded the numbers to the district manager, the regional vice president, and the divisional vice president for approval.

"Every Monday morning," he said, "I would go in and evaluate my sales. I would do what's called 'forecasting.' For example, last year I did $1.2 million in sales. This year I think I can do $1.5 million. So I forecast a conservative percent increase or decrease, whatever my trend is, and then I key that into the computer. The computer spits out a daily payroll figure that is scaled and based on how much volume we did a day last year. It has last year's sales by hour and by department."

The purpose of this formula is to reduce labor costs as sales volumes increase. For example, if a store increased its sales by 7 percent last year compared to the previous year, the goal is to save 0.1 percent of that increase during the next year. The wage bill for the next year could not be budgeted to exceed 6.9 percent of sales. Should sales increase over 10 percent, the manager is required to budget

0.2 percent of sales for wage costs. Based on this estimate, each store manager must budget, on a monthly basis, how many hours to schedule workers.

Thomas's annual compensation, and his future at Wal-Mart, depend on this formula. Store managers get a basic salary. As Thomas put it, "What they do is give you a salary and then you make a bonus and where you make your money as a store manager is in your bonus. How you get your bonus is based strictly on your net profitability for your store. . . . Like the first million of profit you get 1.2 percent and then the next million you get like 0.8 percent and the next million you get 0.4 percent. In the last store 1 made $162,000 [with a yearly salary of $50,000]. That was at the supercenter," Thomas adds. "And I've known guys that have made a lot less, but lower-volume stores typically, like if you're in the $18 million to $25 million range, the person's going to net, but you have to cross a threshold of I think it's a million five to break even, to take a profit out of it."

According to Thomas, store managers are held accountable for sales growth even though sales are not entirely under their control. Their responsibility is to produce "good" sales figures every year and, at the same time, save costs. Wal-Mart provides store managers with a "preferred budget," which would allow them to staff adequately. But no store is actually allowed the preferred budget, which is in excess of the real labor costs that store managers are permitted to spend, i.e., the targeted budget. As a result, the stores are always chronically understaffed. Thomas says, "There is not a store out there that is allowed the run the kind of hours that are needed."

Wal-Mart's wage budget means that managers at every level—from store managers to assistant managers to department managers—have little control over the number of people they can have to run the store. Thomas said he always worked with a "skeleton crew," and constantly struggled to "put out fires." "Things get overbooked. . . . There are three trucks with merchandise that have to be put in the store.

Freight and merchandise sometimes sit on the floors in aisles and boxes. The housekeeping is poor. You will find fire exits blocked, broken pallet jacks and ladders; there are things all over the floor. Floors are dirty and wet and shelves are stacked too high."

Salaried managers—store managers, co-managers, and assistant managers—work as many hours a week as they feel is necessary to get their work done, often sixty to eighty hours. Thomas believes that being a store manager or assistant manager is among the toughest jobs there is because it means taking ultimate responsibility for doing whatever needs to be done, with whatever personnel are allowed. To succeed, i.e., to get a store of their own, managers often work virtually all the time. Yet they also depend on the cooperation of subordinates—department managers, and full-time and even part-time salesclerks—to "get the job done."

Scheduling

In the past, department managers made up work schedules for the people in their departments. Today, Bentonville decides how workers will be scheduled. Recently the home office has introduced its own scheduling formula designed to be used with a computer program created in Bentonville. The technology is extremely agile. According to Mary Roland, a department manager in the jewelry department, "The computer 'knows'" that the store is not very busy on Sunday morning between 9 and 11 A.M. So it will schedule eight people to run the cash registers. But the computer program cannot account for all variations in human behavior. Sometimes on one Sunday it will be very busy during those hours. If there is not enough staff on hand, customers will have to stand in long lines, which Bentonville doesn't like. Because too few cashiers are scheduled to work on Sunday, the store manager will have to call on other sales associates in the stores to run additional cash registers.

At Wal-Mart there are a wide variety of shifts, which makes scheduling even more difficult. Some employees are full-time, scheduled for forty hours. But a twenty-eight or thirty-two-hour week is also considered full-time at Wal-Mart. Part-timers work twelve hours or more a week.

Employees often have to change their schedules, particularly part-time workers who have another job, or students whose academic schedules change frequently. Bill Thomas says that no one can be available 24/7 as Wal-Mart wants everyone to be. If people say they're available, they're lying. Besides, in addition to students, there are family emergencies, such as a sick child or an aging parent, which cause people to be absent from work.

Given these conditions, managers often find it difficult to accommodate employees, who, dissatisfied with untenable schedules, simply quit. This can contribute to additional holes in the store's staffing, putting more pressure on people who are already shorthanded.

Turnover is particularly high at Wal-Mart compared to the retail industry as a whole—35 to 45 percent a year among full-time workers, 56 percent among part-timers. Some claim turnover at Wal-Mart is even higher. According to Douglas Shuit at *Workforce Management*, "Every year 600,000 to 700,000 Wal-Mart associates can walk out the door and must be replaced by fresh faces willing to work for starting hourly wages of $7 to $8. An analysis by Staffing.org shows that the retail industry spends $2,379 for each new hire. At that price, the tab for hiring 600,000 workers would be $1.4 billion."

High turnover, of course, means it becomes more likely that employees fail to learn their jobs properly. Further, regardless of their skill and experience, those working are shorthanded but still remain responsible for doing whatever needs doing, regardless of the time available to them. Managers struggle with skeleton crews, and sales clerks feel the company is insensitive to their needs.

Thomas says, "A lot of the assistant managers get fed up and they get like fire-breathing dragons" at the high rate of turnover. Mary Roland is also irritated by the overwhelming demands of her job. "At Wal-Mart," she says, "you are expected to do the work of three people."

Pressures at Work

The pressures of work at Wal-Mart are revealed by the daily activities workers report. When the goods arrive at the store, Wal-Mart associates remove them. Another worker scans the bar codes with a handheld computer called a "telxon gun." Every stock-keeping unit (SKU), e.g., tube of toothpaste or bottle of shampoo, is followed as it enters the store— whether it is shelved, or damaged and returned to the company, then again if and when it is marked down. It is entered when it is sold and again when reordered. Bill Thomas described the information that could be gathered by Wal-Mart's state-of-the-art computer systems when he said, "I could tell you last year on July 13 between the hours of 7 and 8 P.M. how much [in] sales a store did and how much of it was rung up by Sally Jo, the cashier with the operator number 342, [within] that hour."

The difficulties workers experience at Wal-Mart are illustrated by the demands imposed on them by managers, who themselves are pressured to "get the job done." Katie Mitchell works from 10 P.M. to 6:30 A.M. She starts work after the unloading crew removes the merchandise from the trucks. Her job is to set the merchandise on pallets and bring it to the aisles, where it can be stacked. She has to "inventory" the merchandise after it is unloaded from trucks and remove the shrink-wrap from the packages. Using her telxon gun, Katie counts each item and enters it in the store computer. If she makes an error she has to check with the truck driver's invoice and make the correction. She says that when the truckers arrive they all want to rush to get into the bays and deliver their merchandise. If there is a miscount or an open box, everyone has to wait.

There is always too much work to be done and no one to help her. She often misses work breaks and once missed lunch entirely—that is, she worked off the clock—but she had to get the work done by the end of her shift or be "chewed out" by her supervisor. The biggest problem, though, was that after 10 P.M. the workers were locked in the stores. No one could leave even for an emergency like a sick child. Then, "after you kicked and screamed the supervisor might let you out the back door, which was far from the parking lot where the employee's cars were parked and was unlighted." Wal-Mart, under the pressure of bad publicity, has subsequently changed this policy and does not lock the door at night.

Kate Moroney, employed in a Florida Wal-Mart, works at night, from 10 P.M. to 7 A.M., stocking the frozen foods in the deli department freezers. She also answers the phone and helps customers. After 4 P.M. the department managers leave, so sometimes she is the only one responsible for covering the other departments as well—food, greeting cards, small appliances, housewares, and household chemicals.

Other Wal-Mart employees have also told me that when the store is busy, they are often paged to the front of the store to run the cash register. Then they are required to complete their own work. Recently Kate was asked to train as a cashier, i.e., to study the computer-based learning (CBL) modules, which explain how to operate the store's cash registers, and learn the responsibilities of a cashier. Most training for jobs at the hourly-worker level is done this way. Having passed the test, Kate is now paged frequently to run the cash register. If she is unable to put out her stock for the next day, that job must be finished by the next day's crew, who then get behind on their own work. Billy Draper was a college student who worked part-time at Wal-Mart. He told me that his job was "understaffed," that it was a revolving door and that many people quit. His supervisor often asked him to hurry up with the stocking so Zack could begin to stock the shelves of other departments—often three in one night. The supervisor kept rushing Zack to go faster.

Often about a half hour before closing, just when the staff was ready to clean up and go home, his supervisor would come up with new projects to do, for example, loading soda pop on the shelves on a display in the front of the store. When Billy said that one "couldn't do overtime" at Wal-Mart, his supervisor told him, "Don't clock in until midnight." But Billy said he refused to work off the clock in this way.

Patti Slater works in Wal-Mart's office overseeing financial reports. She said she suffers most when management pulls her from the job she is hired to do, interrupting her work and asking her to "help out" elsewhere in the store. One time the store ran out of computer paper, so Patti was asked to go to a nearby Wal-Mart to get some. Another time a Wal-Mart vice president was scheduled to stop by the store and Patti was asked to go out and buy him some "hometown" souvenirs. Once during the holidays she was asked to clean up a messy Christmas shop. During the back-to-school fall rush, Patti was asked to help customers find copies of the school supply lists that Wal-Mart gives shoppers, a list of items Wal-Mart provides for every grade level in the community schools. When the checkout lines are too long, Patti is sometimes asked to do "line rushing"—to take the telxon gun and scan the customers' merchandise while it is still in their carts. This saves cashiers time, during which more merchandise can be sold. But these extra chores do not excuse Patti from having to finish her own work—and on time—despite what she describes as constant interruptions.

Information Technology

If understaffing generates constant complaints of insufficient time, the speed at which the IT systems allow Wal-Mart to purchase and deliver goods to its stores creates additional problems for Wal-Mart employees. The pressure is generated by both the information technology and the management. Trying to save labor costs, managers push employees to work to the speed of the new machines. Management depends on the large volume of information flows, and on workers who can move merchandise fast enough for the system's efficiency and precision.

All employees are expected to learn how to use the information technology effectively. Yet the proper use of IT itself is problematic. First, the technology is not easy to learn. Second, the high rate of turnover shortens the learning period of many employees. Finally, the detail and quantity of information that must be collected increases the workload and generates mistakes—which take more time to correct.

Patti Slater knows what this means. When I asked her to describe her job she said, "I come in at 6 A.M. I take the reports off the printer, separate them, and start checking them. All the cash received for every item is also input, summed and tallied by category, then printed out on a daily basis. There is a store manager's report, a payroll report, a cash office report . . . about fifty separate reports including ones for department managers." They are checked and tallied on a daily basis. The store manager must review the reports, sign off on them, and send them to the division manager. Then they go up the hierarchy to corporate headquarters, where Bentonville executives examine the payroll and merchandise data from all the stores, districts, and regions to make purchasing and merchandising decisions for all the stores.

When sales workers or department managers make mistakes, Patti must go out on the sales floor to review the problem with them and try to get the numbers to tally. "Sometimes," she says, "the figures can be as much as $1,000 off." The problem, as Patti sees it, is that management does not do a good job of training people to use the telxon guns properly or to manage the inventory. "The CBL modules are the only real training sales associates get in learning to do their jobs," Patti says, but "you can't learn what you need to do the job just by taking the CBLs." High turnover also contributes to this problem.

Patti Slater described her job as so complicated that even her store manager did not have a good understanding of all of Wal-Mart's systems. He often asks her to check out problems she believes were resolved weeks before. She then has to research them all over again in addition to doing the rest of her work. Computers do not make errors, but human beings do. Patti says, "Sometimes the computer says you have more than you can find. Then you have to find it. Was it stolen? Is it in the back room, damaged, lost?"

Sometimes it is necessary to hand-count the items on the shelves, or to look in the back room of the store, where unshelved merchandise is stored. Or damaged goods come into the store and have to be sent back to the vendor rather than be put on the shelves. Then there is employee and consumer theft, or "shrinkage" as it is called, that can also throw off the numbers.

Despite the goal of seeing just the right amount of merchandise in the right size, color, and model on the shelf, there is often too much merchandise. The job of Marty Spinner is to "work the bins at night to find room to put the overstock, which comes into the store in large volumes because a lot is delivered all at once."

Jimmy Forester, a store manager in St. Louis, says that sometimes the buyers get a good price on something, so they buy it, but then it doesn't sell as fast as it is supposed to— maybe thirty items in one week and only five the next. "The merchandise that doesn't fit on the shelves has to be put in the back room. When district and regional managers visit they don't like to see the stockrooms too full, so store managers have to find a way to sell it." They have few options for dealing with this. They can advertise the goods in the local paper or put it on a special display, but they only have the power to mark it down 3.5 percent. The alternative is to store the goods in the back room in the hope of hiding them from the district manager. Jimmy told me that he once covered his overstock of tires with a sheet. Another time he made a display of all the tires to hide his overstocks from the division manager.

Promotions and Staffing

Patti Slater had worked at Wal-Mart for nine and a half years, doing almost every job in the store. When the store opened she was hired at $6 an hour to manage the pet department. Then the manager sent her to open another supercenter nearby to remodel the electronics department. After that she was made manager of the toy department, then the OTC (over-the-counter) drug department, the cosmetics department, and the stationery department. She was finally made a "zone manager," responsible for stationery, pets, paper goods, and furniture, a job which she did for several years. From her latest job, she was promoted to financial clerk.

Instead of being encouraged to pursue management training, a path to salaried management, Patti was put to work in the office. She was also among the highest-paid sales associates, earning $12.40 an hour. Soon after taking this job Patti began having anxiety attacks. She went to the doctor, who put her on medication. "I was taking Valium for breakfast and lunch and it made me sick." The pressure, she believes, "put her over the edge."

One might think that Patti, a competent person, would be offered a chance at the management track. But that was not to be. Wal-Mart promotes few women to salaried managers. Many believe the reason is sex discrimination. At Wal-Mart there are few formal criteria for promotion. Men are often moved up the management ranks through an offer of management training. Then they become assistant managers, store managers, district manager, and above. A full 85 percent of store managers at Wal-Mart are men, often men as young as their early thirties. According to Mary Roland, there don't seem to be any particular criteria for promotion, except being male and having a profitable department. This is confirmed in a study by a consultant to the plaintiffs in the Wal-Mart class-action sex-discrimination suit. Richard Drogin, a statistics professor, found that there were no formal criteria for promotion at Wal-Mart. People, mostly men, are simply "tapped on the shoulder" and moved up—often over the heads of the women who trained them.

Not only does Wal-Mart understaff its stores; when business is slow, management also cuts hours. Anthony Sironno works at a Wal-Mart as a customer service manager. Tony supervises twenty-three people at the "front end of the store," mostly cashiers. Unlike many people, Tony likes his job, appreciating the health insurance and the 401(k) plan. He also expects to be promoted.

He is entitled to a stockholder's bonus, which is dependent on the store's profit. He says his bonus can be anywhere from $0 to $1,700. This year he doesn't expect to get a bonus, because the store's sales have not improved 1.5 percent as was anticipated. He hopes he will next year, if the store's sales increase. Yet later in the interview he told me that the store he works in, on the West Coast, is in a community where there are four Wal-Marts in the area. The store's sales have not improved as projected, he believes, because the area is overstored.

Because of the slow sales, the store started cutting hours three weeks ago. Anthony's were cut from forty to thirty-five, a fact about which he is not happy. He has already started to cut the hours of the people he supervises. He sends one or two people home each week, and they lose two to four hours a person.

Cutting hours when sales fall is a regular practice at Wal-Mart. Sometimes management asks for volunteers to leave early. But others are sent home involuntarily and without warning. According to Katie Mitchell, this happens all the time, a practice confirmed by Jimmy Forester, the manager of the St. Louis Wal-Mart store. Jimmy says, "This is often done by asking someone during a quiet time in the store to simply clock out and go home." The employees are not paid for the lost time.

According to Jimmy, in April 1999 Wal-Mart vice president Tom Coughlin got on the Wal-Mart satellite system and told all store managers that they all had to cut three hours a week of the work time of every employee. At

an average cost of $7.50 an hour, that meant savings of about $20 million per week. Jimmy believes corporate management required this labor cut because it had to send out the first-quarter profit-and-loss statements, and needed these savings to bolster its next quarterly report. This would make the stock price rise, which, of course, favored the executives at the home office.

Store managers are responsible each month for filling out a profit-and-loss statement: sales, labor costs, and other expenses in which managers are expected to increase their sales and cut their wage costs. If they don't, Jimmy says, "the manager's head is put on the chopping block." There are no incentives, just responsibility. He calls it "management by intimidation."

Jed Stone, who worked for Wal-Mart as a store manager from 1983 to 1991 (years that Sam Walton was still the CEO) said that Wal-Mart was unlike any other company he has worked for since. Bentonville's executives continually warned managers, "If you don't beat yesterday [i.e., increase sales, reduce costs], management could have your job at any moment." Bill Thomas had already told me of a "beat-yesterday book" that Sam Walton always used to carry around, which is now on display at the Wal-Mart Museum in Bentonville.

What Stone described was the practice of informally urging managers to break the rules that Wal-Mart formally upheld. To break the rules was a "terminable offense," but not to meet the goals—higher and higher sales, increasing cost reductions—was to lose credibility, to be "coached," demoted, and potentially fired. To "beat yesterday" Jed always had to "cut corners and break the rules." He said it was always a struggle to keep the shelves stacked and the floors shiny, and to get hourly workers to help customers. Inevitably he had to break the rules, mainly having employees work off the clock to avoid paying overtime. He surpassed the acceptable budget for markdowns and worked more than officially allowed, both official reasons for termination.

Senior management, he said, ignored all such offenses when sales were up and profits high. Yet, "as soon as my sales went down, there were audits. Everything I had signed my name to was investigated." Jed said that 10 to 15 percent of all store managers were demoted to assistant manager and moved to another store. Some would be promoted to store manager again. Jed finally left Wal-Mart to take another job. He says, "Store managers are just as much victims of the Wal-Mart system as hourly sales workers, cashiers, and floor cleaners."

A similar approach to the rules was found even at the lowest levels of Wal-Mart's employment structure. Billy Draper, the college student whose first job was to unload stock at night, asked for a day job when his class schedule changed. He was made a cashier. Then Wal-Mart management passed out a statement for cashiers to sign. It described cash scams customers sometimes use. As Billy put it, "The message is, I know and understand the scam. *If I get scammed I realize I will be fired.*"

The Wal-Mart Culture—Squeezing Pennies and Shaming Workers

Much of this behavior is a result of a policy designed to save pennies, because the saved pennies of more than 3,500 stores add up to millions of dollars. The people in the home office feel, to paraphrase Sam Walton, "if you can squeeze more out of a penny," then you should do it, a version of the Puritan ethic that resembles the model of Ebenezer Scrooge instead of Benjamin Franklin. Carolyn Thiebes was the personnel manager in one of Wal-Mart's Oregon stores. She was also a plaintiff in an Oregon wage-abuse case. She told me that the store had no copying machine. The office staff had to go to the local Kinko's if something needed copying. Workers were told that if they needed a pen they should bring one from home. As workers quit or were fired, remaining sales associates were asked to take their dirty smocks home and wash them.

Employees are motivated by constant reminders that they are part of the "Wal-Mart family." Family and team members, of course, pitch in to do what has to be done for the good of the group. Because each employee is "responsible for the whole store," everyone needs to be "flexible." Such an analogy is flawed in two ways. First, Wal-Mart is not a family. Second, family members are not "coached" or "fired." Nor are they held responsible for things that are out of their control.

Carolyn Naster told me that employees are told that at Wal-Mart, "everyone's responsible for everything. A department is everyone's department." Managers can make a person responsible for doing a job about which he or she knows little or nothing, and for which he or she has not been trained. This absolves the manager of responsibility for mistakes and puts the onus on subordinates. Managers delegate work arbitrarily. Should workers fail to complete all they have to do, as former manager Jed Stone described his own difficulties with Wal-Mart, they "take the fall." They can be blamed, even fired, when things go wrong. They discover that the rules Wal-Mart has repeatedly pressed on them are selectively enforced.

Wal-Mart disciplines workers by shaming them. Alan Tripster was treated to this type of punishment. He worked in domestics (bedding and curtains) in a Missouri Wal-Mart. As in other stores, after the Christmas rush management began to cut hours. Instead of laying employees off, however, the managers began to find reasons to fire them. As Alan described it, the managers were "writing up" everyone in his department. "People were getting fired left and right, so everyone tried to walk the straight and narrow." As he saw it, "They would fire people for cause. Then when they needed more help they wouldn't have to take back longtime workers who were making more money and could hire people at the starting wage." Alan remembers a manager saying, in front of a group of associates, "I can get rid of all these people and find others willing to work." The comment, he felt, was deeply humiliating, when spoken to people who needed their jobs so desperately.

Even if shaming doesn't lead to the loss of one's job, at Wal-Mart it is used to discipline workers. As workers are increasingly shamed, made to believe they did something seriously wrong, it becomes easier for managers to "order them around." Prior to being fired in the store where Alan worked, employees were called to the front office on the loudspeaker. Then they would have to walk all the way from the back of the store to the front. Allen called this "the walk of shame." When it happened to him, he said, "it was one of the most horrible experiences of my life." The managers "treat you like you were the worst thing to ever walk the face of the earth."

The same kind of shaming is also found at the top of the organization. Carolyn Thiebes, the personnel manager, had been to Bentonville and toured the corporate offices. She said that each Friday afternoon the management teams in Bentonville have a meeting in a "huge amphitheater" and watch a broadcast where Wal-Mart's CEO and other VPs talk directly to the audience. Executives discuss the week's successes and problems. A manager whose store has sent in a payroll with overtime, which is against company policy, is named and shamed in front of the entire audience.

Harry Borden, another store manager, was also shamed. A man in his midforties, he was somewhat older than the other store managers, and had a heart condition. For the past two years his regional manager had publicly harassed him by making "jokes" about his weight. Harry had a heart condition, but was so "embarrassed and humiliated" by these "jokes" that, without telling his wife, he took diet pills to lose weight, even though the medication was contraindicated for heart disease.

Three months later Harry died from a heart attack. He was carrying a large television set out of the store at a busy time. There were no other associates around to help him. When his wife saw the diet pills in the medicine cabinet she instituted a wrongful-death suit against Wal-Mart, which she eventually won.

Conclusion

As business analysts argue, Wal-Mart saves operating costs and increases its productivity through the use of its innovative information technology and logistics systems. No doubt this is an important goal for all retailers. But how are the labor policies and practices Wal-Mart uses required for the new technologies to be so productive?

In industrial production, advances in technology are frequently followed by employee layoffs: the remaining staff must work faster because they must tend more machines or produce more per hour for the same rate of pay. This productivity increase is made possible not only by the efficiency of the new technology, but by a managerial "speedup." The evidence suggests that Wal-Mart saves money in much the same way. Yet, unlike factory work, the operations of a retail store do not require an increasing number of repetitive tasks. Except for cashiers, the speedup of salesclerks results from Wal-Mart's understaffing, and management demands that all workers do more than what is in their job descriptions, and more work than is possible in the time allotted by their shifts.

Traditionally speedups have been designed to generate more work at the same pay, reducing the worker's real hourly compensation. Wal-Mart has been criticized for its low wages. But its wages may be even lower than they seem. Wal-Mart cuts its labor costs by requiring excessive amounts of work, then making employees work off the clock if they cannot finish in time. As of late 2004 there were thirty-eight lawsuits against Wal-Mart for wage abuse. Wal-Mart also cuts labor costs by cutting hours. High turnover also means constantly hiring new people at the starting wage.

Retail workers at Wal-Mart, unlike factory workers, never know exactly what work or how much work will be asked of them on any particular day. To secure their compliance, Wal-Mart culture is brought to bear. The culture is an effort to "educate" employees to be loyal to the company, to identify with authority, and to accept the demands of an authoritarian regime, a form of management by intimidation. Getting workers to accept this authority makes it possible to manipulate work rules, with employees expected to feel it is legitimate to do the extra work.

Today there are about 1.3 million Wal-Mart employees in the United States. Other retailers and other companies may be using these same methods to speed up their workforce. Despite these tactics, there are many people who believe in the Wal-Mart ethic and like their jobs. There are also many who start working at Wal-Mart with great expectations until they begin to experience the Wal-Mart *modus operandi*. Then a large number feel increasingly angry and betrayed.

THINKING ABOUT THE READING

Rosen describes several practices used by Wal-Mart management to save labor costs. What are some of these practices? How effective are they? Why does Wal-Mart continue to use these practices if so many employees don't like them? Do you think Wal-Mart's employment practices are typical of other large retail outlets? What kind of organizational worker-employer culture do they reflect? Why doesn't Wal-Mart use management practices that might be more favorable to their employees?

Separating the Men From the Moms

The Making of Adult Gender Segregation in Youth Sports

Michael A. Messner and Suzel Bozada-Deas

(2009)

In volunteer work, just as in many families and workplaces, gender divisions are pervasive and persistent. Women are often expected to do the work of caring for others' emotions and daily needs. Women's volunteer labor is routinely devalued in much the same ways that housework and childcare are devalued in the home and women's clerical and other support work is devalued in the professions (Hook 2004). Similarly, men tend to do the instrumental work of public leadership, just as they do in the family and the workplace, and their informal work is valued accordingly.

This article examines the social construction of adult gender divisions of labor in a community volunteer activity, youth sports.

Coaches and "Team Moms"

In 1995, when we (the first author, Mike, and his family) arrived at our six-year-old son's first soccer practice, we were delighted to learn that his coach was a woman. Coach Karen, a mother in her mid-30s, had grown up playing lots of sports. She was tall, confident, and athletic, and the kids responded well to her leadership. It seemed to be a new and different world than the one we grew up in. But during the next decade, as our two sons played a few more seasons of soccer, two years of youth basketball, and more than a decade of baseball, they never had another woman head coach. It is not that women were not contributing to the kids' teams. All of the "team parents" (often called "team moms")—parent volunteers who did the behind-the-scenes work of phone-calling, organizing weekly snack schedules and team parties, collecting money for gifts for the coaches, and so on—were women. And occasionally, a team had a woman assistant coach. But women head coaches were few and far between.

Connell (1987) argues that every social institution—including the economy, the military, schools, families, or sport—has a "gender regime," which is defined as the current state of play of gender relations in the institution. We can begin to understand an institution's gender regime by measuring and analyzing the gender divisions of labor and power in the organization (i.e., what kinds of jobs are done by women and men, who has the authority, etc.).

Institutional gender regimes are connected with other gender regimes. Put another way, people in their daily lives routinely move in, out, and across different gender regimes—families, workplaces, schools, places of worship, and community activities such as youth sports. Their actions within a particular gender regime—for instance, the choice to volunteer to coach a youth soccer team—and the meanings they construct around these actions are constrained and enabled by their positions, responsibilities, and experiences in other institutional contexts. We will show how individual decisions to coach or to serve as team parents occur largely through nonreflexive, patterned interactions that are infused with an ascendant gender ideology that we call "soft essentialism."

These interactions occur at the nexus of the three gender regimes of community youth sports, families, and workplaces.

Research Methods

The low numbers of women coaches in Roseville American Youth Soccer Organization (AYSO) and Little League Baseball/Softball (LLB/S) and the fact that nearly all of the team parents are women gave us a statistical picture of persistent gender segregation. But simply trotting out these numbers couldn't tell us *how* this picture is drawn. We wanted to understand the current state of play of the adult gender regime of youth sports, so we developed a study based on the following question: What are the social processes that sustain this gender segregation? And by extension, we wanted to explore another question: What is happening that might serve to destabilize and possibly change this gender segregation? In other words, are there ways to see and understand the internal mechanisms—the face-to-face interactions as well as the meaning-making processes—that constitute the "state of play" of the gender regime of community youth sports?

First, we conducted a content analysis of nine years (1999–2007) of Roseville's AYSO and LLB/S yearbooks (magazine-length documents compiled annually by the leagues, containing team photos as well as names and photos of coaches and managers). The yearbook data on the numbers and placement of women and men coaches provides the statistical backdrop for our study of the social processes of gender and coaching that we summarized above.

Second, we conducted field observations of numerous girls' and boys' soccer, baseball, and softball practices and games.

Third, Mike conducted several seasons of participant observation—as a volunteer assistant coach or as scorekeeper—of his son's Little League Baseball teams, ranging from six- and seven-year old co-ed T-ball teams to 13- and 14-year-old boys' baseball teams.

Fourth, we conducted 50 in-depth interviews with women and men volunteers—mostly head soccer coaches and baseball or softball managers of both boys' and girls' teams but also a small number of assistant coaches and team parents.

The Coaches' Stories

When we asked a longtime Little League Softball manager why he thinks most head coaches are men while nearly all team parents are women, he said with a shrug, "They give opportunities to everybody to manage or coach and it just so happens that no women volunteer, you know?" This man's statement was typical of head coaches and league officials who generally offered up explanations grounded in individual choice: Faced with equal opportunities to volunteer, men just *choose* to be coaches, while women *choose* to be team parents.

But our research shows that the gendered division of labor among men and women volunteers in youth coaching results not simply from an accumulation of individual choices; rather, it is produced through a profoundly *social* process.

Gendered Pipelines

When we asked coaches to describe how they had decided to become coaches, most spoke of having first served as assistant coaches—sometimes for just one season, sometimes for several seasons—before moving into head coaching positions. Drawing from language used by those who study gender in occupations, we can describe the assistant coach position as an essential part of the "pipeline" to the head coach position (England 2006). One of the reasons for this is obvious: many parents—women and men—believe that as a head coach, they will be under tremendous critical scrutiny by other parents in the community. Without previous youth coaching experience, many lack the confidence that they feel they need to take on such a public leadership task. A year or two of assistant coaching affords one the experience and builds the confidence that can lead to the conclusion that "I can do that" and the decision to take on the responsibility of a head coaching position.

But the pipeline from assistant coaches to head coaches does not operate in a purely individual voluntarist manner. A male longtime Little League manager and a member of the league's governing board gave us a glimpse of how the pipeline works when there is a shortage of volunteers:

> One time we had 10 teams and only like six or seven applicants that wanted to be strictly manager. So you kinda eyeball the yearbook from the year before, maybe a couple of years [before], and see if the same dad is still listed as a[n assistant] coach, and maybe now it's time he wants his own team. So you make a lot of phone calls. You might make 20 phone calls and hopefully you are going to get two or three guys that say, "Yes, I'll be a manager."

The assistant coach position is a key part of the pipeline to head coaching positions both because it makes people more confident about volunteering to be a head coach and, as the quote above illustrates, because it gives them visibility in ways that make them more likely to be actively recruited by the league to be a head coach. To understand how it is that most head coaches are men, we need to understand how the pipeline operates—how it is that, at the entry level, women's and men's choices to become assistant coaches and/or team parents are constrained or enabled by the social context.

Recruiting Dads and Moms to Help

There is a lot of work involved in organizing a successful youth soccer, baseball, or softball season. A head coach needs help from two, three, even four other parents who will serve as assistant coaches during practices and games. Parents also have to take responsibility for numerous support tasks like organizing snacks,

making team banners, working in the snack bar during games, collecting donations for year-end gifts for the coaches, and organizing team events and year-end parties. In AYSO, parents also serve as volunteer referees. When we asked head coaches how they determined who would help them with these assistant coaching and other support tasks, a very common storyline developed: the coach would call a beginning-of-the-season team meeting, sometimes preceded by a letter or e-mail to parents, and ask for volunteers. Nearly always, they ended up with dads volunteering to help as assistant coaches and moms volunteering to be team parents.

None of the head coaches we interviewed said that they currently had a man as the team parent. Four coaches recalled that they had once had a man as a team parent (although one of these four coaches said, "Now that I think about it, that guy actually volunteered his wife do it"). When we asked if they had ever had a team parent who was a man, nearly all of the coaches said never. Many of them laughed at the very thought. A woman soccer coach exclaimed with a chuckle, "I just can't imagine! I wonder if they've *ever* had a 'team mom' who's a dad. I don't know [laughs]." A man soccer coach stammered his way through his response, punctuating his words with sarcastic laughter: "Ha! In fact, that whole concept—I don't think I've ever *heard* of a team dad [laughs]. Uh—there *is* no team dad, I've never heard of a team dad. But I don't know why that would be." A few coaches, such as the following woman softball coach, resorted to family metaphors to explain why they think there are few if any men volunteering to be team parents: "Oh, it's always a mom [laughs]. 'Team mom.' That's why it's called 'team *mom*.' You know, the coach is a male. And the mom—I mean, that's the *housekeeping*—you know: Assign the snack."

Teams are even talked about sometimes as "families," and while we never heard a head coach referred to as a team's "dad," we did often and consistently hear the team parent referred to as the "team mom." This gendered language, drawn from family relations, gives us some good initial hints as to how coach and team parent roles remain so gender segregated. In youth sports contexts, gendered language structures people's conversations in ways that shape and constrain their actions. Is a man who volunteers to be a team parent now a "team mom"?

Gender Ideology and Work/Family Analogies

When we asked the coaches to consider why it is nearly always women who volunteer to be the team parent, many seemed never to have considered this question before. Some of the men coaches seemed especially befuddled and appeared to assume that women's team-parenting work is a result of an almost "natural" decision on the part of the woman. Some men, such as the following soccer coach, made sense of this volunteer division of labor by referring to the ways that it reflected divisions of labor in men's own families and in their community: "In this area we have a lot of stay-at-home moms, so it seems to kind of fall to them to take over those roles." Similarly, a man baseball coach whose wife served as the team parent explained, "I think it's because they probably do it at home. You know, I mean my wife—even though she can't really commit the time to coach, I don't think she would *want* to coach—uh, she's very good with that [team parent] stuff." A man soccer coach explained the gender divisions on youth sports teams in terms of people's comfort with a nostalgic notion of a "traditional family":

> That's sort of the classical family, you know, it's like the Donna Reed family is AYSO, right? . . . They have these assigned gender roles . . . and people in Roseville, probably all over the United States, they're fairly comfortable with them, right? It's, uh, maybe insidious, maybe not, [but] framed in the sort of traditional family role of dad, mom, kids. . . . people are going to be comfortable with that.

Another man baseball coach broadened the explanation, drawing connections to divisions of labor in his workplace:

> It's kinda like in business. I work in real estate, and most of your deal makers that are out there on the front lines, so to speak, making the deals, doing the shuckin' and jivin', doing the selling, are men. It's a very Good Ol' Boys network on the real estate brokerage side. There are a ton a females who are on the property management side, because it's *housekeeping*, it's *managing*, it's like running the *household*, it's behind the scenes, it's like cooking in the kitchen—[laughs]—I mean, I hate to say that, but it's that kind of role that's secondary. Coach is out in the front leading the squad, mom sitting behind making sure that the snacks are in order and all that. You know—just the way it is.

Having a male coach and a "team mom" just seemed normal to this man, "You know, just the way it is," because it seemed to flow naturally from divisions of labor in his household and in his workplace—gendered divisions of labor that have the "the Good Ol' Boys" operating publicly as the leaders "on the front lines . . . shuckin' and jivin,'" while the women are offering support "behind the scenes . . . like cooking in the kitchen." Echoing this view, a man soccer coach said, "I hate to use the analogy, but it's like a secretary: You got a boss and you've got a secretary, and I think that's where most of the opportunities for women to be active in the sports is, as the secretary."

Finding a "Team Mom"

The interview data give us a window into how people make sense of decisions that they have made as youth sports volunteers and provide insights into how gendered language and beliefs about men's and women's work and family roles help to shape these decisions. Yet, asking people to explain how (and especially why) things such as gendered divisions of labor persist is not by itself the most reliable basis for building an explanation. Rather, watching *how* things happen gives us a deeper understanding of the social construction of gender (Thorne 1993). Our observations from team meetings and early season practices reveal deeper social processes at work—processes that shaped people's apparently individual decisions to volunteer for assistant coach or team parent positions. This excerpt from field notes from the first team meeting of a boys' baseball team illustrates how men's apparent resistance to even consider taking on the team parent position ultimately leaves the job in the hands of a woman (who might also have been reluctant to do it):

> Coach Bill stands facing the parents, as we sit in the grandstands. He doesn't ask for volunteers for assistant coaches; instead, he announces that he has "invited" two of the fathers "who probably know more about baseball than I do" to serve as his assistants. He then asks for someone to volunteer as the "team mom." He adds, "Now, 'team mom' is not a gendered job: it can be done by a mom or a dad. But we really need a 'team mom.'" Nobody volunteers immediately. One mom sitting near me mutters to another mom, "I've done this two years in a row, and I'm not gonna do it this year." Coach Bill goes on to ask for a volunteer for scorekeeper. Meanwhile, two other moms have been whispering, and one of them suddenly bursts out with "Okay! She's volunteered to be 'team mom!'" People applaud. The volunteer seems a bit sheepish; her body-language suggests someone who has just reluctantly agreed to do something. But she affirms that, yes, she'll do it.

This first practice of the year is often the moment at which the division of labor—who will be the assistant coaches, who will be the team parent—is publicly solidified. In this case, the men assistant coaches had been selected before the meeting by the head coach, but it apparently took some cajoling from a mother during the team meeting to convince another mother to volunteer to be the "team mom." We observed two occasions when a woman who did not volunteer was drafted by the head coach to be the "team mom." In one case, the reluctant volunteer was clearly more oriented toward assistant coaching, as the following composite story from field notes from the beginning of the season of a seven-year-old boys' baseball team illustrates:

> At the first practice, Coach George takes charge, asks for volunteers. I tell him that I am happy to help out at practice and games and that he should just let me know what he'd like me to do. He appoints me Assistant Coach. This happens with another dad, too. We get team hats. Elena, a mother, offers to help out in any way she can. She's appointed "co-team mom" (the coach's wife is the other "team mom"). She shrugs and says okay, fine. Unlike most "team moms," Elena continues to attend all practices. At the fifth practice, Coach George is pitching batting practice to the kids; I'm assigned to first base, the other dad is working with the catcher. Elena (the "team mom") is standing alone on the sidelines, idly tossing a ball up in the air to herself. Coach George's son suddenly has to pee, so as George hustles the boy off to the bathroom, Elena jumps in and starts pitching. She's good, it turns out, and can groove the pitch right where the kids want it. (By contrast, George has recently been plunking the kids with wild pitches.) Things move along well. At one point, when Coach George has returned from the bathroom, with Elena still pitching to the kids, a boy picks up a ball near second base and doesn't know what to do with it. Coach George yells at the kid: "Throw it! Throw it to the 'team mom!'" The kid, confused, says, "Where is she?" I say, "The pitcher, throw it to the pitcher." Coach George says, "Yeah, the 'team mom.'"

A couple of years later, we interviewed Elena and asked her how it was that she became a team parent and continued in that capacity for five straight years. Her response illuminated the informal constraints that channel many women away from coaching and toward being team parents:

> The first year, when [my son] was in kindergarten, he was on a T-ball team, and I volunteered to be manager, and of course the league didn't choose me, but they did allow me to be assistant coach. And I was so excited, and [laughs] of course I showed up in heels for the

first practice, because it was right after work, and the coach looked at me, and I informed him that "I'm your new assistant." And he looked at me—and I don't know if *distraught* is the correct word, but he seemed slightly *disappointed*, and he went out of his way to ask the parents who were there watching their children if there was anyone who wanted to volunteer, even though I was there. So there was this male who did kind of rise to the occasion, and so that was the end. He demoted me without informing me of his decision [laughs]—I was *really* enthused, because [my son] was in kindergarten, so I *really* wanted to be coach—or assistant coach at least—and it didn't happen. So after that I didn't feel comfortable to volunteer to coach. I just thought, okay, then I can do "team mom."

As this story illustrates, women who have the background, skills, and desire to work as on-field assistant coaches are sometimes assigned by head coaches to be "team moms." Some baseball teams even have a niche for such moms: a "dugout coach" (or "dugout mom") is usually a mom who may help out with on-field instruction during practices, but on game days, she is assigned the "indoors" space of the dugout, where it is her responsibility to keep track of the line-up and to be sure that the boy who is on-deck (next up to bat) is ready with his batting gloves and helmet on. The dugout coach also—especially with younger kids' teams—might be assigned to keep kids focused on the game, to keep equipment orderly, to help with occasional first aid, and to help see that the dugout is cleaned of empty water bottles and snack containers after the game is over. In short, the baseball, softball, and soccer fields on which the children play are gendered spaces (Dworkin 2001; Montez de Oca 2005). The playing field is the public space where the (usually male) coach exerts his authority and command. The dugout is like the home—a place of domestic safety from which one emerges to do one's job. Work happens in the indoor space of the dugout, but it is like family labor, behind-the-scenes,

supporting the "real" work of leadership that is done on the field.

A few coaches whom we interviewed consciously attempted to resist or change this gendered sorting system. Some of the women coaches, especially, saw it as a problem that the team parent job was always done by a woman. A woman softball coach was concerned that the "team mom" amounted to negative role-modeling for kids and fed into the disrespect that women coaches experienced:

> The kids think that the moms should just be "team moms." Which means that they don't take the mothers seriously, and I think that's a bad thing. I mean it's a *bad thing*. I think that's a lack of respect to women, to mothers.

Another woman Little League coach said that most team parents are women because too many people assume

> that's all the women are good for. I think that's what the mentality is. I made it very clear to our parents that it did not have to be a mother, that it could be a father and that I encourage any dad out there that had time to do what team parents are supposed to do, to sign up and do it. But it didn't happen.

Such coaches find that simply degendering the language by calling this role *team parent* and even stressing that this is not a gendered job is unlikely to yield men volunteers. So what some women coaches do is simply refuse to have a team parent. A woman soccer coach said, "I do it all. I don't have a team parent." Another said, "I think in general, compared to the men who coach, I do more of that [team parent work]." This resistance by women coaches is understandable, especially from those who see the phenomenon of "team mom" as contributing to a climate of disrespect for women coaches. However, this form of resistance ends up creating extra work for women coaches—work that most men coaches relegate to a "team mom."

The very few occasions when a father does volunteer—or is recruited by the coach—to be the team parent are moments of gender "crossing" that hold the potential to disrupt the normal operation of the gender-category sorting process. But ironically, a team parent who is a man can also reinforce gender stereotypes. One man soccer coach told me that the previous season, a father had volunteered to be the team parent, but that

> he was a disaster [laughs]. He didn't do *anything*, you know, and what little he did it was late; it was ineffective assistance. He didn't come, he didn't make phone calls, I mean he was just like a black hole. And so that—that was an unfortunate disaster. This year it's a woman again.

The idea that a man volunteered—and then failed miserably to do the team parent job—may serve ultimately to reinforce the taken-for-granted assumption that women are naturally better suited to do this kind of work.

The Devaluation of Women's Invisible Labor

Despite the importance of the work team parents are doing, it is not often recognized as equivalent to the work done by coaches. Of course, the team parent typically puts in far fewer hours of labor than does the head coach. However, in some cases, the team parents put in more time than some assistant coaches (dads, for instance, whose work schedules don't allow them to get to many practices but who can be seen on the field during a Saturday game, coaching third base). Yet, the team parent's work remains largely invisible, and coaches sometimes talk about team parents' contributions as trivial or unimportant. Several coaches, when asked about the team parent job, disparaged it as "not very hard to do," "an easy job." But our interviews suggest that the women team parents are often doing this job as one of many community volunteer jobs, while most of the men who coach are engaged in this and

only this volunteer activity. A field note from a boys' baseball game illustrates this:

> *It is the second to last game of the season. During the first inning, Dora, the "team mom," shows up and immediately starts circulating among the parents in the stands, talking and handing out a flier. The flier announces the "year end party," to be held in a couple of weeks. She announces that she will supply ice cream and other makings for sundaes. Everyone else can just bring some drinks. She also announces (and it's on the flier) that she's collecting $20 from each family to pay for a "thank you gift . . . for all their hard work" for the head coach and for each of the three assistant coaches (all men). People start shelling out money, and Dora starts a list of who has donated. By the start of the next inning, she announces that she's got to go, saying "I have a Webelos [Cub Scouts] parents meeting." She's obviously multitasking as a parent volunteer. By the fourth inning, near the end of the game, she is back, collecting more money, and informing parents on details concerning the party and the upcoming playoffs. Finally, during the last inning, she sits and watches the end of the game with the rest of us.*

Dora, like other "team moms," is doing work before, during, and after the game—making fliers, communicating with parents, collecting money, keeping lists and records, organizing parties, making sure everyone knows the schedule of upcoming events. And she is sandwiching this work around other volunteer activities with another youth organization. This kind of labor keeps organizations running, and it helps to create and sustain the kind of vibrant community "for the kids" that people imagine when they move to a town like Roseville (Daniels 1985).

Sorting and Soft Essentialism

In this article, we have revealed the workings of a gender-category sorting process that reflects the interactional "doing" of gender discussed by West and Zimmerman (1987). Through this sorting process, the vast majority of women volunteers are channeled into a team parent position, and the vast majority of men volunteers become coaches. To say that people are "sorted" is not to deny their active agency in this process. Rather, it is to underline that organizations are characterized by self-perpetuating "inequality regimes" (Acker 2006). What people often think of as "free individual choices" are actually choices that are shaped by social contexts. We have shown how women's choices to become team parents are constrained by the fact that few, if any, men will volunteer to do this less visible and less honored job. Women's choices are enabled by their being actively recruited—"volunteered"—by head coaches or by other parents to become the "team mom." Moreover, men's choices to volunteer as assistant coaches and not as team parents are shaped by the gendered assumptions of head coaches, enacted through active recruiting and informal interactions at the initial team meeting.

Youth sports is a powerful institution into which children are initiated into a gender-segregated world with its attendant ideology of soft essentialism.

In the past, sport tended to construct a categorical "hard" essentialism—boys and men, it was believed, were naturally suited to the aggressive, competitive world of sport, while girls and women were not. Today, with girls' and women's massive influx into sport, these kinds of categorical assumptions of natural difference can no longer stand up to even the most cursory examination. Soft essentialism, as an ascendant professional-class gender ideology, frames sport as a realm in which girls are empowered to exercise individual choice (rehearsing choices they will later face in straddling the demands of careers and family labor), while continuing to view boys as naturally "hard wired" to play sports (and ultimately, to have public careers). Girls are viewed as flexibly facing a future of choices; boys as inflexible, facing a linear path toward public careers. Soft essentialism, in short, initiates kids into an adult world that has been only partially transformed by feminism, where many of the burdens of bridging and balancing work and family strains are still primarily on women's shoulders. Men coaches and "team moms" symbolize and exemplify these tensions.

Our study shows a similar lack of "bad guys" engaged in overt acts of sexism and discrimination. Instead, we see a systemic reproduction of gender categorization, created nonreflexively by "well intentioned, good people." The mechanisms of this nonreflexive informal practicing of gender are made to seem normal through their congruence with the "tacit knowledge" of soft essentialism that is itself embedded in hegemonic professional-class family and workplace gender divisions of labor. The fact that soft essentialism emerges from the intersections of these different social contexts means that any attempt to move toward greater equality for women and men in youth sports presupposes simultaneous movements toward equality in workplaces and families.

NOTE

1. Roseville is a pseudonym for the town we studied, and all names of people interviewed or observed for this study are also pseudonyms.

REFERENCES

Acker, Joan. 2006. Inequality regimes: Gender, class and race in organizations. *Gender & Society* 20:441-64.

Connell, R. W. 1987. *Gender and power.* Stanford, CA: Stanford University Press.

Daniels, Arlene Kaplan. 1985. Invisible work. *Social Problems* 34:363-74.

Dworkin, Shari L. 2001. Holding back: Negotiating a glass ceiling on women's muscular strength. *Sociological Perspectives* 44:333-50.

England, Paula. 2006. Toward gender equality: Progress and bottlenecks. In *The declining significance of gender,* edited by Francine D. Blau, Mary C. Brinton, and David B. Grusky. New York: Russell Sage.

Hook, Jennifer L. 2004. Reconsidering the division of household labor: Incorporating volunteer work and informal support. *Journal of Marriage and Family* 66:101-17.

Montez de Oca, Jeffrey. 2005. As our muscles get softer, our missile race becomes harder: Cultural citizenship and the "muscle gap." *Journal of Historical Sociology* 18:145-71.

Thorne, Barrie. 1993. *Gender play: Girls and boys in school.* New Brunswick, NJ: Rutgers University Press.

West, Candace, and Don Zimmerman. 1987. Doing gender. *Gender & Society* 1:125-51.

THINKING ABOUT THE READING

Messner and Bozada-Deas focus on youth sports organizations as a site in which cultural norms of gender are reinforced. Why are women more likely to be the "team parent" and men the coaches? How do the authors explain the persistence of this gender split? What do they mean by the concept "soft essentialism"? The reading implies that gender norms tend to be reinforced by overlapping social institutions such as work, family, and sports. Discuss this contention and give examples of other situations in which similar patterns are reinforced.

The Architecture of Stratification

Social Class and Inequality

Inequality is woven into the fabric of all societies through a structured system of *social stratification*. Social stratification is a ranking of entire groups of people that perpetuates unequal rewards and life chances in society. The structural-functionalist explanation of stratification is that the stability of society depends on all social positions being filled—that is, there are people around to do all the jobs that need to be done. Higher rewards, such as prestige and large salaries, are afforded to the most important positions, thereby ensuring that the most qualified individuals will occupy the highest positions. In contrast, conflict theory argues that stratification reflects an unequal distribution of power in society and is a primary source of conflict and tension.

Social class is the primary means of stratification in American society. Contemporary sociologists are likely to define a person's class standing as a combination of income, wealth, occupational prestige, and educational attainment. It is tempting to see class differences as simply the result of an economic stratification system that exists at a level above the individual. Although inequality is created and maintained by larger social institutions, it is often felt most forcefully and is reinforced most effectively in the chain of interactions that take place in our day-to-day lives.

The media play a significant role in shaping people's perceptions of class. But instead of providing accurate descriptive information about different classes, the media—especially the news media—give the impression that the United States is largely a classless society. According to Gregory Mantsios in "Making Class Invisible," when different classes are depicted in the media, the images tend to hover around stereotypes that reinforce the cultural belief that people's position in society is largely a function of their own effort and achievement or, in the case of "the poor," lack of effort and achievement.

The face of American poverty has changed somewhat over the past several decades. The economic status of single mothers and their children has deteriorated while that of people older than age 65 has improved somewhat. What hasn't changed is the ever-widening gap between the rich and the poor. Poverty persists because in a free market and competitive society, it serves economic and social functions. In addition, poverty receives institutional "support" in the form of segmented labor markets and inadequate educational systems. The ideology of competitive individualism—that to succeed in life, all one has to do is work hard and win in competition with others—creates a belief that poor people are to blame for their own suffering. So although the problem of poverty remains serious, public attitudes toward poverty and poor people are frequently indifferent or even hostile. Fred Block and his colleagues call this attitude "the compassion gap." In this reading the authors discuss the tendency of intolerance toward the poor in U.S. society. According to their research, this cultural attitude of indifference or disdain is rooted in individualism and a lack of understanding of economic conditions over time (e.g., the relative difficulty of owning a home today as compared with the period just after World War II when much government assistance was available). The authors see the "compassion gap" as an attitude that gets in the way of establishing more workable social policies for the poor.

The United States has the highest rate of teenage pregnancy among all the developed nations. In a comprehensive review of the sociological statistics and literature on the subject, Gabrielle Raley argues that this high rate is largely due to the social conditions of young women in poor communities. These conditions, which include significant economic and social disadvantages and relatively few opportunities for education and life improvement, may contribute to a cultural attitude in which motherhood is seen as one avenue for gaining adult status. Motherhood and adult status may offer a sense of belonging in a world in which these young women are otherwise disenfranchised. Raley's claim is that in order to fully understand teenage pregnancy, we must understand the conditions of disadvantage in which it is rooted.

Something to Consider as You Read

In reading these selections, pay careful attention to the small ways in which economic resources affect everyday choices and behavior. For instance, how might poverty, including the lack of access to nice clothing, affect one's ability to portray the best possible image at a job interview? Consider further the connection between media portrayals and self-image. Where do people get their ideas about their own self-worth, their sense of entitlement, and how they fit into society generally? How do these ideals differ across social class and how are they similar? Some observers have suggested that people in the United States don't know how to talk about class, except in stereotypical terms. How might this lack of "class discourse" perpetuate stereotypes and the myth that the poor deserve their fate? Consider examples of the "compassion gap" in your own life and as reflected in recent news and policy decisions. Does the compassion gap relate to the failure to fully understand social issues such as teenage pregnancy?

Making Class Invisible

Gregory Mantsios

(1998)

Of the various social and cultural forces in our society, the mass media is arguably the most influential in molding public consciousness. Americans spend an average twenty-eight hours per week watching television. They also spend an undetermined number of hours reading periodicals, listening to the radio, and going to the movies. Unlike other cultural and socializing institutions, ownership and control of the mass media is highly concentrated. Twenty-three corporations own more than one-half of all the daily newspapers, magazines, movie studios, and radio and television outlets in the United States. The number of media companies is shrinking and their control of the industry is expanding. And a relatively small number of media outlets is producing and packaging the majority of news and entertainment programs. For the most part, our media is national in nature and single-minded (profit-oriented) in purpose. This media plays a key role in defining our cultural tastes, helping us locate ourselves in history, establishing our national identity, and ascertaining the range of national and social possibilities. In this essay, we will examine the way the mass media shapes how people think about each other and about the nature of our society.

The United States is the most highly stratified society in the industrialized world. Class distinctions operate in virtually every aspect of our lives, determining the nature of our work, the quality of our schooling, and the health and safety of our loved ones. Yet remarkably, we, as a nation, retain illusions about living in an egalitarian society. We maintain these illusions, in large part, because the media hides gross inequities from public view. In those instances when inequities are revealed, we are provided with messages that obscure the nature of class realities and blame the victims of class-dominated society for their own plight. Let's briefly examine what the news media, in particular, tells us about class.

About the Poor

The news media provides meager coverage of poor people and poverty. The coverage it does provide is often distorted and misleading.

The Poor Do Not Exist

For the most part, the news media ignores the poor. Unnoticed are forty million poor people in the nation—a number that equals the entire population of Maine, Vermont, New Hampshire, Connecticut, Rhode Island, New Jersey, and New York combined. Perhaps even more alarming is that the rate of poverty is increasing twice as fast as the population growth in the United States. Ordinarily, even a calamity of much smaller proportion (e.g., flooding in the Midwest) would garner a great deal of coverage and hype from a media usually eager to declare a crisis, yet less than one in five hundred articles in the *New York Times* and one in one thousand articles listed in the *Readers Guide to Periodic Literature* are on poverty. With remarkably little attention to them, the poor and their problems are hidden from most Americans.

When the media does turn its attention to the poor, it offers a series of contradictory messages and portrayals.

The Poor Are Faceless

Each year the Census Bureau releases a new report on poverty in our society and its results are duly reported in the media. At best, however, this coverage emphasizes annual fluctuations (showing how the numbers differ from previous years) and ongoing debates over the validity of the numbers (some argue the number should be lower, most that the number should be higher). Coverage like this desensitizes us to the poor by reducing poverty to a number. It ignores the human tragedy of poverty—the suffering, indignities, and misery endured by millions of children and adults. Instead, the poor become statistics rather than people.

The Poor Are Undeserving

When the media does put a face on the poor, it is not likely to be a pretty one. The media will provide us with sensational stories about welfare cheats, drug addicts, and greedy panhandlers (almost always urban and Black). Compare these images and the emotions evoked by them with the media's treatment of middle-class (usually white) "tax evaders," celebrities who have a "chemical dependency," or wealthy businesspeople who use unscrupulous means to "make a profit." While the behavior of the more affluent offenders is considered an "impropriety" and a deviation from the norm, the behavior of the poor is considered repugnant, indicative of the poor in general, and worthy of our indignation and resentment.

The Poor Are an Eyesore

When the media does cover the poor, they are often presented through the eyes of the middle class. For example, sometimes the media includes a story with panhandlers. Rather than focusing on the plight of the poor, these stories are about middle-class opposition to the poor. Such stories tell us that the poor are an inconvenience and an irritation.

The Poor Have Only Themselves to Blame

In another example of media coverage, we are told that the poor live in a personal and cultural cycle of poverty that hopelessly imprisons them. They routinely center on the Black urban population and focus on perceived personality or cultural traits that doom the poor. While the women in these stories typically exhibit an "attitude" that leads to trouble or a promiscuity that leads to single motherhood, the men possess a need for immediate gratification that leads to drug abuse or an unquenchable greed that leads to the pursuit of fast money. The images that are seared into our mind are sexist, racist, and classist. Census figures reveal that most of the poor are white not Black or Hispanic, that they live in rural or suburban areas not urban centers, and hold jobs at least part of the year. Yet, in a fashion that is often framed in an understanding and sympathetic tone, we are told that the poor have inflicted poverty on themselves.

The Poor Are Down on Their Luck

During the Christmas season, the news media sometimes provides us with accounts of poor individuals or families (usually white) who are down on their luck. These stories are often linked to stories about soup kitchens or other charitable activities and sometimes call for charitable contributions. These "Yule time" stories are as much about the affluent as they are about the poor: they tell us that the affluent in our society are a kind, understanding, giving people—which we are not.[1] The series of unfortunate circumstances that have led to impoverishment are presumed to be a temporary condition that will improve with time and a change in luck.

Despite appearances, the messages provided by the media are not entirely disparate. With each variation, the media informs us what poverty is not (i.e., systemic and indicative of American society) by informing us what it is. The media tells us that poverty is either an aberration of the American way of life (it doesn't exist, it's just another number, it's unfortunate but temporary) or an end product of the poor themselves (they are a nuisance, do not deserve better, and have brought their predicament upon themselves).

By suggesting that the poor have brought poverty upon themselves, the media is engaging in what William Ryan has called "blaming the victim." The media identifies in what ways the poor are different as a consequence of deprivation, then defines those differences as the cause of poverty itself. Whether blatantly hostile or cloaked in sympathy, the message is that there is something fundamentally wrong with the victims—their hormones, psychological makeup, family environment, community, race, or some combination of these—that accounts for their plight and their failure to lift themselves out of poverty.

But poverty in the United States is systemic. It is a direct result of economic and political policies that deprive people of jobs, adequate wages, or legitimate support. It is neither natural nor inevitable: there is enough wealth in our nation to eliminate poverty if we chose to redistribute existing wealth or income. The plight of the poor is reason enough to make the elimination of poverty the nation's first priority. But poverty also impacts dramatically on the non-poor. It has a dampening effect on wages in general (by maintaining a reserve army of unemployed and underemployed anxious for any job at any wage) and breeds crime and violence (by maintaining conditions that invite private gain by illegal means and rebellion-like behavior, not entirely unlike the urban riots of the 1960s). Given the extent of poverty in the nation and the impact it has on us all, the media must spin considerable magic to keep the poor and the issue of poverty and its root causes out of the public consciousness.

About Everyone Else

Both the broadcast and the print news media strive to develop a strong sense of "we-ness" in their audience. They seek to speak to and for an audience that is both affluent and like-minded. The media's solidarity with affluence, that is, with the middle and upper class, varies little from one medium to another. Benjamin DeMott points out, for example, that the *New York Times* understands affluence to be intelligence, taste, public spirit, responsibility, and a readiness to rule and "conceives itself as spokesperson for a readership awash in these qualities." Of course, the flip side to creating a sense of "we," or "us," is establishing a perception of the "other." The other relates back to the faceless, amoral, undeserving, and inferior "underclass." Thus, the world according to the news media is divided between the "underclass" and everyone else. Again the messages are often contradictory.

The Wealthy Are Us

Much of the information provided to us by the news media focuses attention on the concerns of a very wealthy and privileged class of people. Although the concerns of a small fraction of the populace, they are presented as though they were the concerns of everyone. For example, while relatively few people actually own stock, the news media devotes an inordinate amount of broadcast time and print space to business news and stock market quotations. Not only do business reports cater to a particular narrow clientele, so do the fashion pages (with $2,000 dresses), wedding announcements, and the obituaries. Even weather and sports news often have a class bias. An all news radio station in New York City, for example, provides regular national ski reports. International news, trade agreements, and domestic policies issues are also reported in terms of their impact on business climate and the business community. Besides being of practical value to the wealthy, such coverage has considerable ideological value. Its message: the concerns of the wealthy are the concerns of us all.

The Wealthy (as a Class) Do Not Exist

While preoccupied with the concerns of the wealthy, the media fails to notice the way in which the rich as a class of people create and shape domestic and foreign policy. Presented as an aggregate of individuals, the wealthy appear without special interests, interconnections, or unity in purpose. Out of public view are the class interests of the wealthy, the interlocking business links, the concerted actions to preserve their class privileges and business interests (by running for public office, supporting political candidates, lobbying, etc.). Corporate lobbying is ignored, taken for granted, or assumed to be in the public interest. (Compare this with the media's portrayal of the "strong arm of labor" in attempting to defeat trade legislation that is harmful to the interests of working people.) It is estimated that two-thirds of the U.S. Senate is composed of millionaires. Having such a preponderance of millionaires in the Senate, however, is perceived to be neither unusual nor antidemocratic; these millionaire senators are assumed to be serving "our" collective interests in governing.

The Wealthy Are Fascinating and Benevolent

The broadcast and print media regularly provide hype for individuals who have achieved "super" success. These stories are usually about celebrities and superstars from the sports and entertainment world. Society pages and gossip columns serve to keep the social elite informed of each other's doings, allow the rest of us to gawk at their excesses, and help to keep the American dream alive. The print media is also fond of feature stories on corporate empire builders. These stories provide an occasional "insider's" view of the private and corporate life of industrialists by suggesting a rags to riches account of corporate success. These stories tell us that corporate success is a series of smart moves, shrewd acquisitions, timely mergers, and well thought out executive suite shuffles. By painting the upper class in a positive light, innocent of any wrongdoing (labor leaders and union organizations usually get the opposite treatment), the media assures us that wealth and power are benevolent. One person's capital accumulation is presumed to

be good for all. The elite, then, are portrayed as investment wizards, people of special talent and skill, who even their victims (workers and consumers) can admire.

The Wealthy Include a Few Bad Apples

On rare occasions, the media will mock selected individuals for their personality flaws. Real estate investor Donald Trump and New York Yankees owner George Steinbrenner, for example, are admonished by the media for deliberately seeking publicity (a very un-upper class thing to do); hotel owner Leona Helmsley was caricatured for her personal cruelties; and junk bond broker Michael Milkin was condemned because he had the audacity to rob the rich. Michael Parenti points out that by treating business wrongdoing as isolated deviations from the socially beneficial system of "responsible capitalism," the media overlooks the features of the system that produce such abuses and the regularity with which they occur. Rather than portraying them as predictable and frequent outcomes of corporate power and the business system, the media treats abuses as if they were isolated and atypical. Presented as an occasional aberration, these incidents serve not to challenge, but to legitimate, the system.

The Middle Class Is Us

By ignoring the poor and blurring the lines between the working people and the upper class, the news media creates a universal middle class. From this perspective, the size of one's income becomes largely irrelevant: what matters is that most of "us" share an intellectual and moral superiority over the disadvantaged. As *Time* magazine once concluded, "Middle America is a state of mind." "We are all middle class," we are told, "and we all share the same concerns": job security, inflation, tax burdens, world peace, the cost of food and housing, health care, clean air and water, and the safety of our streets. While the concerns of the wealthy are quite distinct from those of the middle class (e.g., the wealthy worry about investments, not jobs), the media convinces us that "we [the affluent] are all in this together."

The Middle Class Is a Victim

For the media, "we" the affluent not only stand apart from the "other"—the poor, the working class, the minorities, and their problems—"we" are also victimized by the poor (who drive up the costs of maintaining the welfare roles), minorities (who commit crimes against us), and by workers (who are greedy and drive companies out and prices up). Ignored are the subsidies to the rich, the crimes of corporate America, and the policies that wreak havoc on the economic well-being of middle America. Media magic convinces us to fear, more than anything else, being victimized by those less affluent than ourselves.

The Middle Class Is Not a Working Class

The news media clearly distinguishes the middle class (employees) from the working class (i.e., blue collar workers) who are portrayed, at best, as irrelevant, outmoded, and a dying breed. Furthermore, the media will tell us that the hardships faced by blue collar workers are inevitable (due to progress), a result of bad luck (chance circumstances in a particular industry), or a product of their own doing (they priced themselves out of a job). Given the media's presentation of reality, it is hard to believe that manual, supervised, unskilled, and semiskilled workers actually represent more than 50 percent of the adult working population. The working class, instead, is relegated by the media to "the other."

In short, the news media either lionizes the wealthy or treats their interests and those of the middle class as one and the same. But the upper class and the middle class do not share the same interests or worries. Members of the upper class worry about stock dividends (not employment), they profit from inflation and global militarism, their children attend exclusive private schools, they eat and live in a royal fashion, they call on (or are called upon by) personal physicians, they have few

consumer problems, they can escape whenever they want from environmental pollution, and they live on streets and travel to other areas under the protection of private police forces.[2]

The wealthy are not only a class with distinct life-styles and interests, they are a ruling class. They receive a disproportionate share of the country's yearly income, own a disproportionate amount of the country's wealth, and contribute a disproportionate number of their members to governmental bodies and decision-making groups—all traits that William Domhoff, in his classic work *Who Rules America*, defined as characteristic of a governing class.

This governing class maintains and manages our political and economic structures in such a way that these structures continue to yield an amazing proportion of our wealth to a minuscule upper class. While the media is not above referring to ruling classes in other countries (we hear, for example, references to Japan's ruling elite), its treatment of the news proceeds as though there were no such ruling class in the United States.

Furthermore, the news media inverts reality so that those who are working class and middle class learn to fear, resent, and blame those below, rather than those above them in the class structure. We learn to resent welfare, which accounts for only two cents out of every dollar in the federal budget (approximately $10 billion) and provides financial relief for the needy,[3] but learn little about the $11 billion the federal government spends on individuals with incomes in excess of $100,000 (not needy), or the $17 billion in farm subsidies, or the $214 billion (twenty times the cost of welfare) in interest payments to financial institutions.

Middle-class whites learn to fear African Americans and Latinos, but most violent crime occurs within poor and minority communities and is neither interracial[4] nor interclass. As horrid as such crime is, it should not mask the destruction and violence perpetrated by corporate America. In spite of the fact that 14,000 innocent people are killed on the job each year, 100,000 die prematurely, 400,000 become seriously ill, and 6 million are injured from work-related accidents and diseases, most Americans fear government regulation more than they do unsafe working conditions.

Through the media, middle-class—and even working-class—Americans learn to blame blue collar workers and their unions for declining purchasing power and economic security. But while workers who managed to keep their jobs and their unions struggled to keep up with inflation, the top 1 percent of American families saw their average incomes soar 80 percent in the last decade. Much of the wealth at the top was accumulated as stockholders and corporate executives moved their companies abroad to employ cheaper labor (56 cents per hour in El Salvador) and avoid paying taxes in the United States. Corporate America is a world made up of ruthless bosses, massive layoffs, favoritism and nepotism, health and safety violations, pension plan losses, union busting, tax evasions, unfair competition, and price gouging, as well as fast buck deals, financial speculation, and corporate wheeling and dealing that serve the interests of the corporate elite, but are generally wasteful and destructive to workers and the economy in general.

It is no wonder Americans cannot think straight about class. The mass media is neither objective, balanced, independent, nor neutral. Those who own and direct the mass media are themselves part of the upper class, and neither they nor the ruling class in general have to conspire to manipulate public opinion. Their interest is in preserving the status quo, and their view of society as fair and equitable comes naturally to them. But their ideology dominates our society and justifies what is in reality a perverse social order—one that perpetuates unprecedented elite privilege and power on the one hand and widespread deprivation on the other. A mass media that did not have its own class interests in preserving the status quo would acknowledge that inordinate wealth and power undermines democracy and that a "free market" economy can ravage a people and their communities.

NOTES

1. American households with incomes of less than $10,000 give an average of 5.5 percent of their earnings to charity or to a religious organization, while those making more than $100,000 a year give only 2.9 percent. After changes in the 1986 tax code reduced the benefits of charitable giving, taxpayers earning $500,000 or more slashed their average donation by nearly one-third. Furthermore, many of these acts of benevolence do not help the needy. Rather than provide funding to social service agencies that aid the poor, the voluntary contributions of the wealthy go to places and institutions that entertain, inspire, cure, or educate wealthy Americans—art museums, opera houses, theaters, orchestras, ballet companies, private hospitals, and elite universities.

2. The number of private security guards in the United States now exceeds the number of public police officers. (Robert Reich, "Secession of the Successful." *New York Times Magazine,* February 1991.)

3. A total of $20 billion is spent on welfare when you include all state funding. But the average state funding also comes to only two cents per state dollar.

4. In 92 percent of the murders nationwide the assailant and the victim are of the same race (46 percent are white/white, 46 percent are black/black), 5.6 percent are black on white, and 2.4 percent are white on black. (FBI and Bureau of Justice Statistics, 1985–1986, quoted in Raymond S. Franklin. *Shadows of Race and Class,* University of Minnesota Press, Minneapolis, 1991, p. 108.)

THINKING ABOUT THE READING

What kinds of messages do people get about wealth and social position from the media? What do these messages suggest about who is deserving and who is not? If these messages are based on inaccurate stereotypes, where can people get more accurate information? Do you think that people in different social classes view themselves and their lives differently based on how they are portrayed in the news and on television? If these portrayals are a significant source of information about one's place in society, do you think these media images affect a person's sense of self-worth and opportunity?

The Compassion Gap in American Poverty Policy

Fred Block, Anna C. Korteweg, and Kerry Woodward,
with Zach Schiller and Imrul Mazid

(2006)

Every 30 or 40 years, Americans seem to "discover" that millions of our citizens are living in horrible and degrading poverty. Jacob Riis shocked the nation in 1890 with a book entitled *How the Other Half Lives,* which helped to inspire a change in public opinion and the reforms of the Progressive Era. In the 1930s, the devastation of the Great Depression led FDR to place poverty at the top of the national agenda. In the early 1960s, Michael Harrington's *The Other America* made poverty visible and paved the way for Lyndon Johnson's brief War on Poverty. In 2005, an act of nature became the next muckraker—Hurricane Katrina, which shockingly revealed the human face of poverty among the displaced and helpless victims of the storm's devastation in New Orleans.

But what makes poverty so invisible between such episodes of discovery? The poor are always with us, but why do they repeatedly disappear from public view? Why do we stop seeing the pain that poverty causes?

Our society recognizes a moral obligation to provide a helping hand to those in need, but those in poverty have been getting only the back of the hand. They receive little or no public assistance. Instead, they are scolded and told that they have caused their own misfortunes. This is our "compassion gap"—a deep divide between our moral commitments and how we actually treat those in poverty.

The compassion gap does not just happen. It results from two key dynamics. First, powerful groups in American society insist that public help for the poor actually hurts them by making them weak and dependent. Every epoch in which poverty is rediscovered and generosity increases is followed by a backlash

in which these arguments reemerge and lead to sharp reductions in public assistance. Second, the consequence of reduced help is that the assertions of welfare critics turn into self-fulfilling prophecies. They insist that immorality is the root cause of poverty. But when assistance becomes inadequate, the poor can no longer survive by obeying the rules; they are forced to break them. These infractions, in turn, become the necessary proof that "the poor" are truly intractable and that their desperate situations are rightly ignored.

The results are painfully clear in our official data. In 2004, 37 million people, including 13 million children, lived below the government's official poverty line of $15,219 for a family of three. The number of people in poverty has increased every year for the last four years, rising from 31.6 million in 2000. Moreover, our government's official poverty line is quite stingy by international standards. If we used the most common international measure, which counts people who live on less than half of a country's median income as poor, then almost 55 million people in the United States, or almost 20 percent of the population, would be counted as poor.

Most distressingly, the number of people living in catastrophic poverty—in households with incomes less than 50 percent of the official U.S. poverty line—has increased every year since 1999. There are now 15.6 million people living in this kind of desperate poverty. This is close to the highest number ever, and it is twice the number of extremely poor people that we had in the mid-1970s, before the cuts in poverty programs of the Reagan administration.

Children, single mothers with children, and people of color—particularly African

Americans and Latinos—make up a disproportionate segment of the nation's poorest groups, with women in each group consistently more likely to be poor than men in that group. But poverty is not unusual or rare—as many as 68 percent of all Americans will spend a year or more living in poverty or near-poverty as adults. Nor is poverty always related to not working; there are still 9 million working-poor adults in the United States.

Moreover, poverty has become more devastating over the past generation. Thirty years ago, a family living at the poverty line—earning a living at low-wage work—could still see the American Dream as an achievable goal (see figure 1). With a bit more hard work and some luck, they too could afford a single-family home, comprehensive health insurance, and a college education for their children. Today, for many of the poor, including many of the faces we saw at the New Orleans Superdome and Convention Center, that dream has become a distant and unattainable vision. Even a two-parent family working full-time at the minimum wage earns less than half of what is needed to realize the dream at today's prices. The old expectation that the poor would pull themselves up by their own bootstraps is increasingly unrealistic.

Figure 1   The Dream Line is an estimate of the cost for an urban or suburban family of four to enjoy a no-frills version of the American Dream that includes owning a single-family home, full health-insurance coverage, quality child care for a four-year-old, and enough annual savings to assure that both children can attend a public, four-year college or university. The Dream Line is not a wage figure because it includes the full cost of health insurance coverage that is often, but decreasingly, offered as a benefit by employers. The figures are national averages and are lower than what people would pay for these services in the largest and most expensive metropolitan areas on the East and West coasts. The housing figure reflects the cost of mortgage payments on the median-priced existing family home at current interest rates. The Dream Line rises so dramatically because the costs of the four H's—housing, health insurance, high-quality child care, and higher education—have risen so much more rapidly than other consumer prices. Dollar figures have not been adjusted for inflation. More details on the way the Dream Divide was calculated are available at http://www.longviewinstitute.org/research/block/amerdream/view.

When the Dream Line is compared to the federal poverty line or to the income that a two-parent family would earn if both parents were working full-time at the minimum wage, it is clear that the dream has become increasingly distant for millions.

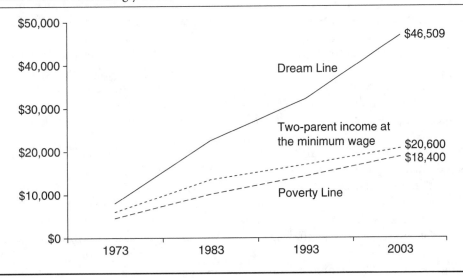

Price rises for the four H's

	Housing	High-quality child care	Higher education	Health insurance
1973 (annual cost)	$1,989	$978	$736	$509
2003 (annual cost)	$10,245	$7,200	$5,000	$8,933
Percent increase	15%	736%	679%	1755%

Despite the growing poor population and the increasing difficulty of escaping poverty into economic security through paid work, the government has been doing less and less to help. Aid to Families with Dependent Children (AFDC) used to be our biggest program to help poor people, but federal legislation passed in 1996 ended AFDC and replaced it with Temporary Aid to Needy Families (TANF). TANF's focus on moving recipients from "welfare to work" has led to a major decline in the number of households receiving benefits and a huge drop in cash assistance to the poor. The average monthly TANF benefit was $393 in 2003, compared to $490 in 1997.

Not only are our programs miserly, they reach too few people among those who are eligible, further reducing the chances that those in poverty can achieve the American Dream. Only 60 percent of eligible households receive food stamps, Despite a commitment to provide health insurance to all children under 18, nearly 12 percent of those children remained without such insurance in 2004, and only 27 percent of all poor families received TANF in 2000. Finally, subsidized housing is provided to only 25 percent of those who need it, and current budget proposals would cut this program dramatically.

Against this backdrop of decreasing spending on most antipoverty measures, the Earned Income Tax Credit (EITC) has become our biggest antipoverty program for the working-age population. EITC aids the working poor by providing an income-tax refund to lift the poorest workers above the poverty line. But for families to benefit significantly from the EITC, someone in the household must be earning at least several thousand dollars per year. Each year, millions of households do not have such an earner because of unemployment, illness, lack of child care, or a mismatch between available skills and job demands. The consequence is a relentless increase in our rate of catastrophic poverty.

Figure 2 shows the combined spending for the two most important cash assistance programs—AFDC/TANF and the EITC. It demonstrates that despite increases in EITC outlays, our total spending on the poor peaked in 1997 and has dropped almost 20 percent since then. Figure 3 takes the further step of adjusting the annual spending for the impact of inflation and the shifting size of the poor population. Spending for each nonelderly poor person peaked at around $1,000 in 1997 and has dropped every year since, with a total decline of close to 30 percent. And if we added food stamps to this chart, the trend would be even stronger, since their real value has also fallen since 1997. There is no clearer evidence that our compassion gap has deepened poverty.

The compassion gap has been greatly increased by the revival in the 1980s and 1990s of the very old theory that the real source of poverty is bad behavior. Since African-American and Hispanic women and men, as well as single mothers of all ethnicities and races, are disproportionately represented among the poor, this theory defines these

Figure 2 Assistance to those in poverty from 1990 to 2004 in billions of dollars

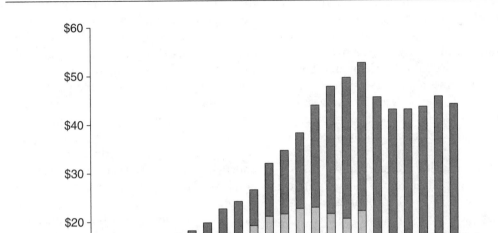

people as morally deficient. Its proponents assume that anyone with enough grit and determination can escape poverty. They claim that giving people cash assistance worsens poverty by taking away their drive to improve their circumstances through work. Arguing that poor people bear children irresponsibly and that they lack the work ethic necessary for economic success, they have launched a sustained war on bad behavior that targets those groups most at risk of poverty.

One of the key events in this war was the passage in 1996 of the Personal Responsibility and Work Opportunities Reconciliation Act (PRWORA), which replaced AFDC with TANF. TANF requires single mothers who receive welfare to find paid work, encourages them to marry, and limits their time on aid to a lifetime maximum of five years. Some states have even shorter time limits. Ultimately, this new program treats the inability to work as a personal, moral failing.

Can Governments Solve Poverty?

The flip side of the premise that poverty is the result of such moral failings is that government actions cannot solve poverty. Yet our own national experience points to the opposite conclusion. For generations, many of the elderly lived in extreme poverty because they were no longer able to work. But the creation of the Social Security system has sharply reduced poverty among seniors by recognizing that most people need government assistance as they age. Yet, rather than celebrating the compassion reflected in this program, the current administration is proposing destructive changes in Social Security that will make it less effective in preventing poverty among this group. And instead of recognizing that most young families also need assistance to survive and thrive, our major antipoverty program, the EITC, leaves out all those families who find themselves squeezed out of the labor market.

Looking abroad also shows that government policies can dramatically reduce poverty levels. The probability of living in poverty is more than twice as high for a child born in the United States than for children in Belgium, Germany, or the Netherlands. Children in single-mother households are four times more likely to be poor in the United States than in Norway. The fact that single-parent households are more common in the United States than in many of these countries where the poor receive greater assistance undermines the claim that more generous policies will encourage more single women to have children out of wedlock. These other countries all take a more comprehensive government approach to combating poverty, and they assume that it is caused by economic and structural factors rather than bad behavior.

Understanding the Compassion Gap: A Misguided Focus on Moral Poverty

The miserliness of our public assistance is justified by the claim that poverty is the consequence of personal moral failings. Most of our policies incorrectly assume that people can avoid or overcome poverty through hard work alone. Yet this assumption ignores the realities of our failing urban schools, increasing employment insecurities, and the lack of affordable housing, health care, and child care. It ignores the fact that the American Dream is rapidly becoming unattainable for an increasing number of Americans, whether employed or not.

The preoccupation with the moral failings of the poor disregards the structural problems underlying poverty. Instead, we see increasing numbers of policies that are obsessed with preventing "welfare fraud." This obsession creates barriers to help for those who need it. Welfare offices have always required recipients to "prove" their eligibility. Agency employees are in effect trained to begin with the presumption of guilt; every seemingly needy face they encounter is that of a cheater until the potential client can prove the contrary. With the passage of TANF, the rules have become so complex that even welfare caseworkers do not always understand them, let alone their clients. Some of those who need help choose to forego it rather than face this humiliating eligibility process.

But this system of suspicion also produces the very welfare cheaters that we fear. Adults in

Figure 3 Spending on poor individuals per person

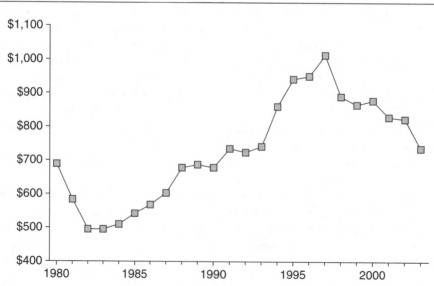

poor households are caught in a web of different programs, each with its own complex set of rules and requirements, that together provide less assistance than a family needs. Recipients have no choice but to break the rules—usually by not reporting all their income. A detailed study from ten years ago, conducted by Kathryn Edin and Laura Lein, showed that most welfare mothers worked off the books or took money under the table from relatives because they could not make ends meet with only their welfare checks. Since then we have reduced benefits and added more rules, undoubtedly increasing such "cheating."

Those who lack compassion have made their own predictions come true. They begin by claiming that the poor lack moral character. They use stories of welfare cheaters to increase public concerns about people getting something for nothing. Consequently, our patchwork of poorly funded programs reaches only a fraction of the poor and gives them less than they need. Those who depend on these programs must cut corners and break rules to keep their families together. This "proves" the original proposition that the poor lack moral character, and the "discovery" is used to justify ever more stringent policies. The result is a vicious spiral of diminishing compassion and greater preoccupation with the moral failings of the poor.

The War on Bad Behavior

The moral focus on poverty shifts our gaze from the social forces that create material poverty to the perceived moral failings of the poor. This shift has led to a war on bad behavior, exemplified by PRWORA, that is not achieving its goals. This war focuses on social problems like teenage pregnancy, high dropout rates, and drug addiction. But research shows that it has been ineffective. Poverty has risen, and punitive measures have had little effect on the behaviors they were supposed to change.

The reduction of teen pregnancy through abstinence-only sex education was one of the main goals of the Personal Responsibility and Work Opportunity Act. Its drafters mistakenly believed that teen pregnancy is one of the root causes of poverty. In fact, if the teenagers who are having children were to wait until they were adults, their children would be just as likely to be born into poverty. But the drafters' other error was ignoring the fact that teen pregnancy rates had already been declining for years when the new law went into effect, primarily because teenagers were using more effective methods of birth-control. (These gains are now threatened by the dramatic expansion of "abstinence-only sex education," which provides no information on birth-control techniques.)

PRWORA also makes assistance to teen mothers contingent on "good behavior." Teen mothers must stay in school or be enrolled in a training program and live with their parents or under other adult supervision in order to receive aid. While it makes sense to help teens stay in school and learn skills, these coercive efforts are failing the children of teen parents. Teen mothers are just as likely today to drop out of school or live on their own as when the act was passed. The only change is that they are now much less likely to receive government assistance: ill-conceived reforms have ensured that children born to teen mothers experience deeper deprivation.

Neither have PRWORA's efforts to control the behavior of the poor had much impact on illicit drug use. Under TANF, states were required to deny benefits to anyone convicted of a drug crime. This was so obviously counterproductive that Congress amended the law in 1999 to allow states to opt out of this ban. Yet neither policy shift appears to have had much impact. According to Justice Department data, adult drug arrests have been increasing relentlessly, from 1 million per year in the early 1990s to 1.5 million in 2003.

But advocates of the war on bad behavior always have a convenient scapegoat for the failure of their punitive policies: they simply shift the blame to single mothers. TANF requires single mothers to work outside the home

Children living in poverty (counting all sources of income, including income from government programs)

Country	Year	Percent of all children in poverty	Percent of all children in single-mother homes in poverty	Percent of all children living with single mothers
US	2000	21.9	49.3	19.5
UK	1999	15.3	33.8	19.5
Canada	2000	14.9	40.7	13.1
Netherlands	1999	9.8	35.1	8.1
Germany	2000	9.0	37.8	12.5
Belgium	2000	6.7	24.5	10.6
Norway	2000	3.4	11.3	14.5

SOURCE: Luxemburg Income Survey: www.lisproject.org/keyfigures/povertytable.htm.

NOTE: This table uses the international convention of measuring poverty as income less than 50 percent of the nation's median income.

regardless of whether work gets them out of poverty. But long hours of work and inadequate child care mean that children are often left with inadequate supervision. When these children get into trouble, the mother gets the blame. Teen pregnancy, drug use, and delinquency are then attributed to the mother's lack of parenting skills. Poor single mothers cannot win; they are failures if they stay home with their kids—providing the full-time mothering that conservatives have long advocated for middle-class children. But they are also failures if they work and leave their children unsupervised. Viewing poverty as the result of bad behavior produces the conclusion that poor single mothers are bad by definition. Since a disproportionate number of these poor single mothers are African American or Hispanic, this rhetoric also hides the racial history that has excluded people of color from opportunities for generations and the systemic racism that persists today.

This war on bad behavior is a deeply mistaken approach to poverty. It ignores the lived reality of people who face crushing poverty every day. It ignores the fundamental wisdom that we should not judge people until we have walked a mile in their shoes. Most basically, it denies compassion to those who need it most.

What to Do? Revitalize the American Dream

Reversing the compassion gap will not happen overnight. We have to persuade our fellow citizens that the war on bad behavior violates our society's fundamental values. We have to show them how far reality has departed from the American Dream, which holds that a child born in poverty in a ghetto or a barrio has the same chance for success and happiness as a child born in suburban affluence. We have to focus national debate on what policy measures would revitalize the American Dream for all of our citizens.

The reason the American Dream is now beyond reach for so many families is that the price of four critical services has risen much more sharply than wages and the rate of inflation: health care, higher education, high-quality child care, and housing. These are not luxuries, but indispensable ingredients of the dream.

Over the last three decades, our society has relied largely on market solutions to organize delivery of these indispensable services, but these solutions have not increased their supply. Instead, we use the price mechanism to ration their distribution; poor and working-class people are at the end of the line, and they find themselves priced out of the market.

We need new initiatives to expand the supply of these key services while assuring their quality. This requires accelerated movement toward universal health insurance and universal availability of quality child care and preschool programs. We need to move toward universal access to higher education for all students who meet the admissions criteria. (We also need to ensure that all our public schools are preparing students for the higher education and training that most will need in order to succeed in the labor market.) And we need to create new public-private partnerships to expand the supply of affordable housing for poor and working-class families. These efforts would restore the American Dream for millions of working-class and lower middle-class families, while also putting the dream within the reach of the poor.

But we also need new policies that target the poor more directly. This requires restoring the value of the minimum wage. Between 1968 and 2002, the purchasing power of the federal minimum wage fell by a third. We need to reverse this trend and assure that in the future the minimum wage continues to rise with inflation. Most fundamentally, we must do what most other developed nations do—provide a stable income floor for all poor families so that no children grow up in horrible and degrading poverty. We could establish such a floor by transforming our present Earned Income Tax Credit into a program that provided all poor families with sufficient income to cover food and shelter. Households would be eligible for a monthly payment even if they had no earnings. Since such payments would target the poorest individuals and families, this would be a cost-effective way to immediately rescue millions of people from catastrophic poverty. Moreover, since payments would be coordinated through the tax system, a household's income would definitely improve as its labor-force earnings rose.

The key to making these policy initiatives feasible is to remind our fellow citizens what true compassion requires. The war on bad behavior offers us an easy way out. It is easy to believe that those in poverty are responsible for their own problems and that ignoring their needs is the best thing for them. It absolves those of us who are better off from the responsibility of caring for others. However, if we want to live up to our national commitment to compassion, we need to recognize that we have a collective responsibility to ensure that in the wealthiest nation in the world there are not millions of people going hungry, millions without health insurance, and hundreds of thousands without homes. Sure, some of those in poverty have made bad choices, but who has not? It is deeply unfair that those who are not poor get second chances, while the poor do not. Rush Limbaugh pays no price for becoming addicted to painkillers, but millions of poor people go to jail and lose access to public housing and welfare benefits for the same offense.

True compassion requires that we build a society in which every person has a first chance, a second chance, and, if needed, a third and fourth chance, to achieve the American Dream. We are our brother's and our sister's keepers, and we need to use every instrument we have—faith groups, unions, community groups, and most of all government programs—to address the structural problems that reproduce poverty in our affluent society.

Dealing with the inadequacies of our current antipoverty programs is a first step in moving the debate in the right direction. Since the fall of 2002, Congress has been stalemated on reauthorizing the TANF legislation that was first passed in 1996. Action in the immediate future seems unlikely because many governors oppose the more stringent work requirements for TANF recipients proposed by the Bush administration and its conservative allies in the House, because those changes would require the states to pay for new work-experience programs.

A compassionate reauthorization of TANF requires four basic steps. First, we must increase assistance levels to rescue families from the deepest poverty and give them enough income to put them over the poverty line. Second, we must abandon the whole system of mandatory time limits on aid, so that families in poverty no longer find the doors to help closed in their faces. Eliminating time limits is particularly important in ensuring that programs serve the many poor women who are victims of domestic abuse. While TANF is supposed to protect such women, too often they are being forced back into the arms of their abusers. Third, we must recognize basic and postsecondary education and training as a "work activity," so that recipients can prepare for jobs that would get them out of poverty. Finally, we need to improve the child-care provisions in TANF. We must do more than provide child-care subsidies to only one out of seven children who are federally eligible. Moreover, we must ensure that TANF children get a head start and are not relegated to the lowest-quality child care.

By themselves, these reforms would not close the compassion gap, but they would mark an end to the futile and destructive war on bad behavior. They could represent an initial down payment on restoring the American Dream.

Postscript

For more than three years Congress was unable to agree on a reauthorization of the TANF legislation that was initially passed in 1996. In early 2006, however, the Republican leadership moved the legislation without debate or discussion by including TANF reauthorization in a large deficit-reduction bill that passed both houses by the narrowest of margins. In fact, the legislation might yet be overturned by the courts because the House and the Senate passed slightly different versions of the bill.

If implemented, the new legislation will widen the compassion gap even further because states are required either to place 50 percent of adult recipients in work-related activities or to reduce the number of families receiving benefits. Since many of those currently on the rolls face multiple barriers to employment, these artificial targets are likely to create considerable hardship. Moreover, the allocation for child care is not enough to maintain the current availability of child care, let alone to keep pace with the new participation requirements.

THINKING ABOUT THE READING

What is the "compassion gap"? Give some examples from recent news stories and your own experiences of this "gap." According to the authors, how does this social attitude contribute to the persistence of social inequality? How do current social policies perpetuate poverty? What is the "dream line"? What kinds of changes are needed both culturally and politically to address the increasing poverty rates in the United States?

Avenue to Adulthood

Teenage Pregnancy and the Meaning of Motherhood in Poor Communities

Gabrielle Raley

(2008)

First the good news: the rate of teenage child-bearing in the United States has been falling since the 1950s, and it has taken a nosedive in the last decade, plunging by 35 percent between 1991 and 2005. Rates of adolescent childbearing are now at historic lows for *all* racial-ethnic groups. And this isn't because more pregnant teens are opting for abortions. In fact, the teenage abortion rate has been falling steadily since the 1980s, a trend that continues today. By 2002, the Guttmacher Institute reports, the teen abortion rate was 50 percent lower than its peak in 1988.

But now the bad news: the United States still has the highest occurrence of teenage childbearing in the industrialized world at just over 40 births per 1000 teenage girls aged 15 to 19. To put that in perspective, the comparable rate is 22 births in Canada, 13 births in Germany, and 4 births per 1000 girls in Japan. Our rates parallel those in many developing countries. And in 2006, for the first time in 15 years, there was a new uptick in teen births. These figures are disturbing because teen childbearing is much more of a problem today than it was in the past, when it was less necessary for girls to postpone motherhood to invest in their education and prepare to make their own living in a competitive labor market.

These figures lead many people to wonder why American teens are so irresponsible. The issue came up recently in a sociology course I teach. We had been discussing how an increasing number of families are feeling the crunch of falling real wages and job out-sourcing, especially in areas of concentrated poverty. "I get that these things make life harder if you're an adult and already have a family," one student interrupted. "But if you're a teenager, why would you *start* a family before you've gotten out of poverty? You're just going to trap yourself and your kid forever. Why don't you just *wait* to have a baby?" Many heads nodded in agreement as she concluded, "It seems so selfish!"

At first glance, the causal relationship between teen childbearing and poverty seems self-evident. Teen mothers are more likely to be poor and to receive welfare, and are less likely to finish high school, than women who delay childbearing. Their children are more likely to be born at low birth weights, have behavioral problems, do poorly in school, and drop out before graduation. Female children of teen mothers are also more likely to end up as teen mothers themselves, while male children have a greater chance of going to prison. One advocacy group estimates that all this costs U.S. taxpayers around $9.1 billion per year in social services.

But if we are further to reduce the rate of teenage childbearing, we need to understand it more thoroughly, looking more closely at its complicated causes and consequences. The first step in this effort is to see teenage pregnancy *in social context*. When we look at the problem in context, we see a very different picture than the stereotype of promiscuous girls popping out babies to collect a welfare check. Instead, we see adolescents growing up in neighborhoods with a long history of limited access to adequate schools and secure jobs—teens whose parents or grandparents paid their dues by holding down menial jobs, only to watch their neighborhoods fall deeper into decay and job prospects for their children dwindle. We see that, in the poorest areas of our country, motherhood may be the only way that an impoverished girl can envision having a future, or a measure of control in her life. Looking at the issue in context, it is not that teenage childbearing represents a *good* choice, but that it is an often *understandable* one, given the lack of better options.

Rather than being the fundamental cause of poverty, adolescent childbearing is often more a result of pre-existing impoverishment, most especially of growing up in concentrated poverty. Experts estimate that 83 percent of teenage mothers come from disadvantaged backgrounds. In fact, teenage childbearing and poverty are so intertwined that taking the 15 states with the highest rates of poverty in the country and comparing them with the 15 states with the highest rates of teenage pregnancy, we find that 11 states appear on both lists.

Looking at teenage childbearing in context suggests the need for social policies much different than the ones pursued in the last two decades. Offering poor unwed mothers "incentives" for marriage or providing teens with better abstinence-only sex education is unlikely to lower our current rates of teenage childbearing because such programs do not address the simple fact that poor teens often do not have much reason to put off childbearing. If we want to help teenagers make different choices about parenthood, we need to give urgent attention to the appalling quality of education offered in poor—usually segregated—schools, the social isolation and lack of decent jobs in areas of concentrated poverty, and the tenacious racism that blames the desperate poverty of main urban populations of color on flawed moral values. If we want teenagers to wait to have kids, we need to give them other options for the future, real incentives to wait.

The rise in unmarried childbearing, its high visibility in many African-American communities, and the socioeconomic consequences attributed to teenage pregnancy fueled the 1996 Personal Responsibility and Work Opportunity Reconciliation Act (PRWORA), which famously ended "welfare as we know it." At the time, public concern over unmarried teenage childbearing was at its peak. In 1995, a year before he signed PRWORA into law, President Clinton called teenage pregnancy "our most serious social problem." Welfare was seen as spawning the rise in female-headed families and encouraging a "culture of poverty" that promoted unwed childbearing, especially among African-Americans. Unmarried teenage pregnancy was singled out for special consideration under PRWORA and its state-controlled block assistance program, Temporary Assistance to Needy Families (TANF). Specifically, TANF mandated that teen mothers live with their parents and stay in school to receive benefits. It also limited them, along with other welfare recipients, to a maximum of five years during which they could receive assistance. Proponents hoped that "getting tough" on welfare recipients would end teen childbearing and reduce poverty.

The fact is, however, that prior to the passage of PRWORA, scholars had been in "widespread agreement" that welfare did *not* cause unmarried childbearing, teenage or otherwise. It is true that there was a rise in unmarried female-headed families from the 1960s to the 1980s. But the real value of welfare payments declined significantly during this same period. If mothers could buy increasingly less with their monthly welfare checks, it's hard to imagine that this was an incentive to create *more* mouths to feed. Sociologist Mark Robert Rank studied 3,000 welfare recipients over eight years; they simply laughed at the suggestion that they would have additional children in order to collect an extra $60–$90 a month in benefits.

Arguments that welfare is the cause of teenage pregnancy generally fail to consider teen mothers' socioeconomic backgrounds *prior* to getting pregnant. Study after study has shown that when background characteristics such as poverty, neighborhood, and social isolation from job networks are controlled for, welfare and race-ethnicity cease to explain variations in teenage pregnancy at all. For example, Christopher Jencks and Susan Mayer found that, controlling for race and family background, sixteen- to eighteen-year-old girls were considerably more likely to bear children while unmarried if they lived in poor neighborhoods than if they lived in economically average neighborhoods.[1]

In another study of the effect of neighborhood on teenage sexual activity, researchers found "the frequency with which youth engage in sexual intercourse, the number of partners they have sex with, and the likelihood of engaging in unprotected intercourse all increase with the level of socioeconomic disadvantage of their communities."[2]

Other researchers found that what had first seemed to be a strong racial-ethnic difference in teenage attitudes about childbearing—with African-American teens far more approving of it than whites—evaporated when they controlled for neighborhood economic disadvantage. Based on their results, they concluded that in fact, "neighborhood economic disadvantage accounts for a substantial proportion of the racial difference in sexual attitude[s]. . . . In short, race is not the explanation for the observed racial differences" in attitudes about adolescent sexuality and childbearing.[3]

So concentrated poverty is a better explanation for teenage childbearing than race-ethnicity or welfare receipt.[4]

Class is not just defined by a person's income or educational status at a particular point in time. It is a *social* relationship that places one group of people in a certain pattern of interaction with other groups and gives group members a set of shared experiences, expectations, problem-solving habits, vulnerabilities, and privileges. It is one's long-term options, not just a particular income or job, that determines class status. This is why a college student who is broke is in a higher and more secure class, with completely different dynamics, than a resident of an inner city, even one who is currently flush. In our country, class has been constructed not just by economic processes but also by racial exclusion and ethnic stratification over a long period of time.[5]

The idea of class as a social relationship must inform our understanding of why teenage childbearing occurs disproportionately among some segments of the population. It is true, for instance, that Latina and African-American teens experience higher rates of childbearing than their white counterparts. But this fact demonstrates first of all the embedded relationship of race, ethnicity, and class in our country, not that racially or ethnically derived values cause disadvantage, as "culture of poverty" proponents maintain.

The tendency to explain teen pregnancy through the lens of "culture" or "values" is itself a hard cycle to break. For instance, researchers often explain Latino teens' lower contraceptive use as a result of cultural patterns or religious beliefs. For example, a qualitative study of teenage-pregnancy practitioners working with Latino youth reported that counseling teens to avoid pregnancy so they could pursue education seemed to be "at odds with traditional Hispanic cultural values," especially with regard to female self-sufficiency.[6]

But while all teens make choices about sex and childbearing in a cultural context, that context is often more complicated than such statements imply. Gloria González-López interviewed immigrant men in Los Angeles about their daughters' sexual activity. She found that while most fathers wanted their daughters to wait to have sex until they were married, "protecting their daughters from a sexually dangerous society and improving their socioeconomic future is of greater concern to these men than preserving virginity per se."[7]

Buttressing an economic rather than cultural reading of Latina teen childbearing, a recent study found that many Latino immigrant youth experience significant structural hurdles to obtaining contraceptives: language barriers make finding and using family planning services difficult, and undocumented teens, in particular, worry that seeking such services will alert the authorities to their illegal status in the country and put their families at risk of deportation. While many non-Latino sexually active teens worry that their parents will disapprove of their actions, most don't have to consider their family's legal and residential security when they seek contraception.

Class, culture, and family background interact in complicated ways. In many studies, poor academic skills and low prospects for educational attainment rank as high as poverty in predicting the incidence of adolescent child-bearing. One study finds that the likelihood that a teen will have a child while unmarried is significantly reduced if she has high grades, high standardized test scores, and plans to graduate from college. Linda Waite and her colleagues at the Rand Corporation found that teen birth rates were highest among girls who had the greatest economic disadvantage and the lowest academic ability. Again however, educational attainment is difficult to disentangle from class and from the long and continuing history of racial segregation in public schools. Although terms such as "academic ability" and "educational aspirations" have a neutral ring, they are factors highly tempered by social privilege.

Most people believe that able and committed children will automatically stay in school, and that their efforts will pay off in an economically stable future. But the social isolation of the poorest of the poor creates neighborhoods with few connections to the job market and few opportunities to get a decent education. To be sure, a gifted student can occasionally, with a little luck, get a good education. But many equally intelligent students run into dead ends, while average students, or less able students who might have succeeded with the extra help available in more affluent communities, fall further behind.

The correlation between educational discouragement and bearing a child in one's teens is striking: high school dropouts are six times more likely than their contemporaries who remain in school to become unmarried parents. In a state-by-state study of school segregation, researchers at Harvard University's Civil Rights Project found that in 2001, only 50 percent of African-American students, 51 percent of Native American students, and 53 percent of Latino students graduated from high school (the comparable rates for whites and Asian-Americans are 75 percent and 77 percent, respectively). A high school teacher in a poor school in East St. Louis explains the connection between poverty, dropping out of school, and bearing a child as a teenager:

> I have four girls right now in my senior home room who are pregnant or have just had babies. When I ask them why this happens, I am told, "Well, there's no reason not to have a baby. There's nothing for me in public school." The truth is, that's a pretty honest answer. A diploma from a ghetto high school doesn't count for much in the United States today. So, if this is really the last education that a person's going to get, she's probably perceptive in that statement.

Just how little does a diploma from a poor high school count? Designs for Change, a Chicago-based research center, found in a survey of the eighteen poorest schools in the country that only 3.5 percent of the students both graduate and can read at the national level. In other words, if 6,700 students enter the ninth grade in these eighteen schools each year, only 300 will make it out with both a diploma and adequate reading skills.

Due to inequitable and antiquated systems of school funding, most schools in impoverished minority communities do not possess the funds to offer college preparatory or advanced classes, even though residents of such communities often tax themselves at higher rates than more affluent areas. Residents of New York's underprivileged

Roosevelt school district have one of the highest property tax rates in the state, for example.[8]

Because educational opportunities are so unequal in the U.S., some experts have argued that schools do much more than prepare kids for future jobs or education, but in fact sort children by their probable class destinations. In schools, both rich and poor, children are instilled with a sense of the opportunities available to them, of their place in the social order. Children who attend poor, segregated schools soon learn to doubt their capabilities as well as their opportunities, giving them little incentive to engage in what middle-class Americans would consider rational planning for the future. Jonathan Kozol, author of some of the most incisive work on public school inequity, found many "industry-embedded schools" in the poor and segregated districts he studies. For example, one inner-city school in Chicago offers a comprehensive "culinary arts" educational track to its high school students to prepare them to work in restaurant kitchens (the program is co-sponsored by Hyatt Hotels, which offers jobs to students upon completion of their training). Sociologist William Julius Wilson argues that most inner-city schools "train minority youth so that they feel and appear capable of only performing jobs in the low-wage sectors."

Such training starts young. One kindergarten Kozol visited had a retail corner in its classroom, complete with a "poster that displayed the names of several retail stores: JCPenney, Wal-Mart, Kmart, Sears, and a few others. 'It's like working in a store,' a classroom aide explained. 'The children are learning to pretend that they're cashiers.'"

Children in inner-city schools are well aware of the inequity of their situation. Students in suburban schools, they realize, don't have to put up with rat infestations, sewage and heating problems, or chronic shortages of books and supplies. They get the message quite quickly about society's assessment of their relative worth. As this Puerto Rican student at a poor high school in New York points out:

If you threw us into some different place . . . and put white children in this building in our place, this school would start to shine . . . They'd fix it fast, no question. People on the outside may think that we don't know what it is like for other students, but we *visit* other schools, and we have eyes and we have brains. You cannot hide the differences. You see it and compare . . .

Poverty, racial-ethnic discrimination, and unfair school funding are great enough burdens for any child or adolescent to shoulder. But teens must also make decisions about sex in a culture that inundates them with sexual commodification at every turn, yet allows them few socially acceptable ways to engage in responsible sex while unmarried.

All adolescents face conflicting messages about sex, responsibility, and future goals. Laurence Steinberg argues that contemporary adolescents have gained access to adult consumption patterns but have lost access to responsible adult roles, a condition he terms "adolescent rolelessness." Furthermore, teens become sexually mature earlier than in the past (currently, menarche occurs at 12 years of age), while the average age at first marriage has risen to almost 26 for women and 28 for men. This presents adolescents with a simple time-management problem. Most will face a decade or more in which they are both sexually mature and unmarried.[9]

Expecting teens to remain abstinent for a decade, or until they are married, is naïve at best.

The results of abstinence-only education have not been encouraging for proponents. According to sociologists Hannah Brückner and Peter Bearman, the majority of teens in grades 7 to 12 who vowed to remain virgins until marriage had nonmarital sex before their follow-up survey six years later. Furthermore, "vow breakers" were less likely than other teens to use condoms when they did have sex. In another study, researchers at Mathematics Policy Research followed middle-school students enrolled in four abstinence programs for five years and found that they had sex at roughly the same age as peers who had not had abstinence education. The two groups initiated sex at the same mean age and had similar numbers of sexual partners. While researchers allow that a small percentage in the recent drop in teenage pregnancy may be explained by fewer teens having sex overall, studies show that approximately 85 percent of the decline in teen pregnancy rates is due to more consistent and effective contraceptive use among teens, not abstinence education.

Yet despite the availability of contraceptive information, impoverished teens continue to have children at much higher rates than other adolescents. A 2005 ethnographic study by Kathryn Edin and Maria Kefalas provides a compelling possible explanation for this variation. Over a five-year period, Edin and Kefalas interviewed 162 low-income black, Latino, and white mothers, most of whom had children as teens. Edin and Kefalas lived in the poor Philadelphia neighborhoods they studied and followed their respondents (and their partners) through the early days of their relationship, through pregnancy, and after the birth of their child(ren).

Only a small number of the women Edin and Kefalas studied *planned* to get pregnant in their teens (nationally about 82 percent of teenage pregnancies are not planned). But neither were their pregnancies entirely unplanned. Most women Edin and Kefalas interviewed described their pregnancies as somewhere in between: "not exactly planned" and "not exactly avoided" (only a few of their respondents were using contraception when they conceived their child).

The explanation for this lack of consistent effort to avoid pregnancy lies in understanding how the social location of these young women shapes their sense of current and future options. With seriously limited opportunities for continued education and future employment, carrying a baby to term is often the one avenue through which low-income girls can assert their grown-up status. Many mothers Edin and Kefalas studied said they wanted someone to love and take care of, while others reported wanting to seal a romance by having a child. For many of these young women, moreover, raising children is the one job for which they've had ample training—most poor kids have had to care for younger siblings. As one eighteen-year-old white mother of two toddlers explained: "When we was living with my mom, I was taking care of my little sister and my little brother anyway. She was working two jobs, so I was taking care of them mostly."

The women interviewed by Edin and Kefalas reported having reasonable access to contraception, but many stopped using it when their romantic relationship became serious. Although they got pregnant earlier than they wanted, many mothers say their timing was off by only a year or two. Most now claim there are advantages to being young and energetic mothers and, in the absence of plans or possibilities for higher schooling, they see few costs to having had a baby in their teens.

It is not that the teens Edin and Kefalas studied do not see pregnancy and motherhood as a challenge. But it is one of the few challenges they believe they can meet. Most residents of the neighborhoods Edin and Kefalas studied said that learning one is pregnant is the first "test" of one's capacity for motherhood. Having an abortion is seen as taking the "easy way" out or as punishing the baby for the mother's mistake. Carrying the pregnancy to term signals that the mother is taking responsibility for her actions and is ready to "grow up." Pregnancy thus symbolizes the beginning of the transition to adulthood for many poor women. Since children are not seen as a roadblock to future success, there is often no reason not to rise to the challenge.

While it is important to acknowledge the complex motivations and personal agency of teens who have babies, we also need to recognize the constrained and deprived situations in which they make their choices. These constraints are not only economic but often sexual. In two out of three births to unmarried teen mothers, the father is not a teen at all but twenty years of age or older, often much older than the mother. It is highly probable that many of these relationships involved some measure of sexual coercion for young teen mothers. One research team estimates that "more than a quarter of teens who had intercourse before age fourteen said they didn't want their first sexual experience to happen." In other cases, much younger women may simply not feel able to negotiate the terms of their sexual relationship, including contraceptive use.

But even for couples whose relationships are truly consensual, there are fewer obstacles to getting pregnant than there are to getting married. Experts estimate that over 50 percent of babies born officially to "single mothers" are actually born to cohabiting couples. Mirroring these findings, Edin and Kefalas report that most of the women in their study lived with their child's father at the time of the birth. And most intended to marry their baby's father . . . later. Indeed, one of the most surprising findings of this study is the high regard for marriage that the women Edin and Kefalas interviewed expressed, and this attitude holds across all racial-ethnic groups they studied. Respondents see marriage as a serious, lifelong commitment that should only be entered into if one plans on staying the course permanently. Given the uncertain and often desperate economic conditions in which they live, this permanence is hard to come by, and many women reported that they did not intend to marry until they had enough economic security with their partners to improve their chance of making it in the long run.

Thus, while motherhood is, as Edin and Kefalas put it, the "primary vocation for young women" in inner-city neighborhoods, marriage is something that should only be entered into if a couple can do it right, and this means attaining a certain level of financial stability and social respectability. Said one young mother of two children, currently living with—though not married to—the father of one of her children, "I want my kids to be stable before I do anything to alter their lives . . . I wanna have an established environment for my kids so that my kids are happy, my kids are healthy, they're safe, they

have their own house, their own toys, their own couch, their own television."

Clearly, such a difference in socially valued avenues of attaining adult status in poor communities puts a strain on teenage relationships. And this strain reinforces the obstacles that women see to getting married, even as it increases the emotional meaning of motherhood in their lives. Contrary to the "culture of poverty" argument, however, this disconnect between marriage and motherhood in impoverished communities reflects the socioeconomic dilemmas facing these young men and women more than it reflects deviant or irresponsible values. Indeed, it is precisely because impoverished young women share so many mainstream values about the importance of marriage and the centrality of breadwinning to a man's "marriageability" that they are reluctant to marry. And it is their lack of access to other fulfilling and rewarding social roles that reinforces their attraction to motherhood and their ambivalence about avoiding pregnancy.

NOTES

1. Christopher Jencks and Susan E. Mayer, "The Social Consequences of Growing Up in a Poor Neighborhood," in Laurence E. Lynn Jr. and Michael G.H. McGeary, eds., *Inner-City Poverty in the United States* (Washington, DC: National Academy Press, 1990), p. 167.

2. Jonathan Crane, "Effects of Neighborhoods on Dropping Out of School and Teenage Childbearing," in Christopher Jencks and Paul E. Peterson, eds., *The Urban Underclass* (Washington, DC: Brookings Institution, 1991), p. 311. Eric P. Baumer and Scott J. South, "Community Effects on Youth Sexual Activity," *Journal of Marriage and Family*, Vol. 63, May 2001, p. 552.

3. Christopher R. Browning and Lori A. Burrington, "Racial Differences in Sexual and Fertility Attitudes in an Urban Setting," *Journal of Marriage and Family*, Vol. 68, February 2006, p. 248.

4. Ibid., p. 248.

5. On the relational nature of class in the U.S. see William G. Roy, *Making Societies: The Historical Construction of Our World* (Thousand Oaks, CA: Pine Forge Press, 2001).

6. Stephen I. Russell, Faye C. H. Lee and the Latin/o Teen Pregnancy Prevention Workshop, "Practitioners' Perspectives on Effective Practices for Hispanic Teenage Pregnancy Prevention," *Perspectives on Sexual and Reproductive Health,* Vol. 36, No. 4, 2004, p. 142.

7. Gloria González-López, "Fathering Latina Sexualities: Mexican Men and the Virginity of Their Daughters," *Journal of Marriage and Family,* Vol. 66, No. 5, p. 1118.

8. Jonathan Kozol, *The Shame of the Nation: The Restoration of Apartheid Schooling in America* (New York: Crown Publishers, 2005).

9. William Cameron Chumlea, Christine M. Schubert, Alex F. Roche, Howard E. Kulin, Peter A. Lee, John H. Himes, and Shumei S. Sun, "Age at Menarche and Racial Comparisons in US Girls," *Pediatrics,* Vol. III, No. 1, 2003. Stephanie Coontz, *Marriage, A History: From Obedience to Intimacy or How Love Conquered Marriage* (New York: Viking, 2005).

THINKING ABOUT THE READING

Raley uses contemporary data and research to dispel several myths about teenage pregnancy. What are some of these myths? According to Raley, what are some of the social conditions that contribute to high rates of teenage pregnancy? Why does Raley make a distinction between low income and lack of life resources? What does she mean when she says that motherhood may be an "avenue to adulthood" for young women who live in poor communities? What are the implications of this research for social policies and public attitudes about teenage pregnancy?

The Architecture of Inequality

Race and Ethnicity

The history of race in the United States is an ambivalent one. Cultural beliefs about equality conflict with the experiences of most racial and ethnic minorities: oppression, violence, and exploitation. Opportunities for life, liberty, and the pursuit of happiness have always been distributed along racial and ethnic lines. U.S. society is built on the assumption that different immigrant groups will ultimately assimilate, changing their way of life to conform to that of the dominant culture. But the increasing diversity of the population has shaped people's ideas about what it means to be an American and has influenced our relationships with one another and with our social institutions.

Sociologists tell us that race is not a biological characteristic but rather a social construction that can change across time and from culture to culture. The socially constructed nature of race is illustrated in "Racial and Ethnic Formation" by Michael Omi and Howard Winant. However, the authors are quick to point out that just because race is socially created doesn't mean it is insignificant. Indeed, our definitions of race are related to inequality, discrimination, and cultural dominance and resistance. Race may not be a purely biological trait, but it is an important part of every social institution.

It has been said that white people in the United States have the luxury of "having no color." When someone is described with no mention of race, the default assumption is that he or she is white. In other words, *white* is used far less often as a modifying adjective than *black*, *Asian*, or *Latino*. As a result, "whiteness" is rarely questioned or examined as a racial or ethnic category. In her article "Optional Ethnicities," Mary C. Waters argues that unlike members of other groups, U.S. whites can choose whether or not to include their specific ancestry in descriptions of their own identities. For whites of European descent, claiming an ethnic identity is a voluntary "leisure-time activity" with few social implications. Indeed, the option of being able *not* to claim any ethnicity is available only to the majority group in a society.

Racial inequality is both a personal and structural phenomenon. On one hand, it is lodged in individual prejudice and discrimination. On the other hand, it resides in our language, collective beliefs, and important social institutions. This latter manifestation of racism is more difficult to detect than personal racism, and hence it is more difficult to change. Because such racism exists at a level beyond personal attitudes, it will not disappear simply by reducing people's prejudices.

In the "Downside of Racial Uplift," sociologist Michelle Boyd provides an example of the intersection of economics, politics, and racial ideologies. "Gentrification" is an urban process that is usually associated with whites moving into and upscaling low-income neighborhoods. This process has resulted in the displacement of many low-income blacks who originally inhabited the neighborhoods. Boyd provides a study of a neighborhood that is being gentrified by middle-class African Americans. These homeowners use an ideology of "lift of the race" to justify urban planning decisions that will increase the value of their homes and the neighborhood. As powerful as this ideology may be (if we help one of us we help us all), the unintended consequence is the displacement of renters whose low-income housing is at risk in the new development plans.

Something to Consider as You Read

As you read these selections, consider the differences between individual prejudice and institutional racism. Is it possible for someone not to be racist and still participate in practices that perpetuate racism? Compare these readings with those in other sections. Consider the connections between access to economic resources, social class, and race How might socioeconomic status influence attitudes and behaviors toward others who may share your ethnicity but not your class position? Think also about how you identify your own race or ethnicity. When you fill out a questionnaire that asks you to select a racial/ethnic category, do you think the category adequately reflects you? When you go somewhere, do you assume you will easily find others of your own race or ethnicity? When you watch television or a movie, how likely is it that the central characters will be people who share your racial background? Practice asking yourself similar questions as a way of enhancing your racial awareness.

Racial and Ethnic Formation

Michael Omi and Howard Winant

(1994)

In 1982–83, Susie Guillory Phipps unsuccessfully sued the Louisiana Bureau of Vital Records to change her racial classification from black to white. The descendant of an 18th-century white planter and a black slave, Phipps was designated "black" in her birth certificate in accordance with a 1970 state law which declared anyone with at least 1/32nd "Negro blood" to be black.

The Phipps case raised intriguing questions about the concept of race, its meaning in contemporary society, and its use (and abuse) in public policy. Assistant Attorney General Ron Davis defended the law by pointing out that some type of racial classification was necessary to comply with federal record-keeping requirements and to facilitate programs for the prevention of genetic diseases. Phipps's attorney, Brian Begue, argued that the assignment of racial categories on birth certificates was unconstitutional and that the 1/32nd designation was inaccurate. He called on a retired Tulane University professor who cited research indicating that most Louisiana whites have at least 1/20th "Negro" ancestry.

In the end, Phipps lost. The court upheld the state's right to classify and quantify racial identity.[1]

Phipps's problematic racial identity, and her effort to resolve it through state action, is in many ways a parable of America's unsolved racial dilemma. It illustrates the difficulties of defining race and assigning individuals or groups to racial categories. It shows how the racial legacies of the past—slavery and bigotry—continue to shape the present. It reveals both the deep involvement of the state in the organization and interpretation of race, and the inadequacy of state institutions to carry out these functions. It demonstrates how deeply Americans both as individuals and as a civilization are shaped, and indeed haunted, by race.

Having lived her whole life thinking that she was white, Phipps suddenly discovers that by legal definition she is not. In U.S. society, such an event is indeed catastrophic.[2] But if she is not white, of what race is she? The *state* claims that she is black, based on its rules of classification,[3] and another state agency, the court, upholds this judgment. But despite these classificatory standards which have imposed an either-or logic on racial identity, Phipps will not in fact "change color." Unlike what would have happened during slavery times if one's claim to whiteness was successfully challenged, we can assume that despite the outcome of her legal challenge, Phipps will remain in most of the social relationships she had occupied before the trial. Her socialization, her familial and friendship networks, her cultural orientation, will not change. She will simply have to wrestle with her newly acquired "hybridized" condition. She will have to confront the "Other" within.

The designation of racial categories and the determination of racial identity is no simple task. For centuries, this question has precipitated intense debates and conflicts, particularly in the U.S.—disputes over natural and legal rights, over the distribution of resources, and indeed, over who shall live and who shall die.

A crucial dimension of the Phipps case is that it illustrates the inadequacy of claims that race is a mere matter of variations in human physiognomy, that it is simply a matter of skin color. But if race cannot be understood in this manner, how *can* it be understood? We cannot fully hope to address this topic—no less than the meaning of race, its role in society, and the forces which shape it—in one chapter, nor indeed in one book. Our goal in this chapter, however, is far from modest: we wish to offer at least the outlines of a theory of race and racism.

What Is Race?

There is a continuous temptation to think of race as an *essence,* as something fixed, concrete, and objective. And there is also an opposite temptation: to imagine race as a mere *illusion,* a purely ideological construct which some ideal non-racist social order would eliminate. It is necessary to challenge both these positions, to disrupt and reframe the rigid and bipolar manner in which they are posed and debated, and to transcend the presumably irreconcilable relationship between them.

The effort must be made to understand race as an unstable and "decentered" complex of social meanings constantly being transformed by political struggle. With this in mind, let us propose a definition: *race is a concept which signifies and symbolizes social conflicts and interests by referring to different types of human bodies.* Although the concept of race invokes biologically based human characteristics (so-called "phenotypes"), selection of these particular human features for purposes of racial signification is always and necessarily a social and historical process. In contrast to the other major distinction of this type, that of gender, there is no biological basis for distinguishing among human groups along the lines of race.[4] Indeed, the categories employed to differentiate among human groups along racial lines reveal themselves, upon serious examination, to be at best imprecise, and at worst completely arbitrary.

If the concept of race is so nebulous, can we not dispense with it? Can we not "do without" race, at least in the "enlightened" present? This question has been posed often, and with greater frequency in recent years.[5] An affirmative answer would of course present obvious practical difficulties: it is rather difficult to jettison widely held beliefs, beliefs which moreover are central to everyone's identity and understanding of the social world. So the attempt to banish the concept as an archaism is at best counterintuitive. But a deeper difficulty, we believe, is inherent in the very formulation of this schema, in its way of posing race as a *problem,* a misconception left over from the past, and suitable now only for the dustbin of history.

A more effective starting point is the recognition that despite its uncertainties and contradictions, the concept of race continues to play a fundamental role in structuring and representing the social world. The task for theory is to explain this situation. It is to avoid both the utopian framework which sees race as an illusion we can somehow "get beyond," and also the essentialist formulation which sees race as something objective and fixed, a biological datum.[6] Thus we should think of race as an element of social structure rather than as an irregularity within it; we should see race as a dimension of human representation rather than as an illusion. These perspectives inform the theoretical approach we call racial formation.

Racial Formation

We define *racial formation* as the sociohistorical process by which racial categories are created, inhabited, transformed, and destroyed. Our attempt to elaborate a theory of racial formation will proceed in two steps. First, we argue that racial formation is a process of historically situated *projects* in which human bodies and social structures are represented and organized. Next we link racial formation to the evolution of hegemony, the way in which society is organized and ruled. Such an approach, we believe, can facilitate understanding of a whole range of contemporary controversies and dilemmas involving race, including the nature of racism, the relationship of race to other forms of differences, inequalities, and oppression such as sexism and nationalism, and the dilemmas of racial identity today.

From a racial formation perspective, race is a matter of both social structure and cultural representation. Too often, the attempt is made to understand race simply or primarily in terms of only one of these two analytical dimensions.[7] For example, efforts to explain racial inequality as a purely social structural phenomenon are unable to account for the origins, patterning, and transformation of racial difference.

Conversely, many examinations of racial difference—understood as a matter of cultural attributes á la ethnicity theory, or as a society-wide signification system, á la some poststructuralist accounts—cannot comprehend such structural phenomena as racial stratification in the labor market or patterns of residential segregation.

An alternative approach is to think of racial formation processes as occurring through a linkage between structure and representation. Racial *projects* do the ideological "work" of making these links. A *racial project is simultaneously an interpretation, representation, or explanation of racial dynamics, and an effort to reorganize and redistribute resources along particular racial lines.* Racial projects connect what race *means* in a particular discursive practice and the ways in which both social structures and everyday experiences are racially *organized,* based upon that meaning. Let us consider this proposition, first in terms of large-scale or macro-level social processes, and then in terms of other dimensions of the racial formation process.

Racial Formation as a Macro-Level Social Process

To interpret the meaning of race is to frame it social structurally. Consider for example, this statement by Charles Murray on welfare reform:

> My proposal for dealing with the racial issue in social welfare is to repeal every bit of legislation and reverse every court decision that in

any way requires, recommends, or awards differential treatment according to race, and thereby put us back onto the track that we left in 1965. We may argue about the appropriate limits of government intervention in trying to enforce the ideal, but at least it should be possible to identify the ideal: Race is not a morally admissible reason for treating one person differently from another. Period.[8]

Here there is a partial but significant analysis of the meaning of race: it is not a morally valid basis upon which to treat people "differently from one another." We may notice someone's race, but we cannot act upon that awareness. We must act in a "color-blind" fashion. This analysis of the meaning of race is immediately linked to a specific conception of the role of race in the social structure: it can play no part in government action, save in "the enforcement of the ideal." No state policy can legitimately require, recommend, or award different status according to race. This example can be classified as a particular type of racial project in the present-day U.S.—a "neoconservative" one.

Conversely, *to recognize the racial dimension in social structure is to interpret the meaning of race.* Consider the following statement by the late Supreme Court Justice Thurgood Marshall on minority "set-aside" programs:

> A profound difference separates governmental actions that themselves are racist, and governmental actions that seek to remedy the effects of prior racism or to prevent neutral government activity from perpetuating the effects of such racism.[9]

Here the focus is on the racial dimensions of *social structure*—in this case of state activity and policy. The argument is that state actions in the past and present have treated people in very different ways according to their race, and thus the government cannot retreat from its policy responsibilities in this area. It cannot suddenly declare itself "color-blind" without in fact perpetuating the same type of differential, racist treatment.[10] Thus, race continues to signify difference and structure inequality. Here, racialized social structure is immediately linked to an interpretation of the meaning of race. This example too can be classified as a particular type of racial project in the present-day U.S.—a "liberal" one.

To be sure, such political labels as "neoconservative" or "liberal" cannot fully capture the complexity of racial projects, for these are always multiply determined, politically contested, and deeply shaped by their historical context. Thus, encapsulated within the neoconservative example cited here are certain egalitarian commitments which derive from a previous historical context in which they played a very different role, and which are rearticulated in neoconservative racial discourse precisely to oppose a more open-ended, more capacious conception of the meaning of equality. Similarly, in the liberal example, Justice Marshall recognizes that the contemporary state, which was formerly the architect of segregation and the chief enforcer of racial difference, has a tendency to reproduce those patterns of inequality in a new guise. Thus he admonishes it (in dissent, significantly) to fulfill its responsibilities to uphold a robust conception of equality. These particular instances, then, demonstrate how racial projects are always concretely framed, and thus are always contested and unstable. The social structures they uphold or attack, and the representations of race they articulate, are never invented out of the air, but exist in a definite historical context, having descended from previous conflicts. This contestation appears to be permanent in respect to race.

These two examples of contemporary racial projects are drawn from mainstream political debate; they may be characterized as center-right and center-left expressions of contemporary racial politics.[11] We can, however, expand the discussion of racial formation processes far beyond these familiar examples. In fact, we can identify racial projects in at least three other analytical dimensions: first, the political spectrum can be broadened to include radical projects, on both the left and right, as well as along

other political axes. Second, analysis of racial projects can take place not only at the macro-level of racial policy-making, state activity, and collective action, but also at the micro-level of everyday experience. Third, the concept of racial projects can be applied across historical time, to identify racial formation dynamics in the past. We shall now offer examples of each of these types of racial projects.

The Political Spectrum of Racial Formation

We have encountered examples of a neoconservative racial project, in which the significance of race is denied, leading to a "color-blind" racial politics and "hands off' policy orientation; and of a "liberal" racial project, in which the significance of race is affirmed, leading to an egalitarian and "activist" state policy. But these by no means exhaust the political possibilities. Other racial projects can be readily identified on the contemporary U.S. scene. For example, "far right" projects, which uphold biologistic and racist views of difference, explicitly argue for white supremacist policies. "New right" projects overtly claim to hold "color-blind" views, but covertly manipulate racial fears in order to achieve political gains.[12] On the left, "radical democratic" projects invoke notions of racial "difference" in combination with egalitarian politics and policy.

Further variations can also be noted. For example, "nationalist" projects, both conservative and radical, stress the incompatibility of racially defined group identity with the legacy of white supremacy, and therefore advocate a social structural solution of separation, either complete or partial.[13] . . . Nationalist currents represent a profound legacy of the centuries of racial absolutism that initially defined the meaning of race in the U.S. Nationalist concerns continue to influence racial debate in the form of Afrocentrism and other expressions of identity politics.

Taking the range of politically organized racial projects as a whole, we can "map" the current pattern of racial formation at the level of the public sphere, the "macro-level" in which public debate and mobilization takes place.[14] But important as this is, the terrain on which racial formation occurs is broader yet.

Racial Formation as Everyday Experience

At the micro-social level, racial projects also link signification and structure, not so much as efforts to shape policy or define large-scale meaning, but as the applications of "common sense." To see racial projects operating at the level of everyday life, we have only to examine the many ways in which, often unconsciously, we "notice" race.

One of the first things we notice about people when we meet them (along with their sex) is their race. We utilize race to provide clues about *who* a person is. This fact is made painfully obvious when we encounter someone whom we cannot conveniently racially categorize—someone who is, for example, racially "mixed" or of an ethnic/racial group we are not familiar with. Such an encounter becomes a source of discomfort and momentarily a crisis of racial meaning.

Our ability to interpret racial meanings depends on preconceived notions of a racialized social structure. Comments such as, "Funny, you don't look black," betray an underlying image of what black should be. We expect people to act out their apparent racial identities; indeed we become disoriented when they do not. The black banker harassed by police while walking in casual clothes through his own well-off neighborhood, the Latino or white kid rapping in perfect Afro patois, the unending *faux pas* committed by whites who assume that the non-whites they encounter are servants or tradespeople, the belief that non-white colleagues are less qualified persons hired to fulfill affirmative action guidelines, indeed the whole gamut of racial stereotypes—that "white men can't jump," that Asians can't dance, etc., etc.— all testify to the way a racialized social structure

shapes racial experience and conditions meaning. Analysis of such stereotypes reveals the always present, already active link between our view of the social structure—its demography, its laws, its customs, its threats—and our conception of what race means.

Conversely, our ongoing interpretation of our experience in racial terms shapes our relations to the institutions and organizations through which we are imbedded in social structure. Thus we expect differences in skin color, or other racially coded characteristics, to explain social differences. Temperament, sexuality, intelligence, athletic ability, aesthetic preferences, and so on are presumed to be fixed and discernible from the palpable mark of race. Such diverse questions as our confidence and trust in others (for example, clerks or salespeople, media figures, neighbors), our sexual preferences and romantic images, our tastes in music, films, dance, or sports, and our very ways of talking, walking, eating, and dreaming become racially coded simply because we live in a society where racial awareness is so pervasive. Thus in ways too comprehensive even to monitor consciously, and despite periodic calls—neoconservative and otherwise—for us to ignore race and adopt "color-blind" racial attitudes, skin color "differences" continue to rationalize distinct treatment of racially identified individuals and groups.

To summarize the argument so far: the theory of racial formation suggests that society is suffused with racial projects, large and small, to which all are subjected. This racial "subjection" is quintessentially ideological. Everybody learns some combination, some version, of the rules of racial classification, and of her own racial identity, often without obvious teaching or conscious inculcation. Thus are we inserted in a comprehensively racialized social structure. Race becomes "common sense"—a way of comprehending, explaining, and acting in the world. A vast web of racial projects mediates between the discursive or representational means in which race is identified and signified on the one hand, and the institutional and organizational forms in which it is routinized and standardized on the other. These projects are the heart of the racial formation process.

Under such circumstances, it is not possible to represent race discursively without simultaneously locating it, explicitly or implicitly, in a social structural (and historical) context. Nor is it possible to organize, maintain, or transform social structures without simultaneously engaging, once more either explicitly or implicitly, in racial signification. Racial formation, therefore, is a kind of synthesis, an outcome, of the interaction of racial projects on a society-wide level. These projects are, of course, vastly different in scope and effect. They include large-scale public action, state activities, and interpretations of racial conditions in artistic, journalistic, or academic fora,[15] as well as the seemingly infinite number of racial judgments and practices we carry out at the level of individual experience.

Since racial formation is always historically situated, our understanding of the significance of race, and of the way race structures society, has changed enormously over time. The processes of racial formation we encounter today, the racial projects large and small which structure U.S. society in so many ways, are merely the present-day outcomes of a complex historical evolution. The contemporary racial order remains transient. By knowing something of how it evolved, we can perhaps better discern where it is heading. . . .

NOTES

1. *San Francisco Chronicle*, 14 September 1982, 19 May 1983. Ironically, the 1970 Louisiana law was enacted to supersede an old Jim Crow statute which relied on the idea of "common report" in determining an infant's race. Following Phipps's unsuccessful attempt to change her classification and have the law declared unconstitutional, a legislative effort arose which culminated in the repeal of the law. See *San Francisco Chronicle*, 23 June 1983.

2. Compare the Phipps case to Andrew Hacker's well-known "parable" in which a white person is informed by a mysterious official that "the organization he represents has made a mistake" and that " . . . [a]ccording to their records . . . , you were to have been born black: to another set of parents, far from where you were raised." How much compensation, Hacker's official asks, would "you" require to undo the damage of this unfortunate error? See Hacker, *Two Nations: Black and White, Separate, Hostile, Unequal* (New York: Charles Scribner's Sons, 1992) pp. 31–32.

3. On the evolution of Louisiana's racial classification system, see Virginia Dominguez, *White By Definition: Social Classification in Creole Louisiana* (New Brunswick: Rutgers University Press, 1986).

4. This is not to suggest that gender is a biological category while race is not. Gender, like race, is a social construct. However, the biological division of humans into sexes—two at least, and possibly intermediate ones as well—is not in dispute. This provides a basis for argument over gender divisions—how "natural," etc.—which does not exist with regard to race. To ground an argument for the "natural" existence of race, one must resort to philosophical anthropology.

5. "The truth is that there are no races, there is nothing in the world that can do all we ask race to do for us. . . . The evil that is done is done by the concept, and by easy—yet impossible—assumptions as to its application." (Kwame Anthony Appiah, *In My Father's House: Africa in the Philosophy of Culture* [New York: Oxford University Press, 1992].) Appiah's eloquent and learned book fails, in our view, to dispense with the race concept, despite its anguished attempt to do so; this indeed is the source of its author's anguish. We agree with him as to the non-objective character of race, but fail to see how this recognition justifies its abandonment. This argument is developed below.

6. We understand essentialism as *belief in real, true human, essences, existing outside or impervious to social and historical context.* We draw this definition, with some small modifications, from Diana Fuss, *Essentially Speaking: Feminism, Nature, & Difference* (New York: Routledge, 1989) p. xi.

7. Michael Omi and Howard Winant, "On the Theoretical Status of the Concept of Race," in Warren Crichlow and Cameron McCarthy, eds., *Race, Identity, and Representation in Education* (New York: Routledge, 1993).

8. Charles Murray, *Losing Ground: American Social Policy, 1950–1980* (New York: Basic Books, 1984) p. 223.

9. Justice Thurgood Marshall, dissenting in *City of Richmond v. J. A. Croson Co.*, 488 U.S. 469 (1989).

10. See, for example, Derrick Bell, "Remembrances of Racism Past: Getting Past the Civil Rights Decline," in Herbert Hill and James E. Jones, Jr., eds., *Race in America: The Struggle for Equality* (Madison: The University of Wisconsin Press, 1993) pp. 75–76; Gertrude Ezorsky, *Racism and Justice: The Case for Affirmative Action* (Ithaca: Cornell University Press, 1991) pp. 109–111; David Kairys, *With Liberty and Justice for Some: A Critique of the Conservative Supreme Court* (New York: The New Press, 1993) pp. 138–41.

11. Howard Winant has developed a tentative "map" of the system of racial hegemony in the U.S. circa 1990, which focuses on the spectrum of racial projects running from the political right to the political left. See Winant, "Where Culture Meets Structure: Race in the 1990s," in idem, *Racial Conditions: Politics, Theory, Comparisons* (Minneapolis: University of Minnesota Press, 1994).

12. A familiar example is use of racial "code words." Recall George Bush's manipulations of racial fear in the 1988 "Willie Horton" ads, or Jesse Helms's use of the coded term "quota" in his 1990 campaign against Harvey Gantt.

13. From this perspective, far right racial projects can also be interpreted as "nationalist." See Ronald Walters, "White Racial Nationalism in the United States," *Without Prejudice* Vol.1, no. 1 (Fall 1987).

14. To be sure, any effort to divide racial formation patterns according to social structural location—"macro" vs. "micro," for example—is necessarily an analytic device. In the concrete, there is no such dividing line. See Winant, "Where Culture Meets Structure."

15. We are not unaware, for example, that publishing this work is in itself a racial project.

THINKING ABOUT THE READING

What do Omi and Winant mean when they say that "race is always historically situated"? What do they mean when they say that everyone learns a system of rules and routines about race that become common sense? Consider some examples of these commonsense rules in contemporary society. How do people learn these rules? How do they unlearn them? Is the idea that race is "natural" one of the rules of the current "race project" in this society? If so, how does this particular rule contribute to social inequality?

Optional Ethnicities

For Whites Only?

Mary C. Waters

(1996)

What does it mean to talk about ethnicity as an option for an individual? To argue that an individual has some degree of choice in their ethnic identity flies in the face of the common-sense notion of ethnicity many of us believe in—that one's ethnic identity is a fixed characteristic, reflective of blood ties and given at birth. However, social scientists who study ethnicity have long concluded that while ethnicity is based on a *belief* in a common ancestry, ethnicity is primarily a *social* phenomenon, not a biological one (Alba 1985, 1990; Barth 1969; Weber [1921] 1968, p. 389). The belief that members of an ethnic group have that they share a common ancestry may not be a fact. There is a great deal of change in ethnic identities across generations through intermarriage, changing allegiances, and changing social categories. There is also a much larger amount of change in the identities of individuals over their lives than is commonly believed. While most people are aware of the phenomenon known as "passing"—people raised as one race who change at some point and claim a different race as their identity—there are similar life course changes in ethnicity that happen all the time and are not given the same degree of attention as "racial passing."

White Americans of European ancestry can be described as having a great deal of choice in terms of their ethnic identities. The two major types of options White Americans can exercise are (1) the option of whether to claim any specific ancestry, or to just be "White" or American, (Lieberson [1985] called these people "unhyphenated Whites") and (2) the choice of which of their European ancestries to choose to

include in their description of their own identities. In both cases, the option of choosing how to present yourself on surveys and in everyday social interactions exists for Whites because of social changes and societal conditions that have created a great deal of social mobility, immigrant assimilation, and political and economic power for Whites in the United States. Specifically, the option of being able to not claim any ethnic identity exists for Whites of European background in the United States because they are the majority group—in terms of holding political and social power, as well as being a numerical majority. The option of choosing among different ethnicities in their family backgrounds exists because the degree of discrimination and social distance attached to specific European backgrounds has diminished over time . . . .

Symbolic Ethnicities for White Americans

What do these ethnic identities mean to people and why do they cling to them rather than just abandoning the tie and calling themselves American? My own field research with suburban Whites in California and Pennsylvania found that later-generation descendants of European origin maintain what are called "symbolic ethnicities." Symbolic ethnicity is a term coined by Herbert Gans (1979) to refer to ethnicity that is individualistic in nature and without real social cost for the individual. These symbolic identifications are essentially leisure-time activities, rooted in nuclear family traditions and reinforced by the voluntary enjoyable aspects of being ethnic (Waters 1990). Richard Alba (1990) also found later-generation Whites in Albany, New York, who chose to keep a tie with an ethnic identity because of the enjoyable and voluntary aspects to those identities, along with the feelings of specialness they entailed. An example of symbolic ethnicity is individuals who identify as Irish, for example, on occasions such as Saint Patrick's Day, on family holidays, or for vacations. They do not usually belong to Irish American organizations, live in Irish neighborhoods, work in Irish jobs, or marry other Irish people. The symbolic meaning of being Irish American can be constructed by individuals from mass media images, family traditions, or other intermittent social activities. In other words, for later-generation White ethnics, ethnicity is not something that influences their lives unless they want it to. In the world of work and school and neighborhood, individuals do not have to admit to being ethnic unless they choose to. And for an increasing number of European-origin individuals whose parents and grandparents have intermarried, the ethnicity they claim is largely a matter of personal choice as they sort through all of the possible combinations of groups in their genealogies . . . .

Race Relations and Symbolic Ethnicity

However much symbolic ethnicity is without cost for the individual, there is a cost associated with symbolic ethnicity for the society. That is because symbolic ethnicities of the type described here are confined to White Americans of European origin. Black Americans, Hispanic Americans, Asian Americans, and American Indians do not have the option of a symbolic ethnicity at present in the United States. For all of the ways in which ethnicity does not matter for White Americans, it does matter for non-Whites. Who your ancestors are does affect your choice of spouse, where you live, what job

you have, who your friends are, and what your chances are for success in American society, if those ancestors happen not to be from Europe. The reality is that White ethnics have a lot more choice and room to maneuver than they themselves think they do. The situation is very different for members of racial minorities, whose lives are strongly influenced by their race or national origin regardless of how much they may choose not to identify themselves in terms of their ancestries.

When White Americans learn the stories of how their grandparents and great-grandparents triumphed in the United States over adversity, they are usually told in terms of their individual efforts and triumphs. The important role of labor unions and other organized political and economic actors in their social and economic successes are left out of the story in favor of a generational story of individual Americans rising up against communitarian, Old World intolerance, and New World resistance. As a result, the "individualized" voluntary, cultural view of ethnicity for Whites is what is remembered.

One important implication of these identities is that they tend to be very individualistic. There is a tendency to view valuing diversity in a pluralist environment as equating all groups. The symbolic ethnic tends to think that all groups are equal; everyone has a background that is their right to celebrate and pass on to their children. This leads to the conclusion that all identities are equal and all identities in some sense are interchangeable—"I'm Italian American, you're Polish American. I'm Irish American, you're African American." The important thing is to treat people as individuals and all equally. However, this assumption ignores the very big difference between an individualistic symbolic ethnic identity and a socially enforced and imposed racial identity.

My favorite example of how this type of thinking can lead to some severe misunderstandings between people of different backgrounds is from the *Dear Abby* advice column. A few years back a person wrote in who had asked an acquaintance of Asian background where his family was from. His acquaintance answered that this was a rude question and he would not reply. The bewildered White asked Abby why it was rude, since he thought it was a sign of respect to wonder where people were from, and he certainly would not mind anyone asking HIM about where his family was from. Abby asked her readers to write in to say whether it was rude to ask about a person's ethnic background. She reported that she got a large response, that most non-Whites thought it was a sign of disrespect, and Whites thought it was flattering:

> Dear Abby,
>   I am 100 percent American and because I am of Asian ancestry I am often asked "What are you?" It's not the personal nature of this question that bothers me, it's the question itself. This query seems to question my very humanity. "What am I? Why I am a person like everyone else!"
>   Signed, A REAL AMERICAN

> Dear Abby,
>   Why do people resent being asked what they are? The Irish are so proud of being Irish, they tell you before you even ask. Tip O'Neill has never tried to hide his Irish ancestry.
>   Signed, JIMMY.
>   (Reprinted by permission of Universal Press Syndicate)

In this exchange Jimmy cannot understand why Asians are not as happy to be asked about their ethnicity as he is, because he understands his ethnicity and theirs to be separate but equal. Everyone has to come from somewhere—his family from Ireland, another's family from Asia—each has a history and each should be proud of it. But the reason he cannot understand the perspective of the Asian American is that all ethnicities are not equal; all are not symbolic, costless, and voluntary. When White Americans equate their own symbolic ethnicities with the socially enforced identities of non-White Americans, they obscure the fact that the experiences of Whites and non-Whites have been qualitatively different in the United States and that the current identities of individuals partly reflect that unequal history.

In the next section I describe how relations between Black and White students on college campuses reflect some of these asymmetries in the understanding of what a racial or ethnic identity means. While I focus on Black and White students in the following discussion, you should be aware that the myriad other groups in the United States—Mexican Americans, American Indians, Japanese Americans—all have some degree of social and individual influences on their identities, which reflect the group's social and economic history and present circumstance.

Relations on College Campuses

Both Black and White students face the task of developing their race and ethnic identities. Sociologists and psychologists note that at the time people leave home and begin to live independently from their parents, often ages eighteen to twenty-two, they report a heightened sense of racial and ethnic identity as they sort through how much of their beliefs and behaviors are idiosyncratic to their families and how much are shared with other people. It is not until one comes in close contact with many people who are different from oneself that individuals realize the ways in which their backgrounds may influence their individual personality. This involves coming into contact with people who are different in terms of their ethnicity, class, religion, region, and race. For White students, the ethnicity they claim is more often than not a symbolic one—with all of the voluntary, enjoyable, and intermittent characteristics I have described above.

Black students at the university are also developing identities through interactions with others who are different from them. Their identity development is more complicated than that of Whites because of the added element of racial discrimination and racism, along with the "ethnic" developments of finding others who share their background. Thus Black students have the positive attraction of being around other Black students who share some cultural elements, as well as the need to band together with other students in a reactive and oppositional way in the face of racist incidents on campus.

Colleges and universities across the country have been increasing diversity among their student bodies in the last few decades. This has led in many cases to strained relations among students from different racial and ethnic backgrounds. The 1980s and 1990s produced a great number of racial incidents and high racial tensions on campuses. While there were a number of racial incidents that were due to bigotry, unlawful behavior, and violent or vicious attacks, much of what happens among students on campuses involves a low level of tension and awkwardness in social interaction.

Many Black students experience racism personally for the first time on campus. The upper-middle-class students from White suburbs were often isolated enough that their presence was not threatening to racists in their high schools. Also, their class background was known by their residence and this may have prevented attacks being directed at them. Often Black students at the university who begin talking with other students and recognizing racial slights will remember incidents that happened to them earlier that they might not have thought were related to race.

Black college students across the country experience a sizeable number of incidents that are clearly the result of racism. Many of the most blatant ones that occur between students are the result of drinking. Sometimes late at night, drunken groups of White students coming home from parties will yell slurs at single Black students on the street. The other types of incidents that happen include being singled out for special treatment by employees, such as being followed when shopping at the campus bookstore, or going to the art museum with your class and the guard stops you and asks for your I.D. Others involve impersonal encounters on the street—being called a nigger by a truck driver while crossing the street, or seeing old ladies clutch their pocketbooks and shake in terror as you pass them on the street. For the most part

these incidents are not specific to the university environment, they are the types of incidents middle-class Blacks face every day throughout American society, and they have been documented by sociologists (Feagin 1991).

In such a climate, however, with students experiencing these types of incidents and talking with each other about them, Black students do experience a tension and a feeling of being singled out. It is unfair that this is part of their college experience and not that of White students. Dealing with incidents like this, or the ever-present threat of such incidents, is an ongoing developmental task for Black students that takes energy, attention, and strength of character. It should be clearly understood that this is an asymmetry in the "college experience" for Black and White students. It is one of the unfair aspects of life that results from living in a society with ongoing racial prejudice and discrimination. It is also very understandable that it makes some students angry at the unfairness of it all, even if there is no one to blame specifically. It is also very troubling because, while most Whites do not create these incidents, some do, and it is never clear until you know someone well whether they are the type of person who could do something like this. So one of the reactions of Black students to these incidents is to band together.

In some sense then, as Blauner (1992) has argued, you can see Black students coming together on campus as both an "ethnic" pull of wanting to be together to share common experiences and community, and a "racial" push of banding together defensively because of perceived rejection and tension from Whites. In this way the ethnic identities of Black students are in some sense similar to, say, Korean students wanting to be together to share experiences. And it is an ethnicity that is generally much stronger than, say, Italian Americans. But for Koreans who come together there is generally a definition of themselves as "different from" Whites. For Blacks reacting to exclusion there is a tendency for the coming together to involve both being "different from" but also "opposed to" Whites.

The anthropologist John Ogbu (1990) has documented the tendency of minorities in a variety of societies around the world, who have experienced severe blocked mobility for long periods of time, to develop such oppositional identities. An important component of having such an identity is to describe others of your group who do not join in the group solidarity as devaluing and denying their very core identity. This is why it is not common for successful Asians to be accused by others of "acting White" in the United States, but it is quite common for such a term to be used by Blacks and Latinos. The oppositional component of a Black identity also explains how Black people can question whether others are acting "Black enough." On campus, it explains some of the intense pressures felt by Black students who do not make their racial identity central and who choose to hang out primarily with non-Blacks. This pressure from the group, which is partly defining itself by not being White, is exacerbated by the fact that race is a physical marker in American society. No one immediately notices the Jewish students sitting together in the dining hall, or the one Jewish student sitting surrounded by non-Jews, or the Texan sitting with the Californians, but everyone notices the Black student who is or is not at the "Black table" in the cafeteria.

An example of the kinds of misunderstandings that can arise because of different understandings of the meanings and implications of symbolic versus oppositional identities concerns questions students ask one another in the dorms about personal appearances and customs. A very common type of interaction in the dorm concerns questions Whites ask Blacks about their hair. Because Whites tend to know little about Blacks, and Blacks know a lot about Whites, there is a general asymmetry in the level of curiosity people have about one another. Whites, as the numerical majority, have had little contact with Black culture; Blacks, especially those who are in college, have had to develop bicultural skills— knowledge about the social worlds of both Whites and Blacks. Miscommunication and hurt feelings about White students' questions about Black students' hair illustrate this point. One of the things that happens freshman year is that White students are around Black students as they fix their hair. White students are generally quite curious about Black students' hair—they have basic questions such as how often Blacks wash their hair, how they get it straightened or curled, what products they use on their hair, how they comb it, etc. Whites often wonder to themselves whether they should ask these questions. One thought experiment Whites perform is to ask themselves whether a particular question would upset them. Adopting the "do unto others" rule, they ask themselves, "If a Black person was curious about my hair would I get upset?" The answer usually is "No, I would be happy to tell them." Another example is an Italian American student wondering to herself, "Would I be upset if someone asked me about calamari?" The answer is no, so she asks her Black roommate about collard greens, and the roommate explodes with an angry response such as, "Do you think all Black people eat watermelon too?" Note that if this Italian American knew her friend was Trinidadian American and asked about peas and rice the situation would be more similar and would not necessarily ignite underlying tensions.

Like the debate in *Dear Abby*, these innocent questions are likely to lead to resentment. The issue of stereotypes about Black Americans and the assumption that all Blacks are alike and have the same stereotypical cultural traits has more power to hurt or offend a Black person than vice versa. The innocent questions about Black hair also bring up a number of asymmetries between the Black and White experience. Because Blacks tend to have more knowledge about Whites than vice versa, there is not an even exchange going on; the Black freshman is likely to have fewer basic questions about his White roommate than his White roommate has about him. Because of the differences historically in the group experiences of Blacks and Whites there are some connotations to Black hair that don't exist about White hair. (For instance, is straightening your hair a form of assimilation, do some people distinguish between women having "good hair" and "bad hair" in terms of beauty and how is that related to looking "White"?) Finally, even a Black freshman who cheerfully disregards or is unaware that there are these asymmetries will soon slam into another asymmetry if she willingly answers every innocent question asked of her. In a situation where Blacks make up only 10 percent of the student body, if every non-Black needs to be educated about hair, she will have to explain it to nine other students. As one Black student explained to me, after you've been asked a couple of times about something so personal you begin to feel like you are an attraction in a zoo, that you are at the university for the education of the White students.

Institutional Responses

Our society asks a lot of young people. We ask young people to do something that no one else does as successfully on such a wide scale—that is to live together with people from very different backgrounds, to respect one another, to appreciate one another, and to enjoy and learn from one another. The successes that occur every day in this endeavor are many, and they are too often overlooked. However, the problems and tensions are also real, and they will not vanish on their own. We tend to see pluralism working in the United States in much the same way some people expect capitalism to work. If you put together people with various interests and abilities and resources, the "invisible hand" of capitalism is supposed to make all the parts work together in an economy for the common good.

There is much to be said for such a model—the invisible hand of the market can solve complicated problems of production and distribution better than any "visible hand" of a state plan. However, we have learned that unequal power relations among the actors in the capitalist marketplace, as well as "externalities" that the market cannot account for, such

as long-term pollution, or collusion between corporations, or the exploitation of child labor, means that state regulation is often needed. Pluralism and the relations between groups are very similar. There is a lot to be said for the idea that bringing people who belong to different ethnic or racial groups together in institutions with no interference will have good consequences. Students from different backgrounds will make friends if they share a dorm room or corridor, and there is no need for the institution to do any more than provide the locale. But like capitalism, the invisible hand of pluralism does not do well when power relations and externalities are ignored. When you bring together individuals from groups that are differentially valued in the wider society and provide no guidance, there will be problems. In these cases the "invisible hand" of pluralist relations does not work, and tensions and disagreements can arise without any particular individual or group of individuals being "to blame." On college campuses in the 1990s some of the tensions between students are of this sort. They arise from honest misunderstandings, lack of a common background, and very different experiences of what race and ethnicity mean to the individual.

The implications of symbolic ethnicities for thinking about race relations are subtle but consequential. If your understanding of your own ethnicity and its relationship to society and politics is one of individual choice, it becomes harder to understand the need for programs like affirmative action, which recognize the ongoing need for group struggle and group recognition, in order to bring about social change. It also is hard for a White college student to understand the need that minority students feel to band together against discrimination. It also is easy, on the individual level, to expect everyone else to be able to turn their ethnicity on and off at will, the way you are able to, without understanding that ongoing discrimination and societal attention to minority status makes that impossible for individuals from minority groups to do. The paradox of symbolic ethnicity is that it depends upon the ultimate goal of a pluralist society, and at the same time makes it more difficult to achieve that ultimate goal. It is dependent upon the concept that all ethnicities mean the same thing, that enjoying the traditions of one's heritage is an option available to a group or an individual, but that such a heritage should not have any social costs associated with it.

As the Asian Americans who wrote to *Dear Abby* make clear, there are many societal issues and involuntary ascriptions associated with non-White identities. The developments necessary for this to change are not individual but societal in nature. Social mobility and declining racial and ethnic sensitivity are closely associated. The legacy and the present reality of discrimination on the basis of race or ethnicity must be overcome before the ideal of a pluralist society, where all heritages are treated equally and are equally available for individuals to choose or discard at will, is realized.

REFERENCES

Alba, Richard D. 1985. *Italian Americans: Into the Twilight of Ethnicity*. Englewood Cliffs, NJ: Prentice Hall.

———. 1990. *Ethnic Identity: The Transformation of White America*. New Haven: Yale University Press.

Barth, Frederick. 1969. *Ethnic Groups and Boundaries*. Boston: Little, Brown.

Blauner, Robert. 1992. "Talking Past Each Other: Black and White Languages of Race." *American Prospect* (Summer): 55–64.

Feagin, Joe R. 1991. "The Continuing Significance of Race: Anti-Black Discrimination in Public Places." *American Sociological Review* 56: 101–17.

Gans, Herbert. 1979. "Symbolic Ethnicity: The Future of Ethnic Groups and Cultures in America." *Ethnic and Racial Studies* 2: 1–20.

Lieberson, Stanley. 1985. *Making It Count: The Improvement of Social Research and Theory*. Berkeley: University of California Press.

Ogbu, John. 1990. "Minority Status and Literacy in Comparative Perspective." *Daedalus* 119: 141–69.

Waters, Mary C. 1990. *Ethnic Options: Choosing Identities in America*. Berkeley: University of California Press.

Weber, Max. [1921]/1968. *Economy and Society: An Outline of Interpretive Sociology*. Eds. Guenther Roth and Claus Wittich, trans. Ephraim Fischoff. New York: Bedminister Press.

THINKING ABOUT THE READING

What is "symbolic ethnicity" according to Waters? Why is this form of ethnic expression optional for some and not others? Based on Waters's thesis, would a campus club for Norwegian Americans be the same as one for African Americans? Consider the slogan "different but equal." Do you think this idea can be applied to racial and ethnic relations in contemporary society? Why are some ethnic and racial groups the subject of discrimination and oppression while others are a source of group membership and belonging? When might an ethnic identity be both? How would you describe the ethnic and racial climate of your college campus?

The Downside of Racial Uplift

The Meaning of Gentrification in an African American Neighborhood

Michelle Boyd

(2005)

On the evening of May 6, 1997, a group of residents gathered in the library of Holy Angels elementary school for the monthly meeting of the Mid-South Planning and Development Commission. Since 1990, Mid-South had overseen a process of neighborhood planning in Douglas/Grand Boulevard, an African American neighborhood on Chicago's south side. The meeting followed its usual format in which the Director's updates were followed by committee reports, presentations, and announcements by residents. The purpose of this information exchange was to keep residents informed about the changes taking place in their community. Among these reports were two that demonstrated the diversity of interests in the neighborhood, the varying meanings of gentrification that emerged from those interests, and the complex challenges they presented.

The first report was given by Linda Tuft, one of three women chairing the committee in charge of Mid-South's upcoming Historic House Tour. This would be Mid-South's third annual tour, which they began both in order to raise money for the organization and to publicize Douglas/Grand Boulevard as an up-and-coming neighborhood. Interest in the event was high—in response to questions, Linda told the group that the tour would feature rehabilitated houses rather than newly constructed ones, including many of the greystone mansions that made the area so distinctive. Then she ended with an appealing offer: those who attended would be rewarded with an outdoor party in the garden of the final house on the tour.

The report immediately following Linda's was quite different. It was given by Elaine Xavier, a resident of Stateway Gardens public housing complex. She spoke not as a member of a formal Mid-South committee, but as a resident actively involved in Mid-South as well as other organizations. She briefly reported to the group that residents of her building had just discovered that the Chicago Housing Authority (CHA) was conducting a feasibility study on the viability of public housing. They had until May 15th, only nine days later, to organize a response to the CHA. Unlike Linda's announcement, which caused a flurry of questions, Elaine's provoked little conversation. Elaine succinctly made her comments and promptly sat back down.

The reports given by these two women reflect the remarkable change in African Americans' role in gentrification over the last 20 years. During the 1970s, blacks were likely to be either victims of or protesters against gentrifying forces. But throughout the 1980s and 1990s they have increasingly moved into poor, urban neighborhoods like Douglas/Grand Boulevard and initiated processes of residential and commercial investment and upgrading. As defined in academic literature, gentrification is the process through which "poor and working-class neighborhoods in the inner city are refurbished via an influx of private capital and middle-class homebuyers and renters" (Smith 1996:32). Where they once identified this process as one of the primary causes of black urban poverty and struggled against its harmful effects, black neighborhood activists now regard it as one *solution* to disinvestment—when, that is, the middle-class residents involved are African American.

These two reports also illustrate that gentrification has different meanings for different blacks: for some residents like Linda, gentrification is a process that will make the neighborhood more attractive to residential and commercial investors and thereby increase the quality of life for both herself and her neighbors. By attracting middle-class blacks to Douglas/Grand Boulevard, these residents hope to avoid racial displacement by whites and maintain the area as an African American neighborhood. Yet Linda's neighbors include low and moderate income residents like Elaine who are neither the initiators, managers nor beneficiaries of gentrification, but instead its observers and its possible victims. Black gentrification, like any other kind, threatens to displace the neighborhood's long-time residents. Thus while Linda is concerned with increasing the return on her investment, Elaine is more concerned with the immediate danger to her home and survival.

In what follows, I examine the framework within which Douglas/Grand Boulevard's gentrification advocates understand the process, and analyze its political implications. I argue that proponents of black gentrification see attracting middle-class investors as a strategy for "uplifting the race." By promoting the presence of the black middle class, gentrification advocates hope to prevent further neighborhood disinvestment and displacement by whites. Yet this framework masks gentrification's differential consequences for blacks of varying economic means. Because it homogenizes the characteristics and interests of the African American population, the uplift frame obscures the necessary conflict of interest embedded in gentrification committed by blacks.

"Who Are the People in Your Neighborhood?" The Douglas/Grand Boulevard Community

Douglas and Grand Boulevard are located on Chicago's south side, at the far northern end of the city's "black belt," where African Americans were segregated throughout the 20th century. Although Douglas and Grand Boulevard are two distinct community areas, the neighborhood redevelopment plan encompasses both. Mid-South, along with the city's real estate entrepreneurs, has refashioned the Douglas/Grand Boulevard area into the single community of Bronzeville—the name by which it is referred in Drake and Cayton's 1945 classic study *Black Metropolis*. In 1990, the year Mid-South was established, most of Douglas/Grand Boulevard's 66,549 residents rented and lived in public housing. Owner-occupied homes made up a mere seven percent of the total housing stock, while public housing units such as Prairie Avenue Courts, Dearborn Homes, Ida B. Wells projects, Stateway Gardens and Robert Taylor Homes made up half of the community's housing. In part because of these units, a significant portion of the residents were quite poor. The median family income in each community was $10,577 and $8,371 respectively. More than half of Douglas/Grand Boulevard families survived on incomes below the poverty line, and 26 percent of residents were unemployed. In addition, the community had a large nonworking population. Thirty-eight percent of its inhabitants were 19 or younger and residents aged 65 years or older constituted 14.5 percent of the community (Chicago Fact Book Consortium 1990).

While these numbers paint a portrait of a uniformly poor neighborhood, such broad strokes hide the significant variation found within the community. Rachel Dean, an architect who was involved with the Mid-South planning process, argues that in the early 1990s the neighborhood's residents were a very dichotomous population in terms of *need*. You've got very, very low income people on the one hand, who have a large need for social services that are not being provided, and other types of neighborhood amenities that were not provided as a result of them being there. And then you had people who had stayed over the years, elderly people. And then you have some young people who are beginning to move back, because of the housing stock itself, and the quality of the buildings.

The neighborhood's location, combined with relatively inexpensive land, deteriorating housing stock, and a population of poor, politically vulnerable blacks, made the Douglas/ Grand Boulevard of the 1990s an attractive site for "reinvasion" by elites of any racial category. To avoid just such an occurrence, several black community organizations began collaborating in 1990 with the city and private institutions for the establishment of the Mid-South Planning and Development Commission. The aim of this organization was to develop a comprehensive economic development strategy for the two neighborhoods. Three years later they produced *Restoring Bronzeville,* a land-use plan that proposes to both revitalize the area and avoid displacement by relying on a combination of historic preservation and racial heritage tourism. From 1997 to 1999, I was a participant observer with Mid-South and three other community based organizations (CBOs) as they attempted to implement the plan. This article draws from ethnographic data, newspaper articles and site documents, as well as informal and formal interviews collected during those years.

Fear and Loathing in Douglas/Grand Boulevard: The Meaning of White Gentrification

At first glance, Mid-South members' feelings about gentrification are unsurprising and straightforward. Community residents fear it, and they agonize over the probability of a

white "invasion" at meetings, rallies, and in casual conversation. Ken Lacey, a resident and business owner in Bronzeville, expressed the views of many when he told me that

> I'm hearing the thing that's going on is . . . the whites coming from the suburbs into the city, and they look at [the neighborhood] and you're walking distance from downtown, McCormick Place [the city's convention center], everything else and they're saying 'Well hey, you know, maybe this isn't that bad after all and we want it back!'

Like many residents, Mr. Lacey perceives whites to be deliberate and purposeful in their attempt to "recover" Douglas/Grand Boulevard from the black residents who live there. In this sense, he expresses both resident concerns and scholarly arguments that gentrification is an example of a "revanchist" desire among racial and economic elites who seek to take back the city from marginalized populations (Smith 1996).

Nevertheless, the members of Mid-South in fact show more ambivalence about the definition and value of gentrification than Mr. Lacey's comment initially suggests. This ambivalence is partly based on the fact that the neighborhood sorely needs economic development. One example can be found in remarks made by Wendy Brown, a resident and non-profit development consultant, at a neighborhood business council meeting. Wendy was leading a discussion encouraging council members to identify their priorities for the community's redevelopment. She suggested that those present form a partnership to insure that, as small business owners, they would be a part of development rather than its victims. They didn't want gentrification, she argued, "because gentrification by its definition means that all of the people who are there will have to move out" and people who had invested in their companies for 20 years should not have to relinquish their businesses. With this comment, Wendy relies on the traditional understanding of gentrification. But as she continues, she argues that, while they did not want gentrification, these small local businesses "did not have the opportunity to grow" due to the present economic conditions in the neighborhood, and that the business council was the body that could work with developers to communicate the needs and priorities of local business owners. Wendy's comments highlight the fact that despite the danger posed by gentrification, the neighborhood is sorely in need of some form of economic development. The residents often complained that the neighborhood needed basic businesses such as a bookstore, sit-down family restaurant, photocopying shop, shoe repair, travel agency, coffee shop and deli.

The need for such services is just one reason that Mid-South's residents are receptive to the idea of attracting the black middle class to the neighborhood. Rachel Dean, the architect who earlier described the stratification in the neighborhood, revealed another reason. She argued that homeowners in particular

> don't care about economic [gentrification]. That would be great! That would enhance their personal property. But, I think, there's a feeling that, hey, we saw the value in this neighborhood first. We moved here. We sunk our dollars here. We worked to try to make it great. We don't wanna get pushed out.

Rachel's comment illustrates that what many residents object to is not gentrification—that is, the influx of the middle class—but displacement. As another resident explained it, they fear that "once the white folks find out that this is really a gem, you know, in terms of its proximity to the Loop and everything else, and they'll want the property and they'll buy it out then."

This contradictory stance towards gentrification is aptly expressed in the Restoring *Bronzeville* redevelopment plan (Mid-South 1993:25). The document insists, on the one hand, that development, in whatever form, should avoid displacement of "indigenous" residents. Thus, it explicitly and repeatedly articulates the importance of providing jobs and economic security for current residents. On the other hand, the plan advocates the development of mixed income housing with a heavy emphasis on owner-occupied units. Rather than demolition and reconstruction, the plan advocates the rehabilitation of existing structures and construction on vacant lots. Residents indeed have a broad-based commitment to the idea of a mixed-income black neighborhood. CBO head Randolph Jeffries asserted the ideas of many when he said that the neighborhood needed "housing to house the working people. And housing to house middle income. Cause you gotta create—in order to create community, you gotta [have] working people, middle income people and upper income people. And then you create community." Thus, while Mid-South members would not use the term gentrification to describe their own activities, the organization explicitly promotes and pursues the revitalization of Douglas/Grand Boulevard through the repopulation of the neighborhood by the black middle class. Using neighborhood historic preservation and racial heritage tourism, Mid-South has sought to make the neighborhood more attractive, not just to investors generally, but specifically to black investors. Given their fears of gentrification by whites, how do Mid-South members distinguish white and black gentrification? How do they understand blacks' behavior and its consequences as different from and more legitimate than that of whites?

Uplifting the Race: The Meaning of Black Gentrification

Comments by Mid-South members illustrate that they understand black gentrification as a strategy for racial uplift. Racial uplift ideology has been defined in many ways throughout history. During the 18th and 19th centuries it referred to "organized social activities which are consciously designed to raise the status of the group as a whole" (Drake and Cayton 1993:716). During slavery, these collective efforts took the form of mutual aid and benevolent societies that opposed slavery and helped blacks support themselves in times of economic crisis (Perkins 1981). In the postemancipation period, they included struggles to educate freedmen and women in preparation for citizenship and political participation (Anderson 1988).

In the late 19th and early 20th centuries however, black elites came to understand racial uplift differently. They defined it not as the collective struggle for equal citizenship rights, but as the individual effort to reform the race, which would prove blacks worthy of equal political status (Gaines 1996). Black elites sought to achieve this reform by adopting and advocating classed and gendered standards of moral behavior and economic success. Booker T. Washington especially championed the view that blacks should focus on achieving economic independence by working as laborers and establishing small businesses. His accommodationist philosophy emphasized the accumulation of capital and eschewed demands for political rights.

Racial uplift ideology still retains its potency in the contemporary period, where it is expressed in arguments that role modeling by the black middle class is the answer to problems of urban decline and economic disinvestment. While previous forms of racial uplift were more focused on convincing whites that blacks deserved citizenship rights, contemporary racial uplift emphasizes the importance of changing the internal behavior and self esteem of blacks themselves (Smith 1999). The crucial assumption of 20th century uplift ideology is that the successes of individual, affluent blacks has a spillover effect, one that either improves the material conditions of all blacks or "'reflects credit on the race'" (Drake and Cayton 1993:716). As a result, modern uplift emphasizes the black middle class' responsibility to use its resources to advance the material status and mental mindset of all African Americans.

Advancing the Race: The Collective Benefits of Gentrification

Many Mid-South supporters express uplift ideas in their interpretations of black gentrification. They often understand middle income residents' personal and financial investment in the community as a *communal* act whose benefits will raise the status of all blacks. Grady Karl, a redevelopment proponent, expressed this widely held opinion in an interview, when he described to me the appropriate role of the black middle class. He said that

> housing directs everything. So, first of all, you've got to come in and anchor the housing. By the black middle class buying these homes . . . two and three hundred thousand dollar houses, that's gonna stabilize the community. . . . Stabilize the community means, to be able to create a tax base first of all, and you do that by creating new businesses that [the] state taxes. You have people being employed, pay taxes, you create a tax base. That tax base supports the redevelopment of the community.

Mr. Karl emphasizes that black gentrification should take the form of residential investment, that is, the purchase of homes that will "stabilize" the neighborhood. With this comment he expresses the fairly conventional assessment that increasing the number of homeowners in a neighborhood establishes a population that will bring disposable and taxable income into a community. This strategy emphasizes a standard benefit that accrues from individual investment.

Yet Mr. Karl also argues that black investment strategies should have a broader purpose. He maintains that it is also the responsibility of the black middle class to come in and buy land; to create development groups; to create investment clubs, investment organizations; to attract new businesses to take care of their needs, in terms of their lifestyle; to establish new businesses to provide these services to the community; to work as part of a team effort to revitalize the commercial business strips.

In this comment, Mr. Karl defines commercial investment as also being a part of the obligation of black gentrifiers. In one sense he sees this establishment of businesses as a self-interested act responsive to the particular needs of the individual. Because residents lack high quality services such as dry cleaning establishments, banks, or grocery stores, CBO leaders expect that affluent blacks will establish these businesses in order to supply themselves with these amenities. Yet at the same time, this vision of investment is a vision of collective self help, in which residents will work in teams pooling resources to meet their needs. According to him, African Americans should take responsibility for more than their personal financial well being; they should also work to increase investment among other residents.

One of the forms of investment that is most frequently encouraged among black elites is the purchase and restoration of historic buildings that are threatened with sale or demolition. Douglas/Grand Boulevard's revitalization hinges on historic preservation efforts that seek to restore the physical and social community of the neighborhood as it existed in the first half of the 20th century, during its supposed "golden age" (Boyd 2000). In addition to their importance as physical structures, the buildings are also significant because of what they mean or represent. This was clearly expressed on a tour of the neighborhood, when resident and community historian Steven Anthony took us by two buildings in which the famous African American newspaper the *Defender* had been housed. When we arrived he announced, "This is the *Defender* Building. This building housed the most influential newspaper in America." Someone on the bus asked him if the newspaper is for sale, and he replied "the whole thing. The whole thing is leaving. And I hope some blacks get together and try to buy it. Cause you know, when I look at the obituaries, I look at the obituaries a lot now, according to the white newspapers, you didn't die. But the *Defender* listed it."

Mr. Anthony argues not only that the building should be saved: he, like Mr. Karl, explicitly contends that African Americans should work as part of a group to save it. This remark reflects racial uplift ideology as well as the knowledge that few blacks in Douglas/Grand Boulevard have the resources to carry out such a venture successfully on their own. This hope—that blacks will invest in the community—is often interpreted as a duty of residents who live in.

At other times, Mid-South members see gentrification and entrepreneurship as a specific obligation of the black middle class. As Grady Karl explained,

> The black middle class, [returning] from its corporate isolation and having done the integration thing, are now saying I need to get back to blackness, cause I'm still being discriminated against. I went out, I found out that I ain't got no more liberation than my money'll get me, and I still don't have a sense of community. So I'm going back. Now, when you get back, are you going to turn on your brother, or are you going to try to use your resources to help empower him? And that's the issue.

Grady, like many Mid-South members, uses the language of return to discuss the physical and financial presence of the black middle class in Douglas/Grand Boulevard. He understands them as returning, not just to the physical community of the neighborhood, but to their essential racial being, to blackness.

Reflecting Credit on the Race: Gentrification and Representation

These comments illustrate what *economic* impact Mid-South members think gentrification will have on the neighborhood. Communal investment strategies are promoted by Mid-South because of their potential effect on the exchange value of neighborhood property, or its worth as a commodity.

While Mid-South members see black entrepreneurship as enhancing African Americans' self-perception, they also see it as having the capacity to shape how outsiders see African Americans. Places are considered dangerous, not just because of the buildings or infrastructure, but also because of the behavior of the people who inhabit them. Likewise, the attractiveness and value of a location is partially based on one's potential neighbors: who they are, and how they behave. Therefore, attempts to re-construct place are fundamentally related to efforts to reconstruct conceptions of the people who inhabit it. Consider, for example, a remark made by Delia Chester, a developer and business owner in the neighborhood. She suggests that it is not just the *existence* of area businesses that matters: equally important is the fact that these businesses are catering to the "better" classes. She tells me that they

> didn't come in and take the project as it was and open the business back up and the same kind of thing. We looked to upscale our neighborhood; to upscale this commercial project and make it stand out to say 'This is us. This is who we are. We want upper-class commercial businesses in here.'

Who they are—and who they tell other people they are—is a well-to-do group of African Americans who have the desire and capacity to revitalize their community. By "reflecting credit on the race," economic investment bolsters the image and self-image of the neighborhood's African American population.

Sliding Down Uplift's Slippery Slope

Racial uplift rhetoric depends heavily upon the notion that the mere investment in commercial and residential properties is of benefit to all neighborhood blacks, regardless of their income level. This argument is based partly on the recognition that racists universalize the behavior of black individuals, attribute the behavior of one to all members of the group. The resulting logic is that improving the circumstance of one individual or sub-group within the black population will improve perceptions of all. But uplift is also based on the assumption that blacks share a common set of racial interests.

Despite their commitment to the uplift framework, Mid-South members realize that not all interests are equally served by the changes taking place in the neighborhood.

Public housing residents like Elaine Xavier have particularly been preoccupied with the issue of the demolition of both the Stateway Gardens and Robert Taylor housing sites. They needed affordable housing, employment, day care and an unchanging cost of living. Because of these different needs, revitalization means something different to middle-income homeowners than it does to those who rented or lived in public housing. Low income residents are afraid that revitalization will once again mean displacement for them and their families, while owners of high-priced housing want to increase the price of housing as well as the quality and cost of neighborhood goods and services. Yet Mid-South members continue to advocate attracting black middle-class residents to the neighborhood, even when they recognize that the black poor are more threatened by their doing so.

This contradictory stance is one of the most distinctive and problematic features of black gentrification. Its advocates do not suggest, in an over-simplified manner, that it is acceptable merely because it is being initiated and led by African Americans. Nor do they express an unabashed dismissal of the concerns of poor blacks. Rather, the problem is quite the opposite. The rhetoric of racial uplift acknowledges the inequality among African Americans while simultaneously minimizing its implications. This tendency reflects a force at play in all urban neighborhoods, and one that is particularly unwieldy in those that have historically suffered from race-based uneven development: whatever their commitment to their marginalized populations, communities are constrained by what Logan and Molotch (1987) refer to as the "Iron Law of Upgrading." Because they are so in need of economic development, they are pushed toward strategies that prioritize their more privileged residents. They are constrained by the fact that "for neighborhoods . . . there is nowhere worth going but up. And going up means attracting, from a finite supply, the prized land users. This locks communities (even poor ones) into the same zero-sum competition across the cityscape. Neighborhoods thereby become wedded to the general rent intensification dynamic, making at least some of them receptive to the entrepreneurs' occasional offers of 'revitalization'" (Logan and Molotch 1987:145). What black proponents of such revitalization strategies add is an interpretive framework that minimizes competing interests and undermines the race-based opposition that would be more likely were the gentrifiers white.

Pressing survival issues, as well as the threat of development, are what preoccupy the most vulnerable members of the neighborhood. Not only were their needs less likely to be discussed, but they experienced a great deal of friction with more affluent residents during the planning process. These tensions surfaced within the Mid-South Planning Group's housing committee. One participant told me that while planning for the land-use document, the housing committee

> had a faction that represented public housing. And there was a faction that had represented the urban pioneers, who came down and purchased a lot of their greystone homes and had invested, you know, considerable amount of money into maintaining them and they felt threatened by all the public housing people and the public housing people felt threatened by these people.

When faced with the issue of mixed income housing, some homeowners vehemently resisted the prospect of having former public housing residents as neighbors. Randolph Jeffries explained that homeowners

> were jumping all over [saying] 'We don't want chose people living next door to us! Hell no!' You know. Oh yeah. Saying, 'Not in my backyard. We don't want those poor people over here. They're going to be breaking into our houses!' Our, you know, sweat and tears going into fixing these houses, these people are gonna break in and steal everything.

Low income residents were as fearful of and hostile toward middle-and upper-income black residents as they were of white outsiders and neighborhood institutions. According to Karl Grady, over the course of the planning process poorer residents "fell away from the table. And the homeowners stayed at the table . . . most of the public housing residents stopped coming because people were not dealing directly with their issues." By homogenizing the needs and interests of the black poor and the black elites, promoters of black gentrification mask the extent to which their strategies differently and disproportionately threaten lower income residents.

Revitalization and Racial Uplift

African American gentrification is most disturbing because of what it suggests about the ultimate purpose of black elite strategies for economic and political advancement. Neither black gentrification specifically, nor uplift ideology in general, seek to disrupt the structures of political or economic inequality that maintain poverty and disinvestment. Instead they hope to help a larger number of blacks participate in those structures from a more advantageous position. The reliance on individual investment as the answer to African Americans' problems is a part of a broader ideological current that suggests that individual class mobility is the answer to racial inequality. Because these strategies tend to gain popularity in times of reduced resources and options, their adoption "is not accidental; rather it signals an ideological and social adjustment to new political-economic arrangements in the United States" (Smith 1999:258). Yet as long as African American elites' goal is confined to ensuring blacks' proportional representation in the middle and upper classes, uplift will remain limited as both a strategy and a goal, unable to challenge new political-economic arrangements in a meaningful, equitable manner.

REFERENCES

Anderson, James. 1988 *The Education of Blacks in the South.* Chapel Hill: University of North Carolina Press.

Boyd, Michelle. 2000 Reconstructing Bronzeville: Racial Nostalgia and Neighborhood Redevelopment. *Journal of Urban Affairs* 22(2): 107–122.

Chicago Fact Book Consortium, ed. 1990 *Local Community Fact Book, Chicago Metropolitan Area.* Chicago: University of Illinois.

Drake, St. Clair and Horace R. Cayton. 1993[1945] *Black Metropolis: A Study of Negro Life in a Northern City.* Chicago: University of Chicago Press.

Gaines, Kevin. 1996 *Uplifting the Race: Black Leadership, Politics, and Culture in the Twentieth Century.* Chapel Hill: University of North Carolina Press.

Logan, John R. and Harvey L. Molotch. 1987 *Urban Fortunes: The Political Economy of Place.* Berkeley: University of California Press.

Mid-South Planning Group. 1993 *Mid-South Strategic Development Plan: Restoring Bronzeville.* Chicago: Mid-South Planning Group.

Perkins, Linda. 1981 Black Women and Racial "Uplift" Prior to Emancipation. In *The Black Woman Cross-Culturally.* Filomina Chioma Steady, ed. Pp. 317–334. Cambridge, MA: Schenkman Publishing Company, Inc.

Smith, Neil. 1996 *The New Urban Frontier: Gentrification and the Revanchist City.* London: Routledge.

Smith, Preston. 1999 "Self-Help," Black Conservatives, and the Reemergence of Black Privatism. In *Without Justice For All: The New Liberalism and Our Retreat from Racial Equality.* Adolph Reed, Jr., ed. Pp. 257–289. Boulder, CO: Westview Press.

THINKING ABOUT THE READING

Racial segregation of neighborhoods has been a long-standing social problem in the United States. What is "gentrification" and how is it related to this segregation? Historically, poorer (mostly black) neighborhoods have been "gentrified" by whites. What are the consequences of this trend for local residents? This reading describes a neighborhood gentrification project being promoted by middle-class African Americans. What is the "racial uplift" ideology and how does it shape this gentrification process? Who is mostly likely to benefit from this neighborhood "renewal"? Who is likely to be displaced?

The Architecture of Inequality

Sex and Gender

12

In addition to racial and class inequality, gender inequality—and the struggle against it—has been a fundamental part of the historical development of our national identity. Gender ideology has influenced the lives and dreams of individual people, shaped popular culture, and created or maintained social institutions. Gender is a major criterion for the distribution of important economic, political, and educational resources in most societies. Gender inequality is perpetuated by a dominant cultural ideology that devalues women on the basis of presumed biological differences between men and women. This ideology overlooks the equally important role of social forces in determining male and female behavior.

Bart Landry explores the intersections of race and gender in "Black Women and a New Definition of Womanhood." Landry examines the difficulties black women have faced throughout history in being seen by others as virtuous and moral. This article provides a fascinating picture of women's struggle for equality from the perspective of black women, a group that is often ignored and marginalized in discussions of the women's movement. Although much of the article focuses on black women's activism in the 19th century, it provides important insight into the intersection of race and gender today. Landry raises an important contrast between the way in which 19th-century middle-class white women and middle-class black women framed the relationship between family and public life.

Gender inequality exists at the institutional level as well, in the law, in the family (in terms of such things as the domestic division of labor), and in economics. Not only are social institutions sexist, in that women are systematically segregated, exploited, and excluded, but they are also gendered. Institutions themselves are structured along gender lines so that traits associated with success are usually stereotypically male characteristics: tough-mindedness, rationality, assertiveness, competitiveness, and so forth.

Women have made significant advances politically, economically, educationally, and socially over the past decades. The traditional obstacles to advancement continue to fall. Women have entered the labor force in unprecedented numbers. Yet despite their growing presence in the labor force and their entry into historically male occupations, rarely do women work alongside men or perform the same tasks and functions.

Jobs within an occupation still tend to be divided into "men's work" and "women's work." Such gender segregation has serious consequences for women in the form of blocked advancement and lower salaries. But looking at gender segregation on the job as something that happens only to women gives us an incomplete picture of the situation. It is just as important to examine what keeps men out of "female" jobs as it is to examine what keeps women out of "male" jobs. The proportion of women in male jobs has increased over the past several decades, but the proportion of men in female jobs has remained virtually unchanged. In "Still a Man's World," Christine L. Williams looks at the experiences of male nurses, social workers, elementary school teachers, and librarians. She finds that although these men do feel somewhat stigmatized by their nontraditional career choices, they still enjoy significant gender advantages.

The social value of a particular activity is often linked to the gender most closely associated with it. Cheerleading, for example, was once an all-male activity. However, recently it has become an icon of American girlhood. Laura Grindstaff and Emily West in "Cheerleading and the Gendered Politics of Sport" explore how the feminization of cheerleading has made it difficult for female participants to obtain any sort of social respect or prestige despite the phenomenal athletic skills it requires. Because cheerleading it is so closely connected to the hypermasculine world of competitive sports (but always in an inferior and supportive capacity), it provides a powerful example of how gender boundaries are created and gender inequality maintained.

Something to Consider as You Read

While reading these selections, think about the significance of gender as a social category. A child's gender is the single most important thing people want to know when it is born. "What is it?" is a commonly understood shorthand for "is it a boy or a girl?" From the time children are born, they learn that certain behaviors, feelings, and expectations are associated with the gender category to which they have been assigned. Think about some of the behaviors associated with specific gender categories. Make a list of stereotypical gender expectations. Upon reflection, do these seem reasonable to you? What are some recollections you have about doing something that was considered inappropriate for your gender? Think about ways in which these stereotypical expectations affect people's perceptions, especially in settings such as school or jobs.

Black Women and a New Definition of Womanhood

Bart Landry

(2000)

A popular novel of 1852 chirped that the white heroine, Eoline, "with her fair hair, and celestial blue eyes bending over the harp . . . really seemed 'little lower than the angels,' and an aureola of purity and piety appeared to beam around her brow."[1] By contrast, in another popular antebellum novel, *Maum Guinea and Her Plantation Children* (1861), black women are excluded from the category of true womanhood without debate: "The idea of modesty and virtue in a Louisiana colored-girl might well be ridiculed; as a general thing, she has neither."[2] Decades later, in 1902, a commentator for the popular magazine *The Independent* noted, "I sometimes hear of a virtuous Negro woman, but the idea is absolutely inconceivable to me. . . . I cannot imagine such a creature as a virtuous Negro woman."[3] Another writer, reflecting early-twentieth-century white male stereotypes of black and white women, remarked that, like white women, "Black women had the brains of a child, [and] the passions of a woman" but, unlike white women, were "steeped in centuries of ignorance and savagery, and wrapped about with immoral vices."[4]

Faced with the prevailing views of white society that placed them outside the boundaries of true womanhood, black women had no choice but to defend their virtue. Middle-class black women led this defense, communicating their response in words and in the actions of their daily lives. In doing so they went well beyond defending their own virtue to espouse a broader conception of womanhood that anticipated modern views by more than half a century. Their vision of womanhood combined the public and the private spheres and eventually took for granted a role for women as paid workers outside the home. More than merely an abstract vision, it was a philosophy of womanhood embodied in the lives of countless middle-class black women in both the late nineteenth and the early twentieth centuries.

Virtue Defended

Although black women were seen as devoid of all four of the cardinal virtues of true womanhood—piety, purity, submissiveness, and domesticity—white attention centered on purity. As Hazel Carby suggests, this stemmed in part from the role assigned to black women in the plantation economy. She argues that "two very different but interdependent codes of sexuality operated in the antebellum South, producing opposite definitions of motherhood and womanhood for white and black women which coalesce in the figures of the slave and the mistress."[5] In this scheme, white mistresses gave birth to heirs, slave women to property. A slave woman who attempted to preserve her virtue or sexual autonomy was a threat to the plantation economy. In the words of Harriet Jacobs's slave narrative, *Incidents in the Life of a Slave Girl* (1861), it was "deemed a crime in her [the slave woman] to wish to be virtuous."[6]

Linda Brent, the pseudonym Jacobs used to portray her own life, was an ex-slave struggling to survive economically and protect herself and her daughter from sexual exploitation. In telling her story, she recounts the difficulty all black women faced in practicing the virtues of true womanhood. The contrasting contexts of black and white women's lives called for different, even opposite, responses.

While submissiveness and passivity brought protection to the white mistress, these characteristics merely exposed black women to sexual and economic exploitation. Black women, therefore, had to develop strength rather than glory in fragility, and had to be active and assertive rather than passive and submissive. . . .

Three decades later, in the 1890s, black women found reasons to defend their moral integrity with new urgency against attacks from all sides. Views such as those in *The Independent* noted earlier were given respectability by a report of the Slater Fund, a foundation that supported welfare projects for blacks in this period. The foundation asserted without argument, "The negro women of the South are subject to temptations . . . which come to them from the days of their race enslavement. . . . To meet such temptations the negro woman can only offer the resistance of a low moral standard, an inheritance from the system of slavery, made still lower from a lifelong residence in a one-room cabin."[7]

At the 1893 World Columbian Exposition in Chicago, where black women were effectively barred from the exhibits on the achievements of American women, the few black women allowed to address a women's convention there felt compelled to publicly challenge these views. One speaker, Fannie Barrier Williams, shocked her audience by her forthrightness. "I regret the necessity of speaking of the moral question of our women," but "the morality of our home life has been commented on so disparagingly and meanly that we are placed in the unfortunate position of being defenders of our name."[8] She went on to emphasize that black women continued to be the victims of sexual harassment by white men and chided her white female audience for failing to protect their black sisters. In the same vein, black activist and educator Anna Julia Cooper told the audience that it was not a question of "temptations" as much as it was "the painful, patient, and silent toil of mothers to gain title to the bodies of their daughters."[9] Williams was later to write on the same theme.

"It is a significant and shameful fact that I am constantly in receipt of letters from the still unprotected women in the South, begging me to find employment for their daughters . . . to save them from going into the homes of the South as servants as there is nothing to save them from dishonor and degradation."[10] Another black male writer was moved to reveal in *The Independent:* "I know of more than one colored woman who was openly importuned by White women to become the mistress of their husbands, on the ground that they, the white wives, were afraid that, if their husbands did not associate with colored women they would certainly do so with outside white women. . . . And the white wives, for reasons which ought to be perfectly obvious, preferred to have all their husbands do wrong with colored women in order to keep their husbands *straight!*"[11] The attacks on black women's virtue came to a head with a letter written by James Jacks, president of the Missouri Press Association, in which he alleged, "The Negroes in this country were wholly devoid of morality, the women were prostitutes and all were natural thieves and liars."[12] These remarks, coming from such a prominent individual, drew an immediate reaction from black women throughout the country. The most visible was Josephine St. Pierre Ruffin's invitation to black club women to a national convention in Boston in 1895; one hundred women from ten states came to Boston in response. In a memorable address to representatives of some twenty clubs, Ruffin directly attacked the scurrilous accusations:

> Now for the sake of the thousands of self-sacrificing young women teaching and preaching in lonely southern backwoods, for the noble army of mothers who gave birth to these girls, mothers whose intelligence is only limited by their opportunity to get at books, for the cultured women who have carried off the honors at school here and often abroad, for the sake of our own dignity, the dignity of our race and the future good name of our children, it is "meet, right and our bounden

duty" to stand forth and declare ourselves and our principles, to teach an ignorant and suspicious world that our aims and interests are identical with those of all good, aspiring women. Too long have we been silent under unjust and unholy charges. . . . It is to break this silence, not by noisy protestations of what we are not, but by a dignified showing of what we are and hope to become, that we are impelled to take this step, to make of this gathering an object lesson to the world.[13]

At the end of three days of meetings, the National Federation of Afro-American Women was founded, uniting thirty-six black women's clubs in twelve states.[14] The following year, the National Federation merged with the National League of Colored Women to form the National Association of Colored Women (NACW).

Racial Uplift: In Defense of the Black Community

While the catalyst for these national organizations was in part the felt need of black women to defend themselves against moral attacks by whites, they soon went beyond this narrow goal. Twenty years after its founding, the NACW had grown to fifty thousand members in twenty-eight federations and more than one thousand clubs.[15] The founding of these organizations represented a steady movement by middle-class black women to assume more active roles in the community. Historian Deborah Gray White argues that black club women "insisted that only black women could save the black race," a position that inspired them to pursue an almost feverish pace of activities.[16]

These clubs, however, were not the first attempts by black women to participate actively in their communities. Since the late 1700s black women had been active in mutual-aid societies in the North, and in the 1830s northern black women organized anti-slavery societies. In 1880 Mary Ann Shadd Cary and six other women founded the Colored Women's Progressive Franchise Association in Washington, D.C. Among its stated goals were equal rights for

women, including the vote, and the even broader feminist objective of taking "an aggressive stand against the assumption that men only begin and conduct industrial and other things."[17] Giving expression to this goal were a growing number of black women professionals, including the first female physicians to practice in the South.[18] By the turn of the twentieth century, the National Business League, founded by Booker T. Washington, could report that there were "160 Black female physicians, seven dentists, ten lawyers, 164 ministers, assorted journalists, writers, artists, 1,185 musicians and teachers of music, and 13,525 school instructors."[19]

Black women's activism was spurred by the urgency of the struggle for equality, which had led to a greater acceptance of black female involvement in the abolitionist movement. At a time when patriarchal notions of women's domestic role dominated, historian Paula Giddings asserts, "There is no question that there was greater acceptance among Black men of women in activist roles than there was in the broader society."[20] This is not to say that all black men accepted women as equals or the activist roles that many were taking. But when faced with resistance, black women often *demanded* acceptance of their involvement. In 1849, for example, at a black convention in Ohio, "Black women, led by Jane P. Merritt, threatened to boycott the meetings if they were not given a more substantial voice in the proceedings."[21]

In the postbellum period black women continued their struggle for an equal voice in activities for racial uplift in both secular and religious organizations. . . . These women's organizations then played a significant role not only in missionary activities, but also in general racial uplift activities in both rural and urban areas.[22] . . .

Black Women and the Suffrage Movement

In their struggle for their own rights, black women moved into the political fray and eagerly joined the movement for passage of a constitutional amendment giving women the right to vote. Unlike white women suffragists, who focused exclusively on the benefits of the vote for their sex, black women saw the franchise as a means of improving the condition of the black community generally. For them, race and gender issues were inseparable. As historian Rosalyn Terborg-Penn emphasizes, black feminists believed that by "increasing the black electorate" they "would not only uplift the women of the race, but help the children and the men as well."[23]

Prominent black women leaders as well as national and regional organizations threw their support behind the suffrage movement. At least twenty black suffrage organizations were founded, and black women participated in rallies and demonstrations and gave public speeches.[24] Ironically, they often found themselves battling white women suffragists as well as men. Southern white women opposed including black women under a federal suffrage as a matter of principle. Northern white women suffragists, eager to retain the support of southern white women, leaned toward accepting a wording of the amendment that would have allowed the southern states to determine their own position on giving black women the vote, a move that would have certainly led to their exclusion.[25]

After the Nineteenth Amendment was ratified in 1920 in its original form, black women braved formidable obstacles in registering to vote. All across the South white registrars used "subterfuge and trickery" to hinder them from registering, including a "grandmother clause" in North Carolina, literacy tests in Virginia, and a $300 poll tax in Columbia, South Carolina. In Columbia, black women "waited up to twelve hours to register" while white women were registered first.[26] In their struggle to register, black women appealed to the NAACP, signed affidavits against registrars who disqualified them, and finally asked for assistance from national white women suffrage leaders. They were especially disappointed in this last attempt. After fighting side by side with white

women suffragists for passage of the Nineteenth Amendment, they were rebuffed by the National Woman's Party leadership with the argument that theirs was a race rather than a women's rights issue.[27] Thus, white women continued to separate issues of race and sex that black women saw as inseparable.

Challenging the Primacy of Domesticity

A conflicting conception of the relationship between gender and race issues was not the only major difference in the approaches of black and white women to their roles in the family and society. For most white women, their domestic roles as wives and mothers remained primary. In the late nineteenth century, as they began increasingly to argue for acceptance of their involvement on behalf of child-labor reform and growing urban problems, white women often defended these activities as extensions of their housekeeping role. Historian Barbara Harris comments, "The [white women] pioneers in women's education, who probably did more than anyone else in this period to effect change in the female sphere, advocated education for women and their entrance into the teaching profession on the basis of the values proclaimed by the cult of true womanhood. In a similar way, females defended their careers as authors and their involvement in charitable, religious, temperance, and moral reform societies."[28] Paula Giddings notes that in this way white women were able "to become more active outside the home while still preserving the probity of 'true womanhood.'"[29] From the birth of white feminism at the Seneca Falls Convention in 1848, white feminists had a difficult time advancing their goals. Their numbers were few and their members often divided over the propriety of challenging the cult of domesticity. . . .

In the late nineteenth century the cult of domesticity remained primary even for white women graduates of progressive women's colleges such as Vassar, Smith, and Wellesley. For them, no less than for those with only a high-school education, "A Woman's Kingdom" was "a well-ordered home."[30] In a student essay, one Vassar student answered her rhetorical question, "Has the educated woman a duty towards the kitchen?" by emphasizing that the kitchen was "exactly where the college woman belonged" for "the orderly, disciplined, independent graduate is the woman best prepared to manage the home, in which lies the salvation of the world."[31] This essay reflects the dilemma faced by these young white women graduates. They found little support in white society to combine marriage and career. . . . Society sanctioned only three courses for the middle-class white woman in the Progressive period: "marriage, charity work or teaching."[32] Marriage and motherhood stood as the highest calling. If there were no economic need for them to work, single women were encouraged to do volunteer charity work. For those who needed an independent income, teaching was the only acceptable occupation.

Historian John Rousmaniere suggests that the white college-educated women involved in the early settlement house movement saw themselves as fulfilling the "service norm" so prominent among middle-class women of the day. At the same time, he argues, it was their sense of uniqueness as college-educated women and their felt isolation upon returning home that led them to this form of service. The settlement houses, located as they were in white immigrant, working-class slums, catered to these women's sense of noblesse oblige; they derived a sense of accomplishment from providing an example of genteel middle-class virtues to the poor. Yet the settlement houses also played into a sense of adventure, leading one resident to write, "We feel that we know life for the first time."[33] For all their felt uniqueness, however, with some notable exceptions these women's lives usually offered no fundamental challenge to the basic assumptions of true womanhood. Residency in settlement houses was for the most part of short duration, and most volunteers eventually

embraced their true roles of wife and mother without significant outside involvement. The exceptions were women like Jane Addams, Florence Kelley, Julia Lathrop, and Grace Abbott, who became major figures in the public sphere. Although their lives disputed the doctrine of white women's confinement to the private sphere, the challenge was limited in that most of them did not themselves combine the two spheres of marriage and a public life. Although Florence Kelley was a divorced mother, she nevertheless upheld "the American tradition that men support their families, their wives throughout life," and bemoaned the "retrograde movement" against man as the breadwinner.[34]

Most college-educated black middle-class women also felt a unique sense of mission. They accepted Lucy Laney's 1899 challenge to lift up their race and saw themselves walking in the footsteps of black women activists and feminists of previous generations. But their efforts were not simply "charity work"; their focus was on "racial uplift" on behalf of themselves as well as of the economically less fortunate members of their race.[35] The black women's club movement, in contrast to the white women's, tended to concern themselves from the beginning with the "social and legal problems that confronted both black women and men."[36] While there was certainly some elitism in the NACW's motto, "Lifting as We Climb," these activists were always conscious that they shared a common experience of exploitation and discrimination with the masses and could not completely retreat to the safe haven of their middle-class homes.[37] On the way to meetings they shared the black experience of riding in segregated cars or of being ejected if they tried to do otherwise, as Ida B. Wells did in 1884.[38] Unlike white women for whom, as black feminist Frances Ellen Watkins Harper had emphasized in 1869, "the priorities in the struggle for human rights were sex, not race,"[39] black women could not separate these twin sources of their oppression. They understood that, together with their working-class sisters, they were assumed by whites to have "low animalistic urges." Their exclusion from the category of true womanhood was no less complete than for their less educated black sisters.

It is not surprising, therefore, that the most independent and radical of black female activists led the way in challenging the icons of true womanhood, including on occasion motherhood and marriage. Not only did they chafe under their exclusion from true womanhood, they viewed its tenets as strictures to their efforts on behalf of racial uplift and their own freedom and integrity as women. In 1894 *The Woman's Era* (a black women's magazine) set forth the heretical opinion that "not all women are intended for mothers. Some of us have not the temperament for family life. . . . Clubs will make women think seriously of their future lives, and not make girls think their only alternative is to marry."[40] Anna Julia Cooper, one of the most dynamic women of the period, who had been married and widowed, added that a woman was not "compelled to look to sexual love as the one sensation capable of giving tone and relish, movement and vim to the life she leads. Her horizon is extended."[41] Elsewhere Cooper advised black women that if they married they should seek egalitarian relationships. "The question is not now with the woman 'How shall I so cramp, stunt, and simplify and nullify myself as to make me eligible to the honor of being swallowed up into some little man?' but the problem . . . rests with the man as to how he can so develop . . . to reach the ideal of a generation of women who demand the noblest, grandest and best achievements of which he is capable."[42]

. . . Black activists were far more likely to combine marriage and activism than white activists. . . . Historian Linda Gordon found this to be the case in her study of sixty-nine black and seventy-six white activists in national welfare reform between 1890 and 1945. Only 34 percent of the white activists had ever been married, compared to 85 percent of the black activists. Most of these women (83 percent of blacks and 86 percent

of whites) were college educated.[43] She also found that "The white women [reformers], with few exceptions, tended to view married women's economic dependence on men as desirable, and their employment as a misfortune. . . ."[44] On the other hand, although there were exceptions, Gordon writes, " . . . most black women activists projected a favorable view of working women and women's professional aspirations."[45] Nor could it be claimed that these black activists worked out of necessity, since the majority were married to prominent men "who could support them."[46]

Witness Ida B. Wells-Barnett (married to the publisher of Chicago's leading black newspaper) in 1896, her six-month-old son in tow, stumping from city to city making political speeches on behalf of the Illinois Women's State Central Committee. And Mary Church Terrell dismissing the opinion of those who suggested that studying higher mathematics would make her unappealing as a marriage partner with a curt, "I'd take a chance and run the risk."[47] She did eventually marry and raised a daughter and an adopted child. Her husband, Robert Terrell, a Harvard graduate, was a school principal, a lawyer, and eventually a municipal court judge in Washington, D.C. A biographer later wrote of Mary Terrell's life, "But absorbing as motherhood was, it never became a full-time occupation."[48] While this could also be said of Stanton, perhaps what most distinguished black from white feminists and activists was the larger number of the former who unequivocally challenged domesticity and the greater receptivity they found for their views in the black community. As a result, while the cult of domesticity remained dominant in the white community at the turn of the twentieth century, it did not hold sway within the black community.

Rejection of the Public/Private Dichotomy

Black women of the nineteenth and early twentieth centuries saw their efforts on behalf of the black community as necessary for their own survival, rather than as noblesse oblige. "Self preservation," wrote Mary Church Terrell in 1902, "demands that [black women] go among the lowly, illiterate and even the vicious, to whom they are bound by ties of race and sex . . . to reclaim them."[49] These women rejected the confinement to the private sphere mandated by the cult of domesticity. They felt women could enter the public sphere without detriment to the home. As historian Elsa Barkley Brown has emphasized, black women believed that "Only a strong and unified community made up of both women and men could wield the power necessary to allow black people to shape their own lives. Therefore, only when women were able to exercise their full strength would the community be at its full strength. . . ."[50]

In her study of black communities in Illinois during the late Victorian era (1880–1910), historian Shirley Carlson contrasts the black and white communities' expectations of the "ideal woman" at that time:

> The black community's appreciation for and development of the feminine intellect contrasted sharply with the views of the larger society. In the latter, intelligence was regarded as a masculine quality that would "defeminize" women. The ideal white woman, being married, confined herself almost exclusively to the private domain of the household. She was demure, perhaps even self-effacing. She often deferred to her husband's presumably superior judgment, rather than formulating her own views and vocally expressing them, as black women often did. A woman in the larger society might skillfully manipulate her husband for her own purposes, but she was not supposed to confront or challenge him directly. Black women were often direct, and frequently won community approval for this quality, especially when such a characteristic was directed toward achieving racial uplift. Further, even after her marriage, a black woman might remain in the public domain, possibly in paid employment. The ideal black woman's domain, then, was both the private and public spheres. She was wife and mother, but she could also assume other roles such as schoolteacher, social activist, or businesswoman, among others. And she was intelligent.[51]

. . . Although many black males, like most white males, opposed the expansion of black women's roles, many other black males supported women's activism and even criticized their brethren for their opposition. Echoing Maggie Walker's sentiments, T. Thomas Fortune wrote, "The race could not succeed nor build strong citizens, until we have a race of women competent to do more than hear a brood of negative men."[52] Support for women's suffrage was especially strong among black males. . . . Black men saw women's suffrage as advancing the political empowerment of the race. For black women, suffrage promised to be a potent weapon in their fight for their rights, for education and jobs.[53]

A Threefold Commitment

An expanded role for black women did not end at the ballot box or in activities promoting racial uplift. Black middle-class women demanded a place for themselves in the paid labor force. Theirs was a threefold commitment to family, career, and social movements. According to historian Rosalyn Terborg-Penn, "most black feminists and leaders had been wives and mothers who worked yet found time not only to struggle for the good of their sex, but for their race." Such a threefold commitment "was not common among white women."[54]

In her study of eighty African American women throughout the country who worked in "the feminized professions" (such as teaching) between the 1880s and the 1950s, historian Stephanie Shaw comments on the way they were socialized to lives dedicated to home, work, and community. When these women were children, she indicates, "the model of womanhood held before [them] was one of achievement in *both* public and private spheres. Parents cast domesticity as a complement rather than a contradiction to success in public arenas."[55] . . .

An analysis of the lives of 108 of the first generation of black clubwomen bears this out. "The career-oriented clubwomen," comments Paula Giddings, "seemed to have no ambivalence concerning their right to work, whether necessity dictated it or not."[56] According to Giddings, three-quarters of these 108 early clubwomen were married, and almost three-quarters worked outside the home, while one-quarter had children.

A number of these clubwomen and other black women activists not only had careers but also spoke forcefully about the importance of work, demonstrating surprisingly progressive attitudes with a very modern ring. "The old doctrine that a man marries a woman to support her," quipped Walker, "is pretty nearly thread-bare to-day."[57] "Every dollar a woman makes," she declared in a 1912 speech to the Federation of Colored Women's Clubs, "some man gets the direct benefit of same. Every woman was by Divine Providence created for some man; not for some man to marry, take home and support, but for the purpose of using her powers, ability, health and strength, to forward the financial . . . success of the partnership into which she may go, if she will. . . ."[58] Being married with three sons and an adopted daughter did not in any way dampen her commitment to gender equality and an expanded role for wives.

Such views were not new. In a pamphlet entitled *The Awakening of the Afro-American Woman*, written in 1897 to celebrate the earlier founding of the National Association of Colored Women, Victoria Earle Matthews referred to black women as "co-breadwinners in their families."[59] Almost twenty years earlier, in 1878, feminist writer and activist Frances Ellen Harper sounded a similar theme of equality when she insisted, "The women as a class are quite equal to the men in energy and executive ability." She went on to recount instances of black women managing small and large farms in the postbellum period.[60]

It is clear that in the process of racial uplift work, black middle-class women also included membership in the labor force as part of their identity. They were well ahead of their time in realizing that their membership in the paid labor force was critical to achieving true equality with men. For this reason, the National Association of Wage Earners insisted that all black women should be able to support themselves.[61] . . .

As W. E. B. DuBois commented as early as 1924, "Negro women more than the women of any other group in America are the protagonists in the fight for an economically independent womanhood in modern countries. . . . The matter of economic independence is, of course, the central fact in the struggle of women for equality."[62]

Defining Black Womanhood

In the late 1930s when Mary McLeod Bethune, the acknowledged leader of black women at the time and an adviser to President Franklin Roosevelt on matters affecting the black community, referred to herself as the representative of "Negro womanhood" and asserted that black women had "room in their lives to be wives and mothers as well as to have careers," she was not announcing a new idea.[63] As Terborg-Penn emphasizes:

> . . . most black feminists and leaders had been wives and mothers who worked yet found time not only to struggle for the good of their sex, but for their race. Until the 1970s, however, this threefold commitment— to family and to career and to one or more social movements—was not common among white women. The key to the uniqueness among black feminists of this period appears to be their link with the past. The generation of the woman suffrage era had learned from their late nineteenth-century foremothers in the black women's club movement, just as the generation of the post World War I era had learned and accepted the experiences of the preceding generation. Theirs was a sense of

continuity, a sense of group consciousness that transcended class.[64]

This "sense of continuity" with past generations of black women was clearly articulated in 1917 by Mary Talbert, president of the NACW. Launching an NACW campaign to save the home of the late Frederick Douglass, she said, "We realize today is the psychological moment for us women to show our true worth and prove the Negro women of today measure up to those sainted women of our race, who passed through the fire of slavery and its galling remembrances."[65] Talbert certainly lived up to her words, going on to direct the NAACP's antilynching campaign and becoming the first woman to receive the NAACP's Spingarn Medal for her achievements.

What then is the expanded definition of true womanhood found in these black middle-class women's words and embodied in their lives? First, they tended to define womanhood in an inclusive rather than exclusive sense. Within white society, true womanhood was defined so narrowly that it excluded all but a small minority of white upper- and upper-middle-class women with husbands who were able to support them economically. Immigrant women and poor women—of any color—did not fit this definition. Nor did black women as a whole, regardless of class, because they were all seen as lacking an essential characteristic of true womanhood—virtue. For black women, however, true womanhood transcended class and race boundaries. Anna Julia Cooper called for "reverence for woman as woman regardless of rank, wealth, or culture."[66] Unlike white women, black women refused to isolate gender issues from other forms of oppression such as race and nationality, including the struggles of colonized nations of Africa and other parts of the world. Women's issues, they suggested, were tied to issues of oppression, whatever form that oppression might assume. . . .

The traditional white ideology of true womanhood separated the active world of men from the passive world of women. As we have seen, women's activities were confined to the home, where their greatest achievement was maintaining their own virtue and decorum and rearing future generations of male leaders. Although elite black women did not reject their domestic roles as such, many expanded permissible public activities beyond charity work to encompass employment and participation in social progress. They founded such organizations as the Atlanta Congress of Colored Women, which historian Erlene Stetson claims was the first grassroots women's movement organized "for social and political good."[67]

The tendency of black women to define womanhood inclusively and to see their roles extending beyond the boundaries of the home led them naturally to include other characteristics in their vision. One of these was intellectual equality. While the "true" woman was portrayed as submissive ("conscious of inferiority, and therefore grateful for support"),[68] according to literary scholar Hazel Carby, black women such as Anna Julia Cooper argued for a "partnership with husbands on a plane of intellectual equality."[69] Such equality could not exist without the pursuit of education, particularly higher education, and participation in the labor force. Cooper, like many other black women, saw men's opposition to higher education for women as an attempt to make them conform to a narrow view of women as "sexual objects for exchange in the marriage market."[70] Education for women at all levels became a preoccupation for many black feminists and activists. Not a few—like Anna Cooper, Mary L. Europe, and Estelle Pinckney Webster—devoted their entire lives to promoting it, especially among young girls. Womanhood, as conceived by black women, was compatible with—indeed, required—intellectual equality. In this they were supported by the black community. While expansion of educational opportunities for women was a preoccupation of white feminists in the nineteenth century, as I noted above, a college education tended to create a dilemma in the lives of white women who found little community support for combining marriage and career. In contrast, as Shirley Carlson emphasizes, "The black community did not regard intelligence and femininity as conflicting values, as the larger society did. That society often expressed the fear that intelligent women would develop masculine characteristics—a thickening waist, a diminution of breasts and hips, and finally, even the growth of facial hair. Blacks seemed to have had no such trepidations, or at least they were willing to have their women take these risks."[71]

In addition to women's rights to an education, Cooper, Walker, Alexander, Terrell, the leaders of the National Association of Wage Earners, and countless other black feminists and activists insisted on their right to work outside the home. They dared to continue very active lives after marriage. Middle-class black women's insistence on the right to pursue careers paralleled their view that a true woman could move in both the private and the public spheres and that marriage did not require submissiveness or subordination. In fact, as Shirley Carlson has observed in her study of black women in Illinois in the late Victorian period, many activist black women "continued to be identified by their maiden names—usually as their middle names or as part of their hyphenated surnames—indicating that their own identities were not subsumed in their husbands."[72]

While the views of black women on womanhood were all unusual for their time, their insistence on the right of all women—including wives and mothers—to work outside the home was the most revolutionary. In their view the need for paid work was not merely a response to economic circumstances, but the fulfillment of women's right to self-actualization. Middle-class black women like Ida B. Wells-Barnett, Margaret Washington, and Mary Church Terrell, married to men who were well able to support them, continued to pursue careers throughout their lives, and some did so even as they reared children. These women were far ahead of their time, foreshadowing societal changes that would not occur within the white community for several generations. . . .

Rather than accepting white society's views of paid work outside the home as deviant, therefore, black women fashioned a competing ideology of womanhood—one that supported the needs of an oppressed black community and their own desire for gender equality. Middle-class black women, especially, often supported by the black community, developed a consciousness of themselves as persons who were competent and capable of being influential. They believed in higher education as a means of sharpening their talents, and in a sexist world that looked on men as superior, they dared to see themselves as equals both in and out of marriage.

This new ideology of womanhood came to have a profound impact on the conception of black families and gender roles. Black women's insistence on their role as co-breadwinners clearly foreshadows today's dual-career and dual-worker families. Since our conception of the family is inseparably tied to our views of women's and men's roles, the broader definition of womanhood advocated by black women was also an argument against the traditional family. The cult of domesticity was anchored in a patriarchal notion of women as subordinate to men in both the family and the larger society. The broader definition of womanhood championed by black middle-class women struck a blow for an expansion of women's rights in society and a more egalitarian position in the home, making for a far more progressive system among blacks at this time than among whites.

NOTES

1. Quoted in Hazel V. Carby, *Reconstructing Womanhood: The Emergence of the Afro-American Woman Novelist* (New York: Oxford University Press, 1987), p. 26.

2. Ibid.

3. Quoted in Paula Giddings, *When and Where I Enter: The Impact of Black Women and Race and Sex in America* (New York: Bantam Books, 1985), p. 82.

4. Ibid., p. 82.

5. Carby, *Reconstructing Womanhood*, p. 20.

6. Harriet Jacobs, *Incidents in the Life of a Slave Girl*, L. Baria Child, ed. (1861; paperback reprint, New York: Harcourt Brace Jovanovich, 1973), p. 29.

7. Quoted in Giddings, *When and Where I Enter*, p. 82.

8. Ibid., p. 86.

9. Ibid., p. 87.

10. Ibid., pp. 86–87.

11. Ibid., p. 87.

12. Quoted in Sharon Harley, "Black Women in a Southern City: Washington, D.C., 1890–1920," pp. 59–78 in Joanne V. Hawks and Sheila L. Skemp, eds., *Sex, Race, and the Role of Women in the South* (Jackson, Miss.: University Press of Mississippi, 1983), p. 72.

13. Eleanor Flexner, *Century of Struggle: The Woman's Rights Movement in the United States* (Cambridge: Harvard University Press, 1959), p. 194.

14. Giddings, *When and Where I Enter*, p. 93.

15. Ibid., p. 95. For a discussion of elitism in the "uplift" movement and organizations, see Kevin K. Gains, *Uplifting the Race: Black Leadership, Politics, and Culture in the Twentieth Century* (Chapel Hill, N.C.: University of North Carolina Press, 1996). Black reformers, enlightened as they were, could not entirely escape being influenced by Social Darwinist currents of the times.

16. Deborah Gray White, *Too Heavy a Load: Black Women in Defense of Themselves, 1894–1994* (New York: W. W. Norton & Company, 1999), p. 36.

17. Quoted in Giddings, *When and Where I Enter*, p. 75.

18. Ibid.

19. Ibid.

20. Ibid., p. 59.

21. Ibid.

22. Evelyn Brooks Higginbotham, *Righteous Discontent: The Women's Movement in the Black Baptist Church, 1880-1920* (Cambridge: Harvard University Press, 1993).

23. Rosalyn Terborg-Penn, "Discontented Black Feminists: Prelude and Postscript to the Passage of the Nineteenth Amendment," pp. 261–278 in Lois Scharf and Joan M. Jensen, eds., *Decades of Discontent: The Woman's Movement, 1920–1940* (Westport, Conn.: Greenwood Press, 1983), p. 264.

24. Ibid., p. 261.

25. Ibid., p. 264.

26. Ibid., p. 266.

27. Ibid., pp. 266–267.

28. Barbara J. Harris, *Beyond Her Sphere: Women and the Professions in American History* (Westport, Conn.: Greenwood Press, 1978), pp. 85–86.

29. Giddings, *When and Where I Enter*, p. 81.

30. John P. Rousmaniere, "Cultural Hybrid in the Slums: The College Woman and the Settlement House, 1889–1984," *American Quarterly* 22 (Spring 1970): p. 56.

31. Ibid., p. 55.

32. Rousmaniere, "Cultural Hybrid in the Slums," p. 56.

33. Ibid., p. 61.

34. Quoted in Linda Gordon, "Black and White Visions of Welfare: Women's Welfare Activism, 1890–1945," *Journal of American History* 78 (September 1991): 583.

35. Giddings, *When and Where I Enter*, p. 97.

36. Estelle Freedman, "Separatism as Strategy: Female Institution Building and American Feminism, 1870–1930," pp. 445–462 in Nancy F. Cott, ed., *Women Together: Organizational Life* (New Providence, RI: K. G. Saur, 1994), p. 450; Nancy Forderhase, "'Limited Only by Earth and Sky': The Louisville Woman's Club and Progressive Reform, 1900–1910," pp. 365–381 in Cott, ed. *Women Together: Organizational Life* (New Providence, RI: K. G. Saur, 1994); . . . Mary Dell Brady, "Kansas Federation of Colored Women's Clubs, 1900–1930," pp. 382–408 in Nancy F. Cott, *Women Together*.

37. Higginbotham, *Righteous Discontent*, pp. 206–207.

38. Giddings, *When and Where I Enter*, p. 22.

39. Terborg-Penn, "Discontented Black Feminists," p. 267.

40. Giddings, *When and Where I Enter*, p. 108.

41. Ibid., pp. 108–109.

42. Ibid., p. 113.

43. Linda Gordon, "Black and Whites Visions of Welfare," p. 583.

44. Ibid., p. 582.

45. Ibid., p. 585.

46. Ibid., pp. 568–69.

47. Ibid., p. 109.

48. Quoted in Giddings, ibid., p. 110.

49. Ibid., p. 97.

50. Elsa Barkley Brown, "Womanist Consciousness: Maggie Lena Walker and the Independent

Order of Saint Luke," *Signs: Journal of Women in Culture and Society* 14, no. 3 (1989): 188.

51. Shirley J. Carlson, "Black Ideals of Womanhood in the Late Victorian Era," *Journal of Negro History* 77, no. 2 (Spring 1992): 62. Carlson notes that these black women of the late Victorian era also observed the proprieties of Victorian womanhood in their deportment and appearance but combined them with the expectations of the black community for intelligence, education, and active involvement in racial uplift.

52. Quoted in Giddings, *When and Where I Enter*, p. 117.

53. See Rosalyn Terborg-Penn, *African American Women in the Struggle for the Vote, 1850–1920* (Bloomington, Ind.: Indiana University Press, 1998).

54. Rosalyn Terborg-Penn, "Discontented Black Feminists," p. 274.

55. Stephanie J. Shaw, *What a Woman Ought to Be and to Do: Black Professional Women Workers During the Jim Crow Era* (Chicago: University of Chicago Press, 1996), p. 29. Shaw details the efforts of family and community to socialize these women for both personal achievement and community service. The sacrifices some families made included sending them to private schools and sometimes relocating the entire family near a desired school.

56. Giddings, *When and Where I Enter*, p. 108.

57. Brown, "Womanist Consciousness," p. 622.

58. Ibid., p. 623.

59. Carby, *Reconstructing Womanhood*, p. 117.

60. Quoted in Giddings, *When and Where I Enter*, p. 72.

61. Brown, "Womanist Consciousness," p. 182.

62. Quoted in Giddings, *Where and When I Enter*, p. 197.

63. Quoted in Terborg-Penn, "Discontented Black Feminists," p. 274.

64. Ibid., p. 274.

65. Quoted in Giddings, *Where and When I Enter*, p. 138.

66. Quoted in Carby, *Reconstructing Womanhood*, p. 98.

67. Erlene Stetson, "Black Feminism in Indiana, 1893–1933," *Phylon* 44 (December 1983): 294.

68. Quoted in Barbara Welter, "The Cult of True Womanhood: 1820–1860," p. 318.

69. Carby, *Reconstructing Womanhood*, p. 100.

70. Ibid., p. 99.

71. Carlson, "Black Ideals of Womanhood in the Late Victorian Era," p. 69. This view is supported by historian Evelyn Brooks Higginbotham's analysis of schools for blacks established by northern Baptists in the postbellum period, schools that encouraged the attendance of both girls and boys. Although, as Higginbotham observes, northern Baptists founded these schools in part to spread white middle-class values among blacks, blacks nevertheless came to see higher education as an instrument of their own liberation (*Righteous Discontent*, p. 20).

72. Ibid., p. 67.

THINKING ABOUT THE READING

How were the needs and goals of black women during the 19th-century movement for gender equality different from those of white women? How did their lives differ with regard to the importance of marriage, motherhood, and employment? What does Landry mean when he says that for these women, "race and gender are inseparable"? What was the significance of the "clubs" for these black women? How does this article change what you previously thought about the contemporary women's movement?

Still a Man's World

Men Who Do "Women's Work"

Christine L. Williams

(1995)

Gendered Jobs and Gendered Workers

A 1959 article in *Library Journal* entitled "The Male Librarian—An Anomaly?" begins this way:

> My friends keep trying to get me out of the library. . . . Library work is fine, they agree, but they smile and shake their heads benevolently and charitably, as if it were unnecessary to add that it is one of the dullest, most poorly paid, unrewarding, off-beat activities any man could be consigned to. If you have a heart condition, if you're physically handicapped in other ways, well, such a job is a blessing. And for women there's no question library work is fine; there are some wonderful women in libraries and we all ought to be thankful to them. But let's face it, no healthy man of normal intelligence should go into it.[1]

Male librarians still face this treatment today, as do other men who work in predominantly female occupations. In 1990, my local newspaper featured a story entitled "Men Still Avoiding Women's Work" that described my research on men in nursing, librarianship, teaching, and social work. Soon afterwards, a humor columnist for the same paper wrote a spoof on the story that he titled, "Most Men Avoid Women's Work Because It Is Usually So Boring."[2] The columnist poked fun at hairdressing, librarianship, nursing, and babysitting—in his view, all "lousy" jobs requiring low intelligence and a high tolerance for boredom. Evidently people still wonder why any "healthy man of normal intelligence" would willingly work in a "woman's occupation."

In fact, not very many men do work in these fields, although their numbers are growing. In 1990, over 500,000 men were employed in these four occupations, constituting approximately 6 percent of all registered nurses, 15 percent of all elementary school teachers, 17 percent of all librarians, and 32 percent of all social workers. These percentages have fluctuated in recent years: As Table 1 indicates, librarianship and social work have undergone slight declines in the proportions of men since 1975; teaching has remained somewhat stable; while nursing has experienced noticeable gains. The number of men in nursing actually doubled between 1980 and 1990; however, their overall proportional representation remains very low.

Very little is known about these men who "cross over" into these nontraditional occupations. While numerous books have been written about women entering male-dominated occupations, few have asked why men are underrepresented in traditionally female jobs.[3] The underlying assumption in most research on gender and work is that, given a free choice, both men and women would work in predominantly male occupations, as they are generally better paying and more prestigious than predominantly female occupations. The few men who willingly "cross over" must be, as the 1959 article suggests, "anomalies."

Popular culture reinforces the belief that these men are "anomalies." Men are rarely portrayed working in these occupations, and when they are, they are represented in extremely stereotypical ways. For example, in the 1990 movie *Kindergarten Cop*, muscle-man Arnold Schwarzenegger played a detective forced to

Table 1 Men in the "Women's Professions": Number (in thousands) and Distribution of Men Employed in the Occupations, Selected Years

Profession	1975	1980	1990
Registered Nurses			
Number of men	28	46	92
% men	3.0	3.5	5.5
Elementary Teachers[a]			
Number of men	194	225	223
% men	14.6	16.3	14.8
Librarians			
Number of men	34	27	32
% men	18.9	14.8	16.7
Social Workers			
Number of men	116	134	179
% men	39.2	35.0	21.8

SOURCES: U.S. Department of Labor, Bureau of Labor Statistics, *Employment and Earnings* 38, no. 1 (January 1991), table 22 (employed civilians by detailed occupation), p. 185; vol. 28, no. 1 (January 1981), table 23 (employed persons by detailed occupation), p. 180; vol. 22, no. 7 (January 1976), table 2 (employed persons by detailed occupation), p. 11.

[a] Excludes kindergarten teachers.

work undercover as a kindergarten teacher; the otherwise competent Schwarzenegger was completely overwhelmed by the five-year-old children in his class. . . .

[I] challenge these stereotypes about men who do "women's work" through case studies of men in four predominantly female occupations: nursing, elementary school teaching, librarianship, and social work. I show that men maintain their masculinity in these occupations, despite the popular stereotypes. Moreover, male power and privilege is preserved and reproduced in these occupations through a complex interplay between gendered expectations embedded in organizations, and the gendered interests workers bring with them to their jobs. Each of these occupations is "still a man's world" even though mostly women work in them.

I selected these four professions as case studies of men who do "women's work" for a variety of reasons. First, because they are so strongly associated with women and femininity in our popular culture, these professions highlight and perhaps even exaggerate the barriers and advantages men face when entering predominantly female environments. Second, they each require extended periods of educational training and apprenticeship, requiring individuals in these occupations to be at least somewhat committed to their work (unlike those employed in, say, clerical or domestic work). Therefore I thought they would be reflective about their decisions to join these "nontraditional" occupations, making them "acute observers" and, hence, ideal informants about the sort of social and psychological processes I am interested in describing.[4] Third, these occupations vary a great deal in the proportion of men working in them. Although my aim was not to engage in between-group comparisons, I believed that the proportions of men in a work setting would strongly influence the degree to which they felt accepted and satisfied with their jobs.[5]

I traveled across the United States conducting in-depth interviews with seventy-six men and twenty-three women who work in nursing, teaching, librarianship, and social work. Like the people employed in these professions generally, those in my sample were predominantly white (90 percent). Their ages ranged from twenty to sixty-six, and the average age was thirty-eight. I interviewed women as well as men to gauge their feelings and reactions to men's entry into "their" professions. Respondents were intentionally selected to represent a wide range of specialties and levels of education and experience. I interviewed students in professional schools, "front line" practitioners, administrators, and retirees, asking them about their motivations to enter these professions, their on-the-job experiences, and their opinions about men's status and prospects in these fields. . . .

Riding the Glass Escalator

Men earn more money than women in every occupation—even in predominantly female jobs (with the possible exceptions of fashion modeling and prostitution).[6] Table 2 shows that men outearn women in teaching, librarianship, and social work; their salaries in nursing are virtually identical. The ratios between women's and men's earnings in these occupations are higher than those found in the "male" professions, where women earn 74 to 90 percent of men's salaries. That there is a wage gap at all in predominantly female professions, however, attests to asymmetries in the workplace experiences of male and female tokens. These salary figures indicate that the men who do "women's work" fare as well as, and often better than, the women who work in these fields. . . .

Table 2 Median Weekly Earnings of Full-Time Professional Workers, by Sex, and Ratio of Female: Male Earnings, 1990

Occupation	Both	Men	Women	Ratio
Registered Nurses	608	616	608	.99
Elementary Teachers	519	575	513	.89
Librarians	489	—*	479	—
Social Workers	445	483	427	.88
Engineers	814	822	736	.90
Physicians	892	978	802	.82
College Teachers	747	808	620	.77
Lawyers	1,045	1,178	875	.74

SOURCE: U.S. Department of Labor, Bureau of Labor Statistics, *Employment and Earnings* 38, no. 1 (January 1991), table 56, p. 223.

*The Labor Department does not report income averages for base sample sizes consisting of fewer than 50,000 individuals.

Hiring Decisions

Contrary to the experience of many women in the male-dominated professions, many of the men and women I spoke to indicated that there is a *preference* for hiring men in these four occupations. A Texas librarian at a junior high school said that his school district "would hire a male over a female":

[CW: Why do you think that is?]

Because there are so few, and the . . . ones that they do have, the library directors seem to really . . . think they're doing great jobs. I don't know, maybe they just feel they're being progressive or something, [but] I have had a real sense that they really appreciate having a male, particularly at the junior high. . . . As I said, when seven of us lost our jobs from the high schools and were redistributed, there were only four positions at junior high, and I got one of them. Three of the librarians, some who had been here longer than I had with the school district, were put down in elementary school as librarians. And I definitely think that being male made a difference in my being moved to the junior high rather than an elementary school.

Many of the men perceived their token status as males in predominantly female occupations as an *advantage* in hiring and promotions. When I asked an Arizona teacher whether his specialty (elementary special education) was an unusual area for men compared to other areas within education, he said,

Much more so. I am extremely marketable in special education. That's not why I got into the field. But I am extremely marketable because I am a man.

. . . Sometimes the preference for men in these occupations is institutionalized. One man landed his first job in teaching before he earned the appropriate credential "because I was a wrestler and they wanted a wrestling coach." A female math teacher similarly told of her inability to find a full-time teaching position because the schools she applied to reserved the math jobs for people (presumably men) who could double as coaches. . . .

. . . Some men described being "tracked" into practice areas within their professions which were considered more legitimate for men. For example, one Texas man described how he was pushed into administration and planning in social work, even though "I'm not interested in writing policy; I'm much more interested in research and clinical stuff." A nurse who is interested in pursuing graduate study in family and child health in Boston said he was dissuaded from entering the program specialty in favor of a concentration in "adult nursing." And a kindergarten teacher described his difficulty finding a job in his specialty after graduation: "I was recruited immediately to start getting into a track to become an administrator. And it was men who recruited me. It was men that ran the system at that time, especially in Los Angeles."

This tracking may bar men from the most female-identified specialties within these professions. But men are effectively being "kicked upstairs" in the process. Those specialties considered more legitimate practice areas for men also tend to be the most prestigious, and better-paying specialties as well. For example, men in nursing are overrepresented in critical care and psychiatric specialties, which tend to be higher paying than the others.[7] The highest paying and most prestigious library types are the academic libraries (where men are 35 percent of librarians) and the special libraries which are typically associated with businesses or other private organizations (where men constitute 20 percent of librarians).[8]

A distinguished kindergarten teacher, who had been voted citywide "Teacher of the Year," described the informal pressures he faced to advance in his field. He told me that even though people were pleased to see him in the classroom, "there's been some encouragement to think about administration, and there's been some encouragement to think about teaching at the university level or something like that, or supervisory-type position."

The effect of this "tracking" is the opposite of that experienced by women in male-dominated occupations. Researchers have reported that many women encounter "glass ceilings" in their efforts to scale organizational and professional hierarchies. That is, they reach invisible barriers to promotion in their careers, caused mainly by the sexist attitudes of men in the highest positions.[9] In contrast to this "glass ceiling," many of the men I interviewed seem to encounter a "glass escalator." Often, despite their intentions, they face invisible pressures to move up in their professions. Like being on a moving escalator, they have to work to stay in place. . . .

Supervisors and Colleagues: The Working Environment

. . . Respondents in this study were asked about their relationships with supervisors and female colleagues to ascertain whether men also experienced "poisoned" work environments when entering nontraditional occupations.

A major difference in the experience of men and women in nontraditional occupations is that men are far more likely to be supervised by a member of their own sex. In each of the four professions I studied, men are overrepresented in administrative and managerial capacities, or, as in the case of nursing, the organizational hierarchy is governed by men. For example, 15 percent of all elementary school teachers are men, but men make up over 80 percent of all elementary school principals and 96 percent of all public school superintendents and assistant superintendents.[10] Likewise, over 40 percent of all male social workers hold administrative or managerial positions, compared to 30 percent of all female social workers.[11] And 50 percent of male librarians hold administrative positions, compared to 30 percent of female librarians, and the majority of deans and directors of major university and public libraries are men.[12] Thus, unlike women who enter "male fields," the men in these professions often work under the direct supervision of other men.

Many of the men interviewed reported that they had good rapport with their male supervisors. It was not uncommon in education, for example, for the male principal to informally socialize with the male staff, as a Texas special education teacher describes:

> Occasionally I've had a principal who would regard me as "the other man on the campus" and "it's us against them," you know? I mean, nothing really that extreme, except that some male principals feel like there's nobody there to talk to except the other man. So I've been in that position.

These personal ties can have important consequences for men's careers. For example, one California nurse, whose performance was judged marginal by his nursing superiors, was transferred to the emergency room staff (a prestigious promotion) due to his personal friendship with the physician in charge. And a Massachusetts teacher acknowledged that his principal's personal interest in him landed him his current job:

> [CW: You had mentioned that your principal had sort of spotted you at your previous job and had wanted to bring you here [to this school]. Do you think that has anything to do with the fact that you're a man, aside from your skills as a teacher?]
>
> Yes, I would say in that particular case, that was part of it. . . . We have certain things in common, certain interests that really lined up.
>
> [CW: Vis-à-vis teaching?]
>
> Well, more extraneous things—running specifically, and music. And we just seemed to get along real well right off the bat. It is just kind of a guy thing; we just liked each other. . . .

Interviewees did not report many instances of male supervisors discriminating against them, or refusing to accept them because they were male. Indeed, these men were much more likely to report that their male bosses discriminated against the *females* in their professions. . . .

Of course, not all the men who work in these occupations are supervised by men. Many of the men interviewed who had female bosses also reported high levels of acceptance—although the level of intimacy they achieved with women did not seem as great as with other men. But in some cases, men reported feeling shut-out from decision making when the higher administration was constituted entirely by women. I asked this Arizona librarian whether men in the library profession were discriminated against in hiring because of their sex:

> Professionally speaking, people go to considerable lengths to keep that kind of thing out of their [hiring] deliberations. Personally, is another matter. It's pretty common around here to talk about the "old girl network." This is one of the few libraries that I've had any intimate knowledge of which is actually controlled by women. . . . Most of the department heads and upper level administrators are women. And there's an "old girl network" that works just like the "old boy network," except that the important conferences take place in the women's room rather than on the golf course. But the political mechanism is the same, the exclusion of the other sex from decision making is the same. The reasons are the same. It's somewhat discouraging. . . .

Although I did not interview many supervisors, I did include twenty-three women in my sample to ascertain their perspectives about the presence of men in their professions. All of the women I interviewed claimed to be supportive of their male colleagues, but some conveyed ambivalence. For example, a social work professor said she would like to see more men enter the social work profession, particularly in the clinical specialty (where they are underrepresented). She said she would favor affirmative action hiring guidelines for men in the profession, and yet, she resented the fact that her department hired "another white male" during a recent search. I confronted her about this apparent ambivalence:

> [CW: I find it very interesting that, on the one hand, you sort of perceive this preference and perhaps even sexism with regard to how men

are evaluated and how they achieve higher positions within the profession, yet, on the other hand, you would be encouraging of more men to enter the field. Is that contradictory to you, or . . . ?]

Yeah, it's contradictory. . . .

Men's reception by their female colleagues is thus somewhat mixed. It appears that women are generally eager to see men enter "their" occupations, and the women I interviewed claimed they were supportive of their male peers. Indeed, several men agreed with this social worker that their female colleagues had facilitated their careers in various ways (including college mentorship). At the same time, however, women often resent the apparent ease with which men seem to advance within these professions, sensing that men at the higher levels receive preferential treatment, and thus close off advancement opportunities for women.

But this ambivalence does not seem to translate into the "poisoned" work environment described by many women who work in male-dominated occupations. Among the male interviewees, there were no accounts of sexual harassment (indeed, one man claimed this was a disappointment to him!). However, women do treat their male colleagues differently on occasion. It is not uncommon in nursing, for example, for men to be called upon to help catheterize male patients, or to lift especially heavy patients. Some librarians also said that women asked them to lift and move heavy boxes of books because they were men. . . .

Another stereotype confronting men, in nursing and social work in particular, is the expectation that they are better able than women to handle aggressive individuals and diffuse violent situations. An Arizona social worker who was the first male caseworker in a rural district, described this preference for men:

They welcomed a man, particularly in child welfare. Sometimes you have to go into some tough parts of towns and cities, and they felt it was nice to have a man around to accompany them or be present when they were dealing with a difficult client. Or just doing things that males can do. I always felt very welcomed.

But this special treatment bothered some respondents: Getting assigned all the violent patients or discipline problems can make for difficult and unpleasant working conditions. Nurses, for example, described how they were called upon to subdue violent patients. A traveling psychiatric nurse I interviewed in Texas told how his female colleagues gave him "plenty of opportunities" to use his wrestling skills. . . .

But many men claimed that this differential treatment did not distress them. In fact, several said they liked being appreciated for the special traits and abilities (such as strength) they could contribute to their professions.

Furthermore, women's special treatment of men sometimes enhanced—rather than detracted from—the men's work environments. One Texas librarian said he felt "more comfortable working with women than men" because "I think it has something to do with control. Maybe it's that women will let me take control more than men will." Several men reported that their female colleagues often cast them into leadership roles. . . .

The interviews suggest that the working environment encountered by "nontraditional" male workers is quite unlike that faced by women who work in traditionally male fields. Because it is not uncommon for men in predominantly female professions to be supervised by other men, they tend to have closer rapport and more intimate social relationships with people in management. These ties can facilitate men's careers by smoothing the way for future promotions. Relationships with female supervisors were also described for the most part in positive terms, although in some cases, men perceived an "old girls'" network in place that excluded them from decision making. But in sharp contrast to the reports of women in nontraditional occupations, men in these fields did not complain of feeling discriminated against because they were men. If anything, they felt that being male was an asset that enhanced their career prospects.

Those men interviewed for this study also described congenial workplaces, and a very high level of acceptance from their female colleagues. The sentiment was echoed by women I spoke to who said that they were pleased to see more men enter "their" professions. Some women, however, did express resentment over the "fast-tracking" that their male colleagues seem to experience. But this ambivalence did not translate into a hostile work environment for men: Women generally included men in their informal social events and, in some ways, even facilitated men's careers. By casting men into leadership roles, presuming they were more knowledgeable and qualified, or relying on them to perform certain critical tasks, women unwittingly contributed to the "glass escalator effect" facing men who do "women's work."

Relationships With Clients

Workers in these service-oriented occupations come into frequent contact with the public during the course of their work day. Nurses treat patients; social workers usually have client case loads; librarians serve patrons; and teachers are in constant contact with children, and often with parents as well. Many of those interviewed claimed that the clients they served had different expectations of men and women in these occupations, and often treated them differently.

People react with surprise and often disbelief when they encounter a man in nursing, elementary school teaching, and, to a lesser extent, librarianship. (Usually people have no clear expectations about the sex of social workers.) The stereotypes men face are often negative. For example, according to this Massachusetts nurse, it is frequently assumed that male nurses are gay:

> Fortunately, I carry one thing with me that protects me from [the stereotype that male nurses are gay], and the one thing I carry with me is a wedding ring, and it makes a big difference. The perfect example was conversations before I was married.... [People would ask],

"Oh, do you have a girlfriend?" Or you'd hear patients asking questions along that idea, and they were simply implying, "Why is this guy in nursing? Is it because he's gay and he's a pervert?" And I'm not associating the two by any means, but this is the thought process.

...It is not uncommon for both gay and straight men in these occupations to encounter people who believe that they are "gay 'til proven otherwise," as one nurse put it. In fact, there are many gay men employed in these occupations. But gender stereotypes are at least as responsible for this general belief as any "empirical" assessment of men's sexual lifestyles. To the degree that men in these professions are perceived as not "measuring up" to the supposedly more challenging occupational roles and standards demanded of "real" men, they are immediately suspected of being effeminate—"like women"—and thus, homosexual.

An equally prevalent sexual stereotype about men in these occupations is that they are potentially dangerous and abusive. Several men described special rules they followed to guard against the widespread presumption of sexual abuse. For example, nurses were sometimes required to have a female "chaperone" present when performing certain procedures or working with specific populations. This psychiatric nurse described a former workplace:

> I worked on a floor for the criminally insane. Pretty threatening work. So you have to have a certain number of females on the floor just to balance out. Because there were female patients on the floor too. And you didn't want to be accused of rape or any sex crimes.

Teachers and librarians described the steps they took to protect themselves from suspicions of sexual impropriety. A kindergarten teacher said:

> I know that I'm careful about how I respond to students. I'm careful in a number of ways—in my physical interaction with students. It's mainly to reassure parents.... For example, a

little girl was very affectionate, very anxious to give me a hug. She'll just throw herself at me. I need to tell her very carefully: "Sonia, you need to tell me when you want to hug me." That way I can come down, crouch down. Because you don't want a child giving you a hug on your hip. You just don't want to do that. So I'm very careful about body position.

. . . Although negative stereotypes about men who do "women's work" can push men out of specific jobs, their effects can actually benefit men. Instead of being a source of negative discrimination, these prejudices can add to the "glass escalator effect" by pressuring men to move *out* of the most feminine-identified areas and *up* to those regarded as more legitimate for men.

The public's reactions to men working in these occupations, however, are by no means always negative. Several men and women reported that people often assume that men in these occupations are more competent than women, or that they bring special skills and expertise to their professional practice. For example, a female academic librarian told me that patrons usually address their questions to the male reference librarian when there is a choice between asking a male or a female. A male clinical social worker in private practice claimed that both men and women generally preferred male psychotherapists. And several male nurses told me that people often assume that they are physicians and direct their medical inquiries to them instead of to the female nurses.[13]

The presumption that men are more competent than women is another difference in the experience of token men and women. Women who work in nontraditional occupations are often suspected of being incompetent, unable to survive the pressures of "men's work." As a consequence, these women often report feeling compelled to prove themselves and, as the saying goes, "work twice as hard as men to be considered half as good." To the degree that men are assumed to be competent and in control, they may have to be twice as incompetent to be considered half as bad. One man claimed that

"if you're a mediocre male teacher, you're considered a better teacher than if you're a female and a mediocre teacher. I think there's that prejudice there." . . .

There are different standards and assumptions about men's competence that follow them into nontraditional occupations. In contrast, women in both traditional and nontraditional occupations must contend with the presumption that they are neither competent nor qualified. . . .

The reasons that clients give for preferring or rejecting men reflect the complexity of our society's stereotypes about masculinity and femininity. Masculinity is often associated with competence and mastery, in contrast to femininity, which is often associated with instrumental incompetence. Because of these stereotypes, men are perceived as being stricter disciplinarians and stronger than women, and thus better able to handle violent or potentially violent situations. . . .

Conclusion

Both men and women who work in nontraditional occupations encounter discrimination, but the forms and the consequences of this discrimination are very different for the two groups. Unlike "nontraditional" women workers, most of the discrimination and prejudice facing men in the "female" professions comes from clients. For the most part, the men and women I interviewed believed that men are given fair—if not preferential—treatment in hiring and promotion decisions, are accepted by their supervisors and colleagues, and are well-integrated into the workplace subculture. Indeed, there seem to be subtle mechanisms in place that enhance men's positions in these professions—a phenomenon I refer to as a "glass escalator effect."

Men encounter their most "mixed" reception in their dealings with clients, who often react negatively to male nurses, teachers, and to a lesser extent, librarians. Many people assume that the men are sexually suspect if they are employed in these "feminine" occupations either because they do or they do not conform to stereotypical masculine characteristics.

Dealing with the stress of these negative stereotypes can be overwhelming, and it probably pushes some men out of these occupations.[14] The challenge facing the men who stay in these fields is to accentuate their positive contribution to what our society defines as essentially "women's work." . . .

NOTES

1. Allan Angoff, "The Male Librarian—An Anomaly?" *Library Journal*, February 15, 1959, p. 553.

2. *Austin-American Statesman*, January 16, 1990; response by John Kelso, January 18, 1990.

3. Some of the most important studies of women in male-dominated occupations are: Rosabeth Moss Kanter, *Men and Women of the Corporation* (New York: Basic Books, 1977); Susan Martin, *Breaking and Entering: Policewomen on Patrol* (Berkeley: University of California Press, 1980); Cynthia Fuchs Epstein, *Women in Law* (New York: Basic Books, 1981); Kay Deaux and Joseph Ullman, *Women of Steel* (New York: Praeger, 1983); Judith Hicks Stiehm, *Arms and the Enlisted Woman* (Philadelphia: Temple University Press, 1989); Jerry Jacobs, *Revolving Doors: Sex Segregation and Women's Careers* (Stanford: Stanford University Press, 1989); Barbara Reskin and Patricia Roos, *Job Queues, Gender Queues: Explaining Women's Inroads into Male Occupations* (Philadelphia: Temple University Press, 1990).

Among the few books that do examine men's status in predominantly female occupations are Carol Tropp Schreiber, *Changing Places: Men and Women in Transitional Occupations* (Cambridge: MIT Press, 1979); Christine L. Williams, *Gender Differences at Work: Women and Men in Nontraditional Occupations* (Berkeley: University of California Press, 1989); and Christine L. Williams, ed., *Doing "Women's Work": Men in Nontraditional Occupations* (Newbury Park, CA: Sage Publications, 1993).

4. In an influential essay on methodological principles, Herbert Blumer counseled sociologists to "sedulously seek participants in the sphere of life who are acute observers and who are well informed. One such person is worth a hundred others who are merely unobservant participants." See "The Methodological Position of Symbolic Interactionism," in *Symbolic Interactionism: Perspective and Method* (Berkeley: University of California Press, 1969), p. 41.

5. The overall proportions in the population do not necessarily represent the experiences of individuals in my sample. Some nurses, for example, worked in groups that were composed almost entirely of men, while some social workers had the experience of being the only man in their group. The overall statistics provide a general guide, but relying on them exclusively can distort the actual experiences of individuals in the workplace. The statistics available for research on occupational sex segregation are not specific enough to measure internal divisions among workers. Research that uses firm-level data finds a far greater degree of segregation than research that uses national data. See William T. Bielby and James N. Baron, "A Woman's Place Is with Other Women: Sex Segregation within Organizations," in *Sex Segregation in the Workplace: Trends, Explanations, Remedies,* ed. Barbara Reskin (Washington, D.C.: National Academy Press, 1984), pp. 27–55.

6. Catharine MacKinnon, *Feminism Unmodified* (Cambridge: Harvard University Press, 1987), pp. 24–25.

7. Howard S. Rowland, *The Nurse's Almanac,* 2d ed. (Rockville, MD: Aspen Systems Corp., 1984), p. 153; John W. Wright, *The American Almanac of Jobs and Salaries,* 2d ed. (New York: Avon, 1984), p. 639.

8. King Research, Inc., *Library Human Resources: A Study of Supply and Demand* (Chicago: American Library Association, 1983), p. 41.

9. See, for example, Sue J. M. Freeman, *Managing Lives: Corporate Women and Social Change* (Amherst: University of Massachusetts Press, 1990).

10. Patricia A. Schmuck, "Women School Employees in the United States," in *Women Educators: Employees of Schools in Western Countries* (Albany: State University of New York Press, 1987), p. 85; James W. Grimm and Robert N. Stern, "Sex Roles and Internal Labor Market Structures: The Female Semi-Professions," *Social Problems* 21(1974): 690–705.

11. David A. Hardcastle and Arthur J. Katz, *Employment and Unemployment in Social Work: A Study of NASW Members* (Washington, D.C.: NASW, 1979), p. 41; Reginald O. York, H. Carl

Henley and Dorothy N. Gamble, "Sexual Discrimination in Social Work: Is It Salary or Advancement?" *Social Work* 32 (1987): 336–340; Grimm and Stern, "Sex Roles and Internal Labor Market Structures."

12. Leigh Estabrook, "Women's Work in the Library/Information Sector," in *My Troubles Are Going to Have Trouble with Me*, ed. Karen Brodkin Sacks and Dorothy Remy (New Brunswick, NJ: Rutgers University Press, 1984), p. 165.

13. Liliane Floge and D. M. Merrill found a similar phenomenon in their study of male nurses. See "Tokenism Reconsidered: Male Nurses and Female Physicians in a Hospital Setting," *Social Forces* 64 (1986): 931–932.

14. Jim Allan makes this argument in "Male Elementary Teachers: Experiences and Perspectives," in *Doing "Women's Work": Men in Nontraditional Occupations*, ed. Christine L. Williams (Newbury Park, CA: Sage Publications, 1993), pp. 113–127.

THINKING ABOUT THE READING

Compare the discrimination men experience in traditionally female occupations to that experienced by women in traditionally male occupations. What is the "glass escalator effect"? In what ways can the glass escalator actually be harmful to men? What do you suppose might happen to the structure of the American labor force if men did in fact begin to enter predominantly female occupations in the same proportion as women entering predominantly male occupations?

Cheerleading and the Gendered Politics of Sport

Laura Grindstaff and Emily West

(2006)

Assumed to exist on the margins of sport (and sport on the margins of "real" life), cheerleading might seem an unlikely subject for academic research. Yet forms of popular culture like cheerleading and sport reveal a great deal about social relations, particularly relations of inequality. Sport has been widely acknowledged as a key institution for examining the production, reproduction, and sometimes contestation of gender inequality. The organization and unfolding of gender relations in a given institution is its "gender regime" (Connell 1987), and, until recently at least, the gender regime of sport tended to buttress notions of male superiority. Scholars generally agree that organized athletics have been central to the construction of what R.W. Connell (1987) calls "hegemonic masculinity," helping to socialize men into business, politics, and war (see Crosset 1990; Kimmel 1990; Messner 1992).

If sport is an arena in which men express and sustain hegemonic masculinity, cheerleading is said to embody the qualities associated with "emphasized femininity" (Connell 1987), notably supportiveness, enthusiasm, and sexual attractiveness (see Kurman 1986). Cast as a feminine auxiliary to sport for the latter half of the twentieth century, cheerleading has served as an icon of normative—meaning white, heterosexual, middle class, and American—girlhood. . . .

The dramatic entry of women and girls into a wide range of sports since the passage of Title IX is well documented (Festle 1996). Cheerleading also changed. It shifted from a primarily female, sideline activity to a more gender mixed, athletic, competitive activity in recent decades. The 1990s witnessed the rapid rise of what is known as all-star cheerleading—private, for-profit cheer programs devoted exclusively to competition and operating independently of schools. There is much debate, both in the media and in the cheer world itself, about whether or not cheerleading should be recognized as a sport in its own right. At the same time, change is never simple or simply progressive, and the debate over cheerleading and sport is about more than increased athleticism; it is also about the gender regime of sports and the historic status of sport as a male preserve. . . .

Historically, women—and middle class white women especially—have found their greatest popular acceptance in the periphery of sport, specifically in "feminine" sports such as gymnastics and figure skating, which are deemed socially acceptable for women but trivialized by the sports establishment (Bryson 1994; Feder 1995). "Feminine" sports mesh neatly with taken-for-granted assumptions that women are "naturally" smaller, slower, and weaker than men but more graceful, flexible, and inclined toward aestheticized or sexualized bodily display— assumptions that work to suppress the actual gender diversity that exists in sport (see Cahn 1994; Kane 1995; Lenskyj 1986). . . .

This paper draws upon ethnographic data to argue that cheerleading, particularly coed college cheerleading, provides a powerful lens through which to examine the relational construction of gender and sexuality in both sport and in society at large. . . .

In Search of Respect

Although cheerleading was once an all-male activity ("invented" in the late 1800s to increase spectator involvement in collegiate football), it was gradually feminized throughout the nineteenth century and has been female dominated since the 1950s (see Adams and Bettis 2003; Hanson 1995). Female involvement changed the nature of cheerleading, shifting emphasis away from character building and leadership to notions of physical attractiveness and sex appeal, which led to a white, middle class bias in the selection of female cheerleaders in the aftermath of desegregation (Grundy 2001; Hanson 1995) and the trivialization and devaluation of cheerleading overall (Hanson 1995). Icons of "ideal" femininity notwithstanding, cheerleading is often considered a trivial activity and female cheerleaders have been negatively stereotyped as dumb and/or sexually promiscuous, particularly as traditional gender ideologies underwent significant change in the wake of second wave feminism (Adams and Bettis 2003; Hanson 1995).

In a real if only partial sense, it was the shift toward sport that "saved" cheerleading from obsolescence and secured its contemporary popularity. If cheerleading lost ground in the post–Title IX era with the rise of feminism and women's sports, it was partly because cultural scripts about femininity expanded during this period to incorporate notions of toughness and physical strength. Cheerleading reclaimed its lost status with women by bringing its performance of femininity up-to-date, combining enthusiasm and sex appeal on the one hand with hard-body athleticism on the other (see Adams and Bettis 2003). The transformation of cheerleading has drawn more men to the activity as well. As a UCA executive put it, "the idea of picking the cutest girl to be on the cheerleading team is so far gone now that guys can migrate back into it and feel good about it."

Today, cheerleading routines incorporate advanced tumbling, stunting, and pyramid building as well as cheering and (sometimes) dance. Cheerleaders call themselves "cheer athletes" and the term "team" is used interchangeably with "squad." While the National Collegiate Athletic Association (NCAA) does not recognize cheerleading as a sport, and while only about half of the nation's high school athletic associations do (Dodd 2004), individual schools may classify cheerleading as a varsity

sport if they wish. Some—including Delta State—award partial scholarships to cheerleaders. . . . Even the slogans on t-shirts and other cheer apparel reflect the bid for sports status: "Girl + Athlete = Cheerleader"; "Hold my weights while I stunt with your girlfriend"; "Other sports use one ball, we use two."

For cheerleaders themselves, the question of whether college cheerleading is a sport, or ought to be classified as a sport, is a complicated one because of the diverse ways that people define sport, the diversity of school cheer squads that exist (coed versus all-girl, competitive versus sideline), the disparate ways that individual schools classify and treat cheerleading, and the difference between believing cheerleading to be a sport and wanting it to be "officially" recognized as such by the NCAA. Regarding this last point, some interviewees were aware of, and supported, the stance of the major cheerleading companies in opposing the classification of school cheerleading as a sport by the NCAA both because of the increased regulation that would ensue and because the sport classification might phase out non-competitive cheerleading altogether. What emerged in the fieldwork and interviews, then, was not a neat calibration of positions for or against the sport designation across all types of cheerleading, much less unanimous support for classifying cheerleading as a sport in a legal sense, but ways of talking about and negotiating the gendered relationship between cheerleading and sport in the search for greater legitimacy. Indeed, the issue of whether or not cheerleading is a "real" sport is a proxy for the issue of respect.

For all the participants in our study, the term "sport" signified high status; cheerleaders knew that playing sports was more prestigious than cheerleading, especially for men, and they complained about being disrespected by the collegiate athletes for whom they cheered. This was true even at Delta State, where the cheer team was the only team in the school's recent history to win a national title. Most of the cheerleaders we interviewed, male and female alike, strongly resented their second class status both in their schools and in the culture at large;

recognizing the cultural legitimacy of sport, they wanted that legitimacy for cheerleading. One Delta State cheerleader was quite blunt about this: "I want it to be considered a sport," she said, "so people can't trash it."

Coed college cheerleaders attempt to bring cheerleading under the umbrella of sport in two main ways: by focusing on the competitive nature of cheerleading, and, related to this, by emphasizing the skill or athleticism of cheerleading. The majority of our interviewees, particularly those on competitive teams, drew firm boundaries between competitive and non-competitive cheer, believing that the former qualifies as a sport but the latter typically does not. The following quote from Jack, a competitive cheerleader on the east coast, is illustrative: "I'm going to say that, for cheerleading to be a sport, it goes from squad to squad. A squad that competes, that has competed in the past, they want to compete in the future, and they're working to compete. I'll say that squad is a sport." Repeatedly we heard phrases such as "a sport is anything where you compete against someone else" (Stanton cheerleader) and "if you're not competing, it's not a sport" (Fairview cheerleader).

At the same time, participants recognize that it is not a competitive orientation alone that puts cheerleading in league with sport, it is also the athleticism and skill presumed to go along with that orientation. Participants routinely characterized competitive cheerleaders as "phenomenal athletes" and emphasized the hard work, dedication, and training required. "If you look at the people who do it, they're not just random people walking in off the street with no ability," said Ruby, a Delta State cheerleader, "they've all been athletes and their bodies are trained. We work hard, it's very dangerous, and we deserve that title [i.e., sport]." Sometimes we heard that cheerleading was *more* demanding athletically than other sports. While interviewees most often compared cheerleading to gymnastics and diving, some also invoked sports in the institutional core. It was Ruby's opinion that "anyone can be a football player, anyone can run with a ball or throw

a ball. Not everyone can do a toss-lib" (a type of partner stunt). Her teammate, Lars, said that his "hardest football practice ever" was still easier than a "mediocre" cheer practice. A young man I met at the Kentucky camp compared cheerleading to his experience playing rugby, hockey, and baseball: "each of those sports is tough," he said, "after practices, you are sore for a bit; [but] after an intense cheer workout, your body is sore for two to three days. Every muscle in your body is used." Because of the premium placed on training and athleticism, a minority of participants questioned competition as the litmus test for sports classification, insisting that sideline-only teams were also engaging in sport if they were highly skilled.

The criteria of competition and athleticism were important for distinguishing squads that "deserved" the sport label from those that did not, and for enabling interviewees to distance themselves from the feminine stigma they associate with earlier generations of cheerleading. Interviewees expressed frustration that outdated, 1950s-era stereotypes persisted and were applied indiscriminately to the whole of cheerleading. Manuel, captain of the Delta State team, insisted that assigning the label "sport" would make little difference unless people also stopped thinking of cheerleading as "just a bunch of ditzy girls on the sidelines who jump around and entertain the crowd." He and others in the study believed that greater knowledge of the activity would breed greater respect. Ben, one of Manuel's teammates, said that "ninety-five percent of the people you meet don't know anything about it . . . as much as cheerleading has changed within the cheer community, for someone on the outside looking in, cheerleading is still the rah-rah skirts and pom-pons kind of thing." Liz, the captain of a competitive Louisiana team, said much the same thing: "People are not willing to accept cheerleading in their brains as a sport. This is based on pure ignorance. They can't accept what they don't know. People think that cheerleading is just a girl's activity or something only girls do." . . .

Obstacles to Respect: The Supportive Function of Cheerleading

Despite the move toward competition and greater athleticism, cheerleading is still strongly associated with its supportive function, best captured by the image of female cheerleaders on the sidelines of (male) sporting events. This image is not as outdated as the cheerleaders we interviewed liked to think. Industry representatives are quick to point out that the "bread and butter" of the business are sideline squads that do little or no competing; since girls and women dominate cheerleading overall, most of these squads are all-girl. Competitive school squads, both coed and all-girl, also uphold the sideline tradition by cheering at sports events, appearing at pep rallies, and performing at school or community functions. The sideline paradigm suggests that cheerleading is central to doing gender in ways that conflate femininity with emotional supportiveness. Insofar as the role of cheerleaders is to express through ritualized performance support for other athletes, they are doing the same kind of "emotion work" in the context of organized sport that middle class women have traditionally done in the interpersonal context of heterosexual marriage (see Cline and Spender 1987; Hochschild 1983).

The sideline function of cheerleading constitutes a major obstacle to its bid for sports status not only among outsiders but also among cheerleaders themselves. As Tarek, one of the Fairview cheerleaders, observed: "how can a sport be something that encourages other sports? Like, if you're there to supplement sports how can you yourself be a sport?" Tarek, like other sideline-only cheerleaders in our study, did not see sideline cheer as a sport because of its supportive dimension, but he also did not see supportiveness and athleticism as mutually exclusive necessarily. Some of the competitive cheerleaders we interviewed disagreed, making comments like, "sideline cheer is easy," "sideline teams don't train like athletes do for other sports," and "they're just out there looking pretty." While we did meet a few competitive cheerleaders who embraced the "spirit" function of cheerleading whole-heartedly, most downplayed their sideline performances as mere practices, or as obligations to fulfill in order that they might participate in the "real" cheerleading that occurs at competitions. When asked whether her cheerleaders would get rid of their sideline obligations if they could, the Delta State coach said, "Oh yeah. Maybe one or two of 'em would say, 'Aw, we don't get to do that anymore?' But the majority of them . . . these kids are all here to compete, and do the things on the side that they have to do."

At Stanton and Fairview, where the cheer teams were non-competitive, the denigration of sideline cheer was accomplished more subtly, by arguing that cheerleading was not just—or even primarily—about supporting other athletes, but an opportunity to display one's skills, improve one's skills, and even compete with the opposing cheer squad on the other side of the field or court. They were not alone in employing such arguments. As the coach of a coed squad in Louisiana put it, "when we go to games, there's a whole competition going on that most of the people in the crowd don't even realize. We believe the football game is just a backdrop for our performance." Male cheerleaders also spoke of competing against male teammates when throwing stunts and basket tosses. "We're competitive," said Heiko, a former member of the Fairview squad. "I used to compete with some of the guys on the team, you know, 'if you drop a stunt you owe me a beer.'" Thus cheerleaders can and do distance themselves from the supportive dimension of cheerleading, assumed to embody outdated expectations for women, by interpreting the sideline role in unexpected and even creative ways that cast cheerleading as competitive and athletic in its own right even in a sideline context.

The gender politics of sideline cheer are further manifest in how strongly male cheerleaders chafe against the sideline component compared to their female counterparts. To be sure, some female cheerleaders expressed deep ambivalence about their supportive role, recognizing its links to an outdated and devalued version of femininity, and, as indicated above, most insisted that their sideline performance was as much "for themselves" as for the athletes they supported. But their ambivalence paled in comparison to the men's, for whom supportiveness is not just devalued or outmoded but gender transgressive. The following comment from Forest, a Delta State cheerleader, is illustrative: "What I don't like? I *hate* the games, *so much*. I hate games. I hate games because I hate being out in front of people in uniform. I've gotten better . . . like, my first year—trying to get the crowd pumped up for some other guys, it was a little weird." Over and over we heard similar comments, even from the men on sideline-only squads. According to John, a Stanton freshman, "if it were up to me, I'd come here and practice three times a week and never ever go to games . . . they want me to do arm movements, do you know how bad that is? They want me to run with the flag and be happy, and that's just horrible, horrible stuff."

Male cheerleaders communicated discomfort with their sideline role in the way they acted during games, holding back from yelling and expressing less enthusiasm than their female teammates. This was true for the men on all three squads observed as well as on teams at the summer training camps (getting men to embrace the sideline function of cheerleading was one of the topics covered in the coaches' seminars that I attended at the camps). At Delta State, roughly half of the men had been on high school cheer teams where they were excused from cheering games altogether. According to Diego, one of the Delta State cheerleaders and a long time UCA instructor, this arrangement had much to do with the successful retention of male cheerleaders at his school: "all we did was compete. And so that made it a lot easier to retain the guys . . . guys hate cheerleading. We hate going to games and standing there and doing motions or yelling. We just want to put the girls up [in stunts]."

Coaches routinely lament the difficulty they face recruiting and retaining boys and men. Some schools, including Fairview, use the term "stunt team" instead of "cheer squad" in an effort to downplay the supportive function and emphasize the athleticism of cheerleading, thereby making it sound more masculine and sport-like. But the part of college cheerleading that involves supporting other teams, whether on the sidelines or when demonstrating crowd skills in a competition setting, undermines its status as a "true" sport, even for participants and coaches who value its athleticism.

More Gender Trouble: The Performative Aspects of Cheerleading

. . . The supportive and performative dimensions of cheerleading are closely related, both in fact and in the eyes of cheerleaders. Appearing before a crowd requires that cheerleaders be enthusiastic, energetic, and entertaining. This is accomplished not just through dancing, tumbling, or eye-catching stunts, but also through the bubbly, peppy, performance of "spirit" in cheerleading—what we call "informal cheerleading." Informal cheerleading is what participants do to express enthusiasm and "rally the crowd," whether on the sidelines or competition mat. It includes smiling, "facials" (exaggerated facial expressions), being in constant motion, jumping, and executing dynamic arm, hand, and head motions—all considered feminine terrain. Performativity is also defined in terms of appearance: how female cheerleaders should look when in front of crowds. In the words of a Stanton cheerleader, "we're told to be in full makeup, to do our hair. Because we're performing. If you're not wearing lipstick, that's the first thing [the coach] will say to you, 'why isn't your lipstick on?'" Being petite is part of the "appearance aspect" for women on coed teams, as is wearing the conventional cheerleader uniform, whose short skirt, tight-fitting shell top (often cropped, exposing the midriff), and hair ribbons suggest a combination of youthfulness and sexual availability. As Connell (1987) so aptly observed: "[emphasized] femininity is performed, performed especially to men" (p. 188).

As a group, the young women we interviewed accepted these feminine accoutrements as "just part of the show," "just for entertainment," and "necessary to please the crowd"—in other words, a taken-for-granted necessity in an activity focused on entertainment and bodily display. While a couple of interviewees expressed discomfort with this state of affairs (as one of the Stanton women put it: "how can it be a varsity sport if you have to have makeup?"), most clearly enjoyed the "girly" aspects of cheerleading and had little interest in trading their short skirts, hair ribbons, and makeup for more gender-neutral attire. Ruby's comment is illustrative: "I think it's fun quite honestly, as a girl I like to do my makeup kind of fun and sparkly and get out there . . . I like wearing ribbons in my hair, it's a girly feminine thing and I think it's something that shouldn't be lost." Regarding the "skimpy uniforms," her teammate, Sidney, said, "I guess it goes back to the whole heterosexual thing, the pretty girls . . . the skimpy uniforms. The guys enjoy it . . . and us looking cute attracts the audience to look at us." She insisted that cheerleading was no different than the rest of popular culture in this regard: "It's the same with being on TV, like, or being a singer. You want them to be cute, you're watching them, you know . . . If you gotta wear the short skirts to make people look at you, then I guess that's what you gotta do." Other interviewees pointed out that cheer skirts are no shorter than skirts worn in tennis or field hockey, and that cheerleading uniforms are modest compared to gymnasts' leotards or swimmers' Speedos. "All sports have kinky outfits," observed Sarah, one of the Stanton women, "why pick on cheerleading?" Female cheerleaders are well aware that cheerleading is trivialized in the larger culture, but they attribute this trivialization not to the short skirts and makeup per se but to people's over-valuation of these elements when assessing the "worth" of cheerleading.

Rather than view the combination of performativity and athleticism as somehow unique to cheerleading, we suggest that female cheerleaders have absorbed the lessons of a culture that strongly emphasizes the display of sexy, athletic bodies (see Heywood and Dworkin 2003) and that this marriage of seemingly contradictory elements is one of the hallmarks of contemporary emphasized femininity (see Adams and Bettis 2003). In absorbing this lesson, female

cheerleaders may be little different than female athletes in more "legitimate" sports or post–Title IX women more generally. As Leslie Heywood and Shari Dworkin (2003) argue, "for much of the younger demographic, exhibiting a hot body is an intense sign of valuation . . . not . . . devaluation," because being sexualized "no longer carries the social stigma it once did" (p. 89). What makes the femininity of cheerleaders "emphasized" relative to that of many other female athletes is the fact that, for cheerleaders, artifice, adornment, and sexual display are not optional characteristics to be adopted off the field or court: they are part of the sport itself. Moreover, the heteronormativity of the girly-girl aspect of coed cheerleading is no small part of the activity's appeal for female participants, as this creates a "safe" outlet for their athleticism—safe because the issue of sexuality appears resolved in the "right" direction. It is telling that while gay men are an acknowledged part of coed cheerleading, lesbians are rarely mentioned and are virtually invisible.

Male cheerleaders are much less sanguine about the performative nature of cheerleading, the increasing sexual commodification of male athletes in the media notwithstanding (see Miller 2001). Commenting on the gender inappropriateness (for men) of cheerleading's "obsession with appearances," Rulond, a Fairview cheerleader, said "never before in my life had I ever been involved in anything where I was so carefully monitored for my [appearance] . . . But image is everything in cheerleading. People were 'Rulond, you need to shave. You need to go in there and comb your hair, young man.'" He explained that this was a turnoff for men. "Usually aesthetics and hygiene and appearance are kind of tertiary and you would rather have your words and actions make your statement about you. I think that's just a nice way of saying cheerleading is too fluffy." As further evidence of his view, Rulond observed, somewhat disdainfully, that "a game face for a cheerleader is a big smile." Indeed, Rulond was one of several men in our study who denied the sport label to competitive as well as sideline cheerleading because the competition is indirect, occurring through the medium of judging, and because the criteria for judging are partly aesthetic. Significantly, these same objections are also raised by male critics of competitive cheerleading in the news media (see Dodd 2004; Morrissey 2004). Thus feminine performativity can prevent competitive cheerleading from gaining legitimacy both when people question the presence of performativity in sport and when this performativity necessitates a "subjective" mode of evaluation.

The performance demands of cheerleading not only undermine its status as a "real" sport, they also expose male participants to homophobia. Male cheerleaders recognize the tension between conventional notions of performativity, coded as feminine, and conventional notions of heterosexual masculinity (also noted by Davis 1990). This tension makes straight men, as well as gay men invested in maintaining a straight image, initially resistant to the more feminized elements of cheerleading, including dancing and jumping, certain cheer motions, and the repertoire of gestures and facial expressions in the informal performance of spirit. Men on coed teams facilitate the visual spectacle of cheerleading, particularly through stunting, tumbling, and pyramid building, but they generally are not asked to smile constantly, bounce up and down, shake pompons, or wiggle their fingers in the air (a gesture known as "spirit fingers"). To do so would risk being labeled gay, a scenario described by one male cheerleader as "the gay cheerleader syndrome."

"Nothing With Hips": Managing the Male Cheerleader's "Image Problem"

. . . To the degree that cheerleading is coded as feminine, and to the degree that femininity (for men) is conflated with homosexuality, male cheerleaders are concerned about managing their gender image. *Everyone* we encountered in this study spoke of the gay stereotype for male cheerleaders. As Ben put it: "most people assume, if you say 'I'm a male cheerleader,' they assume you're gay. It happens all the time. That's why I don't even tell people [that I cheer]. People always ask me if I

play football, and so I just tell 'em 'yeah.' It's not even worth getting into a conversation about." Mandy, a junior on the Stanton squad, spoke of a teammate who was pledging a "hard core, really masculine" fraternity. She predicted he would "quit before rush" because the existing members would never initiate a cheerleader. When asked why, she replied: "because they look at it like, excuse my language, they think it's such a fag thing to do." Sean, a competitive cheerleader from Texas, summed up the reaction he gets when people find out that he cheers, saying, "well um, 'less masculine than most,' 'sissy,' 'fairy'—I've pretty much heard it all."

Male cheerleaders manage the gay cheerleader syndrome in a number of ways, most of which reinforce the notion that being strong and being straight "naturally" go together. For example, some mentioned the importance of throwing impressive stunts as a way to "prove" they weren't gay. "The taunting, I've had it at games," said Jack, a competitive east coast cheerleader. "They call me a fag, and I'm like, 'come on!' and I just shove it in their face. And do a great stunt that they could never do, and shut them up." Others compared themselves to football players—not surprisingly, since football players are widely understood to epitomize hegemonic masculinity. The men on a competitive squad I met at the Kentucky camp lifted weights on the same schedule as their school's football team specifically to impress upon the other athletes their comparable strength. Likewise, Ben, of Delta State, dismissed the assumption that football players were stronger, superior athletes. In his words: "the fact of the matter is, these guys [on the football team] can't do what I do in the gym. Like, I'm more athletic. I have more strength than these guys. It's just, people look at you differently when they find out you're a cheerleader; it takes away from who you are." Sean provides another variation on the football theme when defending his decision to cheer, in the process displaying what we call "compensatory hypermasculinity"—the explicit assertion of heterosexuality in the face of the "discrediting" fact of being a male cheerleader (see Goffman 1963 on the concept of discreditable identities). "Football players roll around in the grass with other males, shower with each other, and slap each other on the butt," he said, "and then you look at me, I'm hanging around with some of the hottest, in-shape young ladies that the school has to offer. I'm touching them and holding them in places you can only dream about. Now let me ask you, who's gay?"

The male cheerleaders in our study knew what gender-appropriate reasons to offer in order to justify taking part in a feminine activity. Unlike female cheerleaders, whose gender identity is confirmed (though not uniformly respected) as a result of their participation, male cheerleaders feel compelled to prove they are "real" men despite being cheerleaders. They do this on as well as off the field by embracing certain parts of the cheerleading repertoire (stunting, pyramid building) and resisting others (smiling, cheering), and in their general demeanor. According to Tom, a freshman on the Stanton squad: "I think if you're a male cheerleader, you tend to try to act more masculine . . . You know, you kind of push out your chest, draw up your shoulders a little bit, look like you're big and tough."

Thus it is not that male cheerleaders refuse to be performative at all while on the sidelines or in competitions, but that they seek out gender-appropriate modes of performance. In fact, when male cheerleaders' performance of masculinity is successful it arguably enhances the image of cheerleading as a tough, athletic activity. Forest described how his attitude toward performativity changed over time, as he came to discover an acceptably masculine approach. He said that in high school he was reluctant to smile and "sell the routine" because he saw that as feminine. "But the more mature I got the more I realized—I saw other [guys] doing it, and you didn't have to do it in a feminine way, you could do it, like, kind of cocky and all pumped up . . . you know, [after a great stunt] hit the crowd, show 'em your guns" (lowering his head toward his biceps in a classic muscle man pose). His teammate, Ruby, who was listening, agreed: "I think the guys, they don't

play it up physically with makeup, but their job is to look good. Like, you have big, strong guys that are muscular and athletic. And they know how to work it in front of an audience."

These comments reveal a "different but equal" perspective on gender relations (including gender performance) that resonates with the views of the young people in our study generally: that the roles of men and women are equally important but organized differently according to gender appropriateness, understood in relation to common sense notions of what looks good for whom. This is underscored in their assessment of male cheerleaders who violate these common sense notions by adopting a feminine—even hyperfeminine—mode of performativity. Bruce, a Delta State cheerleader, explained that it was "okay to be really showy" and to "make the faces," but "only to a certain extent." "[Cheerleaders] do that stuff to make the routine seem more energetic," he explained, "but then there's some people who take it to another level. I mean, they're so flaming the flames are flying off the stage and hitting you on the head!" These "flaming" cheerleaders are, of course, assumed to be gay, and are sometimes resented by other men for perpetuating the "wrong" image of male cheerleaders. According to Ben, "I don't have a problem with gay people, I know a lot of gay people . . . but you get a cheerleader who's, like, flaming, and they take it way too far. Like, the girliest girl I know is not as flaming as guy cheerleaders that are flamboyant about it. It's beyond feminine." When asked why that should bother him, he said, "there's no reason for it, especially if you're going to be in an open forum where it's not just your personal life anymore. Like, this is my life too; this is my cheerleading if you're going to be at a competition I'm at."

At issue here is the *performance of gender* not sexual orientation per se. And the public nature of cheerleading, combined with the fact that cheerleaders are considered ambassadors of their schools, mean that the performance of masculinity is monitored and controlled not just by male cheerleaders but also by coaches, school administrators, and alumni. Diego, of Delta State, said that cheer-leading coaches at the college level were under pressure from alumni to avoid any appearance of homosexuality and that this pressure can lead coaches to pass over men "who don't fit the image of the program." Once a team is constituted, other forms of impression man-agement can occur. Ruth, the veteran coach of a Texas squad, mentioned having a talk every year with the gay men on her team about being too "obvious" with their sexuality dur-ing performances, as she believed this to be "a threat to the squad's respect." Lionel, coach of a Louisiana squad, took a similar approach with the gay men on his team and successfully "toned down" their behavior through "conver-sations about image."

The doing of masculinity in cheerleading is therefore no less a conscious production than the doing of femininity, despite the greater emphasis on artifice and sexual attrac-tiveness for female cheerleaders. What is differ-ent is the degree of variation one sees: performances of femininity are far more con-sistent across squads and across the different cheerleading companies than performances of masculinity, suggesting that within coed cheer-leading at least, masculinity is a less coherent, more polyvalent construct. . . .

What version of masculinity a team embraces is shaped by which cheerleading company a team affiliates with. Despite the commitment to hegemonic masculinity expressed by many of the male participants in our study, it was also understood that, because different companies promote different styles of cheerleading at their camps and competitions, "there is something for everyone" when it comes to male participants, although not in equal proportion: the largest and most prof-itable company, the UCA, is also the most gen-der conservative. As one long-time UCA instructor from the South explained it: "UCA stipulates no toe touches [for men], no girl motions and moves, nothing with hips, no dancing. At camp, the instructors get yelled at if we're just horsing around and the guys are doing those things." She added: "once you

cross that line and let the guys dance like girls you start losing the masculine image you want to project." Participants describe the UCA style as "traditional," "collegiate," and "clean-cut," but also "boring" and "conservative." Dylan, a freshman on the Delta State team, likened the gendered division of labor on UCA squads to a traditional marriage: "In UCA, the guys, they pretty much do the 'men's work.' It's like, the guy goes out and throws the garbage away in a family and the woman cooks dinner. It's like that kind of thing." . . .

What all this suggests is that cheerleading is a contested space for the performance of mas-culinity. The doing of masculinity in cheerlead-ing is a complicated business both because there is latitude in how masculinity gets expressed and because cheerleading continues to be understood as feminine terrain, an inappropri-ate activity for "real" men to pursue. This makes cheerleading a welcoming space for men who do not care to prove their hetero-masculinity, while at the same time prompting compen-satory behavior from men who do. Because cheerleading is a public ritual, staged before an audience, it renders the codes by which gen-dered identities and practices are constructed particularly visible, both to spectators and to cheerleaders themselves, who otherwise might be less conscious of how, exactly, gender gets done. In this sense, the public "display" of gen-der (see Goffman 1976) provides the occasion for reflecting on and negotiating the everyday doing of gender in a broader sense. . . .

Conclusion

Cheerleading is a space where the doing and displaying of gender are particularly visible, and where the gender regimes represented by hegemonic masculinity and emphasized femi-ninity are being negotiated and resecured in the face of alternative regimes. It is a place where the boundaries of gender difference are crossed as well as preserved. To quote Rulond (ironi-cally, one of the men in our study seemingly most committed to hegemonic masculinity):

"[cheerleading] is a way, kind of, of men and women maybe trying on each other's clothes a little bit." Coed college cheerleading is neither a bastion of gender conservatism nor an unfettered space of gender nonconformity; rather, as a mainstream, "feminine" activity seeking legitimacy as a "serious" sport, it expresses and exposes the gender politics at play in a shifting institutional context. In examining these politics, we have been less invested in demonstrating that cheerleading *is* or *should be* considered a sport than in observing the boundary work of participants as they struggle to "match" their doing of gender in cheerleading with their gendered identities and beliefs. . . .

REFERENCES

Adams, Natalie and Pamela Bettis. 2003. *Cheerleader! An American Icon.* New York: Palgrave Macmillan.

Bryson, Lois. 1994. "Sport and the Maintenance of Masculine Hegemony." Pp. 47–64 in *Women, Sport, and Culture,* edited by Susan Birrell and Cheryl Cole. Champaign, IL: Human Kinetics Books.

Cahn, Susan. 1994. *Coming on Strong: Gender and Sexuality in Twentieth-Century Women's Sport.* New York: Free Press.

Cline, Sally and Dale Spender. 1987. *Reflecting Men at Twice Their Natural Size.* New York: Henry Holt and Company.

Connell, R. W. 1987. *Gender and Power.* Stanford, CA: Stanford University Press.

Crosset, Todd. 1990. "Masculinity, Sexuality, and the Development of Early Modern Sport." Pp. 45–54 in *Sport, Men, and the Gender Order: Critical Feminist Perspectives,* edited by Michael Messner and Donald Sabo. Champaign, IL: Human Kinetics Books.

Davis, Laurel. 1990. "Male Cheerleaders and the Naturalization of Gender." Pp. 153–61 in *Sport, Men, and the Gender Order: Critical Feminist Perspectives,* edited by Michael Messner and Donald Sabo. Champaign, IL: Human Kinetics Books.

Dodd, Dennis. 2004. "Colleges Giving Cheerleading a Sporting Chance." *CBS.Sportsline.com,* June 11. Retrieved June 14, 2004 (http://www.sportsline.com/collegefootball/story/7412313).

Feder, Abigail. 1995. "A Radiant Smile from the Lovely Lady: Overdetermined Femininity in 'Ladies' Figure Skating." Pp. 22–46 in *Women on Ice: Feminist Essays on the Tonya Harding/Nancy Kerrigan Spectacle,* edited by Cynthia Baughman. New York: Routledge.

Festle, Mary Jo. 1996. *Playing Nice: Politics and Apologies in Women's Sports.* New York: Columbia University Press.

Goffman, Erving. 1963. *Stigma: Notes on the Management of Spoiled Identity.* New York: Simon and Schuster.

———. 1976. "Gender Display." *Studies in the Anthropology of Visual Communication* 3:69–77.

Grundy, Pamela. 2001. *Learning to Win: Sports, Education, and Social Change in Twentieth-Century North Carolina.* Chapel Hill: University of North Carolina Press.

Hanson, Mary Ellen. 1995. *Go! Fight! Win!: Cheerleading in American Culture.* Bowling Green, OH: Bowling Green State University Popular Press.

Heywood, Leslie and Shari Dworkin. 2003. *Built to Win: The Female Athlete as Cultural Icon.* Minneapolis: University of Minnesota Press.

Hochschild, Arlie Russell. 1983. *The Managed Heart: Commercialization of Human Feeling.* Berkeley: University of California Press.

Kane, Mary Jo. 1995. "Resistance/Transformation of the Oppositional Binary: Exposing Sport as a Continuum." *Journal of Sport and Social Issues* 19:191–218.

Kimmel, Michael. 1990. "Baseball and the Reconstitution of American Masculinity." Pp. 55–56 in *Sport, Men, and the Gender Order: Critical Feminist Perspectives,* edited by Michael Messner and Donald Sabo. Champaign, IL: Human Kinetics Books.

Kurman, George. 1986. "What Does Girls' Cheerleading Communicate?" *Journal of Popular Culture* 20:57–64.

Lenskyj, Helen. 1986. *Out of Bounds: Women, Sport, and Sexuality.* Toronto, ON: Women's Press.

Messner, Michael. 1992. *Power at Play: Sports and the Problem of Masculinity.* Boston: Beacon Press.

Miller, Toby. 2001. *Sportsex.* Philadelphia: Temple University Press.

Morrissey, Rick. 2004. "Glitter? Makeup? Cheerleading is Not a Sport." *Duluth News Tribune,* May 4. Retrieved August 6, 2004 (http://www.duluthsuperior.com).

THINKING ABOUT THE READING

According to the authors, what are some of the ways cheerleading has changed in recent years? What strategies do cheerleaders use to gain respect for their sport? How do these strategies differ between female and male cheerleaders? How does cheerleading reinforce gender stereotypes? How does it challenge these stereotypes?

Global Dynamics and Population Demographic Trends

13

In the past several chapters, we have examined the various interrelated sources of social stratification. Race, class, and gender continue to determine access to cultural, economic, and political opportunities. Another source of inequality that we don't think much about, but one that has enormous local, national, and global significance, is the changing size and shape of the human population and how people are distributed around the planet. Globally, population imbalances between richer and poorer societies underlie most if not all of the other important forces for change that are taking place today. Poor, developing countries are expanding rapidly, while the populations in wealthy, developed countries have either stabilized or, in some cases, declined. When the population of a country grows rapidly, the age structure is increasingly dominated by young people. In slow-growth countries with low birthrates and high life expectancy, the population is much older. Countries with different age structures face different challenges regarding the allocation of important resources.

One form of segregation that people may be less aware of is age segregation—the culture and institutional separation of people of different ages. Social demographers point out that cultural survival is dependent not only on older people sharing traditions and knowledge with younger people, but also on reverse knowledge sharing whereby young people help older people keep up with cultural changes. Current social processes of work/education separation, high rates of mobility, etc., have resulted in a pattern of extreme age segregation in developed countries. Young people rarely interact in a sustained way with older people unless they are related through family ties. Uhlenberg and Jong Gierveld ask how integrated we are across age differences. Using a study based on a Dutch survey, they explore this question by examining personal networks. How many people of varying ages are in your personal network? Although this study is based in the Netherlands, it has strong relevance to most Western nations.

The second reading in this section explores the connections between immigration and generations. Young people translating for their elder family members is a common yet frequently unnoticed aspect of immigrant life. Orellana, Dorner, and Pulida focused their research on immigrant families in Chicago and Los Angeles and documented an extensive pattern of youth translators. The narratives provided by these immigrant youth illustrate that translating is a necessary aspect of everyday life in enabling their families to survive and adapt. This activity also has interesting implications for inter-generational dynamics in the family.

Some other large-scale demographic phenomena affect people regardless of their age. Take, for instance, immigration. As social and demographic conditions in poor, developing countries grow worse, pressures to migrate increase. Countries on the receiving end of this migration often experience high levels of cultural, political, and economic fear. Immigration—both legal and illegal—has become one of the most contentious political issues in the United States today. While politicians debate proposed immigration restrictions, people from all corners of the globe continue to come to this country looking for a better life. An informed understanding of this phenomenon requires an awareness of the reasons for migration and the connection between the choices individuals make to immigrate and larger economic conditions that reflect global markets.

As Arlie Russell Hochschild points out in "Love and Gold," immigration can create serious problems in the families people leave behind. Many destitute mothers in places such as the Philippines, Mexico, and Sri Lanka leave their children for long periods of time to work abroad because they cannot make ends meet at home. Ironically, the jobs these women typically take when they leave their families—nannies, maids, service workers—involve caring for and nurturing other people's families. So while migrant women provide much-needed income for their own families and valuable "care work" for their employers, they leave an emotional vacuum in their home countries. Hochschild asks us to consider the toll this phenomenon is taking on the children of these absent mothers. Not surprisingly, most of the women feel a profound sense of guilt and remorse that is largely invisible to the families they work for.

Something to Consider as You Read

Global or demographic perspectives are big-picture perspectives. As you read these selections, practice thinking about the ways that demographic and global processes may shape individual experiences and choices. For example, consider your personal networks. Do they show signs of age segregation? How has immigration affected your everyday life? Do you know the story of how your family arrived in this country? How many generations have they been here? Is there a substantial immigrant population in your hometown? How has their presence been received by others? How do your personal experiences with immigrants compare to the largely negative images that are often presented in the media? Beyond immigration, think about the ways in which big economic and political changes affect the choices individuals make. Now, add wealth and technology to the equation and consider which countries are going to be in the best position to adjust to these global changes. Who is going to be most affected, possibly even exploited, in this global adjustment?

Age-Segregation in Later Life
An Examination of Personal Networks

Peter Uhlenberg and Jenny de Jong Gierveld

(2004)

Introduction

Margaret Mead (1970) argued that in societies where change is slow and imperceptible, knowledge and culture are passed on from older generations to younger ones. In these traditional settings, she suggested, it is essential for older people to teach newcomers how to function in the society. In contrast, in modern societies where social and technological change is pervasive, it also is necessary for younger people to teach the old. If older people do not interact with and learn from younger people, they risk becoming increasingly excluded from contemporary social developments as they age through later life. Older people may not need or want to know everything that younger ones know, but acquiring some new knowledge is essential to avoid becoming marginalised in later life. The most common example of what the young can currently teach the old is how to use email and the Internet, but many other areas of new knowledge created by cultural change could be described. In either traditional or modern societies, therefore, age-integration is needed if all generations are to be productive participants in the society. Of course there are additional reasons why it would be mutually beneficial for older and younger people to interact with each other. Older people may have resources that could promote the well-being of younger people (and *vice versa*). The absence of interaction, or age-segregation, promotes ageism and insensitivity to the challenges faced by others who differ in age. In general, it seems likely that age-integration

promotes a more civil society. In this paper we take the perspective of older people and explore the level of their integration with, or segregation from, younger adults.

One way to examine the level of age-segregation of older people from younger ones in contemporary society is to examine the age-composition of personal social networks. How diverse are the ages of those with whom individuals interact most frequently and most significantly? Age-integration at the level of personal networks is relevant because network members play an important role in integrating individuals (of any age) into the larger society. Through network members, information and ideas are shared, new ways of thinking and living are discussed, and advice is exchanged. Network members exchange social, emotional, material and informational support that promotes well-being. Through networks individuals are recruited into social movements and organisations, which provide further opportunities for developing personal bonds (Marsden 1988; McPherson, Smith-Lovin and Cook 2001). Thus it is likely that older people whose personal networks lack younger members may be excluded from full participation in the society in which they live.

Forces Promoting Age Homophily in Networks

The social forces that have produced the institutionalisation and age-related stages of the life course over the past two centuries are also likely to have led to widespread age-segregation in social networks (Kohli 1988). Consider, for example, the structured social contexts from which network members might be drawn. A structured pattern of age-segregation begins early in life, for educational institutions use single years of age to group most children throughout childhood, while nurseries and day-care anticipate the age-homogeneity of the school environment from soon after birth. Sports and music for children are often tied to school, and result in age-segregated activities after school and on weekends. Churches imitate schools by establishing Sunday schools, where children are taught in age-homogeneous groups. Laws forbid children to participate in work settings. Specialised doctors see children; specialised therapists counsel and work with children; and special courts deal with children. The separation into homogeneous age groupings is further promoted by television, movies and other forms of entertainment that target children of particular ages. Quite similar institutional forces now largely segregate adolescents and young adults to age-homogeneous networks and activities (Lofland 1968). In these ways a culture that emphasises age-homogeneous groups is established early in life, so that one expects to find a deficit of older people in the personal networks of children and young adults, and *vice versa*. In somewhat similar ways, the age-segregated social institutions encountered by older people encourage age-homogeneity in personal networks through later life.

Work organisations tend to exclude people past age 60 or 65 years from a significant life activity, excluding them from one mechanism that promotes integration and some cross-age interactions with younger adults. Old people continue to be excluded from mainline educational settings (Hamil-Luker and Uhlenberg 2002). When efforts are made to involve older people in educational activities, they often operate from an age-segregationist principle, with separate programmes for old people. Many older people report that participating in church or other religious activity is their most significant social activity outside the family.

But in church people often are grouped on the basis of age for activities, so older churchgoers interact with other old people, and their social networks remain age-homogeneous. Participating in a senior centre or other age-restricted organisation may increase social activity and help expand social networks, but also reinforce age-segregated interactions. Similarly, nursing homes, retirement homes and retirement communities promote extreme age-segregation towards the end of life. In many ways, therefore, older people encounter a society that restricts opportunities for developing age-integrated personal social networks.

Although age-composition has seldom been the focus of studies of personal social networks, several report interesting findings on age homophily (and homogeneity) in networks. A recent review of the literature on homophily in social networks concludes that age consistently creates strong divisions in personal networks (McPherson et al. 2001). In his studies of Detroit men and Northern California residents, Fischer (1977, 1982) reported striking age-homogeneity in non-kin friendship networks. Indeed, 72 per cent of the close friends of the Detroit men were within eight years of their own ages. Similarly, Feld (1984), analysing the Northern California data, found that approximately half of all non-family associates with whom respondents were sociable or discussed problems were within five years of their age. In her analysis of friendship structure, Verbrugge (1977) reported that half of the friends identified by Detroit men occupied the same 10-year age category as the respondent, as did over 40 per cent of the friends of respondents in a German survey. And, as noted above, the GSS study of discussion-partner networks found most non-kin partners to be similar in age (Burt 1991; Marsden 1988). In general, studies have found age-homogeneity in non-kin networks across respondents of all ages, although it is stronger among younger than older people.

As already suggested, however, much less age-homogeneity is observed in kin networks (Burt 1991). This is not surprising, because older people often identify the relationships with their adult children, who tend to be 20 to 40 years younger than themselves, as very important. The 1988 *National Survey of Families and Households* showed that two-thirds of older women in the United States who had children visited a child at least once a week, and over 80 per cent had weekly contact with a child (Uhlenberg and Cooney 1990). Not only do inter-generational ties involve a high level of communication, but also these relationships are generally reported to be emotionally close and significant for instrumental support (for a review see Lye 1996). Furthermore, other kin (parents, aunts and uncles, siblings, cousins, grandchildren, and nieces and nephews) of diverse ages are frequently cited as significant network members. Thus one would expect the age-heterogeneity of personal networks to vary by the number of kin who are included in the network. The primary factor affecting the number of kin in a network is kinship composition. Other family-related events may affect how often older people include kin in their personal networks. In particular, partner status and partner history are relevant, e.g., adult children tend to intensify social interactions with a recently widowed parent who had been in a first marriage (Lopata 1996; Wolf, Freedman and Soldo 1997), and an earlier parental divorce reduces the likelihood that adult children interact frequently with their fathers in later life (Doherty, Kouneski and Erickson 1998; Dykstra 1998; Furstenberg, Hoffman and Shrestha 1995; Jong Gierveld and Dykstra 2002; Lye et al. 1995).

One would expect, of course, that the probability of a network including younger non-kin would increase with the total number of non-kin in the network. More interesting, it is likely that older people have more opportunities to recruit network members of diverse ages when they are active in social contexts that include younger adults. Therefore we anticipate that employed people are more likely than the retired to identify younger non-kin as network members. Similarly, attending church regularly or engaging in volunteer activities might promote greater age-integration, if these occur in age-heterogeneous contexts. The age-composition of the neighbourhood could also be a factor influencing the likelihood of interacting with younger adults. In addition to these structured settings for recruiting non-kin network members, current and past family context may also be relevant. Marital and partner status might be related to the size and intensity of non-kin network relationships. Older adults who are embedded in a large kinship circle, including a partner, children, children-in-law, grandchildren and siblings, need to invest a lot of time in maintaining these social and supportive relationships. In general, therefore, they have less time and energy than others to invest in a varied set of non-kin contacts (Dykstra 1995). Some widowed older adults who live without a partner may intensify contacts with their children, but others may revive latent bonds with others. The latter are to an extent building a new social network of people outside their own household that includes non-kin relationships. Indeed, success has been reported for a special training programme to support widowed older adults to begin new relationships (Stevens 2001). It is not yet known how age-heterogeneous the new relationships formed by widowed persons are.

Adults who divorce and remain without a partner may also compensate for the reduction in the size of the social networks. Personal contacts with new friends, with people 'in the same boat,' may be established in order to rebuild a social network. Those who never formed a partner union and the childless are however in a different position and do not experience the same transition. They often rely on siblings, friends, neighbours and other kin and acquaintances (such as colleagues and co-members of sport and hobby clubs) to maintain social participation and integration (Dykstra 1995). The never-married especially have been found to have a varied network of long-standing non-kin relationships (Wagner, Schütze and Lang 1999).

This interpretation of the literature on networks, kinship and ageing leads to several hypotheses. First, we expect that young adults are under-represented in the personal networks of older people. Second, that the presence of young adults in the personal networks of older people becomes increasingly rare at the more advanced ages. Third, it is expected that a disproportionate number of the younger network members of older people will be kin rather than non-kin. Fourth, the number of living children should be positively associated with having younger kin network members, but not with having younger non-kin network members. Fifth, the likelihood of having younger non-kin network members is higher for those who are employed, attend church, do volunteer work or live in age-integrated neighbourhoods. Sixth, the likelihood of having younger non-kin network members is higher for currently widowed and divorced older adults, who may have renewed and broadened their personal networks, than for those who are currently married, who tend to maintain their past couple-oriented social contacts. Seventh, the larger the number of friends, neighbours and other non-kin in an older person's network, the more likely that there will be young non-kin in the network.

As this study is exploratory, we also include in the analysis two variables of interest but without hypotheses of their effect, namely sex and the educational level of the respondent. One might expect older women from these Dutch cohorts to have less non-family social interaction than men, and hence to have less age diversity in their non-kin networks, but it is also possible that women possess superior social skills that allow them to bridge age barriers more easily than men. Higher levels of educational attainment are associated with higher levels of geographical mobility, so may reduce the breadth of network members that develop over time in a small community. But more education could also be associated with less ageism and greater acceptance of cross-age relationships.

Discussion

Despite the potentially significant implications, previous research has not examined the extent to which people in later life regularly interact with young adults. Using data from The Netherlands, this study has provided evidence on the extent to which older people have age-integrated or age-segregated personal social networks. Further, it has explored the factors associated with diversity in the age-composition of the networks of older people. Several interesting and provocative findings have emerged, and it is hoped that they will stimulate further research.

First, there clearly is a deficit of young adults in the networks of older people. People aged 55–64 years have significantly fewer young adult network members than would be expected if age were not a factor in selection, and the deficit grows even larger for people over the age of 65 years. For example, those aged 75–89 years had only about one-fifth of the number of network members aged less than 35 years that would be expected with complete age-integration. In fact, 68 per cent of the population older than 75 years did not identify any network member younger than 35 years of age.

Second, an overwhelming proportion of the younger network members identified by older people were kin. About 90 per cent of the network members aged less than 45 years old who were reported by people past age 65 years were kin, and a large majority of older people reported no non-kin less than 45 years of age in their networks. Most neighbours, friends and other non-kin associates of older people were old themselves. Thus the most crucial determinant of having younger network members is the size of the kin group, and especially the number of living children. Family building in the young adult phase of the life course turns out to be the major determinant of age-integrated or age-segregated personal networks in late life.

Third, although no segment of the older population appeared to be well integrated with younger adults outside of family relationships, several factors did increase the likelihood that an older person had some significant cross-age interactions. These included participation in organisations that had members of different ages (e.g., work and volunteer settings), and living in a neighbourhood with a high proportion of non-old adults. A plausible explanation for the significance of these factors is that a necessary condition for forming cross-age associations is the opportunity for meeting people of different ages. The failure of church activity to foster more age-heterogeneous relationships may be because church attendance in The Netherlands is much higher among older than younger age groups. In other words, churches may not be strongly age-integrated settings. It also may be that simply occupying common space is insufficient to promote the development of cross-age relationships. Relationships develop when structures promote mutual interaction around a meaningful activity, so while sitting side-by-side in a church service may have no effect, working together on a common project may be highly effective. Further, cultural norms are almost certainly important. When age differences are emphasised and age-stereotypes are prevalent, a significant barrier exists for forming friendships and close associations between young and old people.

Fourth, specific life course events, in particular divorce followed by living alone, increased the likelihood that an older person had some significant cross-age interactions with non-kin. Several studies have shown that shortly after divorce there tends to be a reduction in the number of personal relationships (DeGarmo and Kitson 1996). As time passes after a divorce, however, new relationships are formed. In this process of forming replacement relationships, there is an opportunity for younger non-kin to join the network.

Looking ahead, we anticipate two changes that could significantly increase the age-segregation of the personal networks of older people in The Netherlands. First is the ageing of the population, which will decrease the

relative supply of younger adults as potential network members and increase the relative supply of older ones. Around the time of the NESTOR survey, about 34 per cent of the population aged over 20 years was in the age group 20–35 years, while 17 per cent was aged 65 or more years. By 2050, these two percentages will be reversed—21 per cent of the adult population will be aged 20–35 years, and 33 per cent will be 65 or more years. The second and related change in future cohorts will be a significant decline in the average number of adult children. Because children are the major source of young adult network members, a decline in the number of children could have a large effect. Those aged 65 or more years in 1992 lived out their reproductive years when the Total Fertility Rate exceeded 3.0, but the cohorts entering old age in the near future will have completed family sizes of only about half that level. Further, the increasing prevalence of divorce in future cohorts entering old age may lead to a weakening of the tie between parent and adult child for an increasing proportion of older people (Cooney and Uhlenberg 1990; Dykstra 1998; Jong Gierveld and Peeters 2003). The increase in the number of younger non-kin that is associated with divorce is far smaller than the loss of children from the network. Thus, unless other changes occur, older people in the future are likely to have even less interaction with young adults than they currently do—and as shown above, current levels of interaction are extremely low.

This prospect provokes the question of what changes might divert a trend towards even greater age-segregation of older people. If, as argued in this paper, non-kin network members tend to be recruited from structured social contexts such as workplaces, volunteer settings, educational organisations and neighbourhoods, more attention might be given to increasing the involvement of older people in social structures that include people of various ages. This line of thinking leads directly to the issue of institutional age-segregation, as occurs when chronological age is used as a criterion for participation. Matilda Riley called attention to the structural lags in major social institutions which denied opportunities to healthy and skilled people reaching old age to engage productively in society (Riley, Kahn and Foner 1994). The institutions which are most clearly structured by age are schools and places of work, but the rules and practices of many others create age-group separation. Age is embedded in the formulation and implementation of many social welfare policies and programmes, e.g., nutrition, housing, protective services and recreation. Concerns related to the old often fall under different government programmes and offices than do matters related to children and youth (Hagestad 2002). Even academic disciplines (such as gerontology) tend to sustain separation by age. There is, however, some evidence that the use of chronological age to structure the life course may have peaked.

A recent tendency to break down structural age barriers has been noted in both work and education (Riley and Riley 2000). Retirement in the United States has recently become more flexible, allowing an increasing number of older people to participate in the labour force. The long trend towards earlier age at retirement stopped in the mid 1980s in the United States, and since then labour force participation rates among those aged 55 or more years have been gradually increasing (Clark and Quinn 2002). The long-discussed idea of lifelong learning may now be happening, as an increasing number of people in mid and later life learn alongside younger people (Davey 2002). There are interesting examples in the United States of breaking down the age barriers around schools and creating community learning-centres open to all ages (US Department of Education 2000). In academic programmes, traditional gerontological approaches are being challenged by a life course perspective that views ageing as a lifelong process. If, as suggested by these examples, institutional age-segregation is declining, opportunities for cross-age interaction should increase.

Related to institutional age-segregation is cultural age-segregation, as reflected in age stereotypes and ageist language. In addition to removing the barriers to cross-age interaction, a reduction in ageism and cultural age-stereotyping could facilitate age-integration. The prevalence of age-stereotypes in society hinders the formation of close non-kin relationships between older and younger people (Bytheway 1995; Hummert et al. 1994; Nelson 2002). There is of course some circularity in this association, because age-segregation is a root cause of age-stereotypes. Nevertheless, educational programmes and media efforts to combat ageist stereotypes and language might play a role in increasing understanding and empathy between disparate age groups. Similar efforts to reduce racism and sexism are generally considered to have produced positive results.

Attention is being given not only to ways of reducing structural and cultural barriers between older and younger people, but also to inter-generational programmes that purposely bring diverse ages together. In The Netherlands, a co-ordinated effort to bring older people into age-integrated settings is occurring through an inter-generational neighbourhood development programme at *The Netherlands Institute for Care and Welfare* (Penninx 1999). A notable initiative from this inter-generational programme has involved the Dutch Guilds that exist in about 90 municipalities. People who are aged 50 or more years and who are willing to share their knowledge and skills can form a guild that anyone can contact for assistance free of charge. A request for help, e.g., with car repair, tutoring in school, business advice or care for a disabled child, is referred to an appropriate guild member who then responds directly to the individual needing assistance. Through this matching process, older volunteers and younger people are brought together in a context that is likely to promote positive inter-generational interaction. Other inter-generational programmes described by Penninx include: children visiting older people living in age-segregated institutional settings, older people helping children in local schools, adolescent choreteams helping older neighbourhood residents with various household chores, and older people meeting with immigrant youth to promote their successful integration into Dutch society. Similar inter-generational programmes are developing in other countries. Careful evaluations of the various types of deliberate efforts to bridge age gaps would provide useful information on what structures actually facilitate age-integration.

REFERENCES

Burt, R. S. 1991. Measuring age as a structural concept. *Social Networks, 13,* 1–34.

Bytheway, B. 1995. *Ageism.* Open University Press, Buckingham.

Clark, R. L. and Quinn, J. F. 2002. Patterns of work and retirement for a new century. *Generations, 22,* 17–24.

Cooney, T. M. and Uhlenberg, P. 1990. The role of divorce in men's relations with their adult children after mid-life. *Journal of Marriage and the Family, 52,* 677–88.

Davey, J. A. 2002. Active aging and education in mid and later life. *Ageing & Society, 22,* 95–113.

DeGarmo, D. S. and Kitson, G. C. 1996. Identity relevance and disruption as predictors of psychological distress for widowed and divorced women. *Journal of Marriage and the Family, 58,* 983–97.

Doherty, W. J., Kouneski, E. F. and Erickson, M. F. 1998. Responsible fathering: an overview and conceptual framework. *Journal of Marriage and the Family, 60,* 277–92.

Dykstra, P. A. 1995. Network composition. In C. P. M. Knipscheer, J. de Jong Gierveld, T. G. van Tilburg and P. A. Dykstra (eds), *Living Arrangements and Social Networks of Older Adults.* VU University Press, Amsterdam, 97–114.

Dykstra, P. A. 1998. The effects of divorce on intergenerational exchanges in families. *The Netherlands Journal of Social Sciences, 33,* 77–93.

Feld, S. L. 1984. The structured use of personal associates. *Social Forces, 62,* 640–52.

Fischer, C. S. 1977. *Networks and Places: Social Relations in the Urban Setting.* Free Press, New York.

Fischer, C. S. 1982. *To Dwell Among Friends: Personal Networks in Town and City.* University of Chicago Press, Chicago.

Furstenberg, F. F. Jr., Hoffman, S. D. and Shrestha, L. 1995. The effect of divorce on intergenerational transfers: new evidence. *Demography, 32,* 319–33.

Hagestad, G. O. 2002. Personal communication.

Hamil-Luker, J. and Uhlenberg, P. 2002. Later life education in the 1990s: increasing involvement and continuing disparity. *Journal of Gerontology: Social Sciences, 57B,* S324–31.

Hummert, M. L., Garsta, T. A., Shaner, J. L. and Strahm, S. 1994. Stereotypes of the elderly held by young, middle-aged, and elderly adults. *Journal of Gerontology: Psychological Sciences, 49,* P240–9.

Jong Gierveld, J. de and Dykstra, P. A. 2002. The long-term rewards of parenting: older adults' marital history and the likelihood of receiving support from adult children. *Ageing International, 27,* 49–69.

Jong Gierveld, J. de and Peeters, A. 2003. The interweaving of repartnered older adults' lives with their children and siblings. *Ageing & Society, 22,* 1–19.

Kohli, M. L. 1988. Social organization and subjective construction of the life course. In A. B. Sorensen, F. E. Weiner and L. R. Sherrod (eds), *Human Development and the Life Cycle.* Erlbaum, Hillsdale, New Jersey, 271–92.

Lofland, J. 1968. The youth ghetto. *Journal of Higher Education, 39,* 121–43.

Lopata, H. Z. 1996. *Current Widowhood: Myths and Realities.* Sage, Thousand Oaks, California.

Lye, D. N. 1996. Adult child-parent relationships. *Annual Review of Sociology, 22,* 79–102.

Lye, D. N., Klepinger, D. H., Hyle, P. D. and Nelson, A. 1995. Childhood living arrangements and adult children's relations with their parents. *Demography, 32,* 261–80.

Marsden, P. V. 1988. Homogeneity in confiding relationships. *Social Networks, 10,* 57–76.

McPherson, M., Smith-Lovin, L. and Cook, J. M. 2001. Birds of a feather: homophily in social networks. *Annual Review of Sociology, 27,* 415–44.

Mead, M. 1970. *Culture and Commitment: A Study of the Generation Gap.* Natural History Press, Garden City, New York.

Nelson, T. D. (ed) 2002. *Ageism, Stereotyping and Prejudice against Older Persons.* MIT Press, Cambridge, Massachusetts.

Penninx, K. 1999. *DeBuurt voor Alle Leeftijden [The Neighbourhood of All Ages].* NIZW Uitgeverij, Utrecht, The Netherlands.

Riley, M. W. and Riley, J. W. Jr. 2000. Age-integration: conceptual and historical background. *The Gerontologist, 40,* 266–70.

Riley, M. W., Kahn, R. L. and Foner, A. 1994. *Age and Structural Lag: Society's Failure to Provide Meaningful Opportunities in Work, Family, and Leisure.* Wiley, New York.

Stevens, N. 2001. Combating loneliness: a friendship enrichment programme for older women. *Ageing & Society, 21,* 183–202.

Uhlenberg, P. and Cooney, T. M. 1990. Family size and mother-child relations in later life. *The Gerontologist, 30,* 618–25.

US Department of Education 2000. *Schools as Centers of Community: A Citizen's Guide for Planning and Design.* US Department of Education, Washington, DC.

Verbrugge, L. M. 1977. The structure of adult friendship choices. *Social Forces, 56,* 576–97.

Wagner, M., Schütze, Y. and Lang, F. R. 1999. Social relationships in old age. In P. B. Baltes and K. U. Mayer (eds), *The Berlin Aging Study: Aging from 70 to 100.* Cambridge University Press, Cambridge, 282–301.

Wolf, D. A., Freedman, V. and Soldo, B. J. 1997. The division of family labor: care for elderly parents. *The Journals of Gerontology, 52B,* special issue, 102–9.

THINKING ABOUT THE READING

What is age segregation? According to the authors, what are some of the reasons for age segregation? What are some of the everyday consequences of age segregation? Draw a diagram of your personal networks (e.g., the people you see daily, people you spend holidays with, people you work with) What is the age range of the people in your networks? How many older people do you know who are not your relatives? This reading uses information from a study of Dutch people. How would the findings compare to other cultures? In which social settings would you expect to find the *least* age segregation?

Accessing Assets

Immigrant Youth's Work as Family Translators or "Para-Phrasers"

Marjorie Faulstich Orellana, Lisa Dorner, and Lucila Pulido

(2003)

We begin with Lucila's words as she shares her perspective as a member of our research group as well as the daughter of immigrants from Mexico to Chicago:

> As we're writing this article I look back and remember that before I became involved in this project, I didn't think of translating as something special. To me it was just an everyday part of life. As a kid I translated phone calls, TV shows, bills, letters from the welfare department, visits to the doctor, visits with social workers, interviews; and I filled out applications for health care, welfare, and social security benefits. I did this because I was the only one who could do it. I was the only one in my family who could communicate in both English and Spanish. I became the key to accessing the resources my family needed. As we learn more about the translating experiences of our case study children I realize how many of those experiences are similar to mine. I've come to see what an important and necessary role these children play in the well-being of their families. Whether it'd be filling out an application to receive welfare benefits or telling the doctor what was wrong with my mom, today I realize how my help as a child translator significantly contributed to the survival of my family.

In this article, we draw on a program of mixed-method research in several different immigrant communities to examine how the children of immigrants use their bilingual and bicultural skills to access resources for their families. Influenced by sociologists of childhood who remind us that children are social actors in their own right, we aim to bring new perspectives to the following issues: How do immigrants deal with the challenges of daily life in a new country? How do their children help them access resources, knowledge, and information from the social world outside their homes, and what is the nature of this help?

Para-Phrasing

Invoking a play on the Spanish word "para," we have coined the term "para-phrasing" to signify the various ways in which children use their knowledge of the English language and of U.S. cultural traditions to speak *for* others and *in order to* accomplish social goals. We believe this term emphasizes that what children do is purposeful; they are taking action in the world, not simply moving words and ideas or explicating concepts. At the same time, as with the term "para-professional," para-phrasers may act in capacities for which they have no formal preparation and in which their qualifications are open to question and critique. We examine how such para-phrasing by youth helps immigrant families access knowledge, information, and resources that aid in their settlement.

Methods

This exploration of children's contributions to immigrant households is one part of a larger, multi-method program of research on immigrant childhoods developed in four different communities over the past five years. Our work started with an ethnographic study of families' daily language practices in central Los Angeles, California (see Orellana 2001), a "first-stop" community for immigrants from Mexico and

Central America. Our second community is an ethnic enclave with a long history of Mexican immigration on the southwest side of Chicago, Illinois. The next community currently under study is a more settled one, also in Chicago. In this "second-stop" neighborhood, which we call Regan, we have been working with case study families who have lived in the United States from ten to over twenty years. The large public elementary school in the area is approximately 75 percent Latino (mostly Mexican, from the states of Guanajuato and Michoacán) and 25 percent Polish. Finally, we draw from another on-going ethnographic study of immigrant children and families in Engleville, Illinois, an urban/suburban, mixed-ethnic, mixed-income community near Chicago that has a small but growing population of more recent Mexican immigrants, mostly from the state of Guanajuato.

Gathering data in these various receiving contexts for immigrants has helped us to consider how community institutions shape the needs and opportunities for children to assist their families in connecting to resources outside the home. Through interviews and focus groups with children, parents, and teachers from these neighborhoods, as well as participant observation in the homes and classrooms of 18 case study children, we have been exploring the social processes involved when the children of immigrants act as language and cultural brokers.

Accessing Assets

We begin by presenting results from our domain analyses of the observational, interview, and journal data. These reveal the wide range of ways in which children para-phrase for their families, as well as the varied societal and institutional domains with which they contend. Table 1 gives an overview of some of the specific ways in which children's work helps families to access educational, medical/health, commercial, legal/state, financial/employment, housing/residential, and cultural/entertainment resources, knowledge, and information.

Specialized Encounters and Everyday Ways

When we have presented our work to audiences of teachers, parents, and researchers, people have often voiced concern about the burdens and responsibilities that youth assume through this work. Heightened, marked, dramatic, or "specialized encounters" that may indeed be experienced as burdensome—for example, translating for a parent during a medical exam or at the INS (Immigration and Naturalization Service) office—have received considerable attention in the popular press. Certainly, these encounters with medical, legal, and other institutions make especially visible the role that children play in connecting their families to crucial resources and services. But through our inductive analyses and exploration of survey results, we came to understand that children open up access to resources in multiple, quotidian ways, and that they experience much of their translating work as "just normal." The following excerpts from participants' journals illustrate this juxtaposition of more or less specialized encounters and the more common, everyday para-phrasing efforts of immigrant youth in several domains.

(Everyday; educational/entertainment)

> Today, my dad, my mom and I were watching a movie about babies and how to help them be healthy kids. They mentioned something about two twins that each drew a picture. One drew the picture nice and the other one drew the picture sloppy. The twin that drew the picture nice didn't have any difficulties at birth but in [sic] the other hand the other baby who drew the sloppy picture did have difficulties. My mom didn't understand what they meant. So I translated for her. (Jessica)

(Specialized, legal/state)

> In June 16, 2002, I translated for my mom to the Police. Someone stole(d) her necklaces in the street. So I called the police and describe(d) the man and told my mom what they said. I felt

Table 1 Domains of Para-Phrasing

Educational	Medical/Health	Commercial
• Translate at parent-teacher conferences for themselves and/or siblings, cousins, friends • Visit and evaluate pre-schools for younger siblings • Locate, participate in, and help parents study for their ESL classes • Translate between staff members/teachers and other parents or community members (at random moments, in the hallway, in the classroom, etc.) • Call schools to report their own or siblings' absences • Interpret letters about dress codes/school programs, invitations to apply for programs or other schools, report cards and interim grade reports, consent and field trip forms, notes from teachers, and telephone calls from school staff • Help siblings with homework from school or Sunday school religious course • Translate at community service center that provides ESL, tutoring for kids, babysitting	• Fill out report/give insurance information in emergency room • Translate at doctor's and dentist's offices during family visits • Fill prescriptions at pharmacy • Answer or make phone calls to doctors regarding family treatment • Make appointments or cancel appointments with doctors, dentists • Interpret instructions for medicine, vitamins, other health-care products • Interpret letters asking permission to transfer medical records; appointment reminder cards; information from WIC regarding proper nutrition • Translate details during own and others' operations at hospital	• Shop for or with parents at pharmacies and drug, grocery, home improvement, pet, and computer stores (e.g., BestBuy, Walgreens, Home Depot, Wal-Mart, Mega Mall, etc.) • Complete refund transactions, settle disputes and check for mistakes in sales transactions • Interpret receipts, ads, product labels • Answer phone calls from solicitors and market researchers • Order such services as DirectTV, CallerID, voicemail • Sign for delivered packages • Fill out rental applications (e.g., for musical instrument) • Shop for and buy new homes, cars, etc.

Cultural/ Entertainment	Legal/State	Financial/Employment	Housing/ Residential
• Go to movies, translate plot and dialogue • Obtain discounts at movie theaters • Buy computer games • Interpret at "Six Flags" amusement park • Interpret TV shows, newspapers at home	• Fill out police reports regarding disturbances in neighborhood or home, robberies, etc. • Translate a witness account about a fight at school to guard/police • Call insurance company regarding car damage, car accident • Interpret phone calls and door-to-door sales visits from insurance company representatives	• Cash or deposit checks at the bank or currency exchange • Open bank accounts • Interpret and pay bills • Obtain credit cards • Interpret informational letters from banks and insurance companies, bank statements, and mortgage payment year-end summaries	• Translate between parents and landlords; parents and tenants • Interpret flyers or notices regarding rental property • Talk to managers regarding things broken in apartment

(Continued)

Table 1 (Continued)

Cultural/ Entertainment	Legal/State	Financial/Employment	Housing/ Residential
• Read and translate stories, self-help guides, song lyrics, instructional manuals (for games, videogames, computers and other electronic devices) and jokes for families • Interpret letters about community events (e.g., at church) • Read and interpret letters or e-mail from family • Obtain library card/take books out of library	• Interpret letters from Social Security Office • Obtain welfare or social security by accompanying parents to office, answering questions, etc. • Fill out applications for WIC or welfare • Interpret letters from WIC • Help parents study for citizenship exams • Help to renew MICA, parents' green cards, at INS office • Interpret letters from Congress, representatives, voting materials • Decipher jury summons and other mail from the state • Translate public thank you note/speech for firefighters after 9/11	• Translate financial interactions between parents and tenants • Translate for parents at parent's place of work • Call in sick for parents • Help parents fill out applications for work or for unemployment benefits • Coordinate rides to work for parents • Help with fax machine for contracting work at home • Call to inquire about jobs • Translate between people at their own (kids') work (e.g., golfers and gardeners at a golf course)	• Help to settle rent disputes • Communicate with neighbors (regarding home, property concerns such as leaky gutters)

nervous and I was crying; it was very hard to translate in such a moment. (Amanda)

(Everyday, financial)

Well, I translate to my mom of bills because she do(es)n't understand English that much. We take like an hour. But (it) is worth it cause she learns a lot of stuff. (Monique)

(Specialized, medical)

When I was about 8–9 years old we went to the doctor because my baby brother was 1 month or so. He had to go for a check up and a doctor told (asked) my mom if she was going to give my baby brother milk from he(r) breast, but I did not know what breast meant. So I told the doctor if she could explain what breast meant. She was nice and kind and

said yes of course. She touched her breast and (I) told my mom what the doctor was saying. As far as I can remember this was the scariest translating thing I (had) ever done. I did not translate things that much this week but I did work (a) long time ago translating stuff. Well, I felt so nervous to translate for the doctor because I thought I would not be able to understand the big words doctors use. (Jasmine)

(Specialized, employment; Everyday, commercial)

Today I went to my mom's work. I helped her with her boss because she didn't know what he was saying; she does know, but not that well, so I helped my mom in her work. Then later my dad took me to Home Depot, and he told me to tell the cashier that she marked a thing wrong and I told her. Then she told us I am sorry and my dad told me to tell her that's okay. (Jacqueline)

Educational Domain. The greatest number of observed and reported para-phrasing encounters involve interactions with schools, teachers, or school materials (as also reported by McQuillan and Tse 1995 and Tse 1996). Many of these are "everyday" encounters, including a barrage of written texts that are sent home from school in children's back-packs. The youth in our study help their siblings with homework; assist their parents with ESL homework and to study for citizenship classes; and interpret school materials, report cards, and other informational materials.

Across sites, when children are officially enrolled in a bilingual program, they receive school information in Spanish. But when they exit these bilingual programs, much school information goes home in English only—an institutional practice that seems to confuse the abilities of *families* with those of students, or which simply relies on children's ability to provide the translations. In some cases teachers offer kids a choice of Spanish or English; some of the youth we talked with indicated that if they are given a choice, they will take papers in English, perhaps because of the social stigma attached to "needing" Spanish. In these cases, children have the power to *choose* a linguistic identity, yet their choices (which are influenced by the social prestige value of each language) may leave parents with only indirect access to information about their child's school.

More specialized incidents include translating during parent-teacher conferences, their own as well as those of their siblings. How these transpire varies across schools, classrooms, and grade levels, but in all audiotaped cases (15 conferences), children play pivotal roles not simply in translating *words,* but in interpreting school practices. Children also help their families make decisions about school activities, such as whether siblings should be allowed on specific field trips or to join particular activities, and whether or how teachers should be contacted about particular concerns. Eleven-year-old Jasmine, for example, accompanied her mother as she checked out various pre-schools for Jasmine's brother; she was on hand to translate as well as to weigh in on the school selection decisions.

There was variation across teachers and schools in the tenor of these family-school encounters, but most were non-confrontational and did not appear to be highly charged with power dynamics. Families have numerous opportunities to engage with teachers and schools (though not, perhaps, as much as some educators would recommend), such that any single encounter may not have great consequences for participants. However, the cumulative effect of translator-mediated interactions between immigrant families and schools may be highly consequential for shaping the pathways that the youth and their siblings are able to access. Two of the four adult para-phrasers who were interviewed remembered feeling responsible for shaping their siblings' educational trajectories based on how they had translated during parent-teacher conferences. In one case, the girl's sister was held back a grade. Like Jasmine helping to choose preschools, these youth may have felt empowered *within* the family while taking part in family decision-making, but the families' relationship with school officials may remain unbalanced, and that imbalance may leave children feeling *responsible* for decisions that adults make. Marina remembers:

When I came home, I cried because I felt really bad that they were holding my sister back. I felt bad that I couldn't understand why, that I couldn't explain to the teacher to tell me that my mom wanted to know why. And 'til this day, we really don't know what happened. Because, my sister was not a horrible student, so my mom's convinced that we misunderstood something in the process. Because I'm sure summer school would've been an option for her. And I feel really guilty about it. I do, because I feel like I'm, either I missed something that I didn't articulate to my mom that this nun said. Or, I just didn't get my mom's point across very clearly to her. Because,

I mean, I know summer school would've been an option. I knew kids in my class who were going to summer school.

Medical/Health. The encounters with medical/health domains that we have listed in Table 1 similarly include an array of everyday translations, done as part of everyday life at home (e.g., translating medical labels, instructions for hair care products, and television health programs). More specialized encounters include scheduling and attending routine and non-routine doctor, dentist, and hospital visits, and accompanying family members on trips to the emergency room or for preparations for surgery. Amanda wrote about going with her mother to the hospital when her brother cut himself with a knife: "I was so so nervous. I could almost (not) talk, but I did it." Sammy took charge for himself and his mother during his own hand surgery, including researching information about the surgery on the Internet beforehand. This made him an active participant in his own medical care.

We observed several more routine visits to doctors, and saw as with the school translations, children do much more than move words and ideas between speakers; they are active participants in the presentation of health information and in families' health-related decisions, asking and answering questions, not simply animating their parents' words. Lucila remembers: "I used to have to translate for my mom at the doctor's office so much that it came to the point where the doctor would only talk to me. He wouldn't even look at my mom. Instead he would ask me for updates and symptoms. Afterwards he would give me his recommendations and had me choose what the best options would be for my mom. Often I had to interrupt him to explain what had been going on with my mom and to ask her what she thought, but I must admit that sometimes I made choices for her without asking her first." At the same time, our observations reveal that even when parents do not participate directly in conversational exchanges, they generally track conversations; sometimes their input into medical decisions is made in private conversations with their children, not in the interpretation moments.

Commercial. Many items that families need for daily life are located outside the home, and so parents often enlist their children's help when they go shopping. As Beatríz noted, "my mother has never gone anywhere alone." This is especially true in mixed-ethnic communities, such as Engleville, in contrast with our other sites, where basic items can be secured without interacting with English-speakers. But even in ethnic enclaves, some goods and services cannot be secured from local Spanish-speaking vendors or service providers. Children's interpretation efforts may make a difference in families' willingness to seek out specialized goods and services, such as when Carmen helped her uncle to buy a car, when Estela tried to help her father rent a musical instrument to play in a band, or when Nova helped his family to purchase a computer.

Purchasing and using technology seems to be a domain where children—immigrants and non-immigrants—sometimes exercise power within the family. Yet, the power dynamics within the household are complicated, probably shaped by both gender and age relations. Nova's parents bought the computer principally *for* him and *at his insistence.* While he has helped his family to access the Internet and make use of such technology, he has also constrained their access; the computer is set up in Nova's room, and his eight-year-old sister told us that she rarely gets to use it. We saw this in several other case study families as well, where children's work as interpreters overlapped with their roles as "technology experts," experts who may both facilitate and constrain different family members' use of their computers.

In everyday kinds of commercial translations, children sometimes serve as animators of their parents' words, but more often, they are sent by parents to make inquiries or complete sales transactions on their own. They also assist parents by reading labels and signs, filling out credit applications, checking receipts, cross-checking sales advertisements with prices, and registering complaints about merchandise. At home, they read sales circulars, compare the prices of different products, deal with telemarketers, and help families make decisions about the purchase of items and services, such as long distance phone service.

In commercial transactions in the public sphere, families are consumers, presumably with the rights, power, and privileges of the same. It might seem that such situations would not be particularly burdensome, emotionally laden, or infused with power dynamics. However, several participants in our study recalled shopping expeditions with their parents as moments of embarrassment, humiliation, or shame. Seemingly this is because their identities as poor, working-class or immigrant families were made salient and exposed for public judgment; we see hints of this in Miguel's journal, after he accompanied his father back to the store to obtain a missing part to their newly purchased bunk bed and they were told to "wake up a little": "Today me and my dad went to buy a bunk bed; we got the bunk bed but it was missing a part. We went back to the place again and they told my dad that if top was ready, [sic], it isn't fixed. My dad got angry at him because he told us to wake up a little."

Further hints are evident in Beatríz's recollection of embarrassment when her mother asked many questions while shopping for gloves at a department store: "I thought she was being a nuisance, and I thought, 'I don't want this lady to think this way about my mom.' I saw it as protecting her image." Beatríz also talked about a time when she was sent by her mother to buy cheese at a local supermarket. There, she interpreted a grocer's question about her cheese selections as an interrogation of her ethnicity:

> My mother has never gone to Jewel or Dominick's by herself. She has always gone with someone who can translate for her. I often and still order her cheese and ham from the deli. I recall a mis-communication situation that made my mother upset and made me feel very embarrassed. I was about seven years old. My mother and I were at Jewels. My mother told me

to stand in line while she shopped for other items and order a pound of American cheese from the deli. After about fifteen minutes of waiting my turn, the woman behind the counter asked for my order and I told her that I wanted a pound of cheese. The woman then said, "American, Italian, Swiss . . ." I thought she was asking for my nationality. I responded by saying, "Mexican." In a frustrated tone of voice, she told me that they did not have any Mexican cheese.

Legal/State. In encounters with state and legal institutions, immigrant and social class status may be even more marked. And while some encounters that we have categorized in this domain take place in everyday sorts of ways when societal institutions enter into the home (e.g., translating letters from state officials or election materials), most are deliberate, heightened encounters with authority figures, with very real consequences for families. They include negotiations for citizenship and legal residence, welfare, Women, Infant, and Children (WIC) and social security benefits. The bureaucrats who manage these institutions may view their clients in condescending, paternalistic, and/or confrontational ways, and place the burden of communicating their needs on the clients. Lucila described helping her mother apply for welfare benefits: "It's like ten different things, and they check which ones you need to bring. It would be utility bills and this and this and that, and then your social security card, your birth record, and all these things. . . ."

Through their translations, children partly construct their parents' images vis-à-vis these authority figures. As well, during these interactions, they are potentially witnesses to their parents' humiliation, infantilization, and mistreatment. Lucila recalls the treatment her mother received from a social worker, and the complaint that she registered on behalf of her mother. In this outer sphere encounter, Lucila finds she lacks the power to speak and be heard as an adult, in order to fully express the frustration that she and her mother felt:

> I remember that day and I remember the tension I felt as I listened to my mom angrily

complain about the lady, and the pressure I felt to translate "properly." I didn't know what to say. I wanted the complaint to sound like it came from a grown-up, my mother, but I also wanted to stress how rude (the lady) was, writing that she was very impatient with our situation and that my mom felt very uncomfortable with her and that it was really hard for her to express herself and to understand the lady.

Despite the inadequacies that Lucila *felt* in this situation, however, her willingness to step into the "adult" role and voice this complaint paid off; her mother was assigned a new case worker.

In interactions with institutions that have great power over families' well-being, especially state/legal institutions, children sometimes help their families not by *accessing* information as much as by *withholding* access from others. Elisa reveals this type of discretion, vis-à-vis the research team, when she writes: "Today I translated for my sister a paper but I can't say what was on the paper because it was private"; and more than one student responded to questions about their family on the survey with "I don't want to give you this information." This points to the power inherent in the researcher-researched relationship, but also to children's skills at asserting their own power to resist scrutiny of their families by those who have more societal power than they. When Marjorie asked a group of children if they are ever put in situations where they have to answer questions they don't want to answer, Jocelyn recalled the kinds of questions she has had to answer for her mother, presumably (unstated) to legal/state institutions: "O, ¿cómo (a) cuantos años tuvo a los niños? Por que mi mamá me tuvo bien joven . . . como mi mamá dejo la escuela . . . van a decir que, que para tener un hijo, mejor que se espere más por que va a dejar la escuela." ("Oh, like how old she was when she had kids? Because my mom had me when she was young. Because, since my mom left school . . . they're going to say what, like to have a baby, it would have been better if she had stayed in school.") By not answering such

questions, Jocelyn asserts her power in the outer sphere and protects her mother from critique of her personal life; in describing this to the researcher, she displays her awareness of the judgments that others may make of her mother's choices.

An interesting example that we classified in this category is one that involved Miguel and Nova's mothers, working with a group of neighbors to present a letter of support to firefighters at the local fire station as a response to the World Trade Center attack on September 11, 2001. Certainly, interactions with state services do not have to be heightened, emotional incidents, nor ones where children feel they must shield their families from intrusive institutions. In this case, the youth did not so much access a particular resource in the community for their families, as help to make a personal connection with the fire department, something that may enhance their sense of their own power to access help from such resources in the future.

Financial/Employment. Our decision to combine financial transactions with those specifically related to families' employment in the paid labor force serves to highlight the involvement of our participants in their household economies. Indeed, many of the children we worked with seemed both aware of and well-versed in their family finances. They acquire this knowledge by interpreting bills, helping families decide which bills to pay each month when money is tight, writing checks, reviewing receipts and statements, and mediating transactions in banks.

Most of the examples that we have classified in the "employment" side of this category may seem like relatively specialized encounters to readers, perhaps because in modern U.S. society children's activities are centered in and around schools, not the workplace, but the children who reported these experiences did not necessarily talk about them as unusual. Reported and observed examples include accompanying parents to work where they interpret their parents' words for their bosses and/or co-workers (especially when parents work as domestic laborers or gardeners in private homes), helping parents fill out job applications, making phone inquiries regarding employment possibilities, and assisting with home businesses. In two households, this involves sending and receiving faxed orders, and making phone calls. Two children also talked about calling in to their parents' work to report absences, an interesting reversal of traditional parent-child authority relations vis-à-vis outside institutions. Lucila remembers the complex financial matters she took on:

> I helped my parents fill out job, credit card, and social security applications and income tax forms. I also helped them look for subsidized resources, make major purchases such as domestic appliances, and manage their bank accounts. Not only did I do this for my parents, but I also helped out their friends and other family members in applying for credit or employment.

Housing/Residential. Most of the examples that we have classified as "housing/residential" involve interactions between tenants and landlords or apartment building managers. In one case, a girl whose family owns their own home reported translating for a neighbor who pointed out that their gutter was leaking onto his property. (The girl inquired into the matter and learned "how expensive" gutters are.) In another case, Sammy translates on a regular basis for his mother, who *is* the apartment manager and needs to communicate with tenants who do not speak Spanish. Undoubtedly, families' class positions as tenants, landlords, or homeowners color these translation experiences. It is difficult to discern how children understand social class relations in these reported encounters, and none were directly observed. However, in a journal entry about an interaction with his landlord, Miguel first claims he felt "really good" (a seemingly formulaic response to our request to describe how he felt in translation situations), but then adds a sentence: "And upset because we really don't use (too much) water." He aligns himself with his family, as "we," in their dealings with the

"guy who owns the building," who has the power of surveillance over the family's consumption patterns:

> Today a guy who owns the building came to check the bathroom. Because the water bill came too high, he came to check if there were any leaks. I translated what was happening. I translated to my mom. I felt really good. And upset because we really don't use water.

Cultural/Entertainment. Many of the recorded/observed translations that we have classified as cultural/entertainment took place in the privacy of families' homes, involving only "inner-sphere" participants in the interactions. These were translations of movies, television shows, and radio broadcasts. In these situations, the "outer sphere" enters the home only in the third person, in voices that can be turned on or off at will, and which require no direct response. Through their translations, however, children help their families go beneath the surface of these programs and access deeper understandings. As Miguel describes in his journal:

> Today I translated a part that a guy said in a movie to my dad. It was Independence Day. A black guy told the president that he could ride the spaceship because he knows how to ride almost anything. I felt kind of good because my dad was really paying attention, not just watching the killing.

A few of the events that we have classified as "entertainment" take place outside the home, however, and some do involve interactions with non-intimates (e.g., purchasing tickets for movies and other events). But this work of translating generally took place within the context of fun, in the spirit of group outings, and in situations in which families' working-class, immigrant positions were not particularly marked. For the most part, kids seemed to take their translating work in these situations in stride. Katrina wrote about a family trip to an amusement park: "I was translating and helping people and it was fun."

Conclusion

In this article, we have mapped the domains of immigrant children's para-phrasing experiences in order to demonstrate the wide range of ways in which they help their families to access resources in their new society. We have illustrated how children's everyday and "specialized" para-phrasing helps their families with educational, medical, commercial, state/legal, financial/employment, housing/residential, and cultural institutions. Their efforts have both immediate and long-term effects; and they help their families to access specific resources, knowledge, and information even as they also play a role in *protecting* families from incursions of the outer sphere into their homes and personal lives.

Appendix Study Participants Referenced

Name	Age	Site	Research Method
Amanda	12	Regan	Case Study
Carmen	10	Los Angeles	Interview
Elisa	10	Los Angeles	Interview
Estela	11	Engleville	Interview
Jacqueline	11	Regan	Case Study
Jasmine	11	Regan	Case Study
Jessica	13	Regan	Case Study
Jocelyn	10	Los Angeles	Interview
Katrina	11	Regan	Case Study
Miguel	13	Engleville	Case Study
Monique	12	Regan	Case Study
Nova	14	Engleville	Case Study
Sammy	15	Chicago Area	Case Study
Beatríz	33	Chicago Area	Interview
Lucila	21	Chicago Area	Interview + Co-author
Marina	20	Chicago Area	Interview

References

McQuillan, Jeff and Lucy Tse. 1995. "Child Language Brokering in Linguistic Minority Communities: Effects on Culture, Cognition, and Literacy." *Language and Education* 9:195–215.

Orellana, Marjorie Faulstich. 2001. "The Work Kids Do: Mexican and Central American Immigrant Children's Contributions to Households and Schools in California." *Harvard Educational Review* 71:366–89.

Tse, Lucy. 1996. "Who Decides?": The Effect of Language Brokering on Home-School Communication." *The Journal of Educational Issues of Language Minority Students* 16: 225–33.

THINKING ABOUT THE READING

The authors provide extensive examples of translating activities that immigrant youth do for non-English-speaking family members. What aspects of this reading surprised you? Consider some of the implications of children as "cultural mediators." What impact might this activity have on the typical authority structure of parent-child relationships? What impact might it have on the ways in which immigrant youth understand the cultural backgrounds of their parents and grandparents?

Love and Gold

Arlie Russell Hochschild

(2002)

Whether they know it or not, Clinton and Princela Bautista, two children growing up in a small town in the Philippines apart from their two migrant parents, are the recipients of an international pledge. It says that a child "should grow up in a family environment, in an atmosphere of happiness, love, and understanding," and "not be separated from his or her parents against their will . . . " Part of Article 9 of the United Nations Declaration on the Rights of the Child (1959), these words stand now as a fairy-tale ideal, the promise of a shield between children and the costs of globalization.

At the moment this shield is not protecting the Bautista family from those human costs. In the basement bedroom of her employer's home in Washington, D.C., Rowena Bautista keeps four pictures on her dresser: two of her own children, back in Camiling, a Philippine farming village, and two of her children she has cared for as a nanny in the United States. The pictures of her own children, Clinton and Princela, are from five years ago. As she recently told *Wall Street Journal* reporter Robert Frank, the recent photos "remind me how much I've missed." She has missed the last two Christmases, and on her last visit home, her son Clinton, now eight, refused to touch his mother. "Why," he asked, "did you come back?"

The daughter of a teacher and an engineer, Rowena Bautista worked three years toward an engineering degree before she quit and went abroad for work and adventure. A few years later, during her travels, she fell in love with a Ghanaian construction worker, had two children with him, and returned to the Philippines with them. Unable to find a job in the Philippines, the father of her children went to Korea in search of work and, over time, he faded from his children's lives.

Rowena again traveled north, joining the growing ranks of Third World mothers who work abroad for long periods of time because they cannot make ends meet at home. She left her children with her mother, hired a nanny to help out at home, and flew to Washington, D.C., where she took a job as a nanny for the same pay that a small-town doctor would make in the Philippines. Of the 792,000 legal household workers in the United States, 40 percent were born abroad, like Rowena. Of Filipino migrants, 70 percent, like Rowena, are women.

Rowena calls Noa, the American child she tends, "my baby." One of Noa's first words was "Ena," short for Rowena. And Noa has started babbling in Tagalog, the language Rowena spoke in the Philippines. Rowena lifts Noa from her crib mornings at 7:00 A.M., takes her to the library, pushes her on the swing at the playground, and curls up with her for naps. As Rowena explained to Frank, "I give Noa what I can't give to my children." In turn, the American child gives Rowena what she doesn't get at home. As Rowena puts it, "She makes me feel like a mother."

Rowena's own children live in a four-bedroom house with her parents and twelve other family members—eight of them children, some of whom also have mothers who work abroad. The central figure in the children's lives—the person they call "Mama"—is Grandma, Rowena's mother. But Grandma works surprisingly long hours as a teacher—from 7:00 A.M. to 9:00 P.M.

As Rowena tells her story to Frank, she says little about her father, the children's grandfather (men are discouraged from participating actively in child rearing in the Philippines). And Rowena's father is not much involved with his grandchildren. So, she has hired Anna de la Cruz, who arrives daily at 8:00 A.M. to cook, clean, and care for the children. Meanwhile, Anna de la Cruz leaves her teenage son in the care of her eighty-year-old mother-in-law.

Rowena's life reflects an important and growing global trend: the importation of care and love from poor countries to rich ones. For some time now, promising and highly trained professionals have been moving from ill-equipped hospitals, impoverished schools, antiquated banks, and other beleaguered workplaces of the Third World to better opportunities and higher pay in the First World. As rich nations become richer and poor nations become poorer, this one-way flow of talent and training continuously widens the gap between the two. But in addition to this brain drain, there is now a parallel but more hidden and wrenching trend, as women who normally care for the young, the old, and the sick in their own poor countries move to care for the young, the old, and the sick in rich countries, whether as maids and nannies or as day-care and nursing-home aides. It's a care drain.

The movement of care workers from south to north is not altogether new. What is unprecedented, however, is the scope and speed of women's migration to these jobs. Many factors contribute to the growing feminization of migration. One is the growing split between the global rich and poor. . . .

[For example] domestic workers [who] migrated from the Philippines to the United States and Italy [in the 1990s] had averaged $176 a month, often as teachers, nurses, and administrative and clerical workers. But by doing less skilled—though no less difficult—work as nannies, maids, and care-service workers, they can earn $200 a month in Singapore, $410 a month in Hong Kong, $700 a month in Italy, or $1,400 a month in Los Angeles. To take one example, as a fifth-grade dropout in Colombo, Sri Lanka, a woman could earn $30 a month plus room and board as a housemaid, or she could earn $30 a month as a salesgirl in a shop, without food or lodging. But as a nanny in Athens she could earn $500 a month, plus room and board.

The remittances these women send home provide food and shelter for their families and often a nest egg with which to start a small business. Of the $750 Rowena Bautista earns each month in the United States, she mails $400 home for her children's food, clothes, and schooling, and $50 to Anna de la Cruz, who shares some of that with her mother-in-law and her children. As Rowena's story demonstrates, one way to respond to the gap between rich and poor countries is to close it privately—by moving to a better paying job. . . .

The International Organization for Migration estimates that 120 million people moved from one country to another, legally or illegally, in 1994. Of this group, about 2 percent of the world's population, 15 to 23 million are refugees and asylum seekers. Of the rest, some move to join family members who have previously migrated. But most move to find work.

As a number of studies show, most migration takes place through personal contact with networks of migrants composed of relatives and friends and relatives and friends of relatives and friends. One migrant inducts another. Whole networks and neighborhoods leave to work abroad, bringing back stories, money, know-how, and contacts. Just as men form networks along which information about jobs are passed, so one domestic worker in New York, Dubai, or Paris passes on information to female relatives or friends about how to arrange papers, travel, find a job, and settle. Today, half of all the world's migrants are women. . . .

The trends outlined above—global polarization, increasing contact, and the establishment of transcontinental female networks—have caused more women to migrate. They have also changed women's motives for migrating. Fewer women move for "family reunification" and more move in search of work. And when they find work, it is often within the growing "care sector," which, according to the economist Nancy Folbre, currently encompasses 20 percent of all American jobs.

A good number of the women who migrate to fill these positions seem to be single mothers. After all, about a fifth of the world's households are headed by women: 24 percent in the industrial world, 19 percent in Africa, 18 percent in Latin America and the Caribbean, and 13 percent in Asia and the Pacific. . . .

Many if not most women migrants have children. The average age of women migrants into the United States is twenty-nine, and most come from countries, such as the Philippines and Sri Lanka, where female identity centers on motherhood, and where the birth rate is high. Often migrants, especially the undocumented ones, cannot bring their children with them. Most mothers try to leave their children in the care of grandmothers, aunts, and fathers, in roughly that order. An orphanage is a last resort. A number of nannies working in rich countries hire nannies to care for their own children back home either as solo caretakers or as aides to the female relatives left in charge back home. Carmen Ronquillo, for example, migrated from the Philippines to Rome to work as a maid for an architect and single mother of two. She left behind her husband, two teenagers—and a maid.

Whatever arrangements these mothers make for their children, however, most feel the separation acutely, expressing guilt and remorse to the researchers who interview them. Says one migrant mother who left her two-month-old baby in the care of a relative. "The first two years I felt like I was going crazy. You have to believe me when I say that it was like I was having intense psychological problems. I would catch myself gazing at nothing, thinking about my child." Recounted another migrant nanny through tears, "When I saw my children again, I thought, 'Oh children do grow up even without their mother.' I left my youngest when she was only five years old. She was already nine when I saw her again, but she still wanted me to carry her."

Many more migrant female workers than migrant male workers stay in their adopted countries—in fact, most do. In staying, these mothers remain separated from their children, a choice freighted, for many, with a terrible sadness. Some migrant nannies, isolated in their employers' homes and faced with what is often depressing work, find solace in lavishing their affluent charges with the love and care they wish they could provide their own children. In an interview with Rhacel Parreñas, Vicky Diaz, a college-educated school teacher who left behind five children in the Philippines, said, "the only thing you can do is to give all your love to the child [in your care]. In my absence from my children, the most I could do with my situation was to give all my love to that child." Without intending it, she has taken part in a global heart transplant.

As much as these mothers suffer, their children suffer more. And there are a lot of them. An estimated 30 percent of Filipino children—some eight million—live in households where at least one parent has gone overseas. These children have counterparts in Africa, India, Sri Lanka, Latin America, and the former Soviet Union. How are these children doing? Not very well, according to a survey Manila's Scalabrini Migration Center conducted with more than seven hundred children in 1996. Compared to their classmates, the children of migrant workers more frequently fell ill; they were more likely to express anger, confusion, and apathy; and they performed particularly poorly in school. Other studies of this population show a rise in delinquency and child suicide. When such children were asked whether they would also migrate when they grew up, leaving their own children in the care of others, they all said no.

Faced with these facts, one senses some sort of injustice at work, linking the emotional deprivation of these children with the surfeit of affection their First World counterparts enjoy. In her study of native-born women of color who do domestic work, Sau-Ling Wong argues that the time and energy these workers devote to the children of their employers is diverted from their own children. But time and energy are not all that's involved; so, too, is love. In this sense, we can speak about love as an unfairly distributed resource—extracted from one place and enjoyed somewhere else.

Is love really a "resource" to which a child has a right? Certainly the United Nations Declaration on the Rights of the Child asserts all children's right to an "atmosphere of happiness, love, and understanding." Yet in some ways, this claim is hard to make. The more we love and are loved, the more deeply we can love. Love is not fixed in the same way that most material resources are fixed. Put another way, if love is a resource, it's a *renewable* resource; it creates more of itself. And yet Rowena Bautista can't be in two places at once. Her day has only so many hours. It may also be true that the more love she gives to Noa, the less she gives to her own three children back in the Philippines. Noa in the First World gets more love, and Clinton and Princela in the Third World get less. In this sense, love does appear scarce and limited, like a mineral extracted from the earth.

Perhaps, then, feelings *are* distributable resources, but they behave somewhat differently from either scarce or renewable material resources. According to Freud, we don't "withdraw" and "invest" feeling but rather *displace* or redirect it. The process is an unconscious one, whereby we don't actually give up a feeling of, say, love or hate, so much as we find a new object for it—in the case of sexual feeling, a more appropriate object than the original one, whom Freud presumed to be our opposite-sex parent. While Freud applied the idea of displacement mainly to relationships within the nuclear family, it seems only a small stretch to apply it to relationships like Rowena's to Noa. As Rowena told Frank, the *Wall Street Journal* reporter, "I give Noa what I can't give my children."

Understandably, First World parents welcome and even invite nannies to redirect their love in this manner. The way some employers describe it, a nanny's love of her employer's child is a natural product of her more loving Third World culture, with its warm family ties, strong community life, and long tradition of patient maternal love of children. In hiring a nanny, many such employers implicitly hope to import a poor country's "native culture," thereby replenishing their own rich country's depleted culture of care. They import the benefits of Third World "family values." Says the director of a coop nursery in the San Francisco Bay Area, "This may be odd to say, but the teacher's aides we hire from Mexico and Guatemala know how to love a child better than the middle-class white parents. They are more relaxed, patient, and joyful. They enjoy the kids more. These professional parents are pressured for time and anxious to develop their kids' talents. I tell the parents that they can really learn how to love from the Latinas and the Filipinas."

When asked why Anglo mothers should relate to children so differently than do Filipina teacher's aides, the nursery director speculated, "The Filipinas are brought up in a more relaxed, loving environment. They aren't as rich as we are, but they aren't so pressured for time, so materialistic, so anxious. They have a more loving, family-oriented culture." One mother, an American lawyer, expressed a similar view:

> Carmen just enjoys my son. She doesn't worry whether . . . he's learning his letters, or whether he'll get into a good preschool. She just enjoys him. And actually, with anxious busy parents like us, that's really what Thomas needs. I love my son more than anyone in this world. But at this stage Carmen is better for him.

Filipina nannies I have interviewed in California paint a very different picture of the love they share with their First World charges. Theirs is not an import of happy peasant mothering but a love that partly develops on American shores, informed by an American ideology of mother-child bonding and fostered by intense loneliness and longing for their own children. If love is a precious resource, it is not one simply extracted from the Third World and implanted in the First; rather, it owes its very existence to a peculiar cultural alchemy that occurs in the land to which it is imported.

For María Gutierrez, who cares for the eight-month-old baby of two hardworking professionals (a lawyer and a doctor, born in the Philippines but now living in San Jose, California), loneliness and long work hours feed a love for her employers' child. "I love Ana more than my own two children. Yes, more! It's strange, I know. But I have time to be with her. I'm paid. I am lonely here. I work ten hours a day, with one day off. I don't know any neighbors on the block. And so this child gives me what I need."

Not only that, but she is able to provide her employer's child with a different sort of attention and nurturance than she could deliver to her own children. "I'm more patient," she explains, "more relaxed. I put the child first. My kids, I treated them the way my mother treated me."

I asked her how her mother had treated her and she replied:

My mother grew up in a farming family. It was a hard life. My mother wasn't warm to me. She didn't touch me or say "I love you." She didn't think she should do that. Before I was born she had lost four babies—two in miscarriage and two died as babies. I think she was afraid to love me as a baby because she thought I might die too. Then she put me to work as a "little mother" caring for my four younger brothers and sisters. I didn't have time to play.

Fortunately, an older woman who lived next door took an affectionate interest in María, often feeding her and even taking her in overnight when she was sick. María felt closer to this woman's relatives than she did to her biological aunts and cousins. She had been, in some measure, informally adopted—a practice she describes as common in the Philippine countryside and even in some towns during the 1960s and 1970s.

In a sense, María experienced a premodern childhood, marked by high infant mortality, child labor, and an absence of sentimentality, set within a culture of strong family commitment and community support. Reminiscent of fifteenth-century France, as Philippe Ariès describes it in *Centuries of Childhood*, this was a childhood before the romanticization of the child and before the modern middle-class ideology of intensive mothering. Sentiment wasn't the point; commitment was.

María's commitment to her own children, aged twelve and thirteen when she left to work abroad, bears the mark of that upbringing. Through all of their anger and tears, María sends remittances and calls, come hell or high water. The commitment is there. The sentiment, she has to work at. When she calls home now, María says, "I tell my daughter 'I love you.' At first it sounded fake. But after a while it became natural. And now she says it back. It's strange, but I think I learned that it was okay to say that from being in the United States."

María's story points to a paradox. On the one hand, the First World extracts love from the Third World. But what is being extracted is partly produced or "assembled" here: the leisure, the money, the ideology of the child, the intense loneliness and yearning for one's own children. In María's case, a premodern childhood in the Philippines, a postmodern ideology of mothering and childhood in the United States, and the loneliness of migration blend to produce the love she gives to her employers' child. That love is also a product of the nanny's freedom from the time pressure and school anxiety parents feel in a culture that lacks a social safety net—one where both parent and child have to "make it" at work because no state policy, community, or marital tie is reliable enough to sustain them. In that sense, the love María gives as a nanny does not suffer from the disabling effects of the American version of late capitalism.

If all this is true—if, in fact, the nanny's love is something at least partially produced by the conditions under which it is given—is María's love of a First World child really being extracted from her own Third World children? Yes, because her daily presence has been removed, and with it the daily expression of her love. It is, of course, the nanny herself who is doing the extracting. Still, if her children suffer the loss of her affection, she suffers with them. This, indeed, is globalization's pound of flesh.

Curiously, the suffering of migrant women and their children is rarely visible to the First World beneficiaries of nanny love. Noa's mother focuses on her daughter's relationship with Rowena. Ana's mother focuses on her daughter's relationship with María. Rowena loves Noa, María loves Ana. That's all there is to it. The nanny's love is a thing in itself. It is unique, private—fetishized. Marx talked about the fetishization of things, not feelings. When we make a fetish of an object—an SUV, for example—we see that object as independent of its context. We disregard, he would argue, the men who harvested the rubber latex, the assembly-line workers who bolted on the tires, and so on. Just as we mentally isolate our idea of an object from the human scene within which it was made, so, too, we unwittingly separate the love between nanny and child from the global capitalist order of love to which it very much belongs.

The notion of extracting resources from the Third World in order to enrich the First World is hardly new. It harks back to imperialism in its most literal form: the nineteenth-century extraction of gold, ivory, and rubber from the Third World. . . . Today, as love and care become the "new gold," the female part of the story has grown in prominence. In both cases, through the death or displacement of their parents, Third World children pay the price.

Imperialism in its classic form involved the north's plunder of physical resources from the south. Its main protagonists were virtually all men: explorers, kings, missionaries, soldiers, and the local men who were forced at gunpoint to harvest wild rubber latex and the like. . . .

Today's north does not extract love from the south by force: there are no colonial officers in tan helmets, no invading armies, no ships bearing arms sailing off to the colonies. Instead, we see a benign scene of Third World women pushing baby carriages, elder care workers patiently walking, arms linked, with elderly clients on streets or sitting beside them in First World parks.

Today, coercion operates differently. While the sex trade and some domestic service is brutally enforced, in the main the new emotional imperialism does not issue from the barrel of a gun. Women choose to migrate for domestic work. But they choose it because economic pressures all but coerce them to. That yawning gap between rich and poor countries is itself a form of coercion, pushing Third World mothers to seek work in the First for lack of options closer to home. But given the prevailing free market ideology, migration is viewed as a "personal choice." Its consequences are seen as "personal problems." . . .

Some children of migrant mothers in the Philippines, Sri Lanka, Mexico, and elsewhere may be well cared for by loving kin in their communities. We need more data if we are to find out how such children are really doing. But if we discover that they aren't doing very well, how are we to respond? I can think of three possible approaches. First, we might say that all women everywhere should stay home and take care of their own families. The problem with Rowena is not migration but neglect of her traditional role. A second approach might be to deny that a problem exists: the care drain is an inevitable outcome of globalization, which is itself good for the world. A supply of labor has met a demand—what's the problem? If the first approach condemns global migration, the second celebrates it. Neither acknowledges its human costs.

According to a third approach—the one I take—loving, paid child care with reasonable hours is a very good thing. And globalization brings with it new opportunities, such as a nanny's access to good pay. But it also introduces painful new emotional realities for Third World children. We need to embrace the needs of Third World societies, including their children. We need to develop a global sense of ethics to match emerging global economic realities. If we go out to buy a pair of Nike shoes, we want to know how low the wage and how long the hours were for the Third World worker who made them. Likewise, if Rowena is taking care of a two-year-old six thousand miles from her home, we should want to know what is happening to her own children.

If we take this third approach, what should we or others in the Third World do? One obvious course would be to develop the Philippine and other Third World economies to such a degree that their citizens can earn as much money inside their countries as outside them. Then the Rowenas of the world could support their children in jobs they'd find at home. While such an obvious solution would seem ideal—if not easily achieved—Douglas Massey, a specialist in migration, points to some unexpected problems, at least in the short run. In Massey's view, it is not underdevelopment that sends migrants like Rowena off to the First World but development itself. The higher the percentage of women working in local manufacturing, he finds, the greater the chance that any one woman will leave on a first, undocumented trip abroad. Perhaps these women's horizons broaden. Perhaps they meet others who have gone abroad. Perhaps they come to want better jobs and more goods. Whatever the original motive, the more people in one's community migrate, the more likely one is to migrate too.

If development creates migration, and if we favor some form of development, we need to find more humane responses to the migration such development is likely to cause. For those women who migrate in order to flee abusive husbands, one part of the answer would be to create solutions to that problem closer to home—domestic-violence shelters in these women's home countries, for instance. Another might be to find ways to make it easier for migrating nannies to bring their children with them. Or as a last resort, employers could be required to finance a nanny's regular visits home.

A more basic solution, of course, is to raise the value of caring work itself, so that whoever does it gets more rewards for it. Care, in this case, would no longer be such a "pass-on" job. And now here's the rub: the value of the labor of raising a child—always low relative to the value of other kinds of labor—has, under the impact of globalization, sunk lower still. Children matter to their parents immeasurably, of course, but the labor of raising them does not earn much credit in the eyes of the world. When middle-class housewives raised children as an unpaid, full-time role, the work was dignified by its aura of middle-classness. That was the one upside to the otherwise confining cult of middle-class, nineteenth- and early-twentieth-century American womanhood. But when the unpaid work of raising a child became the paid work of child-care workers, its low market value revealed the abidingly low value of caring work generally— and further lowered it.

The low value placed on caring work results neither from an absence of a need for it nor from the simplicity or ease of doing it. Rather, the declining value of child care results from a cultural politics of inequality. It can be compared with the declining value of basic food crops relative to manufactured goods on the international market. Though clearly more necessary to life, crops such as wheat and rice fetch low and declining prices, while manufactured goods are more highly valued. Just as the market price of primary produce keeps the Third World low in the community of nations, so the low market value of care keeps the status of the women who do it—and, ultimately, all women—low.

One excellent way to raise the value of care is to involve fathers in it. If men shared the care of family members worldwide, care would spread laterally instead of being passed down a social class ladder. In Norway, for example, all employed men are eligible for a year's paternity leave at 90 percent pay. Some 80 percent of Norwegian men now take over a month of parental leave. In this way, Norway is a model to the world. For indeed it is men who have for the most part stepped aside from caring work, and it is with them that the "care drain" truly begins.

In all developed societies, women work at paid jobs. According to the International Labor Organization, half of the world's women between ages fifteen and sixty-four do paid work. Between 1960 and 1980, sixty-nine out of eighty-eight countries surveyed showed a growing proportion of women in paid work. Since 1950, the rate of increase has skyrocketed in the United States, while remaining high in Scandinavia and the United Kingdom and moderate in France and Germany. If we want developed societies with women doctors, political leaders, teachers, bus drivers, and computer programmers, we will need qualified people to give loving care to their children. And there is no reason why every society should not enjoy such loving paid child care. It may even be true that Rowena Bautista or María Guttierez are the people to provide it, so long as their own children either come with them or otherwise receive all the care they need. In the end, Article 9 of the United Nations Declaration on the Rights of the Child—which the United States has not yet signed—states an important goal. . . . It says we need to value care as our most precious resource, and to notice where it comes from and ends up. For, these days, the personal is global.

THINKING ABOUT THE READING

Why do women leave their own families to work in other countries? Why is there such great demand for nannies and other care workers in some countries? Discuss the concept of carework as a commodity available for sale on a global market. What other services are available on a global market that used to be considered something one got "for free" from family members? Before such services were hired out, who, traditionally, was expected to provide them? What has changed? Discuss some reasons why women make up so much of the global labor force today. If these trends in global labor continue, what do you think families will look like in the near future?

The Architects of Change

Reconstructing Society

14

Throughout this book, you've seen examples of how society is socially constructed and how these social constructions, in turn, affect the lives of individuals. It's hard not to feel a little helpless when discussing the control that culture, massive bureaucratic organizations, social institutions, systems of social stratification, and population trends have over our individual lives. However, social change is as much a part of society as social stability. Whether at the personal, cultural, or institutional level, change is the preeminent feature of modern societies. Social change occurs in many ways and on many levels (e.g., through population shifts and immigration, as illustrated in the previous chapter). Sociologists are also interested in specific, goal-based social movements. Who participates in social movements? What motivates this participation? How successful are they? Social movements range from neighborhood organizers seeking better funding for schools to large-scale religious groups seeking to influence law and politics regarding issues such as abortion, same-sex marriage and immigration. Social movements come in all shapes and sizes. The readings in this final chapter provide three examples of very different forms of social movements.

Different groups are affected differently by significant historical events. In the aftermath of 9/11, Muslim Americans found themselves the subject of extreme cultural vilification and harassment both from the public and from government agencies. Sociologist Pierrette Hondagneu-Sotelo provides a detailed account of the ways in which Los Angeles–based Muslim Americans have organized and are working collectively to protect their image as decent Americans who deserve the same civil rights as all Americans. Muslim American activists are working not only to correct the extreme images of terrorism portrayed in the media but also the fear and lack of education regarding civil rights in their own communities.

In the end, the nature of society, from its large institutions to its small, unspoken rules of everyday life, can be understood only by examining what people do and think. Individuals, acting collectively, can shape institutions, influence government policy, and alter the course of society. It's easy to forget that social movements consist of flesh-and-blood individuals acting together for a cause they believe in. In "Challenging Power," Celene Krauss examines the process by which white, working-class women with very traditional ideas about women's roles in the family became community activists in toxic waste protests. She shows how these women became politicized not by the broader ideology of the environmentalist movement but by the direct health threats toxic waste posed to their children. This article provides an important corrective to the common notion that large-scale social movements are based in ideology. In this case, as is so often the case, these women were motivated by the material conditions affecting the immediate lives of their families. This can be a powerful motivator.

In the final selection, sociologist William I. Robinson suggests that the current immigrant labor protests reflect more than temporary opposition to immigration policies. According to Robinson, these protests are indicative of a growing awareness regarding global capitalism and the exploitation of immigrant labor. Robinson traces the necessity of immigrant labor in the new global markets and asks us to consider the possibility that a global social movement is forming based on the issue of immigrant labor rights.

Something to Consider as You Read

As you read these selections, consider the connection between people's ideas, beliefs, and goals and the motivation to become involved in social change. Participation in a social movement takes time and resources. What do you care enough about to contribute your time and money? In thinking about the near future, which groups do you think are "worked up" enough about something to give a lot of time and energy in trying to create social change? If these groups prevail, what do you think the future will look like?

Muslim American Immigrants After 9/11

The Struggle for Civil Rights

Pierrette Hondagneu-Sotelo

(2008)

There is a new movement to make people in Muslim, Arab, and South Asian immigrant communities become politically engaged and informed American citizens, but unlike the civil rights movement of the 1950s and 1960s, religion is delicately interwoven into these current efforts. I was introduced to part of this movement on a bright Saturday morning in December 2002 when two thousand people convened at the gargantuan Long Beach Convention Center for the annual convention of the Muslim Public Affairs Council (MPAC). The large convention halls, the registration desks, the speakers dressed in expensive suits and business attire, and the prominent MPAC banners—in red, white, and blue and featuring stars and stripes—prompted my student and me to think we had stumbled into a Democratic or Republican Party convention. All that was missing were balloons, booze, and major television media.

In the wake of 9/11, many non-Muslim South Asians and Christian Arab American immigrants became both victims and activists, as did some Latinos and Asian Americans of various religions. White, U.S.-born Christians and Jews were generally not targets, but many of them, particularly those in the clergy, also worked tirelessly in interfaith dialogues and formed new alliances with these groups. In this chapter I focus particularly on the Muslim response, but also on the collective South Asian and Arab American immigrant response to 9/11. I provide a snapshot of what these community organizations and leaders did in Los Angeles and Orange Counties to restore civil liberties and how, in this process, they renegotiated religious and racial identity with media and government realities. The leaders and organizations discussed in this chapter constitute part of a new movement for immigrant civil rights and for Muslim American identities in the United States.

Muslim citizens and immigrants are a growing and increasingly visible part of the population in all Western, industrial, and postindustrial societies. Syrian immigrants from what is today Jordan and Lebanon, most of them Christian, came to the United States, mostly to the Midwest, during the late nineteenth century as labor migrants and peddlers. Racist exclusionary laws in the 1920s curtailed midcentury immigration from Asia and the Middle East. But the 1965 immigration act, with its preference system for highly educated, skilled migrants and its lifting of the racist exclusionary immigration laws, reopened the doors. Consequently, in the 1970s highly educated, urban-origin Muslim immigrants began coming to the United States from nations as diverse as Pakistan, India, Iran, Indonesia, and Jordan. They were seeking economic and academic opportunities in the United States and fleeing political violence. Many came as students and started student organizations, such as the Muslim Student Association and the Islamic Society of North America, to keep their religion alive in their families and communities. Shared religious identity allowed them to forge connections even though they came from diverse nations. Since the census does not collect data on religious affiliation, the precise number of Muslims in the United States is disputed, but a population of 6 million Muslims is the figure most often cited. About one-third are African American, with the remainder split among Arabs and South Asians.

A plethora of Muslim organizations, most of them built in the 1980s and 1990s, emerged in the forefront of the response to post-9/11 backlash against Muslim, Arab, and South Asian American immigrant communities. I studied a handful of these organizations in Los Angeles and Orange Counties, which is where approximately six hundred thousand Muslim Americans reside. Most of these organizations are directed by first-generation immigrant men who were educated in U.S. universities, many of them in the sciences or business. These men are the antithesis, in substance and physical appearance, of the dominant media representations of bearded, bomb-throwing, foreign, Muslim masculinity. They are clean-shaven and telegenic, they wear exquisite business suits, and they appear equally adept at speaking at press conferences, on panels with the FBI or officials from the Department of Homeland Security, or with Christian interfaith groups. They are not formally trained Islamic religious scholars or imams but savvy, eloquent spokesmen for Islam in America, and they were already making optimistic headway into mainstream American politics before 9/11.

These Muslim American leaders seek to work within the system. They threw their support to the Bush-Cheney ticket in the 2000 presidential election, driven in part by Bush's campaign promise of less support for Israel and by Bush's pledge to repeal the 1995 Antiterrorism and Effective Death Penalty Act—which allows the government to use secret evidence against non-U.S. citizens. While these groups gained momentum in the 1990s, it is the post-9/11 assaults on their communities that propelled them headfirst into the struggle for civil rights. These Muslim organizations, built on the model of modern, professional organizations—with executive directors, public relations specialists, administrative support, newsletters, websites, boards of directors, and small but skilled staffs—were well positioned to take political action, and

they were joined by other groups, as I detail further below.

As I see it, this collective effort constitutes a traditional struggle for civil rights and civil liberties. The goal of these activists is both discursive, to carve out an identity as American Muslims (or as American Arabs or South Asian Americans, as the case may be), and instrumental, to end racial and religious discrimination, detentions, profiling, and harassment based on religion, race, and nativity. In this regard, the struggle waged by Muslim, Arab, and South Asian immigrants in the United States runs parallel to the civil rights movement waged by African Americans in the 1950s and 1960s. It is also parallel to the experience of Japanese Americans during World War II internment. Here, it is instructive to pause for a moment and contrast the religious contours of these movements.

In the Steps of Black Americans and Japanese Americans?

There appears to be much in common between the experience of Japanese Americans during World War II and Muslim Americans in the current era. In both instances, the United States government responded to violent attacks from outside the nation by seeking to define and retaliate against an enemy within the nation. Both instances rely on racial discrimination against citizens and immigrants of Japanese or Muslim, Arab, or South Asian origins. And not surprisingly, in the post-9/11 period, there has been an outpouring of support from Japanese American organizations to Muslim, Arab, and South Asian American communities affected by the post-9/11 backlash and new affiliations between these groups.

What happened to Japanese Americans is well known. Soon after Japan attacked Pearl Harbor on December 7, 1941, President Franklin Delano Roosevelt signed Executive Order 9066. Everyone of Japanese ancestry on the West Coast was subjected to curfew and, eventually, forced removal from their homes, schools, and workplaces. Entire families were freighted into internment in camps in remotely located rural places in Utah, Idaho, and Montana and deserts in California. Approximately 110,000 people of Japanese descent, 70,000 of them American citizens, spent the duration of World War II living in cheaply constructed wooden barracks in places like Manzanar or Topaz, with armed sentry guards posted along the barbed wire enclosure fences.

The contemporary Muslim struggle for civil rights shares much with the goals of the civil rights movement of the 1950s and 1960s. These Muslim American leaders want to put an end to unfair treatment and discrimination against their communities, and they want the right to claim a Muslim American identity, just as blacks sought to become fully enfranchised American citizens. Religion, however, gets used differently by these groups. In the contemporary instance, religion is the central basis for discrimination and is a primary means of mobilization, but religion does not serve as a rationale for making claims for the restoration of civil liberties. While civil rights leaders in the 1950s and 1960s regularly quoted the Bible to give religious relevance to social injustices, the contemporary Muslim, Arab, and South Asian civil rights leaders do not appeal to Islamic sacred scriptures to claim their rights. Instead, they evoke the American Constitution as a textual source of justice. The Quran is not the warrant for making claims about inclusion in the American polity, nor is it a means of motivating people to social action. Rather, as we will see, the Quran is used variously, as a text that helps unify Muslim organizations and Muslim collective identity, and when it is engaged in public discourse, to show that American values and political traditions are compatible with Islam's major tenets.

Religious freedom is a foundation American narrative. The central struggle for these groups, however, is not the right to practice Islam but to lay claim to rights and civil liberties as Americans and as immigrants who are racialized, "alienized," and oppressed because of their religious identification. While these groups claim to share experiences of minority subordination with other U.S. racial-ethnic minorities, especially with Japanese Americans who were also held suspect during World War II, their struggle is to disestablish Christianity as a precursor to American national identity. To be clear: They are not against Christianity. In this regard, their goals go right to the heart of the origins of the United States.

For the first- and second-generation immigrants active in this project, religion and ethnicity act as an organizing net. But in an era when being foreign, Islamic, and Middle Eastern is conflated with "terrorist," they cannot deploy religion in overt, highly visual public ways. Organizations such as the Council on American-Islamic Relations (CAIR) and MPAC seek to represent themselves as both Muslims and Americans, while the South Asian Network (SAN), the American-Arab Anti-discrimination Committee (ADC), and the Palestinian American Women's Association (PAWA) are also working to represent themselves as Americans. In this struggle for recognition and self-definition, they use established, institutional modes of political engagement. These include town hall meetings, conventions, press releases, and formal meetings and collaborations and informal meetings with federal, state, and local government and law enforcement authorities. They organize as members of racialized immigrant groups, and in the post-9/11 era, they establish coalitions and working relations with other groups, such as Japanese Americans and Christian clergy as well as government representatives from the FBI, the Department of Homeland Security, and the local sheriff's office. They seek to influence public opinion and the state, but they refrain from bringing highly visible expressions of Islam to the political arena.

"We Should Be Able to Define Ourselves"

Constructing and promoting an identity is at the heart of the struggle for all the ethnic-religious organization leaders I interviewed. For the leaders of CAIR, MPAC, PAWA, ADC, and SAN, civil rights is, at core, a discursive struggle. This is their primary challenge. At stake in the post-9/11 era is who will control the image of Muslim Americans, Arab Americans, and South Asian Americans. What will be included in the content of this identity? And will this identity be used to promote inclusion or justify exclusion? These groups want inclusion, and they are actively seeking a place in the American polity and society that reflects their position both as Americans and as immigrants who will no longer be racialized and persecuted because of religion and phenotype. They want to contest the images of them that circulate through the media.

These groups seek inclusion as Americans, but not an inclusion that compromises being Muslim. Their remedy focuses on educating the larger society, to show that they are American *and* Muslim. As Salam Al-Marayati, the Los Angeles director of MPAC, told me, "We're stressing the American Muslim identity. We're trying to be more vocal and set America straight."

Know Your Neighbor, Know Your Rights—and Show Yourself to the FBI

Immediately after 9/11, organizations like CAIR and MPAC were thrown into high gear, initially responding reactively, defending and protecting members of their communities, and then proactively, educating and informing members of the Muslim immigrant communities and other Americans as well. The aperture of collective self-definition opened up as it never had before, and the leaders saw this as a new opportunity and obligation. The Islamic-identified organizations were most deeply affected by these imperatives. They set about the task of educating Americans about Muslims and of informing their own ethnic communities about civil rights. We can think of these, respectively, as

"Know Your Neighbors" and "Know Your Rights" campaigns.

The executive director of the Muslim Public Affairs Council told me that in the Los Angeles area, MPAC had sponsored or participated in over four hundred public forums and outreach events between September 11, 2001, and February 2002, the time of the interview. MPAC sought not only to inform and protect community members, but also to educate the government and the larger public.

How did organizations with small, already stretched paid staffs accomplish this? They dipped into their general membership to develop a new pool of leaders. As Samer Hathout, a lawyer, MPAC board member, and daughter of a key leader reflected, "We feel so behind, so overwhelmed. There's so much to do now. . . . Everyone wants to know about Islam, so there is this overwhelming demand for speakers and appearances." MPAC developed new spokespeople during this period, and she noted, "People that didn't necessarily want to do public speaking are finding that it's not as scary as they thought it was. So it's really brought out some more leaders for us."

At the Council on American-Islamic Relations office in Orange County, the response was initially reactive and service oriented—taking reports of hate crimes, employment discrimination, and school and workplace harassment—but it also did proactive work aimed at information and outreach. Speaking of the immediate post-9/11 months, the executive director of CAIR, Hussam Ayloush, said, "We've been doing the same thing for the last almost eight years nationwide, and the last six years in Southern California. But what's happened is the degree or the amount of what we were doing has changed—the intensity. In the past maybe we used to give one presentation at a church maybe every two months, at a school every two months; we would deal maybe with twenty cases of discrimination. Within a few months after September 11th, we had to deal with over—if I'm not mistaken—close to two hundred cases in our area of hate incidents." Like other organizations, CAIR was not equipped for this barrage of activity. "As a small office," explained Ayloush, "we weren't prepared to deal with a flood of phone calls." They brought in more volunteers and hired new staff, but this required devoting more resources to training.

More time and resources were subsequently devoted to civil liberties issues. CAIR, for example, has continued to issue "action alerts" through the Internet, alerting Listserv recipients to instances of prejudice, discrimination, and violence against Muslims. For affluent, literate, educated, professional-class immigrants, the Internet is a useful resource. One observer has called this "action alert activism."[1]

Instead of a policy of noncooperation with government authorities, the groups decided to participate in town hall meetings, which brought together Muslim, South Asian, and Arab American community leaders and members with FBI, INS, and Department of Justice functionaries. I attended the second in the Southern California series of town hall meetings in January 2002, four months after 9/11. It was officially sponsored by the U.S. Department of Justice Community Relations Service, through the efforts of Ron Wakabayashi, a Japanese American with a long history of civil rights activism. The meeting was held on a Saturday afternoon in a ballroom of a Holiday Inn in La Mirada, a city just off Interstate 5, near the industrial area where northern Los Angeles and southern Orange County meet. There were over one hundred people, most of them Arab American or Muslim, and a handful of Sikhs. In the lobby, where various groups set up tables to distribute leaflets, I saw newspapers in Arabic, but I was most struck by how prosperous the people looked. In fact, I remember wishing that I had dressed up a bit more. The men—and it was mostly men—wore suits and ties, and the women wore professional attire. Many women wore headscarves that matched their outfits. Once in the ballroom, the audience mostly listened attentively—but sometimes heckled—as speakers from the FBI, INS, and the Department of Justice addressed questions of

concern. Joining the three white middle-aged men representing the government were four community representatives, including one woman, and the moderator, Tareef Nashashibi, who introduced himself as president of the Arab American Committee of the Republican Party of Orange County. He began on an upbeat note, celebrating and thanking the FBI for incarcerating Irv Rubin of the Jewish Defense League, who bombed offices in 1985, killing Alex Odeh, and he emphasized the rights of citizens and the importance of working together with government. "We are aware," he stated at the outset, "of the FBI looking closely at us, and we want to look back at them." He identified the use of secret evidence as a major threat, and he said, "These issues are important to us, the recent immigrant group. We are all citizens of this country, and we need to be treated alike." At the meeting, the government representatives addressed questions from the audience about the use of secret evidence, racial profiling, detentions, and visas. The INS representative claimed that the term "racial profiling" had been abused by the media in "unsettling ways," and he tried to allay fears by saying that less than one hundred people in the INS western region had been detained due to post-9/11 investigations. The audience response varied, from polite questions and nodding heads to outright heckling.

The diversity of views expressed by the community organization speakers and the audience was also evident among the leaders I interviewed. Some of them saw the town hall meetings as important for building relations with local government bureaucrats and for educating government officials about their communities. They saw these meetings as "building bridges," as ways to keep their own communities abreast of developments, but also as educational efforts, so that government officials "will know that Arabs and Muslims are not what they see on TV." As one leader said to me in an interview: "We wanted to make sure that people do not have this fear of the FBI, so we arranged several town hall meetings with the FBI, the INS. . . . They had very pleasant people working with them. . . . It helped us both, both communities. I think it helped them realize that as they attended those meetings they saw that the Muslim community was not just a bunch of bearded men shouting, 'Death to America!'"

Other community leaders found little to celebrate in these new collaborations. One critic had this to say: "We had three town hall meetings with the FBI, the INS, and the Justice Department, and I felt like it was group therapy. We talked . . . they listened and they did not do anything. There's still a lot of people being detained, still a lot of people going to jail. The idea about democracy that we are innocent until proven guilty no longer stands. There is no due process for the Arabs or the Muslims."

These internal conflicts speak to the diversity of Muslim American, Arab American, and South Asian American immigrant communities. Just as there is no monolithic voice in the Muslim world, there is no monolithic voice among these various communities in the United States. One interviewee candidly noted that the diversity of the Muslim community makes the advocacy work a challenge. Some members favor traditional party affiliations and congressional causes, while others advocate grassroots connections with labor and civil rights organizations; others bitterly disagree about the relative merits and dangers of participating with the FBI, INS, and Department of Justice. Fighting domestic surveillance of Muslim American immigrant communities and yet working with the federal government is the tightrope these groups walk. The groups want to work with the government, but they want to stop government surveillance based on racial-religious profiling and unspecified standards. While there are disagreements on approaches, they all agreed that a big part of the problem is the United States' ignorance of their communities.

Of the organizations I examined, none were as explicitly focused on the project of addressing imagery in media and among opinion makers as CAIR and MPAC. Within MPAC, no one was out on the frontlines more than Sarah Eltantawi. Freshly out of graduate school, female, and still in her twenties, she had only been on the job for a few months before 9/11. Suddenly, she found herself on Fox News and CNN. By February 2002 she had debated Daniel Pipes on the *Greta Van Susteren Show* and had been on the *O'Reilly Factor* three times. "The first time was with John Gibson," she said. "That was absolutely horrific. . . . I was supposed to go on and talk about American Muslims' response to 9/11, and as soon as I got on there, he immediately started screaming at me about 'Why do you people have a problem with the United States after all we've done for the Palestinians? After all we've done for the peace process, you ungrateful, blah, blah, blah.' I mean, he really just screamed at me, wouldn't let me get a word in edgewise." From her experience, she concluded, "O'Reilly's people just want Muslims up there, like sitting ducks." That television appearance was followed by more where she was often pitted against so-called terrorism experts like journalist Steve Emerson and Daniel Pipes, editor of the *Middle East Quarterly*. Both of these men frequently write and speak about the dangers of radical Islam and promote the view that Arab and Muslim American communities harbor terrorist sleeper cells. As Eltantawi recalled of the news shows, "The question of who Muslims are and who Arabs are is never approached objectively, but more like, The Quran says this and this about infidels. What do you have to say?' We're always on the defensive, always having to answer questions that are posed with a certain kind of bias in mind."

Moderate, peaceful Muslim Americans do not fit the narrative or what is profitable to print, and this determines, in part, how these communities come to be viewed by society at large. During the first few months after 9/11, a counternarrative appeared in the media news, as we saw the debut of a series of "human interest" stories on Muslim American families. These constituted the mass media's approach to the "Muslim moment." On the one hand, these stories presented humanizing quotidian portraits of Muslim American families. The features focused on Muslims as average American families, were typically shot in the domestic sphere of kitchens and dining rooms, and showed glimpses of all-American mortgages, children with homework, and family members gathered around a dining table for an evening meal. On the other hand, these portraits may have played into the new American paranoia of sleeper cells. Regardless of how these "American family" narratives were ultimately read by viewers, they did present a significant departure from the media-as-usual representations of Muslim and Arab Americans. Ra'id Faraj, the public relations director of CAIR, was among the most charitable in his assessment of the media. "The mainstream media," he said, "has been okay. After all, they've definitely worked with us on all kinds of stories. We've assisted them on stories, we gave them numbers and statistics, and we helped them to find individuals in the communities [to feature]." Nader Abuljebain of the ADC was less sanguine with his succinct assessment: "So I'm glad at least they know we exist, and we don't all have tails, and we are not all terrorists or millionaires or belly dancers."

In 2002 CAIR debuted a series of billboards along Southern California freeways showing photos of smiling, multiracial Muslims—the photo was reminiscent of a Benetton ad—with the text "Even a Smile Is Charity," to suggest that Muslims might be kind and compassionate rather than dangerous. CAIR also invested in getting books and videos with accurate portrayals of Islam into public and school libraries. MPAC members were encouraged to write letters to the editor, and they did, and some of these were published in the *Los Angeles Times*. In the post-9/11 period, MPAC actively encouraged members to become media spokespeople. "We are learning to do the sound-bite thing," explained Samer Hathout.

A long-term route to remedy media distortion involved getting more Muslim Americans and Arab Americans into media

jobs. This is part of the larger Muslim American project of cultivating leaders in the second generation. As one leader said, Muslims should be "encouraging more Muslims in those fields, fields of media, journalism, communication, educating members of the media, sensitizing them." First-generation Muslim immigrants and their children tend to concentrate in science and engineering jobs, so as one interviewee said, "encouraging them to be journalists or [in] any area of the liberal arts . . . to consider politics as a career" is part of the solution.

In at least one instance, Hollywood stars were mobilized to fight prevailing negative Hollywood images. In the immediate aftermath of 9/11, the Los Angeles County Commission on Human Relations sought to deter hate crimes with the help of Hollywood celebrities. Robin Toma said that after the movie star Patricia Arquette, herself the daughter of a Muslim American father, came forward to volunteer "to do something about what she saw was the anti-Muslim, anti-Arab backlash in this country," celebrities were recruited to do radio public service announcements against hate. Arquette visited public schools to talk with youth and apparently used her personal networks to recruit celebrities for the radio spots. Hollywood was also rewarded by MPAC for fair and non-stereotypical portrayals of Muslims. To encourage fair representations in film, MPAC had already introduced a media awards program. Past winners now include Denzel Washington, Morgan Freeman, Spike Lee, George Clooney, Kevin Costner, and Yusuf Islam (formerly known as Cat Stevens).

Leaders of these organizations worked hard to allay fears and anxieties and to inform their communities of their civil rights. It was a tough sell. Fear prompted people to stay away from mosques and Islamic centers and to withdraw their financial contributions to Islamic charities. Randall Hamud, a third-generation Arab American civil rights attorney and ADC board member who was defending detainees, reported at an ACLU-sponsored public forum his frustration with raising bail money—no one now wanted to take the risk of association with detainees, even though they were not proven to be guilty of anything. Hamud also reported accompanying clients from San Diego who were asked to come forward for questioning. The FBI asked them, "Why were you trying to change your license plate?" Neighbors had reported seeing Hamud's client changing his license plate at night, but the client had merely been tightening a license plate that was coming loose.[2] In this context of surveillance and accusations, community members were less likely to volunteer information and were reluctant to report hate crimes out of fear and stigma.

As Hamid Khan, executive director of SAN, put it, "Right now we feel besieged, because of detentions, because of dealing with the FBI, we are having extreme difficulty in documenting needs because people are unwilling to share stories, but they tell us, 'We just had a raid.'" Michel Shehadeh of ADC concurred: "The community is not coming out to join organizations and to fight back. This is a scared community, and the challenge is to empower the community." Most agreed that the fear was greatest among the foreign-born.

In the aftermath of 9/11, the organizations discussed here devoted a good deal of their outreach and educational efforts to their own communities, particularly first-generation immigrants. Large public forums at Islamic centers, churches, town hall meetings, and hotels attracted thousands of people. Informational materials were distributed at these meetings and in ethnic newspapers. Yet the community leaders reported that immigrants in the Muslim American, Arab American, and South Asian American communities presented particular challenges: ignorance of their rights and entitlements in the United States; the legacy of having grown up under despotic rulers and being unaccustomed to freedom; and intensified fear and anxiety due to government repression following 9/11.

If information is power, knowledge of basic civil rights and entitlements, the leaders reasoned, may help deter abuses. Toward this end, the organizations distributed thousands of "know your rights" brochures and cards. The pocket-sized, fold-up cards such as the ones distributed by CAIR, for example, included titles such as "Know Your Rights as an Airline Passenger," "If the FBI Contacts You," "Your Rights as an Employee," "Your Rights as a Student," and "Reacting to Anti-Muslim Hate Crimes." These were brilliantly prepared, informative, pithy documents and included simple, sequential steps to take in a variety of problematic circumstances. Similar brochures and cards were distributed by the other organizations, and they were translated into multiple languages, including Arabic, Farsi, and Hindi. Some of the organizations set up websites. MPAC, for example, featured one with information ranging from First Amendment rights, Miranda rights, and the rights of due process for noncitizens to the difference between hate crimes and hate incidents, including online forms for downloading hate crime reports. The document on hate crimes instructed the aggrieved to do the following:

- Report the crime to your local police station immediately. Ask that the incident be treated as a hate crime. Follow up with investigators. Inform CAIR even if you believe it is a "small incident."
- Document the incident. Write down exactly what was said and/or done by the offender. Save evidence. Take photographs.

"Know Your Rights as an Airline Passenger" advised people of their rights and told them what to do in instances of racial profiling:

- As an airline passenger, you are entitled to courteous, respectful and non-stigmatizing treatment by airline and security personnel.
- You have the right to complain about treatment that you believe is discriminatory. If you believe you have been treated in a discriminatory manner, immediately:
  o Ask to speak to a supervisor.
  o Ask if you have been singled out because of your name, looks, dress, race, ethnicity, faith or national origin.
  o Ask for the names and ID numbers of all persons involved in the incident.

○ Ask witnesses to give you their names and contact information.

○ Write down a statement of facts immediately after the incident. . . .

○ Contact CAIR to file a report.

As the reader will observe, this information does not make reference to God, the Quran, or religion. Not only do the materials urge nonviolent responses, they are all based on protections offered by the U.S. Constitution and U.S. laws. The materials instructed the aggrieved to take proactive steps, to remain calm and seek witnesses, to gather evidence and documentation that might be used in court, and to contact legal advocates and start a paper trail of documentation. These efforts, however, sometimes fell on *frightened ears.*

In spite of these obstacles, the crisis galvanized an upsurge of public engagement among Muslim American immigrants and the advancement of a particular collective identity.

Conclusion: The Moderate Mainstream

Muslim American immigrant organizations responded to the post-9/11 backlash leveled at their communities through public engagement, civic participation, and outreach to their own communities and beyond. In all these efforts, they put forth an image of community members as moderate mainstream, middle-of-the-road, middle-class Muslims. Based on what leaders of these organizations told me and what I observed of their organizations' activities, I came to see four dimensions to this collective Muslim American— and sometimes, more expansively, Middle Eastern, Arab, and South Asian—identity project: (1) showing involvement with national domestic issues; (2) promoting moderate political views; (3) avoiding overt forms of religious piety in the public sphere; and (4) regularly offering public declarations of American patriotism and denouncements of Islamic fundamentalist violence and terrorism.

NOTES

1. www.mpac.org, accessed January 26, 2007.

2. The forum where Randall Hamud reported this information, "Racial Profiling after 9/11," was held at a Jewish venue, the University Synagogue, in Brentwood, California, on March 12, 2002.

THINKING ABOUT THE READING

What are some common myths and stereotypes about Muslim Americans, especially since 9/11? What are some of the similarities between contemporary Muslim Americans and Japanese Americans living in the U.S. after the bombing of Pearl Harbor? What are some of the ways in which Muslim Americans are organizing to dispel these stereotypes? What are some of their main concerns and strategies? What role does religion play in their organizing activities? Why are they so focused on education about civil liberties?

Challenging Power

Toxic Waste Protests and the Politicization of White, Working-Class Women

Celene Krauss

(1998)

Over the past two decades, toxic waste disposal has been a central focus of women's grassroots environmental activism. Women of diverse racial, ethnic, and class backgrounds have assumed the leadership of community environmental struggles around toxic waste issues (Krauss 1993). Out of their experience of protest, these women have constructed ideologies of environmental justice that reveal broader issues of inequality underlying environmental hazards (Bullard 1990, 1994). Environmental justice does not exist as an abstract concept prior to these women's activism. It grows out of the concrete, immediate, everyday experience of struggles around issues of survival. As women become involved in toxic waste issues, they go through a politicizing process that is mediated by their experiences of class, race, and ethnicity (Krauss 1993).

Among the earliest community activists in toxic waste protests were white, working-class women. This [article] examines the process by which these women became politicized through grassroots protest activities in the 1980s, which led to their analyses of environmental justice, and in many instances to their leadership in regional and national toxic waste coalitions. These women would seem unlikely candidates for becoming involved in political protest. They came out of a culture that shares a strong belief in the existing political system, and in which traditional women's roles center around the private arena of family. Although financial necessity may have led them into the workplace, the primary roles from which they derived meaning, identity, and satisfaction are those of mothering and taking care of family. Yet, as we shall see, the threat that toxic wastes posed to family health and community survival disrupted the taken-for-granted fabric of their lives, politicizing women who had never viewed themselves as activists. . . .

This [article] shows how white, working-class women's involvement in toxic waste issues has wider implications for social change. . . . These women . . . fought to close down toxic waste dump sites, to prevent the siting of hazardous waste incinerators, to oppose companies' waste-disposal policies, to push for recycling projects, and so on. Their voices show us . . . that their single-issue community protests led them through a process of politicization and their broader analysis of inequities of class and gender in the public arena and in the family. Propelled into the public arena in defense of their children, they ultimately challenged government, corporations, experts, husbands, and their own insecurities as working-class women. Their analysis of environmental justice and inequality led them to form coalitions with labor and people of color around environmental issues. These women's traditional beliefs about motherhood, family, and democracy served a crucial function in this politicizing process. While they framed their analyses in terms of traditional constructions of gender and the state, they actively reinterpreted these constructions into an oppositional ideology, which became a resource of resistance and a source of power in the public arena.

Subjective Dimensions of Grassroots Activism

In most sociological analysis of social movements, the subjective dimension of protest has often been ignored or viewed as private and individualistic. . . . [Contemporary theories] show us how experience is not merely a personal, individualistic concept: it is social. People's experiences reflect where they fit into the social hierarchy. . . . Thus, white, working-class women interpret their experience of toxic waste problems within the context of their particular cultural history, arriving at a critique that reflects broader issues of class and gender. . . .

. . . This article focuses on the subjective process by which white, working-class women involved in toxic waste protests construct an oppositional consciousness out of their everyday lives, experiences, and identities. As these women became involved in the public arena, they confronted a world of power normally hidden from them. This forced them to re-examine their assumptions about private and public power and to develop a broad reconceptualization of gender, family, and government.

The experience of protest is central to this process and can reshape traditional beliefs and values (see Thompson 1963). My analysis reveals the contradictory ways in which traditional culture mediates white, working-class women's subjective experience and interpretation of structural inequality. Their protests are framed in terms of dominant ideologies of motherhood, family, and a deep faith in the democratic system. Their experience also reveals how dominant ideologies are appropriated and reconstructed as an instrument of their politicization and a legitimating ideology used to justify resistance. For example, as the political economy of growth displaces environmental problems into their communities, threatening the survival of children and family and creating everyday crises, government toxic waste policies are seen to violate their traditional belief that a democratic government will protect their families. Ideologies of motherhood and democracy become political resources which these women use to initiate and justify their resistance, their increasing politicization, and their fight for a genuine democracy.

Methodological Considerations

My analysis is based on the oral and written voices of white, working-class women involved in toxic waste protests. Sources include individual interviews, as well as conference presentations, pamphlets, books, and other written materials that have emerged from this movement. Interviews were conducted with a snowball sample of twenty white, working-class women who were leaders in grassroots protest activities against toxic waste landfills and incinerators during the 1980s. These women ranged in age from twenty-five to forty; all but one had young children at the time of their protest. They were drawn from a cross section of the country, representing urban, suburban, and rural areas. None of them had been politically active before the protest; many of them, however, have continued to be active in subsequent community movements, often becoming leaders in state-wide and national coalitions around environmental and social justice issues. I established contact with these women through networking at activist conferences. Open-ended interviews were conducted between May 1989 and December 1991, and lasted from two to four hours. The interview was designed to generate a history of these women's activist experiences, information about changes in political beliefs, and insights into their perceptions of their roles as women, mothers, and wives.

Interviews were also conducted with Lois Gibbs and four other organizers for the Citizens Clearinghouse for Hazardous Wastes (CCHW). CCHW is a nation-wide organization created by Gibbs, who is best known for her successful campaign to relocate families in Love Canal, New York. Over the past two decades, this organization has functioned as a key resource for community groups fighting around toxic waste issues in the United States. Its leadership and staff are composed primarily of women, and the organization played a key role in shaping the ideology of working-class women's environmental activism in the 1980s. . . .

The Process of Politicization

Women identify the toxic waste movement as a women's movement, composed primarily of mothers. As one woman who fought against an incinerator in Arizona and subsequently worked on other anti-incinerator campaigns throughout the state stressed: "Women are the backbone of the grassroots groups, they are the ones who stick with it, the ones who won't back off." Because mothers are traditionally responsible for the health of their children, they are more likely than others within their communities to begin to make the link between toxic waste and their children's ill health. And in communities around the United States, it was women who began to uncover numerous toxin-related health problems: multiple miscarriages, birth defects, cancer, neurological symptoms, and so on. Given the placement of toxic waste facilities in working-class and low-income communities and communities of color, it is not surprising that women from these groups have played a particularly important role in fighting against environmental hazards.

White, working-class women's involvement in toxic waste issues is complicated by the political reality that they, like most people, are excluded from the policy-making process. For the most part, corporate and governmental disposal policies with far-reaching social and political consequences are made without the knowledge of community residents. People may unknowingly live near (or even on top of) a toxic waste dump, or they may assume that the facility is well regulated by the government. Consequently, residents are often faced with a number of problems of seemingly indeterminate origin, and the information withheld

from them may make them unwitting contributors to the ill health of their children.

The discovery of a toxic waste problem and the threat it poses to family sets in motion a process of critical questioning about the relationship between women's private work as mothers and the public arena of politics. The narratives of the women involved in toxic waste protests focus on political transformation, on the process of "becoming" an activist. Prior to their discovery of the link between their family's health and toxic waste, few of these women had been politically active. They saw their primary work in terms of the "private" sphere of motherhood and family. But the realization that toxic waste issues threatened their families thrust them into the public arena in defense of this private sphere. According to Penny Newman:

> We woke up one day to discover that our families were being damaged by toxic contamination, a situation in which we had little, if any, input. It wasn't a situation in which we chose to become involved, rather we did it because we had to . . . it was a matter of our survival. (Newman 1991, 8)

Lois Gibbs offered a similar account of her involvement in Love Canal:

> When my mother asked me what I wanted to do when I grew up, I said I wanted to have six children and be a homemaker. . . . I moved into Love Canal and I bought the American Dream: a house, two children, a husband, and HBO. And then something happened to me and that was Love Canal. I got involved because my son Michael had epilepsy . . . and my daughter Melissa developed a rare blood disease and almost died because of something someone else did. . . . I never thought of myself as an activist or an organizer. I was a housewife, a mother, but all of a sudden it was my family, my children, and my neighbors. . . .

It was through their role as mothers that many of these women began to suspect a connection between the invisible hazard posed by toxic wastes and their children's ill health, and this was their first step toward political activism. At Love Canal, for example, Lois Gibbs's fight to expose toxic waste hazards was triggered by the link she made between her son's seizures and the toxic waste dump site. After reading about toxic hazards in a local newspaper, she thought about her son and then surveyed her neighbors to find that they had similar health problems. In Woburn, Massachusetts, Ann Anderson found that other neighborhood children were, like her son, being treated for leukemia, and she began to wonder if this was an unusually high incidence of the disease. In Denver, mothers comparing stories at Tupperware parties were led to question the unusually large number of sick and dying children in their community. These women's practical activity as mothers and their extended networks of family and community led them to make the connection between toxic waste and sick children—a discovery process rooted in what Sara Ruddick (1989) has called the everyday practice of mothering, in which, through their informal networks, mothers compare notes and experiences, developing a shared body of personal, empirical knowledge.

Upon making the link between their family's ill health and toxic wastes, the women's first response was to go to the government, a response that reflects a deeply held faith in democracy embedded in their working-class culture. They assumed that the government would protect the health and welfare of their children. Gibbs (1982, 12) reports:

> I grew up in a blue-collar community, I was very patriotic, into democracy . . . I believed in government. . . . I believed that if you had a complaint, you went to the right person in government. If there was a way to solve the problem, they would be glad to do it.

An Alabama activist who fought to prevent the siting of an incinerator describes a similar response:

> We just started educating ourselves and gathering information about the problems of incineration. We didn't think our elected officials knew. Surely, if they knew that there was already a toxic waste dump in our county, they would stop it.

In case after case, however, these women described facing a government that was indifferent, if not antagonistic, to their concerns. At Love Canal, local officials claimed that the toxic waste pollution was insignificant, the equivalent of smoking just three cigarettes a day. In South Brunswick, New Jersey, governmental officials argued that living with pollution was the price of a better way of life. In Jacksonville, Arkansas, women were told that the dangers associated with dioxin emitted from a hazardous waste incinerator were exaggerated, no worse than "eating two or three tablespoons of peanut butter over a thirty-year period." Also in Arkansas, a woman who linked her ill health to a fire at a military site that produced Agent Orange was told by doctors that she was going through a "change of life." In Stringfellow, California, eight hundred thousand gallons of toxic chemical waste pumped into the community [water supply] flowed directly behind the elementary school and into the playground. Children played in contaminated puddles yet officials withheld information from their parents because "they didn't want to panic the public."

Government's dismissal of their concerns about the health of their families and communities challenged these white, working-class women's democratic assumptions and opened a window on a world of power whose working they had not before questioned. Government explanations starkly contradicted the personal, empirical evidence which the women discovered as mothers, the everyday knowledge that their children and their neighbors' children were ill. Indeed, a recurring theme in the narratives of these women is the transformation of their beliefs about government. Their politicization is rooted in a deep sense of violation, hurt, and betrayal from finding out their government will not protect their families. Echoes of this disillusionment are heard from women throughout the country. In the CCHW publication *Empowering Women* (1989, 31) one activist noted:

> All our lives we are taught to believe certain things about ourselves as women, about democracy and justice, and about people in positions of authority. Once we become involved with toxic waste problems, we need to confront some [of] our old beliefs and change the way we view things.

Lois Gibbs summed up this feeling when she stated:

> There is something about discovering that democracy isn't democracy as we know it. When you lose faith in your government, it's like finding out your mother was fooling around on your father. I was very upset. It almost broke my heart because I really believed in the system. I still believe in the system, only now I believe that democracy is of the people and by the people, that people have to move it, it ain't gonna move by itself.

These women's loss of faith in "democracy" as they had understood it led them to develop a more autonomous and critical stance. Their investigation shifted to a political critique of the undemocratic nature of government itself, making the link between government inaction and corporate power, and discovering that government places corporate interests and profit ahead of the health needs of families and communities. At Love Canal, residents found that local government's refusal to acknowledge the scope of the toxic waste danger was related to plans of Hooker Chemical, the polluting industry, for a multimillion dollar downtown development project. In Woburn, Massachusetts, government officials feared that awareness of the health hazard posed by a dump would limit their plans for real-estate development. In communities throughout the United States, women came to see that government policies supported waste companies' preference of incineration over recycling because incineration was more profitable.

Ultimately, their involvement in toxic waste protests led these women to develop a perspective on environmental justice rooted in issues of class and a critique of the corporate state. They argued that government's claims—to be democratic, to act on behalf of the public interest, to hold the family sacrosanct—are false. One woman who fought an incinerator in Arizona recalled:

> I believed in government. When I heard EPA, I thought, "Ooh, that was so big." Now I wouldn't believe them if they said it was sunny outside. I have a list of the revolving door of the EPA. Most of them come from Browning Ferris or Waste Management, the companies that plan landfills and incinerators.

As one activist in Alabama related:

> I was politically naive. I was real surprised because I live in an area that's like the Bible belt of the South. Now I think the God of the United States is really economic development, and that has got to change.

Another activist emphasized:

> We take on government and polluters. . . . We are up against the largest corporations in the United States. They have lots of money to lobby, pay off, bribe, cajole, and influence. They threaten us. Yet we challenge them with the only things we have—people and the truth. We learn that our government is not out to protect our rights. To protect our families we are now forced to picket, protest and shout. (Zeff, 1989, 31)

In the process of protest, these women were also forced to examine their assumptions about the family as a private haven, separate from the public arena, which would however be protected by the policies and actions of government should the need arise. The issue of toxic waste shows the many ways in which government allows this haven to be invaded by polluted water, hazardous chemicals, and other conditions that threaten the everyday life of the family. Ultimately, these women arrived at a concept of environmental injustice rooted in the inequities of power that displace the costs of toxic waste unequally onto their communities. The result was a critical political stance that contributed to the militancy of their activism. Highly traditional values of democracy and motherhood remained central to their lives: they justified their resistance as mothers protecting their children and working to make the promise of democracy real. Women's politicization around toxic waste protests led them to transform their traditional beliefs into resources of opposition which enabled them to enter the public arena and challenge its legitimacy, breaking down the public/private distinction.

Appropriating Power in the Public Arena

Toxic waste issues and their threat to family and community prompted white, working-class women to redefine their roles as mothers. Their work of mothering came to extend beyond taking care of the children, husband, and housework; they saw the necessity of preserving the family by entering the public arena. In so doing, they discovered and overcame a more subtle process of intimidation, which limited their participation in the public sphere.

As these women became involved in toxic waste issues, they came into conflict with a public world where policy makers are traditionally white, male, and middle class. The Citizen's Clearinghouse for Hazardous Waste, in the summary of its 1989 conference on women and organizing, noted:

> Seventy to eighty percent of local leaders are women. They are women leaders in a community run by men. Because of this, many of the obstacles that these women face as leaders stem from the conflicts between their traditional female role in the community and their new role as leader: conflicts with male officials and authorities who have not yet adjusted to these

persistent, vocal, head-strong women challenging the system.... Women are frequently ignored by male politicians, male government officials and male corporate spokesmen.

Entering the public arena meant overcoming internal and external barriers to participation, shaped by gender and class. White, working-class women's reconstructed definition of motherhood became a resource for this process, and their narratives reveal several aspects of this transformation.

For these women, entering the public arena around toxic waste issues was often extremely stressful. Many of them were initially shy and intimidated, as simple actions such as speaking at a meeting opened up wider issues about authority, and experiences of gender and class combined to heighten their sense of inadequacy. Many of these women describe, for example, that their high-school education left them feeling ill-equipped to challenge "experts," whose legitimacy, in which they had traditionally believed, was based on advanced degrees and specialized knowledge.

One woman who fought to stop the siting of an incinerator in her community in Arizona recalled: "I used to cry if I had to speak at a PTA meeting. I was so frightened." An activist in Alabama described her experience in fighting the siting of an incinerator in her community:

> I was a woman ... an assistant Sunday School teacher.... In the South, women are taught not to be aggressive, we're supposed to be hospitable and charitable and friendly. We don't protest, we don't challenge authority. So it was kind of difficult for me to get involved. I was afraid to speak. And all of a sudden everything became controversial.... I think a lot of it had to do with not knowing what I was.... The more I began to know, the better I was ... the more empowered.

Male officials further exacerbated this intimidation by ignoring the women, by criticizing them for being overemotional, and by delegitimizing their authority by labeling them "hysterical housewives"—a label used widely, regardless of the professional status of the woman. In so doing, they revealed an antipathy to emotionality, a quality valued in the private sphere of family and motherhood but scorned in the public arena as irrational and inappropriate to "objective" discourse.

On several levels, the debate around toxic waste issues was framed by policy makers in such a way as to exclude women's participation, values, and expression. Women's concerns about their children were trivialized by being placed against a claim that the wider community benefits from growth and progress. Information was withheld from them. Discourse was framed as rational, technical, and scientific, using the testimony of "experts" to discredit the everyday empirical knowledge of the women. Even such details as seating arrangements reflected traditional power relations and reinforced the women's internalization of those relations.

These objective and subjective barriers to participation derived from a traditional definition of women's roles based on the separation of the public and private arenas. Yet it is out of these women's political redefinition of the traditional role of mother that they found the resources to overcome these constraints, ultimately becoming self-confident and assertive. They used the resources of their own experience to alter the power relations they had discovered in the public arena.

The traditional role of mother, of protector of the family and community, served to empower these activists on a number of levels. From the beginning, their view of this role provided the motivation for women to take risks in defense of their families and overcome their fears of participating in the public sphere. A woman who fought the siting of an incinerator in Arkansas described this power:

> I was afraid to hurt anyone's feelings or step on anyone's toes. But I'm protective and aggressive, especially where my children are concerned. That's what brought it out of me. A mother protecting my kids. It appalled me that money could be more important than the health of my children.

A mother in New Jersey described overcoming her fear in dealing with male governmental officials at public hearings, "When I look at a male government official, I remember that he was once a little boy, born of a woman like me, and then I feel more powerful." In talking about Love Canal, Lois Gibbs showed the power of motherhood to carry women into activities alien to their experience:

> When it came to Love Canal, we never thought about ourselves as protestors. We carried signs, we barricaded, we blocked the gates, we were arrested. We thought of it as parents protecting our children. In retrospect, of course, we were protesting. I think if it had occurred to us we wouldn't have done it.

In these ways, they appropriated the power they felt in the private arena as a source of empowerment in the public sphere. "We're insecure challenging the authority of trained experts," notes Gibbs, "but we also have a title of authority, 'mother.'"

Working-class women's experiences as organizers of family life served as a further source of empowerment. Lois Gibbs noted that women organized at Love Canal by constantly analyzing how they would handle a situation in the family, and then translating that analysis into political action. For example, Gibbs explained:

> If our child wanted a pair of jeans, who would they go to? Well they would go to their father since their father had the money—that meant we should go to Governor Carey.

Gibbs drew on her own experience to develop organizing conferences that helped working-class women learn to translate their skills as family organizers into the political arena.

> I decided as a housewife and mother much of what I learned to keep the household running smoothly were skills that translated very well into this new thing called organizing. I also decided that this training in running a home was one of the key reasons why so many of the best leaders in the toxic movement—in fact, the overwhelming majority—are women, and

specifically women who are housewives and mothers. (Zeff 1989, 177)

Of her work with the CCHW, Gibbs stated:

In our own organization we're drawing out these experiences for women. So we say, what do you mean you're not an organizer? Are you a homemaker—then God damn it you can organize and you don't know it. So, for example, when we say you need to plan long-term and short-term goals, women may say, I don't know how to do that. . . . We say, what do you mean you don't know how to do that? Let's talk about something in the household—you plan meals for five, seven, fourteen days—you think about what you want for today and what you're going to eat on Sunday—that is short-term and long-term goals.

Movement language like "plug up the toilet," the expression for waste reduction, helped women to reinterpret toxic waste issues in the framework of their everyday experience. "If one does not produce the mess in the first place, one will not have to clean it up later," may sound like a maternal warning, but the expression's use in the toxic waste context implies a radical economic critique, calling for a change in the production processes of industry itself.

As women came to understand that government is not an objective, neutral mediator for the public good, they discovered that "logic" and "objectivity" are tools used by the government to obscure its bias in favor of industry, and motherhood became a strategy to counter public power by framing the terms of the debate. The labels of "hysterical housewives" or "emotional women," used by policy makers to delegitimize the women's authority, became a language of critique and empowerment, one which exposed the limits of the public arena's ability to address the importance of family, health, and community. These labels were appropriated as the women saw that their emotionalism, a valued trait in the private sphere, could be transformed into a powerful weapon in the public arena.

What's really so bad about showing your feelings? Emotions and intellect are not conflicting traits. In fact, emotions may well be the quality that makes women so effective in the movement. . . . They help us speak the truth.

Finally, through toxic waste protests, women discovered the power they wield as mothers to bring moral issues to the public, exposing the contradictions of a society that purports to value motherhood and family, yet creates social policies that undermine these values:

We bring the authority of mother—who can condemn mothers? . . . It is a tool we have. Our crying brings the moral issues to the table. And when the public sees our children it brings a concrete, moral dimension to our experience. . . . They are not an abstract statistic.

White, working-class women's stories of their involvement in grassroots toxic waste protests reveal their transformations of initial shyness and intimidation into the self-confidence to challenge the existing system. In reconceptualizing their traditional roles as mothers, these women discovered a new strength. As one activist from Arizona says of herself, "Now I like myself better. I am more assertive and aggressive." These women's role in the private world of family ultimately became a source of personal strength, empirical knowledge, and political strategy in the public sphere. It was a resource of political critique and empowerment which the women appropriated and used as they struggled to protect their families.

Overcoming Obstacles to Participation: Gender Conflicts in the Family

In order to succeed in their fights against toxic wastes in their homes and communities, these women confronted and overcame obstacles not only in the public sphere, but also within the family itself, as their entry into the public arena disrupted both the power relationships and the highly traditional gender roles within the family. Divorce and separation were the manifestations of the crises these disruptions induced. All of the women I interviewed had been married when they first became active in the toxic waste movement. By the time of my interviews with them, more than half were divorced.

A central theme of these women's narratives is the tension created in their marriages by participation in toxic waste protests. This aspect of struggle, so particular to women's lives, is an especially hidden dimension of white, working-class women's activism. Noted one activist from New York:

> People are always talking to us about forming coalitions, but look at all we must deal with beyond the specific issue, the flack that comes with it, the insecurity of your husband that you have outgrown him. Or how do you deal with your children's anger, when they say you love the fight more than me. In a blue-collar community that is very important.

For the most part, white, working-class women's acceptance of a traditional gendered division of labor has also led them to take for granted the power relations within the family. Penny Newman, who was the West Coast Director of CCHW, reflected on the beginnings of her community involvement:

> I had been married just a couple of years. My husband is a fireman. They have very strict ideas of what family life is in which the woman does not work, you stay at home. . . . I was so insecure, so shy, that when I finally got to join an organization, a woman's club, . . . it would take me two weeks to build up the courage to ask my husband to watch the kids that night. I would really plan out my life a month ahead of time just to build in these little hints that there is a meeting coming up in two weeks, will you be available. Now, if he didn't want to do it, or had other plans, I didn't go to the meeting. (Zeff 1989, 183)

Involvement in toxic waste issues created a conflict between these traditional assumptions and women's concerns about protecting their children, and this conflict made visible the power relations within the family. The CCHW publication *Empowering Women* (1989, 33) noted that:

> Women's involvement in grassroots activism may change their views about the world and their relations with their husbands. Some husbands are actively supportive. Some take no stand: "Go ahead and do what you want. Just make sure you have dinner on the table and my shirts washed." Others forbid time away from the family.

Many of these women struggled to develop coping strategies to defuse conflict and accommodate traditional gender-based power relations in the family. The strategies included involving husbands in protest activities and minimizing their own leadership roles. As Lois Gibbs commented: "If you bring a spouse in, if you can make them part of your growth, then the marriage is more likely to survive, but that is real hard to do sometimes." Will Collette, a former director at CCHW, relates the ways in which he has observed women avoiding acknowledged leadership roles. He described this encounter with women involved in a toxic waste protest in New York:

> I was sitting around a kitchen table with several women who were leading a protest. And they were complaining about how Lou and Joe did not do their homework and weren't able to handle reports and so on. I asked them why they were officers and the women were doing all the work. They said, "That's what the guys like, it keeps them in and gives us a little peace at home."

In a similar vein, Collette recalled working with an activist from Texas to plan a large public hearing. Upon arriving at the meeting, he discovered that she was sitting in the back, while he was placed on the dais along with the male leadership, which had had no part in the planning process.

As the women became more active in the public arena, traditional assumptions about gender roles created further conflict in their marriages. Women who became visible community leaders experienced the greatest tension. In some cases, the husbands were held responsible for their wives' activities, since they were supposed to be able to "control" their wives. For example, a woman who fought against an incinerator in Arkansas related:

> When the mayor saw my husband, he wanted to know why he couldn't keep his pretty little wife's mouth shut. As I became more active and more outspoken, our marriage became rockier. My husband asked me to tone it down, which I didn't do.

In other cases, women's morals were often called into question by husbands or other community members. Collette relates the experience of an activist in North Dakota who was rumored to be having an affair. The basis for the rumor, as Collette describes, was that "an uppity woman has got to be promiscuous if she dares to organize. In this case, she was at a late-night meeting in another town, and she slept over, so of course she had to have had sex."

Toxic waste issues thus set the stage for tremendous conflict between these women and their husbands. Men saw their roles as providers threatened: the homes they had bought may have become valueless; their jobs may have been at risk; they were asked by their wives to take on housework and child care. Meanwhile, their wives' public activities increasingly challenged traditional views of gender roles. For the women, their husbands' negative response to their entry into the public sphere contradicted an assumption in the family that both husband and wife were equally concerned with the well-being of the children. In talking about Love Canal, Gibbs explained:

> The husband in a blue-collar community is saying, get your ass home and cook me dinner, it's either me or the issue, make your choice. The woman says: How can I make a choice, you're telling me choose between the health of my children and your fucking dinner, how do I deal with that?

When women were asked to choose between their children and their husbands' needs, they began to see the ways in which the children had to be their primary concern.

At times this conflict resulted in more equal power relations within the marriages, a direction that CCHW tried to encourage by organizing family stress workshops. By and large, however, the families of activist women did not tolerate this stress well. Furthermore, as the women began openly to contest traditional power relations in the family, many found that their marriages could not withstand the challenges. As one activist from Arkansas described:

> I thought [my husband] didn't care enough about our children to continue to expose them to this danger. I begged him to move. He wouldn't. So I moved my kids out of town to live with my mom.

All twenty women interviewed for this article were active leaders around toxic waste issues in their communities, but only two described the importance of their husband's continuing support. One white woman who formed an interracial coalition in Alabama credited her husband's support in sustaining her resolve:

> I've had death threats. I was scared my husband would lose his job, afraid that somebody's going to kill me. If it weren't for my husband's support, I don't think I could get through all this.

In contrast, most of these activists described the ongoing conflict within their marriages, which often resulted in their abandoning their traditional role in the family, a process filled with inner turmoil. One woman described that turmoil as follows:

> I had doubts about what I was doing, especially when my marriage was getting real rocky. I thought of getting out of [the protest]. I sat down and talked to God many, many times. I asked him to lead me in the right direction because I knew my marriage was

failing and I found it hard leaving my kids when I had to go to meetings. I had to struggle to feel that I was doing the right thing. I said a prayer and went on.

Reflecting on the strength she felt as a mother, which empowered her to challenge her government and leave her marriage, she continued:

> It's an amazing ordeal. You always know you would protect your children. But it's amazing to find out how far you will go to protect your own kids.

The disruption of the traditional family often reflected positive changes in women's empowerment. Women grew through the protest; they became stronger and more self-confident. In some cases they found new marriages with men who respected them as strong individuals. Children also came to see their mothers as outspoken and confident.

Thus, for these women, the particularistic issue of toxic waste made visible oppression not only in the public sphere, but also in the family itself. As the traditional organization of family life was disrupted, inequities in underlying power relations were revealed. In order to succeed in fighting a toxic waste issue, these women had also to engage in another level of struggle as they reconceptualized their traditional role in family life in order to carry out their responsibilities as mothers.

Conclusion

The narratives of white, working-class women involved in toxic waste protests in the 1980s reveal the ways in which their subjective, particular experiences led them to analyses that extended beyond the particularistic issue to wider questions of power. Their broader environmental critique grew out of the concrete, immediate, everyday experience of struggling around survival issues. In the process of environmental protest, these women became engaged with specific governmental and corporate institutions and they were forced to reflect on the contradictions of their family life. To win a policy issue, they had to go through a process of developing an oppositional or critical consciousness which informed the direction of their actions and challenged the power of traditional policy makers. The contradiction between a government that claimed to act on behalf of the family and the actual environmental policies and actions of that government were unmasked. The inequities of power between white, working-class women and middle-class, male public officials were made visible. The reproduction within the family of traditional power relationships was also revealed. In the process of protest these women uncovered and confronted a world of political power shaped by gender and class. This enabled them to act politically around environmental issues, and in some measure to challenge the social relationships of power, inside and outside the home.

Ideologies of motherhood played a central role in the politicizing of white, working-class women around toxic waste issues. Their resistance grew out of an acceptance of a sexual division of labor that assigns to women responsibility for "sustaining the lives of their children and, in a broader sense, their families, including husband, relatives, elders and community." . . .

The analysis of white, working-class women's politicization through toxic waste protests reveals the contradictory role played by dominant ideologies about mothering and democracy in the shaping of these women's oppositional consciousness. The analysis these women developed was not a rejection of these ideologies. Rather, it was a reinterpretation, which became a source of power in the public arena. Their beliefs provided the initial impetus for involvement in toxic waste protests, and became a rich source of empowerment as they appropriated and reshaped traditional ideologies and meanings into an ideology of resistance. . . .

REFERENCES

Bullard, Robert D. 1990. *Dumping in Dixie: Race, Class and Environmental Quality.* Boulder, CO: Westview Press.

Bullard, Robert D. 1994. *Communities of Color and Environmental Justice.* San Francisco: Sierra Club Books.

Citizen's Clearing House for Hazardous Wastes. 1989. *Empowering Women.* Washington, DC: Citizen's Clearinghouse for Hazardous Wastes.

Krauss, Celene. 1993. "Women and Toxic Waste Protests: Race, Class and Gender as Resources of Resistance." *Qualitative Sociology 16*(3): 247–262.

Newman, Penny. 1991. "Women and the Environment in the United States of America." Paper presented at the Conference of Women and the Environment, Bangalore, India.

Ruddick, Sara. 1989. *Maternal Thinking: Towards a Politics of Peace.* New York: Ballantine Books.

Thompson, E. P. 1963. *The Making of the English Working Class.* New York: Pantheon Books.

Zeff, Robin Lee. 1989. "Not in My Backyard/Not in Anyone's Backyard: A Folklorist Examination of the American Grassroots Movement for Environmental Justice." Ph.D. dissertation, Indiana University.

THINKING ABOUT THE READING

Krauss describes how ordinary women became mobilized to construct a movement for social change when they felt their children's health was being threatened. Did their traditional beliefs about motherhood and family help or hinder their involvement in this protest movement? What effect did their participation have on their own families? Why do the women Krauss interviewed identify the toxic waste movement as a women's movement? Why don't men seem to be equally concerned about these health issues? How did the relative powerlessness of their working-class status shape the women's perspective on environmental justice?

"Aquí estamos y no nos vamos!"
Global Capital and Immigrant Rights

William I. Robinson

(2006)

A spectre is haunting global capitalism—the spectre of a transnational immigrant workers' uprising. An immigrant rights movement is spreading around the world, spearheaded by Latino immigrants in the US, who have launched an all-out fight-back against the repression, exploitation and racism they routinely face with a series of unparalleled strikes and demonstrations. The immediate message of immigrants and their allies in the United States is clear, with marchers shouting: "*aquí estamos y no nos vamos!*" (we're here and we're not leaving!). However, beyond immediate demands, the emerging movement challenges the very structural changes bound up with capitalist globalisation that have generated an upsurge in global labour migration, thrown up a new global working class, and placed that working class in increasingly direct confrontation with transnational capital.

The US mobilisations began when over half a million immigrants and their supporters took to the streets in Chicago on 10 March 2006. It was the largest single protest in that city's history. Following the Chicago action, rolling strikes and protests spread to other cities, large and small, organised through expanding networks of churches, immigrant clubs and rights groups, community associations, Spanish-language and progressive media, trade unions and social justice organisations. Millions came out on 25 March for a "national day of action." Between one and two million people demonstrated in Los Angeles—the single biggest public protest in the city's history—and millions more followed suit in Chicago, New York, Atlanta, Washington DC,

Phoenix, Dallas, Houston, Tucson, Denver and dozens of other cities. Again, on 10 April, millions heeded the call for another day of protest. In addition, hundreds of thousands of high school students in Los Angeles and around the country staged walk-outs in support of their families and communities, braving police repression and legal sanctions.

Then on the first of May, International Workers' Day, trade unionists and social justice activists joined immigrants in "The Great American Boycott 2006/A Day Without an Immigrant." Millions—perhaps tens of millions—in over 200 cities from across the country skipped work and school, commercial activity and daily routines in order to participate in a national boycott, general strike, rallies and symbolic actions. The May 1 action was a resounding success. Hundreds of local communities in the south, midwest, north-west and elsewhere, far away from the "gateway cities" where Latino populations are concentrated, experienced mass public mobilisations that placed them on the political map. Agribusiness in the California and Florida heartlands—nearly 100 per cent dependent on immigrant labour—came to a standstill, leaving supermarket produce shelves empty for the next several days. In the landscaping industry, nine out of ten workers boycotted work, according to the American Nursery and Landscape Association. The construction industry suffered major disruptions. Latino truckers who move 70 per cent of the goods in Los Angeles ports did not work. Care-giver referral agencies in major cities saw a sharp increase in calls from parents who needed last-minute nannies or baby-sitters. In order to avoid a total shutdown of the casino mecca in Las Vegas—highly dependent on immigrant labour—casino owners were forced to set up tables in employee lunch-rooms and hold meetings to allow their workers to circulate petitions in favour of immigrant demands. International commerce between Mexico and the United States ground to a temporary halt as protesters closed Tijuana, Juarez-El Paso and several other crossings along the 2,000-mile border.

These protests have no precedent in the history of the US. The immediate trigger was the passage in mid-March by the House of Representatives of HR4437, a bill introduced by Republican representative James Sensenbrenner with broad support from the anti-immigrant lobby. This draconian bill would criminalise undocumented immigrants by making it a felony to be in the US without documentation. It also stipulated the construction of the first 700 miles of a militarised wall between Mexico and the US and would double the size of the US border patrol. And it would apply criminal sanctions against anyone who provided assistance to undocumented immigrants, including churches, humanitarian groups and social service agencies.

Following its passage by the House, bill HR4437 became stalled in the Senate. Democrat Ted Kennedy and Republican John McCain co-sponsored a "compromise" bill that would have removed the criminalisation clause in HR4437 and provided a limited plan for amnesty for some of the undocumented. It would have allowed those who could prove they have resided in the US for at least five years to apply for residency and later citizenship. Those residing in the US for two to five years would have been required to return home and then apply through US embassies for temporary "guest worker" permits. Those who could not demonstrate that they had been in the US for two years would be deported. Even this "compromise" bill would have resulted in massive deportations and heightened control over all immigrants. Yet it was

eventually jettisoned because of Republican opposition, so that by late April the whole legislative process had become stalled. In May, the Senate renewed debate on the matter and seemed to be moving towards consensus based on tougher enforcement and limited legalisation, although at the time of writing (late May 2006) it appeared the legislative process could drag on until after the November 2006 congressional elections.

However, the wave of protest goes well beyond HR4437. It represents the unleashing of pent-up anger and repudiation of what has been deepening exploitation and an escalation of anti-immigrant repression and racism. Immigrants have been subject to every imaginable abuse in recent years. Twice in the state of California they have been denied the right to acquire drivers' licences. This means that they must rely on inadequate or non-existent public transportation or risk driving illegally; more significantly, the drivers' licence is often the only form of legal documentation for such essential transactions as cashing cheques or renting an apartment. The US-Mexico border has been increasingly militarised and thousands of immigrants have died crossing the frontier. Anti-immigrant hate groups are on the rise. The FBI has reported more than 2,500 hate crimes against Latinos in the US since 2000. Blatantly racist public discourse that, only a few years ago, would have been considered extreme has become increasingly mainstreamed and aired in the mass media.

More ominously, the paramilitary organisation Minutemen, a modern day Latino-hating version of the Ku Klux Klan, has spread from its place of origin along the US-Mexican border in Arizona and California to other parts of the country. Minutemen claim they must "secure the border" in the face of inadequate state-sponsored control. Their discourse, beyond racist, is neo-fascist. Some have even been filmed sporting T-shirts with the emblem "Kill a Mexican Today?" and others have organised for-profit "human safaris" in the desert. One video game discovered recently circulating on the internet, "Border Patrol," lets players shoot at Mexican immigrants as they try to cross the border into the US. Players are told to target one of three immigrant groups, all portrayed in a negative, stereotypical way, as the figures rush past a sign that reads "Welcome to the United States." The immigrants are caricatured as bandolier-wearing "Mexican nationalists," tattooed "drug smugglers" and pregnant "breeders" who spring across with their children in tow.

Minutemen clubs have been sponsored by right-wing organisers, wealthy ranchers, businessmen and politicians. But their social base is drawn from those formerly privileged sectors of the white working class that have been "flexibilised" and displaced by economic restructuring, the deregulation of labour and global capital flight. These sectors now scapegoat immigrants—with official encouragement—as the source of their insecurity and downward mobility.

The immigrant mobilisations have seriously threatened ruling groups. In the wake of the recent mobilisations, the Bush administration stepped up raids, deportations and other enforcement measures in a series of highly publicised mass arrests of undocumented immigrants and their employers, intended to intimidate the movement. In April 2006 it was revealed that KBR, a subsidiary of Halliburton—Vice-President Dick Cheney's former company, which has close ties to the Pentagon and is a major contractor in the Iraq war—won a $385 million contract to build large-scale immigrant detention centres in case of an "emergency influx" of immigrants.

Latino immigration to the US is part of a worldwide upsurge in transnational migration generated by the forces of capitalist globalisation. Immigrant labour worldwide is conservatively estimated at over 200 million, according to UN data.[1] Some 30 million are in the US, with at least 20 million of them from Latin America. Of these 20 million, some 11–12 million are undocumented (south and east Asia are also significant contributors to the undocumented population), although it must be stressed that these figures are low-end estimates.

The US is by far the largest immigrant-importing country, but the phenomenon is global. Racist attacks, scapegoating and state-sponsored repressive controls over immigrants are rising in many countries around the world, as is the fightback among immigrant workers wherever they are found. Parallel to the US events, for instance, the French government introduced a bill that would apply tough new controls over immigrants and roll back their rights. In response, some 30,000 immigrants and their supporters took to the streets in Paris on 13 May 2006 to demand the bill's repeal.

The Global Circulation of Immigrant Labour

The age of globalisation is also an age of unprecedented transnational migration. The corollary to an integrated global economy is the rise of a truly global—although highly segmented—labour market. It is a global labour market because, despite formal nation state restrictions on the free worldwide movement of labour, surplus labour in any part of the world is now recruited and redeployed through numerous mechanisms to where capital is in need of it and because workers themselves undertake worldwide migration, even in the face of the adverse migratory conditions.

Central to capitalism is securing a politically and economically suitable labour supply, and at the core of all class societies is the control over labour and disposal of the products of labour. But the linkage between the securing of labour and territoriality is changing under globalisation. As labour becomes "free" in every corner of the globe, capital has vast new opportunities for mobilising labour power where and when required. National labour pools are merging into a single global labour pool that services global capitalism. The transnational circulation of capital induces the transnational circulation of labour. This circulation of labour becomes incorporated into the process of restructuring the world economy. It is a mechanism for the provision of labour to transnationalised circuits of accumulation and constitutes a structural feature of the global system.

While the need to mix labour with capital at diverse points along global production chains induces population movements, there are sub-processes that shape the character and direction of such migration. At the structural level, the uprooting of communities by the capitalist break-up of local economies creates surplus populations and is a powerful push factor in outmigration, while labour shortages in more economically advanced areas is a pull factor that attracts displaced peoples. At a behavioural level, migration and wage remittances become a family survival strategy (see below), made *possible* by the demand for labour abroad and made increasingly *viable* by the fluid conditions and integrated infrastructures of globalisation.

In one sense, the South penetrates the North with the dramatic expansion of immigrant labour. But transnational migratory flows are not unidirectional from South to North and the phenomenon is best seen in global capitalist rather than North-South terms. Migrant workers are becoming a general category of super-exploitable labour drawn from globally dispersed labour reserves into similarly globally dispersed nodes of accumulation. To the extent that these nodes experience labour shortages—skilled or unskilled—they become magnets for transnational labour flows, often encouraged or even organised by both sending and receiving countries and regions.

Labour-short Middle Eastern countries, for instance, have programmes for the importation (and careful control) of labour from throughout south and east Asia and north Africa. The Philippine state has become a veritable labour recruitment agency for the global economy, organising the export of its citizens to over a hundred countries in Asia, the Middle East, Europe, North America and elsewhere. Greeks migrate to Germany and the US, while Albanians migrate to Greece. South Africans move to Australia and England, while Malawians, Mozambicans and Zimbabweans

work in South African mines and the service industry. Malaysia imports Indonesian labour, while Thailand imports workers from Laos and Myanmar and, in turn, sends labour to Malaysia, Singapore, Japan and elsewhere. In Latin America, Costa Rica is a major importer of Nicaraguan labour, Venezuela has historically imported large amounts of Colombian labour, the Southern Cone draws on several million emigrant Andean workers and an estimated 500,000 to 800,000 Haitians live in the Dominican Republic, where they cut sugar cane, harvest crops and work in the *maquiladoras* under the same labour market segmentation, political disenfranchisement and repression that immigrant workers face in the United States and in most labour-importing countries.

The division of the global working class into "citizen" and "non-citizen" labour is a major new axis of inequality worldwide, further complicating the well-known gendered and racialised hierarchies among labour, and facilitating new forms of repressive and authoritarian social control over working classes. In an *apparent* contradiction, capital and goods move freely across national borders in the new global economy but labour cannot and its movement is subject to heightened state controls. The global labour supply is, in the main, no longer coerced (subject to extra-economic compulsion) due to the ability of the universalised market to exercise strictly economic discipline, but its movement is juridically controlled. This control is a central determinant in the worldwide correlation of forces between global capital and global labour.

The immigrant is a juridical creation inserted into real social relations. States create "immigrant labour" as distinct categories of labour in relation to capital. While the generalisation of the labour market emerging from the consolidation of the global capitalist economy creates the conditions for global migrations as a world-level labour supply system, the maintenance and strengthening of state controls over transnational labour create the conditions for immigrant labour as a distinct category of labour. The creation of these distinct categories ("immigrant labour") becomes central to the global capitalist economy, replacing earlier direct colonial and racial caste controls over labour worldwide.

But why is this juridical category of "immigrant labour" reproduced under globalisation? Labour migration and geographic shifts in production are alternative forms for capitalists to achieve an optimal mix of their capital with labour. State controls are often intended *not to prevent* but to *control* the transnational movement of labour. A *free* flow of labour would exert an equalising influence on wages across borders whereas state controls help reproduce such differentials. Eliminating the wage differential between regions would cancel the advantages that capital accrues from disposing of labour pools worldwide subject to different wage levels and would strengthen labour worldwide in relation to capital. In addition, the use of immigrant labour allows receiving countries to separate reproduction and maintenance of labour, and therefore to "externalise" the costs of social reproduction. In other words, the new transnational migration helps capital to dispose of the need to pay for the reproduction of labour power. The inter-state system thus acts as a condition for the structural power of globally mobile transnational capital over labour that is transnational in actual content and character but subjected to different institutional arrangements under the direct control of national states.

The migrant labour phenomenon will continue to expand along with global capitalism. Just as capitalism has no control over its implacable expansion as a system, it cannot do away in its new globalist stage with transnational labour. But if global capital needs the labour power of transnational migrants, this labour power belongs to human beings who must be tightly controlled, given the special oppression and dehumanization involved in extracting their labour power as non-citizen immigrant labour. To return to the situation in the US, the immigrant issue presents a contradiction for political and economic elites: from the vantage points of dominant group interests, the dilemma is how to deal with the new "barbarians" at Rome's door.

Latino immigrants haw massively swelled the lower rungs of the US workforce. They provide almost all farm labour and much of the labour for hotels, restaurants, construction, janitorial and house cleaning, child care, gardening and landscaping, delivery, meat and poultry packing, retail, and so on. Yet dominant groups fear a rising tide of Latino immigrants will lead to a loss of cultural and political control, becoming a source of counter-hegemony and instability, as immigrant labour in Paris showed itself to be in the late 2005 uprising there against racism and marginality.

Employers do not want to do away with Latino immigration. To the contrary, they want to sustain a vast exploitable labour pool that exists under precarious conditions, that does not enjoy the civil, political and labour rights of citizens and that is disposable through deportation. It is the *condition of deportability* that they wish to create, or preserve, since that condition assures the ability to super-exploit with impunity and to dispose of this labour without consequences should it become unruly or unnecessary. The Bush administration opposed HR4437 not because it was in favour of immigrant rights but because it had to play a balancing act by finding a formula for a stable supply of cheap labour to employers with, at the same time, greater state control over immigrants.

The Bush White House proposed a "guest worker" programme that would rule out legalisation for undocumented immigrants, force them to return to their home countries and apply for temporary work visas, and implement tough new border security measures. There is a long history of such "guest worker" schemes going back to the *bracero* programme, which brought millions of Mexican workers to the US during the labour shortages of the Second World War, only to deport them once native workers had become available again. Similar "guest worker" programmes are in effect in several European countries and other labour-importing states around the world.

The contradictions of "immigrant policy reform" became apparent in the days leading up to the May 1 action, when major capitalist groups dependent on immigrant labour—especially in the agricultural, food processing, landscaping, construction, and other service sectors—came out in support of legalisation for the undocumented. Such transnational agro-industrial giants as Cargill, Swift and Co, Perdue Farms, Tyson Foods and Goya Foods, for instance, closed down many of their meat-packing and food processing plants and gave workers the day off.

Neoliberalism in Latin America

If capital's need for cheap, malleable and deportable labour in the centres of the global economy is the main "pull factor" inducing Latino immigration to the US, the "push factor" is the devastation left by two decades of neoliberalism in Latin America. Capitalist globalisation—structural adjustment, free trade agreements, privatisations, the contraction of public employment and credits, the break-up of communal lands and so forth, along with the political crises these measures have generated—has imploded thousands of communities in Latin America and unleashed a wave of migration, from rural to urban areas and to other countries, that can only be analogous to the mass uprooting and migration that generally take place in the wake of war.

Just as capital does not stay put in the place it accumulates, neither do wages stay put. The flip side of the intense upsurge in transnational migration is the reverse flow of remittances by migrant workers in the global economy to their country and region of origin. Officially recorded international remittances increased astonishingly, from a mere $57 million in 1970 to $216 billion in 2005, according to World Bank data. This amount was higher than capital market flows and official development assistance combined, and nearly equalled

the total amount of world FDI (foreign direct investment) in 2004. Close to one billion people, or one in every six on the planet, may receive some support from the global flow of remittances, according to senior World Bank economist Dilip Ratha.[2] Remittances have become an economic mainstay for an increasing number of countries. Most of the world's regions, including Africa, Asia, Latin America and southern and eastern Europe, report major remittance inflows.

Remittances redistribute income worldwide in a literal or geographic sense but not in the actual sense of *redistribution*, meaning a transfer of some added portion of the surplus from capital to labour, since they constitute not additional earnings but the separation of the site where wages are earned from the site of wage-generated consumption. What is taking place is a historically unprecedented separation of the point of production from the point of social reproduction. The former can take place in one part of the world and generate the value—then remitted—for social reproduction of labour in another part of the world. This is an emergent structural feature of the global system, in which the site of labour power and of its reproduction have been transnationally dispersed.

Transnational Latino migration has led to an enormous increase in remittances from Latino ethnic labour abroad to extended kinship networks in Latin America. Latin American workers abroad sent home some $57 billion in 2005, according to the Inter-American Development Bank.[3] These remittances were the number one source of foreign exchange for the Dominican Republic, El Salvador, Guatemala, Guyana, Haiti, Honduras, Jamaica and Nicaragua, and the second most important source for Belize, Bolivia, Colombia, Ecuador, Paraguay and Surinam, according to the Bank. The $20 billion sent back in 2005 by an estimated 10 million Mexicans in the US was more than the country's tourism receipts and was surpassed only by oil and *maquiladora* exports.

These remittances allow millions of Latin American families to survive by purchasing goods either imported from the world market or produced locally or by transnational capital. They allow for family survival at a time of crisis and adjustment, especially for the poorest sectors—safety nets that replace governments and fixed employment in the provision of economic security. Emigration and remittances also serve the political objective of pacification. The dramatic expansion of Latin American emigration to the US from the 1980s onwards helped to dissipate social tensions and undermine labour and political opposition to prevailing regimes and institutions. Remittances help to offset macroeconomic imbalances, in some cases averting economic collapse, thereby shoring up the political conditions for an environment congenial to transnational capital.

Therefore, bound up with the immigrant debate in the US is the entire political economy of global capitalism in the western hemisphere—the same political economy that is now being sharply contested throughout Latin America with the surge in mass popular struggles and the turn to the Left. The struggle for immigrant rights in the US is thus part and parcel of this resistance to neoliberalism, intimately connected to the larger Latin American—and worldwide—struggle for social justice.

No wonder protests and boycotts took place throughout Latin America on May 1 in solidarity with Latino immigrants in the US. But these actions were linked to local labour rights struggles and social movement demands. In Tijuana, Mexico, for example, *maquiladora* workers in that border city's in-bond industry marched on May 1 to demand higher wages, eight-hour shifts, an end to "abuses and despotism" in the *maquila* plants and an end to sexual harassment, the use of poison chemicals and company unions. The workers also called for solidarity with the "Great American Boycott of 2006 on the other side of the border" and participated in a protest at the US consulate in the city and at the main crossing, which shut down cross-border traffic for most of the day.

The Nature of Immigrant Struggles

Labour market transformations driven by capitalist globalisation unleash what McMichael calls "the politics of global labor circulation"[4] and fuel, in labour-importing countries, new nativisms, waves of xenophobia and racism against immigrants. Shifting political coalitions scapegoat immigrants by promoting ethnic-based solidarities among middle classes, representatives of distinct fractions of capital and formerly privileged sectors among working classes (such as white ethnic workers in the US and Europe) threatened by job loss, declining income and the other insecurities of economic restructuring. The long-term tendency seems to be towards a generalisation of labour market conditions across borders, characterised by segmented structures under a regime of labour deregulation and racial, ethnic and gender hierarchies.

In this regard, a major challenge confronting the movement in the US is relations between the Latino and the Black communities. Historically, African Americans have swelled the lower rungs in the US caste system. But, as African Americans fought for their civil and human rights in the 1960s and 1970s, they became organised, politicised and radicalised. Black workers led trade union militancy. All this made them undesirable labour for capital—"undisciplined" and "noncompliant."

Starting in the 1980s, employers began to push out Black workers and massively recruit Latino immigrants, a move that coincided with deindustrialisation and restructuring. Blacks moved from super-exploited to marginalized—subject to unemployment, cuts in social services, mass incarceration and heightened state repression—while Latino immigrant labour has become the new super-exploited sector. Employers and political elites in New Orleans, for instance, have apparently decided in the wake of Hurricane Katrina to replace that city's historically black working class with Latino immigrant labour. Whereas fifteen years ago no one saw a single Latino face in places such as

Iowa or Tennessee, now Mexican, Central American and other Latino workers are visible everywhere. If some African Americans have misdirected their anger over marginality at Latino immigrants, the Black community has a legitimate grievance over the anti-Black racism of many Latinos themselves, who often lack sensitivity to the historic plight and contemporary experience of Blacks with racism, and are reticent to see them as natural allies. (Latinos often bring with them particular sets of racialised relations from their home countries.)[5]

White labour that historically enjoyed caste privileges within racially segmented labour markets has experienced downward mobility and heightened insecurity. These sectors of the working class feel the pinch of capitalist globalisation and the transnationalisation of formerly insulated local labour markets. Studies in the early 1990s, for example, found that, in addition to concentrations in "traditional" areas such as Los Angeles, Miami, Washington DC, Virginia and Houston, Central American immigrants had formed clusters in the formal and informal service sectors in areas where, in the process of downward mobility, they had replaced "white ethnics," such as in suburban Long Island, the small towns of Iowa and North Carolina, in Silicon Valley and in the northern and eastern suburbs of the San Francisco Bay Area.[6]

The loss of caste privileges for white sectors of the working class is problematic for political elites and state managers in the US, since legitimation and domination have historically been constructed through a white racial hegemonic bloc. Can such a bloc be sustained or renewed through a scapegoating of immigrant communities? In attempting to shape public discourse, the anti-immigrant lobby argues that immigrants "are a drain on the US economy." Yet, as the National Immigrant Solidarity Network points out, immigrants contribute $7 billion in Social Security a year. They earn $240 billion, report $90 billion, and are only reimbursed $5 billion in tax returns. They also contribute $25 billion more to the US economy than they receive in health-care and social services. But this is a limited line of argument, since the larger issue is the incalculable trillions of dollars that immigrant labour generates in profits and revenue for capital, only a tiny proportion of which goes back to them in the form of wages.

Moreover, it has been demonstrated that there is no correlation between the unemployment rate among US citizens and the rate of immigration. In fact, the unemployment rate has moved in cycles over the past twenty-five years and exhibits a comparatively lower rate during the most recent (2000–2005) influx of undocumented workers. Similarly, wage stagnation in the United States appeared, starting with the economic crisis of 1973, and has continued its steady march ever since, with no correlation to increases or decreases in the inflow of undocumented workers. Instead, downward mobility for most US workers is positively correlated with the decline in union participation, the decline in labour conditions and the polarisation of income and wealth that began with the restructuring crisis of the 1970s and accelerated the following decade as Reaganomics launched the neo-liberal counterrevolution.

The larger backdrop here is transnational capital's attempt to forge post-Fordist, post-Keynesian capital-labour relations worldwide, based on flexibilisation, deregulation and deunionisation. From the 1970s onwards, capital began to abandon earlier reciprocities with labour, forged in the epoch of national corporate capitalism, precisely because the process of globalisation allowed to it break free of nation state constraints. There has been a vast acceleration of the primitive accumulation of capital worldwide through globalisation, a process in which millions have been wrenched from the means of production, proletarianised and thrown into a global labour market that transnational capital has been able to shape. As capital assumed new power relative to labour with the onset of globalisation, states shifted from reproducing Keynesian social structures of accumulation to servicing the general needs of the new patterns of global accumulation.

At the core of the emerging global social structure of accumulation is a new capital-labour relation based on alternative systems of labour control and diverse contingent categories of devalued labour—sub-contracted, outsourced, casualised, informal, part-time, temp work, home-work, and so on—the essence of which is cheapening and disciplining labour, making it "flexible" and readily available for transnational capital in worldwide labour reserves. Workers in the global economy are themselves, under these flexible arrangements, increasingly treated as a sub-contracted component rather than a fixture internal to employer organisations. These new class relations of global capitalism dissolve the notion of responsibility, however minimal, that governments have for their citizens or that employers have towards their employees.

Immigrant workers become the archetype of these new global class relations. They are a naked commodity, no longer embedded in relations of reciprocity rooted in social and political communities that have, historically, been institutionalised in nation states. Immigrant labour pools that can be super-exploited economically, marginalised and disenfranchised politically, driven into the shadows and deported when necessary are the very epitome of capital's naked domination in the age of global capitalism.

The immigrant rights movement in the US is demanding full rights for all immigrants, including amnesty, worker protections, family reunification measures, a path to citizenship or permanent residency rather than a temporary "guest worker" programme, an end to all attacks against immigrants and to the criminalisation of immigrant communities. While some observers have billed the recent events as the birth of a new civil rights movement, clearly much more is at stake. In the larger picture, this goes beyond immediate demands; it challenges the class relations that are at the very core of global capitalism. The significance of the May 1 immigrant rights mobilisation taking place on international workers' day—which has not been celebrated in the US for nearly a century—was lost on no one.

In the age of globalisation, the only hope of accumulating the social and political forces necessary to confront the global capitalist system is by transnationalising popular, labour and democratic struggles. The immigrant rights movement is all of these—popular, pro-worker and democratic—and it is by definition transnational. In sum, the struggle for immigrant rights is at the cutting edge of the global working-class fight-back against capitalist globalisation.

NOTES

1. Manuel Oruzco, "Worker remittances in an international scope," *Working Paper* (Washington, DC, Inter-American Dialogue and Multilateral Investment Fund of the Inter-American Development Bank, March 2003), p. 1.

2. For these details, see Richard Boudreaux, "The new foreign aid; the seeds of promise," *Los Angeles Times* (14 April 2006), p. 1A.

3. Inter-American Development Bank, *Remittances 2005: promoting financial democracy* (Washington, DC, IDB, 2006).

4. Philip McMichael, *Development and Social Change: A Global Perspective* (Thousand Oaks, CA, Pine Forge Press, 1986), p. 189.

5. In a commentary observing that mainstream Black political leaders have been notably lukewarm to the immigrant rights movement, Keeanga-Yamahtta Taylor writes: "The displacement of Black workers is a real problem—but not a problem caused by displaced Mexican workers . . . if the state is allowed to criminalize the existence [of] immigrant workers this will only fan the flames of racism eventually consuming Blacks in a back draft of discrimination. How exactly does one tell the difference between a citizen and a non-citizen? Through a massive campaign of racial profiling, that's how . . . In fact, the entire working class has a stake in the success of the movement." She goes on to recall how California building owners and labour contractors replaced Black janitors with largely undocumented Latino immigrants in the 1980s. But after a successful Service Employees International Union drive in the "Justice for janitors" campaign of the late 1980s and 1990s, wages and benefits went up and the union's largely Latino members sought contractual language guaranteeing African Americans a percentage of work slots. See

Taylor, "Life ain't been no crystal stair: Blacks, Latinos and the new civil rights movement," *Counterpunch* (9 May 2006), downloaded 18 May 2006 <http://www.counterpunch.org/taylor0508 2006.html>.

6. See the special issue of NACLA *Report on the Americas,* "On the line: Latinos on labor's cutting edge" (Vol. 30, no. 3, November/December 1996).

THINKING ABOUT THE READING

What is the "global circulation of immigrant labor"? What are some of the issues and concerns that face immigrant workers? According to Robinson, recent immigrant labor demonstrations reflect the growing consciousness of a "global working class." Who or what are the "global working class" described in this reading? What are some of the ways they resist global capitalism? What will be some of the implications of these strategies if they are successful?

Credits

Chapter 1

From *The Sociological Imagination* by C. Wright Mills, copyright © 2000 by Oxford University Press, Inc. Reprinted by permission of the publisher.

From *Invitation to Sociology* by Peter Berger, copyright 1963 by Peter L. Berger. Used by permission of Doubleday, a division of Random House, Inc.

From "The My Lai Massacre: A Military Crime of Obedience," by Herbert Kelman and V. Lee Hamilton. In *Crimes of Obedience* (pp. 1–20), edited by Herbert Kelman and V. Lee Hamilton. © 1989 by Yale University Press. Reprinted by permission.

Chapter 2

From *Culture of Fear* by Barry Glassner. Reprinted by permission of Basic Books, a member of Perseus Books Group.

From Chapter 1, pp. 11–28, "Researching Dealers and Smugglers" from *Wheeling and Dealing* by Patricia A. Adler. Reprinted by permission of Columbia University Press.

Chapter 3

From *Observing Ourselves: Essays in Social Research* by Earl Babbie, copyright © 1986. Reprinted with permission of Waveland Press, Inc. All rights reserved.

From "Sense and Nonsense About Surveys" by Howard Schuman from *Contexts*, Summer 2002. Reprinted by permission.

Chapter 4

From "Body Ritual Among the Nacirema" by Horace Miner. *American Anthropologist* 58:3, June 1956, pp. 503–507.

Excerpts from "The Melting Pot," from *The Spirit Catches You and You Fall Down: A Hmong Child, Her American Doctors, and the Collision of Two Cultures* (pp. 181–209) by Anne Fadiman. Copyright 1997 by Anne Fadiman. Reprinted by permission of Farrar, Straus, and Giroux, LLC.

From *Golden Arches East, McDonald's in East Asia,* 2nd ed. Edited by James L. Watson. Copyright 1997, 2006 by the Board of Trustees of the Leland Stanford Jr. University. All rights reserved. Used with the permission of Stanford University Press, www.sup.org.

Chapter 5

From "Life as the Maid's Daughter: An Exploration of the Everyday Boundaries of Race, Class, and Gender" by Mary Romero, from *Feminisms in the Academy* by Mary Romero, Abigail J. Stewart, and Donna Stanton (eds.) (pp. 157–179). Copyright © 1995. Used by permission of The University of Michigan Press.

From "Introduction: The Making of Culture, Identity, and Ethnicity Among Asian American Youth," by Min Zhou and Jennifer Lee from *Asian American Youth Culture, Identity, and Ethnicity* by Jennifer Lee and Min Zhou (eds.) (pp. 1–30). Copyright 2004. Used by permission of Routledge.

Chapter 10

From "Making Class Invisible" by Gregory Mantsios from *Race, Class, and Gender in the United States: An Integrated Study, 4th ed.* by Paula S. Rothenberg. Copyright © 1998 Gregory Mantsios. Reprinted with permission.

From "The Compassion Gap in American Poverty Policy" by Fred Block, Anna C. Korteweg, and Kerry Woodward with Zach Schiller and Imrul Mazid from *Contexts*, Vol. 5, No. 2, Spring 2006, pp. 14–20. Copyright 2006 by University of California Press. Used with permission.

From "Avenue to Adulthood: Teenage Pregnancy and the Meaning of Motherhood in Poor Communities" by Gabrielle Raley from *American Families: A Multicultural Reader* by Stephanie Coontz (ed.) (pp. 338–350). Copyright 2008. Used by permission of Routledge.

Chapter 11

From "Racial and Ethnic Formation" by Michael Omi and Howard Winant from *Racial Formation in the US.* Copyright 1994. Reprinted by permission of Routledge via Copyright Clearance Center.

From "Optional Ethnicities: For Whites Only?" by Mary C. Waters from *Origins and Destinies: Immigration, Race and Ethnicity in America,* 1st edition by Pedraa/Rumbaut. 1996. Reprinted with permission of Wadsworth, a division of Thomson Learning (www.thomson rights.com).

From "The Downside of Racial Uplift: The Meaning of Gentrification in an African American Neighborhood". Reproduced by permission of the American Anthropological Association from *City & Society* by Michelle Boyd, Vol. 17, No. 2, 2005, pp. 265–288. Not for sale or further reproduction.

Chapter 12

From "Black Women and a New Definition of Womanhood" by Bart Landry, from *Black Working Wives: Pioneers of the American Family Revolution* by Bart Landry. Berkeley: University of California Press. Copyright © 2000 by the Regents of the University of California. Reprinted by permission.

Excerpts from *Still a Man's World: Men Who Do "Women's Work"* (pp. 1–5, 81–108) by Christine L. Williams. Berkeley: University of California Press. Copyright © 1995 by the Regents of the University of California. Reprinted by permission of University of California Press in the format Textbook via Copyright Clearance Center.

From "Cheerleading and the Gendered Politics of Sport" by Laura Grindstaff and Emily West from *Social Problems,* 53:500–518. Copyright 2006. Reprinted by permission.

Chapter 13

From "Age-Segregation in Later Life: An Examination of Personal Networks" by Peter Uhlenberg and Jenny de Jong Gierveld from *Ageing and Society*, Vol. 24, No. 1, 2004, pp. 5–28. Copyright 2004 Cambridge University Press. Used with permission.

From "Accessing Assets: Immigrant Youth's Work as Family Translators or 'Para-Phrasers'" by Marjorie Faulstich Orellana, Lisa Dorner, and Lucila Pulido from *Social Problems,* 50:505–524. Reprinted by permission.

From "Love and Gold" by Arlie Russell Hochschild from *Global Woman: Nannies, Maids, and Sex Workers in the New Economy* by Barbara Ehrenreich and Arlie Russell Hochschild. Copyright 2002. A version of "Love and Gold" appeared in *The American Prospect* in 2000. Reprinted by permission of Henry Holt and Company.

Chapter 14